MID-TERM REPORT

MID-TERM REPORT

Phil Redmond

CENTURY · LONDON

Published by Century 2012

2 4 6 8 10 9 7 5 3 1

Copyright © The Publishing & Licensing Agency Ltd 2012

Phil Redmond has asserted his right under the Copyright, Designs
and Patents Act 1988 to be identified as the author of this work

This book is a work of non-fiction based on the life, experiences and recollections of the
author. In some limited cases names of people, places, dates, sequences or the detail of events
have been changed to protect the privacy of others. The author has stated to the publishers
that, except in such minor respects not affecting the substantial accuracy of the work, the
contents of this book are true.

First published in Great Britain in 2012 by
Century
Random House, 20 Vauxhall Bridge Road,
London SW1V 2SA

www.randomhouse.co.uk

Addresses for companies within The Random House Group Limited can be found at:
www.randomhouse.co.uk

The Random House Group Limited Reg. No. 954009

A CIP catalogue record for this book
is available from the British Library

ISBN 9781846059841

The Random House Group Limited supports The Forest Stewardship Council (FSC®),
the leading international forest certification organisation. Our books carrying the FSC
label are printed on FSC® certified paper. FSC is the only forest certification scheme
endorsed by the leading environmental organisations, including Greenpeace. Our paper
procurement policy can be found at www.randomhouse.co.uk/environment

Typeset in Bembo by Palimpsest Book Production Limited,
Falkirk, Stirlingshire

Printed and bound in Great Britain by
Clays Ltd, St Ives plc

To the kids . . .
And those that didn't make the final cut

Contents

Acknowledgements

This has been a difficult tale to write, not least due to the number of things I wanted to include, but mainly because despite having been fortunate enough to have had three highly visible television programmes, I have also managed to maintain a strict separation between my public and private lives. Often, this has been like managing two completely separate existences, a line I will continue to walk throughout this book and which, I hope, I will be able to explain along the way. I also hope to explain a bit more about the programmes I am known for, some that I am not, and other aspects of the media . . . one of which is that media is about box office and circus, and no circus is complete without a few clowns. However, having guarded my own privacy for years, I also appreciate its value to others. Consequently, I have tried to avoid naming the clowns who contributed to my own media circus. If they want to stand up and identify themselves, that is, of course, their right.

Still, just as there were clowns, so too there were people who helped me and to whom I owe a lot. Those I would like to acknowledge publicly are:

- Alexis – for finding me when I found her and for becoming my partner in every way imaginable . . .
- Family – for always being there especially when I wasn't . . .
- My various PAs, ever at the centre of the storms, especially Helen, Carmel and Diane, and Janet who carries the domestic burdens, but most notably Donna who still exercises controlled calm in dealing with the mood swings and perpetually changing diary . . .
- John Cleese – for taking time to meet me, showing me how to open a milk carton and instilling in me the idea that the only fun part is the moment of creation. The rest was, is, and always will be, sheer hard work . . .
- Brian Finch, unfortunately now the late Brian Finch, a writer from Wigan who told me not to get on the treadmill before I knew what I wanted to grind out . . .
- Susan Sandon – for initially responding to a daft email and then hanging on and on and on, far beyond what I would have done, until . . .
- The Cast of Characters found in the book for sharing parts of your lives with me, for good or bad . . .
- The millions of viewers who have watched my programmes over the years and especially the loyal band of *Brookside* fans who stayed with the programme to the final episode, defying Channel 4's schedulers by tracking and returning to the programme every time they shifted its slot to throw you off the scent. I hope this book gives you some insight into the process of getting *Brookie* into your living rooms . . .
- And, probably not said often enough, thanks to Alan Emtage, Bill Heelan, and J. Peter Deutsch, while students at McGill University in Montreal in 1990, for inventing the concept of the search engine that enabled Larry Page and Sergey Brin to develop one of the greatest tools available to any writer: Google. Without it the task would have been a lot harder and taken a lot longer.

The danger, of course, in making any list, lies in overlooking the obvious. 'Team effort' is a great way to cover it, and many will have heard me say that I couldn't have done what I have without great teams around me. I always meant it. I still do.

Acknowledgements

And, lastly, as with any television audience, thanks to you, whoever you are. Because if you are reading this, in one form or another, you have made this process complete.

Phil Redmond, June 2012

1

The Setup (1949–60)

'Who made me? God made me' – Catholic rote learning from
Penny Catechism

'Hi, Jeremy,' I said. 'I'm Phil Redmond and I did *Grange Hill*. If
what you've just said is true, would you let me have characters
who could say f★★★ at eight o'clock at night?'

Well, it was something like that. The expletive was there. It was
January 1981. The Royal Institution was a hubbub. Hundreds of
potential and wannabe independent producers had crowded into its
august lecture theatre to hear Jeremy Isaacs, the new Chief Executive
of the UK's soon-to-be Channel 4, outline his vision for the future.
He had done his stuff and was working the room like a Roman
Emperor massaging the Senate when I managed to block his way.

It felt like a time-freeze moment. The babble appeared to die
away as those around us waited for his response. He gave me an
imperial stare for a moment, looked me up and down in my jeans
and trainers, and probably thought the Visigoths had arrived at the
gates of Rome. But like a true patrician he grinned amicably and
said, 'Come and see me. We'll talk.' So I did and the rest, as they
try to say, is history. Sort of.

I found him camped out at the headquarters of the then television regulator, the IBA (Independent Broadcasting Authority). As
television regulators seem to do, they had grand offices. Not quite
so grand as the home of the current regulator Ofcom, overlooking

the Thames, but the building was in Knightsbridge and right opposite Harrods so no doubt handy for picking up the weekly shop.
The Emperor, though, was tucked away down a long corridor at
the back of the building. He was on his own in a classic transient
set: desk, phone, a couple of chairs and a huge poster for the film
he had recently produced, *A Sense of Freedom*, propped against the
wall.

It was a far cry from the image projected at the Royal Institution,
but I guessed that if he had the bottle to take on a Glaswegian
headcase like Jimmy Boyle, whose autobiography the film was based
upon, he would be up for trying to develop an up-to-date version
of *Coronation Street*. And so it turned out.

We chatted through what he wanted to do with the channel and
what I wanted to do with a new twice-weekly. He asked me why
he should do it and I responded that every channel in the world,
no matter how radical, needed to be promoted, and the best way
to do that was with a twice-weekly. We were still avoiding the word
'soap' as that would have been unworthy of Channel 4. And, after
all, Granada, where Jeremy had earned his wings, still referred to
'The Street' as a twice-weekly. It was a habit we ourselves stuck to
for many years as I shared Granada's view. The Americans produced
and sold soap; we made drama. It was only after the media explosion of the late 1980s, that I switched to saying that I didn't care
what people called it, so long as they watched. It was easier.

Jeremy Isaacs said he agreed and would love to have a long-runner,
but his key question was, how could he afford it? He was working
with an average slot cost of around £30k an hour and we both
knew *Coronation Street* cost a lot more than that. I replied, as I often
did, and still do actually, that it shouldn't. How can you bring down
the costs? he asked. I told him I used to be a quantity surveyor. The
ethos was not about saying, 'If that's what you want, this is what it
costs,' but more, 'If that's all you've got, this is what you can have.'
The secret lay in finding the right technology and an innovative
approach to fixed overheads to remove costs.

This philosophy is as true today as it was back then, and if it
were applied across the board to organisations like the BBC and
Channel 4, they would still be able to expand their public-service
offer, rather than continually contracting it. The underlying reason
why they do not is also exactly the same as it was back then: too

many people being paid too much to protect the status quo. But we will get to that later in the story.

In 1981, I had been writing for television for eight years, having spent the five before that working as a quantity surveyor, one of the people who actually count the bricks and copper pipes and everything else that goes into every building project. It seemed to me that the television production process was similar, bringing people and resources together at a particular time to perform particular tasks to deliver a particular outcome. Both were labour-intensive, relied on technology and were susceptible to the weather. On the other hand, the driving philosophies of both industries could not be farther apart.

In the construction industry competition for funding or market share was the imperative, which forced a constant search for new ideas, new technology and new efficiencies; while in television it seemed the approach was constant expansion, unlimited resources and spend as you want. The BBC's licence fee was almost guaranteed to rise above inflation due to something known as 'broadcasting inflation'. For ITV, with a state-sanctioned monopoly on advertising, it literally was, as Roy Thomson, the Canadian founding chairman of Scottish Television, once famously said, a 'licence to print money'. Ten years later in 1991, when MerseyTV teamed up with Yorkshire and Tyne Tees Television to have a go at the Granada licence, things had changed, a bit. The then finance director of Yorkshire Television, Alan Harding, had a moment of nostalgia on top of the old Barings Bank Tower one night, reflecting on the way things had gone. 'Back in the seventies and eighties,' he mused, 'we used to be walking around in cash up to our knees. Now, it's only up to our ankles.' We nearly all sighed.

That's another part of the journey I'll get to later, but back in 1981 Channel 4 was eyed suspiciously by the TV establishment, both management and unions, as some form of Thatcherite Trojan Horse designed to drive down costs and change working practices. They were right. And as with all forms of social upheaval there was a simultaneous common-sense private acknowledgement of the need for change, running alongside the publicly stated contrary view that the status quo must be preserved. It is a peculiarly British way of doing things.

OK, said The Emperor, I understand all that, and I'd love to have a twice-weekly to promote the rest of the channel around, but how could you actually deliver it within that £30k slot cost? Simple, I said, by buying all the houses and technology upfront. Amortise the costs over three years, thus removing two of the biggest cost centres – set construction and equipment hire. As I started to get into the groove about wiring up the entire estate, I could see that patrician stare again. Was I speaking Visigoth? Apparently not, as he then told me he had persuaded the almost legendary David Rose to come across from the BBC to take on the role of Commissioning Editor for Fiction, a title that in itself sent out the signal that Channel 4 was going to be different.

I knew of David Rose as he had produced *Z Cars* back in the 1960s. Although allegedly about a fictional place called Newtown, we all knew it was really about Kirkby where I was going to school at the time, especially as its theme tune was an adaptation of the Everton FC anthem, 'Johnny Todd', that is still played as the team comes out. By the time I took my first tentative steps towards television in the early 1970s, David had taken on the role of Head of English Regions Drama, Birmingham, soon seen as *the* place for script innovation. Alan Bleasdale's *Boys from the Blackstuff* came from there, as did Philip Martin's *Gangsters*, and *Empire Road*, the first British television drama to be written, directed and acted by a black cast and crew. Then there were the one-offs by Alan Plater, David Hare, Mike Leigh, and the other great Scouse playwright, Willy Russell.

Sometimes knowingly, sometimes not, I had probably watched almost every programme he had had a hand in by the time we sat and chatted in another empty office at the back of the IBA. Yet on a few occasions before this I had tried unsuccessfully to get to see him in Birmingham. In fact, once I was turned away by one of his script editors and branded a fascist. Why? Because I wanted to write a play about the theological concept of angels. It was, he thought, totalitarian paternalism.

I tried pointing out that I was actually from what many viewed as the Socialist Republic of Merseyside and the angels were used metaphorically to show the way society was beginning to face challenges to the status quo. No luck. I then tried pointing out that I was actually from the Catholic Republic of Merseyside and it could be looked upon as a re-examination of the use of metaphor in religious teaching as, perhaps, some of the miracles may well have been. The interpretation of the Ten Commandments was getting a bit fuzzy in an age of equal rights, as where did coveting or desiring a neighbour's live-in partner fit? And they appeared to remain silent on getting wasted on a Saturday night too.

It didn't cut any ice with David's acolyte. Not only was I not allowed near the Drama Department at BBC Pebble Mill, but he met me in reception to deliver his homily and then, metaphorically, cast me out into the drama wilderness. More baffled than annoyed or dispirited, I made my way back to Marxist Merseyside and wrote in my diary: 'Guy today – clown.' Our paths did not cross again for nearly twenty years, when I discovered he was working for me. Unknown to me, someone had hired him as a director. When we were introduced I don't think he remembered me. I never reminded him. Until now, perhaps.

David probably didn't know any of this, nor that I had also been rejected by his successors at *Z Cars*, as by the time I met him I had become Phil Redmond who created *Grange Hill* and won the Writers' Guild of Great Britain's Best Newcomer Award. That was a very proud moment in my life and happened before awards ceremonies became a staple of the industry. Instead of the now typical mantel-piece ornament all I got was an envelope, but within it was a cheque for £150. I went out and bought a fantastic sound system. Brushed aluminium stacking modules, speakers you could sleep on, and rows of knobs and switches to twiddle. It's still in use, thanks to the patience and skill of MerseyTV's techies who, with great forbear-ance, resurrected it a couple of times over the years. I can still remember seeing their shoulders sag as I walked in with one of the various bits under my arm. On reflection, looking across at all the other bits of paper, metal and glass that line the mantelpiece, that cheque was probably the best award I ever had. The music that came out of it stimulated the writing of every other 'award-winning' project.

What I didn't know about David at the time, which he told me in later years, was that everything I had been saying about buying properties to act as sets and installing technology to reduce costs was what he had been trying to do at the BBC. He had wanted to buy an old manor house somewhere in Birmingham, to shoot a drama there. Like me he'd had the idea of buying, not renting, and then having an asset to sell off at the end of the production. The BBC bureaucracy couldn't cope with the common sense of it all, but he knew he could probably do it at Channel 4. So instead of Jeremy's pointed question about how I would produce this proposed long-runner, David's main query was what would it be about?

I said it was probably an update of *Coronation Street*, then becoming known affectionately as *Corrie*, and to some extent his own *Z Cars*, as although both had started out as radical dramas, alongside others like Ken Loach and Tony Garnett's *Days of Hope* and the seminal *Cathy Come Home*, television drama recently had started to become a little less raw. A little more safe. I wanted to do what I had with *Grange Hill* and write about Britain in the 1980s, not some rose-tinted, romanticised view of what life used to be like in the 1950s.

I wanted to explore the drama in real people's lives. I remember when *Corrie* first started, the famous class-conscious scenes of Ken Barlow going to university and coming back having changed, to give his parents a hard time because they had a sauce bottle on the table. Or moments like *Z Cars'* Fancy Smith, played by Brian Blessed, throwing his dinner at the wall. Drama about affairs, pregnancy, divorce or 'anyone for tennis' seemed easy to come by, but what about the tensions in contemporary religion around divorce and contraception? And alongside these great themes, what about the more mundane dramas in life that affect us all? The harshness of unemployment, encapsulated brilliantly by Alan Bleasdale's *Blackstuff*, was one thing, but no matter how brutal times were, unemployment itself was not the main issue.

Of greater anxiety to the 88 per cent of the workforce still in a job, was the *fear* of unemployment. On Merseyside, this was a daily anxiety, affecting everyone. Not finding a job, but keeping the one they had. I was interested in these daily anxieties. Things such as depending on your old car to get you to work and then one day it doesn't pass the MOT test – a not-too-distant memory in my own case as I'd spent many a Sunday afternoon patching up the exhaust on an old 1966 Ford Zodiac MkIII, the posh version of the Zephyr model used in David's own police series, on which I relied to reach my job. The drama in all this was attached to the poverty trap. The inability of people to break the cycle of debt. Neither able to afford a reliable car nor have enough to repair the old one properly.

These were the things I talked to David about. He smiled through that great grey bushy beard of his and suggested I had better put it all down on paper. From that moment I became what I later used to describe, tongue-in-cheek, as the third longest-serving member of Channel 4's workforce. It seemed then, as I had discovered with *Grange Hill* a few years earlier, not just a case of finding myself in the right place, with the right idea, at the right time, but of having the good fortune to be with the right people. That doesn't happen often in life, let alone in television. How it all happened for me and why I ended up sitting in that office with David Rose goes all the way back to 1949, the year I was born, and to the first response learned by rote from the *Penny Catechism*: 'Who made me?'

That theological position survived until the onset of puberty when the creation of life suddenly seems a little more complicated than a spare rib and a bit of magic. By then I also knew that I was 'made in 1949', as part of the post-World War II baby boom during the so-called return to normality after six years of war. How much of a part God played in my creation is open to debate, but according to my parents he kept them both safe during the conflict, despite my dad's having served with Wingate's Chindits in Burma behind Japanese lines. As part of the baby-boom generation I would agree that we have experienced something of a golden age. Although as I write this there is great uncertainty about the world economy, it is highly unlikely that we will fall to the same level of deprivation, or see the global wars, that our parents and grandparents witnessed.

When I started school, in September 1954, at St Dominic's Roman Catholic Infants School in Huyton, just outside Liverpool, the reverberations from the 1939–45 conflict were still being felt and the Cold War was shaping up. Food rationing had only just ended and my most vivid memory of that traumatic first day is refusing to let go of a Bounty Bar my mother had given me for break, in case anyone nicked it.

I guarded it with my life, keeping it between my legs while working at a desk so that by the time break came it was a soggy mess, but tasted great. It wasn't simple fear of losing my treat that motivated me so much as the thought of what it represented. Despite both my parents working, money was always tight. Besides the cash that had undoubtedly been spent on my new school uniform, my mother had found more money to buy chocolate for me, in an attempt to ease my path into this alien world.

There were prayers before and after everything and constant monitoring of attendance at mass, confession, communion and that catechism, as the slow process of piling on the guilt for merely being alive was applied to us. My family would now be described as economic migrants from Wexford, and during that Catholic upbringing it was emphasised by some in the family that we were Irish, not Roman Catholics, with the presumed link to Irish Republicanism kept subdued.

With the benefit of life's only exact science, hindsight, there were signs and stories at family gatherings, but our parents kept it away from us, having, I presume, accepted their own parents' decision to leave and forge new lives in Liverpool. Like many of my generation, I am thankful for those parental decisions that allowed me to have lived in the time and place I have – otherwise I am sure the sense of natural justice that burns in most Scousers would have led me to a very difficult answer to the 'Irish question'.

I did however once congratulate Tony Blair on bringing the end of the 800 years of conflict at least within sight, given that, like an Irish mile, that has still to be determined by the passage of time. In itself this is something often overlooked by those seeking to understand Irish relations: time. While the Irish never forget, the English never remember. Yet I suspect that Tony Blair's real legacy as Prime Minister will be more connected to his chapter in the UK's long and turbulent history with the island of Ireland than to anything else.

My own family came over around 1918 but by 1949 found them-selves among the socially cleansed, those people moved from the city centre during the great post-war slum clearances that swept across the UK to create vast new towns like Basildon, Hemel Hempstead and Welwyn Garden City, as well as swamping old settle-ments with overspill estates like Easterhouse and Castlemilk in Glasgow, Wythenshawe in Manchester, and Kirkby, Skelmersdale and Huyton in Lancashire, but all just outside Liverpool.

We ended up in Huyton, where Stevie G of Liverpool FC, and Joey Barton, and Alan Bleasdale, and, for those of a certain age, Dickie Davies and Rex Harrison, all come from. It is in these towns that you will find and hear some of the strongest Scouse accents. They are hard-core as there is a certain sense there of being sent to colonise the outlying districts. These communities appeared positioned almost like Roman forts, as if to protect the mother city itself from the advance of the Woollybacks of St Helens, Ormskirk, Widnes and, of course, the old foe in Cheshire.

To understand this you have to try and understand Liverpool not just as a place or bureaucratic administrative area, but as a state of mind. Once described as the second city of Empire, but only in London, it is a city that has as its centre-piece one of the finest Neo-classical buildings in the world, according to Prince Charles, in St George's Hall, where carved marble statues of the city's movers and shakers are depicted in senatorial togas. Instead of the Roman SPQR, *Senatus Populusque Romanus* (The Senate and People of Rome), the inscriptions round this temple to nineteenth-century civic splendour read SPQR.

This was no idle vainglory, for by the middle of that century 80 per cent of UK trade and 50 per cent of world trade was flowing through its docks, which stretched for nearly eleven miles at the century's end compared to London's meagre run of two. There was more wealth in Liverpool than anywhere else on earth, one of the reasons why the city still has a rich and deep cultural legacy in its museums, galleries, universities and entrepreneurial spirit. It retains them because it had oligarchs before the term was invented. Then, as now, if they wanted something, they simply bought it.

Why is all this important to my own tale? Because it is hard to grow up in and around a city like Liverpool without absorbing not simply its rich history, but the attitude that built it. The ability to ride the waves, the good and not so good, as prosperity ebbs and flows like the tides of the great river on whose northern bank the city sits. Liverpool has always been on the periphery of everything, while at the centre of nothing. It has seen things come and go, the carpetbaggers pass through, and it has, as any port will, taken its cut and commission and survived by its wits, knowing that for every time of prosperity, austerity will follow, so get what you can while you can.

This is what gives the Scouser their ability to find an angle on any ball, and learn to read between the lines before learning to read; what creates their typical toughness, sometimes harshness, which is too often mistaken for being aggressive or quarrelsome. It is what gives them the need and the ability to face up to and speak about inconvenient truths. This is what Tony Blair accused his wife Cherie of being: a bolshie Scouser. That term dates back to 1911 when fear of trades union strikes caused the then government to send a gunboat up the Mersey to quell the 'Bolshevik Scousers and their general strike'.

Yet, with this hard edge comes a softer, almost sentimental, side that knows life can be brutal, jobs will come and go, but when they do, people should still be treated fairly and with decency. It is, in short, a respect for natural justice. That ability to argue the same point from opposite sides, within the same sentence, and not see the contradiction.

People often say that they find Liverpool a difficult city to work in. What they mean is that it's not an easy city to exploit. If you are open, honest and fair, no matter how pragmatically decisive you have to be, then it is a relatively easy place to be. It is a city that respects the truth, no matter how harsh, but that respect has to be earned. It cannot be bought, as Michael Heseltine found out in his relationship with what many now regard as the People's Republic of Merseyside.

My earliest memory predates that school Bounty Bar but is perhaps linked to it. I was around the age of three when I learned to protect, or at least keep a firm grip on, the things I held most precious. Mum and Dad had taken me and my brother Larry and sister Kathy, by bus and ferry, yes, across the Mersey, for a day out to what was once a great local landmark, New Brighton Fairground. With its own tower and ballroom, venue for all the Merseybeat bands, this was one of the great summer treats that filled the family holiday periods long before the notion of Billy Butlin's holiday camps, never mind package trips abroad.

I had been on one of the fairground stalls and won a large pencil rubber. How, where and at what seems to have escaped the family's collective memory, but they do remember me dressed to the nines and carrying the obligatory bucket and spade. I do not remember anything of the bus and ferry trips, the sandcastle-building on the beach, or the donkey rides, deckchairs, ice-creams and bingo stalls that filled these days out, but I do quite clearly remember walking along the pier towards the ferry and looking admiringly at my now cherished trophy – until someone barged past and knocked it from my hand. Another of those moments you shoot in slow motion as the prize dropped towards the pier decking, to do what you could never reproduce on camera – glide straight through the gap in the wooden decking.

I remember standing staring at the spot, probably incapable of rationalising what had happened except that my trophy was gone. My mum told me many years later I was somewhat upset yet I do not remember that. Only that I had learned a very valuable lesson: keep tight hold of what you cherish.

The next thing I learned was not to walk round the house in my socks when my mum was doing what most mums seemed always to be doing – altering or adjusting our clothes. No binning and a quick trip to Matalan or Primark for her. Recycling then meant knowing how to 'make do and mend'. There were usually needles and pins everywhere, which may have been the inspiration for, or at least created the empathy with, The Searchers' great number of the same name. Still, one day I was wearing no shoes and I stood on a sewing needle.

I didn't actually realise for a day or two. My foot was sore, but not too troublesome until I suddenly felt a sharp pain in it and couldn't put it flat on the floor. Informing my mum and dad of this, long after the sewing basket had been put away, I was told I had probably stood on something, right, and it would pass in a day or two, wrong. It was only when my mother found me crawling, literally, on hands and knees to a neighbour's house to watch what was then the first television set in our road, that she suspected there might be something badly wrong. It was also, perhaps, the first indication of my future, though neither of us realised it.

A visit to the GP, and an examination which would probably now contravene international conventions on interrogation techniques, had me both in tears and on my way to Alder Hey Hospital where an X-ray revealed I did indeed have a needle in my foot. Not only that, but it had gone in at such an angle and to such a depth that the only way it was coming out was by surgical removal. Parental guilt trips all round.

The stay in hospital is a bit hazy in my mind except that I remember waking up one time and being able to see the stars in the night sky. My bed had been moved on to an open-air balcony, presumably as it was believed the fresh air was good for me or it may have been due to overcrowding. No one explained and no one asked. You didn't in those days. You just got on with things. Made do and mend.

This even extended to the games we played and, yes, I am going to repeat the point many others of a certain age have made: that we could play out in the street without fear or hindrance from either antisocial behaviour orders, curfews or passing cars. There were the usual squabbles, and harassment from neighbours when the games got too loud, boisterous or invasive as, looking back, it must have been really irritating to have spent a whole weekend working on your garden, only to have a football constantly decimating the dahlias and roses. Official regulation, though, was a distant concept.

Instead, social order was maintained by the usual threats of bursting the ball or telling our parents, but by and large the neighbours were reasonably tolerant. They knew that their own kids were probably involved or, if they weren't, would be indoors shattering the peace there. In fact many was the time, especially during school holidays when both our parents were working, that we were told to go out and play and not to come back until teatime.

This meant we often roamed miles from home, living as we did in what was then the last street of the urban conurbation. At the end of our road the city stopped and the countryside began, so I grew up drifting between urban vandalism and countryside high spirits. Damming drainage ditches to create makeshift swimming ponds or swinging on trees and snapping a branch is high-spirited. Hanging round street corners or swinging on a lamppost is antisocial vandalism.

In the 1950s cars were still few and far between and food was bought from farmers selling door to door, a form of mobile farmers' market, I suppose. We were able to play football or rounders or impro- vised games of chase that revolved around various mechanisms like knocking down piles of broken roof tiles or kicking an old tin can to start and finish the games. Perhaps every hour or so we would all stop to let an occasional car pass, but then get right back to the game.

This unrestricted access to the road as a playground did have unfortunate consequences for me personally, though. I became prob- ably one of the first traffic statistics on our estate when, running out from behind a farmer's van, I was knocked down by one of those infrequent passing cars. Again, I don't remember much about it except waking up in my 'dad's chair', wrapped in one of those massive red blankets all ambulances carried then. That was it. No after-checks. No X-rays. No MRI. Just a quick check over and a firm, 'He'll be all right.' Then a really good telling off for causing so much trouble for the nice ambulance men, and a visit to church to thank God and my Guardian Angel for looking after me. It occurred to me to wonder at the time, if the Guardian Angel was that good, why couldn't he have warned me about the car? Like losing my prized rubber, I assumed it was meant to teach me a lesson. And it did. Look right, left, and right again.

If this parental response to childhood trauma seems a bit harsh these days, it didn't then. My mum and dad, as in most households locally, both had to work, and therefore anything that either interrupted or threatened their working patterns had to be dealt with quickly. There was never any question of charging off to sit in A&E for hours on end. It was usually Mum, again as in most of the local households, who would be around in these times of trauma as I didn't see that much of my dad. He worked variously as a bus driver, ambulance driver and bread delivery man, and his shift working patterns meant he was often up and out before we got up, or else he would have gone out when we got back from school. Even when he was working a typical sort of day, it meant an early start, and then in the evening he would be out at some form of church-related function.

This is one reason I think the theory of the male role model, or lack of it, being connected to all society's ills is a bit suspect. Yes, perhaps to some it is relevant, but the working-class model then was that dads were seldom seen and matriarchal authority ruled. 'Wait until your father gets home' was almost a catchphrase, but although you knew he would enforce discipline, you also knew it was your mother's discipline he would be enforcing. I'm not sure much has really changed there.

There was, however, respect for the wartime experiences of our male relatives. We knew, even if they refused to talk about it, that they had endured things during the war that we only saw in films. My dad served in the King's Regiment (Liverpool), which helped form Wingate's Chindits. They were sent deep into Burma, to cause as much disruption as possible to the Japanese while fighting their way out again.

He would occasionally, but very rarely, give us glimpses of that time when talking about a three-month march through the jungle, losing his wedding ring crossing the Irrawaddy river, or coming up against what they thought was the Japanese Imperial Guard. The latter he would always say with a chuckle, because they had been told that all Japanese were around five foot tall, but he found himself face to face with none under six foot. I have since learned that this was a popular misconception, and size was not a pre-requisite for joining the Imperial Guard. Other Japanese units, like the 58th Infantry Regiment that operated close to India, would have had well-built six-footers in their ranks.

What was beyond doubt, though, was my dad's dislike of chicken, Winston Churchill and Errol Flynn, with the common factor being Burma. Churchill because he treated it, as my dad and many others thought, as the forgotten war. Errol Flynn because of the film *Objective Burma*. Hollywood then, as it still does today, in true 'never let a few facts get in the way of a good story', approached the subject matter simply as a good yarn, in which Errol almost single-handedly liberates the country without a British accent to be heard. The film was actually banned in Britain when first released for this very reason. There was outrage at the way it completely ignored the British role in the campaign, and, of course, the high death and casualty rates in units like my dad's.

That was one memory that stayed with me as I began to take a more than passing interest in film and TV production, one of the reasons *Grange Hill, Brookside* and *Hollyoaks* were always very well researched. No matter what tale you want to tell as a writer, there is a certain obligation to be as truthful and respectful as possible to the real people whose lives you may be fictionalising.

My dad's dislike of chicken stemmed from having to eat it every day for a year while recovering from his time in the Burmese jungle. He once told me that he and the rest of his squad were so fed up with eating jellied chicken out of tins that one day when they spotted a monkey on the edge of the camp, a mission was organised to capture, cook and eat it. He said he had no recollection of what it tasted like except that it wasn't chicken. His dislike of it was something that stayed with him for the rest of his life and, whenever catering for Dad, chicken was never on the menu.

Another legacy of the war was the residual resentment, bordering on racism, felt towards anything either German or Japanese. My mum felt more strongly about the Germans because she had lived through the bombing of Liverpool, even down to having been strafed by the Luftwaffe while she and a friend were running for an air-raid shelter. Dad obviously felt more animosity towards the Japanese, especially as his brother, my Uncle Paddy, had been at the Fall of Singapore and was held in the infamous Changi jail for most of the war. We never got to the bottom of what exactly Uncle Paddy went through there, but even in the heat of those English summers we still reminisce over, he would sit huddled in front of a three-bar electric fire, trying to keep warm.

Being exposed to these influences left a deep impression on us as a family and meant we never bought Japanese or German goods. This was something that stayed with me until I went back to university as a so-called mature student and studied economic history in more depth, eventually starting to accept that as part of any peace process there needs to be trade between old enemies. If we hadn't helped rebuild the German and Japanese economies, as the then allies failed to do after the First World War, they would soon have become breeding grounds for extremist politics and we would have been back in conflict once again.

It is interesting that even though our politicians espouse this theory in support of our continuing engagement in areas like Iraq, Afghanistan and now, no doubt, in Libya, they seem unable to make the obvious connection with the events of 2011 when large areas of our inner cities saw the outbreak of riotous looting. People need to feel the sense of purpose and community that comes with widespread employment. That applies to our own inner cities as much as it did to post-war Germany and Japan. In fact the post-war overseas economic rebuilding policy was so successful that by the time *Brookside* came along all the equipment was Japanese and my car was German.

Although in recent years the local authority ward where I was born, Page Moss, has become one of the most deprived in Europe, never mind the UK, at the time I was growing up, we never thought of ourselves as 'deprived'. Compared to now we probably weren't. We had gardens and privet hedges and trees, all well kept by the neighbours and ourselves, while the council seemed to do a reasonable job of keeping the streets and pavements in good condition. Crucially, all our parents were employed and the council was reasonably well funded. The area started to decline as the jobs started to decline, and with that came the twin pressures of poverty and increased social need. At the time, though, it seemed to me a good place to live, far from the stereotypical Scousology of grimy terraces and dingy night clubs. That was why I set *Brookside* a mile or so away from where I was born and raised: to reflect the greener side of living in a post-war garden city suburb. I used to go home for lunch as it was cheaper and we didn't qualify for free school meals, although even if we had I doubt my parents would have applied. There was a certain stigma attached to the 'free schoolies'. I remember at an early age thinking this odd, especially as my parents were very active in raising money for the church and helping run things like the second-hand clothes shop and mother and baby groups. It only came to me later that they were making that same distinction we all make throughout life: helping those who need it, but baulking at those who simply expect to be given it.

Going home for lunch also exposed me to lunchtime TV, for since my pavement crawl we too had our own rented set, and many a lunchtime I sat in front of it with a bowl of tomato soup, dunking bread and watching one of the many BBC interludes, the short films showing waves, or kittens, or a potter working at his wheel, that were transmitted between the real programmes. There was one in particular that used to fascinate me no matter how many times I saw it: London to Brighton in 4 Minutes.

It was simply a high-speed film shot from the front of a steam train as it left London and travelled to Brighton. I was so taken with this piece of film-making that in the mid-1980s I actually began making an updated version, but from Liverpool to London – partly, I confess, to keep reminding the London mob that Liverpool was not on the far side of the universe. This time though, to reflect societal change, we would shoot from the front of a train, bus and plane. Halfway through we discovered the BBC had already remade the London–Brighton journey in 1983. Being too tied up with launching *Brookie* we had missed this, so the project was shelved as, in a four-channel age, there would have been no buyer. Today of course we would have found another outlet, if not online or by download. If you want to see both the original and the 1983 versions, they are on YouTube. But what isn't?

I still think a film mixing rail, road and air travel would be cool, and my fascination with this film was probably another early clue as to where my future career lay, but at the age of eight my life was dominated by being an altar boy: serving mass, benediction, and mastering the art of a five-chain incense thurible. (Not so long ago I attended the funeral of one of my many Irish cousins. It was one of those occasions when the dwindling clan gathers and promises to stay in touch, though lack of time always seems to prevent it, and I took the opportunity to see if I could still handle the thurible. I was delighted to find that I could.) The cassocks and surplices we boys wore were home-made, and even with these religious garments fashion was everything. Who had the best pleats and lace in their surplice and whether the cassock was of wool, cotton or man-made fibre. Whatever, the only way to get the candle wax off the material was with a hot iron and brown paper.

Status was all. Who was senior to whom determined which function you performed during the various ceremonies, with the main prizes being thurible at benediction and communion during mass when, ungodly though it was, you had the opportunity to stare at the various cleavages bending over the altar rail. Along with the angels comedy I also wrote a play about my time as an altar boy but this time the then Head of Plays at the BBC, James Cellan Jones, decided it was too offensive to Catholics. When I again pointed out that it was actually about my own Catholic upbringing, he switched his objection to the fact that 'others would feel obliged to be offended on Catholics' behalf'.

This was obviously interpreted by my still Marxist-influenced Scouse mind as establishment rejection. Another case of not what the system wanted. After all, Cellan Jones was wearing sandals to work, without socks, and, above all else, a cravat. It is more than likely that in reality the play was not good enough and he was introducing me gently to the BBC's way of never actually saying no, while never actually saying yes.

Like all good bureaucracies the BBC relies on the passage of time and user-fatigue to sidestep the awkwardness of having to say no too often. This is why I always found it easier to deal with ITV, as you could see the knife coming straight for your chest. The Americans are even better at it. They say no before you even finish the ask, which helped me deliver my own production mantra: the second-best answer is always a very fast no. Because then you are free to move on and focus on other things.

One of the perks of my being on the altar was the weekday requiem masses that took place from around 8.30 a.m. This meant that the mass and funeral rites would finish around 9.15 a.m. and then you would travel with the priest to the cemetery for the interment. Depending upon the size of the family turnout and cortège, this could take until 10.30, meaning you wouldn't get back into school until breaktime. No questions asked.

It did mean however that you were exposed to a lot of other people's grief. You also learned how to spot which one of the mourners was likely to try and throw themself on the coffin as it was lowered into the ground, and be out of the way in time. The undertakers were, naturally, quite tuned into all this and at every funeral one would always be at the spouse's elbow, just in case. It also meant that while I was able to miss the first few lessons occasionally, usually catechism, I was also learning some of the more pragmatic details about funerals.

While waiting for the priest to give me a lift back to school, I would stand and watch the gravediggers get back to work as soon as the last mourner left. Quickly the trappings, or what I would now term the set dressings, of the interment scene were pulled back. The flowers and wreaths were set to one side, the boards around the grave were lifted, and sometimes one of the gravediggers would drop down into it to remove the ornate handles from the coffins, which would be handed back to the undertakers to reuse.

Like everything in life, though, perks have to be paid for somewhere along the line, and my payback came when I got to the ripe old age of ten and was deemed old and reliable enough to serve the 6.30 a.m. mass – at the cemetery. This was provided for those who wanted to attend daily mass but had early starts and couldn't attend the scheduled 8.30 a.m. mass at the main church. It wasn't that bad in the summer, but I'm sure forcing a ten-year-old to wander through a gothic cemetery in the darkness of winter would now qualify as child abuse.

Yet I and a few other boys just got on with it. There was no question of getting a lift or catching a bus the three miles to the cemetery. My dad would have left around 4.00 a.m. as at that time he worked delivering bread to the shops, so I would be woken about 5.30 by my mum. She was a school cleaner and had to start work at 6. She didn't have as far to go, so I would leave before her without breakfast, so I could take communion, and then be given a lift back home from the priest. On many occasions I had to stay on for a funeral and although I got into school late, it was never quite the same after getting up at 5.30 and not having breakfast. This early ritual would serve me well in later years, though. You can get so much done in the hours before the rest of the world wakes.

★

Being involved early on with the Church meant that I was soon on the path of many a young male Catholic: towards the priesthood. Around my tenth birthday the call came. As the eldest boy, it was time for me to be offered to the Church. So off I went along with practically my whole class, to an open or induction day at the Upholland seminary, St Joseph's, to the north-east of Liverpool, another marathon journey for those without a car.

I remember being very impressed with the college itself, which was set in around 200 acres of parkland, and the hard (but soft) sell about what a great life it was in the clergy. I was nearly won over by the setting and snooker tables, until they showed us the communal showers and casually threw in the fact that we would be expected to shower in cold water. No way! If there was one thing I hated about our life at home, it was the constant rationing of hot water and only being able to have a bath once a week. The horror of living with cold showers for years was compounded by the fact that there was talk at home of our soon having hot water 'at the flick of a switch'.

I won't repeat the often-told working-class tales of waking up to find the curtains frozen to the window or ice in the toilet but yes, it was outside. Suffice to say, hot-water rationing was still the greatest deprivation we knew. Even having the toilet outside wasn't as bad for us as others had it, as at least ours was in a porch as part of the house. Worse than that was having the coal cupboard in the kitchen. This meant that if my mum wasn't hovering on the coal-man's shoulder when he dumped the coal into it, the whole kitchen would disappear under a black coal-dust cloud. It would then be our fault, and our job to clean it up.

Then came the white-heat technology of the 1950s nuclear age when we were promised unlimited electricity at virtually no cost. Instant heat. Instant hot water. It meant we could take out our gas-heated dolly tub and replace it with a twin-tub washing machine. And we would no longer have to wait for my dad to build up the coal fire so the back boiler would heat up the water. An electric immersion heater would be doing that instead. No matter what the Church said about duty, I was not going to give this up for a life of cold showers. I would rather risk being damned, I decided.

While I may have baulked at the cold showers, the impression St Joseph's made stayed with me – its marble-clad chapel, cloisters, and atmospheric, medieval-looking library, the sort depicted in films like

The Name of the Rose or the Harry Potter series – to the extent that forty years later, while looking for premises in which to expand MerseyTV, on hearing that St Joseph's was up for sale, Alexis and I tried to buy it. But it turned out it was too near the flight paths for Manchester Airport; shooting there would have been a nightmare. End of romantic circle. And, of course, my rejection of life at the seminary probably owed more to my growing doubts about the faith itself than the seminary's lack of hot water.

These doubts started when I was serving at the biggest occasion in the Catholic calendar, the Paschal or Easter Vigil at Midnight Mass. This is when all the pomp, ceremony, regalia and theatre of the Church is on display, in celebration of Christ's resurrection.

The Easter Midnight Mass was the great occasion for those of us still serving as altar boys and there was both fierce competition and huge resentment about who did what. Everyone wanted to play one of the key roles, like carry the incense thurible or processional crucifix, or act as the holy water carrier or one of the acolytes. To our constant annoyance our dads and uncles from the Catholic Men's Club would frequently take these plum jobs from us. We were sent to the back as makeweights in the procession. Where were all this lot when I was walking through the cemetery at six in the morning? I wondered.

All this was turning over in my head one Easter as we processed round the packed church which could hold over a thousand people, or more when they were crammed in at the back and sides. There we were in all our finery: new or freshly cleaned, pressed and starched cassocks and surplices. The priest in his gold-embroidered chasuble and silk humeral veil, carrying the benediction monstrance beneath a silken canopy, all to the accompaniment of singing from the choir and congregation. It was a splendid piece of liturgical theatre but at one particular moment, around the fifth or sixth of the fourteen Stations of the Cross, the depiction of Christ's final hours that adorns all Catholic churches, I looked across to see the silk-clad priest being blessed with holy water and incense, and wondered how all this pantomime fitted with the tales the missionaries told us of pagan rites and devil-worship ceremonies that they had had to exorcise from the continents of Africa, India, Asia and South America.

They would show us slides of faraway exotic tribes that they had civilised by bringing them the Catholic bible and catechism. Among these slideshows there would invariably be examples of the sort of

20

pagan practices and ceremonies they had banished, but none of them appeared anything like as elaborate as our own performance that night.

By the time the procession reached the ninth or tenth Station, my almost sacrilegious thoughts had progressed further. If God is omniscient and omnipresent, as we were taught, why do we have to do all this stuff? I asked myself. In fact, why do we have to walk through cemeteries or even get out of bed on Sunday morning to tell him we love him? Wouldn't he just, well, know?

If they had let me take the five-chain thurible I would have been too preoccupied to puzzle out all this. As it was, by the time we got to the side chapel where the holy water was to be consecrated, I was on a bit of an intellectual roll. There was also, on reflection, another early sign that a life of TV production lay ahead of me. The parish priest was officiating and two of the other priests had opened the ornately carved oak chest where the water was kept, and lifted out what looked like a galvanised zinc tank similar to the one that stored cold water in the loft at home. Against all the other finery, pomp and procession, this seemed a bit of a let down. They could have done with a better 'prop'.

Once blessed, the water was to be lowered back into the tank but I noticed a strange expression on one priest's face. It was a look almost of ecstasy – and then I saw that he had cut his hand on the tank's metal handle. Blood was running down and dripping into the water, to be diluted into spidery trails. I realised that he was undergoing a form of religious experience as the organ and the singing reached their crescendo, no doubt sharing some of Christ's own suffering on the cross. This may be my later writer's or producer's interpretation, but what I do know was clearly in my mind then was, 'I'm not going to bless myself with that water any more.'

Needless to say, my theological doubts received short shift at home. It took me until my eighteenth birthday before I was finally able to confront my mum and tell her I was no longer attending mass. I wasn't struck down from above either. Although it strained our relationship for years to come.

While being on the altar did have its perks, like cleavage spotting and getting in to school late, it also had its problems, the main one being that it marked you out as a perfectly legitimate target for the school bullies. Most of these you could shrug off, but there was one guy we used to call Digger. The name was appropriate, never questioned, and always avoided in conversation with him if possible.

One time he decided that everyone should kneel before him and be lightly whacked on the head with a dinner tray. The alternative was much worse, so gradually he worked his way through the ranks until one day I found myself cornered by him and his crew. Taking a look at the odds I decided I had better conform, but instead of a light whack he really cracked me round the head, bringing tears to my eyes. This was obviously a better reaction than expected so soon I found myself cornered once again by his hunting party.

It was one of those stand or fall moments I later included in every teenage drama, when you literally have your back to the wall, no way out, caught between the rock and the headcase. The only thing I could do was pick up a house brick which was lying nearby and threaten Digger with it. For a moment there was a stand off between us, with the typical feints and lunges to test what each other would do. However, the street instinct in him knew I was panicking and not really up for a fight, so he lunged at me. I decided to throw the brick over his head, hoping he would jump to one side, creating enough of a gap for me to get away. It almost worked. But not quite.

As I threw it, he jumped backwards, not sideways, and took the brick right on his head. He went down with blood flowing everywhere. By this time the usual gang had been attracted to the scene and word was going round that 'Reddo's bricked Digger'. The staff soon arrived, Digger went to hospital for stitches and I was sent to the Headmaster.·

Fortunately, because I was the altar boy and Digger was the school bully, I got off with a severe tongue-lashing. I'd also like to report that Digger never bothered me again, which he didn't, in school. That came a couple of years later and was an autobiographical detail I later included in the teenage drama series *What Now?*

At the time of that initial confrontation I was approaching the other thing I had been groomed for, apart from the seminary, the eleven-plus examination. Although I wasn't exactly a swot, I never had any trouble with exams and was always in the top half-dozen or so, to the extent that, along with a couple of my friends, I was put forward a year at the age of nine, to spend two years in what would now be called Year 6. By the time the actual examination came round it didn't seem like such a big deal, except for one thing: my elder sister, Kathy, had taken it and failed.

She was considered 'cleverer' than me so expectations were not that high. When I passed everyone was delighted, including Kathy, but a few years later my younger brother, Larry, also failed. I was no brighter than either of them, and it was Kathy who won the prizes at school for English and Larry who brought home the sports trophies . . . a perfect example of how imperfect education selection processes can be.

Having cleared this selection hurdle, I was also expected to go to one of the two Catholic grammar schools in Liverpool, St Edward's (The Eddies) or St Francis Xavier's (SFX). However, this too was not to be. Instead, in the Socialist Jerusalem of Huyton, I was selected to be part of a group that would form the basis of the top quartile, or grammar stream, in the great comprehensive experiment of the 1960s. I was to be among the first 2 per cent selected to go through the comprehensive education system. I only fully understood the significance, and tragedy, of this years later when studying the sociology of education.

While my parents were delighted that I had passed the eleven-plus, they were slightly anxious about the suggestion I should go to the planned St Kevin's Roman Catholic Comprehensive School for Boys (aka St Kev's), because it was in Kirkby, twelve miles away from our home in Huyton. The parish priest convinced them this was in fact the best thing that could happen to me, which was, as time would prove, actually true if not perhaps in the way he'd envisaged. As we were often told, God moves in mysterious ways.

What it meant in practice was that I would have to be bussed in to school. That in turn meant I would be back to early starts. Every day. As Mum and Dad left for work early, I was expected to get myself up and be out of the house by 7.15 for the two-mile walk to the bus pick-up point. I would join thirty other transportees for the fifty-minute journey to school, to be deposited there at around quarter to nine, in time for morning assembly. The return journey would result in my getting home around 5.30.

This meant that in the seven years I was at St Kev's, I saw very little of my parents, while my brother and sister, who went to the local secondary modern, could roll out of bed at 8.30 and later on be home by 4. I often regretted passing that exam, pondering on how clever my siblings really were!

As with the cemetery walks, in the spring and summer months the journey was not that bad, but in winter and autumn the hardship began as soon as I got out of bed. First thing, along with the frozen curtains, came the freezing cold floors. Covering the floorboards was cheap linoleum, except in the kitchen which had hard quarry tiles. Although our house was not the classic two up, two down, for we had four rooms upstairs counting the bathroom, they were all cold and inhospitable at 5.30 in the morning.

As the toilet was outside, I would gather up my school uniform and mountaineer my way from the bedroom to the kitchen, trying not to put my feet on the cold lino or quarry tiles. As I grew taller, I could actually get from bedroom to kitchen by using a 'chimneying' technique to straddle the wooden skirting boards, so narrow were the stairs and hallway. I would then light the grill to warm the kitchen, and get washed in the sink, hoping my mum had flicked the switch for a bit before she left. If not, cold water.

When in 1960 I learned I was going to St Kev's though, I was just happy that I got an extra two weeks' holiday as, apparently, the school wasn't quite ready. This turned out to be a bit of an understatement. They had only just started to build it. It was finally finished and formally opened in 1966, by the then Prime Minister and our local MP, Harold Wilson.

I was by then in the Lower Sixth. England had won the World Cup. We took more notice of that, and the only thing I was mildly impressed by was the fact that the Prime Minister was actually the bloke my mum had introduced me to once in our hall at home. He had obviously been out canvassing and on the knocker, even if he did seem even posher than our Headmaster and priests.

After that extra two weeks, jubilant at having escaped the clutches of the Jesuits, I discovered I would be facing an even more formidable force: teachers who had been *rejected* by the Jesuits. It is an old Catholic joke that sadistic teachers are those deemed too cruel even for the Jesuits, but the religious zeal displayed by some of our St Kev's teachers put many of the local priests to shame. It was probably this fervour that led many of us to question, and eventually reject, the formalised notion of religion. It was also where my real education began. And where *Grange Hill* came from.

2

The Backstory (1960–66)

'Well, Redmond, I would never have put you down as someone with ambition.' – *Skull Nelson, sixth-form tutor*

A question often asked of me over the years was whether *Grange Hill* was autobiographical. I often sidestepped it by saying that I couldn't answer as I needed to protect both the innocent and the guilty. However, like sponges, writers absorb everything – to be squeezed out again at some future date, to help form a believable character or give a plot some texture. Perhaps, on first meeting, we should give the same sort of warning the police do when arresting someone: 'Everything you say or do may be taken down and used in a work of fiction . . .' As one of the first educational pioneers, perhaps guinea pigs, in the comprehensive system, this was bound to be a formative influence on me. Yet I can honestly say only a couple of my real-life school adventures were used as storylines – most of them wouldn't have been allowed under broadcasting regulations.

I used one early on: in Episode 4 of Series 1 of *Grange Hill*, the now infamous internet hit about the class running wild in the swimming pool. It's also on YouTube, if you want to see it. The storyline had Tucker & Co. sneaking back into the pool after the teacher had taken an injured classmate to the medical centre, and proceeding to run riot. It created a bit of a furore at the time, with a representative of the National Union of Teachers complaining that it showed teachers in a bad light.

I remember the union's letter of complaint saying something like, '. . . *even if a child had had a leg torn off, a teacher would never leave other children alone near water*'. At the time it left me wondering what sort of ethical position that was, suggesting they'd leave a child to bleed to death rather than break a rule. Yet, thirty years on, we are all familiar with stories of police officers accused of allowing a child to drown in a pond, or fire officers not rushing to rescue people, for fear of breaking their Health & Safety procedures. But at my secondary school our sports teacher did break the rule about leaving pupils unsupervised and no one criticised or complained. Our classmate was treated properly and the rest of us had a great time. Then we all got detention.

It is interesting reflecting on that episode now, for the irony is that although I shared the kids' frustrations about what could and couldn't be shown, it is doubtful that sort of episode would now get made for fear of breaching the regulations on taste, decency, imitable behaviour and so on. What I did try to do at the time though was to present an approximation of what life at school was like for the majority, never mind whether it was at comp, grammar, or even a private school. *Grange Hill* worked in this way because it wasn't about education as such, but about all the social inter-actions formed by the comings and goings between lessons or on the way to and from the school itself.

The aim was always to give an impression of what it was like to transfer from the junior school to the 'big school'. Regardless of whether the true-to-life swearing was missing, or the slang was not quite right locally, the emotions were universal. Which people, lessons or teachers you liked or didn't, which liked you or didn't, and, naturally, who fancied whom and who didn't.

But while many of Tucker Jenkins's escapades were, if not auto-biographical, then hugely derivative of my time at St Kevin's, and while, on reflection, it may have been the best thing that ever happened to me, at the time it felt far from that. It felt as though I'd been lifted out of my own community and deposited in a totally alien landscape. Like that Bounty Bar on my first day at primary school, my memories of the first morning at St Kev's are still vivid. In the case of the latter it seemed more like the opening of a post-apocalypse sci-fi movie.

Our bus pulled up in a road opposite what appeared to be a

building site. This was the 'not-quite-ready' school, now shrouded in smoke from a huge fire around which a clutch of Neanderthal-like shapes appeared to huddle, prodding and poking and throwing odds and ends into the flames. As the bus pulled away thirty fresh-faced eleven-year-olds were left behind in their sparkling uniforms, short trousers, polished satchels and regulation peaked caps. Perfect victims.

As though smelling fresh meat, the Neanderthals began to stand erect and make their way towards us through the swirling smoke. As they drew closer they seemed even more menacing as their leather jackets and jeans and teddy-boy quiffs became apparent. Today they'd be described as feral youths. We were soon to learn that they were the Fourth Form, but didn't want to be.

It was not long before our caps were being tossed hither and thither and an impromptu Health & Safety demo made it clear why a) a satchel should never be worn on your back, unless you like being dragged down the street by it, and b) you should beware of the hard peak of a folded cap as it was a very efficient weapon. Fortunately it was also not long before a couple of teachers emerged from the smokescreen and uttered a phrase I would get to know quite well over the years: 'You boys, put that lad down!'

In September 1960 St Kevin's was a twelve-form entry school, which meant it took about 360 new pupils every year, eventually growing both in square footage and number of inmates until, with around 2,000 pupils, it became the biggest boys' school in the UK. It was a massive vision and a flagship project for the Catholic Church, perhaps then at the zenith of its influence on post-war Britain. It also epitomised the early and almost evangelical madness of the comprehensive system, as part of the 'big is beautiful boom' of the 1960s.

Everywhere you looked there were big schools, big hospitals, big housing estates. St Kevin's itself, in the heart of Kirkby new town, stood opposite a row of five twenty-two-storey tower blocks. It was part of the great socialist utopia, and that was the problem. Everything was too big. Building on that scale made things too expensive and difficult to maintain. It wasn't the ideology that was wrong, simply the fact that the technology was not then available to service or sustain it – now common things like LED lighting and computer-managed lift systems with auto-call-out for maintenance were not even dreamt about. Today, nearly every monument to this building boom has been, or is in the process of being, demolished and replaced with buildings on a more human scale, including those embedded in the early *Brookside* title sequence. Three of the five tower blocks opposite my old school have gone, and even the school itself closed in 1987, to be replaced with low-rise housing. One of the roads is named St Kevin's Drive as a historical reminder.

That closure probably says more about the decline of the Catholic Church than it does about the turmoil so often visited upon education in the name of progress, like the Building Schools for the Future programme that saw first Knowsley and then Liverpool replace all its existing schools with Learning Centres. Now, as then, the call is for better facilities, amenities, teaching, education and opportunity. In fact, St Kevin's had all those things. It eventually had fantastic facilities and great staff, but it was simply too big. Not just in terms of its physical size, but in the gulf that existed between the policy-makers, teachers, pupils and parents. They all circled the same sun of equal educational opportunity, while living on separate planets.

The policy-makers were looking for a quick and efficient way of delivering mass education. The Catholic Church was looking for a flagship project to project Catholic values. The pupils and parents were looking for a decent education that would lead to better jobs. And, as I soon found out, like the old saying about Britain and America, the policy-makers and staff were separated from kids and parents by a common language. They all agreed the priority was education, education, education. Well, who wouldn't? But for the kids and their parents that meant training for jobs, while for the teaching staff and policy-makers it meant a more rounded education. The kids and parents wanted jobs. The staff and policy-makers wanted qualifications. The staff and parents realised there were no jobs to be had. The staff and policy-makers realised there was a skills shortage. The pupils and parents knew there was no hope. The teachers and policy-makers decided a new policy was required. Sound familiar? It should do. It is the same debate we are having now, and the same one that underpinned the 1870 Education Act, regarded as having laid the foundations for the model of state education.

In 1960, though, we were on the threshold of a socialist Jerusalem and in thrall to new technology, so even if our school wasn't finished we were going to participate in another brave new world. It was all part of the great renewal programme for Britain and we were going to be the first to benefit from it, even if this was a bit difficult to believe on that first day.

Although supposedly a new model for schooling and state-of-the-art for the 1960s, St Kevin's still had all the structures and trappings of an old-fashioned grammar. It had houses, house halls, prefects, sets and streams. The Head even wore a scholar's gown. What it didn't have was proper classrooms. These turned out to be the house halls themselves, subdivided by hardboard partitions so that you could hear what was going on in the next class at all times. We also ate lunch there, so that when you came back for the first lesson of the afternoon you learned to check the desks and chairs for custard and cabbage spills.

The houses were all named after saints and I was designated to St Gregory, on which I didn't have any opinion, but the house colour was Manchester City blue, on which I did. By this time my dad had done the usual Scouse thing of introducing my brother and me, for it was still a man's game back then, to the football, and as was also the custom we went to Liverpool one week and Everton the next, when he could afford it. There was never any money for away trips so everyone just alternated between the home matches. My dad was a Red so I followed him, but my brother, probably from typical sibling rivalry, chose to become a Bluenose and follow Everton. So Manchester City blue? Ah, well, I'd put it down as a penance and offer up the suffering to God.

Geography lessons were always the bright spots in the timetable as our teacher agreed with us that it was terrible trying to teach and learn in hardboard classrooms, and would instead set us tasks, like sketching out maps of Kirkby so we would get to know the area. We all enjoyed these lessons, especially as the teacher, Mr McGough, was not like the other members of staff. He was younger, more fun, wore brightly coloured striped scarves and had mad hair. He would also spend a lot of time sitting quietly at the front of the class, writing in an exercise or rough workbook. Later I discovered that Mr McGough was *the* Roger McGough, and we came to know each other better nearly fifty years on when I was able to call upon the old school network and persuade him, without much difficulty, to help us during Liverpool's Capital of Culture year in 2008.

Most of the school was still a huge construction site. The staff and administration block was complete, as was part of the ground floor of the general teaching block, a huge three-storey building that would one day contain around thirty classrooms. Initially this was home to the Neanderthals and somewhere the rest of us avoided. Other promised buildings, like the sports hall, swimming pool, assembly hall, science and arts and crafts blocks, were in various stages of construction, and to get from one side of the site to the other we were supposed to walk round these construction areas. Needless to say, we often took the most direct route, usually while following one of the teachers across the building site. Health & Safety was a thing of the future.

We were also taught survival skills. Informally in the playground, but more formally in the classroom we were forced, quite literally, to do woodwork, metalwork, and in my own case engineering workshop, theory and practice. Here you were taught what damage everyday tools like chisels, saws and electric drills can do to the human body – although looking back on some of the guys at school, while this was welcome knowledge to them, for society at large it may not have been such a good idea.

However, it did instil in us both an understanding of and a respect for safety, and without our having to be lectured, hectored, or dressed up like the still-to-be-invented Duplo Men and Bob the Builder. You only cut or burned yourself, or switched on a lathe with the tightening key still in the chuck, once. When you had felt and seen that key fly out of the lathe and embed itself in the concrete-block walls, you quickly realised that 'sir' might, after all, have a point.

Amazingly, among all the lathes, metal presses, cutters and forges there were very rarely casualties. The more devout put this down solely to God's beneficent watchfulness. The less devout put it down to sheer luck and the fear of having to go home and tell your parents you had maimed either yourself or someone else.

Still there was one occasion that brought both believers and doubters together in wondering about a higher purpose when, above the din made in the workshop, a huge crash was heard inside the metal storeroom. Silence . . . then a general rush to see what had happened. We found that the racking that held all the steel bars had collapsed. Not forward but sideways, so that the racks full of steel bars and rods, varying in thickness from one-eighth to two inches (it was around 1964 and pre-decimalisation), had slid sideways and were now pinning an extremely white and shaking classmate to the wall. Unharmed.

How he had escaped without a graze, never mind being impaled, remains a mystery considering that probably a ton of metal had come flying straight at him, but the incident was soon being used to illustrate the mysterious way in which the Lord works His wonders. Ironically, although it had seen fit to spare a boy's life, divine inter- vention did not stretch so far as to protect the hapless victim from being berated and beaten for going to get a piece of steel without permission. He also had a hard time at home once his parents heard how 'stupid' he'd been. In those days we learned what the word 'accident' meant the hard way. Now an incident like that would be a court case and/or a TV drama. No one did it again though.

The informal part of our training was the natural outcome of St Kev's being the biggest all-boys school in the UK. With that amount of teenage testosterone about, life became, if not exactly a battle for survival, something pretty close to it. This was not merely the result of our being an all-male institution, but also stemmed from the tribal differences. There were boys from the various districts of Kirkby itself, like Northwood, Southdene and Tower Hill. Then there were the likes of us from Huyton, Prescot and the outlying districts of Liverpool. Each tribe had its own rivalries and pecking orders, and for the first year or so these differences were played out in the corridors, playgrounds and especially after school. Hardly a night passed without some score or other being settled 'outside'.

Reflecting on this now, it seems ironic that instead of typical form designations, 1A, 1B etc., ours were based on the ethos '*Pax Dominus Vobiscum*: Peace and the Lord be with you', although the unsaid 'or else' was always implied. Just as every day and every lesson began and ended in prayer, and every piece of paper had to have the inscription AMDG in the top left margin, the Jesuitical '*Ad Majorem Dei Gloriam*: For the greater glory of God'. It is, of course, a senti- ment every warring tribe takes into battle.

Then there was the school motto itself, '*Respice Finem*: Look to the end'. We were told that it meant we should think carefully about whatever we did and consider the consequences. That could easily have been interpreted as the end justifying the means, especially taking into consideration God's mysterious ways, and the fact that the Catholic Church has a chequered history of tolerance and persecution. However, to be fair, it was drummed into us that it meant think before you act, and was therefore perhaps more in line with Google's present-day motto: 'Don't be evil.'

I'm not sure I really took any notice of the school motto when I was actually there. How many pupils do? But on reflection, even with a bit of post hoc rationalisation, I was struck by how apt the words appear to have been in relation to my own life and career. In fact, I have always found that same question come to mind whenever I am contemplating something new: 'What is the point?' Not in a negative, let's not do it way, but rather attempting to define the real purpose and likely outcome of any situation. *Always look to the consequences*. Perhaps I was listening after all.

Respice Finem may well have been something the school planners themselves should have taken into account, for it could also mean 'just because you can do something, doesn't mean you should'. Like the huge social engineering projects that saw whole communities torn up and scattered to the outer reaches of our cities during the big-is-beautiful boom. It may also help explain why, later on, I found it easy to stand on a platform with David Cameron to help launch the Big Society principle.

Back at school, though, *Respice Finem* did not act as much of a deterrent to the various extra-curricular fighting clubs still trying to settle whatever the daily score was. Sometimes these scores were with the staff and, as we made our nightly evacuation to the relative safety of our own home patches, we would see the gathering of the clans outside the school gates, waiting for whoever was that night's target. There was never anything serious reported the following morning, as obviously the staff drove in and out, and curiously, at least initially, the aggression was always focused on 'after school', the unwritten code being that what went on in and out of school were two entirely separate issues. Of course, the staff and the police gradually brought these fight nights to an end.

In school staff members tended to patrol in twos – in our minds for fear of ambush or of being unable to summon help. This was probably mere teenage fantasy, although the assassination attempt on the Headmaster did raise a few eyebrows. Whether that too was deliberate or simply stupid could never be determined, and it came to rank alongside the conspiracy theories surrounding the assassination of JFK. (It was also yet another story I would never have got through the script-editing process and into *Grange Hill*.)

The known facts are these. The ground-floor corridor of the general teaching block ran the full length of the building. The upper floors were reached by three staircases, one at each end and one in the centre, but there were no interlinking corridors on the upper floors. All traffic filtered down and up the main central staircase. At the changeover bell the scene was the typical bedlam illustrated in every school drama, with familiar staff and prefect shouts of 'Keep to the left' and 'Walk, don't run'.

At the bottom of the central staircase you were at the centre of these human tidal surges, and it was here that the Head would occasionally stand to observe and be observed. You were also in full view of anyone leaning over from the upper landing and, as such, a prime target. On the fateful day, he was in position when a full milk bottle was dropped from above. Fortunately for everyone it only grazed his shoulder and then shattered on the floor. For a moment bedlam was suspended.

An eerie silence followed as everyone took in what had happened. And the implications. Then bedlam of a different kind broke out as both staff and prefects were sent to seal off the building. No one was allowed out as the upper floors were scoured for the attempted assassin, but in the days before CCTV cameras and swipe cards, the blind eye ruled.

No one ever admitted to being involved, which led to the belief that it was either an irrational act such as many teenagers are capable of – as in the 2010 student demonstrations when someone threw a fire extinguisher off the top of an office block on to the crowd below, or the 2011 looting spree – or even an accident. But who would be likely to own up to either? Especially as you could go to confession and receive absolution for it in any case, which for me had become another perceived flaw in Catholic doctrine. You could do anything so long as you later confessed and said sorry. As for the Head, he continued to take up his position. But only occasionally. And just slightly under the first-floor overhang.

★

Something else develops in a testosterone-fuelled all-male environment; camaraderie, the part of the male psyche that turns even mild-mannered professionals into potential lager louts and football hooligans once they're out with the lads. Something similar is displayed on hen nights, of course, but there are few females who would plan a journey of twelve miles three days in advance in order to avenge a perceived slight to their dignity and self-respect. As I discovered when going into school the morning after my primary school Nemesis, Digger, had publicly 'settled up' with me for our old differences.

It had been another classic, almost clichéd scene. Two guys, me and my mate Howey, were walking along with two girls. As we approached a darkened doorway, we felt rather than saw a couple of shadowy figures. Our group instinctively moved aside to create a defensive gap. The figures waited until we passed, and then stepped out. 'Got the time, mate?' Turning back, I recognised one of them immediately. 'You don't come from round here, do you, Reddo?' The implication was obvious. What are you doing with our girls? By which time the gap had closed and any retreat was cut off. The girls were pushed away. The gap closed completely as head met head, followed by fist. If we went down we knew feet would follow, so we didn't. It was as quick as it was hard, and then they were gone. The girls' presence had shortened the attack. No one liked having witnesses.

Digger had obviously seen this as payback for our confrontation in the junior school playground. The next day my schoolmates in Kirkby saw the split lip and black eye as an insult, in need of avenging, especially as Howey was also one of my St Kevin's mates. They immediately started to organise the logistics of how and when to travel the twelve miles to Huyton, in search of Digger. This was an interesting and tricky diplomatic situation, fully illustrating the difficulties of trying to balance a life spent in two, if not three, separate communities, as my co-victim in the assault also travelled to St Kev's with me on the school bus. He lived on the infamous Hillside Estate in the Parish of St Columbus. He was one of four brothers who 'ruled' their particular part of the estate and had already had to persuade them not to take a team across to sort out Digger the previous night.

Eventually we managed to talk the Kirkby contingent down, said it was our fault for being in the wrong place at the wrong time with the wrong girls, and if they went across, Digger would only retaliate. My mate's brothers would then get involved and we would not only end up with a three-area gang war, but me and my mate would never be able to walk the streets again. And we wanted to, because we really fancied those girls. This seemed to swing it for us. Although disappointed, our school mates agreed to back down and we all, literally, lived to fight another day. The lesson I took from it was that you need to stand up to bullies, but must always remember they have long memories. And that, if you are not careful, violence can escalate. We never did get the girls, though, who probably also wanted to walk their own streets again.

Our raging testosterone levels were not helped by the education planners who had decided, in their wisdom, to locate the city's biggest Protestant comprehensive, Ruffwood, right next to the biggest Catholic enclave. It didn't matter whether sectarianism was an issue or not, the fact that the barrier separating the two schools was a massive spoil heap left over from building them meant that pitched battles were frequently waged over who controlled this particular high ground. It probably also had a lot to do with the fact that Ruffwood was mixed, so that protagonists on both sides were out to impress.

If you go to Google Maps and search for 'Roughwood Drive, Kirkby', you will find a satellite image of exactly where my school used to be, complete with an eerie outline of its Olympic-standard running track. It's like looking at an archaeological survey of an old Saxon or Roman settlement, adding further weight to the feeling that my schooldays there were spent manning the forts in defence of the homeland.

Two roads leading off Roughwood Drive, Everdon Wood and Badby Wood, have been built over the former entrances to the school. Opposite them you will see the two remaining tower blocks with below, on the corner of Roughwood Drive and Old Rough Lane, the site of the Protestant Ruffwood Comp with whom we fought for control of the dividing spoil hill. This too has disappeared, after becoming All Saints Catholic Centre for Learning, itself formed by merging St Kev's with our sister girls' school, St Gregory's. So, we won in the end. Mysterious ways, eh?

Alongside the survival skills, St Kev's offered a much steeper learning curve. What I would later identify as the socialisation value of education. Learning to mix with, accept and befriend people from outside your own social circle, race or creed. In other words, being thrown together and forced to get on with each other. Like all imposed social policies, this is fine in theory, but difficult in practice. People do not, naturally, come together unless they share a common aim or goal.

Being educated in one area and living in another means having two centres of gravity, two sets of friends, a point often overlooked by our policy-makers. They forget, or perhaps ignore, the shared bond that exists in communities, centred on things like a common employer, skill, craft or faith. The community spirit so often sought and espoused by politicians can only be forged through these bonds, a shared past bringing shared values. They may be of faith, but could equally arise from a local industry, as seen in a mining village or steel town or shipping city, that gives the area its sense of common purpose. This is also what underpins the success rates at faith schools, and is something too often overlooked when policy-makers talk about building community cohesion and support. It is not the faith itself but the shared common values that build community spirit.

Once the bond of faith or shared values starts to decay through the rise of secularism, or closing of mines or steel mills or docklands, then communities also start to decay and splinter. Where we have gone wrong in social policy, not just in the UK but elsewhere, as in the so-called 'rust belt' in the Mid-West and North-Eastern states of the USA, is in not recognising early enough that the challenge is not about replacing one form of job with another, but replacing one form of common purpose with another. We should be looking at what individual communities need, down to a neighbourhood level, rather than simply trying to find one large employer to replace another.

Later on, one of the guiding principles of *Grange Hill*, *Brookside* and *Hollyoaks* would be the way people living in the same community interact with each other. While characters would have different backgrounds, all of them would share a common purpose. This later came to be known as 'precinct drama', where the same characters inhabit the same central set. With *Grange Hill* it was the school, *Brookside* was obviously about life at home, while *Hollyoaks* was more about the itinerant lifestyle that goes with being a teenager, but soon had the college, pub and shops that evolved into Hollyoaks Village. No matter what life or the scriptwriters threw at them, the common purpose lay in how the characters reacted with each other on that central set.

Moving from junior school to secondary school had changed my own central precinct set. While I was at St Dominic's, school, church, home and social life were inevitably interlinked. Once I went to St Kevin's, the twelve-mile distance meant that the common bonds were broken, especially since going to St Kev's now took ten hours of my daily life, Monday to Friday. I would see my mum and dad for about two hours over tea before they went off on some church-related activity. I would then be left with my siblings to kill the three to four hours before bed, which often included making and stapling bingo books for use in the church club. One sheet of red, blue, brown, green, buff, staple. One red, blue, brown . . . and so on. We must have made thousands over the years, and we fret about child labour now.

Soon, though, St Kev's became my main central set. At St Dom's Juniors I was always in the top six. At St Kev's my first set of exam results saw me in the top six of what was the top form in the top stream in the school. By the second year the results started to decline. Although still in a faith school, for me the underlying foundations of community, church and social mix were starting to crumble.

From spending most of my waking hours at school, the focus of my friendships started to shift and be formed with a new sense of common purpose: my mates now were the guys who shared the daily bus ride.

That bus gave me my first real sense of being out on a limb. Being outside the norm, as the socio-psychologists like to say, and having to forge a new life and new friends. I suppose I had been through this before, from my time spent as an altar boy and from having been moved up a year in Junior school, but I was too young then to really appreciate any sense of difference. Now I did, and in a big way. One I would not fully appreciate until twenty-two years later, when *Brookside* was launched. How life cascades. How that programme couldn't have existed without that first fateful trip on the school bus. Without that time I would never have ended up with the real-life education I was to receive. Without that, *Grange Hill* would never have happened, let alone been as successful as it was. Without that, Channel 4 would never have commissioned *Brookie*. And you would not be reading this.

During the summer leading up to my sixth-form year at St Kevin's I discovered how tight the household budget really was when we awoke in the middle of the night to find the house full of black smoke. It was from the paraffin heater my dad had started leaving on in the kitchen to keep the chill off overnight. The two things that were the bane of our lives were making sure the heater was always topped up and that the wick was trimmed. If either of those jobs was neglected, the wick rather than the paraffin would burn. And fill the house with smoke.

By the time we got down and put out the heater, my mother was distraught to discover the kitchen and hall were covered in black soot on a scale no amount of careless coalmen could have managed. We all went back to bed and the clean-up began the following day. By this time my dad had passed on to me one of life's most valuable lessons, whether intentionally or not I do not know: never do something you hate properly or you'll be asked to do it again.

In his case it was anything to do with DIY. He was the classic gammy-handed carpenter. If Mum nagged him to do something round the house, he would duck and dive until she would do something like rip a whole piece of wallpaper from the wall, or take a hinge off a door so it would be left hanging and unusable, trying to shame him into sorting it out. Sometimes it worked, but more often than not he would drag across one of his extensive network of friends from the church club to do it for a few quid. It was how the local economy worked. Each would help the other with their particular skill.

My dad's was football as he had been a handy player in his youth and was always proud of having played for his Regimental football team. He organised and ran the teams attached to the church club, as well as the billiard and snooker teams, and had a great network of mates who could help out with almost anything.

Another valuable lesson my dad passed on was never to be shamed into doing anything. He wasn't. Things would get done when he wanted them to be done, and until then we had to live with sagging doors and bits of missing wallpaper. Until I started engineering workshop, theory and practice, and realised that I could do most of this stuff, and the few quid my dad was paying his mates could then come my way. Which it did, but with a newly introduced family discount. Still, it was cash.

Cleaning up after the heater scare meant that the entire kitchen had to be decorated. To get things like this done quickly and with minimal disturbance or interruption, I would do them overnight when everyone else went to bed. The kitchen was re-done while I listened to the just-released Beatles album, *Revolver*, stopping every twenty minutes or so to turn over the vinyl album while carefully protecting it and the old record player from the dust, paint or paste. Oh, for an iPod and Bluetooth headset in those days.

Just as I was finishing and about to get ready to go off to school, I moved a dish that had some papers in it and noticed one of my dad's pay slips among the pile. Curious, I took it out and was astonished to see how little he was earning. I think it was around £11 after tax. I remember being staggered by that, especially as I was listening to a Beatles album that had cost about £1. I was paying for it on the drip at the rate of five shillings, or 25 pence, a week, which I got for doing things like the redecorating round the house.

It stayed with me for days, trying to figure out what we had, what things cost, and even with my mum's wages as a school cleaner I couldn't quite figure out how she and Dad could afford it all. Especially the car. Until I put the dots together and realised that, just like me, they were obviously paying for things on credit, and managing the household budget amazingly efficiently. Which explained why we weren't allowed simply to flick that hot water switch.

It was probably also around this time that the penny dropped about the tallyman, the guy coming to the house every Friday night to collect money, as like most teenagers I was living in my own universe. It took the shock of seeing my dad's wage slip to snap me out of it. This guy was obviously coming to collect the hire-purchase payments on the debts my parents had run up at his clothes shops. Predating credit cards, this was the only way they could have got credit, although I hate to think what sort of rates they would have been paying just to keep up with that great working-class tradition of making sure the kids were all well turned out. It wasn't something I could discuss with them, as I wasn't supposed to know, but it somehow didn't seem fair that they were expected to survive on such a low income. It did, however, explain why we were almost among the last in our area to get things like the TV, the phone and the car – even if that was an old second-hand Standard 10 Estate.

I still remember the excitement when Dad took my brother and me into town to collect it from the second-hand dealer's. The car was far from luxurious, but it was clean and tidy and to us was probably the best thing that had ever happened. It made a big difference to my dad, as it meant he could leave home later and be home from work earlier, not that that made much impact on my life as I was still bound to the daily hike to and from the school bus. It did, however, mean that we were able to do more things as a family at weekends, but with cash still scarce this usually meant spending more time with my numerous aunts, uncles and cousins.

The other impact my discovery had was on my recent decision not to find a job, but to stay on at school for the sixth form. Now that didn't feel quite right. I thought I should be doing what some of my friends were doing and finding a job to help out with the family budget. I mentioned this to Mum and Dad and neither of them hesitated in saying that was not what they wanted. They wanted me to go on and get to university. To be the first in the family to do so. When I pushed them as much as I could on how they would manage, the reply was as stoic as it was simple. We always have. It must have been a massive decision, though, for my mum and dad to go on supporting me. While I had been busily exploring more of the informal than formal channels for acquiring an education at school, I had ended up with a reasonable clutch of O-levels so I suppose the collective opinion was that I showed enough promise to get into university if I applied myself. As it turned out, I did – but not in the way that was expected.

What did start to happen was that I gradually took over the maintenance of the car, both to keep the running costs down and, by doing so, to get a few quid off my dad and his friends every now and then. By the time I was old enough to drive I could strip and rebuild any type of common engine, but for me the paraffin heater accident and discovering my dad's pay packet probably had more of an impact in developing my entrepreneurial instincts.

It was probably these same ambitions that were stirred when a quantity surveyor came to visit the school and talk about how project management and cost control were the tools that would one day rule the world. That sounded good to me, and while on reflection I should perhaps have tried for architecture, this kind of thinking and my five years' training as a QS were things I would later take into the creation of MerseyTV and *Brookside*. To get there, though, I first had to pass my A-levels.

As my time at St Kev's started to come to an end, I had gone through all the university application processes and applied to the required six universities, although I already knew that even if I were offered a place, I would probably not go. It wasn't about money, as the student grants then available would have given me, ironically, more than I ever had while living at home. It was about self-confidence. I just did not feel able to take on the challenge of living away from home, or to enter what was still the very middle-class world of higher education. If university lecturers were all like my teachers at school, I knew I would never cope.

This is the great flaw in education: the value gap that is so often apparent between teachers, pupils and parents. The difference between idealism and pragmatism. The difference between telling someone they can make a difference and showing them how. The difference between what *could* be on offer and what actually *is* on offer. The difference between looking over the horizon and looking out of the window. The difference between what the staff have seen elsewhere and what the kids and parents experience every day. These differences are what build or sap an individual's confidence. All children are born naturally bright, inquisitive and creative. That is nature's contribution. Everything that happens later is down to nurture, and by far the biggest influence is not family, as many politicians would dearly like us to believe, but where that family lives, because it determines who and what they are.

No matter what education system the state puts in place – whether comprehensive, grammar, academy or faith-based – the major influence on it is the same as with real estate: location, location, location. Next in importance is a good head teacher, but the location of a school is the ultimate determinant of its long-term success or failure, for it is the location that determines the social mix of pupils, staff and parents. Is this an area where the mobile middle class choose to live, or one where the immobile working class are forced to stay? And, equally important, what are the shared values and common purpose that come from living in this particular neighbourhood and community?

Too often one of these elements is out of balance, and a child's education suffers as a result. In my own case there was a mismatch between the aims of the teaching staff at St Kev's and those of their pupils and the pupils' families. While pupils and parents shared common goals and aspirations, the teachers might as well have come from a different planet. They didn't understand the social pressures to which we were vulnerable. This is why private schools, usually in prime locations, continue to succeed. Staff and pupils share a common value system, which boosts confidence and understanding on both sides. Kids in this environment are conditioned to believe that they can achieve if they want to. Whereas in working-class communities the intentions and aspirations might be the same, but are totally undermined by that all-important walk to and from school.

A good head can make a great difference, but only during their tenure and only if they can attract the right calibre of staff, something that in itself is affected by the location of the school. This will always be a hotly contested debate, but I have seen no significant advances in the education system between 1954, when I entered it, and 2009, when I chaired the Knowsley Youth Commission, looking at what life had in store for young people in the same area as I was born. It still seems to be a case of higher skills on offer, but only half an education. The jargon has changed, the system has not. The last Labour government's Building Schools for the Future programme was no different from the renewal programme of the 1960s that saw me go to a brand new comprehensive school, but perhaps the fact that the school no longer exists is the real clue to the efficacy – or not – of these policies.

St Kevin's was built as part of a joint national policy for government and church, and was doomed to fail even before the next educational buzz words, 'academies' and 'building renewal', started to be heard. Buildings in themselves mean nothing. It is what goes on inside them that matters. Education is about people, their intellectual potential, and the needs of the economy that surrounds them. National curriculums playing into national policies based on perceived national needs can never share the same sense of common purpose or shared values as a local neighbourhood or community.

It comes down to this. If national policy is to shift away from large-scale, labour-intensive manufacturing towards importing cheaper goods from abroad, then what happens to all the local communities built specifically to provide the labour for the old, displaced factories? It was a question never asked in cities and towns like Liverpool, Knowsley and Huyton. If it had been, then perhaps someone would have answered: the jobs are exported but the people are left behind. As are the derelict factories. It's all very well saying kids need to be better skilled, but for what if their community is being asset stripped around them?

That was exactly what was going round in my head when I reached the end of my time at St Kev's. I was being encouraged to go to university, but for what? Like my choice of A-levels, it wasn't what I *wanted* to do but what I *could* do, according to my previous exam results. I had wanted to study Maths and Economics in the sixth form but, despite passing my Maths O-level a year early, I was told I couldn't because I had opted out of Physics two years earlier and the Maths I had studied was 'the wrong sort of Maths'. Having the 'wrong sort of experience' was something I would hear from various bureaucratic apologists down the years, but back then I was left wondering what that was all about, and then taking A-level English, Economics and General Studies.

To take this argument of separation by a common language further, I later discovered that English and Economics was not a combination popular with university admissions officers, and that to have any hope at all of passing General Studies I needed a foreign language, which I hadn't studied since my second year at school. I was though, on paper, sitting three A-levels, the results of which were as predictable as they were confusing. General Studies was a joke. Nothing I had revised for Economics came up, and I could only attempt answers to three of the required four questions. In English everything I'd revised duly appeared and I ran out of paper. General Studies went as expected, but I also unexpectedly failed English and passed Economics. Surprising at the time but, on reflection, perhaps the perfect preparation for a career in television.

Without even waiting for this contrary result, I decided the best avenue open to me was to join those quantity surveyors who were going to rule the world. I started scanning the local paper's job adverts, and on 10 July 1967 began work as a trainee quantity surveyor, ten days before I was officially supposed to leave school. No one seemed to notice or be bothered.

My last memory of my time at St Kev's is of a sixth-form post-A-level get together with our sixth-form tutor, whom we affectionately referred to as Skull Nelson due to his often gaunt appearance. As part of this he had to tick a few boxes and have a quick one-to-one discussion with us on what we were planning for the future. I told him I didn't have any great plans except perhaps to try quantity surveying, or any job to start earning money, but that I definitely didn't want to end up like my dad, just a cog working in a large machine. He asked what I had in mind long-term and I explained that I had sometimes gone out with my dad, helping him deliver bread to shops. I enjoyed that, and because I was by now quite good at car mechanics, I might, when I could afford it, get a van and try and build a delivery business.

I can still see the look on his face and hear his final words to me: 'Well, Redmond, I would never have put you down as someone with ambition.' This was the guy who was supposed to have been in charge of my pastoral care for two years . . . but I didn't take it too personally. How little they knew us. But then, how could they? By the time I left, the school had close to to 2,000 kids, and 150 staff who never had time to get to know anyone. That was probably the only conversation I had with my tutor, not that I held it against him. I had never known how to speak to him. It was my own lack of self-confidence. Something I would be forced to overcome and in so doing would take me on a circuitous route to university.

3

Character Development (1968–72)

'Only the moment of inspiration is fun. Having the idea. The rest of it is bloody hard work' – *John Cleese, Hungry Years Restaurant, 29 April 1972*

I found my first job advertised in our local paper, the *Liverpool Echo*, and went for an interview some time in June. The firm was called Everiss & Blundell and was situated in a small Dickensian mews, Chapel Walks, among the maze of warehouses near the waterfront. It was obviously part of the city's great maritime history. The guy interviewing me, his name long since over-written in my memory bank, was the senior partner and somewhat Dickensian himself, with round tortoiseshell glasses and a shirt with a stiffly starched wing collar. He was even posher than Harold Wilson and had the air of a venerable cleric about him. I had no trouble imagining him in cassock and surplice, or even an abbot's robe. I don't know what he saw in a nervous, thick-accented youth from Huyton but he asked me if I would be able to start in two weeks.

He must have known the school term hadn't ended, but he also probably knew that we were in that strange period of drift that always follows A-levels and was testing how sincere I was. My immediate response of yes might have been enough to convince him to give me the job, although I later discovered that the clerical impression I'd received might not have been far off the mark as he was the only Catholic partner in the firm. He might then have been sympathetic to the great educational experiment that was going on out at St Kevin's, something he would have been made aware of from the sheer scale of the building project.

I also soon learned a lot more about his collars as it was part of my duties to make the weekly trip to the specialist cleaners where I would swap a box of used for a box of fresh. The smell of starch was also a weekly reminder of my own time in the vestry, laying out the priest's freshly starched surplices, but none had had the sharp edges of those collars. No wonder period characters are often portrayed as straight-backed and stiff-necked.

Whatever it was that got me through that interview I ended up with a job, and if my parents were disappointed by my decision not to go to university, then it was more than compensated for by my getting a job in a profession. It was definitely another first for the family and would later lead to the only really difficult period I had with my dad, when I decided to 'throw it all away', to use his words. 'And for what? Some daft idea of becoming a writer?'

However, on 10 July 1967, following the weekend the Beatles released 'All You Need Is Love', I started work as a trainee quantity surveyor, or QS, earning a predecimal £4.16.10d per week (£4.84-ish), around two-thirds of today's hourly minimum wage. This was about a third of what my dad earned, so for my own needs it was more than enough. And it was payback time. It was expected that once you had a job you would contribute to the family budget, so I handed over £2 a week to my mum. Although she often gave me some if not all of it back as I was still head of household mainte-nance.

I was earning a lot less than some of the guys who had left school at the end of the fifth form and followed the path of what Harold Wilson . . . yes, him again . . . described as 'the white heat of tech-nology', to become part of a highly skilled labour-force for the new highly skilled telecommunications economy. Sound familiar?

For the geeks, the late-1960s also saw the first steps toward building the internet, in something called the ARPANET (Advanced Research Projects Agency Network). This was a network connecting the University of California at Los Angeles (UCLA), Stanford Research Institute, the University of California at Santa Barbara and the University of Utah, using a standard phone 50Kbps line. In other words, the way we used to have to 'dial-up'. Really slowly. Contrary to folklore it wasn't conceived and built for the military to provide a bomb-proof control and command system, it was devised for general data exchange and to cope with the unreliability of the then existing components. It was during the Cold War that the military spotted its potential.

With yet further resonance for our current obsession with the internet and mobile phones, just as 2011 saw the Beatles appear in the iTunes store for the first time, in 1966 the BBC commissioned them to write and perform a song for the world's first global satellite link, to be watched in forty countries. It was 'All You Need Is Love'.

Telecommunications were, therefore, cool, and we were just as in thrall to technology then as we are today, just as we were bombarded by the gee-whizz marketing of what this or the other device would do for us, how labour-saving it would be and how it would change our lives. Some things did, of course, like immersion heaters and washing machines, reducing the time it took to wash clothes. Central heating eliminated the mess and inconvenience of coal deliveries and automated manufacturing techniques made producing goods quicker and cheaper. All of this gave something else. Time. People were now finding spare time on their hands. They needed things to occupy them. Television would fill the void.

The downside to all these new advances were the unforeseen implications. If automated manufacturing techniques could produce goods faster and cheaper, making skilled craftsmen like panel beaters and engineering machinists unnecessary, then production could be shifted to places where the last vestiges of human labour required, brute strength or dexterity for fetching, carrying and packaging, could be bought at much cheaper rates. Just as we have seen the internet rapidly change the way we do everything today, the seeds of the UK's de-industrialisation began with the sector that was then sucking in most of my friends from school; telecommunications. But I didn't want to climb up a pole in December or to risk 50-volt shocks. It was quantity surveying for me.

Having made the decision not to go into factory work but to try the professional route, I had soon to start navigating what my parents, and countless others, have referred to as 'the university of life'. I discovered that, just like school, work was about socialisation and receiving both formal and informal education. What to do and what not to do in the office and around my new colleagues. Quantity surveying, like most other professions, I suspect, was riddled with the same sort of petty hierarchies and status struggles as the Church. My role was to be at the bottom, on call to fetch and carry, whether it be starched collars for the senior partner, milk and sugar for the office tea or the end of a tape measure in the muddy part of a building site. Dogsbody, basically.

This didn't particularly bother me, as I quite liked having the freedom to wander around the city centre on my various errands, especially as I was now enjoying an extra hour in bed every morning and getting home from work around the same time as I had from school. Nothing, I also thought, could be as bad as getting up to do that cemetery walk . . . until I was taken out to the city's infamous tenement blocks. As well as the massive 1930s quasi-Art Deco blocks of flats common in most inner cities, Liverpool also had them dating back to the nineteenth century, as it had been the first city to build council housing as far back as 1869. It was in these tenements that some of the most deprived council tenants still had to survive until the introduction of a government-funded programme to bring all council properties up to something called the Parker Morris standard.

After a report of 1961, with the typically catchy name *Homes for Today*, six years later standard recommendations were set for all new housing, and in 1969 for all council housing. I was to discover that the house where I had grown up did not meet the new minimum legal standard. Although we had our own toilet, a mandatory requirement, and 3.2 cubic metres of storage in the kitchen including the coal cupboard, something Parker Morris might have quibbled over, we most certainly didn't have the heating system suggested, as my morning mountaineering ritual to avoid the freezing quarry tiles would testify.

Still, our house was nothing like some of the tenements I visited to start measuring up for the improvement work. It astonished me how people used to let us straight in when we knocked on the door, and if there was someone still in bed they would just tell us to get on with things and try not to wake them. This was, of course, only after they had ascertained we were not actually from the council.

From these visits I learned that I was not the only one who had to share a bedroom, and was quite fortunate it was only with my brother, not brothers, or sisters, or the dogs, cats and the occasional monkey we came across. I saw the apocryphal coal in the bath in a two-bedroomed flat on the sixth floor. After all, with no balcony and your front door opening on to a communal walkway and, the topper, with no hot water on tap or available at the flick of a switch, what else would you use it for? I even ended up going to measure up some houses in Darwen in Lancashire that still had earth floors in the kitchen – in the late 1960s. And there was me, having done everything I could to avoid walking on cold lino.

Apart from sowing the early seeds for *Brookside*, which started with Bobby and Sheila having worked hard to 'get off the estate', my interest in wider social issues probably stems from these further excursions outside the comfort zone of my family, friends and community. It was probably the scale of the problem rather than the need for improvements that hit me, as it seemed nearly every council house in the city needed to be upgraded. I could also see the same sort of separation by a common language that I had experienced in Kirkby and Huyton, as the council policy-makers were about to inflict the consequences of their good intentions on the less than enthusiastic population. Residents of one estate of terraced houses in Garston argued that even with the new Parker Morris standard, their houses would be less comfortable than they had made them themselves through their own hard work and cash. They didn't want to be improved. They liked their houses as they were, and why couldn't the council go off and 'waste the money on something else'.

We would get earfuls of this when we were out measuring up, despite trying to hide behind the 'only following orders' line. I would then find myself arguing on the tenants' side when we got back to the office, especially against a middle-class lad who had started working there not long after me, straight from one of the Protestant grammar schools. He lived in one of the posher neighbourhoods that don't really like to admit they are actually in Liverpool, and had an accent that could cut glass, but that wasn't what set us apart. He had gone the approved route and never moved outside his own comfort zone. He didn't have anything in common with the people of Garston. He couldn't even speak to them. To his way of thinking they should just be grateful for what they got. After all, no one ever gave his family anything. They just didn't know what was good for them . . . and so on. Eighteen going on forty-five.

I would learn in later years to make allowances for these sorts of cultural differences as none of us should be blamed for where and to whom we were born. Michael Caine once famously said that he'd been poor and he'd been rich, and he knew which he'd rather be. I can empathise with that, but I've also learned that it is much better to start at the bottom and go up rather than try to navigate a route down. Yet it is this sort of cultural apartheid that still permeates our society, regardless of the talk about social mobility and the idea that we are all somehow either classless or, conversely, middle-class.

That argument is as daft now as it has always been, for our society is riven with divisions. It might be termed something else, like 'the digital divide' or 'postcode lottery', but it always comes back to location, location, location, which means certain types of people living in certain areas in certain conditions. My middle-class grammar-school contemporary might have believed that his family never asked for or received anything from anyone, but he entirely missed the point that *they didn't need to*. He was also completely oblivious to the fact that with one of his parents working in the public sector, his own family was in receipt of state benefits – the deferred benefit of the state pension fund. Still, although I then saw the world from a black-and-white teenage perspective, we should not judge him too harshly. For him as for millions of others, the point about the deferred state benefits did not come into focus until the 2008 crash. And even then it was through a soft filter.

If the seeds of *Brookside* were sown by my early experiences in Kirkby, then the world of work further expanded my social horizons and conscience. This first entry into working life would also help me later on when working on the sit-com *The Squirrels*. All the comedy of office politics was there, alongside the harsher truths of employment – the main one being that it wasn't simply a way of receiving glorified pocket money, but that it had all the same relent-lessness as school: authority system, social hierarchy, bullying, boring work, and results that relied purely on effort. More importantly, you were only allowed to mess it up a few times before you were out. No sports master or indulgent form tutor offering pastoral care, whether you wanted it or even knew it existed, to explain how much your talent was valued.

And so it was that I learned I was allowed to be late, once. That I couldn't go missing for too long while delivering mail or picking up those starched collars. That it was not my place to query why it was me and not the grammar-school bloke who had to go and get the toilet rolls and tea bags. Sometimes it was like being back on the altar. You did the cemeteries and the tenements with three to a bed while the others grabbed the High Mass and private home renovations with three cars in the garage. I also discovered that while I was working towards a qualification from the Institute of Quantity Surveyors (IQS), my grammar-school colleague was going for the more prestigious Royal Institute of Chartered Surveyors (RICS), the logic being that I was working-class and therefore an employee, while he was middle-class and therefore destined to be a partner.

I also learned the need for concentration and hard work while slaving over one of the grindingly boring chores newcomers were given, checking the increased cost sheets, a task designed to test your mental stamina to the extreme. The prime role of a QS was first to cost a project, and then to monitor those costs throughout the build, so as to be able to agree the final account at the end. This meant, bluntly, needing to count every brick, bag of cement, length of copper tube and light switch. With labour being the biggest cost, as in most businesses, the real problem lay in keeping an eye on variations made to the contract. This is where contractors can make huge amounts in extras, as anyone who has ever 'had the builders in' will know. Whether it is a small kitchen extension, loft conversion or £70 million museum, as I would discover much later in life as Chair of National Museums Liverpool, the game may be on a different pitch, but the rules are the same. Agree a price, agree a mechanism for changes – and then watch them like a hawk.

Quantity surveyors are professional hawks, and theoretically supposed to be impartial arbiters, but since we were employed by the architect on behalf of the client it didn't take long to figure out who the enemy was supposed to be. The increased cost sheets used to arrive as part of the monthly valuation of work to date and, as the name suggests, would detail every change above the agreed contract sum and include the hourly rates for every worker on the site, as well as the materials used. The materials were quite straightforward, provided you went out to the site and physically counted everything, constantly making sure that the contractors or the subcontractors were not double-counting stuff you had already paid for, or even having stuff delivered to one job that was really for another, simply to get the cash out of you for their own cash flow.

Checking the workers' hours, though, was something else again, assuming that there was already an agreed Variation Order authorising the work. Not only did you have to make sure that they were claiming the right rate, that for example a labourer wasn't being billed as a joiner, and that any union or various increases in National Insurance were correct, there were also the tricky issues of whether the time spent matched the job, or even if the names matched the people on site, let alone whether the scale of the job matched the time claimed. Given the old principle that work expands to fit the time available, part of my job was to query why it would take, for instance, six men to excavate a hole to find and divert a drain when you knew the hole would only have needed two men with spades; or why three of the men on the sheet were also simultaneously recorded as being at the far end of the site installing a staircase, and one of the three was also an electrician who shouldn't have been there in the first place. And why were they all called O'Grady?

On the other hand, sometimes you had to make the case on behalf of the contractor, aka the enemy, for work that the client and/or architect had changed their mind about. In these cases, the contractor had undertaken the aborted work under a clear directive from the architect and therefore should not be penalised simply because someone had changed their mind. This often didn't make you the most popular person in the site hut, especially as it was always the client who had to pick up the bill even if the fault was the architect's, as it very often was.

As I became more experienced, it also became more apparent to me that the real enemy was in fact the architect. While many of them are good at design, few are actually very good at the practical and project management side of the business. Hence the need for quantity surveyors. One invaluable piece of advice passed to me by an older QS was: always look above door-height for cost savings. Architects tend to look at the whole building, and therefore every piece, segment and surface is of equal significance and creative interest to them, whereas the public, the users of the building, tend never to look above head-height. It is something you can test yourself on by thinking about how many buildings you go into. What do you remember most? The doors? Wall coverings? Floors? And . . . ?

The best moment I ever had with an architect was while working on a Catholic convent. I was sent to attend a site meeting and told to expect a bit of tension as the Mother Superior was not best pleased with the new chapel. Arriving at the site I found the architect, also a Catholic, in a bit of a state. He asked me to try and explain to the nuns that the new altar was indeed in the original design, tender and contract, and was therefore a legitimate expense. I thought that a fair point, but though by that time technically non–practising, did not relish the idea of trying to face down an angry Mother Superior.

We were shown into the new chapel by a novice nun, the sort who as teenagers we always fancied, just because we knew we shouldn't, and always wondered why they had taken the cloth. The architect was obviously beyond such thoughts, in a state of high agitation and ageing by the minute. It soon became clear why when Mother Superior glided in, her box-like habit creating the impression of an ecclesiastical Dalek. As soon as she said, 'It's a monstrosity. An affront to God. It must go,' I knew we were lost.

The 'monstrosity' was still carefully wrapped in protective sheeting, which was soon wrenched aside to reveal a huge piece of marble. On closer inspection I found this was to be the new altar for the chapel, and had been carved in one piece from one of the Carrara quarries that had been supplying the Vatican for centuries. I have to admit it was a stunning piece of sculpture and, according to the architect's stammering explanation, a figurative interpretation of the stone at the sepulchre that rolled back to allow Christ's resurrection.

Mother Superior fixed her eye on him and for a moment we didn't know which way it was going to go. Was her fixed quizzical gaze considering his theological reasoning, or was he simply confirming her impression that he was an idiot? 'It's a monstrosity.' He was an idiot. I started to speak, but she held up her hand. I nodded. She then slowly and carefully explained to the hapless architect that we, two men, were only in this building at all because it had not yet been consecrated or devoted to God, but if we cared to look round we would notice the sparsity of the design, the frugality of the fittings. Their order embraced chastity, asceticism, and the rejection of worldly goods. All they required was a simple altar. Two uprights and a plank across the top, I think she said. Then she definitely said that what they did not want, nor would have, nor would pay for, was some self-indulgent, ornately carved work of art. I remembered my own early thoughts during Easter High Mass about graven images. I could see her point.

With that she turned and glided out. End of meeting. I looked at the architect, now with his mouth popping soundlessly like a goldfish's. We left and it was later resolved, as the minutes recorded, that he would cover the cost of the altar himself. I changed jobs shortly afterwards and never knew what happened next. Whether the nuns graciously took the unwanted monstrosity as a gift, or whether they still have their plank altar and there is now a magnificent barbecue erected somewhere in the garden of an architect-designed house. What we all learned, though, is that it is extremely difficult to enforce a contract with the handmaidens of God.

To qualify for the IQS I had to get at least two A-levels, which I was expecting to achieve, but when the results came out in the August, I didn't. This meant that I had to go into work and tell them, with the risk that they would then ask me to leave. It was not something I was looking forward to, but it had to be done as I was expected to apply to the IQS for membership and then go to the College of Building once a week to study for my professional exams. There was only one course a year so it would mean having to delay everything for 12 months, until I could resit an A-level, and I was certain they wouldn't agree to that. However, I must have done something to impress them as they agreed to let me stay provided I made sure I did the resit in time to enroll next year.

This was a surprise and, I felt, generous of them, although having made the journey from employee to employer myself subsequently, I can now see it may just have been a pragmatic response, to do with the firm's workload and the hassle involved in finding someone else to do my job. Even at dogsbody level, often the devil you know is worth hanging on to.

Whatever it was, I was grateful and determined to make sure I got the necessary A-level, especially as the grammar-school kid sailed through his exams, of course, to continue his planned route through life. I then signed up for a correspondence course, what later became known as distance and online learning, though back then everything went back and forth by post, or snail mail. I'd decided that if I had to spend another year studying, I would do it in a new subject. Something we weren't allowed to do at school. I was also still a bit deflated by my failure in English, so I chose Economic and Social History instead.

Living at home and sharing a bedroom with my brother was not the best environment for home study: neither was the challenge of trying to keep in touch with the guys from school, especially as we were now scattered throughout the city and no longer had the classroom to keep us together. By the time the following June came round I felt a bit more confident but again I came away with nothing, for the same reason as I had before. Not enough time spent studying.

Now I was in a real bind. It wasn't just the thought of losing my job; for the first time in my life, I really felt that I had let my parents down. The first one in the family to get a professional job, and I had blown it. I could blame the harshness of my English A-level result on some unknown and anonymous examiner, but I had no one to blame but myself for not applying myself this time round. Then it started to dawn on me that if I lost my job, not only would I lose what income I had and become a burden on my mum and dad again, but I would also have to start looking for another job. Any job. And that was not what I wanted to do. I would not go so far as to say that I enjoyed what I was doing, but it seemed a lot better than what my mates were doing, even if they were getting more cash.

There was one particular job I had already worked on that really brought this home: Stanley Abattoir, the biggest slaughterhouse in the North West. I used to pass it every day on the bus home, and I knew that every week thousands of animals would be taken there to be killed and butchered. Its two biggest claims to fame at the time were that it had been closed in 1957 when Foot and Mouth Disease had been found in the cattle, and in the same year the Quarrymen, John Lennon's band that later morphed into the Beatles, had played one of their early gigs at the Social Club there. I don't think the two were connected, or that Lennon ever went back there, but when you are starting out, you take anything.

Which was why I one day found myself having to borrow my dad's old Army coat, to try and keep warm in the sub-zero temperatures of the freezer rooms. I was there to measure up the place so we could do a rough estimate of what a refurbishment would cost. This was a long and slow process as it was impossible to stay in the freezers for very long. Measure one wall, get out. Measure another and out into the warmer, if still freezing, passageways. After an hour or so you had to go out into the daylight to thaw out a bit, and every couple of hours nip over to the powerhouse to get a cup of tea.

Another reason not to stay in the freezer spaces for too long was the smell. One of those smells, or at least its memory, that stays with you. Even today. At the risk of hyperbole, it was, to me, the smell of death. Imagine sour milk. Then imagine that ten times stronger, and you might just begin to get close. How the guys who worked there stood it I do not know, but I respected them for doing it and made sure I took plenty of breaks. It was on one of these short warm-up interludes, walking between the receiving sheds and the slaughter sheds, that I noticed what I thought was a sheep standing in a hole.

Only its head was visible and its eyes seemed to be staring at me as I approached. I was trying to figure out how it had got in there, or if it was actually in one of the underground storage rooms and was popping its head out of a ventilation grid, when I realised it was, well, a sheep's head. Lying in the middle of the roadway. I looked round to see if I could find out where it had come from and there to my left was a huge pile of similar heads. It was about three metres high and this one had obviously rolled off to land perfectly upright on its severed neck.

Although not squeamish by nature, it did put me off lamb for a while, especially as one of the slaughtermen walked by while I stood there and scooped up the head and tossed it back on the pile without even breaking step. To him it was no longer an animal but a product. And a job. The sort of job I knew had to be done, but not something I could ever do myself. These were the thoughts going through my head while I was trying to figure out what to do about not getting that extra A-level. It wasn't just a case of letting my mum and dad down . . . what would I end up doing instead? There was only one thing for it. I'd have to fib.

So that is what I did. I went in and told them at work that I had indeed passed my resit and would be applying for the IQS and college course for next year. I had found out that I didn't actually need to apply for the IQS until I was ready to take the professional exams, which would be at least two years away. So, provided no one asked to see the actual A-level certificates, I would be OK. I would definitely get them next time round. Which I did, thankfully.

Not only that, I also picked up another O-level, in commerce.

I'd tagged this on to the A-level entry fee as I'd realised the main examination cost lay in paying the fees at the centre where you sat the exam, rather than for the subjects themselves. Perhaps it was another pointer to the career ahead of me. Meanwhile I'd belatedly realised that what they'd always said at school was true: $R = \frac{(E + A)}{T}$ where R is for Reward, E for effort, A for Application over Time. What, as parents, we are always trying to get across to our kids. You get out what you put in. So from September '68 until June '69 I became a regular visitor to the Reading Room in Liverpool's Picton Library, another of nineteenth-century Liverpool's architectural gems.

In those days the library was open until 9 p.m. so I could stroll across there after work and spend a couple of hours working before heading home or out for the evening. Nowadays, with the ever-increasing pressure on public funds, this great resource is no longer available after 5 p.m. This is undoubtedly also tied to the rise of the internet as a research tool, therefore lowering the demand for phys-ical copies of books or research material, but it has masked the role of the library, any library, as a quiet safe haven for people to study in. With increased concern in recent years about how formal educa-tion is failing in many areas, allowing libraries to slide down the social agenda may be something that comes back to haunt us. Certainly I would not have been able to get that A-level without them.

Something else I picked up over this year was my first car, all £25 worth, as my weekly wage had rocketed to £7. Like my dad I had found an old Standard 10 from a typical second-hand car dealer who, basically, lied through his teeth about the state of it. As I knew the model inside out by then, I managed to nurse it back to health with many a cut knuckle, curse and incantation to the saints, as my mum preferred to class her own occasional frustrated, 'Jesus, Mary and St Joseph'. If you heard that you knew you were in trouble. I was able to take it apart and put it back together again and then to offload it for a half-decent Austin A55, that before long I had decided wasn't and eventually rebuilt.

The car brought me what Henry Ford had promised: greater mobility and a wider travel-to-work radius. This was something I would learn more about during my sociology era, but it comes down to the fact that all our towns and villages have developed on the basis of how far people are prepared to travel. The typical journey was, and still is, about 45 minutes long. At a good walking pace that equates to about 3–4 miles. So any settlement considered anyone living within 3–4 miles as one of 'us', whereas anyone living further out would become one of 'them'. That still holds up today if you stop and think about where you actually live.

What Henry Ford's 'any colour so long as it's black' Model T did was extend the distance people could travel in 45 minutes, from 3–4 miles to 30–40 miles. Hence, villages grew into towns, towns into cities, and the great urban sprawl traced the development of transport systems. Having my own car meant I could now look for work in places that were not reached by the bus route at the corner of the road. That meant, instead of following the bus and tramlines into the city from Huyton, I could turn the other way, as I once did for school, and head out into Woollyback land for my second job.

This was completely different from the first. Instead of the rundown Dickensian offices among the dockland warehouses, it would be in a rather grand house on the main road into St Helens, right opposite Pilkington's Glass Headquarters. From the city that had dominated world trade to a town that was dominated by the world's glassmaker, the local joke being that St Helens was a little town just outside Pilkington's – or Pilks, as it was colloquially known.

I had decided to move with an almost clear conscience now that I had achieved the necessary second A-level required for IQS membership. I was restless and I wanted to earn more money. After two years of poring over increased costs sheets and measuring bricks and drains and holding tapes and theodolite poles on various building sites in all weathers, I wanted a bit more than the light relief of fetching and carrying toilet rolls. Later on in life, of course, when I had my own company, I would realise that this is the most important management function of all. That all business comes down to toilet rolls, parking and canteens.

What I really wanted was to start taking more responsibility for working up the Bills of Quantities that were central to all construction jobs. Taking the architect's drawings and figuring out how many bricks, bags of cement and so on would be needed. Unfortunately my Dickensian firm in its Dickensian offices still had a Dickensian attitude to training, progress and pay. Chatting to other people at the

College of Building, I realised our pay scales were behind most, especially in the contracting sector where there was not so much fuss about qualifications if you could do the job. I started to look around and eventually found a job on offer out in St Helens. For me this was even easier than getting into the city centre so I applied. And got the job. And the money? It went from £7 to £11 per week.

The job turned out to be with a much smaller firm, Rex Snowling Associates, that in fact turned out to consist of Rex himself and one other QS. There were two girls in the office, and another lad had just been taken on, with whom I soon discovered I had something in common. He came from Kirkby but had gone to the school right next-door to St Kev's, Ruffwood. Life there was very different from at my old city-centre firm. Rex was a lot younger and therefore more dynamic than the partners I had known previously. We were no longer just quantity surveyors, but construction cost consultants. This sounded much more twentieth century – and there wasn't a wing collar in sight.

Something else that fired me up was Rex's approach to standardised systems. He had worked out that most Bills of Quantities contained almost the same descriptions over and over again. Every building has to have the site cleared, the ground prepared, foundations laid, drains installed, walls, floors, staircases, windows, roofs, paint, etc. I got this straight away. Just as my childhood toys of Meccano and Bayko, a system of steel rods and brick tiles that predated Lego, had taken their inspiration from common building types, why couldn't buildings, especially similar buildings like schools, hospitals, libraries, etc., not be costed according to standardised terms and descriptions? In other words, life would be made to imitate the toys.

These 'quantities descriptions' would be things like, 'internal door, flush finish, half-hour fire-resistant, size 6'6" x 2'6" x 2"; no. 6'. Each door would then require items to be costed for forming the opening, the door frames, the hinges, handles, locks, finishes and so on. The only thing that would change from job to job would be the numbers and sizes. Why not then simply have a standard form printed with all the usual descriptions, and we would then fill in the sizes.

Although this may sound obvious now, as we are all familiar with auto-fill functions on computers and websites, in the late 1960s and early 1970s the internet geeks were, remember, only just starting to strap the ARPANET together over in California. Back in the real world, we were still having to type everything over and over, and if you wanted a copy of anything you had to ask at the time of typing for a carbon copy, the inked sheets slipped between pieces of paper in a typewriter. I think the maximum you could go to was six, and even this depended upon the strength of the typist's wrists as it needed a certain amount of pressure to make the last copy legible.

This quantities system would later be extended to something called the SCOLA system, at which I became an expert. SCOLA stood for the Secondary Consortium of Local Authorities, and the principle was relatively simple. If local authorities all agreed to build from an agreed manual of components, then the combined buying power would reduce the overall cost. It is exactly what drives today's numerous price comparison or 'groupon' websites, where large numbers of users come together to get the best deal on various items. Like St Kev's being the biggest all-boys school in the UK, the basic principle was fine, but way ahead of the technology needed to control and monitor it.

Out in St Helens, then, we were on the cutting edge, pushing hard at the twentieth-century technological frontier by having our quantities pre-printed and simply filling in the variables by hand. Any number of copies could then be produced quickly through the various design, planning and discussion stages, and sent to a professional printer for the tender copies. This removed hours, days, if not weeks from the preparation process, which meant, as I am sure Rex figured, we could actually take on more work and earn our increase in pay. He also took the view that if you could handle the work he would let you, and so by the time I was twenty-one I was managing contracts at a cost and involvement level that my previous employers had kept for partners. But if I learned a great deal about standardised systems and project management out in St Helens, I also ran straight into the establishment wall that made me vow that, as soon I could, I would never wear a tie again. The status quo was alive and well, and living out in Widnes.

Widnes is one of those towns that, as a Scouser, you're never quite sure about. It just seems to be on the way to and from everywhere else, without having any obvious reason for being there. Both the Romans and the Vikings gave it a miss, and although it is actually home to the world's first railway dock, where goods could be offloaded directly from train to ship, this was merely a stop on the world's first commercial railway, the Liverpool to Manchester. Perhaps it was because it was just a stop on the way to somewhere else that it found its niche as the centre of the UK chemical trade. There was no one already there to complain about the smell. Apparently, according to an official history of the town published by the then Widnes Corporation in 1961, by the end of the nineteenth century it was described as 'the dirtiest, ugliest and most depressing town in England' and a 'poisonous hell-town'.

I remember finding out all this during the Liverpool Capital of Culture year in 2008 when we ran a project to find out how Scousers really defined their city limits. Not the kind of lines that Roger McGough had us drawing around Kirkby, but where people saw their natural communities as lying. While Runcorn, on the opposite, southern bank of the Mersey to Widnes, and linked by what is known, tellingly, as the Runcorn Bridge, was felt to be part of the greater Scouse nation, Widnes was still classed as belonging to another world. Probably Lancashire. And it was here, in 1970, that the establishment wall went up against me.

I had been to an early meeting at the Education Offices to talk about a school project we were working on. I had been informed one of the senior officers would be present. We were doing a lot of work with schools at that time, preparing for something known as ROSLA: Raising of the School Leaving Age from 15 to 16 in September 1972. Most of the work revolved around making sure there were enough classrooms and toilets to cope with the extra numbers to be detained in education.

The substance of the meeting is long lost, but I do remember being told to make sure I was properly turned out and not dressed as if to meet a contractor on a building site. I came in my best shirt and tie and the only suit I possessed. We went through what we needed to do and I headed back to St Helens, where I was met by a stony-faced Rex with the classic drama line, 'My office.' I looked at the others present but they all shook their heads.

'Is that what you were wearing at the meeting?' he asked, as I walked into his office, but before I could even respond he carried on. He had, he told me, just taken a call from the senior officer at Widnes who had complained that I had turned up inappropriately dressed. I looked down. I had on my favourite and, I might add, highly fashionable blue knitted tie and pink shirt. What was inappropriate about that? He obviously read my expression and said that while he personally didn't mind, it was what the clients thought that counted. If they thought it was inappropriate, then inappropriate it was deemed to be. 'Don't let it happen again. Now get out.' I did, and started looking for a job elsewhere.

I think it is safe to say that I have never been a fashion victim, something else I put down to a lack of cash in my formative years, with the emphasis being on trying not to look out of place, rather than aiming for cutting edge. I suppose that was the key issue in Widnes. While I thought I was dressing to impress, I clearly wasn't. To me this was another example of the cultural divide, so I vowed that as soon as I could I would never again wear a piece of clothing made obsolete once the automated buttonhole machine was invented. I get the point about using a tie to express oneself, or to signify membership or support for certain groups, clubs, schools or regiments and such like, but why do it with a piece of cloth that dangles from your neck like a ready-made noose? (A lesson absorbed, perhaps, from my engineering theory and practice class.)

Since leaving quantity surveying in 1972 I have probably only worn a tie on half-a-dozen occasions, excluding things like black-tie events, which fall under the category of fancy dress anyway. While tieless, I have met the Queen, various Prime Ministers, Presidents, Bishops, clerics and dignitaries, and never had as much trouble as I have had trying to get into a few restaurants, clubs or even race tracks, which are all, in their various ways, peddling the social drugs of alcohol and tobacco but feel affronted if someone doesn't want to wear a Health & Safety hazard round their necks.

The daftest example of this I ever came across was after I had written an article for the *Daily Telegraph* suggesting that the National Lottery could do more with their cash to help culture and the arts. I was duly invited to lunch by Camelot to 'share views', at one of the old London clubs. I asked my PA, Donna, to point out that I never wore a tie and would that cause an issue? The answer came back that they had negotiated a special dispensation, provided I wore a silk polo-shirt. The lunch never happened. It actually made the point about them not understanding the real cultural needs of society.

It would be another year or so before I could abandon ties though, as I moved on to my third and, as it turned out, final term as an employee in 1971. By this time I had moved out of the family home in Huyton and had a flat in the city centre, which meant the journey out to St Helens was now reaching the outer limits of the travel-to-work theory.

I stated to look for a job in the city centre and, amazingly, I found one just along the road in Rodney Street, the Harley Street of the North West, where medics of every description lived cheek by jowl, or perhaps cheek by bowel. Amongst them was a smattering of architects, engineers and, naturally, quantity surveyors. So while I lived at number 12, I would go to work at number 38 for Houghton and Stackpoole (H&S).

It was not long before I became frustrated. Not by the work I was given, but by the fact that I could get through a day's worth in ninety minutes. Having leaped from the nineteenth-century world of Chapel Walks to the latter part of the twentieth century in St Helens, I now found myself dragged back to somewhere in the 1950s, where the prevailing state of mind was about knowing there were big technological challenges coming, but not knowing how to deal with them. This was not specific to my new employers, nor to quantity surveying in general, but was something being felt right across British industry, and further compounded by the fear of losing what had already been hard won. Result, inertia.

H&S was another large firm with several partners and therefore, due to the need for collegiate decision-making, worked at a much slower pace than I had become used to at Snowling's. There was a feeling that they needed to modernise but were not quite sure how, and no doubt some of the partners did not want to change the lifestyle it had taken them so long to acquire. This was something else I would become familiar with in the coming years, the realisation that dinosaurs procreate too. Having waited for so long to take over the stomping and roaring, the baby dinos did not want to face up to extinction just yet.

A great irony was that the reason I got the job with them was because of my experience with standardised systems, and in partic-ular the new SCOLA system. It was, so we thought at the time, the future, and I discovered this carried more weight with a prospective employer than my lack of IQS qualifications. It must have done as I found my salary increased from £14 per week to the princely sum of around £17. My thoughts turned towards a new – or perhaps more correctly, different – car. This time something less practical, which is when the Zodiac MkIII arrived, affordable because I would now be walking to work, something that would also make my dizzying new wage increase go even further.

To find the purchase cost I sold my by then lovingly rebuilt A55 to one of the guys at the new office, on condition I took his old battered wreck in part-exchange. I can't quite remember what the car was but it was something like a Hillman Minx. There was a real art to starting it, and once running it sounded like a right bucket of bolts being shaken about, but I thought it would make a reasonable runabout once the engine was sorted.

This was not quite as easy as it used to be living at my parents', where I could pull a car round the back of the house and leave it there while working on it. Living in the North West's Harley Street, I guessed the other residents wouldn't take too kindly to me stripping down an old car by the side of the kerb, so I tucked it away temporarily up a side street, Maryland Street, right opposite the flat so I could keep an eye on it. Every time I had a chance to take it up to my mum and dad's, I could never get the thing to start. This went on for a few weeks or so until one day I was walking down the road to get a newspaper when I suddenly heard a familiar sound. It was the bucket of bolts starting up.

I turned back to look and, sure enough, the Hillman came tearing round the corner from Maryland Street. There were two young guys inside and they had probably used a nail file or something, as you could do, in the worn locks to get in and start it. Without thinking, I stepped out into the road and roared at them, 'That's my car, you b★★★★★★★!' which was enough to make them instinctively swerve, hit the kerb, bounce on to the pavement and crash into the side of Notre Dame Convent on the corner. I ran towards them but they scarpered up and over a wall, into the convent grounds and away.

The bucket was now dented and bent at the front end, making the easy fix and nice little earner unrealistic. So ended my potential career as a used car salesman and I eventually flogged it off as scrap for £10. On top of this, the thing wouldn't start and I had to get help to push it back down the road. I never found out what happened to the *Fast and Furious* duo. They would just have had to take their chances of bumping into Mother Superior.

However, the postscript to this tale came from the guy to whom

I'd sold my precious A55. He changed jobs not long after and went to work at Cheshire County Council, where he was allowed to park in a car park near the river. One day he forgot to put the handbrake on and all my months of blood, sweat and toil ended up as a photo story in the *Chester Chronicle*. Up to its windows in water, the A55 too had to be scrapped.

This convinced me that despite my mechanical interest and ability, and despite my telling my sixth-form tutor that I wanted to be a man with a van, perhaps vehicles were not going to provide an alternative path to quantity surveying, with which I was becoming more and more frustrated. While I did enjoy wrestling with the complexities of the SCOLA system and coming up with solutions to unforeseen design challenges, I found the pace of work too frustrating. I began to understand what it must have been like for Roger McGough all those years before.

Eventually I went in to see one of the partners and asked if there was anything else I could do, explaining that I had had a lot more responsibility in my previous job. He listened but basically told me that he couldn't give me anything else, as that would put me on a par with some of the older and, pointedly, better qualified staff. He couldn't justify either that or the pay rise that would go with it. So, with a metaphorical pat on the head, I went back to completing what I had to do in an hour and a half and then, quite honestly, frittered and fretted the days away until I got so depressed at the thought of wasting more time that I decided to pack it all in.

This kind of decision sounds dramatic when summarised, but I had been thinking about it for a long time. I had also been trying to write comedy sketches after selling one to Mike and Bernie Winters while writing with a friend from school. It was called 'Breakfast in Bed' and featured Mike as a hotel manager showing Bernie to his room. Bernie asked if breakfast in bed had been arranged as requested and Mike confirmed it had, whereupon Bernie threw back the bed covers and leaped into . . . a bowl of porridge. Boom, boom. The best part about it was that we received £7.10s in old money from Thames Television, and a young and fit Cilla Black made a guest appearance as a French maid. For a couple of Scousers, how good could it get?

Although we split the money it was, on a pro rata basis, still far better than even the £21 per week that I was now earning, and I think I must have trodden the same familiar path that most aspiring writers do by writing to anyone and everyone, asking for advice. One person who responded was the one and only John Cleese, who agreed to meet and chat over lunch, why I do not know. We met at the Hungry Years Restaurant in Earls Court on 19 April 1972 and he proceeded to give me a master class on how to write comedy, as well as teaching me how to open the then newly introduced individual milk cartons.

Despite having the nerve to send off the initial letter, I was so nervous to be meeting an already cult figure that my hands were shaking while I struggled to find a way to open this strange pyramid of plastic that Londoners used for their milk. John noticed and calmly reached over, took the carton and demonstrated 'the knack', without comment or judgement. It was a small, yet at the same time memorable, moment, as without even knowing it he had shown me that it was possible to bridge the class divide. Here was the product of an archetypal Scouse comprehensive sitting having a burger and chips with an archetypal product of Oxbridge. For me it was probably the first real step towards realising that life is not about where you come from but rather who you are. It is not about structures but about people and their ideas. It is ideas that bond people, not class.

I can't recall which ideas I had sent him, or everyone else for that matter, as it is comparatively easy to sit within the sanctuary of your bedroom and randomly fire off ideas to the world, which is why so many people blog on the internet, but it is something else when someone replies, 'Let's meet.' Whatever it was, there must have been something in it to spark his interest, so no matter how insecure, nervous or apprehensive I felt, I kept telling myself that this was John Cleese. Of *Monty Python*. It might be my once-in-a-lifetime moment. As it turned out it was . . . to hear the two valuable pieces of advice he gave me over that lunch.

The first appears as the heading to this chapter. The only really enjoyable moment is the moment of creation. That moment in which you make yourself laugh or giggle or find yourself unable to find the words fast enough to explain the idea to others. My wife Alexis talks about frequently having to stand and wait for me to go through this phase, often without her understanding a word of the disjointed half-sentences I speak at the time, knowing it will all fall into place later after – and this was the main point of John's advice – the hard work has been put in.

A lot of people have ideas. Many have good ideas, a few have great ideas, but fewer still can actually deliver them. Great ideas don't get to the screen by chance, but only after a long and usually slow process that starts with convincing everyone else your moment of hysteria is not just idle self-indulgence. That it will appeal to a wider audience. That it can be made. That it will achieve great ratings. The demographic will be spot on. The writing will be compelling. The casting perfect. The direction empathetic. Camera work will be high-definition. Sound will be digital. Design will be fantastic. Costumes evocative. Music moving. Titles intriguing. Marketing perfectly focused. Scheduling targeted. And all of that will bring great reviews. Or not.

John's second piece of advice: take the reviews with a pinch of salt. Do not let one negative review overshadow everything else. No matter if you have nine rave reviews, someone somewhere won't like it on the old basis of 'you can't please all the people, all the time'. Yet it can be the one negative review out of ten that stays with you. This might well have been an insight into John Cheese's own character, but it also went to the basic human need to seek universal favour. Even when we know that this is impossible, we would all like everyone to love us and appreciate what we do, often forgetting that at other times we ourselves are the ones passing judgement on others.

As with many past events, I have no memory of what exactly we went on to talk about, but I came away feeling both grateful and inspired. We met a few times after that, once when the Python stage show came to Liverpool, but our career paths diverged and I am not sure if John knows how influential that chat was for me. Apart from those two nuggets of advice about hard work and keeping the reviews in balance, I learned how to open a milk carton and about the value of giving young talent an opportunity. Things I would take into the future when establishing MerseyTV.

Apart from this moment of clarity and support, what was also emerging from the responses to my avalanche of letters and submissions to all and sundry was a familiar Catch-22 situation: I needed to spend more time writing but I couldn't because I had a full-time job to hold down, but that wasn't progressing because I wasn't putting in the time for the professional examinations. A choice had to be made. The typewriter and phone or bricks and cement? I had to concentrate on one or the other. But how many QS-es had had lunch with John Cleese? I sat down and wrote my resignation letter.

People have since said to me that they thought it was a very brave thing to do, but my response has always been twofold. One, it didn't really feel like a risk as back in the 1970s there seemed to be plenty of jobs available if things didn't work out. And second, linked to the first, is the fact that you often achieve great things through sheer naivety. I probably didn't really know what state the economy was in back then, and since 2008 have wondered if many of us, or anyone for that matter, actually does.

But my decision was made based on what I thought were the best options at the time. So off I went to work the next day, ready to make the grand gesture, only to find there was nobody there to accept my resignation. None of the partners would be in that day. Even an extra day's reflection did nothing to change my mind, however, so a month later, on 28 July 1972, I ended my career as a QS and started life as an aspiring, soon-to-be struggling, writer.

4

Storyline Development (1972–76)

'Don't get on the treadmill until you have learned what it is you want to write' – *Brian Finch, Wigan, March 1976*

As with most journeys, whether of a thousand miles or not, the one to Brookside Close included a series of stepping-stones. From project to project. Lesson to lesson. Learning the craft. Gathering the skills, and scars, but always gaining experience. The final two stepping-stones were *County Hall* and *Going Out*, one a great experience, the other not so great. Both served me equally well. Further back on the path were stops at *Doctor in Charge, The Kids From 47A, The Squirrels, Sally Ann, Together, Horse in the House*, and *Potter's Picture Palace*. Oh, and a brief appearance at *Coronation Street*. Before them all there was Harry Secombe.

Upon making the decision that I no longer wanted to stay a QS, having handed in my slide rule and SMM (Standard Method of Measurement), I decided I wanted to write comedy for a living as by this time the much talked about golden age of comedy was in full flow. Following the BBC's 1960s series like *Hancock, Steptoe and Son* and *Till Death Us Do Part* came sit-coms like *The Likely Lads, Bless This House, The Lovers, The Liver Birds* from Liverpool, the great variety shows like *Morecambe and Wise, The Two Ronnies*, and, of course, *Monty Python's Flying Circus*.

If television was the new rock 'n' roll then comedy was heavy metal, but with only that Mike and Bernie Winters sketch behind me, the next few months were spent in a constant round of submissions and rejections, until towards the end of the year I sold an equally daft sketch to Yorkshire Television's *Harry Secombe Show*. This one had Harry being interviewed by a straight man about his pet talking octopus. I can't remember much about the content or punchline, except that it involved Harry wearing a comedy wetsuit, and gallons of water sloshing about as he kept ducking his head into a large water tank to consult the octopus.

One thing I clearly remember, though, is that this was my first fight over fees and rights. Yorkshire offered around £30 for a two-minute sketch, which was twice my weekly wage as a quantity surveyor. As the other established writers were paid around £60 per sketch, I figured that as a new writer they were trying to underpay me. My Scouse gene kicked in. I wanted parity. They told me to take it or leave it, and fully expected me eventually to take it as they went ahead, recorded and transmitted the programme.

It was probably more their high-handed attitude than anything else that made me dig my heels in, as I was desperate for the credit as much as the money, but I said I would leave it and what would they do about breaching my copyright? This focused their corporate mind and eventually they grudgingly paid me the £60, and in so doing taught me two even more valuable lessons. One was immediate: the value of copyright. The other hit home a decade later when I started *Brookside*, as early as Episode 7.

We had been fortunate enough to get Liverpool legend Peter Kerrigan to play Bobby Grant's union boss, Arthur. One of the primary directives to both casting and legal was that no one could come on set or be recorded without first having signed their contract accepting the standard *Brookside* terms. This was partly as a result of my old tussle with Yorkshire, but more to do with later wrangles with the BBC Copyright Department over *Grange Hill*, around the recurring theme of them threatening to cancel the programme if I did not sign the annual licensing contract by a certain date. It was a common tactic within the industry to try and delay sending back the contract until the work had been done, and then ask for an uplift.

And so it was with Peter. No sooner had we started on Episode 7 than I heard that he was now demanding his 'usual fee', not the *Brookside* Equity minimums that everyone else had signed up to. It was a simple but frustrating decision, especially as, only three weeks into the shoot, the production schedule was by this time almost a work of fiction in its own right. Arthur, rather than Peter, had to go.

I adopted what was to become a familiar routine over the years: went back to my office and rewrote the episode. While Arthur was originally supposed to bring news that the union would not officially back Bobby Grant's wildcat strike, thus precipitating its collapse, I now had a van race up to the picket line sounding its horn. Bobby walked over, everyone looked anxious, and Bobby returned to the men, ashen-faced. Arthur was dead; he'd had a heart attack. Just as Arthur's heart had given out, so the heart went from the picket line and Bobby went home to have an even better emotional scene with his wife, Sheila.

It was not the only emotional scene. Peter was obviously upset, as were a few folk around him, and there was a brief creative exchange around my right to kill off 'his' character. I stuck to the position, from which I never wavered over the years, that the programme itself is the star and no one is bigger or invaluable. It seemed to work. We moved on and no one was ever again allowed to set foot on a set until the contract had been signed, returned and the signature witnessed.

Back in 1972 though, I didn't quite appreciate that the fight over a comedy octopus would be the first skirmish in a never-ending war over copyright retention. Nor that I would go on to battle on almost every front in this war, quickly and profitably learning that copyright is infinitely divisible, which makes anything both potentially valuable yet almost impossible to quantify. Any potential value relies solely on the ability to sell it, either in its original life state or else recorded on any existing or yet to be invented technology platform in the now known or any future universe. See, it rolls off the tongue, doesn't it? It's a mindset that perfectly suits a Scouser's ability to argue both sides of the same argument in the same sentence, and remain oblivious to any irony or conflict. We were born to argue over social justice and copyright, and my next fight was only a stepping-stone away. The 'big break', *Doctor in Charge*.

I had given myself six months to see if I could become a writer. On the Monday following my leaving quantity surveying, I signed on the dole and was delighted to discover that it was no normal dole queue for me. I was eligible to join the Professional and Executive Register. I'm not sure if we got a few quid extra, but it was a 'nicer queue' with 'nicer people' than the one where all the brickies and flaggers had to go. The first thing I had to do was attend an interview so they could assess how to help me find the right job. They were 'nice', if perplexed, when I told them I didn't want to be a QS any more, but be a television scriptwriter instead. I might as well have said that I fancied a crack at being a brain surgeon but, as in all good bureaucracies, regulations somewhere said that if I, a Professional or Executive, wanted to seek a career change, then I had to be given an aptitude test. So an aptitude test I was given.

I was left alone in a room with a multiple-choice questionnaire. In the days before touch-screen or optically scanned forms, to complete this you had to punch a hole next to the appropriate question. An inner sheet would then be pulled out a bit more after each question, so the holes would eventually form a pattern across it. The questions were things like:

Q: if you ran over a dog, would you:
    a) drive on and hope no one had noticed?
    b) stop and try and administer first aid?
    c) stop and report it immediately to the police? Or,
    d) reverse back over it to make sure it was dead?

I figured that the pattern of holes, literally joining the dots, must eventually indicate what sort of career you were suited for, so I pulled out the inner sheet and looked at the back where, sure enough, there was a whole range of jobs and professions listed. I found the one most similar to my goal, which I think was Advertising Copywriter, punched all the holes leading back to it, joined the dots in reverse order, refolded the inner sheet and waited for them to return. They then took the form away and came back a short while later saying they would see me in six months, just to check how I was getting on. I'm sure they knew I'd used my initiative, shall we say, but perhaps that was what they expected from those on the Professional and Executive Register. I'm also sure that reverse-engineering the form had me opting for d) reverse back over the dog.

By Christmas 1972, my self-imposed deadline was rapidly approaching and, despite now knowing a lot of people's phone numbers and their PA's first names, the only thing to show for it was the Harry Secombe sketch for Yorkshire. I decided to give it another three months, as the £60 I'd eventually been paid would help stretch things and by this time I had also got to know Humphrey Barclay who was producing the *Doctor in Charge* series at London Weekend Television (LWT). At that time the writing team included Graham Chapman from the Pythons, Bill Oddie and Graeme Garden from *The Goodies*, and the actor Jonathan Lynn who would later go on to do *Yes Minister* with Anthony Jay.

It was illustrious but intimidating company, so the mere fact that Humphrey kept encouraging me to send in ideas gave me the confidence to extend that six-month deadline. However, as is typical in the 'hurry up and wait' media atmosphere, by the following February there was still no sign of a commission. I started the process of digging out my slide rule and SMM and applying for jobs.

I was scheduled to go back to being a QS with Unit Construction on Monday 26 March 1973, when Humphrey called me the Friday before that. He was going to commission one of my ideas: 'The Garden Fête'. The fee was to be £400, five months' QS salary, and soon a second and third commission followed, so that by June I had another year's income already in the bank. There is an entry in my diary for that day that reads: 'HB Called. Commissioned. Hurrah.' Very Scouse. Very reverse snobbery but the relief is plain. I was on my way.

The idea for that first script came straight out of my own past experience in helping my mum and dad raise money for the church through what we called the annual Gala Days, when the parish would come together and mount stalls, organise games, etc. A carry over from trades unions Gala Days, no doubt, but with a typical village fête and fundraiser atmosphere. The script's plot followed the usual student medic hi-jinks with the punchline being that one of the donkeys from the Donkey Derby runs amok and ends up crashing through a tent just in time be crowned Miss St Swithin's, instead of the love interest and heart-breaker Angharad Rees, probably better known for *Poldark* and more lately as a jewellery designer. This was also my first experience of the press giving away the storyline as the *TV Times* featured a great picture of the donkey already wearing the winning sash.

My other episodes were about an epidemic – with hilarious consequences, of course – and, in line with my developing interest, an early examination – with more hilarious consequences, of course – of patients' rights in trying to challenge the bureaucracy and busybodies running the hospital, in particular the omnipotence of the main authority figure, consultant Sir Geoffrey Loftus, played brilliantly by Ernest Clarke.

If I'd thought life couldn't get any better than having Cilla Black in that Mike and Bernie Winters sketch, then this was on another level. To reach for a well-worn cliché, it is hard to describe the moment when you see your first credit board. When your name goes up on the studio monitors, and then later at home, that 'Written by . . .' moment is very, very special. So much so that I asked Humphrey if I could have the actual board, for that was exactly what all the credits were like then. Black boards with white lettering on them that were stacked on an easel and then quickly removed one by one in front of the camera. I still have that first one. It hung in my MerseyTV office for thirty years.

This first experience of the production process was also a steep learning curve, or I made it so since I was as hungry to learn more about the art of writing comedy as I was interested in the business of producing it. On the comedy side the biggest lesson was to maintain faith in the original idea. As John Cleese had said, the fun was in the creation: the rest was hard work. And one of the biggest dangers for a writer is losing faith in the original script. If it is funny on first read-through, the writer's job is to protect it from the creative team's natural desire to 'improve things'. This takes a great amount of confidence and discipline as by the time you have heard a joke six times it is no longer funny. The temptation then, to be firmly resisted, is to embellish things, forgetting that your audience will be hearing it for the first and only time.

The production week would start with a read-through and then slowly proceed through the script, rehearsing each scene until the day of recording in front of a live audience. This would probably be six days later, so by that time both cast and crew were so familiar with the lines that the temptation to make it 'funnier' by ad-libbing or inserting other gags was enormous, but had to be resisted. As a writer you would be hovering on the sidelines trying to protect your sacred words, but at that time writers were very much the bottom of the pile. Once the script was accepted and put in the hands of a producer you were history. There was as yet no automatic right for a writer to be able to attend any part of the production process. You were tolerated, but ignored.

This was one of the things I helped change as part of the Writers' Guild of Great Britain Television Committee. We eventually won the right to attend the read-through and rehearsals of our work, and be paid an attendance allowance to do so, like every other member of the production process. While it may sound like nothing more than common sense to have the person who actually wrote the script hanging around to answer questions, that fails to take into account both the history of television and the egos of producers and directors, something I would later do battle with and which eventually drove me on to create MerseyTV in a classic example of Marxist theory: seizing the means of production from the bourgeoisie.

To understand why writers were at the bottom of the heap you need an understanding of the balance of power within broadcasting, and the status quo in the 1970s. Although this is a subject in its own right, already covered by many others, I'll try and summarise it very briefly under three headings: public service, box office and unions.

The public-service element came from the foundation of the BBC in the 1920s when the then developing commercial radio industry was nationalised under the principle that broadcasting was too important to be left to a 'combine of commercial companies'. This was the original BBC, the privately owned British Broadcasting Company, and the combine was the six large telecommunications companies that owned it: Marconi, Radio Communication Company, Metropolitan-Vickers, General Electric, Western Electric, and British Thomson-Houston Electric Company. Like Apple creating iTunes to shift iPods, these companies had come together to make content for the radio sets they were manufacturing.

The government though, as governments do, started to fret about the power of mass communication, and so did what governments also do: formed a committee to look into it all. The 1926 Crawford Committee then came back with the 'right decision', which was that it should be state-owned and funded, and who better to run it than the guy who had been running the commercial company? Thus John Reith became the BBC's first Director-General. Or, as the BBC, under its mantra 'Inform, educate and entertain', gradually became the high church of public-service broadcasting, perhaps he should be seen as its first Pope.

Although Reith himself is said not to have taken to television, believing its moving images would lead to frivolity and distraction from the high tone set by radio, the values and moral standards he put in place cascaded into the new medium in the 1930s. These values and moral standards were, of course, also those of government and the governing classes – what became known as 'the establishment'. He was right in predicting that television's moving images would demand more than talking heads, but the clipped vowels and evening dress of the early years made it clear that this was still an up-market operation for an up-market clientele, comparable to a night at the theatre rather than a trip to the musical hall or dance palais, which it probably was as the number of televisions could be counted then only in thousands and cost more than a car, themselves still comparatively rare throughout Britain.

The next great step forward in television's development came in 1954 when, along with an end to rationing of food, there was an end to TV rationing with the arrival of ITV. The post-war government, as governments do, set up another committee under Lord Beveridge. Having already laid down the foundations of the modern welfare state in his 1942 report, he turned his attention to the future of television. Although the committee recommended that broadcasting should stay in the hands of the BBC as a state monopoly, a minority report came out that favoured creating other broadcasters to compete with it. This was authored by Conservative MP Selwyn Lloyd, later to become Foreign Secretary and Chancellor of the Exchequer. Lloyd's minority report proposed several changes: a Commission for Broadcasting to oversee the BBC, but only as a radio broadcaster; a separate Television Corporation; competition to be provided by another or possibly two other national commercial broadcasters for radio and television, and a potentially large number of local radio stations. Apart from not removing television from the BBC's remit, this proved to be a fairly accurate outline of what happened over the following sixty years.

A new Conservative government was elected in 1951 and soon got to work on the ideas that Selwyn Lloyd had proposed, culminating after much controversy and heated debate in the 1954

Television Act. A new Independent Television Authority (ITA) was charged with awarding licences, on fixed terms and 'in the interests of good taste'. This was because the only other existing examples of commercial television were in the United States, and were widely considered 'vulgar', especially as coverage of the Queen's Coronation, the event I had crawled up the street to watch, had been interrupted in the US by advertisements. Not only that, but one of the breaks had apparently featured a celebrity chimpanzee known as J. Fred Muggs. You can see the point, but because of this fear of 'vulgarity', advertising slots were, as they still are, strictly limited, and a clause was included in the 1954 Act banning breaks during any broadcasts featuring the Royal Family. I wonder if it still exists, and if Sue Johnston, Ricky Tomlinson and Caroline Aherne know about it?

With the scene now set for commercial television funded by advertising, the next thing was to find the right sort of people to run it. People who would know how to attract large audiences that would appeal to large advertisers. People like theatre impresarios or cinema owners, already feeling threatened by this new form of moving-image entertainment. So it was that the likes of show-business agent Lew Grade ended up with a licence for Associated Television in London; theatre and cinema owner Sidney Bernstein with Granada in Lancashire; and Associated British Cinemas (ABC) in the Midlands and North. Television's second element was therefore box-office entertainment.

The third historical element that contributed to the way television was run in the 1970s came about as a reaction to the first two. Big government created first a big corporation for a public-service broadcaster, then second, insisted on competition from big commercial companies with big ideas for mass marketing. In such a scenario the value of each programme slot is inevitably less important than the overall schedule, and in turn individual contributors become, well, simply cogs in the greater machine. That then creates tension with the third strand of the operation, the unions, as big companies inevitably promote and then provoke big unions, to the extent that industrial relations often become a more dominant production concern than the cost or quality of the product itself – a lesson brutally learned in the 1980s.

These three historic elements, or pressures, of public service, box office and unions are what exercised the money men up on the top floors of whatever tower block they inhabited. They might have enjoyed a particular programme personally, but in corporate terms whether a line here and there stayed or went was of little concern to them. What did matter was the number of beans in the sack. If you paid a bunch of writers to attend every programme rehearsal and recording, all those beans soon added up to expensive sackfuls, alongside potential parity claims from other unions. Best then just to say no to writer participation.

That sort of corporate mentality in ITV played to the cultural legacy of its founding fathers. In theatre and film, the producers and directors were gods. Writers were initially courted and fêted but there were always plenty more of them, both established and aspiring. In television the problem was exacerbated as the development of series required teams of writers rather than the single-authored voice of a play or serial. More series meant more writers. They also meant more producers. Each series would have one producer, a big cog, with more status. And it would have more writers, smaller cogs, of lower status. Writers became seen as hired pens brought in to get the job done. And if there were not enough writers, or time, or inclination to go out and find them, then producers or script editors would simply do it themselves. How hard could it be?

All of this was becoming apparent to me while I worked on the *Doctor in Charge* series, but was really hammered home when I later went to work on *The Squirrels* at ATV. This was a sit-com set in an office environment and had been created by Eric Chappell who had also written *Rising Damp* for Yorkshire. Eric was too busy to write all the *Squirrels* scripts so I managed to get myself on to the writing team for the third series, and in doing so met a writer called Brian Finch, then probably the highest-paid writer in the UK and earning well into six figures.

Brian is, sadly, no longer with us but was, in my opinion, from what little time I spent with him, both a great man and a great writer. He was best known as the guy who could write anything at short notice. He had started out as a journalist, did a spell on *TV Times*, and through that moved into television. He told me it was his journalistic training that meant he could sit down at his typewriter and bash out anything to a quick deadline. In fact, he also said he found it difficult to work any other way. He had to have a deadline to focus upon.

John Cleese had given me that early advice on the moment of creation and the importance of hard work. Brian reinforced this but also gave me a masterclass on what being a professional television writer was all about. Delivering what was asked within the restrictions set. That was the job you accepted. You could argue for the art when it was your own show, but if you accepted a commission on someone else's show, just do it. Otherwise they will just get someone else. But there was a caveat that stayed with me as the second most important bit of advice I ever received. Don't get on the treadmill until you have learned what it is you want to write.

He gave me this bit of advice one night at his home in Wigan, waving his arm to indicate his very comfortable house and telling me that, although he was very well paid and had a great life, he had earned so much and created such a lifestyle for himself that he now found it difficult to stop and find the time to write what he really wanted to write. He felt pigeonholed as a 'series writer', the guy who could write and fix anything but had not yet established himself as an individual creative talent. The sadness and regret this talented man felt resulted from the still elitist nature of the television business at the time. ITV was seen as vulgar, downmarket, the place you went to make money, as against the higher purpose of the BBC's public service. Series were downmarket to serials, which in turn ranked below single dramas in the artistic merit league. Today Brian would be fêted and his talent could have revived a lot of creaky dramas over the years. I left Wigan for the trip back to Liverpool feeling I had been privileged to spend an evening with a wise and generous man.

To give Humphrey Barclay due credit, he was slightly ahead of the industry in always encouraging his writers to be part of the production process. You could attend his read-throughs, rehearsals, studio and even location recording, even if you wouldn't be paid for doing so. The trade-off was that it allowed you to grow quickly. To learn how the business operated, if you wanted to. There were many who didn't, as the BBC and ITV negotiators would point out in our union negotiations. Why give right of access to people who were not interested anyway? The counter-argument was that they were, but couldn't afford to take time off paid work to do so.

I did want to attend and used every opportunity I had to watch and learn about the process. What would and what wouldn't work.

As with school and quantity surveying, it is often the stuff you learn informally, by simply observing what is going on, that proves the most valuable. This was brought home to me quite clearly when I was allowed to attend the recording of a new pilot LWT were making as a potential vehicle for a new rising star called David Jason.

Sir David, as he now is, had been an irregular character in the *Doctor* series and it was obvious he had a brilliant talent for comedy. One of the writers on the programme, Bernard McKenna, had written a script called *The Top Secret Life of Edgar Briggs* in which Jason played an inept personal assistant to the head of the British Secret Intelligence Service. It was a bit like the US series *Get Smart* where the clueless operative still manages to solve every case and save every day. I had asked if I could attend the recording as I had picked up a copy of the script and read it on the train back to Liverpool.

I thought it was the funniest thing I had read, really making me laugh out loud on the train. I was therefore filled with anticipation while sitting in the studio audience and . . . it was terrible. The recording seemed to bear little resemblance to the script I had read and was now full of 'embellishments', which were perhaps funny to those jaded after the week's rehearsals, but not to everyone else. Although going into production, it never survived the first series, while the future Sir David's talent was recognised a year later in *Porridge* and *Open All Hours*.

All these productions and recordings were like informal training seminars for me. Crucially, while attending a recording of one of my own episodes, my interest and understanding of copyright was stimulated after meeting Richard Gordon, the original author of the novels on which the *Doctor* films and television series were based. Chatting to him, I discovered that while I was being paid £400 per episode, he was getting a similar amount just to license the copyright to London Weekend. It was obvious where I needed to be.

The next seminar topic was back to the rate for the job, after finding out that The Goodies and Pythons were being paid around £700 a script. Even accepting that they had a more established track record, the disparity still seemed disproportionate. I made my case to Humphrey and the contracts folk who were, as people, sympathetic. But, being good cogs in the larger machine, they pointed out that their hands were tied as there was actually a government pay freeze on at that time.

When the next series came round I got an uplift, but also a very painful and sharp lesson on the realities of the business. Having done two series from each of the first two books, *Doctor in Charge* and *Doctor at Large*, Humphrey then wanted to move on to *Doctor at Sea* and had come to a deal with cruise-ship operator Fred Olsen to shoot on board one of their cruises. The only trouble was that we had to fit in with their cruise schedule, which meant things had to be put together much faster than previously.

The writing team was called in to a late-night script-planning meeting on top of the LWT tower on the South Bank, and there a plan was formulated as to how we could get the scripts turned round in time. I was asked if I would write one episode individually and co-write the opener with another rising star, Gail Renard. We agreed and were set impossible delivery deadlines but with strong assurances from Humphrey that all he wanted to see was a structure and the logistics required. The opener was duly written and delivered and then I set to work on my own episode just before Christmas, with a deadline of 31 December. I remember not being happy with it, as I had rushed it as requested, but with those reassurances ringing in my ears, I sent it off with a note saying I knew it was far from perfect. Humphrey agreed. And rejected the script.

I was devastated. So much for the reassurances, although even at the time I was more annoyed that I had sent in a script I was not happy with than I was with the rejection. And the failure of the script might not even have been down to the shortage of time, for as I have learned over the years, state of mind is far more important than the number of hours a writer spends at the desk.

Possessing the Scouse gene for sniffing out conspiracy – we learn to read between the lines before we learn to read – I did have a few suspicions at the time that I'd been knocked back because I was being 'too difficult' in asking for more money, but it probably wasn't the case. When I later learned to play the four-dimensional game of media politics, I discovered the scriptwriting business is relatively straightforward. It comes down to what Brian Finch told me. It is about delivery. If you deliver the goods, almost anything will be forgiven. I didn't. Simple as that. Learning curves can have a few rough edges.

My biggest mistake probably lay in growing too complacent. As I had been taken into this fantastic comedy academy and written three of the previous series' sixteen episodes then, obviously, I was the next big thing. On top of this I was also beginning to get my name about since, through getting the break on *Doctor in Charge*, I had cracked Catch-22 and found myself an agent, Fraser & Dunlop, one of the biggest. By Christmas I was working on *The Kids From 47A*, courtesy of Gail Renard who was script editing, and had a series in development with Thames Television. Considering that nine months earlier I was on the verge of returning to quantity surveying, I was now a legend in my own lunchtime. By the New Year it was all falling apart.

The Thames development came to nothing except a long-term relationship with the Executive Producer for Drama, Lewis Rudd, who would eventually commission *Going Out* at Southern Television. *The Kids From 47A* was an interesting premise, predating by many years the US hit *Party of Five*. 47A was the number of a flat where three siblings were having to fend for themselves, although I don't think it was ever explained what had happened to Mum and Dad. While a great premise, because what kid doesn't want to live alone without their parents, an area Channel 4 tried to mine more recently with its reality TV show *Boys and Girls Left Alone*, at the time I think the prevailing wisdom was not to upset the audience with any thoughts about parental death. So, don't mention it.

It was a fun series to work on, with the kids always having to stay one step ahead of the authorities to keep their independence. One of the episodes I did revolved round the fifteen-year-old big sister, and now mum figure, Jess, played by Christine McKenna of *Flambards*, trying to explain to her nine-year-old brother why he was in trouble for picking flowers in a public park. How the concept of 'public' does not mean the flowers are available for everyone to pick. Despite my still strong desire to write comedy, this was another early indicator of the sort of drama I was later to become interested in. What *47A* really did though was introduce me to Lew Grade's ATV, ITV's powerhouse of showbusiness and variety.

While going to the BBC was a bit like going to the HQ of a nationalised industry, a visit to Granada in Manchester felt like calling in at the Prudential as Sidney Bernstein had developed it specifically to sell off as offices if the television company failed. Thames felt like the old Crawford biscuits factory my mum had worked at for a time, but ATV, based out in Elstree, near Borehamwood, was known as the 'British Hollywood'. Since the 1920s, it had been home to several film studios like ABC and MGM, while ATV had taken over the former British National Studios, still known to the locals as 'The Douglas Fairbanks studios' as he had once owned them and planned to make films for Hollywood there. With their green-tiled roofs, the buildings could have been on any studio lot in Burbank.

My links with this piece of Hollywood continued through to the *Grange Hill* years after ATV sold the studios to the BBC. Initially bought for a training base, the BBC soon moved production there, including building Albert Square for *EastEnders*. It all became a bit institutionalised after that, but back in its ATV days you often saw big Hollywood names like Bing Crosby, Bob Hope and Julie Andrews wandering the studio corridors. It was also, perhaps inevitably, staffed by more of the Oxbridge bunch, and not long after the LWT experience, my residual insecurity began to resurface. For me, it was a bit like being back with the grammar-school nerds as a QS.

Any competitive social pack will hunt for weakness and soon I found that the gaps in my education were starting to show. While it was too late to start catching up on the past participle in French – or *le participe passé*, apparently, a challenge one ex-Cambridge script editor did throw at me – two things became clear. One was that if I wanted to succeed in this world then, to use a construction term, I needed to backfill those education gaps. That, in turn, should help boost my levels of confidence and self-esteem. So I decided to see if I could do what my mum and dad had originally wanted: go to university.

In September 1974 I went along to Liverpool University and made my case to the then Head of Social Studies, Peter Davies, saying I wanted to restart my education. I explained I wanted to carry on being a writer and to use the university course for what it should be used for: filling gaps, expanding horizons and extending knowledge. To my surprise and delight he was sympathetic, to the point of creating a space for me in that year's intake, and then becoming something of a Guardian Angel to me during my time there. I had retained an interest in economic and social history, which probably helped as he was an economic historian himself, so with his assistance I was able to put together an eclectic degree mix of Sociology, Politics, and Economic and Social History. It was a great pleasure for me to be able to thank him publicly in 2010, while receiving an Honorary Doctorate from the University of Liverpool, for having the faith first to create that space for me thirty-five years earlier, and then for looking after me over my time there, especially during the final year when *Grange Hill* was taking so much of my attention. I should have been thrown out, but he knew that the reason I had approached him in the first place was to make myself a better writer, and *Grange Hill* was in fact a product of my course work.

Social Studies was perfect for me, as was the grant that came with it. At the ripe old age of twenty-five I was classified as a so-called mature student, which meant I also qualified for a mature student's grant of around £800 per year, plus the ability to sign on the dole during the vacations. It would be fair to say that my writing career benefited from state subsidy, just as it would be easy, with all the recent unease about tuition fees, student loans and debt, to look back on this period through rose-tinted glasses as the golden age of education. Perhaps it was in some ways, but it would be a mistake to fall into the trap of thinking that education then came free. It didn't, we simply paid for it in arrears rather than upfront. We have changed the mechanism of fee collection from taxes to loan repayments and, while there are arguments against that, vociferous opponents would do well to go back and look at the average taxation rates in the 1970s against what they are now.

Social Studies was also perfect for me because within a few weeks the 'ghost of university lost' was laid, mainly, ironically, because of my age and background. Although I found myself out on a limb again – too old for the average student crowd and too young for the middle-agers who were there as part of their career development – I was able to challenge the largely middle-class lecturers about the real causes of things like crime and gang violence on the estates. If I had found the path I wanted to follow, in television, then I had also discovered how I would navigate it confidently: through sociology. Instead of fretting about class conflict, I would write about it.

Sociology is always conflicted, between the empirical and rhetorical, the observation against the postulated theory, or perhaps more correctly, quantitative versus qualitative research. My background in Huyton, Kirkby and quantity surveying had given me a real understanding of the social relations, stratification, interaction, culture and deviance of the working-class communities that so fascinated my middle-class tutors, epitomised perhaps by the vogue piece of the day, Howard Parker's *A View From the Boys*. This was what is referred to as a participant observation study, where the sociologist tends to mix with and become accepted by those under scrutiny.

A View From the Boys had Parker running with and being assimilated into a gang on the sort of estates and tenement blocks I had refurbished as a QS. The places where the monkeys and five in a bed shared the coal in the baths. Or so he thought. It was obvious to me, reading this great work, that the boys were enjoying playing with their newly found best mate. I appreciate I may be doing Parker a disservice, as he did admit at the time that it was a subjective rather than objective piece of work, but to me it was all tosh. Exactly the same sort of scenario we see every now and then on TV when the out-of-town, usually middle-class media folk roll up to get down and dirty with the boys in the hoods. The lads see them coming a mile off, turn it on for the cameras and then play them like rats in a barrel, especially if there are any 'arrangement/facilities fees' on offer.

As we should all know by now, after a decade or so of reality TV, no one acts normally on camera and media-baiting has been going on since Outside Broadcast (OB) units were invented. The best example I have seen was during the inner-city riots. Not in 2011, but back in 1981. The disturbances in Toxteth in Liverpool, like those in St Paul's in Bristol, Handsworth in Birmingham, and Chapeltown in Leeds, unlike the 2011 riots, resulted from racial tension and inner-city deprivation. This was a dangerous and difficult time, but after a few days of the same footage of missile-throwing, police charges, cars and buildings burning, the media started to look for underlying reasons and causes. Naturally, for balance, they needed to get a few of the actual rioters on camera to counter the establishment view, and I remember watching a late-night live news programme that appeared to have a ring leader explaining the conspiracy that lay behind it all.

'What conspiracy?' said the eager reporter. 'It's, like, big business and that, isn't it?' offered our riot expert. The reporter looked a bit surprised. 'Big business? What do you mean?' 'Well, it's just them out to make us do it, isn't it? Use the petrol in the bottles. The more we do it, the more they make, see. It's just a conspiracy.' You could see the reporter mentally shifting gear from bafflement to excitement, already writing the Bafta speech for this great scoop, until . . . 'It's Esso and Pilkington's, isn't it?' The potential Bafta, along with any pretence at serious journalism, evaporated faster than warm petrol as the 'rioters' all fell about laughing. Gotcha!

The same sort of wind up, or perhaps media class-gulf, was on display during the 2011 riots coverage, only this time the media were probably victims of their own spin. Having spent the last thirty years first building the myth that television's primary function was news and current affairs, they then fell into the trap of rationalisation and centralisation, becoming convinced that everything flows and can be explained from London. That national news is the capital's news. This has led, over the past decade or so of cost-cutting, to an unhealthy concentration of resources on the comings and goings of government, so that relationships within the Westminster media village became too cosy, to be thrown into stark relief by the phone hacking scandal that broke around News International in 2011.

This slow erosion, almost implosion, of real national and regional perspectives in news coverage had also bred the idea that every news story can be viewed through the lens of party politics. Hence the complete nonsense spoken about the 2011 riots. The news agenda at the time was geared towards austerity cuts and simmering concerns about policing tactics at various demonstrations, like those around tuition fees and the G8 conference. When the first riots started in Tottenham, where there was a long history of racial tension going all the way back to the 1981 riots, the police were probably right to stand back and figure out what it was they were really facing.

This led to an instant knee-jerk reaction in the Westminster media village, with accompanying political and media criticism about the police 'getting it wrong again', while at the same time broadcasting the clear information that the North London cops were indeed taking a hands-off approach. This then appears to have encouraged copycats and opportunists to have a go elsewhere, and when they met with little resistance, social media did the rest until soon it appeared to be open season on every high street. This was more organised flash-mobbing smash and grab than real rioting. The usual suspects dutifully started popping up across the news channels, claiming every reason under the sun for this breakdown in civil order, with Opposition Shadow Ministers claiming that the anti-social behaviour was both a symptom of and a reaction to twelve months of Coalition rule. Even Paxo on *Newsnight* thought this was daft. What exactly was supposed to be going on? Libraries are closing, so let's grab a pair of trainers as compo?

No matter what the post-mortem inquiries tell us, the socio-logical interest of the 2011 riots lies in the fact that the smash-and-grab raids even took place, so what caused people to feel either angered or emboldened enough to risk it? The explanation probably comes down to the very same thing that Parker's study seemed to overlook in his 1970s record of areas like the Bullring tenement block in Liverpool: playing the percentages on being caught. The Bullring, as its name suggests, is a huge semi-circular 1930s block of flats. All the stairways, balconies and front doors overlook the central area, and this, according to sociology researchers, created a sense of village. One community facing inward to support itself against the rest of the city. This sense of belonging was, apparently, why crime and antisocial behaviour rates were lower there than elsewhere in the city.

Well, perhaps, as my own parents came from this sort of inner-city community, which could be intimidating to 'non-residents', but the fact that every front door and every front window over-looked the other 400 flats had another consequence, not noted by the social scientists. As we knew from experience, you only nicked the records at parties where no one knew you. It wasn't just a matter of friendship or community, but of weighing up the chances of being identified and caught. It's sociology, not rocket science. If people think they can get away with something, they will be tempted to try. Whatever it is. All businesses build in a set percentage for 'staff losses', something I would later have to come to terms with myself as a large employer. Go on, try this test. What have you 'borrowed' from someone or somewhere?

This sort of empirical analysis from a 'participant practitioner', rather than an observer, didn't go down too well with the younger tutors, some of whom were around my own age. I got straight As, though, from Professor J. B. Mays, senior lecturer, holder of the Eleanor Rathbone Chair, and a leading name in the field of youth, education and juvenile delinquency. Some of the young turks had decided he was 'out of touch'. I think they meant 'no longer naive'.

Mays' work can be summarised as pointing out that a lot of what we now call antisocial behaviour is '. . . not so much maladjustment, as . . . adjustment to a sub-culture in conflict with the culture of the city as a whole', and it 'draws attention to the interrelationship of family and neighbourhood'. In other words, wanting and trying to fit in. To share the common purpose or values, be one of the crowd. Exactly what most of the participants said after being collared by CCTV after the 2011 smash-and-grab riots. They invariably said they were simply swept along. This is not to condemn or condone, simply to try and understand. That above all is what sociology is about. And once there is understanding, then perhaps solutions may be worked towards or, at the very least, preventative support can be offered.

If Criminology and Urban Sociology helped me understand the world a bit better, the sociology of education explained exactly what had happened to me after passing that eleven-plus exam, and why I was now back studying. It was all down to political and social engineering. Although I have since been back to the university to give a guest lecture at the School of Sociology, describing my time as a member of the Marxist Appreciation Society, it became more and more obvious to me during my studies there that class conflict lay at the heart of society's dysfunction; policy-makers of one social class not quite understanding the class or classes for whom they were, or are, framing policy.

Why else would you herd people together in large tower blocks? Or displace 70,000 people from an inner city to dump them in the middle of a rural landscape without basic amenities like schools and shops? Why else would you carve out huge tracts of land to create roads that allow industry to exit faster than it can enter? Why else would you close local hospitals and force people who are not in the best of health to travel greater and greater distances in search of treatment? Why else would you force householders to have homes renovated to a lower standard than those they already have? Why would you do any of these things unless you categorised people merely as statistics or numbers?

Yet, it is not just the bulldozer of state legislation that clears the path for political intervention. What is known as neighbourhood gentrification also plays its part, when property markets overheat and both developers and homeowners look for greener pastures, too often literally, where they can capitalise on lower land prices and Henry Ford's travel-to-work legacy. Before long, traditional working-class or rural communities are swallowed up by a fast-expanding middle class, whose demands soon start to change the local pub, restaurants, and even what's on the supermarket shelves. There is nothing wrong with this; it is part of the inevitable growth in any society. In many ways it is far preferable to the enforced social cleansing and suburban clearances we have seen in the past, except for one thing. What happens to those who are displaced by it?

We now have areas of our cities and countryside rendered virtually inaccessible to large tranches of the population simply because they can no longer afford to live there. Every developer knows that in order to gain planning permission they must provide affordable or social housing as part of the development plan. But is providing a few token cheap houses in an otherwise expensive district really the solution — or is that just a way of providing cheap property for the servant class to live in?

Is there still a Marxist edge to this multi-millionaire writer's voice? No, because this argument is not really about politics or class or social creed or even Marxism — now just one of sociology's fashion labels — but more about common sense. If you allow a community to grow up around one employer or industry, then it should be just a matter of common sense to provide some form of insurance for if, or when, that sole source of employment shuts up shop. As the great Liverpool philosopher George Harrison wrote, 'All Things Must Pass'.

The point is that central planning anywhere, from Moscow to Milton Keynes, inevitably ends in disaster, as the dictates of centralised agendas and political careers are incapable of recognising, let alone responding to, local need. New housing is better than slums. New schools and hospitals are better than old ones. Immigration is good for the economy. European integration is good for financial, personal and military security. No one can argue with these policies, only with the ways in which they are implemented. How can merging three local schools into one be good for the three communities that once revolved around them? How can merging hospitals be an improvement for the patients and their visitors forced to travel miles and pay through the nose to park when they arrive? How can a new house without access to public transport be seen as an improvement? Immigration without integration can only cause tensions. Just as European rather than national sovereignty will only cause resentment. The USA has been involved in this process for nearly 250 years and is still a long way from achieving social harmony.

These are the kind of arguments I raised in urban sociology, where the overriding view was that cities were dead and people wanted to live in suburbia. I argued the exact opposite, already living as I was in the centre of the city and right next-door to campus. Given the choice, many more would like to live in cities so that there would be no travel costs and all amenities would be reachable on foot. At this time most of the lecturers, naturally, lived in the leafy suburbs with their sandstone villas, and the students travelled in from the pastoral halls, also based out in the suburbs. Today, in common with most university towns, Liverpool city centre is dominated by student halls, including, in another of life's great ironies, the once infamous Bullring. From once feared tenement block, it has now been refurbished to become desirable student accommodation. En-suite bathrooms, broadband and Sky pre-installed. How's that for the evolving face of a city?

In 1997, after the arrival at Channel 4 of Michael Jackson as Chief Executive, I found myself once again engaged in this argument around *Brookside* and *Hollyoaks*, though this time arguing on the other side. Jacko and his crew had fallen for New Labour's idea that 'we are all middle-class' and 'suburbia is dead'. There I was, sitting in our production base in a leafy suburb of Liverpool, making a programme about people who lived in the suburbs, for the majority of our audience who also lived in the suburbs – and here was a bunch of metropolitans telling us that suburbia was dead! The future was all about loft living apparently, so *Brookie* should move to the docks. That suggestion was daft and led to what turned out to be the opening skirmish in the Long and Winding Road to *Brookie's* extinction.

By the third year of my Social Studies degree, I had managed to sell the idea of *Grange Hill* to Anna Home, then Executive Producer of Children's Drama at the BBC. I had been trying to maintain the momentum of my writing career but, just as when I was working full-time, my inability to be in London and able to 'drop in' on people was a handicap. I had even followed everyone's advice to 'get yourself an agent'. In fact, by the time I got to *Grange Hill* I had tried three. Large, medium and small, but no size fitted as I always ended up frustrated by either the lack of doors being opened to me, or the fact that I was always 'on hold' while they dealt with the likes of Tom Stoppard and Alan Bleasdale first. I could understand that, but not the idea that it seemed to be left to me to find the work, and them stepping in to negotiate the contract and then taking 10 per cent.

It soon occurred to me that this was a one-way arrangement as they would have to up every fee offered by about 20 per cent to make my retaining them worthwhile, especially as I had no need of late-night or early-morning counselling sessions. I'd had all the therapy I'd need just growing up in Huyton: Life gets tough; live with it.

It wasn't until I moved to the other side of the production desk that I started to appreciate that if agents didn't exist we would have to invent them. If media, and television in particular, were created as the pilot scheme for care in the community, as I have often said, then agents are the community nurses. There are plenty of folk who need that paid-for friendly voice at the end of a phone, either to calm them down or to talk some sense into them. But for me, it was a 10 per cent overhead I didn't want to carry.

The light-bulb moment for *Grange Hill* occurred as I was walking into the dole office in Hardman Street during the Easter vacation in 1976. Now only a student and no longer on the Professional and Executive Register, this meant queuing up with the 'real people'. I was now in the second year of studying the sociology of education and we had recently been looking at the work of Ivan Illich and John Holt.

Holt's work, *How Children Fail*, was a hot topic. It argued that children fail primarily because they are too often fearful, bored, and confused at school. This, combined with well-intentioned but often misguided teaching strategies, within a school environment that is disconnected from reality and 'real learning', results in a school system that kills children's innate desire to learn. From the earlier comments I have made in this book you can imagine that this had a real impact on me. My own early experience was clearly reflected in Holt's work.

The fear is the fear of failure and/or humiliation and disapproval. This affects the ability to grow intellectually and, as in my own case, stunts rather than promotes confidence. Ongoing motivations like house points or gold stars actually reinforce children's fears of failing exams and receiving disapproval from the adults in their lives. Rather than learning the actual content of the lessons, students learn how to avoid such embarrassment. How often have we heard this in recent years? That kids are taught to pass exams rather than learn.

The other major point Holt made was that all children are born with tremendous curiosity and capacity for learning, understanding and creativity. Ask any parent. However, by the age of three adults start to stifle that intellectual capacity and creativity by imposing too many rigid rules and guidelines, designed to force the growing infant to 'conform to the norm'. More often than not creative capacity is restricted by making our children afraid to be wrong. The more disturbing side to this is that by the age of seven, the old Jesuit threshold for taking the child and showing the man, children have learned the social codes to such a degree that they know how they are being ranked or perceived in life's pecking order. No matter how schools try to disguise things, kids soon work out whether the 'green' or the 'squirrel' table is actually 'top' or 'bottom'. They figure it out by who is on it and the body language of the staff when interacting with pupils, and then they start performing to the level where they sense they have been put.

Illich's work, *Deschooling Society*, was even more radical, seminal and simple. Instead of trying to deal with the reasons why children fail in institutionalised education, he argued, we should simply remove the problem by refocusing our efforts and scrapping schooling altogether except for teaching people how to read, write and learn. This would then lead to a system of self-education driven by interest and need, moderated and mentored by peer networks. Illich's idea was that we could embrace new technology so that people with similar interests, aims and objectives could identify each other through computer networks and support each other in their learning. This was radical bordering on the revolutionary in 1971. Today we would probably call it social networking or closed-user group activity.

While both of these works still have great resonance with current concerns over education, common to both was the implicit assumption that education should be viewed as similar to taxation, a universal curse no one could avoid. If this was so, and I was looking for a television idea that would appeal to most people, and most people had to go to school in one form or another . . . then surely *that* was the common bond. As the light bulb came on, everything else became clear to me. Comprehensives were the new big thing, I had been among the first 2 per cent of pupils to be educated in one, my speciality as a QS was schools, I was studying the sociology of education, and my mum had been a school cleaner for most of my life. Why not write a series about a school?

I seem to remember also getting ideas for the first few episodes while I was still waiting in the queue to sign on. The opener would be the inevitable first day. Episode 2 would be about making new friends, Episode 3 about hating games, Episode 4 the swimming-pool incident. Then another one about messing about on a building site . . . I was letting my mind run away with these thoughts when I noticed we were not making any progress towards the front. Leaning to one side to take a look, it seemed like there was a guy getting a really hard time from the girl behind the counter. They looked to be about the same age but there was an obvious status game going on as she was, after all, an official of the state while he was, well, just a dolite.

'Hurry up,' she kept saying. 'Just sign it.' He was muttering some form of explanation or apology, but whatever it was it was not impressing the state Tsarina, as the fateful words were then heard: 'It says here, you have to. If you don't sign, you don't get your money.' Whereupon the guy, who was covered in tattoos before they were fashionable, hunched up and started to sob. 'What's up now?' came the unsympathetic query. The guy eventually scribbled something on the form and shoved it across the counter. The Tsarina looked at it. 'That's just a scribble. It doesn't match what I have here. Do it again.' But this was the breaking point. The guy straightened himself up, glanced back at those of us waiting in the queue and wiped his eyes with the back of his hand. 'I know it doesn't match, you f***ing b****, 'cos I can't write, can I? Happy now?'

With that he turned and walked out, not caring what it did to her precious systems. She just watched him go, looking slightly puzzled. I don't know what she'd been expecting but it wasn't that. She looked at the form, then signed it herself. No doubt it said somewhere in the regulations that she could do that. Next.

By the time I had got up front to sign, she had moved on, as though the incident had never happened. Perhaps it was a regular occurrence for her, but I already had it down for an episode in its own right and a lifelong commitment to supporting literacy campaigns began there, reaching its height twenty years later with the Brookie Basics project. That helped over 30,000 adults improve their literacy and was used in twenty-six prisons. I never saw either the guy or the girl again but that one trip to the dole office saw me on a roll. I had the basics for *Grange Hill* and had found the natural route for my writing: social reality.

Having only worked with ITV companies, that seemed a logical place to pitch my new idea. The only ITV companies that were making children's drama were ATV, Thames and Yorkshire. At the same time, they were also part of the so-called Big Five among the ITV companies that pretty much dictated the ITV schedule. The amount of programming each could make for the national network was determined by how much value each brought to the overall schedule in terms of advertising revenue. How much they contributed to the overall programme budget. This meant companies like Granada, which contributed *Coronation Street*, carried more influence than, say, Channel Television or Southern Television.

The machinations behind the ITV Network have always been worthy of a drama in their own right, including the episodes that saw MerseyTV having a tilt at Granada, and while everyone always vehemently denies that there has ever been any form of cartel in operation at any time, a lot of decisions have been deemed 'right' by the 'right people'. But what do you do if you are the only regulated monopoly in town? You have to make up your own rules. So how can you not be 'right'? How else would a small, rurally based ITV company, for instance, be able to afford to make and show drama when their audience consisted of a few holidaymakers, farmers, and cattle? They couldn't. But what they could do was chip into the overall programme budget and then just take what they were given and transmit it at the same time as everyone else, to make sure the network advertising policy held. Without being a cartel, of course.

To get a children's programme made then, there had to be a sponsoring ITV company that would take it to the Children's

Committee for approval and funding. While this was theoretically open to all ITV companies, it wasn't hard to work out that ideas from the Big Five sponsors would get a more favourable hearing. That was the plan then. I would start with ATV, thanks to my contacts from *The Kids From 47A*, and then work outward. They said no. I then tried Thames who said they liked the idea, but no. Eventually I got to see Joy Whitby who was then at Yorkshire Television but Chair of the Children's Television Committee. She said no together with the comment, 'Why on earth would kids want to watch a programme about school when they have been there all day?' Obviously, she hadn't foreseen the rise of reality TV.

Fed up with ITV, I then approached the BBC and met Anna Home, then Executive Producer of Children's Drama, and she said yes. Just like that. But why?

5

Scripting (1977–81)

'We know how to handle our characters, Phil' – *Harry V. Kershaw*
Coronation Street, *1977*

After Anna Home said yes to *Grange Hill* at the BBC, there were
only two major stepping-stones to *Brookie*: *Going Out* and *County
Hall*. However, as Michael Caine impersonators are likely to say, not
a lot of people know this but there was an even bigger one lurking
just below the surface: *Coronation Street*.

Having met Brian Finch on *The Squirrels*, he put my name forward
to Producer Bill Podmore who had just taken over running *Corrie*,
which was then regarded as an ailing soap. The posh drama lot had
their tongues out, knives in, and, this being ITV, their eyes on the
slot and budget that would be free if they succeeded in ousting it.
In reality there was not much wrong. It was just going through a
cycle I would come to know quite well in the future. It had drifted
away from its original intent – something that happens with all
long-runners. It's partly to do with audience familiarity, partly fatigue,
but more often due to a change in personnel, who sometimes take
the programme in a new direction that doesn't suit either its production intent or its audience.

When later on I was asked to go in and 'have a go at *Emmerdale*',
it was obvious, to me, that the folk running it at the time had started
watching what the other programmes were doing, rather than asking
what their audience actually wanted and expected. For instance, the

audience for *Brookie* was expecting social realism, gritty, harder-edged than the other twice-weeklys, and with a suburban take on life. The audience for *EastEnders* was looking for something similar, but with an inner-city feel. *Emmerdale* had to deliver a softer focused view of life, and from an idealised image of the countryside, something most people like to look at but not actually to visit or smell. By the time I got there it was full of metropolitan issues and everyone seemed to be inter-married or about to be. This might have been the metros' view of the countryside actually, everyone being inbred and wishing they were really living in Chelsea.

The same thing appeared to have been going on with good old *Corrie* in the mid-1970s. It had shifted slightly away from what had become its USP towards the end of the 1960s: its heart-warming sense of Northern community. Perhaps it was a rose-tinted view of the North, with everyone popping in for cups of sugar and calling 'Cooooeee' before they did. If they had tried that in any of the communities Howard Parker's *A View From the Boys* had looked at, they would probably have ended up in A&E. Or worse. Nevertheless this was what its audience expected, not political discourse on the politics of Northern Ireland. It had moved away from the harshness of Ken Barlow slagging off – sorry, admonishing – his father about the sauce bottle on the table. By the early-seventies it had settled into a comfortable groove, offering its ageing audience a reassuring and slightly comical take on life, not just as they would like it but how they were starting to remember it.

There was, and is, nothing wrong with this, as a long-runner's relationship with its audience is a bit like a marriage. They fall in love when young, fit and looking for excitement; they share a great honeymoon, and then settle into a life of common values, stories and events, to share later with the kids and grandkids. Fading eyesight means neither of them notices the other's wrinkles. It is only when someone else comes along, often younger, less sympathetic and less knowledgeable about the past, and opens up a window on to the world that the harsh light of reality shines in and shows up the wrinkles. This is what had happened to *Corrie*, and Bill Podmore was brought in as the counsellor with the anti-wrinkle cream.

Corrie was no longer in the Top Ten, not because the writing, acting or production values had changed, but because the storylines had taken on a more realistic edge under the previous producer,

Susi Hush. Having grown up with the early episodes, I personally found this period really interesting as it was more in tune with what I wanted to do with my own writing. Susi later went on to work on both *Grange Hill* and *Brookside*. Still, no matter what we writers or producers like or want, the people who count are the viewers and they had passed judgement in the most telling way. They simply switched channels.

By the time I ended up in Bill Podmore's office, he was the relatively new broom doing what I would end up doing on my own account on an almost regular five-year cycle: revitalising the show. I was probably put forward by Brian as new blood, and I am sure I was only invited because of the respect in which he was held. Whatever the reason, I found myself attending storyline meetings in a large conference room somewhere near the top of the insurance-like office block Granada called home. It had the typical huge table, great views over Manchester, and around this vast expanse of veneer sat the likes of Julian Roach, John Stevenson, Leslie Duxbury, and of course the doyen duo of Adele Rose and Harry Kershaw, who had been with the programme since its beginning.

There is not much in the memory bank about the whole process, except that there was a small telephone booth attached to this conference room that the writers appeared to use on a rota basis. I suppose this was in the days before mobiles and people still had the universal need to keep in touch with the outside world, as well as pass on the bill for doing so to Granada. At one end of the long table sat Bill, flanked by note-takers who turned out to be the storyliners. They would later issue fully worked-up storylines from which the writers would produce commissioned scripts. Number of scenes, who was in the episode, when it took place, etc. While I was impressed with the standardised nature of the system, which reminded me of the Bills of Quantities that Rex Snowling had introduced me to and was something I would later adapt for *Brookie*, this committee process seemed a little stifling for the writer. Still, if that was the job, inserting dialogue, and you got paid for it, who was I to argue? Exactly. A view that was soon hammered home to me.

Despite the return to university to overcome my sense of educational insecurity and lack of self-confidence, being across the table from the likes of Harry Kershaw was even more intimidating than working with the Pythons and Goodies. Never mind the affectionate nickname *Corrie*, this was, even then, *The Street*. I'd read John Holt. I knew my lowly position at the end of the table indicated my place in the pecking order. However, having sat on my hands for a while, I couldn't contain myself when they started talking about the Queen's Jubilee episode.

The overall story was that they would organise their own street party and a community float for the carnival parade, with the idea being that the lorry for the float, naturally, in true soap style, would not start and therefore throw everything into jeopardy. The debate around how this would happen seemed to go round and round in circles, with all the usual and, as I would also learn later, typical fantasy and lack of technical knowledge from the production teams. I don't know why this is, but it always seems to be the way. Most people in the arts haven't got a clue how anything technical works, never mind how to fix it if it goes wrong. Does one come before the other? You don't understand stuff so you seek a career to avoid it? Or is the creative mind wired differently? Perhaps 'wired' is not the right word for technophobes. Then again . . .

Anyway, there were all kinds of ideas, including, I am sure, the driver being abducted by aliens, but no one had thought of the obvious until the Scouse petrol head asked. 'What about . . . ?' No one heard. 'What about . . . ?' A bit louder. No one noticed. I was resisting actually putting my hand up. 'I have an idea . . .' Louder. It seemed to catch Bill's attention. 'Young Phil has an idea.' All heads turned in my direction. Oh, yes. I was still there. 'How about,' I offered, 'Harry Hewitt just forgets to turn the lights off?' They looked puzzled. 'You know, if you leave your lights on . . . and they drain the battery . . . your car won't start. Harry could do that.' Silence. 'That's happened to me,' someone confirmed. It might have been Brian, helping me out. They all turned and looked at Bill. He smiled. They all looked back at me, and smiled. 'Well done, young Phil.' And my idea made it through the storyline process, into the script, through production and on to the screen. I still consider this to be one of my finest achievements, helping Bill add that pivotal moment when *The Street* regained both its sense of comedy and realism. Others may disagree, of course.

Flushed with this heady success, by the time of the next meeting, my confidence had greatly increased. So by the time the team got round to discussing the big dramatic storyline, I felt ready to enter into debate with them. The story had Deirdre and Ray Langton leaving their baby with Ena Sharples while they went off for the weekend. This would be the first time away from the baby and, while they would have a great time, on the way home their train would be delayed. Ena would then fall down the stairs and put the baby in jeopardy. They loved it. I hated it. My argument – reasonable, I thought, as I was still young Phil – was that no couple in their twenties would ever leave their first-born with a septuagenarian neighbour. 'They just wouldn't do it!' I heard myself exclaim. Heads turned towards the lower end of the table. They wouldn't? 'No young person would.' Emphasis on *young*.

They all stared at me. Was I really questioning their collective experience and wisdom? Emphasis on *experience*. Heads then turned back towards the top of the table where Bill Podmore sat staring at me, a quizzical expression on his face. Not smiling. Then the senior writer, Harry Kershaw, leaned over and said in what I assumed was a friendly, avuncular, Don Corleone manner, 'We know how to handle our characters, Phil.' Emphasis on *our*. Other heads nodded. Bill stared at me. I stared back. He raised an eyebrow. Enough said? I nodded and sat back. Sighs of relief all round and off they went, plotting one of the most ridiculous stories I had ever heard. It stayed in. I didn't.

At lunchtime there was the expected tap on the shoulder. 'Shall we have a word, Phil?' It was Bill. I was history. And, later, very grateful both for that and the whole experience of sitting round that table for a few meetings. If I'd stayed, who knows? There might have been a body under the Rover's. But we both seem to have got on without each other. And once again, like a sponge, I had absorbed everything I could, to squeeze it out later at *Brookie* and *Hollyoaks*. There potential writers would have to shadow at least three story meetings, to see if they blended in with the rest of team and that they really understood what the programme was about. How to handle 'our' characters.

This setback was followed soon afterwards by the re-emergence of the debt cycle, triggered once again by my trusty Ford Zodiac, which had recently become less trustworthy. It kept overheating. I'd probably worked it too hard, flogging up and down to London on all those occasions when I 'just happened to be passing' so could I drop in. This was one of the real advantages of living in Liverpool as producers in London thought it was on the far side of the planet

– most still do actually. In those days it really was a slog to get up and down, so they were more inclined to give you five minutes if they thought you'd made that arduous journey.

I should have known the Zodiac was on its way out when those London trips took longer and longer as it kept dying, often in the outside lane of the motorway. I would then spend a while on the hard shoulder, trying to figure out what was wrong, until eventually I traced it to a tiny crack in the radiator. Although that was fixed, I found myself falling back into the poverty cycle. Not having enough cash to replace this old car, I was spending too much time and money trying to keep it going, and not enough getting on with pushing the script ideas out the door.

It turned out the car needed a new cylinder head, way beyond my means then. It had to go. It was now worth more as spares than anything else, so I took it down to the dump, dismantled as much as I could and then let the crusher have it, selling and recycling the bits as and where over the next few years. You could do that back in the seventies too. If a bulb blew on your indicators, you could actually change it yourself. No need for an engineering degree or to buy a whole new light cluster. However, while still finishing off at university and not yet having received a commission, it was back to public transport for me, a day or two of which soon makes you appreciate what Henry Ford was going on about.

The only way to avoid these cycles of debt, I figured, was to get the Richard Gordon prize, owning my own series copyright, which at the time I still thought would come through comedy. I was bombarding everyone I knew, and those I had yet to know, with ideas for sit-coms. There was one about a soldier leaving the army and trying to adjust to civvy street; a young couple on the eve of their wedding discovering they have to become guardians to teenage siblings; the guardian angel idea that had me thrown out of BBC Birmingham, now re-worked into a sit-com; a small building company; an undertaker's. You think of it, I probably worked up a format for it. Almost every day a new idea went out, including one about kids at school. And almost every day a rejection came back, but at least people were remembering my name.

At the same time I was still trying to keep up at university, and as well as getting me in to see Bill Podmore, Brian Finch got me on to his children's sit-com, *Potter's Picture Palace*. It was being produced in Manchester as part of the BBC Children's output in the North and revolved around the running of a small independent cinema. I never quite got why they thought this would appeal to kids in the 1970s, children of the electronic age, as even the early ITV founders had seen their cinema audiences being lost to television. Then again, it was slightly anarchic and slapstick, and in the same vein as *Rentaghost*, helping to broaden the BBC Children's Department's output.

In typical BBC fashion, although programmes are often made outside London, they are editorially controlled from the capital, with the same sort of 'branch economy' mentality that saw many corporate HQs drift to London while the factories stayed in the Midlands and North. Profits to the centre. Sweatshops in the regions. It was no surprise to discover that although Potter's Picture Palace was to be made in Manchester, the producer and director would come up from London to put the show together.

This was not surprising as BBC Children's Department was based in London, although I felt this approach was short-changing regional audiences. Everything tended to get 'polished' back to a London-centric acceptance of the world. It was this that made me constantly vigilant on *Grange Hill* to make sure that neither London tubes nor buses featured in the first series, so that kids would not immediately assume it was a London-based programme. Of course, the actors spoke with their own natural twangs, something that created controversy in its own right, but the audience accepted that, especially those North of Watford. They knew that even in their own areas there was often a mix of accents – but they didn't have a tube and they didn't have red buses that had London Transport all over them. Both stayed out of the programme until 1982, when I was busy setting up *Brookside*. A new producer was drafted in by the BBC, and obviously couldn't see the point of not showing them. It was produced in London, wasn't it? So what? The producer's name was Susi Hush. We had a much bigger falling out later, on *Brookside*.

It may have been the fact that I was working on *Potter's Picture Palace*, even though it was in Manchester, that got me to the eyrie on top of the BBC's East Tower that housed the Children's Department. I went to see Anna Home in June 1976, a few days after finishing my second-year university exams. We talked about comedy and what should or shouldn't be on screen, but then I told her that what I really wanted to do was a series about a comprehensive school, for all the sociological reasons I may already have bored you with. I wondered how she would react because if I was the scally from the comp, Anna was definitely the Head Girl from the local grammar at least. However, she grinned and slowly reached into a drawer to take out a file. It had something like 'School Series' written across the front. She opened it to reveal it was empty. I was, as I would be with David Rose, in the right place, at the right time, with the right idea and with the right person. She then asked me to put something on paper – and the rest, as cliché would tell us, was one creative battle after the other.

I went back up to the flat in Liverpool and spent a few weeks putting all those thoughts I'd had in the dole queue down on to paper, at times using an ironing board as a desk due to lack of space. This image has often come back to me, especially when doing things like Chairing the Merseyside Entrepreneurship Commission and listening to public-sector quangorins, the quango equivalent of Whitehall's mandarins, talking about wasting taxpayers' money on 'serviced office space' or 'creative hubs' for would-be entrepreneurs. Any real entrepreneur knows that you do not build the temple until you establish the religion, and will work off kitchen tables or ironing boards, in bedrooms or garages, to get started.

Having bashed it all out on my fifteen-year-old Olympia SG-1 typewriter, with extra-long carriage to allow wider or several documents to be typed in one pass, I sent the outline down to Anna. On 15 July 1976 she called to commission the first script and eight storylines. Incredible. Was this my Richard Gordon moment?

The great news needed to be celebrated in the only way fitting. I went out and found a proper desk, but at the weekly auctions that went on behind my city-centre flat where I had bought the typewriter for about three quid. I can't remember what I paid for the desk but it wasn't much, then I got down to work and sent the first script and storylines to her on 6 September. It was only while writing this that I realised it was the same date on which we started shooting *Brookside* in 1982. Spooky, eh? Perhaps not. Anna called me on the ninth and said she liked it and would put it up to Monica Sims, then Head of Children's Programmes. And so began that anxious wait for the yes, or more usual no.

By the time I had got in to see Anna, four years since giving up my QS job a few doors down from the Rodney Street flat, I had already learned a lot about this from the number of rejections and bad reactions I had received: from the straightforward rejection letters, sometimes even only a compliments slip, to the extreme reactions of that script editor in Birmingham. I was beginning to learn that although acting like a literary brush salesman and cold calling on the knocker would not often get you a commission, it might just give you a good idea of what the broadcasters were looking for. It also taught me that the second-best media answer is a very quick no. That means you can put whatever it is you were pinning your hopes on behind you, and focus on something else. There always has to be something else on the go.

I never thought at the time that I was driven, but after reflecting on and reviewing my life throughout this period it is obvious in hindsight that I had discovered the path I had been unable to articulate to my sixth-form tutor. I'd got so far and I was determined not to go back. I couldn't. I still had my dad on my back about 'throwing it all away'. Having come to accept my not going to university back then, he now could not see the point of my giving up the safety, as he saw it, of a profession like quantity surveying.

This was partly why I never told him or the rest of the family what I was up to most of the time. It was also partly due to the fact that what I was doing was outside their life experience and expectations. And that was tied to the traditional working-class thing of not 'getting above yourself'. Why did I think I was better than or different from all my mates who had gone straight into industry? Even my brother Larry was now working at a proper job, as a BT engineer. Despite the huge pay differential between selling a script and receiving a weekly wage, he got fifty-two of those a year and I was averaging one script sale. So I never told them about going for a trial on *Corrie*, in case it didn't work out. As it didn't. It was the same with *Grange Hill*. It might never happen.

This habit was to become deeply ingrained in me over the years as I felt much more comfortable telling people what I had actually done, rather than what I would like to do. For me, success was always about seeing something on the television in my living room, not a promotional piece in a trade magazine, and as the chances of success were still small, I felt I had to be constantly looking beyond the letterbox that only admitted rejection letters. This is one of the things I often say to aspiring writers: not to pin their hopes on one idea, no matter how great or unique they think it is. It won't be.

For one thing, whenever *you* have an idea, you can guarantee that six other people will have shared the same experience, event or emotion that sparked your own creative process. That is why there is no such thing as copyright in an idea. It is not actually the idea that is important, but the execution of that idea. The individual 'take' on it.

It is another axiom of business that only bad news comes by mail. Good news makes the phone ring, and ring for me it finally did, on Friday 22 October at 3.50 p.m. It was Anna. They were going to put the programme into production. The fact that I still have a note of the exact time she called may give some indication of how big a moment that was for me. It was not just amazement I felt, but also a deep sense of relief. Especially because now I had something really positive to tell the family.

However, with another deep cut from the learning curve, the sense of euphoria did not last long, as another well-known broadcasting mantra was demonstrated to me: never believe anything in television until you see the credits go up on screen – on the repeat. Within days I received a call from ATV. Although they had turned down my school idea, they had stumbled across, quite by accident they said, one of their staff producers who happened to be working up a school series. It was purely coincidental, but they wondered if I would like to work on it for them.

What did someone say? There is no copyright in ideas. I took a deep breath, suppressed the Scouse conspiracy gene in me and told them that I better hadn't, as I was now working on it for the BBC. I then started to worry that the BBC might get cold feet as ATV would air their series first. Anna was not put off at all. This was what she wanted to make and she would. But no matter how confident she felt, or how confident I was now becoming, I knew we would be testing the notion that it is the execution and delivery, rather than the idea, that matters. And we did. And the other school series only lasted a year. Another valuable lesson learned. Once the BBC decides to do something, it does it well.

Getting back to my ironing board, I wanted my characters to sound as well as look like typical kids in a typical school anywhere in Britain, with the always added caveat that there was no such thing as a typical school. So I came up with Jenkins, Benson, Yates, etc. and then grafted on their Christian names. Patrick for Tucker, perhaps to give a hint of Irish, but also because I could then call the main female protagonist Patricia, with some early idea that in the long term the two 'Pats' would get together, through a shared respect derived from their earlier antagonism. It was one of those writer's flights of fantasy. Pure Hollywood, nineteenth-century melodrama, or simple observation of how many teenagers get together after first being school friends? To mask this, of course, they had their nicknames of Tucker and Trisha.

Class was an obvious consideration, given that one of the primary goals of the comprehensive system was to push together people of varying social backgrounds and needs. These differences were to be illustrated by the way the characters looked, behaved, dressed, spoke, and of course were named. Tucker, Trisha and Benny were working-class; Justin and Julie were middle-class. There were no toffs, as I don't think it had at that date become fashionable to be seen to send your kids to the local comp.

Next in difficulty to naming the characters, choosing a programme's title is a tricky art, as while you want it to be instantly recognisable, you don't want to get too tricksy so that if it runs for a few years it sounds either dated or daft. *EastEnders* is a good title, while an earlier BBC attempt, *The Newcomers*, was not. You can always be an East Ender, but how long do you remain a newcomer? I decided then that, like *Coronation Street*, the title should actually indicate what the programme was about, and therefore be the name of the school. And it needed to be something that would work in any part of the country, not too geographically specific. Thinking back over all the schools I had visited during my time as a QS was not helpful, but the place where we occasionally went for lunch in St Helens was, a pub-restaurant that had the perfect name: Grange Park. And so it was as *Grange Park* that the programme was originally commissioned. Nine months later I was told the title must be changed.

The BBC were concerned that someone, somewhere would try and claim that the programme was modelled on their existing or previous school, and sue for libel. I understood this. What I didn't understand was why it had taken their legal team so long to reach this conclusion. I can't remember now whether the reason was that there were too few or too many schools called Grange Park, which might heighten the risk of complaint, but the decision was taken that we had to change the name.

There was another complication. Because it had taken so long for this decision to be reached, the production had been ploughing on. The programme now had an official programme code, and this was not an easy thing to change. Today, when we are starting to get used to computers just doing what we tell them by voice recognition, this may not seem like a big deal. But when you consider that the BBC at that time had a whole building tucked away behind Shepherd's Bush Green that housed its then cutting-edge mainframe computer, it was a very big deal. Not only would it take days to re-programme the computer but there was no other way to go back over the previous records except laboriously by hand. However, there was a plan. As the programme code was something like *GRANG 08484*, the task was to pick any other name beginning with 'Grange' from a list they had checked against the Department of Education record of UK secondary schools.

This had names like Grange Brow, Grange Pond, Grange Valley, Grange Hill, Grange View and Grange Road. I opted for Hill and crisis was averted. Four years later I was travelling to the BBC by tube and glanced at the map displayed in each carriage. There, on the Central line, was a station called Grange Hill. Damn, I thought. After all my work to make it a non-London school, the name had been a London one all along.

Originally this issue had only arisen because the BBC's logistics meant that the series had to be produced in London. I had wanted to set the series somewhere on Merseyside, which had, as it always seems to, been leading the charge to the new system of education. It seems odd now looking back, but even in 1976, nearly ten years after I had left St Kev's, comprehensive schools were still a relatively new concept, especially to those working in television who had, by and large, come through the grammar or public school route.

Jumping forward thirty years, I faced the same sort of education lag when MerseyTV took over producing the programme and I wanted the storyline to include the school being granted specialist status in media studies. Despite MerseyTV's having previously helped six Merseyside schools achieve specialist media, arts or drama status, the BBC folk had great difficulty getting their heads round what it was all about, and how much better resourced Merseyside's schools were compared to the ones where they had previously been shooting. That great North–South divide again.

Back in 1976, the appointment of Colin Cant as *Grange Hill*'s producer and director gave me a new slant on that, as he was a Scot and suddenly I felt like the Southerner. Until we were both in front of Anna. I also found a new car. Still with the 'make do and mend' mentality, I had taken an old Morris 1800 off one of my aunties. Although it had great engineering it was not exactly cool. Colin was selling his MGB GT, which was cool, except in summer when the heater never quite closed down. It did however have manually switched overdrive, an electric radio aerial and a windscreen-washer system. You had to pump it with your thumb, but at the time this was cutting edge.

Apart from the car, Colin also brought with him the ideas of using news crews to shoot the location film inserts and bringing the camera down to the kids' eye-level. Using news crews meant the footage would have a different, more realistic look, something else I would take forward to *Brookie* when I opted to use the same camera technology then used by the *News* and *Match of the Day*. This instantly gave *Brookie* that sense of realism that the audience identified with but couldn't quite put their finger on, while bringing the camera down to the kids' eye-level was a touch of creative genius, as it instantly made the programme appear to be shot from their point of view. The camera would be looking up at the teachers, rather than down at the kids.

Colin also brought the programme a sense of authenticity through deliberately looking for young actors who, even if coming from stage schools, had retained their own accents. This would immediately create a sense of empathy with the intended target audience, even if it also meant it would increase the complaints about the 'language' used, or not used, in the programme. Although he was a bit nervous of the character-focused scripts, thinking they were a bit light compared to the traditional plot-driven dramas he had been working on up until then, he immediately 'got it', and would sometimes find himself caught between Anna and myself as we slowly teased out our cultural differences into full-blown creative arguments.

These started innocuously enough with the usual North–South divide on the use of language. One of the most common questions asked by kids about *Grange Hill*, when comparing their experiences at their own school, their own social reality, was: where is the swearing? But as a programme going out on children's television, no swearing was allowed – despite the many claims and criticisms about 'bad language' over the the years.

While it is fair to say that *Brookside* did get a reputation in its early days, as it did use every word except those beginning with 'f' and 'c', what was the bad language people were complaining about in *Grange Hill*? Nothing more than slang and working-class accents. While Tucker's favourite line, 'Flippin' 'eck, Benny,' became almost a catch-phrase, this was the first time such accents had featured on television. For some, it was a dropped vowel too far.

The only time a real swear word was heard on *Grange Hill* was by accident. It was an actor, messing about off-camera during a recording when he called out something like 'you daft sod'. This happened to be picked up on the sound recording, but at such a low level that both recording and sound engineers missed it. When the complaint came in the post-production team had to work hard to find it, so how the complainant heard it, we never knew. Anyway, the offending word was eventually found and edited out in time for the repeat.

The word 'sod' featured in an early discussion with Anna too. I had had one of the characters say something similar to the actor caught off-mic, along the lines of 'you silly sod', meaning 'as thick as a clump of earth, or sod'. It was only then that I discovered that Southerners related this to a far more earthy interest in sexual deviancy and the word was cut. What a sheltered life I had led.

There were also other gentle reminders that I should try and refrain from calling children 'kids', as the BBC did not consider their audience to be the offspring of goats, as well as more brutal interventions like adding a few lines here and there to soften the harshness of the language.

The best example of this was Episode 5, a story about Trisha and Julie looking after the school hamster. I had written this as a comedy episode about losing the hamster then trying to replace it, with hilarious consequences, but also as a vehicle for exploring the themes of friendship and authority. Working-class Trisha and middle-class Julie would come together through this unfortunate adventure, as well as falling foul of the authoritarian Miss Clarke, who would have a go at Trisha for, as usual, wearing earrings. The episode would come to an end on a feel-good, 'Phew, got away with that!' and a shared joke about their form teacher, Mr Mitchell, smelling of drink after lunch, a common occurrence across society at that time, but the point was to have the two girls noticing and making friends across the class divide.

However, the BBC felt we shouldn't mention teachers having a drink at lunchtime, so I amended it to a joke about doing a piece for the magazine, with Trisha saying to Julie, 'You still doing that piece for the school magazine on animals?' 'Yes. Why?' 'You'll have to include Miss Clarke, then.' 'Why?' Then, on Trisha, close-up for punchline and end of episode: 'Because she's a cow!' Cue music, roll credits and leave the audience grinning.

On the day of the recording, I was sitting in the gallery all day with Colin watching the programme being slowly put together. Towards the end Anna came down from the East Tower eyrie to sit in and watch. I did not think too much of this and was watching the last scene go through, waiting for the great punchline. And it came. And went. And not in close-up, but in a wide two shot as Trisha and Julie walk away from camera babbling on. 'Oh, Trisha, you are awful,' said Julie. 'Well, she deserves it. Because babble, babble, babble, babble . . .' Bleed in music and roll credits, leaving the audience barely smiling.

The next voice I heard was Colin's. 'That's it, everyone, thank you.' I turned to where Anna was sitting, but, to use the Irish, there she was, gone. The seat was empty and the exit door still swinging. I turned back to Colin, who was now very busy tidying up his scripts. Others started to drift away. 'What just happened, Colin?' I asked. 'Ah,' he said, and then told me that there had been some concern expressed about the ending. That it wasn't felt appropriate to end a BBC children's programme with the word 'cow'. Some children, of the non-billy goat variety, might have been left disturbed.

No doubt Anna had had to rush off to do something, but I was annoyed at the way they went about dealing with the problem. Having just got through the swimming-pool episode, which I had felt would be a bit on the edge for some, why make such a fuss over one word? If they had spoken to me about it, I would have crafted a better ending than the wishy-washy tail-out they had cobbled together.

★

Naturally, in the writing business everything comes down to rows over words, and there is no better word for getting people excited than copyright. Not long after the cow episode I was very excited. It was one of those good news, bad news moments, with the good news being, good, great and amazing, but all wiped out by the bad news being absolutely terrible. Horrendous even. It also turned out to be the make-or-break moment of my career. Whether I would actually achieve my Richard Gordon goal or not.

It started as a typically pleasant media lunch, with Anna taking me to the posh bit of the BBC restaurant and canteen, where we probably laid the cow issue to rest and started talking about the next series. Good. How they were so pleased with things they wanted to commission the next series even before transmission of the first. Great. They also wanted to increase the number of episodes from nine to eighteen and transmit twice a week. Amazing. I was delighted. This was a real step change apparently, not just in children's television, but across the business. So that was the good, great and amazing bit.

Then came the bad news. Following the old ATV logic on *The Squirrels*, with so many scripts to complete in a limited time, other writers would be necessary. I myself could probably do four, possibly five, of them. My face and then my mouth said it all. Not happy. This is my series. No, it's not, it's the BBC's. Oh? Yes. The BBC wanted a school series and commissioned you to write it. No. *I* wanted to write a school series and came to you with the idea. Right place, right time, right idea, remember? Yes, but that could be argued either way. Needless to say, this didn't help the pudding go down.

At the time my still smouldering class-consciousness was probably a key factor in all this. While on the one hand it immediately triggered a kneejerk view that the middle classes were out to exploit me, it probably also propelled the argument to a more fundamental difference of opinion over the relationship between broadcaster and writer. From the BBC's and ITV's perspective, they were employing me. From my point of view, coming from the professional fee-based background of quantity surveying, they were a client to whom I was providing professional services. While they had a right to expect those services to be delivered promptly and competently, they did not have any other form of ownership or control over me, as they would over an employee.

To be fair to Anna, she was simply looking at the production logistics and had worked out that having four or five writers would be better than placing me under added pressure, especially as I had struggled a bit towards the end of Series 1 to deliver the scripts to length. This was partly due to inexperience and partly due to the pace of the drama. The scripts were initially timed on a traditional page count of around thirty seconds per page. This was fine for plot-driven or period drama, but due to my detailed stage directions reinforcing the character-driven stories, my scripts tended to come out at around twenty seconds per page. The phone would often go and I'd be told, 'We need two more minutes.' This meant I would have to write an extra scene or two to get close to the running time.

A lot of directors don't like writers giving stage directions, as they feel they are responsible for the look and choreography of the show, but I hold the opposite view for two reasons. One, it should at least help the director to understand what was in the writer's head, even if they wish to deviate from it. The second reason is tone. Only the writer should decide what the tone of the episode should be, and that should be spelled out on the page for everyone to see, from design to sound as well as the director. To assist this process further we added an extra meeting to the usual production processes for *Brookie* and *Hollyoaks*, the writer-director meeting, when the director had to sit and talk to the writer, whether they wanted to or not.

I obviously couldn't articulate it like that back in 1976, but I still felt it was important to write as much as I could into the script, to try and get my intention across. Anna was probably weighing all this up while looking ahead to the next series. But I also felt strongly that I wanted to embed my original intent behind the series and maintain its momentum before allowing too many diverse voices and opinions to start influencing its development. By the time we had finished coffee we had agreed that I would do at least nine episodes, with possibly only one other writer to work on the rest, and I would work harder at getting the script timings right. Having sorted out the editorial and production problems, we still had to resolve the rights issue, which I had to take up directly with the appropriately named BBC Copyright Dept.

It was customary in those days for the contract to assign full copyright in the script to the writer, as is still often the case, but the BBC

contract I had signed was unclear as to who owned the actual characters and format. Even though they had copyright in the physical
recording, the contract appeared to give them no rights to commission anyone else to use the characters I had created. My argument
therefore was that they had to acquire these rights separately and,
while I would agree to license the format and characters as they
needed them, I was not going to assign them full copyright. Even if
it meant they wouldn't go ahead? I was asked. Even so, I said.

Those around me thought I was mad and that I should just grab
what I could. Who knew what would happen? The first series might
fail anyway. Why didn't I just take what was being offered and, of
course, not upset the biggest employer in the market? It was one
point of view, but in my opinion wrong. Whether it goes all the
way back to my early Catholic upbringing or having run-ins with
bullies like Digger, the one thing that always makes me dig my heels
in is anything I perceive as, well, intimidation, if not bullying. The
BBC was trying to use their market domination to make me concede,
in just the same way as YTV had tried to do over Harry Secombe's
octopus. From the BBC's point of view, I suppose they simply saw
it as maintaining the status quo and protecting themselves against
precedent. Somewhere there would be a guideline: 'It says here . . .'
But that was my point. In the contract, it didn't. After several months
of arguing back and forth we finally reached the day before transmission. It was the BBC that conceded.

We had gone right down to the wire but they finally acknowledged that there could be no copyright in an idea, only a fully
developed proposal, and the format and characters did indeed belong
to me. That was a great moment for me. A great feeling and a great
day. Probably my biggest day ever. I had won the Richard Gordon
prize.

And just when I thought that life couldn't get any better, it did.
After I had endured some pretty rainy days over the three-month
copyright argument, the sun shone down on me even more brightly.
I finally received a commission from Thames Television for, with
great social irony, *Horse in the House*. On the one hand I had just
won a long battle to retain the rights to a series that was sold on
the basis of not being about 'kids with ponies', and here I was being
commissioned to write an episode in a series about . . . kids with
ponies. Did I hesitate? No. I had got to know the producer, Ruth

Boswell, really well, she had supported me and helped me develop over the years, and I wanted to work with her. And *Grange Hill* had still not hit the screen. It might not work. The long fight over the copyright might turn out to be meaningless. Never believe anything, until you see the repeat.

A few days later though, after the first episode went out and received a favourable response, I sent in the outline storyline for Series 2. Life was now starting to get very busy for me. This was the first time I found myself working on overlapping projects, including a mini-series for ATV. It proved that the years spent courting Thames and ATV, bombarding them with ideas, had been worthwhile. And it introduced me to the crazier end of the business when I ended up writing 50 per cent of a trilogy.

When I'd had a call from ATV a few months earlier, I'd been a bit surprised to be asked would I come in and talk to Roy Clark. Er, yeah, I said. This was Roy Clarke who had written *Open All Hours* and *Last of the Summer Wine*, even in 1977 a huge hit. I thought I could give him ten minutes or so. It turned out to be a familiar ATV scenario. They wanted to turn a play he had recently written, *The Bass Player and the Blonde*, into a mini-series, but as with Eric Chappell and *The Squirrels* the author was too committed on his other sit-coms. I went up to Elstree to meet him and a producer called Dennis Vance. We had lunch and I obviously passed the audition as I was asked to write one of three scripts, but never saw Roy again. Dennis was the man.

And what a man he was – a legendary figure at ATV, with a long list of credits that stretched back to the 1948 film *Scott of the Antarctic*, where he'd started out as an actor. Since then he seemed to have directed almost every major production ATV had done. From a series of single plays with Douglas Fairbanks Jr. and *Armchair Theatre*, to series like *The Power Game* and *Van Der Valk*, there seemed to be nothing Dennis hadn't done, including ATV's afternoon soap opera *Crossroads*. If I wanted to keep learning about the business, he was a walking masterclass. One of the first and most important lessons he taught me was: keep the drinks cupboard locked. Not that, in my case, it was ever a temptation.

Spike Milligan was quoted as saying that many people die of thirst, but only the Irish are born with one. Having grown up in the Irish culture of weddings and wakes, by the time I got to the age of 'learning to like it', I couldn't see the point. I did the dutiful thing and went with my dad and uncles to the local church clubs and tried the various brews on offer, but apart from not actually liking the taste of alcohol, in my mind I could never quite get beyond seeing that pay slip of my dad's. While I was full of admiration for what my parents had achieved on a limited income, I couldn't help but wonder how much further things would have gone if they didn't spend so much on alcohol and tobacco.

This particular point was hammered home when my dad had a health scare and was forced to give up smoking. The money he saved paid for his first car. Initially we thought he had lung cancer but fortunately, if I can put it like that, it turned out to be a small droplet of diesel oil that had somehow got into his lungs from the time he spent as a bus driver, siphoning fuel from one vehicle to another. Although needing major surgery to remove it, along with two-thirds of one lung, he survived to die in his late seventies of a heart attack. As he himself would have said, a much better way to exit.

Having made the decision not to drink, I then had to put up with all the flak from the other addicts. How could I not? What was wrong with me? Just try this . . . try that . . . I can honestly say that by my mid-twenties I had probably tried nearly every form of alcohol known to mankind, just to shut people up. The only one I could mildly tolerate was Ouzo, but again that same question would come up. What was the point? Like alcopops today, it seemed to have been invented to help people who didn't like the taste of alcohol get drunk – and why would they want to do that? Something else a lifetime of Irish weddings and wakes gives you is an observer's view of the results, consequences, and often loss of the day after. I don't know how many times I have used the dramatic or comedy moment when a character uses some derivative of the question, 'What happened to my jacket last night?'

It seems incredible that back in the 1970s alcohol was as free-flowing in the media workplace as filtered and bottled water are now, and working out meant how far you had to walk to the company bar. All script meetings seemed to start at around 11.30, for introductions and catch-ups, and then were immediately relocated to the canteen or restaurant. Everyone would get back to the office about four-ish to check if there were any messages or calls to be ignored. A teetotaller like myself couldn't understand why the companies condoned it, let alone provided the means. It felt like a raft of fear floating on a sea of white wine. The fear, naturally, was about missing the next great hit, so nobody would deviate from the status quo. It had always been like this. It seemed to work. Don't rock the raft.

Even when Channel 4 came along in the 1980s and decided not to have a canteen, they did provide open access to the wine cupboard. Gradually this was tightened up, starting with restricting access until after 6 p.m., which might have been why quite a few meetings seemed to take place around 6.30. If you ever needed to go in later in the evening, which was when we used to do a lot of the negotiations for *Brookie*, there was often, to my teetotal eye, that sea of opened wine bottles stretching across the open-plan offices.

But ATV was always the fun place to be, simply because you never quite knew what would result from the stardust Lew Grade sprinkled across the place through his ITC film production arm. Apart from bumping into Julie Andrews in the corridor, you could suddenly find Jim Henson and the Muppets getting into the lift with you and rehearsing a complete show between floors, or follow the strains of a full orchestra to discover Tony Bennett or Val Doonican recording a special for the US networks. One of the most magical moments I had there was stumbling across Bing Crosby recording a Christmas show for the US.

It was one of the hottest summers on record. As we left a script meeting to weave our way across the lot we noticed a crowd gathered outside the open dock doors of one of the studios. It was so hot the air conditioning couldn't cope so they had opened the studio doors to increase air flow. Going over to look, we were met with the incongruous sight of a forest of Christmas trees, fake snow falling, and in the middle of it all Bing was singing. 'White Christmas', of course. This might have been the first time I experienced the power of production to transcend reality. When, for a few moments, you are drawn into a suspended state where fiction and fantasy become the universe. It's most common when you shoot in something like a nightclub during the day. While you are inside with all the extras, actions, lights and sounds of the club, it becomes whatever time the fiction demands. You can then face a moment's disorientation when someone calls tea or lunch break and you walk out of the noise and gloom of a club at 2 o'clock in the morning to discover bright midday sunlight. Just like it was after standing watching Bing do his stuff for a while. We turned away from this fantasy winter scene with one of the world's biggest entertainment legends, headed back into the blazing heat of reality and went off in search of our sausage and chips.

In the showbusiness world of ATV, characters like Dennis appeared to be part of the fabric, but soon I was introduced to the other writers who would be working on the project. One was a guy called Ian Lindsay, another new talent ATV was cultivating, but the other was a household name, Geoffrey Lancashire, who had just done *The Cuckoo Waltz* for Granada, and before that *The Lovers*. They were both huge hits at the time. Once again I found myself in exalted company, or so I thought until we were all summoned to dinner at Dennis's 'place in town'. It was in one of those large redbrick mansion blocks favoured by TV and film folk at the time. Although we all turned up on time, Dennis was a bit late. By about two hours.

On arrival he appeared already to have had a starter somewhere else and went into pure film producer mode, holding court and asking us all what we intended to do with our scripts. Then he seemed to fasten on to Geoffrey when he appeared a little hesitant in his response, to the extent that he started battering him about the head with his script folder. I'm sure it was all meant in good humour, but I felt thankful Dennis hadn't worked for Widnes Council when I wore that blue tie with my pink shirt. Geoffrey didn't seem to be enjoying the joke, and neither was anyone else.

Who was this lunatic and why were they letting him get away with it? 'It's just Dennis,' came the response from one of the production team. 'And it's for Lew.' What was? Apparently, although a legend within the company, 'just Dennis' had hit personal problems and was now being given a helping hand to get back on his feet from none other than Lew Grade himself. As such everyone was being tolerant and, while I could sympathise, I knew if he ever tried the script folder gag on me, even if he was friends with the Pope, he would get a good robust Scouse response. I also decided never to have a meeting with him after lunch.

It turned out that Dennis was not the only one with a reputation for being late, as Geoffrey too was known for having trouble in meeting deadlines. Not being a day or two late, as we all were, but just not delivering. There were a few apocryphal stories, like the one included in his *Guardian* obituary in 2004, about how Thames Television had to enlist another writer and friend of his, John Finch, to go and find him at a hotel where he was struggling to deliver a script for their series *Man at the Top*, a business-based drama. Another story was that even after delivering a script to Granada, he then went back to the script office after hours and took it back. This might have been an extreme example of every writer's dread of letting anyone see the first draft, but on *Bass Player* he seemed to have done it again. I got a call from ATV. Geoffrey had withdrawn, so would I split his script down the middle with the other writer, Ian?

I was still on my mission to follow Brian Finch's advice of doing as much as I could, anywhere, any way, as well as the bit about always being a professional. If they are paying you to do a particular job on someone else's series, do it. Otherwise they will get someone else, like they were doing now with Geoffrey. Then I wondered how many other writers could say they had written 50 per cent of a trilogy. Why not? I did it, stayed out of range of Dennis's script file, watched the programme being recorded, transmitted, and then put it to the back of my mind, filed away as another great learning experience. Until 2011, when I got a letter asking if I would agree to its being released on DVD, and answered in the same way. Why not?

Grange Hill finally hit the screens on 8 February 1978, and although audience measurement and research was nowhere near as sophisticated as it is now, it was soon clear that the series was a hit. As the BBC said, it seemed to be filling a great need. At the time, BBC ratings were as hard to come by as the alchemist's gold, not to be shared with programme-makers or ITV, but there was talk of attracting around 8 million viewers. No matter which way it was considered, *Grange Hill* appeared to be the most successful launch ever of any new children's series.

The first series was relatively tame. Apart from the small furore over the swimming-pool episode, and the BBC's internal concerns over kids and cows, it was pretty much standard comedy capers and *Boy's Own* adventures for Tucker & Co. Series 2 became more controversial as I started to push the storyline more towards what life was like in a typical comprehensive, bearing in mind that there is no such thing. In came things like shoplifting, fighting with neighbouring schools, and student protests about uniforms, the canteen, and the fact that those on free school meals had to sit on separate tables. Having said that the series was not directly autobiographical, it is probably obvious where a lot of the influences came from.

Series 2 is key in any production. It is the make or break time. You have to take the opportunity to do what you really want to do then. If it is a success you have established the formula. If it is a flop you don't get another chance. I decided to push it and it was not long before there were accusations and complaints about Marxist subversion of children's programmes. I'd come, it seemed, full circle in political extremism. There was also an often-quoted report that 'questions were asked' in Parliament about whether the BBC should be transmitting this sort of programme and questions were put to the then Home Secretary, William Whitelaw, about whether this Marxist subversion was an appropriate programme for the BBC to be producing. In time-honoured fashion he replied that it was up to the BBC to decide what programmes it made, although that did little to assuage the time-honoured protests that dragged in celebrities to say they had banned their children from watching. I am still meeting people today who tell me they did so, just as I am still meeting many people who said they were prevented from watching at home so, also in time-honoured fashion, they simply went somewhere else to watch it away from their parents.

The Students' Action Group, SAG, which took up most of the kids' causes on the programme, was the focus of much of the outrage and protest because, ironically, the kids were seen to be being outraged and protesting. I wanted to write about how disempowered kids felt by their own education, as well as how easy it is to be swept along by protest movements. It is still a current concern, but at the time that is what was deemed to be Marxist subversion – the fact that I showed challenges to authority – despite the fact that I always had the figures of authority, like the Head, Mr Llewellyn, prevail. This was, and always remained, one of the overriding guidelines: that while the kids could challenge the status quo or demonstrate their feelings of injustice, it would always be the figures of authority who facilitated, not provided, the resolution.

This was different from the typical deus ex machina resolutions that were common in other children's dramas, when it was always a fairy godparent or figure of authority that would provide the solution. What I was keen to portray was the growing interest in student democracy, and the idea that active debate and compromise is a far better system of governance. Sounds a bit pompous, but effective democracy can be. It was, after all, a work of fiction with some room for artistic licence. At the same time, while developing my interest in socially relevant drama, the easiest way to court controversy, I was illustrating how the world actually is, rather than the way policy-makers would like it to be. I always felt an obligation at least to offer a possible solution to whichever issue was featured. It might not always have been the right one, but I felt that was better than simply writing about how bad things were, without at least trying to stimulate a debate.

That was probably what upset the chattering classes. The student demonstrations we featured were viewed as showing a blueprint for how to disrupt schools up and down the country. But the critics always overlooked certain key points. One was that there was never anything in the series that hadn't already happened somewhere else. Before each new series I would go to at least six different schools and talk to the kids about the programme. What they thought about it. What was good, bad or indifferent. Which characters they liked. Whether it was like their school or not. And, always, what they would like to see in it. If I heard a similar tale from the majority of schools on uniforms, homework, school councils, day trips, magazines or whatever, I would consider this a legitimate area to develop. Which then led to the conundrum of who was actually influencing whom?

Another thing often overlooked by those claiming the programme was provoking dissent and bad behaviour was that these things had existed before *Grange Hill* came along, and still only occured in a minority of the 30,000 or so schools in the UK at the time. It is never the programme, or any programme for that matter, 'wot made me do it', but whether the social conditions for anti-social behaviour pre-exist. Sorry, more sociology again, but out of many examples let me include two.

After the shoplifting episodes in Series 2, I got a call one day from BBC Legal. There were two boys on trial in Bristol for shop-lifting and part of their defence was that they had been influenced by *Grange Hill*. What's that got to do with me? I asked. It seemed like an obvious question. Nothing, came the reply, but we're not sure whether we have the right to issue a script to the Court. You own the copyright, remember.

I'm not sure how the law stood then. Nowadays, although it is still a bit of a grey area on non-broadcast material, I am sure it would simply be sent under the various anti-terrorism provisions, but as it was I gave my assent for the script to be telexed to Bristol. The kids got banged up because the Judge had obviously read *Oliver Twist*.

The other is a more heartening tale and involved a typically Tory mum I met in Teddington High Street. You are that *Grange Hill* chappy, aren't you? she challenged. The vowels were so clipped they nearly cut me in half. Er . . . yes. Well, I just want to tell you that I was shocked to find my children watching that dreadful programme of yours. Ah. I could have told her about the letter I'd received from the Head Boy of Eton, saying it was the favourite programme at the school, but instead I began my usual line of explanation, never defence. I appreciate it may be out of your experience, but . . . She cut me short. Oh, I know, and there's no need to give me all that sociology mumbo-jumbo, I've read your interviews. No, I just wanted to tell you that I was horrified by what I saw, but when I asked my children, 'Surely that's nothing like your school?' do you know what they said? Er . . . It wasn't? I guessed. Exactly. They told me their school was far worse. And do you know what I have done now? Joined the PTA. I'm going to shake them up. So, thank you for that dreadful programme. She then spun on her heel and went off down the high street. With no doubt in my mind that she would shake up whichever school she was now taking on, I went home with a broad smile on my face. Unexpected consequences, or the Lord's mysterious ways?

With the success of *Grange Hill* I had also done another time-honoured thing and followed many another Merseysider to London. I found myself living in what was then the closest the UK came to Southern California, the media village that centred around Twickenham where the word 'Marxist' meant a fan of the Marx Brothers and the political divide was between Tory and Liberal. This was definitely not *Grange Hill* territory and when people found out who I was there would often be a politely raised eyebrow.

This was illustrated one day by the postman, knocking on the door holding a bundle of scripts from the BBC that wouldn't fit through the letterbox. He handed them to me and turned away, but stopped halfway down the path. ''ere, you that Phil Redmond?' 'Er, yep.' 'You're infamous, aren't you?' I grinned. 'Sounds like I am now.' He went off laughing. 'They'll love you round here.' He obviously had not met the Tory mum.

While it was quite fascinating moving from the socialist North to a well-heeled metropolitan suburb, for me there was not really any of that sense of disconnect or detachment I have heard others facing this transition talk about. This was probably because 'party animal' is another phrase that people would not immediately associate with me. While I may now be able to network, I have never been a natural networker. I think that dates back to my *always* having had a sense of disconnect, to the extent that it is now a form of normality for me. Set apart as an altar boy, travelling to St Kevin's, being the first in my family to join a profession, jobs in different towns, starting to write, going to university . . . all of these stages in my life meant losing friends while gaining others, but all were transitory.

It had also meant that while I'd had the typical teenage loves and losses, I had done so without having any of the deeper ties that are forged through teenage group culture. This might also have had something to do with my Irish Catholic background, where family is the keystone and makes you automatically look inward for comfort and solace. It was definitely this that caused me most anguish when the furore around the success of *Grange Hill* broke out.

For some unknown reason, a temporary member of staff at the BBC gave out my address and phone number, and as a consequence my family became targets for some quite unpleasant harassment until the source of this was identified and dealt with. The BBC's Legal Department was very helpful to me at this time, for which I will be eternally grateful. From that moment on I have never spoken about my private life, do not give out my telephone numbers, and do not participate in any social media. My colleagues, generally, have been respectful of that. I have never used family or property or friendship for publicity. Once invited into your private life the media can never be uninvited, and the adage remains true: the only way to keep a secret is never to tell anyone.

This is the reason that some people may find sections of this book a bit thin on detail, but I have tried nevertheless, difficult though it has been at times, to give insights into the major events that formed me and helped to shape my career. At times, even my own children have found this 'media blackout' policy frustrating as they have grown through the typical teenage desire to be famous. However, they have told me that the older they got, the more they appreciated the reasons behind it, especially when reaching the stage most children of successful parents reach, when they just want to be taken for who they are themselves, rather than as the son or daughter of . . .

Typically at family gatherings, though, it is my brother Larry who tells the best tale about this phenomenon from the period he spent working at MerseyTV. Whenever Dad phoned to speak to him there, he would always tell the receptionist that he was 'Phil's dad, wanting to talk to Larry'. When Larry asked him if there was something he needed to know about who his own father might be, Dad laughed and told him, 'Sorry, lad, but you get better service if you're related to the boss!'

The debate and furore around Series 2 continued, and to give the BBC credit they didn't waver, despite Edward Barnes, who had taken over from Monica Sims as Head of Children's Programmes, telling me that he had only been in the job five minutes when he was deluged with letters demanding his resignation. His calmness under fire might have had something to do with the biggest cultural driver in media: ratings. They went up. By around 20 per cent, the alchemists said. A need was definitely being satisfied and the decision to commission a third series was made. There were only two problems. Would I agree to modify the programme's vision? And to tone down the content?

There has never been any such thing as censorship in television, although sensible people do, occasionally, come to 'the right decision'. I knew this because before meeting Anna and the team to discuss the third series of *Grange Hill*, I had stumbled across an example of it for myself.

I had been commissioned to write a script for a series of pilots ATV were going to make in an attempt to find the next big sit-com. I had chosen to do the one about the ex-sergeant major who leaves the army after twenty years and tries to adjust to the sloppy and seemingly anarchic world of civvy street. A sort of *Bless This House* meets *The Good Life*.

All was going well until shortly before the planned recording date when I got a call asking if I would change the script. Why? Because the plot revolves around British Gas not turning up to connect the cooker. Er . . . that's the point. Something almost everyone in the UK had suffered in the great housing boom of the 1960s and '70s as well as the nationwide conversion from coal to natural gas. Something the military mind could neither understand nor accept, with hilarious consequences, of course. Yes, we know, but it's come down from 'upstairs'. What's upstairs? Sales. And apparently British Gas is one of our biggest customers and they don't want to upset them, so can they be waiting for a sofa instead? Sofas aren't funny. They could be. But . . . but it's about logistics and how big organisations, like the army, can manage them, and others, like British Gas, find it impossible to arrive at a set place at a set time to do a set task. I was sounding like a QS. We know. But can we change it? Then it came. *Respice Finem* – or it might not get made, which would be a shame. I said I didn't want to change it. They said they understood. They'd leave it with me. Let me think about it. Obviously hoping I would come to the 'right' decision.

I didn't, as although I would like to say that I went back and reviewed Brian Finch's advice and decided to make a stand nevertheless, I never got the chance. I had another call soon afterwards to say the series was being postponed. Money was tight. Whether it was because I'd prevaricated or really for financial reasons I never found out, but one thing I did learn was that advertisers had no need to influence programme-makers. They did it themselves, on the advertisers' behalf. That, I discovered, is how regulation *really* works.

So going into the BBC to discuss the content of Series 3 was not that stressful. By now I was becoming more pragmatic, perhaps tempered by the first few turns of the treadmill Brian had warned me about, but I was doing what I'd realised I wanted to do when I was back in the Liverpool dole office. I was writing drama that really connected with its intended audience. And now that I had been given the chance, supported by the BBC; had watched, listened and taken part in debates about the programme, and in debates about the debates in the programme; had had the experience of being stopped in the street by the Tory mum and others like her, and had the postman recognise me as a writer, not an actor, in a programme; had been out and talked to and listened to the kids in schools, and had realised what a powerful force a continuing drama serial actually is, I realised that one episode of *Grange Hill* was reaching almost as big an audience as the BBC's prestigious single dramas, and I could do it twice a week. I didn't want to give it up. This was where I wanted to be. So I listened.

The sixth floor, the BBC's 'upstairs', needed a positive response from me to the next series, I was told. They had fully supported Series 2, its ideals and principles, but if the heat didn't subside they couldn't go beyond Series 3. OK, I got it. Series 3 should be rooted more in community than conflict. The school would be seen as cohesive rather than divisive. Instead of SAG, the School Council would become a much more positive force as the whole school came together to fund and build an Outward Bound centre, then one of the vogue ideas in education. Get city kids out amongst the trees and hills, and point out strange things like real pigs and cows. Idyllic. Inspirational. Almost. It seemed like the right decision at the time.

Before each series I would write the overall storyline, the story arc from Episode 1 to Episode 18. Who would be in which episode and how they would overlap. Because of the strict regulations on when children could and couldn't work, I would put this together as a critical path analysis or project production schedule, in much the same way that I would have done for a construction project as a QS. Actors under eleven could only work for something like forty days: 11 to 14-year-olds could do sixty days and 14 to 16-year-olds eighty days. For every hour they worked they had to have an hour's education, which meant that on every production day they could be scheduled for only one half-day's use. What this meant in practice was that Tucker, say, could only be in eleven out of eighteen episodes, so the trick was to try and make it look like he was in more. I did this by always having him featured in the first two and the last episodes of a series, then in the middle, and after that stagger him across the rest with more weight towards the end of the series so that the audience always felt they had seen a lot of him.

Alongside this I would overlap, say Benny, Alan and Trisha talking about him as though he had just left the room or been in the last lesson. This was done for all the characters, and attached to the actual storylines I would deliver these character-appearance schedules on an A3 spreadsheet. With all the episodes appearing across the top and the character names listed down the side, like a football fixtures sheet, it was easy to see when the characters were in and overlapping as well as where any potential gaps would be. It acted as a guide and when the actual schedule was prepared they might find Trisha was only committed for thirty-five of her forty days, so we could add her to other episodes. This was another system I took with me and refined for *Brookside* and *Hollyoaks*.

Although *Grange Hill* was always transmitted across February and March, I used to start each new series as though it was September, and feature events like Christmas, the school play, exams and sports day to give an overall feel of the school year. It also set the pattern of renewal that saw a new first year arrive every other series. With Series 3 and Tucker, Trisha & Co. moving into the third year, before it became known as Year 9, the school saw the arrival of the entrepreneurial Pogo Patterson. Similarly, Series 5 would see the arrival of Gonch and Hollo, Fay, Claire and Precious, and of course Zammo, Roland and Gripper Stebson, all getting ready to take on the mantle being left behind by the 'oldies', Tucker, Benny, Trisha, Cathy, Alan, Justin, and Doyle & Co.

In every series I would also try and include a story based around a school trip or the events of the holidays, to give an impression of life outside school. In Series 2 it was a camp; in Series 3 it was to be the Outdoor Centre. This went down well with everyone on the sixth floor and so the third series storyline was written to show how kids, staff, parents and teachers came together to fund-raise, acquire and refurbish the centre. It was going to be a great example of positive community action. Cohesion not division . . . until the typical phone call came.

You know we all decided how fantastic the Outdoor Centre would be? Yep. Well, it isn't. Oh, why? We've just had the budget cut, we can't go. Oh, so you want to change the storyline to be studio- rather than location-based? No, just cut it. But we have fifteen episodes building up to visiting the centre in Episodes 16 and 17. Yes, but we no longer have those episodes. We stop at 16 this year. Ah, that sort of budget cut. Yes, sorry. OK, leave it with me. Great, by tomorrow? Of course.

I was learning. The art of television is to get the art in on time – and on budget. Remember that, young Phil. But not always . . . as I would discover when I got the next call from ATV. How would I fancy having a go at dramatising the great 1950s comic-book hero, *Dan Dare*?

6

First Draft (1981–82)

'Either he goes, or I go' – *Producer's ultimatum*, County Hall, *1981*

When compiling a series of reflections like this, it is surprising how events shift about in your memory. How things you always thought took part in one era were actually part of another. The memory of Bing Crosby in the last chapter, for example. I had always thought it was part of my *Dan Dare* period at Elstree, but that happened in 1980/1 and Bing died in 1977. What I also didn't appreciate was that although 1982, the year of *Brookside*'s launch, would be a life-changing year for me, the most formative year of my career was probably 1980, when working on *Dan Dare, Going Out* and *County Hall* simultaneously taught me what television was really all about. Three different programmes that gave me the cumulative experience and confidence to take on the challenge of *Brookside*, even if I didn't fully appreciate what a huge challenge it was at the time.

A year later, 1981, I had that Writers' Guild Best New Writer award, my new hi-fi, *Grange Hill* had won three Baftas *and* The Multi-Coloured Swap Shop Award three times. I'd survived Dennis Vance, *Grange Hill* Series 5 was in production, *Going Out* had been commissioned, scripted and produced by Southern TV, *Dan Dare* hadn't, but the *Grange Hill* Christmas annuals and novels were now making me more money than even Brian Finch had made.

The annuals were published by IPC, home to the *New Musical Express, Shoot, Woman's Own* and nearly every other magazine you could think of. IPC ended up publishing them because BBC Publications were then a bit sniffy about the idea of publishing spin-off books. BBC Merchandising later got into a bit of a state when they realised the annuals were selling in the hundreds of thousands and they weren't getting anything back from a BBC programme. But that was the point. It wasn't theirs to sell. I'd learned my copyright lesson well from Richard Gordon, and they had turned down the chance to publish. It was the same story with the *Grange Hill* original novels. They ended up being published by Fontana and sold in similar numbers, even out-selling the likes of Frederick Forsyth on the bestseller lists. With a nod towards public service, the BBC did publish a special collection of short stories with the aim of trying to encourage reluctant readers. However, still hidebound by the notion that their core activity was television, not commercial enterprise, the eventual sales proved the wisdom of my building a relationship with the UK's biggest magazine publisher. That probably did more to encourage kids to read than anything BBC Publications had planned.

While the *Grange Hill* publishing empire was booming, *Brookside* was slowly evolving with Channel 4, *Going Out* was in production at Southern and I was working on *Dan Dare*. Which only went to prove that when you are hot in media, the phone never stops. So, I decided to get away from it all for a bit, spend some time with the family and go down to Cannes. And go to MIPCOM, one of the biggest television sales, co-production and distribution markets in the world. Well, what else would you do to relax? But not for long. The BBC sent a script editor to track me down on holiday.

County Hall was the final stepping-stone before *Brookside*, and while it was a vital and formative experience, and while it was a vital and formative experience, it was not a happy one. It was so unhappy, in fact, that it even defies an initial Google search, suggesting that in the age of instant websites and nostalgic forums it hardly rates a mention in the collective consciousness. You will have to work hard to find any real detail about the programme, but perhaps the summary of Episode 7 could provide a clue: *Tony and Les get into an argument over the new time clock.* Obviously heady stuff. Compared to student militancy, bodies under the patio or the *Hollyoaks* babes, would you set Sky+ on series link? You can be honest, for that summary concisely illustrates the basic problem with *County Hall*. How do you transfer an abstract democratic ideal on to screen? How do you personify faceless bureaucrats?

One way of not doing this is to appoint people to produce it who don't have a clue what they are actually working on, and because of that, don't really want to be working on it anyway. Which is exactly what the BBC did, which meant I was likely to experience some creative friction. This became increasingly apparent as the series progressed.

There is as much denial within the BBC as there is opinion outside about what its role and function should be, but even a cursory reflection on its drama output from the early 1960s to the present date reveals a slow but continuous retreat from the front-line engagement with social issues it showed with *Z Cars* and the hard-hitting single dramas like *Cathy Come Home*. This is not a function or inevitability of structure or resource, but a casualty of wrong decision-making, often by the wrong people with the wrong motivation, even if driven by good intent. It is part of the 'telly for telly's sake culture' that has appeared, particularly over the past ten to fifteen years, rather than a vocational desire to deliver public service.

I think the first indicators of that shift in culture were there in the making of *County Hall*, when the production process became driven not by the needs of the drama, but by corporate perception and risk aversion. It was originally conceived at the end of 1979 to follow the *Grange Hill* model of two episodes per week over thirteen weeks, the standard drama season run. It was commissioned in this format at the beginning of 1980. By the time I delivered, I discovered a series producer had been appointed to make thirteen weekly episodes. Why had no one bothered to mention this to me?

It seemed the decision had been taken to split the allocated budget and hedge bets with another series by the more established Ted Whitehead, called *World's End*. Although notionally set in a small local community, it sounded to me a lot like life round the pub of the same name in the King's Road, Chelsea. While I wanted to write something that impacted on the lives of nearly everyone in Britain, county politics, the London brigade typically seemed to want to eulogise their local boozer.

To establish a long-runner it is necessary either to give it enough time to build momentum, twenty-six episodes, or to increase resources so as to heighten the drama. To hold an audience's interest for a week until the next episode needs more impact than hooking them for a day or so. By making what was probably thought to be a shrewd each-way bet, splitting the resources between two programmes, both programmes were condemned to failure. They each ran for one series and never saw the light of day again. I don't know how Ted felt about it but even before I heard that knock on the door in Cannes, I knew I was in the wrong place with the wrong person with the wrong idea.

My new producer had previously invited me over to his place to talk through the series, and the moment he opened the door I knew this was going to be tricky. That gut two-second, seven-second rule. Body-language experts will tell you the first two seconds is when we make an instinctive decision about whether we like someone or not, and the next two seconds confirm it. After that it is very rare, if we are honest, that we ever change our opinion. He might well have had the same reaction although, on reflection, I was still fighting my own inbred reverse snobbery as he looked a potential Oxbridge Don, taking a day off. But it wasn't his fault he appeared to have had a socially sheltered and therefore narrow education. I decided to give him the benefit of the doubt and took him through the history of the project.

I had sold the original idea to the then Head of Drama, Graeme MacDonald, as the BBC's return to socially relevant twice-weekly programmes like *Z Cars* or *The Newcomers*, and then spent almost a year researching the project. I even told my new producer how Graeme turned grey when I first told him what I wanted to write about, but then said, 'OK. You're the one with the track record.' I hoped 'the Don' got the point. He didn't. He listened politely, but I got the sense that the history of the project was not important to him, especially as Graeme had now moved on to become Controller of BBC2 and would be barred from having any direct connection or influence over individual programmes. Perhaps, the Don ventured, that was why I had not been informed of his own appointment, but from now on I would have to work only through him.

That seemed logical, if not encouraging, so then I explained that I had decided to look at three different types of county politics: in an urban conurbation, a rural or 'shire' county, and in London. No matter which form of bureaucratic structure you look at, it tends to break down into those three distinct forms. The towns and country where most people live and London as something on its own. Outside the Greater London Council (GLC) I chose Merseyside and Cheshire, partly because I already knew a little of how they worked, as well as people from my days as a QS, and also because I knew I would get a spread of political opinion. Merseyside County Council would inevitably have a left-leaning tendency. Cheshire County Council, in almost perfect counterpoint, would lean to the right, being one of the great Tory heartlands, especially within what was known as the 'arc of prosperity' that stretches from Chester to Macclesfield. It still does. A lot of the old money there was made and emigrated from Liverpool. London, of course, would give me its own peculiar take on everything.

The Don nodded and said that sounded reasonable, but as we now only had thirteen episodes, we would need to 'get to work on the scripts'. I agreed, but with a real feeling that chalk had just met cheese.

There were smaller stepping stones between *Grange Hill*, *Going Out*, and *Dan Dare*, like *Sally Ann* and *Together*, both at Southern Television with Lewis Rudd whom I had got to know while he was at Thames Television. There he created *Magpie* with Sue Turner, but we had never managed to work together. When he moved to Southern I kept in touch and, as part of the now Redmond–Finch philosophy of trying to write on anything and everything to broaden my experience as fast as possible, I found myself working on afternoon and early-Sunday evening drama.

With regulatory permission to expand television broadcasting into daytime still a recent development, the screens had to be filled with something other than test cards and potter's wheel interludes. This led to the development of afternoon drama. Granada had started running *Crown Court* in 1972 as a lunchtime offering; ATV had *The Cedar Tree* and Thames had *Rooms*, which was then almost a *Who's Who* of British television series writing talent, including John Finch, Paula Milne, Leslie Duxbury, Fay Weldon and Willis Hall. Dennis Vance pops up in the directors list and Tony Holland, who went on to devise *EastEnders* with Julia Smith, as script editor.

All these programmes had proved popular with their audiences and I suppose Southern, not one of the ITV's Big Five, were looking for gaps in the schedule that they could occupy. Their afternoon offering was *Together*, a soap set in a retirement community, then a relatively new concept. I guess the idea was to appeal to an ageing afternoon demographic, but it never quite worked as Southern had never had access to the Wenham Report, the one that said all programme slots have the same demographic as the *Sun*.

One reason might have been that Southern decided, for some reason, to record it live. This might well have been in the hope that if it was successful they could drive the costs down while achieving the same success as ATV's infamous late-afternoon offering, *Crossroads*.

If so, they also forgot why video recording was invented. That while 'going live' can be a great adrenalin rush for the crews and actors, it increases the pressure on the production and puts the same strains on 'quality' that led to the IBA ordering ATV to reduce the number of *Crossroads* episodes from five to four and then to three. On the other hand, the programme was second in the ratings only to that other so-called ailing soap *Coronation Street*, probably another indicator of the gulf between regulators, producers and audience. While the regulators hated the production quality, the producers loved maximising resources to give their audience what they wanted. Something non-challenging to wind down to at the end of the day. Wobbly walls and all.

Together then, despite having Cleo Laine singing the title song and a cast that included Sarah Greene, of *Blue Peter* and *Saturday Super Store*, alongside John Burgess, who much later became our own 'Bing' Crosbie in *Brookside*, didn't get it together. Neither did *Sally Ann*, but for a different reason. Usually when you write a drama it can be boiled down to the old Hollywood shorthand of good guys and bad guys. White hats and black hats, as they used to say in the Westerns. For a long-runner you need all the shades in between, but the basic ingredient mix of goodies and baddies, or heroes and villains, still holds true. Even when they're villains we love to hate. *Sally Ann* was about the Salvation Army so, without diluting the basic concept and straying outside your precinct set and established characters, the dramatic tensions seemed to be about real goodies and really really goodies. It couldn't even be about goodies and not so goodies, as why would they be in the Salvation Army at all if they were less than a goody?

★

There was no ambiguity about goodies and baddies in *Dan Dare*. Dan was the goody. The Mekon was the baddy. Simple. Straightforward. By the time I got the call from ATV Scripts I had learned just to go with the flow and see where it took me. Wherever it was, it was bound to be interesting. I wasn't disappointed. From having lunch with a *Playboy* centrefold to inviting a British screen legend to sleep in my spare room and having Elton John lined up to do the music, this was a typical Lew Grade stardust-sprinkled production, even if he probably never knew anything about it. It was some form of co-production deal between ATV and, well, I was never quite sure who. The producer, Leon Clifton, was American, and one of the exec producers was Paul de Savary, brother of Peter, the property developer. They seemed to operate out of a plush Georgian mews house just behind the US Embassy; I was commissioned by ATV, and the production offices were out in Elstree.

When the call first came I was asked if I knew anything about Dan Dare. Probably like most boys who grew up in the 1950s and 1960s, I had been a regular reader of the *Eagle* comic in which he was the star character. Despite money being tight at home we always had the *Eagle, Bunty, Dandy* and *Beano* every Friday. Perhaps that was my parents' way of doing what we are still urging children to do, 'just read anything', and perhaps this also laid the foundation for my interest in visual story-telling and technology. Apart from Dan's spaceships, ray-guns and teleporters, another regular and popular feature of the *Eagle* was its own version of the centrefold: cutaway graphics of cars, trains, ships and planes. It was probably also considered a safe read as, although written and illustrated by among others Frank Hampson, it had been commissioned by the Reverend Marcus Harston Morris, who would later become Deputy Chairman of the National Magazine Company and have the highest accolade in UK magazine publishing named after him, the Marcus Morris Award. Past recipients have been Tony Elliott for *Time Out*, John Brown for *Viz* and his customer publications, and Michael Heseltine for *Haymarket*. But in 1949, Morris was seen as a campaigning vicar based in Birkdale near Southport, just north of Liverpool, who was concerned about the corrupting influence of the rising number of imported American comics. Like my own tale of hawking *Grange Hill* round every ITV company, Morris visited every Fleet Street publisher, trying to interest them in the idea of providing something more uplifting and wholesome for British youth. My mum and dad would probably have approved. So, yes, I did know all about Dan, Digby, their boss Sir Hubert and, of course, the very wholesome and feminist Professor Jocelyn Peabody.

To add a bit of glamour, it was decided to cast a Playboy Playmate as Professor Peabody, and while this might have been a great box-office idea, that it could ever have been described as 'wholesome' in the way the Reverend Morris stipulated is debatable. Whether values change as time moves on or casting Miss Playmate as Prof. Peabody was opportunistic, inspired, or just because the guys on the team wanted to meet her, I never knew, but I have to admit I've been in more arduous casting sessions.

The script process was more daunting, not just because I was being asked to take on and adapt one of the UK's best-loved popular culture figures, but also because I was coming in under the usual ATV scenario. They already had a pilot script but weren't happy with it, so they were looking for another writer. I asked who had written the pilot and they wouldn't tell me until they had seen my script. They also said if I took the commission, I couldn't tell anyone until it was handed in and accepted. Or rejected. I agreed.

So I went off and started to ponder what had changed since Dan first blasted off into the future in 1950. Then, he was launched into a post-war period when all heroes were in uniform and a grateful nation would look upon them with unwavering admiration. Evil dictators and despots would be brushed aside, as The Mekon and his Martian cronies were yet another thinly disguised metaphor for Nazi Germany. By the 1980s we had been through Korea, Suez, the slow dismantling of Empire, the Arab-Israeli War and Vietnam, while the Cold War was still underway. The popular view of the military had shifted slightly. Biggles and eulogising war movies of the 1950s had given way to the darker viewpoint of *The Deer Hunter, Apocalypse Now* and *The Dogs of War*. Dan's former stiff upper lip and public school morality would appear incongruous to a 1980s television audience.

Instead of this, I thought it would be interesting, and funny, to show him having to fight on two fronts: saving the world while also having to dodge the bureaucracy and cost-analysis that all armed forces endure in peacetime, something that we have seen with even greater severity in recent times. So I had Dan ordered back to

Spacefleet with all possible speed, only to be stopped by the space cops hiding behind an asteroid with their speed ray-gun. Then having to negotiate flight paths with British Spaceways and not having enough fuel, so trying to use his Amex card – a gag that later popped up in the spoof movie *Airplane*, proving once again that every time you have a good idea, someone else will have it as well. ATV loved the script. Then they told me who I would be replacing – none other than Dick Clement and Ian La Frenais. These guys were high on my admiration list as the creators of *The Likely Lads* and *Porridge*. I didn't believe it at first, thinking it was a wind up, but the script department confirmed it and, as life somehow arranges these things, going out to celebrate that evening, who ended up on the next table? Dick and Ian. They didn't know me. I didn't know them. It probably wasn't the best time to say hello.

So pre-production started. And the typical madness. The first script would be made as a pilot and I was asked to attend a script meeting out at Elstree. I was also asked to take extra copies of the script with me as it would take days to get things through the ATV script process. Remember, this was still 1981, electric typewriters were only just available and photocopying was a black art known only to the Xerox Company. On the way out to Elstree I stopped at a Xerox copy shop, the only place to go before they sprouted on every high street. The 1980s equivalent of phone shops. But like early mobile phone prices, they were ridiculously expensive. It cost around £15 per script, at 1981 prices (probably around £150 now), but that's what ATV had asked for. Until I got there and gave them the bill. Another media lesson. Always test the 'urgency' of a situation by suggesting whoever makes the ask should pick up the bill. This was especially true in the pre-fax, pre-email days of 'biking things over'. If things were urgent, the habit was to get things collected and delivered by motorbike delivery services. In a 'hurry up and wait' industry, i.e. hurry up, I want it – now wait until I have time to read it, this was a very costly habit.

The trick was always to suggest that if they needed it that urgently, *they* should send the bike. It was amazing how often they decided that the good old Post Office would do after all. This time, though, they did need the scripts that day. So I took them in, got an earful about the cost, and then sat back and listened to our music man explain he had been back and forth to New York half a dozen times already to see Elton John, Paul McCartney, Eric Clapton, Frank Zappa, and probably Elvis and Buddy Holly too, and all on Concorde. No one mentioned the cost.

The theme music was going to be a rework or adaptation of Chopin's Étude No. 3 in E major, Op. 10, we were told. Everyone nodded authoritatively but our music man wasn't fooled. He knew we were all bluffing, so up came one of those still new-fangled ghetto-blasters from under the table, and instead of its usual playlist of Black Sabbath or Led Zeppelin (he looked the type, and hip-hop and breakdance were still to come), out came this great piece of music, accompanied by his commentary on how the titles would run against it. If you don't know the piece, find it. If you do know the piece, you have to imagine it starting over slow shots of Dan, Digby and Prof. Peabody suiting up; 10 to 12 seconds in, the typical NASA shots heading out to the spaceship; 20 seconds and shots of them taking seats; 25 seconds, nervous tension waiting for ignition; 30 seconds and shots of Sir Hubert and ground staff; 35 seconds, thumbs up and ready to go; 40 seconds, final checks; 45 seconds and 5–4–3–2–1 ignition; 50 seconds, smoke trails and fire plumes; 55 seconds and the great ship rises, slowly then faster; 60 seconds and we are in space and floating. Or so ran the commentary. And it worked. Or would have worked. Re-worked. Adapted and cut down to television's 30-seconds format. By Elton John.

Next up was the costume design. Early estimates were in and the helmets alone looked like they would cost about £3,500 each (£35,000 per helmet now). Someone whistled. Another voice asked, 'If the helmets cost that much, what are the suits going to cost?' A mutter from somewhere else. 'Thought we were pretending to go to the moon, not actually going there.' 'And we can't go near the suits either,' another voice added. 'That's non-negotiable. It's become an industrial relations issue.'

This was almost like a death-ray hitting the room as it was only a few months since a ten-week strike had brought ITV to a stop and blank screens to viewers' living rooms. Inflation was running very high at the time and the companies had offered a 9 per cent pay rise. The unions, however, wanted 25 per cent. With inflation around 13 per cent, ITV eventually agreed to 17.5 per cent, back-dated to 1 July 1970, with the promise of another 7.5 per cent in January 1980 and a further 15 per cent the following July. This was

ITV in the days of cash up to its knees, but no one wanted to risk upsetting still-fragile industrial relations. If 1980 was a key year for me, it was also crunch time for the television unions who had crossed Margaret Thatcher's sights.

Another aspect of the unions was how strictly they enforced the closed shop, and restrictions on where and with whom they would work. This meant that most productions had to be staffed and resourced from within the companies, including the building, manufacture or making of sets, props and costumes. A costume drama had been allowed to rent its props only on the understanding that in-house staff were also fully employed, and that the next production would be fully crewed, staffed and resourced from staff union members. *Dan Dare* was that next production, which perhaps explains the cost of those helmets in-house.

With the spectre of the unions casting a shadow more sinister than The Mekon's, all heads then turned to me to ask how many times I thought Dan and Digby would need to be in spacesuits. Quite a bit, I said. I felt like suggesting they turn to their relatively cheaply photocopied scripts, but I was already picking up on where the real priorities lay. The record company would offset the music budget and the design costs were an IR issue. However, skimming through the scripts, one keen-eyed producer noted that Dan and Digby were only in one or two scenes together in suits. How about rewriting the script to make sure they were never in the same scene in space? Then they could share a suit. Yeah. Why not?

Why not indeed? Mainly because Dan Dare was supposed to be about 6'3" tall and fit, while Digby was supposed to be, well, not. Small and round-ish. Then, someone said, What about Professor Peabody? She'll have to have a different cut. She's a scientist, someone else cut in. Can't she stay indoors? You mean, in the spaceship? Whatever. She was also supposed to be a symbol of equal opportunity. They had that in the original 1950s comic strips. She couldn't just 'stay indoors'. At £3,500 a helmet? Can't she always be away at some feminist conference? And what about the boots? someone chipped in. What! If the helmets cost that much, how much are the boots going to cost? And Prof. Peabody . . . she's a woman. Women and shoes. She'll need more than one pair, won't she? It was decided to park that issue until we knew who was actually going to play the various roles, something that became apparent over the next few weeks. As would the actual number of suits, helmets and boots needed. Casting was about to start.

While *Dan Dare* was heading for film industry glamour, *County Hall* was seeking out *Guardian* readers with leather patches on the elbows of their cardigans. I would spend days shadowing people to get a feel for what their daily routines and typical agendas were. From the Leaders and Chief Executives, down to the post-room workers and, in Cheshire's case, the gardeners. I attended council meetings, committee sessions, caucus groups. One day I shadowed Sir Horace Cutler, the then Conservative Leader of the GLC, meeting him at his home for breakfast, and leaving my trusty new car, Colin Cant's old MGB GT, in his driveway until we returned around midnight. If the Don had appeared to be the epitome of the middle-class, then at first sight Sir Horace appeared to be the epitome of a Northerner's Tory caricature. Sharp suit, bow tie and well-trimmed beard. As we talked he evolved into a dramatist's dream: the multi-faceted character.

Although coming from a wealthy family and despite going to grammar school, he never went to university but worked as a carpenter in the family business. When his father died unexpectedly, he had to take on the running of it, and had gone into politics for a reason not dissimilar to why I wanted to write about it: the extent to which local politics impacts on our lives. For him, and for the family business, it had repercussions on the building trade, an issue I was familiar with from my own days as a QS. The writing sponge was soaking all this up, especially his ideas for 'privatising' many of the GLC's functions, including giving tenants the right to buy their council homes, all long before the term 'Thatcherism' had been heard.

It was an interesting day, moving from meeting to meeting, observing the way people reacted to him, how he reacted to them, and how those I already knew changed in his presence. It was probably the first time I had considered the power of office. What a badge of authority bestows on the wearer, and how fleeting the effect can be. The following year the former carpenter, now Sir Horace, was out after losing the election to Labour.

After leaving him that night to head home I was pondering all this and how I would use it in *County Hall*, but more importantly how cool it was that he had a radiotelephone in his car. It was obviously a new gizmo as he was doing what people tend to do now on their mobiles: call the office to say they are on the train or, in our case, the car. I did wonder how many other people he would actually be able to phone. Since the radiotelephone was the size of a small suitcase, it was doubtful there were more than a few hundred in the entire country. But now that the MGB GT was becoming my second skin, I was rapidly finding out that when you were dashing from meeting to meeting across London, the constant dilemma was whether to stop and find a phone box to say you were running late, or just to press on knowing that that was what they had already assumed. To be able at least to call the office and get them to call ahead . . . *that* was the future. I decided that as soon as I could afford it, I'd get one. And a bigger car to fit it in. I did both a couple of months into *Brookie*.

Another thing that stuck with me after my meeting with the GLC leader was the way a car could be turned into a mobile office or even a communications centre. One of the biggest drama clichés of the time, from *The Planemakers* to *The Brothers*, had to be the fat-cat capitalist being driven to the office while reading the *Financial Times*. Once you have been at the sharp end of running your own business, you soon realise that the best thing about a 9 to 5 job is that you know what you will be doing at 5 p.m. As a business owner there are very few hours in the day when you have the luxury of time to sit back and read the newspaper. It's usually a quick glance here and there or else listening to a digest of what you need to know.

On the ride in and out of London with Sir Horace, I immediately grasped the point of having a driver. It converts what would normally be dead time into something more productive. The drive out to his place and the drive back were two hours in which I could have been busy writing up my notes which, over the week, meant I could have gained an extra working day. This was something nearly everyone in the land cottoned on to when mobile phones appeared: the fact that you can carry on your life while driving. In fact, this was so obvious, and so useful, that everybody did it, everywhere and anywhere, to the point that it has now had to be regulated.

Over the years my use of mobile technology evolved along with the business. As soon as I could afford it I did get a phone in the car and, even if it was mostly used for calls back to the office, there were always answerphones (later, voicemail) so that, no matter what time of day or night, wherever I was, I could leave messages or reminders to be picked up on later. As technology improved, mobile communication platforms evolved into virtual offices and portable viewing facilities. Travelling back and forth to London, I would often edit the *Brookie* and *Hollyoaks* scripts, watch rough cuts, casting and location tapes, and clear the in tray. I probably got through at least three times the amount of work I would have done on the train, and didn't have to lug it all through a crowded station either. Being driven became my preferred way of travelling and, actually, over time the cheapest. It isn't the obvious door-to-door cost, nor the time saved, but the extra time it gives you, the extra work that can be done, the extra opportunities it throws up.

That is why I am constantly amazed at the way government chips away at things like official cars, drivers, taxis etc. as an easy way of being seen to be cost-saving. They are not really, they are penny-pinching – or what the Americans call nickel 'n' diming. Trying to be seen to be frugal and set a good example, they are actually only demonstrating that they don't understand the value of time. Obviously the key factor here is how we value our own time. When I was at the centre of *Brookside*, I was the one everyone wanted answers from. I was the one everyone was waiting for scripts from. Or decisions on casting. Or locations. Or talking to the press. The one responsible for driving things forward. Driving myself from A to Z as well wasn't the most effective use of time.

I chatted to Cherie Booth about this once after being at a Labour Party event in Bolton with Tony. There he was, the Prime Minister, having travelled from London for a day of government engagements in the North West plus attending a Labour Party rally in Bolton, about to be driven up to Scotland to give a speech to the Scottish Labour Party. And after that he would be driven all the way back to London. This was not an isolated example but a fairly regular occurrence for him. Accepting that there has to be a clear separation between government and party business, I couldn't help thinking that most people would appreciate that their Prime Minister was also a politician, and might just prefer that the person with their finger on the launch codes was not so knackered all the time. They might also think we could afford an official helicopter every now and then, for our Prime Minister.

An even dafter example was when I once bumped into Wirral MP Linda Chalker, later Baroness Chalker, on the plane up from

London to Liverpool. She also happened to be Minister of State at the Foreign and Commonwealth Office and was therefore considered a possible target after the IRA Brighton Bomb attack on Margaret Thatcher. I was sitting on the plane when I noticed some blue lights travelling across the tarmac. Two official cars stopped at the steps to the plane and after a moment a flak-jacketed, armed police officer walked into the cabin, followed by another carrying the Ministerial bags. Linda then came through and sat down in the seat next to me. The cops relaxed when they realised we knew each other – then nodded and said, 'Have a good weekend, Minister. See you on Monday morning.'

On the flight up I asked her if she would have a similar escort waiting for her in Liverpool, obviously being a bit closer there to the boys in Ireland. She said no. As soon as she got on the plane in London she ceased being a Government Minister and became a constituency MP, thereby failing to qualify for protection. I took a quick glance round the plane, hoping the IRA understood the difference, and then ended up carrying the Ministerial bags across the tarmac for her in Liverpool.

Worlds away from *Dan Dare*'s Hollywood glamour and *County Hall*'s sensible shoes and cardigans, *Going Out* was aiming for a teenage audience living a life of council-estate grunge. Just as I had initially had difficulty trying to interest people in the idea of making a series about school, the notion of teenagers actually carving out time to sit and watch TV was met with similar disbelief despite *Grange Hill* already developing a sizeable teenage audience. Because of this I was pushing the BBC to think about extending *Grange Hill*'s range beyond the fifth form. ITV were already doing it, the new Channel 4 might be doing something, so surely it was obvious that the BBC should capitalise on an asset it had already created. We had spent five years building an audience, so why not keep the characters and actors and retain that audience, rather than throw it all away simply because the actors outgrew the remit of the Children's Department? No other industry would spend so much on R&D, marketing etc and throw away its market share.

This was part of my pitch when I got to meet the then BBC2 Controller Brian Wenham, trying to persuade him to commission a teenage spin-off of *Grange Hill*. He was interested but this was in the days before brand value and extension and, as always, money was finite. Unlike ITV, there would be no extra income, just a reallocation of resources, and it would mean a huge gamble to go against the idea that teenagers didn't watch TV. To make his point he showed me a copy of an internal BBC report into audience composition, commissioned to prove to the government what great value it was for the licence fee, especially as there was a new fourth channel on the horizon that would probably start carving out some of his audience from BBC2.

Unfortunately, the research didn't quite support the thesis, with its overarching point that no matter what BBC slot, whatever channel or time, the audience composition was exactly the same as Britain's template for populist taste, the *Sun* newspaper. End of strategy for special pleading and Brian put a copy of the report theatrically in the bottom drawer of his desk where, I knew, it would always remain. It did though, I think, help convince him that if we made a good teenage programme the audience would find it. From that, eventually, came *Tucker's Luck*.

Meanwhile Southern TV, like the rest of the UK, was rocking to Olivia Newton John and John Travolta in *Saturday Night Fever*. This film started to change the popular perception of what teenagers wanted to watch. It certainly made an impact on Southern Television's then Director of Programmes, Jeremy Wallington, who asked Lewis Rudd to find him a 'British *Saturday Night Fever*'. This was in line with Southern's logic of trying to identify programme areas that the other ITV companies were not already occupying. Afternoon drama had recently been vacated by ATV and Thames, which had cancelled both *The Cedar Tree* and *Rooms*, an area in which they hoped to place *Together*. *Sally Ann* was planned for the early-evening Sunday God slot, so perhaps teenage drama might be a fruitful new niche.

Lewis and I agreed that if the programme was to resonate with teenagers it had to be as realistic as *Grange Hill* in terms of British culture, and as realistic as *Saturday Night Fever* in its use of everyday language. He told me to go for it, saying we would have the arguments about content once we had sold the initial idea to Jeremy. So I did, focusing on the six weeks that eventually face all school leavers, their first summer of freedom without the certainty of that return to school in September. The end of the beginning of the transition from childhood to adulthood. From school kids to kids on the block. The teenage rites of passage.

The first episode was almost a bookend to the first episode of *Grange Hill*. Just as we followed Tucker into an alien world of higher education and authority, from the more relaxed atmosphere of his primary school to the harsher world of an organised education factory, *Going Out* opened with its central characters about to leave this institutionalised world to negotiate a more uncertain, often chaotic life, lacking its former routine. Whereas in school Tucker and every school kid in the UK knew where the lines of authority were drawn, the *Going Out* characters, like most school leavers, soon discovered that these lines can shift, sometimes on a daily basis, and you are left to fend for yourself. At least in school there is someone to turn to. At least in school everyone knows who the nutters and bullies are, be they staff or pupils. In the wider world the first challenge is figuring out who you're up against and who can be trusted to help you.

This moment is brought home to our central characters early in Episode 1. Roger, the Jack the Lad of the group, has a typical run in with the caretaker on their last day at school when he drops some litter. The caretaker comes back with the usual line from authority: 'Pick that up.' Roger replies, 'We're finished with this place, Parky, which means there's nothing you can do – got it?' He then turns to the rest of his gang with a huge grin on his face. That's told him, eh? They all laugh, until the caretaker steps forward. 'Yeah. It also means I can push your teeth so far down your throat, you'll have to stick your hand up your arse to bite your nails. You got that, sonny?' The blood and bravado drain from Roger's face. The group all look suitably chastened and Roger picks up the litter. Caretaker nods, and goes on his way. Welcome to the real world, kid. Within that one exchange the whole premise and tone of the series was established and, to use the same realistic language, the s*** hit the fan.

The phone went. Phil, love the script. Great. It's terrific. Thanks. Everything we asked for. But? Er, yes, but . . . we have a problem with the language. You asked for *Saturday Night Fever*. Yes, yes, I know but . . . You have seen the film? Er, yes. But it's, well, the language. You have seen the film? I have, but . . . Ah. You've seen the 'X'? Yes. And Jeremy might have only seen the 'A'? Possibly.

And there we had it again. That gulf between the programme commissioners, the producers and the audience.

When *Saturday Night Fever* hit the cinemas and became one of the biggest teenage hits of all time, if not the biggest, it was seen as representing their life. Even if it was only a fictional representation, the emotions and language it contained seemed to be realistic. English could be heard in the bits between the swearing. This of course resulted in it receiving an 'X', or 18 Certificate as it is now. The studio, as they do, had originally underestimated its potential appeal, hence the X-rating. They then realised, as they do, that this was locking out a huge potential audience in the low- to mid-teens, plus lucrative television sales. So, as they do, the studio re-cut the film and released a cleaned-up 'A' version, Adult Supervision or PG. In other words, no swearing. We were now convinced that Jeremy Wallington, from whom we needed the green light, had only ever seen the 'A' version and had therefore missed the same point as Joy Whitby had on *Grange Hill*. We needed to come up with something about, for and of the audience's own world.

There was nothing else for it. We would have to have a meeting. See if we could come up with a compromise. A solution for Jeremy. The right decision. Ahead of this Lewis sent me what I dubbed the 'defuckification memo', another example of there being no censorship in British television, only considerations of taste and decency. So long, of course, as we come to the right decision about whose taste and decency. The memo was a page-by-page schedule of all the problematic words, terms and phrases throughout the script. Needless to say, the realism I'd been encouraged to include was challenging taste and decency on every page, and we soon got down to haggling over whether I could keep three 'bloody's for every 'bugger' sacrificed.

Despite my unofficial classification of the memo itself, my own form of self-censorship, taste and decency meant there were no f's or c's. These are the two expletives that cause most widespread offence, so unless it is a highly charged or very specific moment, I can see no point in deliberately alienating most of your intended audience. The interesting point about different regional sensibilities came up this time in relation to one character referring to another as 'shitface'. This seemed to exercise the sensibilities of the South East in particular, whereas the Londoners' bête noire of 'sod' didn't register with them.

Meanwhile over at Elstree the wrangling about how many spacesuits they could get away with was occasionally interrupted by other production considerations, like music and special effects. At another script meeting we heard which rock idol our music man had Concorded off to meet this time. One thing was guaranteed. If it ever came off, the musical score and accompanying album would be, as our music man kept saying to our accompanying groans, out of this world. So too would be the special effects, and we were due to look at a test tape of footage the RAF had shot for the production. At that time they were not spread across the globe on peacekeeping missions so, as part of their regular exercises, they had agreed to use a low-level training flight over the Arctic to shoot some footage for us using infra-red film. The hope was that this would make it resemble the Martian landscape, which we could then use as a backdrop. The viewing of the RAF footage was scheduled for the same studio in which I had watched Bing Crosby a few years earlier. Again, for the time, the material looked terrific. This may have something to do with the fact that ATV and its associated company ITC had a good track record in special effects from working with the likes of Gerry Anderson who created *Thunderbirds, Space: 1999* and *Terrahawks* – a title I would later parody for Imelda and her Terrorhawks in *Grange Hill*. Even if Gerry wasn't working on *Dan Dare*, a lot of the technicians and crew who had worked with him would be.

After watching the RAF footage I was asked whether I would like to sit in on one of the Playboy Playmate lunches. The old philosophy of 'Why not?' came into play. Again I got to sit behind the rope in the posh area of the canteen. Although these things can sound more glamorous than the reality, this time – with the long legs, big hair, big eyes, polished nails and perfect teeth all on display – it really was. Probably more so because of the reaction from everyone else at the studio. *Dan Dare* was the next big show. We were it. Except for *The Muppets*. No one could upstage Kermit and Miss Piggy. And just recently they had surpassed themselves.

Whenever you went into ATV's canteen block, someone would point out the mural painted on the end wall above the entrance doors. Legend had it that it was of *Swan Lake* as Lew Grade had wanted to film the famous performance of Rudolf Nureyev and Dame Margot Fonteyn. While trying to persuade them to agree to this, he had their heads painted on to the figures in the mural. Whether this is true or not, the point was that the great man loved this mural. Then, one night, *The Muppets*, aka Jim Henson & Co., broke into the canteen and painted over the figures with likenesses of Kermit, Miss Piggy, and a few others. The staff were outraged and fearful of what Lew would think. Word spread. Soon the legend himself appeared with his legendary cigar, took one look and said, 'I like it. Keep it.' No Playmate could upstage that, but after lunch we all agreed we would now need at least two spacesuits. Prof. Peabody would definitely have to have her own. Tailored.

This led on to consideration of who would play Dan and I was asked if I would meet someone they had in mind, talk them through the script and explain how I saw the rest of the series developing. Sure. Who was it? It's a big name. Well, used to be big. Massive. Colossal. Who is it? You'll know the name. Amazing actor. Biggest in the world once, then gave it up. Found God. The whole commune thing or something. I knew I was being wound up. This could be his comeback. All down to you . . . Go on then, I said. Ever heard of a guy called James Fox? Er, of course. How far was the wind up going? It's him. He's interested. This *is* a wind up? No. He wants to get back in the business and he's interested in being Dan Dare. Wouldn't that be great? It would. So, we thought you'd be great at talking him through it. That OK? Er, yeah.

And so from having lunch with the Playmate they thought would be ideal for the Reverend Morris's wholesome feminist Prof. Peabody, I was about to have dinner with the man we all then regarded as an ex-druggie, now born-again Christian New Ager. How much crazier could this programme become? Of course, like so much else, that was all part of the media circus nonsense. In Fox's previous film, *Performance*, he had acted alongside Mick Jagger and his Rolling Stones partner's partner, Anita Pallenberg. The heady mix of rock music, the film business and a movie about sex, drugs and violence had all contributed to the myths surrounding Fox's own decision to 'quit the business'. He appeared to have adhered to the 'tune in, turn on, drop out' philosophy of psyche-delic drugs advocate Timothy Leary, and put his acting career on hold, while he subsequently went off to find God somewhere. A typical casualty of the celebrity culture of the late sixties and early seventies.

This all seemed perfectly plausible in the 1960s, when he had been on the verge of international stardom with films like *The Servant*, *King Rat* and *Thoroughly Modern Millie* before he decided to, well, drop out. However, arrangements were made with James and he offered to come to my place in Teddington and talk things through. I asked him where he was staying and he said he hadn't thought about it, so I offered to put him up if he didn't mind sleeping on a camp bed in my spare room. It was one of those things you say, like 'we must do lunch', not really expecting anyone to say yes. But he did.

When the doorbell rang I wasn't quite sure whether there would be a long-haired hippy or a robed druid standing on the other side. Either way it would do my reputation for infamy with the neighbours a power of good. The reality was worse. There stood this amazingly smart, well-kempt, fit and polite man. He looked closer to a Mormon, a tax inspector or a CID officer than a drop out. My God, I thought. They'll think I'm respectable.

Throughout the evening James proved to be both charming and well informed about the project. He told me that despite the gossip about his wild and colourful past, he had simply got fed up with the business and sought spiritual comfort after his father died. One thing led to another and he'd spent the last six or seven years working with a religious group and re-examining who and what he was. Now it was time for him to get back to work. He asked me who we had in mind for the other characters. Rodney Bewes of *Likely Lads* fame had been suggested for Digby, perhaps the suggestion of my predecessors, Clement and La Frenais. I told James this and he seemed to approve. I wondered whether to tell him about Prof. Peabody, and decided not just then. I went to bed thinking, I've got the legendary James Fox sleeping on a camp bed in my spare room. How amazing is that? And he's around six foot . . . We're definitely going to need three spacesuits.

If *Dan's Dares*, as I was now privately calling the project, had become one of the first pilot programmes for Care in the Community, my life at the time seemed to be becoming equally crazy. Like many of my Scouse predecessors building a career in the media, I found myself not on any yellow brick road, but a

British Rail train about twice a week. When *Grange Hill* took off, I decided to move south to cut down the weekly travel. No sooner had I done it than I found myself working with Southern on *Going Out* in Southampton and researching *County Hall* back on Merseyside and in Cheshire. At least I could sometimes time the Northern trips to allow me to stop off at Elstree for *Dan Dare* on the way up or down.

My days were getting longer and longer; my early training for the graveyard shift helped. When back home, literally, I stayed with my mum and dad, although that meant sleeping in what seemed to be a constantly shrinking room. Had I really shared it with my brother when we were both in our late teens? Did I really mountaineer down those few stairs and chimney along the hall to avoid the lino tiles, now covered by wall-to-wall carpet? I tried to balance on the skirting boards, just as I used to when I was eleven, but couldn't. Either I'd lost the knack or my legs were too long to get them at the right angle. On each visit my dad would ask me when I was going to get a proper job.

On Merseyside or in Chester, where Cheshire County Council was based, I found that the items under discussion differed from those I'd heard aired by the GLC, but the protocol and power plays remained the same. Politicians were still, well, politicians. Although the politics was not as intense or as febrile in Cheshire as at the GLC or Merseyside, with their late-night deals and corridor coups, the Cheshire Tories seemed to have a simple mechanism for getting things through. They did it without the opposition being present to slow things down.

On one shadowing day I was escorted by the PR guy to sit in on a planning committee meeting that was dealing with the contentious issue of 'gypsies'. Since the 1960s there had been an obligation on local authorities to provide sites for gypsies and travellers. There is a legal difference between the two. Romany gypsies trace their ethnic origin back to migrations, probably from India, taking place at intervals since before 1500. Travellers break down into Irish travellers and any other group that elects to lead a 'nomadic or seminomadic lifestyle'. Like Romany gypsies, Irish travellers were only recognised as a distinct ethnic group under the Race Relations (Amendment) Act of 2000, although they have been coming to England since the nineteenth century.

Left: My official Holy Communion photo, aged 7. A closer look reveals the family teeth – the gap shared with both Mum and Dad! I only had the teeth for four more years…

Right: A Redmond family day out. I lost my rubber – and I think the girl on the right is wondering why my sister Kathy has no hands…

Below: Me and 'Sir' – now aka Liverpool's own Poet Laureate, Roger McGough. He was as fun, and poetic, a Geography teacher as anyone could wish for.

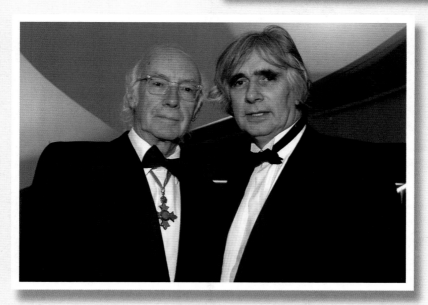

Above: The original VT machine I taught myself to use in the early days.

Above and right: Although the annuals sold
well, there was never anything to beat that
original sausage image – iconic.

Above: Tucker (aka Todd Carty) & Co with his famous leather jacket.

Left: A few terms later we were back at Grange Hill (aka Childwall), but probably both wishing we could get back into those leather jackets…

Right: A *Grange Hill* script meeting. From left to right: Andrew Corrie, my script assistant; Albert Barber, then director but later producer; Ron Smedley, then producer; Leigh Jackson, *Grange Hill* script editor who would take over from, on right, Anthony Minghella.

Brookside Close started out like this…

went to this…

and ended like this.

The drama started out with gritty Scouse gits…

went to a Scouse wedding…

and ended up with C4 glamour babes.

Above: Sue Johnston during Sheila Grant's rape storyline.

Above: The best seat in the house (with/on Ricky Tomlinson, aka Bobby Grant).

Left: Sue and Ricky in what was to become a famous position – twice over.

Right: Brookside's first Script to Screen session with *(front row, L–R)*: Brian Regan (aka Terry Sullivan); Dorothy Hobson, academic; Barry Woodward, writer from beginning to end, as was Andy Lynch *(back row, far left)*. Next *(L–R)* is Bill Dean (aka Harry Cross), me and David Rose from C4.

Mal Young and I started on *What Now?*…

and ended up as part of the establishment!

Below: My best friend Richard Foster with his wife, now Lady Mary Foster, after his knighthood. Alexis and I threw a lunch for him; the 'knight's' suit of armour came from a TV prop company.

Above: The closest I came to a dog until Capital of Culture – on *Waterfront Beat.*

Right: Off-screen drama: what could have been my last ride home…

Below: An early attempt at community sponsorship and my dad's church footie team ends up going up against my brother's…

Oh brother! A family at war

THERE will be a family at war to-night when the Liverpool Challenge Cup final is played at Prescot Cables' Hope Street ground (kick-off 6.30 p.m.).

For the Redmond family will be very much involved as the teams, St. Dominic's and H. B. and H. Newton, battle it out.

The Saints, whose president is Lawrence Redmond senior, have been sponsored this season by the Mersey Television Company, who run the Brookside series. The TV company's chairman is Lawrence's son, Phil.

But when Newton step out to-night they will be led by Phil's brother, Lawrence junior, who is player-manager.

Treble chance

There will be more at stake, too, for the Saints.

Already this season they have won the County Combination first division title and also the Lancashire Amateur Cup, so they will be chasing a treble success against the team from the North-West Counties League division three.

There'll certainly be no love lost for the 90 minutes among the Redmonds, but when it's all over there will be a celebration drink to toast the victors.

The picture (above), shows left to right: Lawrence junior, Phil and dad Lawrence.

● Inside: Focus on the local soccer finals.

Despite the legal obligation to provide campsites, Cheshire's provision was limited, faced as they always were with local residents' opposition. The intended users' objections probably matched the level of opposition, as the designated areas were usually where the travellers didn't want to go, which in turn led to trespass when they found somewhere they preferred. In Cheshire, a county of landed Tories, this was not something that would receive a sympathetic hearing. For me, as a dramatist, this had all the ingredients for powerful and passionate confrontation, as we have more recently witnessed in Essex with the Dale Farm evictions and to some extent New York's Wall Street and London's St Paul's Cathedral 'occupations'. The meeting in which the Council would decide whether to grant or deny further campsites promised to provide some good material, especially as the committee membership reflected the basic premise of the series. What would it be like to be the Independent candidate who held the balance of power on a hung Council? I was about to find out years before anyone had heard of Nick Clegg.

Along we went to the designated committee room and met some of the waiting opposition Labour members. Like myself down in Teddington, they were a rare breed in Cheshire, and had formed an alliance with a couple of Independents on the Committee. If they could unite they might just have enough votes to force the County Council to fulfil its obligations and overrule the objectors, as well as provide better facilities for the traveller sites. It promised to be a big event. I watched as they started to get ready, slightly nervous but businesslike. Reading their notes. Checking all papers were in order. Then we waited. The starting time for the meeting came and went. The small talk continued, nervousness being replaced by puzzlement. Where were the committee officers, never mind the other members? Puzzlement turned to irritation at the discourtesy. The PR guy, probably more conscious of what a shambles this looked to me than to help the members, went off to find out what was happening. Irritation turned to anger as he returned looking shaken. The meeting had been moved to a room upstairs.

After a mad scramble to gather papers, bags and coats, an angry crocodile of councillors charged up the stairs, only to be met by the ruling majority filing out of the room. All done. Protests upheld. Planning permission denied. Anger turned to fury. Insults were hurled. I made notes. This was somewhere between *Yes Minister* and *The Power Game*. It would make great *County Hall*.

The Don agreed. But . . . It all seems so remote. That's the point. But it's about faceless bureaucrats. That's the point, to personalise them. Real people making strategic decisions that affect other real people who don't know anything about what's going on. They would if it was about a pedestrian crossing outside their homes. Can't we do that? No, no. That's district politics, not county. Whether to have Belisha beacons or a pelican crossing is not the same as the racial connotations attached to gypsies and travellers, I argued. Drama is about people not issues, he countered. What? Anyone for tennis or an affair or both? It's people who create the issues, I countered. However, when I discovered he had commissioned a title sequence based on a pinball rolling around a maze of anonymous corridors it confirmed my suspicion that he had totally missed the point.

We agreed to resolve things as the scripts developed and I went off thinking that he would see sense once he did a bit more reading and got into the characters, storylines and scripts. He probably went off thinking the same thing about me. He was the producer. His opinion was what counted. Which was true. It did. Which is why the arguments intensified as the project developed, to culminate in that ill-judged decision to send a script editor all the way to Cannes to chase script delivery.

To this day, despite having had any number of media lunatics cross my path, I can't quite fathom how they ever thought, on the one hand, that flying someone to Cannes was a sensible use of the BBC's money, or on the other why it would do any good. They might have thought I was late delivering, but I didn't, and even if I had been cavalier enough to take off for a week, was it likely I would then pack my bags and go home to write a script, simply because someone with a posh voice came to chastise me in the South of France? The more recent phrase 'What planet were they on?' was not then in use, so instead the BBC emissary got five minutes of Scouse philosophy and was sent packing. I then went across the road to the MIPCOM conference centre, to the BBC Enterprises stand, and having remembered the *Corrie* writers' tip, asked if I could use their phone to call BBC UK.

While my original BBC patron might have gone, my *Dan's Dares* adventure had paid off in an unexpected way. The new Head of

Drama at the BBC had arrived – from ATV. It was David Reid and I had already got to know him out at Elstree. I called and explained where I was and why I was calling. Shall we fix a meet? Great. When are you back? Tuesday. Tuesday it is.

By the time the meeting came round I had been through the usual cycle of wondering if I had over-reacted. Had the Don been right after all to send his script editor? But then I'd thought back over all the conversations we'd had about the project and the scripts, ever since that first meeting when he'd asked why I had written twenty-six storylines. We were definitely not 'gelling'. Nor was the relationship with the script editor that good even before our unexpected rendezvous in Cannes. All she had been trying to do was change the scripts, not edit them. To make me rewrite them into the programme they wanted to make – a not uncommon complaint from writers across the industry, and something that would help push me towards taking an active role in the Writers' Guild of Great Britain (WGGB).

Arriving at Threshold House, the home of BBC Drama, I had rehearsed the whole thing in my mind several times and kept coming back to the two same points of principle I've held throughout my career: the BBC didn't employ me and they were commissioning my idea, not an idea from the producer and his oppo. That did not rule out creative collaboration, or accepting good advice and ideas, but neither did it mean anyone had the right to ride roughshod over my work simply because they thought they could. It does all come down to a matter of opinion, and I have not been slow in using the 'and unfortunately it's mine that counts' line, but if you are not the creator, or even the initiator, of the idea, your role is to facilitate it or pass. It is the converse argument to Brian Finch's 'they'll get someone else'. At times, producers too have to accept that an idea may simply not be for them, and pass it on to someone more sympathetic. Before someone else moves them on.

David Reid was always a quiet, gentle man, very similar to the 'clerical' partner in my first quantity surveying job, so the planned mediation meeting started at least in an atmosphere of serenity – which lasted about thirty seconds. It was all over in about ten minutes, or that's what it felt like. The tension between me and my producer was obvious. I thought he had acted both unreasonably and irresponsibly. He accused me of doing the same. He said I didn't understand that this was adult drama. I accused him of the same thing. This was social realism not escapism. He said . . . I said . . . until eventually I think I might have come out with a line about him being nothing more than a glorified BBC administrator, so why didn't he just accept that and get on with it? Up out of his chair he leaped. 'That's *it!*' He headed for the door, flung it open, turned back to David and issued the immortal line, '*It's either him or me. Either he goes, or I go.*' And out he went, slamming the door. I turned to look at a now bemused David. He pondered for a moment and then said quietly, 'Looks like I'm stuck with you.'

In reality life had probably already moved on. I will always fight to protect something that is right and viable, but I am also extremely good at cutting, running and abandoning lost causes. It's the Scouse pragmatism gene again. I think, in both my head and my heart, I knew the project was doomed as soon as I discovered the budget had been halved and my new producer was never going to be a soul-mate. The other thing that probably didn't help was that while everything that could go wrong was going wrong on *County Hall*, on *Going Out*, everything that could go right seemed to be going right. True, it wasn't adult drama, but neither was it for kids.

While Lewis Rudd, like Anna Home with *Grange Hill*, might not initially have known what he was getting, or letting himself in for, after seeing the script he went looking for the right producer-director – something the adult drama folk hadn't even considered doing with *County Hall*. Just as Anna had found Colin Cant, so Lewis found another Colin, Colin Nutley. More recently a huge name in Swedish cinema, at the time he had just finished a children's series, *Noah's Ark*, an adaptation of John Rowe Townsend's novel. This was set slightly in the future and had as its theme the social and moral decline of Britain due to economic collapse. Inflation is rife, and deprivation and desperation lead to lawlessness. The story deals with how one family try to cope, by turning an old manor house into their castle.

There are many resonances with today, as although the novel was originally written in 1976, the television series hit the screens in 1980 when Britain had just come out of the 'Winter of Discontent' and we were in the midst of great social and economic change. The word 'Thatcherism' was about to enter the language. It was a tough and uncompromising production for the time, and after all the furore around *Grange Hill's* second series, Lewis must have felt that Colin and I would work well together. He was right. Yet even before we met, I had already had to negotiate the minefield of taste, decency, authenticity and copyright.

Now that I had ruined *Saturday Night Fever* forever for Lewis Rudd's boss, the defuckification memo that followed gave the impression that Southern were passing the *Going Out* script round in plain brown paper envelopes. They were so concerned about the content that they had decided, again without telling me, that if they were going to go ahead with the project then they had better be sure that they would be able to stand up and defend its authenticity, both to the ITV Big Five who would have to pay for it and to the regulators. By this time I thought I had the ultimate credentials with the people who really mattered: the audience. With *Grange Hill* having had the best response of any new children's programme launch, the ratings for the controversial second series had gone up by around 20 per cent. Then, even for the toned down, 'positive' but truncated third series, the ratings had gone up yet again. This meant that with the greatest cultural test passed, increased ratings, at least *Grange Hill* was safe and vindicated. It had been the right decision to tone things down a bit. That surely should have been enough for Southern. But no. They had a better idea. They would ask a teenager.

This might have been one of the early symptoms of the debilitating disease later identified as market testing that gradually hobbled the industry. When instead of relying on their own guts and track records; and instead of going back to their founding fathers; instead of remembering how Sidney Bernstein and Lew Grade relied on circus and box office; and instead of giving the audience what they wanted . . . they started to try and second-guess what the audience would ask for. Bernstein and Grade always knew that what the audience really wanted was not what they already had, but something new. The secret of circus and box office is surprise.

This is why ideas like audiences voting for the way a drama should unfold come and go. The audience doesn't really want to know how it turns out, or not until the end. True, part of the fun and enjoyment is going back and unpicking it and discussing how it could have gone this way or that way. But that is always after the event. Storytelling is about suspense. Keeping the audience guessing.

Keeping them hooked. Playing to expectation by pointing to a probable outcome, and then going against that expectation to deliver the twist at the end. It is difficult to do, but when it works it is the most satisfying experience for writer and reader, director and audience, producer and box office. To play to expectation is to find what the audience knows, understands and can interpret, like kids in school or people in work, and then graft on the things that they might have heard about but never actually seen, or might have thought about but wouldn't actually do. Escapism, as I tried to explain to the Don during one of our sparring bouts, is watching other people doing your job. And, hopefully, making a hash of it.

Fortunately, the teenage tester gave my script the thumbs up, high five, wicky shake, said it was cool, hot, bad, sad, sound, fit, awesome or whatever, and so Jeremy Wallington relaxed, Lewis smiled, and we could all go to the network and regulators and say that the script was liked by one teenager in one seaside town in the South of England. It had been thoroughly market tested. It was authentic. Solid. Wonder what Jeremy would have made of *The Inbetweeners*?

I can now see that 1980 was probably the pivotal year in my original quest to become a television writer. It might not yet have been the proper job my dad was still hoping for, but I had been voted Best Newcomer by the Writers' Guild; I had commissions on two potentially long-running series at Southern TV, *Sally Ann* and *Together*, as well as my own six-part teenage series in development, *Going Out*. At ATV I was helping to develop *Dan Dare*. At the BBC *Grange Hill* was still going from strength to strength, and I had the commission to develop and write the twenty-six-part *County Hall*. The only real issue was how I would cope if they all succeeded. How would I find the time to write them when my life was already fully occupied, with virtually no time left for socialising?

I needn't have fretted: 1980 was also the year of applications for the renewal of the ITV franchise licences. The regulators got to work. Both Southern and ATV lost their franchises. Southern were just kicked out and replaced by TVS. ATV had to reorganise and evolved into Central. On ITV's judgement day in 1980 they lost their businesses, and I lost *Sally Ann*, *Together* and *Dan Dare*.

With *Dan Dare* I came to the view that all that craziness was probably nothing more than the political manoeuvrings of an ITV company trying to demonstrate in its franchise renewal application that it had listened to the harsh criticism over its too-popularist output, like *Crossroads*, and was looking to make more programmes of 'quality'. And that is another nebulous term that I will be returning to, as it still casts its stifling shadow over the industry. In its pursuit, was *Dan Dare* nothing more than a gambit in the franchise game? While I was in that restaurant sitting next to Clement and La Frenais, fretting that they might be cheesed off because I had replaced them, had they already seen the writing on the wall, that the project was a non-starter, and bailed out, leaving the naive newcomer to flog the stalking horse? Perhaps, but even so it was great while it lasted. It was brilliant to have experienced a Lew Grade, high-octane, big-budget project. It was great to have spent some time in Britain's Hollywood.

Going Out was already in production but because Southern were now dead men walking, they lost any chance of negotiating a decent network slot as all the ITV companies knew they had to transmit by 31 December 1981. As a result the programme went out in various late-night graveyard slots across the country, to tiny audiences . . . most of whom I seem to have met over the years.

That left *County Hall*, but after the BBC stifled it at birth by first halving its budget to fund *World's End* and then throwing the Don in my direction, I was back to *Grange Hill*, and never, ever believing anything until seeing the credits go up – on the repeat. Yet, there is one last postscript to the story of *County Hall*. Looking back through my research files, I found a note that simply read, 'Derek Hatton and Ken Livingstone – two to watch in the future.' I subsequently got to know 'Degsy' in Liverpool, I've still to meet Red Ken, but if the series had continued I'm sure many of his exploits, including his leadership coup, would have proved as inspirational as Degsy did. And none of us had yet heard of Boris Johnson. *West Wing* in the East End?

For me it turned out to be an amazing feast-and-famine year . . . if you can call being left with the most successful eighteen-part children's television programme plus its associated publishing income 'famine', but everything becomes relative in the end.

Each of these projects gave me incredibly valuable experience, but what is also intriguing about reflecting on that year is wondering what would have happened if they had all come off. How busy and, more to the point, how hungry would I have remained to take on the challenge of *Brookie*? I suspect I would still have gone for it, but wonder if Channel 4 would have done. I was, actually, perilously close to being on that treadmill Brian had warned me about. As it turned out, 1980 was pivotal, not just for showing me what to do, but also showing me what not to do. I had learned a lot. The television business was about politics, money and ratings. Is it acceptable? Can we afford it? What sort of ratings will it get?

These were all valuable lessons to take forward, with the most important being that I needed to take more control over my work. Initially I thought I should write and direct, but there was always a producer above the director, above the producer an executive producer, and above them a departmental head, then channel controller, and ultimately director of programmes. This was probably when the idea of using the Marxist ethic of seizing the means of production first came into my mind. I decided I had to have my own production company. That meant looking towards Channel 4, which was why I ended up alongside all the wannabe independent producers crowded into the Royal Institution in January 1981, to listen to the newly crowned Emperor launching the next golden age of British television. *Brookside* beckoned, and with it the discovery of my real soul-mate and future partner, Alexis.

7

Second Draft (1949–60)

'How much are those houses?' '£25,000.' 'Right. I'll take thirteen.'
– *Croxteth sales centre, Liverpool, 1981*

If *Grange Hill* had drawn upon my time at a comprehensive school, *Going Out* on my time as a teenager and *County Hall* was the result of my years as a quantity surveyor, then *Brookside* was where they all came together: kids, teens, work and family. It was also time to update *Corrie*. Then over twenty years old, it was no longer an accurate reflection of British life, with its row after row of back-to-back Victorian terraces.

Thinking about how an updated *Corrie* would look involved a similar process to *Dan Dare*. How had the world changed since its launch? What had happened over the intervening years? How had people changed over that period? Apart from obvious things like colour tellies and washing machines, phones for all and cheap cars, the new working-class environments were Parker Morris-standard council estates, high-rises and vast private estates of identical houses. Home ownership was starting to become more accessible, especially for two groups, young people and council tenants, as Sir Horace Cutler's GLC Right to Buy plan had been taken up and implemented by the Conservative government.

The national figure for home ownership was around 60 per cent in 1981 and would rise to approximately 73 per cent in 2005. Ownership among 20 to 24-year-olds, to become Channel 4's target demographic, was increasing and would go from 31 per cent in 1981 to around 40 per cent in 1991, when the dream faded during the 1990–92 recession and home ownership became too costly. By 2005 the figure had fallen back to 20 per cent among this age group. Within those statistics you can see both the reasons for *Brookie*'s early success and the seeds of its eventual demise. In 1981 it was relevant and appealed to young people wanting to own their own homes. By 2005, 50 per cent of Channel 4's target audience rented private accommodation. They had become the *Hollyoaks* generation.

Naturally, life's never quite that straightforward, but the basic premise that you have to stay not just with, but slightly ahead of your audience, still holds. You have to keep surprising them. In my last years as a QS I could see that developers were starting to move away from the model of having 200 or 400 identical homes on one estate. It was easier and cheaper to build like that, but it was also dependent on selling to one market segment. As times began to get tougher towards the end of the 1970s that was going to be a risky strategy, so developers started to look at ways of selling to mixed communities. The one-bedroomed starter homes, next to the two- and three-bedroomed semis, in with four-bedroomed detached prop- erties. Some with garages, some without. Some middle-class, some not. Sound familiar? It soon would be. This was what the new *Corrie* would look like, the sort of mixed-housing communities starting to pop up all over the UK, no longer defined by one socio-economic group or class, but becoming manufactured microcosms of the country itself.

Just as with *Grange Hill* and *County Hall*, I now knew what I wanted to write about and what my fictional world would look like. Now I had the setup, I next needed to decide who would inhabit it. The characters and their backstories. The sort of charac- ters who would appeal, be relevant and make it 'typical', bearing in mind, as usual, that there is never any such thing. Characters who would represent the main issues and themes of the day, and come together or clash in the same way they would in a wider society. Characters who would, by economic circumstance, be thrown together in a neighbourhood community while separated by social and political differences. Manufactured microcosms that would throw up opportunities for dramatic conflict, tension and humour.

With Britain making the shift, whether it liked it or not, from a manufacturing to a services-based economy, the big themes were around trades unionism, deindustrialisation and the emergence of young professionals, or 'yuppies', alongside the development of a black or informal economy. In short, as manufacturing went overseas, factories closed and people had to look at other roles to play. This had been on the cards since the first sightings of radios, televisions and cars from Japan and Germany in the early 1970s. Initially, perhaps as with my own parents, a residual reluctance, even resentment from the 1939–45 war meant that people did not take this new economic threat seriously enough, but probably more to do with that sense of denial people embrace when anything challenges the status quo. Unfortunately, denial is never enough as the same rule that says no bureaucracy ever deconstructs itself, also says that it is new technology rather than political shift that is the disruptive force. Thatcherism, as it became known, was more a consequence and result of technological advances than the primary cause of the huge economic and social changes that were about to sweep across Britain – waves of social change driven by a tsunami of technological innovation that would make much of what Britain manufactured obsolete.

This, once again, is hindsight. At the time people were simply trying to cope, using the only methods they knew. On the one side there seemed to be the trades unions, embedded in socialism and command-and-control economic idealism; on the other a conservative government wedded to the policies of capitalism and laissez-faire. Let the market prevail. Between them were the majority of people, trying to make sense of it all on a daily basis, just getting on, surviving as best they could. As in *County Hall* I wanted to personify the typically faceless, or even demonised, caricatures of the union vs. management conflict. The news media was constantly featuring one dispute or other, with trades union leaders becoming household names, like Derek 'Red Robbo' Robinson at the car-maker British Leyland, home of the original Mini; Arthur Scargill of the National Union of Miners (NUM); Jack Jones, from Liverpool, the General Secretary of the Transport and General Workers' Union (TGWU). On the world stage there was Lech Wałęsa, who founded Solidarity, the first independent trades union in Communist Poland, and went to jail as a result, but later won the 1983 Nobel Peace Prize before becoming President of Poland in 1990.

What interested me about these 'household names' was that our perception of them as 'characters' was coloured by what they were doing or perhaps how it was being interpreted by the news media. We might have heard of them, could recognise them, but we knew hardly anything about them. Like the unseen officers in county politics, they were anonymous but exercised huge influence over all our lives. But what were they like away from the cameras? When they came away from the picket-line confrontation with police, media interviews and negotiations at Number 10? Did they arrive back home and still have beans on toast, change light bulbs and have someone call them Dad while someone else nagged them about leaving their coats on the back of a chair? Probably.

To explore and personalise things, I wanted to feature an active trades unionist and their family, hence Bobby and Sheila, Barry, Karen and Damon Grant. But they would also epitomise something else: the new affluence of the working class, something that had been growing since the 1970s when, for the first time, car workers and other white-goods production line workers had started to earn more than a subsistence wage. This section of society was becoming aware of the concept of disposable income, i.e. that not taken by housing, food, clothes and travel to work, to be spent on things like leisure, home decoration and holidays. For the first time many had enough money to pay more than a basic rent. They could afford a mortgage to buy their own homes. For Bobby and Sheila this meant getting off the council estate and moving on to one of the new mixed-housing developments. I pushed it a bit by giving them number 5, the biggest house on The Close. Although it was still only a small-ish three-bedroomed house, it was detached and had an integral garage. As one of the leaders of Scargill's NUM responded, when quizzed by the media as to why he was travelling first-class during a miners' strike, 'Nothing's too good for the working class.'

My own off-screen interests also informed my writing about trades unionism both before and after setting up the company; before as a writer and member of the WGGB, and later as an employer. I can't remember how or when I actually became active in the WGGB, although I do remember trying to find its offices, for the first meeting of the Television Committee I attended. From memory it felt as if it was over a launderette or something similar in a row of shops on Edgware Road in London. It took me about twenty minutes to find the side door and hidden nameplate, then climb up a rickety stair-case into a couple of ramshackle offices. Unlike the actors' union Equity, which had a comparatively palatial Georgian property in Harley Street, this seemed entirely appropriate to those apparently considered at the bottom of the broadcasting food chain.

That was probably the main reason I became involved. It seemed both wrong and frustrating to me that writers, especially series writers, were held in such low esteem by the producers, script editors and directors with whom they worked. On everything I had worked on, from *Doctor in Charge* to *Grange Hill*, there had been not just creative discussion, but stand-up fights about what should or should not be in the scripts. While I had always been able to fight my own corner if necessary, and been willing to compromise or even change if I thought it improved the script, I would not be brow-beaten into change for change's sake. It was the attitude that they had the right to do what they liked with a script that was most galling. Especially in the closed-shop, one-man-one-job world of the tele-vision unions. No one would ever contemplate hiring a musician, actor or director who was not a member of the Musicians' Union (MU), Equity or the Associated Cinema and Television Technicians (ACTT), let alone fiddle about with their work or roles. That would mean 'all out' and the production 'blacked'.

However, when it came to the scripts, well, it seemed anyone could write. No need for membership of the WGGB, and if a producer, script editor or director felt like writing an episode or two, then why not? A nice little earner for them. What's to stop them? Exactly. A writer could not direct their own work if not a member of the ACTT closed shop, but any member of the ACTT could write a script. This was what rubbed up against the Scouse justice gene. One set of rules for some. No rules for others.

It is not hard to see, on reflection, where these attitudes stemmed from. For the original founders of television, their reference points would have been theatre and film, where the box office prevailed and it was the productions themselves, with their star names, spec-tacle and circus-barker marketing, that drew in the crowds. From the unions' perspective, the early technology was big and cumber-some and needed a lot of people on low wages and poor conditions to service it. As the ITV impresarios started to build up cash piles from their licences to print money, the unions first wanted their fair share, then protected what they had, and finally started extracting as much as they could. It is a predictable cycle, but again, so long as they were all wading round in cash up to their knees, what was the problem? Don't rock the raft. And writers? Well, there's a bunch of them on every show, isn't there? If they don't like it . . .

None of this is to deny any of the outstanding work that was done by television writers, or that some, myself included, were treated better than others if they were perceived as stepping over the line from being just a hired pen, to actually creating the box-office interest. Generally, though, with the great British talent for creating class barriers, single plays ranked above serials, which ranked above series. It was a caste system and it seemed wrong to me. Having been through all the various arguments and travails about writers' rights with the BBC and various ITV companies on my own account, it felt like a natural step for me to become more involved in the union that negotiated the basic writers' agreements. The ones that contained all those precedents I always seemed to be pushing against.

I climbed the stairs to the meeting room, to find myself sitting down with the likes of Trevor Preston who had recently written two of my favourite series, *Out* and *Fox*; Troy Kennedy Martin who had co-created *Z Cars* and written the Michael Caine version of *The Italian Job*; and Paula Milne, then a very hot writer in TV, creator of the medical drama *Angels* for the BBC. This had Julia Smith as producer and Tony Holland as script editor, the partnership that would go on to create *EastEnders*. There seemed to be a general meeting of minds among us all, and over the next few years we made major improvements to the writers' agreements. We improved access provisions for writers to attend the rehearsal and recording of their work; forced a bit more respect for the writer's position; pensions, script-fee rates, and negotiated the first royalty-based agreement in the UK: the BBC Videogram Agreement. All of this was won through bargaining through the sheer weight of our combined credits and reputations. More the others than mine, I admit.

BBC Video was set up to take advantage of the developing video-cassette and disc market. The idea was to take the BBC output, both recordings from the library and future productions, and make them available for retail sale. But it was also a great example of how people can become enthralled by technology, to the extent of convincing themselves that others will automatically 'get it' and, in television's case, go on to pay for what it originally viewed for only the cost of the licence fee. Thirty years later, the same issue still faces every section of the media. Trying to figure out how to make money or, in the jargon, monetarise the net. Why *should* anyone pay for anything that was initially given away free? As I've already touched on, you can find almost anything from television's back catalogue on YouTube, so why would you think of buying a copy from the original broadcaster? It is a reasonable question, especially if you are under thirty and have grown up with the culture of the internet being 'free'. For those of us who have had to fight hard to learn the Richard Gordon lesson, it does not seem that reasonable – until you stand back and think about the way technology and government regulation has artificially controlled and then distorted the market-place.

To do so necessitates going all the way back to the 1926 Crawford Committee and its belief that broadcasting was too important to be left to commercial companies. That, in essence, proposed nationalising the developing commercial radio market to create the BBC as a state-owned, funded and, the key point, controlled broadcasting industry. While the market would be free to manufacture and sell radios, the content, or programmes to be received by the technology, would remain firmly under government control, no matter how impartial or benign the intention. What this meant was that the tone, range and geographical access was then limited to what the state could either afford or allow. As the duty of government is to provide services to the greatest number of people at the lowest possible cost, large transmitters broadcasting over huge distances to large population areas became the policy norm. That set the pattern, philosophy and mindset that still dominate today's media.

Left to the 'combine of companies' that John Reith feared so much, broadcasting would probably have developed in a completely different way, moving much quicker than it has towards locally based services, similar to local newspapers. But it didn't, and the legacy of state control is something we are still trying to shake off in order to find a way to promote, or even allow, local television services. This is a huge hole in social policy, depriving large conurbations, like Liverpool, of a television service that could act as a powerful tool for social cohesion and economic regeneration. Just as DIY, gardening and cooking have been stimulated by national programming, imagine if that potential to stimulate interest could be harnessed in each of our cities, to help support and promote local agendas. It can still be done, also as. a legacy of the Crawford Committee, through the BBC, but that is a bigger debate. It needs to be underpinned by an understanding not just of how broadcasting, and television in particular, developed as a government-controlled and -regulated industry, but also how the people within it became complacent, both about competition and the pace of technological change.

Remember those geeks out in California who had been working on the ARPANET since the 1960s? Broadband and the internet were sneaking up on broadcasting and every other form of data transfer, which eventually led to downloading of music and films. Yet the broadcasters should have been better prepared because they were already doing it themselves. To transfer programmes across the networks, or take live feeds from, say, the Grand National in Liverpool, and transmit them across the nation, they had built their own closed network of dedicated phone lines. Long before the public was allowed to watch live football matches on TV, there were a privileged few within the broadcasting engineering network who could watch their favourite teams every week, while the recordings for *Match of the Day* were fed across the network to Television Centre in London. And they got paid to do it.

As with all these tales about the past it is easier to join the dots later, especially as the technology was often divorced from the board-room by six or seven floors. While the engineers knew what was possible, management upstairs was too preoccupied with industry politics and how to wade through all that cash. It was both impossible and unnecessary to worry about competition, because none was allowed under government regulation and, paradoxically, neither was diversification. The BBC was prohibited from commercial activity, while ITV could not capitalise on their television licences by promoting associated commercial interests. Even then, they were taxed at 98 per cent on everything they earned, so where was the incentive for change?

But there were people who could see the future, not in broad-casting itself perhaps, but in the growing facilities companies, which provided extra camera, recording, sound, crane and lighting equip-ment, which started to appear in the late 1970s. Like the film industry, television had started hiring in extra or new technology and specialist services, due to the high cost of purchase. It also meant that rather than have to maintain studios and outside broadcast units that could cope with any form of production, from a live news feed to recording a football match, facilities companies could be hired on a daily rate to fill the gaps.

It was not long before these companies realised that they could actually make the programmes themselves, if they could build relationships with the creative talent. Which is how I got to know one of the biggest – yet another link back to ATV Elstree. While working on *The Kids From 47A*, *The Squirrels* and *Dan Dare*, I had also got to know Nigel Plaskett, one of the puppeteers who worked on *The Muppets*, *Pipkins* and later *Spitting Image*. He was keen to try and set up his own production company in some shape or form and had got to know the guys who owned the facilities company that supplemented a lot of ITV's production capacity. Together we hatched a plan. If we could pull the creative talent together, the facilities house would put in the technical equipment, then all we needed was the cash flow from the ITV companies and we could produce programmes for them at a rate they couldn't match in-house.

So we set to work, called ourselves London Pictures because even then we could see the growth of videocassette recorders would stimulate a demand for non-broadcast content, and created four projects, with four promotional or 'taster tapes' to show the buyers. It was great fun, the promos were good, the technical quality was better than the broadcasters' as we had access to the latest equipment – including a Quantel image manipulator, a piece of kit every broadcaster wanted but could not afford. It was the first time anyone could twist, rotate, bend, and shape a full-screen picture – something that soon became de rigueur on *Top of the Pops* and every music video. Christine McKenna, star of *Flambards*, joined us after acquiring the rights to make a further series. ITV had decided to drop it while the audience still wanted more, another typical 'Buggins' turn' broadcasting casualty. Richard Bramhall from *The Kids From 47A* directed and produced that, while Colin Nutley from *Going Out* directed a contemporary thriller. Nigel created a great pre-schools concept called *Alphabet House* that featured musical letters of the, well, alphabet who all lived together in a, well, house. We also had a new sci-fi concept based around the Lancelot legend, featuring Brian Capron who played the very popular Mr Hopwood in *Grange Hill* and went on later to become known for his role as serial killer Richard Hillman in *Coronation Street*.

We were trying to create an updated, British version of United Artists, and while it was a fantastic way of learning how things could be done, and for what cost, we had forgotten the most obvious point: the barrier to market entry. We were dealing with ITV. Why would they let anyone else muscle in on their patch? Even more significant, what was the point? We might save them 30 per cent of the programme costs, but 98 per cent of that would simply disappear in tax so, like *Dan Dare*'s spacesuits, why would they risk antagonising their in-house unions? End of production dream. And then along came Channel 4. It would be set up as a publisher, with no production capacity of its own, with the aim of acquiring its programmes from independent suppliers. In a typically British compromise the duopoly was about to be broken. Almost. In a typically British way. A curate's egg? More like a dog's breakfast.

The notion of introducing competition into broadcasting had been around since the 1948 Beveridge Television Committee. Ever since ITV started in 1955 there had been constant dialogue between broadcasters, would-be broadcasters, the BBC and politicians on how and what sort of competition should be introduced. In fact, the idea of a second commercial channel was so widely anticipated that many television sets sold in the 1970s and early 1980s already had a designated fourth channel button marked 'ITV 2'. If it had been left to the marketplace to decide, this was probably what would have happened, but with the Crawford philosophy about broadcasting still needing to be controlled dominant, the political debate dragged on, and on, and on, until finally, three decades after the Beveridge-Lloyd Report, the Broadcasting Act 1980 created the framework to introduce the long-awaited fourth channel.

The result was a totally independent Channel 4. Neither ITV nor BBC, it was both a pragmatic and an inspired compromise that could have succeeded save for another age-old issue: vested interest. Unlike the dinosaurs wandering around unfettered and unchallenged, dominating the planet but unable to predict or prevent the impact that destroyed them, the duopolysaurs of ITV and BBC had been staring at that ITV2 button for years. They had been in on the debates, they had influenced policy, so what finally emerged was something the canal owners might have dreamed up to fight off the railways. In the nineteenth century, the joke was that if it were left to the canal owners, steam engines on rails would simply have replaced the horses used to haul the barges. The same appeared to be true of the new ITV2. Although it was called Channel 4, the plan was to add another tax on ITV's licences to print money. Each ITV company would pay a percentage of its advertising revenue to Channel 4, which would then use that cash to make its programmes. In return the ITV companies would transmit Channel 4's programmes but collect for themselves the advertising revenue for slots in and around those programmes. Still with it? If you are, you're ahead of the Department of Trade (DTI) officials I later sat before in Manchester, trying to explain why they should give me a job-creation grant towards the costs of setting up *Brookside*. I'll come back to them, as I had to do many times, including showing them the actual 1980 Broadcasting Act that established Channel 4, as they couldn't quite get their heads round it initially. They were not alone.

From the BBC's public-service point of view, the one area it was weak on, as I had helped highlight with *Grange Hill* and the attempts to expand it beyond the fifth form, was programmes for late-teens and twenty-somethings. Children were reasonably well catered for by both ITV and BBC, but that only extended to around the 16-year-old age group, *Grange Hill*'s fifth form. The BBC's general audience then, as now, was probably above 35. ITV's was, and still is, older. The obvious gap for any new channel to enter was the mid-teens to mid-twenties age group. And so Channel 4's remit became to cater for audiences not already served by the existing broadcasters. On the one hand sensibly filling a perceived gap; on the other, the classic regulatory fix of making sure that the new entrant would not directly challenge, and therefore upset, the existing status quo. So, 'independent' Channel 4 was charged with reaching minorities not already served. I looked at this closely. I could help with that. Once they opened up shop.

Like most people in the industry, though, I had to wait for Channel 4 to emerge, so I was still exploring other avenues. Apart from London Pictures, I had also started thinking about the possibility of producing a *Grange Hill* film, where the only barrier to market was money. If I could raise the finance, the film would be made. With my publishing results behind me, I went back to BBC Enterprises and suggested that this time they should actually be involved from the outset. After all, they had not long before launched BBC Video. I managed to get all the way up the chain to Managing Director Byron Parkin and found him to be very straightforward, businesslike and, most importantly, forward-looking. With the success of the television programme, books and Christmas annuals, the idea of making a *Grange Hill* film seemed an obvious follow-on project, but Byron knew he would have a difficult time financing it fully as his remit was mainly to raise money to help support internal programming by exploiting what the BBC owned, not to invest in third-party projects. *Grange Hill*, of course, was owned by me not the BBC.

However, there was a logic in the BBC contributing to the project as any returns they made could then be put into future television production. He agreed to support the idea of BBC Enterprises putting up half the budget, provided I could find the rest and market research backed up everything I said. It did. It found that 98 per cent of all children polled watched *Grange Hill*, with an approval rating of 95 per cent, and 68 per cent of them would definitely go and see the film. This equated to around 3.5 million ticket sales, when the average film viewing figure at the time was 1 million, so it looked like a no-brainer. Even with the distributor taking their 70 per cent cut, this would generate £5–6 million, on top of which the BBC would acquire the TV and, naturally, video rights. Then there was the book of the film, the posters and badges, and anything else they could squeeze out of it.

My next stop was the publicly funded British Film Institute and the National Film Development Fund, both theoretically there to help fund and promote British films, but one said the script was not 'experimental enough', while the other said it was *too* experimental. Ah, well, only opinions, but no return for the taxpayer there, so I went off to the commercial sector and, having talked to EMI, Columbia and a host of smaller distributors, one of which said that while 'TV spin-offs' were not something they would consider, they 'hadn't seen such a sure-fire hit outside porn'. It might have been this that pushed me towards George Walker, the ex-boxer and owner of Brent Walker Pictures, which had made Joan Collins's *The Stud* and *The Bitch*, until finally I met Fred Turner who ran Rank Film Distributors. They took a look and eventually agreed it would make a great summer release. They said they would match the BBC, if the BBC followed through. Great. Back to Byron. Great. He would put the 'no-brainer' to the next Board meeting so we could hit the summer timeframe. We both felt confident. But the Board said no. No return to the taxpayer there either.

The only other time I have heard such deep disappointment in someone's voice was ten years on, when John Fairley of Yorkshire Television was with me when we heard from the ITC that we had had our bid for Granada rejected. If Byron was disappointed, I was angry at what I felt was a typical and shortsighted bureaucratic attitude. It was, and is, something not confined to the BBC, but having initially tried to claim the copyright in *Grange Hill*, then complained they were not receiving any publishing return for 'their programme', when they were offered what both their own research and a commercial distributor had agreed was a sure fire 5:1 return, they simply refused to do it.

The rationale given was that BBC Enterprises should not be investing in films, which was BBC-speak for 'turf war'. There was an internal debate going on about whether the BBC should make films for the cinema and, if so, who should do it, and was that an appropriate use of the licence-fee income? I have no doubt that there was a high moral principle in all this, but from the outside it looked, as it often does, like an interesting intellectual debate about how to spend taxpayers' money, rather than addressing an innovative way of raising revenue on behalf of those taxpayers. I had seen this so often as a QS. It had helped form my desire to do *County Hall*, but I had also learned by now to recognise bureaucratic or corporate mindset, the 'not invented here' syndrome, from which you can spend a lot of time and energy trying to woo, coax and cajole its adherents . . . or else cut and run. Without the BBC, Rank felt they couldn't go alone and so there was a different decision to be made. Start again, or park the project. I decided to park it and try again the following year. Which I did, for the next twenty-seven years. Channel 4 was now on the horizon.

It was still 1981. *County Hall* was going nowhere. *Going Out* had gone and *Dan Dare* had been vapourised. *Grange Hill* was still building but, as the film deal had demonstrated, BBC decisions were based on corporate policy not business sense. Apart from which, as I had discovered on Series 3, budgets could suddenly disappear. I had, after all, like the BBC itself, only an annually renewable twelve-month contract. I was much too dependent on them; still felt driven by the need to find something more long-term. Something that would provide greater security and, through that, greater freedom from the fear of Brian Finch's treadmill. Something that would also give me more creative control. This feeling could have stemmed from the *Grange Hill* movie experience as I still have no doubt that it was a 'no-brainer' and could have grown into a yearly franchise. But as that was not to be, I turned my mind towards Channel 4.

Unfortunately so did everyone else, including the likes of David Puttnam, so it didn't take me long to realise that – just as when I went in search of an agent, to discover I would end up around 250-something in the queue behind the likes of Tom Stoppard – now I would end up at the back of a queue stretching out of Channel 4, down the street and round the block. I would be just another pedlar of ideas. I would need something more than 'I'm Phil Redmond and I've done . . .' to stand out from the crowd. Something that no one else could offer. Something that had not been done before. Anywhere in the world. Hence my initial approach to Jeremy Isaacs. Which eventually led to David Rose, which eventually led to a raging maelstrom . . . and a real understanding of the old adage: be careful what you wish for.

Perhaps I should have sensed what was coming when I was on my way to a meeting with the small band that made up Channel 4, then still camped at the back of the IBA building in Knightsbridge. Not yet having the benefit of a radiotelephone like the one Sir Horace Cutler had, I was facing the usual London traffic-delay dilemma of whether to waste even more time by stopping and telephoning to say what everybody already knew. I was running late. The usual decision was taken. Press on. The speed and manoeuvrability of the MGB GT was helping me make up time. Until I came over the brow of a hill . . . and found a wall of metal and red brake lights sliding to a halt in front of me. I just about managed to stop, only to be shunted from behind. Crunch. Everyone blamed everyone else, but especially the now long-gone pedestrian who had dashed across the road to cause the first car in line to brake.

Unlike today, though, everyone exchanged details and went on their way. No calls for police forensics units to seal off the neighbourhood in case the incident was linked to a terrorist-inspired insurance scam to launder money. I took a look at the MGB. Front grille gone. Headlight cracked. A water leak at the front, and bent bumper and smashed lights at the back. But, drivable. Off I went and arrived in Harrods car park, engine steaming and with the temperature gauge nudging the red. Funny looks. Sort that later. Off to the meeting. Sat down. Got the commission confirmed. Back to the car with some water. And started to feel my ribs. Ouch! Adrenalin is one of nature's best assets and something I would definitely need plenty of in the future. Especially for the real car crash that lay ahead for me.

Nursing the MG out of Harrods car park marked the beginning for me of a two-year white-knuckle ride as events started to cascade and merge into each other once my life picked up speed. My appointments diaries for this period were of limited use while writing this memoir as there are large sections left blank or simply blocked out under generic headings like Channel 4; Liverpool; *Flambards*; banks; MERCEDO; *Grange Hill*; Manchester; Alphabet House, Department of Trade; accountants; Maidenhead; technicals; *County Hall*; interviews; *GH* film, test shoot; USA, lawyers. There were lots of 'lawyers' throughout 1981 and 1982. I obviously knew at the time what I was doing day-to-day, but too often one day rolled into the next as, in the pre-word-processing days, we started getting into cycles of meeting in the evenings, going through contracts, then returning to our offices to review them, have them retyped, to then meet early the following morning to carry on negotiating.

At its height I once stopped about 3 a.m. one day and looked across at the 'contracts table', which held a separate contract for everything from the initial format to the leases on the *Brookside* houses. I picked them all up and spread them across the floor. A 3- by 4-metre contract rug. I knew them all line by line, clause by clause, sub-section by sub-section . . . and we still hadn't got anywhere near production. All the talent negotiations, contracts and rights issues were yet to come.

By this time I had progressed from working on the ironing board at my Olympia typewriter, had gone through a phase of writing in a garden shed, and was now working out of a one-bedroomed flat I had bought in Teddington. I could even afford a PA who had a cutting-edge electric IBM golf ball typewriter which could do rapid and continuous keystrokes for underlining, had a correction ribbon built in, and had additional golf ball print heads to change the font. For the first time ever we could have *italics*. How neat was that? All thanks to the *Grange Hill* publications income.

Technology has always played a key role in everything I have done, whether seeking out the latest and most productive typewriter to opting for solid-state recording for *Hollyoaks*, but as the maelstrom gathered force it was gaining increased momentum from the discussions, debates and arguments raging over which technology would be used to make *Brookie*.

Having in my time stood around enough air-conditioned and soundproofed boxes, otherwise known as television studios, and compared being in them to the experience of being out on location with a film crew, one thing was immediately apparent to me. The location shoots appeared to be far more efficient than studios. They might have cost more to set up, but they also returned more in terms of content, quality and look. There was a better sense of camaraderie on a film shoot, a sense of all being in it together. The same feeling and atmosphere that develops on school trips or conferences or anywhere people are allowed to turn their backs on rules, regs and procedures. Conversely, a studio imposes a different mindset. That sense of corporate familiarity. The place itself is not as interesting as a different location and there is always something else requiring attention other than the group itself. Soon everything becomes systemised, procedurised and boring.

While *Grange Hill* was being recorded I often used to wander round Television Centre between the takes, popping in to the different studios to see what else was going on and how they were doing it. This was the pre-surveillance and anti-terrorism society, when you could just drive into the BBC, find somewhere to park and make your way to whomever you wanted to see. My backstage wanderings had made me think about the dead atmosphere of those soundproofed boxes, as well as, paradoxically, the benefits they could bring to a production. On a studio multi-camera shoot the big saving is time, as the programme or show is edited as it is recorded by cutting between cameras. This reduces the need for post-production time and facilities, which means that typically in a studio twenty-five minutes per day can be recorded, compared to around five minutes on location. To be able to do this meant that each scene had to be rehearsed to the point where, when it was time for the 'magic five minutes', in every hour, cast, crew, sound and cameras would know their lines and cut points, which would enable the vision mixer, who cut between the cameras, to edit at the right moment. This meant there was always an atmosphere of restrained tension on set. No one wanted to make a wrong move in case they made a sound, cast a shadow, knocked a piece of equipment or, as on *Crossroads*, made the scenery wobble. Actors were especially conscious of not slamming doors too hard to express anger, or overlapping their lines in case an important piece of dialogue was misunderstood. Everyone knew it was difficult to edit out the mistakes as post-production was extremely limited.

This had developed into an art form in its own right by the time I got to *Emmerdale* years later, when I discovered that the actors had got into a routine of leaving almost a second at the end of their lines to help the vision mixer make the edits. What it meant for the viewer was a very measured, sometimes laboured, form of delivery that lacked any real passion. You can't have an all out row and leave one-second gaps between the lines. Out on location, when shooting single-camera, you could afford to let the actors ramp up the passion, slam doors, fall or throw each other against walls without any worries because they were real and solid. Because single-camera has to go through post-production to stitch all the single shots and soundtracks together, it means you can deliberately overlap the dialogue, as in any real argument. For drama, it is the best way of shooting.

From high in some of the viewing boxes at Television Centre, you could look down into the studio and see a lot of very expensive equipment, equally expensive people, and a lot of intellectual potential, all sitting or standing about waiting for the magic five minutes in every hour when everything comes together for a take. In the other fifty-five minutes, back in familiar surroundings, that intellectual potential had to be channelled elsewhere – all too often into talks about pay and conditions, which is the downside of having a highly educated workforce. There had to be a better way to harness it and I spent a fair amount of time mulling this over until the answer appeared to be as simple as it was obvious. What was needed was something that could offer both the control and speed of the studio, with the vibrancy, energy and realism of location shooting. What was needed was a hybrid. It didn't exist. It would have to be created. But how?

By applying the basic principles of the construction industry: new ideas, new technology; and, location, location, location. The first thing to decide upon was the technology.

The television standard then was to record on 2-inch-wide video-tape in studio and 16mm film on location. However, having already worked with Nigel and the others in London Pictures, with access to the latest equipment at the facilities house, what I had in mind was shooting everything on what was regarded as new and revolutionary 1-inch C-format. This meant everything was lighter, faster, and, of course, cheaper. The only real downside being a big one: mindset. It was new. Therefore it meant change. Therefore the industry was still reluctant to adopt it. As with all innovative technology, it is incredibly hard for most people either to see or hear the differences that the geeks spend hours, days, months, or even years arguing over. While you may watch or listen to a new TV or hi-fi in a specially set up viewing suite, when you will hear the squeaking of the bow and breaths being drawn by the performer, unless you then go home and spend a six-figure sum on installing a similar suite at home, you will never again hear them above the ambient noise of traffic, central heating, cooking and chatting that prevails in most homes.

Industry opinion was framed by the technology priests, whose jobs depended on regulating and maintaining technical standards. Their sacred instrument was the oscilloscope. Revered almost as much as a five-chain thurible, to them this was the only thing that mattered as it measured and analysed the video signal. No matter what it looked like artistically to the naked eye, if it didn't hit the industry benchmark it was unacceptable. Sometimes these guys didn't even watch the picture, but they could tell you exactly when the camera cuts took place, when they were filming indoors or out, and even what the characters were wearing, just from watching the various gamma, black and luminance levels as they passed through. As 1-inch tape was obviously half the size of 2-inch, it was in their eyes immediately suspect. Less surface area. Less quality.

I was in for a fight.

The argument, in the end, coalesced around the same issue I had run into over the *Grange Hill* film: not invented here. Channel 4, as a new broadcaster, was initially being advised by specialist engineers who had decided that the 1-inch C-format was only good enough for location news and sport. Not drama. That should only be recorded in studios with 2-inch machines or on film on location. However, I wanted to blend the two. Be on location, but have the control of a studio shoot. I also wanted to try and recreate what Colin Cant had done with *Grange Hill*: give the programme a look of realism by using news equipment and news techniques.

Having learned the mindset lesson at BBC Enterprises, I decided to enlist a bit of help in the technical argument. Through the facilities house I was introduced to their supplier, Sony, who in turn put me in touch with someone who would become Channel 4's technology priests' Nemesis: Colin McKeown. He was as evangelical about moving forward as they were about maintaining the status quo. And, he was not just a fellow Scouser, he also came from Huyton.

He'd worked at ITN News and had just returned from Saudi Arabia where he had helped organise the first television broadcast of the annual Hajj pilgrimage to Mecca. Forbidden as a non-Muslim from entering the holy site, he'd had to do most of this through remote instructions. I reasoned that if he could handle that, he could probably handle the Channel 4 advisers, and soon he was tackling the project in the swashbuckling way with which he always seemed to approach life: coaxing, cajoling, and sometimes simply sweeping people along the path he wanted to go.

While the technicals went back and forth, David Rose wanted to see more scripts. However, the biggest challenges were not the creative elements, as the talent was there to find and hire, but getting the costs down to match the tough financial target of £30,000 per hour. At the time, average set construction costs alone were running at around £13,000 per half-hour, so two half-hours a week meant £26,000 of the budget would be accounted for if we built the set using traditional techniques. The estimated cost of hiring the camera, sound, lights and editing equipment would be around £5,000 per day. We would need to shoot two episodes a week working over five days, giving a weekly cost of £25,000, And this was without adding in all the other staff costs like catering, admin, finance, maintenance, security . . . and that was only to set up and stand waiting actually to shoot something. There were writers, directors, cast and crew still to arrive on location. Did balancing the books seem impossible? No. As a QS I knew the answer. Eliminate the cost. Across everything. This took me back to location, location, location.

By the time I got to the sales centre in Croxteth Park I had already met several other developers and looked at various sites, but I knew what Broseley Homes had on the former estate of the Earls of Sefton would be ideal. The estate itself comprised the historic Croxteth Hall and around 1,000 acres of farmland and woodland, handed to the city as part of an Inheritance Tax settlement. There was an understanding that it be kept as a 'working estate', which, in the People's Republic, had been interpreted as meaning an 'estate for working people', so around half of it was sold off for housing development while 500 acres were retained as a country park surrounding the historic hall. It is still a Green Flag park, the national standard of excellence, with Liverpool having more of these than anywhere else outside London. It was both idyllic and an ideal situation for location production. I had by then worked out the characters I wanted in the programme and the size of the technical and administration square footage we would need. So by the time I got to the sales centre I was ready with the question: 'How much are those houses?' '£25,000.' 'Right, I'll take thirteen.'

Initially this was met with the sort of response you would expect, but after telling them who I was, that *Grange Hill* fella, and why I wanted the houses, it wasn't long before I was sitting in their Head Office in Leigh, near Wigan, being stared at by two builders straight from central casting. They were Broseley's founder Danny Horrocks and Regional Manager Graham Baker. Their argument was simple. Where I wanted to put my fictional cul-de-sac, they wanted to build twenty one-bedroomed flats. So long as they got the cash they were expecting from these, they would help me. No haggling. OK. What do you want to build? they asked me. Houses for my characters, and technical and admin facilities. Let's see. I showed them the outline. We'll get Marketing to take a look, then the architects will sketch out what sort of houses and configurations we would use. OK. When's it likely to happen? I needed them by June 1982 at the latest. Nine months ahead. They looked at each other. This Channel 4 . . . they good for the cash? I hope so. They're owned by the government, I told them. They exchanged wary looks. As we would in 'the Republic'. Did government promises really mean anything? And you did *Grange Hill*? Yeah. Another look. OK, leave it with us.

I knew when I left they'd be up for it as the recession was starting to bite and £325,000 in sales would do no harm to their cash flow. I also knew that once we moved on a bit, 'the cash they were expecting' would be the profit line. The sales pitches at the time heralded the age of '100 per cent mortgage and everything thrown in.' This meant carpets, and fully-fitted kitchen. If we stripped those out, as well as removing their finance costs on the mortgage lending, I knew I would be able to push the price down. Until Channel 4 decided to take over.

It was a perfect meeting of Northern nous and Southern sophistication. Broseley said they wanted the full price. Channel 4 said OK. I think the Liverpool lad would have been given a better discount.

Even at the full cost of £25,000 a house, this meant that taking the average set construction cost of £13,000 per half-hour episode, we would only need to shoot twenty-six episodes, the equivalent of thirteen weeks' output, to have, in effect, paid them off. This also meant the full cost, £325,000, compared very favourably with the projected £450,000 it would have cost in location facility fees, every year. After thirteen weeks we would remove the set costs for, as it turned out, twenty-one years ... at a price of £9.44 million for anyone counting, less inflation. Not a bad deal. The same thinking went into the equipment costs, then projected at around £1.1 million per year to hire, at a discounted block deal. To buy outright cost around £650,000. The slot cost was coming down, but even with the house deal negotiated, we still had to get planning permission.

This was the most tense period of my life. I had been working with Channel 4, the television unions, Sony, the Liverpool Development Agency, the Merseyside Economic Development Organisation (MERCEDO), Broseley, and had even talked the Department of Trade into offering a £195,000 job-support grant, but everything was conditional on everyone else saying yes. And that was conditional on being given planning permission. I felt like a juggler balancing on a ball, with three other jugglers on my shoulders. If the planning ball beneath me was kicked away, we would all come tumbling down. It finally rested on which way Liverpool City Council would vote. Nobody could predict that. At first I hoped they hadn't heard that the independent production sector was being hailed by Margaret Thatcher as a sunrise industry, or that if they had, Scouse pragmatism would prevail. However, then as now, you can never be certain. All we needed was that planning permission. And all we could do was wait, including for the date of the planning meeting itself. Even that was uncertain.

My own Scouse pragmastism had me looking forward. What next? If this all collapsed around me, as the *Grange Hill* film had done, what would I do then? I was beginning to feel that I had to move on from writing. I really enjoyed deal–making. I didn't want to go back and have to sit in rooms arguing over my scripts with producers and directors on subjective points of perception! With 20/20 hindsight, I realise it was more to do with creative control than anything else. I didn't want to go back to anything approaching the torrid time I had had on *County Hall*.

All of this was going through my mind during a short trip I took to New York, theoretically to try and 'take a break' and unwind, which, inevitably, means you get more time to think about all the things that could go wrong. To try and counter this, I had arranged to see the BBC Enterprises guys there, to show them copies of *Going Out* and the pilot tapes we had shot with London Pictures, already converted and transferred to the US 525 TV system. The idea was to show them the kind of quality we could shoot with the new emerging Sony technology. It worked. They thought it was 35mm and we started to plan how we could start producing for the US market, but it never got much further than that as although, unlike Cannes, I didn't get someone turning up at the hotel door demanding to know where the scripts were, I did get a call to say that the *Brookside* planning permission meeting had been brought forward. It was Monday. The planning meeting was Tuesday, the following day.

After a dash out to JFK Airport, an overnight flight to Heathrow and a connecting flight to Liverpool, I managed to make it in time to join Graham Baker from Broseley at the meeting. My PA also managed to get the four box files of background information to me there, although I don't know how as all this took place in the days before mobile phones. We settled in at the back of the Council Chamber while they ploughed through the order of business. From memory we were about halfway down the list, which seemed to range from the consideration of large-scale factories to new shop signs, one of which was scheduled shortly before us. After a while, even the intricacies of Points of Order and procedure could not keep me from fretting about what might or might not be, depending upon the outcome of what was decided in this room. After twelve months of spinning plates it might all come down to what one or two councillors thought about television, or whether they let their kids watch *Grange Hill* or not. Such is the inconvenience of democracy. I was getting nervous, but when I looked at Graham he seemed totally relaxed. He was busy killing time working through a file of paperwork. Multi-tasking at meetings predated the BlackBerry era.

My mind drifted to how we had got this far and how everything starts with someone, somewhere having an idea and then dragging everyone along with them. In this case, quite literally, as only a few weeks before, when Channel 4 had decided to come up and meet Broseley, I had first taken David Scott, the broadcaster's Director of Finance, out to see the planned location. Although officially classed as parkland within the old Sefton Estate, it was nothing more than a water-logged field and an MGB GT is not the best off-roader. There was nothing for it but for David to get out, ankle-deep in mud, and push, while I slowly edged the car forward. The last thing I wanted was a Norman Wisdom moment, leaving Channel 4's Director of Finance face down in the mud. It was a bonding process, and I doubt many independents could say that they were ever given such a helpful push by their broadcaster.

Bringing my attention back to the meeting, I looked at the order of business. We were only a few items away from consideration. Judging by the amount of time they were devoting to a new sign over something like a chip shop, I wondered how long it would take them to wade through what we were planning to do, what no one anywhere in the world had done, in amongst the residential development out in Croxteth.

As the shop sign discussion turned to the brightness of the neon, the Council Chamber doors burst open. It was the tea trolley, which seemed to have a point of order all of its own: get the orders done with and then out again, ASAP. Soon the room was filled with murmurs of: 'Cup of tea, Chairman? Sugar with that? Pass a biscuit to the Chairman, love.' And as the cups and saucers and sugar and biscuits were passed back and forth, Graham suddenly got to his feet. I looked up at him. Let's go. What? It's done. We're through. And with that, he left. I looked back at the running order and he was right. They were on to the item after *Brookside*.

So that was it. After I'd flown all the way back from New York, it was accomplished as the Chairman was handed his tea. We then went out to take a look at the site. The place where a few weeks ago David Scott had had to push the car out of the mud was now covered in foundation slabs and drainage runs. I looked at Graham, puzzled.

'We took a flyer. We wouldn't have had them ready in June for you, if we hadn't.'

I asked if that was why the planning was brought forward, but he just shrugged. I then asked him what would have happened if the Council had said no. He just gave me another Lancashire grin and went over to talk to his site foreman. The QS in me knew enough not to go any further. Right place, right time, right idea, with the right person.

I stood for a moment and looked across the muddy field dotted with slabs of pristine concrete. It was now real. Absolutely brilliant. And I was now even more determined. My days of being 'just a writer' were gone. And I was not going back. It was 2 February 1982.

8

Rehearsals (1982)

'I won't tell you how to run the production, if you don't tell me how to manage the finance.' – *Justin Dukes, Managing Director, Channel 4*

The euphoria around the granting of planning permission soon turned to feelings of deep relief. There was no Plan 'B' simply because we were now only eight months away from Channel 4 going on air. We had to start delivering two episodes a week, according to one of the provisions in that contract rug, six weeks ahead of transmission. That was now a little over six months away, and all I had so far was a small band of still unpaid, still uncontracted 'helpers' and a lot of conditional agreements. And a few slabs of concrete in a muddy field. David Rose was getting impatient too. It was all very well arguing about what sort of cameras we would use, but what would they be pointing at? He wanted to see more than the four scripts and original storylines the commission, and C4's multi-million-pound investment, were based upon. It was time to turn the conditional 'yeses' into firm commitments.

Once again I began to appreciate the legacy from those early-morning trips to the cemetery as I began a work routine that still endures. Writing is done in the cool and quiet early-morning hours. At that time, always on W. H. Smith Jumbo plain-paper pads with medium-thick black Pentel pens, or red for editing. In later years I would force myself on to the computer screen, but back then the hand-written drafts were dropped with my PA to be collected typed at the end of the day, for overnight revision. A technique I developed, or perhaps more correctly learned, was always to stop writing at a point when I was still in full flow and knew exactly where the story or character point would go next. It was then just a matter of picking up where I'd left off.

A lot of writers talk about the creative process being the time when every light bulb in the house gets changed, every weed removed from the garden or every office 'tidied up' . . . anything other than actually getting down to that blank page. This is part of the creative displacement process, that allows your brain to filter and reorganise all the research or emotional clutter and arrive at the 'light-bulb moment', when 'the characters take over'. I have often said that, for me, this was how MerseyTV materialised: anything rather than actually sit at the desk and do the hard work John Cleese warned me about. So while I was pinballing between meetings about whether we really needed an Aston Character Generator, which we did to put the titles and credits on the end of the programme; or central heating in the houses as the production lights would actually provide too much heat – we decided against but then wished we hadn't; or whether we could negotiate better terms with the unions – which we did but then later lost . . . at the back of my mind I was always thinking about things like what Sheila Grant would say to Bobby about Karen's latest unsuitable boyfriend.

First, though, despite David's desire for more scripts, there was still that contracts rug to tackle. From my point of view, there was no sense in writing more scripts until I knew we had the deal in place. While he would ask, 'What are we going to shoot?' I would respond, 'What am I writing for?' At the centre of all the negotiations was my long-time lawyer, Leon Morgan of Davenport Lyons. I had met Leon years earlier when both *Grange Hill* and my own aspirations began to outgrow the services offered by literary agents. Davenport Lyons was based in Soho Square in London, something of a centre for the film industry at the time where you would find the likes of 20th Century Fox, Disney, Sony Music, and a host of smaller production and distribution companies, including Paul McCartney's MPL. The ACTT union also had its headquarters there. In some ways that mirrored what I wanted to do with Bobby Grant: show that the unions could now afford to live in the same real estate

as management. It also reflected the respective status of the technicians, who could afford a property on Soho Square, and the writers,
who hung out above a launderette on the Edgware Road.

I got to know the café in Sutton Row, just off the square, very
well, as Leon and I would often reconvene there for our early-
morning contract sessions, before anywhere else was open. By this
time Channel 4 had moved from the IBA offices in Brompton Road,
via a couple of offices in Avenfield House on Park Lane, to Haddon
House on Fitzroy Street, while waiting for their new headquarters
at number 60 Charlotte Street, just down the road, to be finished.
While we met in a caff, their senior management canteen turned
out to be Bertorelli's Restaurant and it was in there that I bumped
into another Colin from the BBC, this time Colin Leventhal, my
old sparring partner as Head of Copyright. He grinned and told
me he had just moved to Channel 4, to get away from me, only to
find I was already there ahead of him. He asked me what were the
main outstanding issues on the *Brookside* contract. The same as on
Grange Hill. Money and copyright. He rolled his eyes and grimaced.
Not again.

He would later say, quite objectively, that no matter what anyone
offered me, I would never be satisfied. And from a broadcaster's point
of view, he was right. Unless, or until, a television company can
offer the same level of exploitation and return as a major film studio,
then my view remains unchanged. They should only acquire what
rights they need for their own business and market. To broadcast on
television, they don't need to own the entire copyright.

Colin was part of a growing band now arriving at the channel,
or C4 as it was starting to be known, to join Jeremy Isaacs and
David Rose. Justin Dukes had arrived from the *Financial Times* to
become Managing Director, bringing with him Frank McGettigan,
who had something of a reputation for being tough with the unions.
C4's new offices were now established at Charlotte Street, and with
coloured letter-heads in place of the sticky labels they'd used every
time they changed temporary base camp, they were fast becoming
a real bureaucracy. Soon Colin, Leon and I would start forging a
copyright path few had travelled before us. The fledgling bureaucracy
immediately defaulted to the mindset of the BBC and ITV by trying
to sweep up all copyright. I was determined this was not going to
happen, so it was probably fortunate for me that it was Colin who

came in as Head of Legal at C4, as without our *Grange Hill* relationship and shared experience we probably would have parted ways over precedent and principle at an early stage. This was put to the test during one late-night session.

We already had the basis for a three-year deal, with a break clause for either side after twelve months. Although we were still arm-wrestling on copyright, the biggest issue was the agreed contract price. In every deal this figure goes back and forth as much as up and down, until there is nothing left to argue over and you reach the deal or no deal moment. We were there, about £150,000 apart, which doesn't sound too much, now, but then it was breaking point. And, just as with Yorkshire and Harry Secombe's talking octopus, for me it was about principle, not cash.

The point in contention revolved around the £195,000 job-support grant I had managed to secure from the DTi. With the existing support of the regeneration agencies on Merseyside and in Liverpool, this was supposed to symbolise the fact that even the government backed the idea of creating new jobs in television. We had factored it in to our cashflow projections, but C4 thought *they* should be the beneficiaries, reducing the contract sum commensurately. I thought this was wrong. It had nothing to do with them but was part of the establishment costs of MerseyTV, a point confirmed by the government in a classic Kafka-esque bureaucratic trap. The £195,000 had to go to MerseyTV, but as income, and therefore subject to taxation. As soon as we received it, we would have to pay back £60,000 in tax. Some grant that was, and a prime example of why people get so frustrated and fed up with stealth taxation. Why didn't the government just reduce the original amount to £135,000, or even £130,000, and save the cost of the paperwork? The bigger issue, though, according to my 'rithmetic, was that if C4 then chipped the contract price by £150,000, because of the DTi grant, MerseyTV would in effect lose £150,000 plus £60,000 in government clawback. That would be a loss of £210,000 in all. Er, no way. No deal.

Having reached this impasse, we had agreed to meet after Jeremy, Justin and David Scott got back from one of their road shows, flogging the channel to the advertisers. Leon and I had our prelim meeting, or dinner, in one of the restaurants in Charlotte Street, and he made me focus on how serious I was about the budget figure.

Was I sure I couldn't find another way of funding the shortfall? I knew I couldn't without thinking about relinquishing control of the project, which would be the price of taking in investment from somewhere else, even if we could find it. The principle of control was too important to me for that. We then went across to wait for them to get back, which turned out to be quite late as their plane had been delayed. This, of course, gave the nagging doubts time to ferment and rise to the surface. Was Leon right? Should I just go with what was on offer and try and find the cash elsewhere? Should I do the film thing and mortgage the house or take out a loan?

I went for a wander round the deserted open-plan offices, the detritus and empty wine bottles of the day's activity not yet swept into history by the cleaners. In and out of the toilets, smiling to see how only C4 would put style over Health & Safety by choosing Italian taps, marked 'C', for Caldo. Hot water when non-Italian speakers would be expecting cold. I thought about taking on debt but the memories of my early days were still strong. It was not long before I came to the conclusion that I was comfortable enough as I was. While I really wanted this deal, I was not desperate. If it didn't happen, I wouldn't exactly be destitute. And one other thing crystallised for me as I looked out of the C4 windows down into Charlotte Street, watching the restaurant clientele coming and going, eating meals that cost more than the average weekly wage on Merseyside. I was not going to put into jeopardy what I had already achieved. If C4 wouldn't finance the real cost of the programme, then neither would I.

By the time the others arrived none of us really wanted to get into a long session so we quickly ran through the point under dispute. I couldn't, nor would I, proceed without the £150,000. They said no. That was it. I said OK, no deal. They asked was I sure? I said yes. I couldn't do it without that money. I needed that leeway. Even then it would be tough, but I would make it work, somehow. But not without.

They asked for a breakout to discuss it and Leon immediately went to work on me, asking me to consider it one last time, leaving aside the emotion felt. The deal was a good one. Its potential was amazing. Was I sure I wanted to walk away if they didn't agree? I told him that it was good advice, and I didn't want to walk away, but I felt too exposed without that £150,000. While I remember how real it felt at the time, on reflection both now and soon after

I could see what both Justin and Leon were probably thinking. The amount was only around 3 per cent of the total figure we had been talking about. Was it worth pushing the deal to the brink on that sort of margin?

Put like that, probably not, but I suspect it revolved around something much deeper for me. Around commitment. And principle. We had got to this point because I had brought them the project. Shown them how they could have their own version of *Corrie*, as both promotional vehicle and cash cow. Told them how it could be done. How it could be made. I'd found the new technology, the government grant and local support, the site and house builder, and had even opened dialogue with the unions. True, I was doing it for my own benefit too, but it was by this stage not the deal I had originally taken to them – which had included a share for me of the advertising revenue in and around the programme. Equally true was the fact that this precedent was one they would never allow, as their whole business was built on standard terms and conditions, which distilled down to production companies accepting a fixed fee unrelated to the commercial success of the television programme on offer. I could accept that, as it was something I would have done myself and would go on to do with MerseyTV. Consequently, over the months, we had shaped a deal that related to the size and risk of the project. It was a good deal for me but not the one I'd originally wanted. I would receive my writer's fee and royalties on a similar level to *Grange Hill* on all the episodes, plus the production fee for the company. That was the principle of the deal, but an element of irritation had crept in on their side as they constantly totalled up what I personally would end up receiving as programme creator, writer, producer, and of course, sole proprietor of the production company. If I had been developing the idea for one of the other new independents, had partners or even been working for ITV, this wouldn't have been an issue. Everything would have been seen and judged differently. But because everything was flowing back to Phil Redmond, they even had a schedule prepared to remind them of this when we were negotiating. Leon and I would exchange smiles as the 'Redmond Schedule' was passed back and forth, with the occasional, 'Don't you realise how much you personally are set to gain from all this?' Er, yes, that was why I was there.

I was never sure whether this was any one person's particular concern, or just simply a part of the bureaucratic mindset which becomes focused more on perception than reality. What people perceive is going on rather than what is actually going on. I don't know what they really expected. That I would simply say, Oh, OK, tell you what, I won't take a production fee so you can give more to another producer to employ another writer. Or, Shall I not write my own programme but spend all my time editing someone else's scripts? Whatever it was, by the time we all got together for the 'take it or leave it' chat, I think in my head I felt they were just trying to chip away that £150,000 so I would have to put it up, and then they would be able to put a cross through a line on the Redmond Schedule. What I was pushing for, I suppose, was another point of principle. Their commitment. Regardless of the figures on the Redmond Schedule, what I wanted them to recognise was that they were getting a great deal.

After what seemed like a long period, but was probably only 10 or 15 minutes, we got the call to reconvene. Jeremy had left the room and gone back to his office. David Scott was still there but looking quite exhausted, which he probably was, we all were, but also strangely subdued, as though exercising self-restraint. Something had clearly gone on in that room. You could sense it in the air. But Justin was his usual calm and precise self. He spoke slowly and deliberately, to let me know that we were indeed at the 'take it or leave it' point. They would agree not to make a call on the grant aid and to reinstate the £150,000, but as a contingency amount only. That was it. No coming back. I looked at Leon; he nodded. I then smiled and nodded at them. Deal.

There has been much written about Jeremy Isaacs's role in shaping C4 and nothing can be taken away from that, but just as I had Alexis at my side throughout everything, Justin Dukes was immensely important to the channel in those early days. As Managing Director of C4, Justin 'got it' and was responsible for everything and anything not 'creative', yet probably his greatest contribution lay in forcing the creative community to start treating television as a business and not simply a form of club where everything was done by patronage, friendship and Buggins' turn.

Although regarded by many as just a 'suit' and a bit of a management guru, with his love of charts, graphs and critical-path analyses, he immediately grasped the potential of the new technology and different working practices. He was leaving newspapers and Fleet Street, which seemed to be in the same level of denial and resistance to change that the then-disappearing car, motorbike and television-set manufacturers had exhibited in the late 1960s and 1970s.

Looking back, while he certainly brought a new discipline into the world of independent production, this was probably one of the reasons he never achieved his ambition of succeeding Jeremy Isaacs as Chief Executive. I actually think it would have been a good appointment, for both the channel and the industry, as Justin was above all a facilitator. He saw the roles of administration and finance as providing the solid framework within which creative people could work. This was similar to the philosophy we built at MerseyTV, and was borrowed from the BBC I had experienced in the late 1970s and early 1980s, pre-John Birt, where metaphorical padded cells were constructed within the corporate structure, in which 'creatives' could rattle around at will, doing no harm either to themselves or the organisation, every now and then emerging with a brilliant idea.

However, by 1988 Justin had only been at C4 seven years, which was not enough time to change the industry mindset completely. It was always going to be a hard act to follow the first Emperor, especially as Jeremy and Justin had become such an established double act. Jeremy was the heart and passion of the channel and carried the torch for the arts, while Justin was the calm, rational, strategic fixer. They became, like Alexis and me later, almost yin and yang, with the sum greater than its two halves. I soon learned that if there were any difficulties ahead, I should speak to Justin first. He would then, calmly, break the news to The Emperor. And deal with the emotional response.

Although Justin Dukes was not destined to become Chief Executive of C4, he certainly played a part in shaping it. Even before we reached the deal or no deal moment, we had been eyeball to eyeball on how to finance the purchase, rather than hiring, of the technical equipment. I was planning to lease it all over three years. The banks, as we know, are not charities, but they did have a valid point when asking what would happen if either side invoked the twelve-month break clause in the three-year contract? Where, they wondered, would the cash come from in the second and third years to finance the loan? 'It'll be OK, honest,' didn't seem to work for them, so I went back to Justin. Would he put the cash upfront so we could buy equipment outright? No. Why not? You did with the houses. They are an appreciating asset, the equipment isn't.

We then got into a 'debate' about the relative merits to both sides of different ways of moving forward, with my point always being that I was prepared to squeeze costs everywhere, including reducing my own fee levels, in return for a proper production fee, part of which lay in the ownership of the houses and equipment.

The point was that if things didn't work out after twelve months, I would have to wind up everything, but would at least be left with a production base. Justin's counter-argument was that he didn't think there was much incentive for me to work my hardest if I could just 'walk away' with a comfortable cushion at the end. I won't, I protested. It'll work. Then you could always mortgage your house to pay for the equipment. Oh, right, you don't want to buy a depreciating asset, but it's OK for me to do it, is it? I'd been listening to Mother Superior.

Back and forth it raged until eventually we got to the 'take it or leave it' moment when I said that I didn't care how he paid for it, I wanted the equivalent of the cost of the houses and equipment and he should do that by doing as he had done with the houses and simply put the money upfront as a one-off payment and then we could maintain the £30,000 slot cost. That was when he came out with the line, '*Phil, I won't tell you how to run the production, if you don't tell me how to manage the finance. OK?*' We agreed to sleep on it, as there was by this time no indication from either of us that we wanted to walk away. We wanted to find a compromise, which we eventually did, revolving around us leasing and C4 guaranteeing any outstanding payments if the programme was pulled after twelve months.

Eventually then, with Leon Morgan's good counsel, in every sense of the word, we framed a contract with Channel 4 that gave both sides what they wanted. They had all the copyright control they needed to protect the precedents they were desperate to establish across the industry, while I received guaranteed returns, consultation, and reserved all the rights they didn't need for broadcast. We also developed the principle of 'mutuality': that each side would recognise that we now had a shared mutual interest in the success of the programme and that we would work together to develop and exploit it.

★

With the Heads of Agreement in place, it was time to focus on getting the site ready. Thanks to the foresight and planning of Graham Baker at Broseley in taking the risk of laying the concrete slabs and drainage ahead of planning permission, we already had six weeks' start. He still had only five months in which to get all the houses and gardens, the pavements and road, ready in time for us to start installing the technical equipment, so that we could start camera tests and technical runs before shooting began in September. Graham was the archetypal gruff, no-nonsense Northern builder, an act he probably played up to. He had his project plan as we had our critical-path analysis, two bits of paper that constantly had to run in parallel. But while ours ended up being amended on an almost daily basis, Graham just pressed ahead, brushing aside what he probably thought of as the flappings and faffings of arty-farty folk. This was the upside of the fixed-price, staged-payment deal Broseley had struck with C4. Graham knew exactly what he was getting, when and how much profit he was making, so he got on with things at a rate probably impossible in normal circumstances as he would have been building to a marketing and sales plan, meshing in with cash flow. The other thing it enabled him to do was build the rest of the properties around what would become Brookside Close.

Where he had originally planned twenty one-bedroomed flats, the thirteen houses I had asked for in the sales centre were quickly emerging. Six would be configured to suit the various characters, one four-bedroomed house would become the canteen, three would form a terrace for technical, wardrobe and make-up, with the other three being configured back-to-back, to form the administration and production offices.

When I had originally outlined my plans to him there were two essential points: that we needed to be on a cul-de-sac, so there would be no through traffic for us to contend with, and that our set should be built before the rest of the surrounding houses, so that we would appear on any future neighbour's land search as the TV company at the bottom of the garden. As with living next to any factory, gas works or electricity pylon, if they bought when we were up and running they would have no grounds for future complaint. That didn't stop a couple of them trying over the years, of course, especially when negotiating a rates discount, but by and large we had very good relationships with our neighbours, not least because our

24/7 security meant we had the lowest burglary rate in the UK as there was always someone watching over the area. Though even that, in a pre-surveillance society, brought the odd complaint over the years. Odder still was the complaint that there was too much security, in the form of the police cars that used to park up during the night. The council had given us planning permission to build a mini-bungalow to act as our security lodge at the entrance to the site, which had to remain in keeping with the surrounding houses. Knowing our security guys had this cosy little nest, the local cops often dropped in overnight for a cup of tea. In case they were needed, they would leave their patrol car doors open and turn up their radios so they could hear them, which unfortunately meant the neighbours did too.

I doubt any of this was in Graham's mind as he ploughed on with the building, but what he also demonstrated was the same thing I had been part of as a QS. How to squeeze as much as possible and make every pound do the work of two. Although I had had to spend a great deal of time trying to convince the TV and film technical priests that there were different ways of doing things, like getting rid of the nests of snaking cables that littered most production sets, Graham with his construction background got it straight away: reducing time saves cost. The biggest cost is labour. So when I talked him through the idea of having all the houses cabled back to one central point, he got it straight away and just drew a couple more lines on his site plan for the JCB to scratch out a few more drainage trenches.

For most people today the idea of networked buildings is probably commonplace, but not back in 1982. Personal computers were just about to make an appearance and the majority of people still worked outside an office environment. In fact, 1982 was dubbed 'IT82' by Kenneth Baker, then Minister for Industry and Information Technology, in trying to raise awareness of new technology. The BBC Microcomputer started to appear in schools, the one with the big red buttons on the keyboard, as well as Clive Sinclair's ZX81. I wanted to be ready for the opportunities this new technology would offer, but no matter how 'hi-tech' it all was, it would still need old-fashioned pipes or ducts to carry the cables from each house back to the central technical facilities area.

This was exactly what both the BBC and ITV did with the big

soundproofed boxes they called studios, although they then built their sets inside the boxes and still had cables snaking everywhere. Every one of which took time to lay, reset and pull back each night. On location the time taken to rig and derig would amount to ninety minutes in the morning, and sixty minutes in the evening. It actually said so in a lot of the local union agreements. Which meant out of every ten-hour shooting day, you lost 25 per cent before you even started. If I could eliminate that time by having everywhere already cabled, we would gain an extra day a week in shooting time. No doubt you can see the common sense of the idea. But you probably don't have a 1982 mindset. This was not a studio. This was not a location.

That was a big problem I had to overcome. It was, well, new. No, it was not a studio, just as it wasn't a location either. It was something between the two, the control of a studio with the vibrancy of a location. C4's technical guru wanted to soundproof all the houses by double cladding the walls and filling the gaps between the first-floor joists with sand. This would have doubled the cost of construction, so we settled on extra plasterboard, double-glazed windows and everybody standing still during a take. It was a location after all. For cable ducting they wanted to lay studio-quality, purpose-formed concrete ducts with removable tops, which would have been both impractical, as they would have to have been visible across the gardens and paths, and doubled the cost. We settled for Graham's trenches, drainage pipes and manholes. Every five years or so we had to replace cables that had corroded or been eaten by rats, but that was nowhere near as expensive as the ducting superhighway Channel 4's techies wanted us to have. It wasn't a studio.

To try and give an example of the costs involved, there were two camera cables, six sound lines, and two constant-phase electrical supplies to each house, in the 'meter cupboard' under the stairs. Each camera cable cost around £30 per metre, but the connections at each end for the cameras cost £1,500 each. That meant a 10-metre cable from the camera to the wall plug cost £300 plus £3,000 for the end connectors. We then needed 10 of these, running from around 30 metres to 150 metres in length. At those costs it was obviously better to have most of them buried. Why did the ends cost so much? Partly because they had something like 30 separate wires within them, but also because you could only get them from one place, Sony. Until in later years we discovered the military used the same connectors and, for once, the Department of Defence was spending less than broadcasting on its kit. We then started buying our mobile recording vans too from military suppliers, not just because they undercut the broadcast providers, but because they were built to a higher spec. Theirs had to survive the impact of a nuclear pulse, the electromagnetic shockwave that fries all electronics after a nuclear explosion. Fortunately, we never had to test this.

Other things we did with the houses was move all the hot-water cylinders from the cupboard on the top of the stairs into the lofts, so that we could use the cupboards for storage or a camera position. They were made removable so the cameras could be placed on the remaining platform to shoot characters coming up the stairs and on the landings. This was not so successful: back to the same rigging and derigging issue, it simply took too long, as well as the fact that the cameras were still too bulky at the time. What was more successful, though, was removing the party wall between the two main bedrooms and replacing it with a double-sided wardrobe that could be opened to shoot from one bedroom to another, allowing the camera to get further back from the action. In one of the houses, number 7, home to nurses Sandra Maghie, Kate Moses and hospital porter Pat Hancock, but later home to the Chois, Harry Cross, Farnhams and Dixons, all the walls were left out upstairs, to provide a larger space where we could build mini-sets and cheat locations. It was here that Bobby had a union office, Heather Huntington visited her account-ancy clients, and Billy Corkhill's first wife, Doreen, had a dodgy liaison with a dentist, as well as becoming some of the first sets for *Hollyoaks*.

The early months were spent trying to marry the need to get the site finished with making sure we managed to squeeze in as many amendments as we could that would help cut production time, and therefore cost. We had holes, or camera traps, cut in walls between the kitchens and living rooms, or between bedrooms and bathrooms, that would be hidden by pictures, mirrors or bookcases, presaging the advent of *Big Brother*. One idea that never quite worked was to have a tarmac strip built adjacent to the pavement so that a cameraman, as they were at the time, could be pushed in a wheel-chair along a smooth surface without any of the troublesome bumps between paving flags. It was a film trick, but never quite worked because most of our camera crew were influenced by television and simply wanted glacial-smooth studio floors or proper tracks and dollies to run on. It was a mindset push too far, and by the time we got everyone to accept what we did as 'different', the ground had moved to the extent that the tarmac was too bumpy anyway. By this time we also had female camera crew, which meant that the camera shoulder mounts had to be adapted slightly, having been designed by and for a gender without breasts.

The difficulty of changing people's mindset should never be under-estimated. It is, I think, the biggest, yet most rewarding, challenge that faces any manager. To get people to change what they have 'always done' takes time, perseverance, stamina, patience, and some-times even diktat, but nothing brings bigger rewards and more success than introducing new thinking. Nowhere is that challenge more evident than in industrial relations, usually because most trades unions have fought hard to achieve the ground they occupy on behalf of their members. Any change to the status quo is going to be met with utmost caution. On *Brookside*, with the initial costs of the houses and technical equipment dealt with by C4, and having worked with Broseley to engineer out the construction costs, negotiations were continuing with the television unions. There were three major areas up for discussion: which production agreement we would operate; manning levels; and the level of repeat and residual fees for the talent unions.

On the first point, we agreed to recognise and operate the basic principles of the ITV national agreements, as everyone was still working on the basis that C4 was, in reality, ITV2. While on the face of it that may not seem like a great concession, at the time every ITV company was paying way above the national rates. Our local ITV company, Granada, was paying around 25 per cent more, while London Weekend Television (LWT) were paying their staff around 60 per cent above the national rates. While this concession on the national rates would, therefore, result in a great saving for us, it would still mean we would be offering jobs to people in the locally depressed economy at two or three times the average wage.

That point was not lost on the national union officials who also agreed to relax their stance on holidays. The industry standard for holiday entitlement was 25 days. We wanted it to be 20. And we wanted everyone to take it in August, a return to the old Northern idea of wakes weeks, when everyone would be off work at the same time to allow for maintenance and refurbishment work to the factory or plant. The union agreed to this

On the second point, manning levels, each of the television companies had their own agreed crewing level for both studio and location work. These roughly followed the 4+4+4 film system for camera, sound and lights, itself a hangover from the era when the pieces of equipment used were so big and heavy that they needed four-man crews to move them. Over time, as technology changed, the focus went from basic need to protecting employment, which is not a problem in an ever-expanding revenue business. However, as soon as revenue starts to fall, the whole system stutters and then starts to implode. As we have seen in public services over the past few years. Fortunately, the unions accepted the point that as this was a completely new venture, using completely new technology and techniques, there would be no minimum manning levels from the outset, but crewing would be determined by need and new technology.

From the talent unions came the third concession. They were willing to talk about reducing the guaranteed repeat fee from 100 to 50 per cent of the original fee. At the time neither *Corrie* nor *Emmerdale* was repeated, but although the channel's schedule was a closely guarded secret, David Rose and I had spoken of putting the two weekly episodes together to form an Omnibus edition at the weekend. There was already some precedent for what was deemed a 'narrative repeat', or something repeated within the same week. Also, I had not missed the obvious point that any Omnibus edition meant spreading the cost across two hours in the weekly schedule – something that helped ease the original target of getting everything into the £30,000 slot cost. Now it was £60,000. It was achievable, provided we got all the concessions we needed from the unions. I was still juggling in the maelstrom.

Every change or development inevitably meant another clause or change to the contracts rug, so what was crucially important from the outset was to get my own company legal structure right. Although I had by now formed a limited company to manage the control and copyright in *Grange Hill*, called Phil Redmond Enterprises to have a bit of fun at the expense of BBC Enterprises, the size and scale of *Brookside* meant I had to have something a bit more sophisticated. More legal advice and the Mersey Television Co. Ltd (known as MerseyTV) was formed as the main holding company, which would then have a subsidiary to manage the project, and through which all legal contracts, obligations, etc. would flow, so that in the event of disaster it would be the subsidiary, rather than the holding company, that would go down. This was a typical business arrangement, but in all the optimism about a new technological era and the advent of the 'sunshine industries', I wanted to make sure that whatever structure we put in place would also allow for future growth and ambition. People often used mistakenly to refer to the company as Merseyside Television, whereupon I would explain that I deliberately chose to use 'MerseyTV', as the river, not the country, went all the way from Liverpool to Salford and it was intended to send a message along the Manchester Ship Canal to Granada TV: the Scousers were coming.

All this was with the idea of growing into the developing world of IT82, when a fibre-optic IT Superhighway would replace the copper telephone system and within a few years we would have radio, television and 'data services' delivered to our houses. Soon there were cable consortiums mushrooming all over the UK to take advantage of this new boom. Canals, railway tracks and even sewers suddenly had more value as they acted as the IT Superhighway's roadbeds. Billions were invested, poured into or wasted on the project, depending upon your view of history and technological development, by being dropped into the gap between the government rhetoric in thrall to the technical geeks on one side and the harsh realities of the marketplace on the other. And isn't it always so? While the government wanted the UK to become the first fully cabled society, and take the lead on the information revolution that lay ahead, it did precious little to encourage it, except for spending a few million here and there on campaigns and putting the BBC Micros in schools. In the marketplace BT, still only a few years from changing its name from the old General Post Office (GPO), was under-resourced, underfunded, in need of reinvestment and preparing for privatisation as a means of resolving that. The potential content providers, the film industry, BBC and ITV, were too busy worrying about losing market share to the new Channel 4 – and therefore almost 90 per cent of the cable that was laid in this period remains dark and unused to this day.

Off-stage, to one side and quietly working away, was that pesky Australian the regulators had already chased away from ITV, Rupert Murdoch. He had tried to 'rescue' LWT back in the 1970s by buying a majority share and improving its performance and ratings by changing its schedules. That was too much for the regulators who declared him unfit to run a British television company on the grounds that he was, despite being an Australian and member of the Commonwealth, well, still a foreigner. Undeterred, and probably a little irritated, he had decided to buy into the coming satellite technology. As the UK was ignoring satellite and cable and bracing itself for a fight over Channel 4, Rupert Murdoch was slowly working away getting ready for the technological revolution the government was predicting. And isn't that also always so?

I could see the changes coming and wanted to be ready.

Within the MerseyTV structure were companies named Mersey Cable, Mersey Video, Mersey Music and Mersey Sound. Mersey Cable was for the cable revolution that never happened. Mersey Video was for the videogram market, which didn't happen until the 1990s. Mersey Sound was for the expected expansion of local radio, which didn't happen until the 1990s but ended up being hobbled in the same sort of regulatory market regime as the ITV franchises, with only Mersey Music becoming active in recording and licensing music for exclusive use within our own programmes. During my time at ATV and *Dan Dare*, I had learned all about the costs of music specially recorded for a TV programme, which was practically all we talked about. These were astronomical, even more than the dreamed-of spacesuits for Dan, Digby and the Playboy Playmate. Using the regular MU agreements for theme music, the title music would have cost more than the production budget for an entire episode, and would have had to be renewed after every thirteen episodes.

Like all such agreements it was originally designed to stop exploitation of both composers and musicians and allow them to share in any potential secondary market sales. Eventually, though, the original costs became so prohibitive that the TV companies got round them by opting for already recorded music available from music libraries. This was music written and performed speculatively, with the intention of being used only in the background. I discovered this when Colin Cant didn't like the original music written for *Grange Hill* and, at the last moment, simply plucked a track from a music library – plucked being the appropriate word as it was called 'Chicken Man' by Alan Hawksworth, and apparently written one hour before it was recorded. Nevertheless, that familiar da–da–da–dat–da opening became synonymous with *Grange Hill* over its entire run, despite different producers trying to introduce different theme tunes. The fact that it was a library track, and not original to *Grange Hill*, was why it also ended up on Michael Aspel's *Give Us A Clue* daytime charades programme.

Music was one of the two biggest potential costs to the channel, as for ourselves and every other independent. The other was ITV's unions cost base. The idea with Mersey Music was that it would record and then license the tracks to Mersey Productions and we would then collect the Performing Rights Society (PRS) income that was paid by broadcasters under a blanket licence to the publishers and composers of any music included in their programmes, in the same way that every café, shop or church hall has to have a PRS licence to play recorded music. The Mersey Music library would provide a source of sound-a-like music for the programmes, but also provide a circular revenue stream back to Mersey Television. This was another idea lifted from the BBC and ITV companies who all had book or music publishers for the same purposes, and with our own model about to provide an additional source of revenue, things were finally looking manageable. That is, until Channel 4 started negotiating on its own behalf. While they drove their costs down, they caused ours to rocket.

They announced that they had done a deal with PRS which meant they would only have to pay around 12.5 per cent of what the BBC and ITV did for a blanket music licence. Great news for the channel's cost base, terrible for Mersey Music's revenue forecasts, as our projected income would be cut by 87.5 per cent.

And it got worse, as on the union front we heard that Jeremy, in what was probably meant to be a tough message to the unions, gave a speech somewhere saying that while C4 would support independents cutting costs wherever they could, the channel would not undercut the national agreements. Hearing this was a gut-wrenching moment for me. I looked at the phone. It would soon start ringing. Sorry, Phil. I know what we said, but . . . like to help, but we can't any more. It's the national agreements or nothing. Your boss just said so. And so, with a sentence or two, Jeremy had stripped away any chance of our own specifically tailored local agreement, and added 25 per cent to the budget.

Just the requirement to allow people 25 days' holiday instead of 20 and the right to spread them across the year meant we needed almost 20 per cent more staff to cover the shoot and be in production for 52 weeks instead of 48. Maintenance would have to be done overnight or at weekends, and the actors and writers would receive 100 per cent repeat fee instead of 50 per cent. We managed to hold on to a few things round the edges, like having Merseyside, rather than the Brookside site, as our 'base', for the calculation of travel time and costs, but I had to put a call in to Justin Dukes. Did he realise what The Emperor had just done? And the PRS deal? He was not sympathetic about Mersey Music and the PRS issue, that was our profit and therefore our risk, but fully took on board the consequences of the unions position and agreed a budget uplift to cover any unforeseen costs. That became another principle, another clause, written into the *Brookside* and *Hollyoaks* contracts: that any additional costs resulting from national union agreement negotiations, to which we were not party, would be underwritten by the channel. This was invoked a couple of times over the years. The music position, though, would be something else that would come back to haunt us.

These moments would become a regular part of life, reinforcing the company ethos of always having the next iron in the fire. No sooner had something been achieved than something unforeseen arrived, demanding our immediate attention. There never appeared to be any time to enjoy moments like seeing the real-life buildings take shape in that muddy field. Not that there was much time anyway, as from seeing the bare concrete slabs to finding the roofs being lowered into place was something like eight weeks, during which I had had to think about getting a permanent roof over my own head once production started. I was beginning to ponder how I would manage this as time was such a scarce commodity, when I happened to drive past a house in Mossley Hill, Liverpool, with a For Sale board outside. It was in one of the 'desirable roads', so I stopped, reversed back and looked in through the open double gates. There stood a classic white stucco, three-storey, Georgian merchant's house, complete with gas lamp to one side of the steps leading up to the double entrance doors. Perfect. I'm not sure I'd say I fell in love with this house, but the Scouse 'That'll do for me' sprang to mind. Waiting until I could find a phone, I then called the estate agent's, asked how much it was, and said I'd buy it. Don't you want to see it? I just did. Don't you want to look round inside? Only once the survey tells me it's worth the cash. And it was. So I bought it, with the hardest part of the deal being hanging on to the gas lamp outside the front door. The owner didn't want to sell it, it became a deal-breaker, and in the end I always said I bought the gas lamp and got the house free.

I also nearly made a mate for life as the owner kept coming back for bits and pieces that he suddenly remembered were of great 'sentimental value'. One day I came home to find my dad in a bit of a state, as he had called round to discover the previous owner taking away a section of sandstone wall. They had exchanged a few words, and in the end I had to get the lawyers to 'ask him' never to come back. That finally cured his sentimentality, but having kept that house for over twenty years, long after moving out and letting it be used for staff housing and the first set for Kurt Benson's house in *Hollyoaks*, I too developed a soft spot for it. Not least because it became home to Alexis and me, was where we celebrated our marriage, and the place where my dad finally conceded I had a proper job after all. It was not long after the incident with the previous owner, and my dad was round one weekend when I found him standing at one of the floor-to-ceiling lounge windows, staring out across the lawn with misty eyes. I asked if he was OK and he turned to me, still misty-eyed, and said he was. Then he told me how he used to drive buses down this road, looking at these houses and never thinking he'd live to see the day when one of his own could afford to buy one. He gave me a hug – and never again asked when I would get a proper job. I got a bit misty-eyed myself.

The other great thing about that house was that it marked another great shift in my life from Mr Fixit to Mr Organisit. While I had both the time, in between commissions, and the inclination to refurbish my house in London for myself, what this house needed was beyond me. It was the biggest property I had owned, and I had neither the time nor the inclination to tackle it myself. To get that done, I turned back to the family tradition and brought in a few of my dad's mates. When it came to the final plastering, though, an art not easily mastered as anyone who has tried will know, there were none better than some of my cousins, who came and did a fantastic job.

In case the petrol heads have been wondering how the MGB GT was coping with the Liverpool–London commute, it wasn't. A new house was also followed by a new car. The MG was brilliant for getting round London, but not so good for a long journey, especially in summer with the heater that never quite turned off. Still missing the size and comfort of the old Ford Zodiac, I wanted something similar to go up and down the M1–M6 corridor. I opted, naturally, for the Zodiac's successor, a low mileage five-year-old Ford Granada Ghia MK II V6 with a 3-litre engine. It also had electric screen washers and retrofitted air-conditioning, something even cooler (well, why not?) than the MG. This just ate up the motorway with no problems except for a slight prop-shaft rumble and vibration at around 60 m.p.h., which usually occurs if the shaft is slightly out of balance or the universal coupling joints are worn. I replaced both shaft and couplings but still that vibrating rumble persisted, easily solved by always travelling below or, usually, above 60 m.p.h.

As more people started working with me they kept asking why I was driving this old beast. I'd go on about the V6 engine, the air conditioning, etc., but they would then mention the prop-shaft rumble. The real reason I hung on to it was what I later discovered is known as wealth anxiety. When people suddenly find themselves a lot wealthier than their friends and family. When they don't have the same level of worries about paying the bills. When they get a bigger and better house and, of course, better cars. The worry is that people will start reacting differently, as they invariably do.

This went on for quite some time as although I had been able to afford almost anything I wanted since the *Grange Hill* annuals had started selling, and it was not an issue in a relatively comfortable area of London like Richmond and Teddington, I was still not fully comfortable with my wealth back home. Until I was stuck on the side of the M6 at 4.00 in the morning, steam obscuring both me and the Granada from the passing traffic. After a few hours of this, the working-class angst was exorcised by pragmatism and a visit to BMW soon followed. I ended up with not just one brand new red BMW 323i, the hot car of the moment, but a deal that also included a new black one and an old 'pre-owned' lime green

BMW 2002, which would serve as one of the pool cars. It was a deal I was talked into, without much resistance I have to admit, by the production manager who had come from the *Grange Hill* movie project and who ended up with the black BMW. As this character features a bit more in the *Brookside* story, and to ease the typing, I'll use the abbreviation GHPM (*Grange Hill* Production Manager). The deal itself was done while we were still operating from Teddington and because of that the new cars were delivered to Thames Ditton, with standard-issue plates, which no one noticed at the time but would come back to bite me when the press blitz hit later. The biggest immediate impact the 323i made was in Liverpool. One reaction, from friends and family, was that it was about time I had a decent car, the money I was on. The other reaction was from the cops.

Having grown up on the streets of Huyton and Kirkby I had, like many of my contemporaries, got used to being stopped occasionally by the police. Just in case. Just checking, etc. But as I grew older and became a motorist I discovered that it was only pedestrian scallies who were stopped, while motorists were obviously a cut above the estate. Provided the car fitted.

The first time I went to visit my mum in my new, gleaming red 323i, I was pulled over. Just checking, we don't get many of these round here, mate. You mean, you thought I'd nicked it? Yeah. At least they were honest. And then we spent a petrol-head thirty minutes talking about the car and its capabilities, one of which was to travel just below the sound barrier – something I often put to the test in the days when you could travel the motorways at certain times and not see another car, cop or speed trap. Which is a great irony as the car crash that nearly killed Alexis and me happened when I was driving at 69 m.p.h. We got hit from behind in that 323i and its safety cell did what they said in the ads. Saved our lives. Something that made me slightly sceptical about the 'speed kills' lectures. It doesn't. Like leaving a chuck key in a lathe, it's not the machines themselves but people not operating them properly that is the biggest risk.

A press storm had been building since the beginning of 1982 as the channel went off on its advertiser recruitment road show. Then the reality of a second commercial channel stepping into the market began to dawn on Fleet Street. For some reason I didn't even get then, never mind now, the view formed that Channel 4 was somehow going to steal all the advertising revenue from both ITV and the colour supplements of the weekend press – perhaps because they were still a relatively new development in publishing or because of the mixed ownership with ITV, but it was probably nothing more than the typical fear of change and loss. Or market control at work. Whatever it was, the press had voted against Channel 4. What this meant was that everybody who had a complaint, gripe or whinge against the new channel was sure of a press platform from which to attack.

Outside our discussions of a special deal for *Brookside*, the unions were all trying to maintain the over-used cause of parity with ITV, and a big issue was the rates paid to actors for the television commercials. These were so well paid that there was a small community of actors who never did anything else. In fact they couldn't under the terms of their contracts, as they were seen by the advertisers as 'the faces' of their products, a fact that supported Equity's view that they should be paid well. Channel 4 and ITV, who would be selling the ad-space, wanted lower rates as the new channel would have a much lower reach than ITV. It had a 10 per cent share of the audience as a target, only reached a few times during The Emperor's reign, instead of ITV's then 50 per cent. Equity dug in and instructed their members not to work on ads specifically for Channel 4, so for the first few years there were often programme captions or promos on screen instead of ads. Needless to say, a lot of people liked that. From our point of view, the wider media interest put us firmly in the spotlight as *Brookie* was going to be the channel's biggest commission and, of course, the programme that would become their own *Corrie*, attracting a large share of the advertising income. The *Corrie* tag was something else that would come back to haunt us.

Word was out that the channel had awarded a contract for a soap, but because I was not unknown on the production circuit, most of our meetings had taken place out of hours. It took a while for the press to find out what was going on. Eventually, though, the call came, from Sue Summers at the *Evening Standard*. Could she come and interview me about *Grange Hill* and any future plans? She had already been tracking Channel 4 and there was no real reason to look at *Grange Hill* just then, so I figured this was a fishing exercise, especially as she was insistent on coming out to Teddington to see me in my office. I could have said no but in medialand that would have been the same as 'no comment'. In other words, damn, you found out. So we cleared the office of everything *Brookside* and Channel 4 and littered it with more *Grange Hill* merchandise than you could find in the BBC shop. Except for one thing.

During one late-night session at C4's squat in Avenfield House, I had insisted that David Scott give me a cheque to cover some of the development costs. He had agreed and actually went personally to a huge cheque-issuing machine and typed the cheque out himself. I later had it framed and hung in the office. Which was why we missed it. It had become a part of the fabric. While Sue was waiting she obviously spotted it, but waited until she was about fifteen minutes into the interview before asking me if I was doing anything with Channel 4. Not really. Then why do you have a framed cheque for £17,500 hanging on your wall? Doh.

The press were then alerted and soon found out that Susi Hush had come on board as producer after Channel 4 had been nagging me to get some 'production experience' on the team. It did make sense to have someone else looking at the creative side of the programme: scripts, cast and directors. I actually tried to persuade Colin Cant, but he was still finishing off *County Hall* and probably felt one Phil Redmond warzone was enough. Susi was working as the current producer of *Grange Hill*, and despite her putting London buses into the programme I had quite liked what she had done, as I had actually liked what she had tried to do with *Corrie* a few years earlier, despite that not proving successful for Granada or the ITV audience. Then again, I hadn't, in the eyes of Harry Kershaw and Bill Podmore.

After the usual creative dance about where editorial control would rest since I would be both executive producer and proprietor, as well as the writer with a reputation for arguing with producers, we managed to find the words that would get us across the line and she went off to start the talent recruitment while I got on with all the other aspects. Like suddenly discovering that I was facing another programme name change.

Although I have referred to *Brookie* as, well, *Brookie* and *Brookside*, up until this point it was in fact originally called *Meadowcroft*, a name I thought much more pastoral and in keeping with the fashion at the time for country-sounding names like Apple Croft, Fox Meadows,

Barley Mow, Wheatsheaf, all conjuring up a sense of suburban idyll. Then the phone went.

Phil, we have a slight problem with the programme. What's that? The name, *Meadowcroft*. What? Could you change it? Why? We've just discovered we've commissioned another programme with a similar name. And then I thought, We've been talking for over a year so how come . . . never mind. What's the other name? *Meadow Lark*. Is it a drama? No, a comedy based on a character in a West End play. Right, and how long will it be on for? Hard to say, initially six weeks. So you want me to change the name of the drama programme we have been talking about for over twelve months, that everyone in the world now knows about, even the Department of Trade and Industry, and which will be on twice a week, hopefully, for at least ten years, because of a six-part comedy show? That's it, yes, any chance?

I knew this would probably go on and on, and *Grange Hill* had had to change. Perhaps this was some sort of omen. Mysterious ways even. I looked out of my new office window, the bedroom of number twelve, down to where they were erecting the fence that would separate us from the River Alt. What about *Brookside*? I suggested. Sorry? Brook-side. We have a small river, stream or brook flowing past. We are on the side of a brook. *Brookside*. Hmmmm, I'm not sure I . . . Do you want to change the name or not? Yes. Great name. Love it. Thanks. Fortunately computers had moved on. It was now easier to change the contracts and stationery.

I'm not even sure *Meadow Lark* even made it to screen but another soundalike did: *Broadside*. That ran for two series and the channel often used to mix up our ratings data with theirs. And as if that wasn't enough to confuse anyone, just after the first anniversary of *Brookside* I received a letter from the channel dated 17 November 1983, saying they had read my submission *Meadowcroft* but had regretfully decided not to pursue it. I framed that one too and wrote back suggesting a better response would have been, 'we already have something similar on air'.

So *Meadowcroft* became *Brookside*, and the road itself became Brookside Close after Broseley did what they'd promised not to do and named the rest of the development Brookside. They thought it would be a selling point, but for us it opened a whole minefield of potential litigation if any of our future neighbours decided we were basing our storylines on them. As the road name had now been officially registered with the Land Registry, we then had to hastily arrange to have The Close itself unadopted, as on buying the houses Channel 4 had done just that, bought the houses but not the road itself. This meant that anyone would have had right of way into The Close, the very thing I had set out specifically to prevent.

Susi Hush had by this time met a lady called Janet Goddard through the Liverpool Playhouse and Everyman Theatre and together they were starting to recruit local writers, following our standard policy of Liverpool first, then the North West, the Celtic fringes, followed by the rest of the UK with London last. Remembering what had happened to my initial vision of *Grange Hill* (née *Park*) being set on the outskirts of Liverpool, I wanted to make sure we weren't sucked back into the metropolitan view of the world. *Brookside*, as it was now officially called, would have a bit of magic to it as it would be coming from Liverpool and following on from *Z Cars* to *Blackstuff*, from *Days of Hope* to *Liver Birds*, but it would be about the UK as a whole, and definitely not London-centric.

I knew I had to write the first batch of scripts so that everyone would understand that we would be dealing with national, not local issues and themes. I wanted to write about unionism, but from a national perspective, not simply about the decline of a port city; I wanted to write about deindustrialisation but including the newer opportunities in the service industries and new technology; I wanted to write about the hardship felt in the management offices as well as on the shop floor; about the black or informal economy alongside the benefit culture; and above all I wanted to write about family life, and how kids and teens were an integral part of that, not mere appendages to it. I knew I had to write the scripts to illustrate this; to illustrate the drama and sit-com that could be found in everyday incidents like neighbours' gardens and parking disputes. I wanted to write about community as much as character. I knew I had to write those scripts. Everyone knew I had to write those scripts. The biggest problem was, when? Where would the time come from?

Things started to pick up speed again as the roofs went on and equipment and people started to arrive with nowhere to go and Susi needed an office but Colin McKeown had figured it would be best to hire experienced heads of department and then train everyone else, as we were boldly going where no engineers had been before and all that, so why not do the same with crews – but check when the tarmac was being rolled and the pavement laid in case the wiremen needed more improvised ducts to pull the cables through to avoid induction issues across mains video and sound while being careful not to get tangled with BT or the alarms that were tripping over Council road inspectors and building regulation officials and landscapers who were still trying to figure out how and where all the trees should be never mind the equipment as the rooms couldn't take real desks so kitchen counter tops would be fitted when we go down to Maidenhead to talk to Sony about the equipment spec as they could do everything from camera lens to monitor screen except vision mixing and sound dubbing but before that where are are the contracts for the staff; is this the editor's chair; is that colour right for the Grants; will we ever build upstairs in number seven; which union do gardeners belong to; what do you think of these lights for reception; are we doing CCTV; how are the scripts coming; how many phone lines; which is the production office; and admin; and accounts; and site management? And DTi want you to meet Michael Heseltine about Baker's IT82 fibre optic drive, but before that do you want plain or Artex ceilings?

And so it went on and on, the maelstrom picking up energy as more and more people arrived asking more and more simple questions that needed more and more complex answers. And all the time bouncing between London for *Grange Hill* and Channel 4, Maidenhead for Sony, Manchester for the DTi or demonstrations of a 'revolutionary' fully integrated word processing and script-printing system that would cost more than the houses, up to Carlisle to see a production training centre then back to the Slaughterhouse pub in Liverpool to meet writers. And each time I would leave a pile of answers only to come back to find the questions had multi-plied exponentially, including the usual requests from television traditionalists like Susi for more office space and first class rail travel. It was always no to first class, with the line that I wanted everyone to mix and get to know their intended audience, but the point about office space was taken. We simply didn't have enough, so I started thinking about buying a few of the flats that were to be built overlooking the back of the set. Another visit to Broseley and another 'I'll take seven' moment.

Yet solutions were also appearing, like the arrival of Brigid Kilgallen, a no-nonsense solid Scouse matriarchal figure who people crossed at their peril. Originally arriving to cover reception, she ended up being the only person Broseley's Graham Baker would speak to and stayed with us for many years as site manager. Colin appeared to declare that he had found the solution to not only the electrical phase distribution load issue – something we all always want to know, right – but also to one of our biggest problems, heat dissipation from the lights: we should omit the central heating from the houses. The lights would do it and we would make a saving. Great. It was beginning to look like I could go off and work on the long-delayed scripts, as well as admire the plasterwork at home . . . until Susi decided she wanted out.

Ostensibly she told me she couldn't function as producer without scripts, but underneath it all was the fundamental problem of old meets new. I think she had arrived too late in the process. By the time she came on board, I just couldn't give her or the scripts the time I would have liked to, nor did she have the time to switch from the old mentality, of having the support of BBC or ITV resources, to what we were trying to do in a matter of months. We decided to part ways, during which I made a casual remark to the trade press that I thought she had decided life in Liverpool was not for her and wanted to spend more time back in London with her own business and the family. Bad mistake. Big lesson. It was meant to be a typically bland deflection away from my real feelings, that she couldn't cope with us not being able to provide her with the typical empty office, desk, phone and PA straight away. I also assumed she would prefer to be cast as human rather than a wally, so I walked straight into it. She took this as a sexist slight on her professionalism and invoked the whole grievance procedure through the ACTT.

This meant we all had to adopt formal positions and in doing so ended up in a full ACAS (Advisory Conciliation and Arbitration Service) procedure that basically ended up with us paying her a relocation allowance of £2,500 and her pay for the time she was with us of around £4,500. That, I thought, was the end of it, but she taught me another valuable lesson: get your retaliation in first. No sooner had we concluded the hearing than the press was full of how she and the ACTT had 'forced' *Brookside* to compensate her. We weren't forced, but I was always careful from that moment on

to have our own media strategy in place, to watch what I said about
anything, and fall back on the sharpest weapon always being the
truth. What I should have done was release the comments from the
ACAS hearing which record the ACTT as saying this: '. . . *ACTT
would like to make it clear that, with the notable exception of the matters
in question, relationships between* Brookside *and ACTT are good, and
the industrial relations record of the company is considerable.*' And the
Arbitrator saying this: '. . . *the company, being new, did not have the
resources of an established television enterprise. All of these points were fully
known and made the job of a line producer significantly different to comparable functions in e.g. the BBC or an established ITV company.*' Exactly.

The major point though is that it taught me a lot about communication and how you can never assume people understand anything,
especially something completely new, until they see it demonstrated.
Experience itself, as Colin had recognised on the technical side, is
often the biggest inhibitor. While, given time, we could probably
have worked out our differences, life was too pressurised then for
old and new mindsets to meld instantly. The biggest challenge came
a few weeks later, though, when the *Sunday Times*, now owned by
that pesky Australian who the British TV regulators had chased away
once, decided to turn its sights on Channel 4.

9

Tech Runs (1982)

'*Brookside* – all fur coat and no knickers' – Sunday Times, *1982*

People were now arriving at a constant rate to populate The Close, the real inhabitants ahead of the fictional characters who would follow. Everywhere you went someone was installing or testing something. Legs were sticking out of manholes and hanging from ceiling hatches, with the most alarming sight for me occurring on a visit to the tech block to discover Colin McKeown in the CAR (Central Apparatus Room), reaching up into the loft space while standing on our brand new £55,000 portable 1-inch recorder to do it. 'Stress test,' he immediately said on seeing my expression. 'They're built for this, but we'd better test it before taking it out.' Then scuttled off somewhere else. The other guys just grinned and turned back to weaving another batch of electronic spaghetti. We were only weeks away from the planned test shoots and things had to be brought under tighter control.

We had been flying on adrenalin and enthusiasm, but when you go over the line from planning to production something else happens. All those numbers on cash flows and budgets start changing as people actually start converting numbers into real money then spending it. This is when you discover that, just like with kids, there are two currencies in the world, their money and yours. One of the things that had precipitated Susi's departure was the realisation that she was no longer dealing with BBC or ITV budgets, but real cash.

If you went over budget at the BBC or ITV, they had the opportunity to move things from one cost centre or programme to another. Ultimately, they could also ask for either a licence fee or ad-rate hike. Our budget was actual cash, real money, my money, that once spent was gone. Any overspend on the budget would come out of the production fee.

We had argued long and hard with Channel 4 over this, but not unreasonably they took the view that they also did not have ITV budgets, only the cash given to them. They had to live within whatever was handed over from ITV. They also, again not unreasonably, reminded me that I was the one who had always claimed he could do it within the budget, especially with the £150,000 'uplift' they had already generously provided. It was a fair point. Made over and over and over and over, to the extent that after Alexis arrived she turned it back on them and suggested that we keep any under-spend. The principle of mutuality, perhaps? Which became academic as her budgets were always accurate and never went into unforeseen overspend throughout the programme's entire history.

The real cash argument began around tables, chairs and rail fares. GHPM, the production manager I had taken on from the *Grange Hill* movie, and C4 were all still in the metropolitan mindset. Whereas my priority was the production budget. More Habitat than Bauhaus.

It used to grate on the QS in me that C4 had been set up with such a high specification for its offices, compared to what I had seen across ITV and the BBC, something that carried over into the Richard Rogers' Crystal Palace they now inhabit. As Chair of National Museums Liverpool, I can see and support the argument for public buildings being, in themselves, pieces of public art or inspirational venues. But they are open to the public and planned to last for a hundred years, not for the exclusive use of people working for a public corporation with a public-service remit. Nor should anyone have expected C4 to last a hundred years in 1981, given the publicity surrounding the IT82 sunrise industries. While that fundamental change might have been delayed, we are now approaching the threshold of technological change past which it will be difficult to preserve broadcasting's status quo through political will and market manipulation. Considering how Sky and Virgin Video established themselves, in industrial sheds in Isleworth or converted canal warehouses somewhere near Ladbroke Grove, and then the doomed launch of British Satellite Broadcasting, with its

Squarial and temple at Marco Polo House, was there any need for C4 to build itself such a grand temple? Or even to stay in London? The answers are: from the North, 'no'. From the capital, 'of course'.

Alexis has always counselled me that you can run your own business any way you want to, but how others fund their business is up to them. Fair point, except we both agreed it isn't exactly C4's business. As a state corporation, somewhere down the line our taxes are propping it up, as with the BBC.

In terms of cost control then, no one had ever attempted to do what MerseyTV was about to do: run a production on the scale and size of *Brookside* outside a traditional broadcasting structure. It was important therefore to have robust and sustainable procedures in place. So very early on in 1982, Standing Order No. 1 came into effect: NO—— until any further Standing Order. This was scribbled on a piece of paper and pinned up behind my desk where it stayed until the company's sale in 2005. Standing Order No. 2 soon followed: There will be NO further Standing Orders.

Saying that no one else had ever done what we were attempting might seem a bit of an exaggeration, or perhaps a use of dramatic licence, but it was true. To the extent that Sony asked me to fly out, first-class, to their High Technology Centre in Palo Alto, California, probably at about the time Steve Jobs and Bill Gates were hatching their world-domination plans. Sony were interested in what I had in mind as the post-production equipment we were ordering had been designed only with news coverage in mind. The proposal that it could be used for drama was of huge interest to them, especially the idea of using it on location. Typically, though, I had to squeeze this trip in between everything else, which meant flying to the West Coast . . . for lunch.

When I arrived at Palo Alto they took me straight to the lab to show me the world's first Sony 3000 Editor prototype. Designed for gathering news, it was meant as a simple cut-and-butt editor for compiling footage to be inserted into the studio news broadcasts. The sort of thing you see every day when a reporter is out and about somewhere. Shot of location, couple of set ups of what's going on, with reporter doing voice over, last shot of reporter, and then out shot of location ready to hand back to studio. With no multiple edits to take different angles or cut between characters, the memory was small and there was no provision for mixing or fades.

We then headed off for lunch in a typically geeky utilitarian windowless canteen, where I spent a few hours with their techies, talking through how I saw the drama, what kind of effects I would want to use and how many edits we were likely to expect. In a typical studio recording you might have as few as twenty to thirty edits, if that. Most of the work cutting between cameras is done by the vision mixer so each scene is complete when finished. The post-production job was simply to join those scenes together on one tape, add titles, credits and end-of-part captions as necessary, taking a couple of hours at most.

What we were proposing was something more in line with film, when there could be up to twenty to thirty edits per scene, each taking between five and ten minutes. In the event, it was not unusual for *Brookie* to have a couple of hundred edits per episode. In other words, there were not enough hours in a working week to edit two episodes manually. The answer was to use Sony's new 'computer-controlled' editing facility. Without getting too geeky about it, it was the difference between fast-forwarding to a favourite scene on a videotape against chapter-searching on a DVD. For those too young to remember that, it was perhaps more like looking in a telephone directory than dialling a 118 number . . . Too young for that? It was a heck of a lot quicker.

The techies paying for lunch had the computer code on the table in front of them: a thick continuous stream of punched computer paper that they eventually spread across the floor of the canteen, going back and forth scribbling notes against the relevant line of code that would have to be changed every time I talked about something they had not thought of, like mixes. After a few intriguing and entertaining hours we were done, they went back to the lab to start the modifications and I headed back to the airport.

On the way out one of them took me into his office, opened his drawer and took out a small plastic disc, about the size of a 45 rpm vinyl disc. He passed it to me and said did I know what it was. I said no, but it looked a bit like a laser disc. Nah, they're crap, he said, and that thing in your hand can hold much more data. What are you going to do with it? Dunno. Just know they'll be big one day. It was of course an early DVD, a few months before even CDs were available. It was to be ten years before DVDs found their way into the shops.

Because of all the changes they decided to make to the 3000 Editor, Sony couldn't get it into manufacturing in time for us, so they sent the prototype, and a free engineer for six months, who would sit in the edit suite and, every time it crashed, take it apart and solder another component on the back, all the time feeding this information back to Palo Alto. When they eventually got into production they came to swap out our central processor board, and I asked if I could have it. It had hundreds of integrated circuits arranged in a grid pattern that looked like a piece of electro–pop art representing an American city grid. At the time it was valued at £3,000 but they reckoned we had given them much more than that in field tests and product design. That too stayed on my wall and the relationship with Sony stayed in place for a good number of years. Every time I went over to California I would drop in to say hello, not least to pick up a few spare push switches for the 3000 Editor. We were going through them on a regular basis and they were costing over $100 each, so they used to give me a bagful, saying it was something else they hadn't predicted in the design. Although, apparently, only we and the Japanese destroyed so many switches.

Arriving back in the UK, it would have been nice to crash for a while, but it was straight from the airport and back into the mêlée, with a quick stop at the BBC for a *Grange Hill* script meeting and back on up to Liverpool. For me sleep was becoming something that happened in the minutes between meetings. Although the critical path analysis had us taking possession of the houses in June (which happened thanks to Graham Baker), installing equipment in July (which nearly happened), and tech running and shooting in August – that didn't happen. For one thing we had yet to receive all the gear, including two expensive new mixing desks. Another thing was, we needed a few actors.

With the guiding hand of an established producer removed, Janet Goddard was asked to carry on what she had begun doing with Susi and start the casting trawl. Scripts were now coming in from the writers I had already recruited, plus the PR guy I had come across at Merseyside County Council, Barry Woodward. The first writers' meeting was held not at *Brookside*, but where I had originally said 'Right. I'll take thirteen' – right behind Broseley's Sales Office. They had a row of show houses and, when I told them I was looking for more space, said I could have one of those. At a discount. So I bought what would become, although I wasn't supposed to know it, the staff party house, Whitebeam. The idea was to use it both as early office space and to provide cheap accommodation for staff we would need to bring in from outside the area. It was obvious that buying a house and then renting it out to freelance staff at subsidised rates was going to be cheaper for us than paying hotel bills. It provided some sense of community for people who might only be with us for a short time and would otherwise be left on their own in a bedsit or small hotel somewhere. It worked amazingly well. Too well probably, as the 'party house' designation may indicate.

It was probably as bizarre a setting for the writers as it was for me, meeting in the kitchen-diner of a four-bedroomed detached house in the middle of a housing estate. Especially as the guy calling himself the executive producer knelt on a chair to make a point and found his knee go right through the Habitat rattan seat. So much for our cost cutting. That wouldn't have happened with Channel 4's Bauhaus chairs.

My new writing team would attempt the next twelve scripts following on from my initial ten, which probably weren't finished even then. Andy Lynch wrote six of those as he already had some experience of writing comedy: the anti-smoking campaigner Allan Swift wrote three; and I thought I'd try out the teacher, Jimmy McGovern, on two, and give one to the PR guy from the County Council. Len Rush and his wife Helen, along with Frankie Clarke, brother to Margi Clarke and later of *Letter to Brezhnev* fame, came in the second wave. While none of the latter stayed the course, Barry Woodward eventually went on to write 400 episodes, more than any other writer, Andy Lynch did 174, Allan Swift 82, and all of them stayed to the end. Jimmy McGovern wrote 80 episodes and went on to write *Prime Suspect, Cracker,* and to become *the* Jimmy McGovern, eventually coming almost full circle in making *The Street* for the BBC. Well, since the 1960s launch of *Corrie,* it has been an enduring format.

What also started here was the establishment of 'the writer's' company. There would be no script editors. Nor would producers be allowed to fiddle with the script. If there were changes to be made, then the writers would be asked to do them to their own scripts. Having suffered over and fought long and hard against other people 'fiddling' with or trying to insert or piggy-back their opinions on to my scripts, I was determined from the outset that this would not happen at *Brookside*. Unless I was the one to do it. But that was different. It was my idea. It was also what would keep the sense of authorship around the programme. As time progressed and the script process became more formalised and structured, these principles became embedded. It was designed to be, and I think it remained, a writer's company.

All writers would attend the six-monthly long-term planning meeting and the monthly storyline conference. The writers asked to write that month's scripts would then all attend a commissioning meeting, then a first draft meeting where all the scripts would be discussed. This was a very tough process for people to get used to, as, like the directors' first rough-cut, this is a very sensitive time for any writer. The first time they and their work are exposed to the world.

There was always the problem of month-to-month continuity, but making sure the first and then second draft scripts were delivered ahead of the following month's storyline conferences helped minimise the frustration of someone's 'great idea' falling foul of someone else's. Soon my life revolved around a four-weekly script pattern: week 1 storylines; week 2 script commissioning; week 3 first drafts; week 4 second drafts.

With the writing team in place and scripts underway, it was now time for me to think seriously about who would play the characters. A lot of the early casting for *Brookie* was done in the Playhouse rehearsal rooms, due to Janet Goddard's links there. My method then, as it always remained, was never to focus on what actors had already done, but to concentrate only on whether they were right for the part. Did they feel, sound, think and, most importantly, look right? This is one of the most brutal parts of the job. Usually you are looking for a type rather than an individual. When a character appears on screen, the audience has to believe instantly that what they are seeing seems 'right'. It's why Sean Connery and Daniel Craig really are James Bond, while Timothy Dalton and Roger Moore, for all their respective talents, always appeared to be playing James Bond. I know, it's not an exact science and Roger will appeal to different audiences, but it always worked in casting, for me, and I was always open and truthful about it.

Too often I had sat in on casting sessions where a producer and director had engaged an actor in conversation for about an hour, talking about this, that and the other, when we all knew as soon as the five-foot, eight-stone anorexic had shuffled into the room that they would never convince anyone they were the six-foot-six rugby prop we were looking for. The politically correct thing was to give everyone an equal opportunity to convince those casting of their ability, and see if the part could be adapted to suit their talents. The fact that no rugby team on earth would put in a five-foot anorexic was overlooked, and soon the creative compromises would begin.

Partly to help prevent this sort of non-productive 'detour', I soon learned to look at a current, not posed or publicity, photograph of the actor first, to check the look. If that wasn't possible, as was often the case when starting something like *Brookside* and *Hollyoaks*, when you are looking primarily for new faces, then the next best thing was to be honest with the actor as soon as they came through the door. Explain that we were doing an initial trawl and that a lot of it would depend on looks. Not just how they looked individually, but since we were casting family groups, whether the potential characters all looked as though they came from the same gene pool. I feel strongly that an actor desperate for a part, particularly the new faces, should not be kept hanging about chatting, all the time thinking that the longer they stay, the better their chances are. It is almost immoral and borders on the cruel to keep people hanging on, which is why I keep saying the second best answer in life is always a very quick no.

In the early casting for *Brookside*, the unions' closed shops meant no one could act in film or TV without an Equity card. On Merseyside no one would challenge this sort of edict. When Equity rejected my first choice to play Bobby and Sheila Grant's oldest lad, Barry, as not having a card, we had to go through the motions of looking at every other registered Equity member in the North West. If we hadn't found someone, I am sure Equity would have relented and allowed our initial choice. However, even that attracted controversy as I was attacked for not looking at members in the Afro-Caribbean Register. Strikes and blacklisting (yes, an unfortunate term, in use at the time) were threatened until I dug my heels in and pointed out that I was looking for the eighteen-year-old son of a white Roman Catholic couple in their forties of Irish descent.

If their son turned out to be Afro-Caribbean that, in the 1980s, would be a bigger story than the one I was intending to portray.

Common sense prevailed and on the Saturday morning before shooting began I met the man who would later help turn Barry Grant into one of the most successful TV characters in the UK, Paul Usher. Paul, although having an Equity card by virtue of his band, had not done a lot before and was due that morning to be on the set of *Yentl*, Barbra Streisand's movie, which was shooting some scenes down on Liverpool's famous waterfront. He chose to come and see what we were up to instead, and in a small office in one of the *Brookside* houses I knew serendipity had played its hand.

The actor we couldn't get was Joe McGann, of the McGann acting clan, the only one in the family still to get his Equity card. What would have happened to *Brookside*, Paul and Joe if Equity had not initially blocked his participation may be being played out in an alternative universe, but it did reinforce my belief in not compromising the drama until you really, really have to, something I would later drive various producers and our casting department to the edge of despair over in the future. Like finding Kurt for *Hollyoaks*. Even if it meant re-jigging or holding up the production schedule for a few days, I would not compromise until I felt we had exhausted all avenues or serendipity had decided not to smile on us. A long runner is not like a one-off. Every decision you make you have to live with for years.

Those early casting sessions had some magical moments, like watching Amanda Burton's mass of hair come up the stairs, and hearing the soft Irish lilt that I knew would captivate at least 49 per cent of the audience. Then Doreen Sloane as *Brookie*'s own answer to Margaret Thatcher and *Woman's Own* pin-up who would captivate all those in the audience of a certain age. Then her complete opposite in class and politics, Ricky Tomlinson, walking in with a casualness I hadn't seen in other actors anxious to get a part. Although he was not an established actor, Janet was very keen that I should meet him and he'd already got his Equity card through the variety route, playing ukulele and doing stand-up round the pubs and clubs. Janet was right about one thing. He looked like Bobby Grant should look with his unkempt hair, beard, and what from memory I think was the classic working-class attire of a donkey jacket, although I may be doing Ricky a sartorial injustice.

After a bit of chat about what he'd been doing and getting a couple of shrugs and a few 'this and that, lad's, and 'you know's, I gave him some background about Bobby being a trades union official and asked him to do an improvisation for me. About Christmas morning. He hadn't found either the time or bottle to tell his wife that he wouldn't be there for the family Christmas lunch, because 'management' had asked for urgent talks, and they chose Christmas to test the union resolve or else to manipulate the media by reporting that they wouldn't agree to meet. He said, 'OK, lad,' and went off into a monologue that had both Janet and me transfixed as he talked to his fictional and invisible wife about his love and respect for her, the family, and how he didn't want to let them down, but what else could he do in such a case, where the management were deliberately using the situation to create stress and disharmony in the union, knowing that while he was a paid official, the people he represented were out on strike, losing wages, unable even to afford Christmas dinner, so if he didn't turn in they would use that as a wedge to try and force a split so he hoped she would support him as she had always done and see that social justice had to come ahead of his turkey dinner?

At the end of it he said, 'That any good, lad?' I said, 'Yep, I'd let you out of Christmas dinner if I was married to you.' He gave one of the loud cackling laughs I would come to know well over the coming years, stood up, shook my hand and left as casually as he had arrived. I turned to Janet and said, that's him, but don't tell him yet. I want to find Mrs Grant first.

I left that session feeling buoyed up by discovering someone so empathetic with the part, and told a few people how amazing 'this guy' had been. It was not until the programme was transmitted that I found out why, when the calls started to come in demanding that 'the Marxist agitator' be sacked. I at first thought it was my old *Grange Hill* non-fan club after me again, until it became clear exactly who Ricky was: one half of the Shrewsbury Two, building workers who had been convicted of conspiracy and sent to prison in 1973 for helping to organise strikes and flying pickets. Although there were a lot of other people involved, only Ricky Tomlinson and Des Warren were actually sent to prison, Ricky for two years and Warren for three. It caused outrage in the trades union movement then, and since there has been suspicion that the whole process was politically manipulated due to the tensions building in the country following the first miners' strike in 1971. During their time in prison both Ricky and Warren had gone on hunger strike and refused to wear prison uniform, opting for wearing only blankets and being treated as political prisoners. No wonder Ricky was empathetic with Bobby Grant. And no wonder he had taken to the clubs with his ukulele, as he later told me both he and Warren were 'blacklisted' by the construction industry. There is a great film to be found in that story, and if I had known it at the time I would still have offered him the part. To their credit, Channel 4 took the same supportive line.

With my trades unionist then cast, the search for his wife went on, but ended as soon as Sue Johnston walked in. Even before she got to the table where we were sitting I knew, just as I had with Mandy and Ricky. Sue was giving the impression of casualness, but there was also a sense of authority about her. A controlled dignity. This might have been controlled nervousness or simply because she wanted the part. There was something else about her as she walked towards me: she could easily have been one of my Irish cousins, a Catholic matriarch or a Mother Superior, carrying that air almost of grace that led me to give her the nickname 'St She'. Like Ricky, I pushed her a bit on who and what she was, and Sue herself later said that it was more like a job interview than the sort of casting session she was used to. Because it was. I was looking for people who would stay the course. Be able to think on their feet and get on, or put up, with those around them for what would become a five-day-a-week commitment. She could, would and did.

The next stage in the casting was the mix and match. Putting all the possible permutations together and seeing who gelled, who didn't and who might. I used the same process for all the major characters and, whenever possible, within the set they would inhabit. The aim was to let them work together, improvise off each other, start talking, hanging about, waiting around together. Would they be able to stand each other during the long hours spent on set and location, waiting for the magic moment to arrive?

The final mix and match sessions for *Brookie* took place at Brookside itself and there were many scenes of unbridled joy, the sort of moments that make the business a bit special, but the best reaction I ever saw was when we agreed to take on a young school leaver, Francis

Harcombe, as a runner – the industry term for dogsbody. Straight from school, he had no real qualifications but was a solid Scouse, willing to do anything to get a job. When we told him his eyes almost popped out in excitement and then he asked could he use the phone to call his mum? When we said yes, he ran the length of the office we had rented in Liverpool and called her, practically shouting down the phone, 'Mum, Mum, I've got a job!' And so he did, and one which took him from dogsbody, to living in the bungalow with the Rank Xerox machine printing all the scripts, to eventually moving across to the shoot to become senior floor manager or first assistant director. The guy who actually runs the shoot. He's the one who saves or costs you money. He also later became Frannie. Well, he was in show business by then.

By July we were getting ready to move from temporary offices in the city centre to Brookside itself when I discovered the down-side to the great management mantra 'delegate'. My GHPM had signed a five-year lease. Why? So we would have a city-centre base. For what? One of the advantages of coming to a city built for 80,000, with a population of 400,000, was that you could get from anywhere in ten minutes. And the city we'd be dealing with most was London. Money wasted. So I began watching the delegated power and used the offices as a location, occasionally. Soon the newcomers at Brookside outnumbered those from the city centre and the place was a hive of activity as the legs disappeared from manholes and loft openings and the camera tests and tech runs began; when new systems, new equipment, new cast, new crews and, above all, new ideas started to come together. And clash rather than mesh. I started to learn that the media, the great communication industry, is hopeless at communicating. That was when I first began to hear the phrase I would come to dread, 'I just thought . . .' I just thought we were doing it this way. I just thought you said, knew, agreed or whatever. I just thought it could or couldn't do that. There was no one particular problem, just a combination of misunderstandings, assumed knowledge, and underlying it all lack of belief in the new systems. One example of this I'd expected. The other came as a total surprise.

I'd expected that the established union members would display the old mindset, insisting that things should be done in particular ways and on particular equipment. But no one had ever shot drama in this way before, never mind out of the back of an old Volvo estate car on a portable recorder. This was more like home movies than a proper Outside Broadcast with furniture van-sized vehicles. What were the manning levels? Who pressed which button? Was this bit of cable sound or vision? And who should drive the cars – ACTT, EEPTU or NATTKE? The answers to these quandaries usually came from the newer members; by simply getting on with things. Although having been given cards to enter the hallowed closed shop, another of the 'concessions' we had won, they had no previous experience of these sort of one-man-one-job demarcation traditions, and thought they were daft.

This was the surprise to me – that the newer entrants led the way. Even the electricians, traditionally the most militant of the TV unions, were a breath of fresh air. This was partly due to my following the advice I'd been given by the union itself, recruiting from general industry rather than TV, and partly down to the Head of Department, Steve Griffiths. Although himself coming from an established TV lighting company, he was forward-thinking and pragmatic, as indeed were most of the working-class members of the company. These were people who understood, like the national officials, the value of the jobs we were creating, and especially of the wage rates dicated by the television union agreements compared to what they could find in the declining local economy.

The niggles, when they did come, were usually from the middle-class armchair socialists who ended up in shop-steward roles because no one else wanted to fill them. It would be they who, intellectually rather than out of need, tried to maintain the weekly shop meetings demanded of the union, together with the separate office, with telephone and locked notice board, that all the agreements insisted on. We didn't have the space for that but said they could use the actors' Green Room, a space upstairs in number 4, the canteen house, reserved for the actors during the shoot. However, they would have to organise their own rota, and although there was a phone there we were not going to supply them all with individual locked cabinets. We were not ITV. They accepted this. Another concession.

Weekly union meetings arose from the Marxist theory of organised cells. A regular meeting allows constant reinforcement of the party line but also needs a regular agenda, therefore members have to be active in seeking out issues to populate this. It was not long before we saw the need for another structure as not all staff actually needed, or wanted, to belong to the unions. Admin, accounts, reception and anyone deemed 'management' were outside the collective bargaining arrangements, which was a bit daft anyway as we were all excluded from influencing the national agreement negotiations. Nevertheless we all maintained the union shop-management principle and engaged in the typical mind games. The union reps would constantly refer to 'management', and as sole proprietor, despite now employing professional managers, this was always odd for me to hear. I suppose my own working-class background and journey still made me feel at odds with the term management, it being synonymous with the middle classes, just as years later I had a go at a journalist for describing me as a media mogul. I told him that I was still a writer and exec producer, doing a real job on the production, not some ITV or BBC manager swanning round from conference to conference or lunch to lunch.

With scripting and casting underway, and crew and staff recruitment continuing, the other creative element we needed was directors. A legacy from Susi Hush was an old school director whose credit list extended from *Coronation Street* to *Blake's 7*, but also included *Dr Who* and two of my own favourite BBC programmes, *The Brothers* and *Survivors*. The idea of having this older figure was that he would bring a bit of experience to the production process, which he certainly did. It was an amazing experience and probably not one Susi envisaged when she started calling him the 'senior director', a title he seemed to take to heart. We also had two younger new directors, Chris Clough and Keith Washington, to shepherd along. At least that was the idea.

Chris came across from Granada, stayed with us for a while and then moved off to *EastEnders*. More recently he has produced *Skins*. Keith came to us from the BBC series *Angels*, later went on to things like *Jonathan Creek* and *Casualty*, but had previously been an actor and, from memory, had performed as Jesus in *Jesus Christ Superstar*. That might just have been someone winding me up, but if he didn't he certainly looked as though he should have done, with his piercing eyes and biblical beard. Chris, on the other hand, although also bearded, was a quiet, gentle teddy bear of a man who soon won over both cast and crew. Although our older director was supposed to be the shepherd, it soon emerged that it was he who needed shepherding, and while Keith probably brought more acting flair to his performance as director, Chris soon emerged as the one to take on the responsibility of shooting the opening episodes.

We planned a launch event for August which, for me, turned into another bitter-sweet moment in the whirl of that first year. It's a moment often found in production, in fact – where you look back at the photos of what went on and can see you were there, but you can't quite recall all the details. When everybody else seems to be enjoying themselves, and you may even be smiling or laughing along, but afterwards cannot recall what you were feeling or what was said. And then you wish you hadn't been quite so distracted or counting the clock down quite so hard so as to get on with something else. It's the same feeling I sometimes get when looking at the production stills from our shoots in Rome, Spain, Ireland, London or wherever, and remembering I was probably sitting in a crowded room at the time and arguing with Jimmy McGovern and/or Frank Cottrell Boyce and/or Allan Swift or Kay Mellor, or any permutation or combination of the writing team, but usually thoroughly enjoying it all the same.

The launch was on 10 August and we even had a podium for speeches. We all stepped up to say encouraging words, as you do at these events. Channel 4 congratulated me; I congratulated them and Broseley and the Council and Merseyside County Council, the DTi and all those who had taken the leap of faith to join us. Or at least I hope I did. We also ceremonially signed the contract that Leon had been working on for the past year. Well, we didn't actually, we faked it as we were still arguing about a few things and I don't actually think the original contract ever did get signed. In the end it became a game with Alexis and me to see how long we could hold off signing, knowing very well that we were committed, and the legal principle of 'acting upon' was definitely in play. I think it was only in 1990, when the channel had to change its formal statutory position of being a subsidiary of the IBA to become a stand-alone public corporation, that David Scott locked us in his office until we formally wrapped up the outstanding paperwork.

One memory that stands out for me, and one that may explain why I was distracted, was showing round Liverpool's Lord Mayor and the Chief Executive of the County Council and noticing that all the dividing walls between the bedrooms had huge areas marked with crosses, about two metres square. I pulled Colin to one side and asked what they were and he told me that was where the camera guys wanted to cut a few more traps to make it easier to shoot. They're a bit concerned about space and want to . . . He saw my face. A bit OTT then? OTT? They're not traps, they're great gaping holes! And it won't make anything easier to shoot if the houses fall down around them. A quick chat with Graham from Broseley confirmed that while we could cut out small areas, as they had done during the build in the kitchens and bathroom, taking out huge sections would cut through the bracing rods and compromise the integrity of the buildings' structure. Enough said. The holes were never cut, so at least the launch served one useful purpose.

These sorts of events I found more draining than enjoyable, but always understood their importance in building and maintaining good community relationships. It was with a weary, and wary, sense of responsibility that I went along with everyone else to a lunch in our honour hosted by Merseyside County Council. They were pleased to have another television presence in the region other than what was considered the Manchester-centric Granada. The lunch was held at nearby Croxteth Hall and there were more speeches in which we told each other how marvellous we all were, but this time, being a purely local event, it seemed to have a much more relaxed and friendly atmosphere. It is, though, another bitter-sweet memory as from that lunch would develop my lasting relationship with Liverpool Museums, later to become National Museums Liverpool, of which I would become Chair in 2008.

Lunch was held in one of the Hall's grand but crowded rooms, although having been back there many times since I've never quite been able to recall which one. I do remember being presented with a special Croxteth Hall tea service, because it remained in pride of place in my office for twenty-five years. It might have been because we didn't have to organise that lunch, or that I wasn't worried about the reactions of the people wandering around The Close, or perhaps the event itself was a distraction from the maelstrom of the production process, but I relaxed enough to get chatting with the then Director of Museums, Richard Foster, another quiet and calm man, like David Reid at the BBC, who would, over the years, became my best friend.

It is always difficult to say why we connect with certain people but with Richard it was because we never asked anything of each other, except an occasional sympathetic ear to purge the frustrations of our different careers. Superficially we might have seemed worlds apart, the comprehensive kid and the public-school scholar, but we found a common cause and shared humour in satirising the pomposity of many of the people populating the bureaucratic and regulatory systems within which we operated. It is still one of life's great puzzles to me why perfectly rational people begin to act like the cast of *Yes Minister* when they join a committee. Any committee. We shared this sense of puzzlement and fun until Richard's tragic death in 2001. My 'official photograph' now hangs on a museum wall near his, and every time I see it I smile at the memory of times we shared, knowing that he would be pleased that the relationship with the city's museums he encouraged in me back then is still so strong. I miss those irreverent sessions.

For me, Richard's friendship was a welcome, perhaps sought-after, relief from a world where everyone seemed to want something from me. Or, worse, was trying to take something from me. Whether real or imagined does not matter, as even before *Brookie* had got into production I felt as though whatever I did, or whichever way I turned, someone, somewhere, was trying to exploit me. I know this sounds like the typical Scouse stereotype but, like all clichés, it only exists because it is based on truth. This was a point I would later make to many writers, anxious about discussing their great idea in case someone stole it. That is almost the price of admission. You have to get 'ripped off' once in order to learn how the game is played.

On my own journey I had the skirmishes with Yorkshire over that octopus, the BBC while they were trying to claim the *Grange Hill* copyright, ATV on coincidentally discovering a similar school series, agents trying to take a slice of things they had nothing to do with, and even C4 attempting to divert the DTi grant. Now, as an employer, I was beginning to get a sense that people thought I worked for them, not the other way round. My job was to provide their job. Fair enough, up to a point. That was what I wanted to do. It was what I was prepared to do. But I also wanted them to do what *I* wanted them to do, not what they kept thinking I should do. Or what I should give them. Like 20 per cent of the company, perhaps?

9: Tech Runs

It was another stereotypical corporate mugging. Part of Justin Dukes' compact about leaving me to run the production if I let him sort the finances was a demand that I should bring in a good Financial Director to manage our financial reporting. The person I turned to was connected to the London Pictures venture. When the decision was made to buy rather than hire equipment, he told me he would leave his existing job and come and join me. We met at the London Kensington Hilton to discuss the deal. He said he knew how much weight C4 placed on the need for an experienced FD and gave me a piece of paper on which he'd listed his terms. A five-year fixed-term salary at £150,000, car, private health insurance, etc., etc. Oh, and that 20 per cent of the company. We looked at each other. Shook hands. And parted company.

I suppose that was an easy decision to make in hindsight, as what was the point of working so hard to achieve total creative control only to give it away to anyone who asked for a cut? Yet, against the backdrop of C4 wanting to see some form of traditional structure around me, it felt like another stumble on an already rocky road. It was with some trepidation that I went back to tell Justin what had happened. However, he was as pragmatic as ever and told me my preferred candidate had not passed his own two-second, seven-second test, but he had been prepared to go along with it if I was convinced. Justin said he would ask David Scott to help me find someone else, which he did. And that, it would turn out, would be another story.

There was one other thing we had to do in terms of local relations, and that was to invite in all the local residents now starting to encircle us, as more and more of the surrounding houses were sold. It was also the first sign of the rising intensity of the media storm that was about to engulf C4. The press were still prodding and jabbing at the channel in the fight over the colour-supplement ad revenue, and *Brookside* was now on the front line so there were constant forays on to our turf looking for negative stories. A mini-squall had blown up around the fact that we would be shooting in the middle of a housing estate, suggesting that we would have high lighting towers, like football floodlights, and a public address system like Crewe Station, to make our neighbours' lives a misery. Despite our having tried to forestall this by finding a site where we would be there first and the fact that our planning permission restricted

227

the number of times we could shoot after midnight, there was also the small point of its being absolute nonsense. But, as we should all know by now, why let a few journalistic facts get in the way of a good freelance fee? We got the neighbours in for a barbecue and demonstrated all the lights. We told them how we would use them and explained that noise was actually the last thing we wanted. All anxieties were allayed and we always kept up a good dialogue with the neighbours, including mince pies at Christmas.

Elsewhere, media interest was gathering fresh energy when the *Sunday Times* decided to run a big piece, focusing on Susi Hush's departure, as proof that Channel 4, and *Brookside* in particular, was in chaos. Susi was depicted as the experienced producer to whom I refused to listen since I was concerned only with keeping absolute dictatorial control, which was probably true in many ways. The newspaper reported that she couldn't cope with such chaos and came out with the quote that MerseyTV and *Brookside* was 'all fur coat and no knickers'. I assumed this was some middle-class put down, but couldn't help thinking about the Wenham audience demographics rather than the *Sunday Times* readership and wondering a) if they would ever read this, and b) if they did, whether it might actually excite their curiosity in the programme.

As a way of further illustrating how dictatorial I was, they high-lighted the fact that I had banned alcohol from the site, which I had, and also had a quote from Jimmy McGovern, which I still consider to be one of my better sound bites. He was late delivering his first script and had told Janet that he had a bad toothache. When she told me, I said off the cuff, 'Tell him he doesn't write with his teeth.' It was a typical Scouse riposte, and Jimmy had obviously told them this. It still makes me smile now, but the *Sunday Times* obviously took it as an example of me being beastly to writers, and added it to their story of the perceived woes going on 'up North'.

The killer, though, was that first-ever new car. My brilliant red BMW 323i. The one with that number plate I hadn't taken much notice of at the time since it was a simple regional designation for Walton-on-Thames. It started with EGO and ended in 1, before the yearly suffix 'X'. This was reported as though I had gone out and bought a flash new BMW and then gone and found the plate EGO 1 to stick on it. Partly true, but somehow, EGO ★★★X doesn't quite sound the same, does it? It was meant to be another stitch up, but from it we all learned a bit more about handling the media, it strengthened our relationship with Channel 4, and back on site the feeling was that if the Londoners were out to get us, then we must be doing something right. I still have that number plate. Not because of all this, but because it was once on the car that saved both Alexis's and my life. It really is a cherished plate.

With the ceremonial duties out of the way, we now had our production centre, most of our equipment, most of our cast, the houses were finished and were being dressed and furnished ready for their fictional owners to arrive, turf was laid on the front lawns, a security barrier was in place, directors were dissecting the existing scripts, writers were scribbling away on new ones, and the admin department was waiting, like the production and edit suites, sitting quietly humming, ready for the onslaught. Which was put back a week, then another until we could prevaricate no further. In order to meet the one immovable point in our schedule, the transmission date of 2 November, we would have to start shooting on 6 September 1982.

10

Shoot – Part 1 (1982)

'Under the Companies Act the Directors do have the power to remove you as Chairman' – *Management coup, October 1982*

6 September 1982: The Close stood ready. Actors were in Make-up and Wardrobe. Cameras, sound, lights were deploying round the site. The engineers were firing up the recording machines and production gallery. The canteen was peeling and chipping. Everyone was getting ready to start recording what would become a familiar sight to viewers in the years to come. Walking on to The Close that morning you would have found:

Numbers 1–3: The Technicals (sunshine industry), ground floor – Wardrobe and Make-up; first floor – Technical Facilities
Number 4: The Caterers – Canteen
Number 5: The Grants (working-class, union aspirations), Sheila, Bobby, Barry, Karen and Damon, already established, socially mobile from local council estate
Number 6: Young Francis (working-class), script-printing
Number 7: Vacant, first floor – micro-set building space
Number 8: The Collinses (middle-class – management redundancy), Annabelle, Paul, Lucy and Gordon – on their way, downsizing, from Wirral
Number 9: The Huntingtons (professional classes – aspiring), Heather and Roger Huntington, on first rung of property ladder

Number 10: The Taylors (entrepreneurial working-class – informal economy), Gavin, Petra, and second-hand cookers stacked on the front lawn

Numbers 11–13: The Admin Block (mixed-class – new economy), ground floor – Reception at Number 13; Admin at Number 11; Production at Number 11. First floor – Finance and Personnel across Numbers 13 and 11; my office at Number 12, overlooking The Close

Everything looked ready to go, but if I thought I had been at the centre of a maelstrom before we heard that historic first 'roll tape', then it soon seemed to have been a period of relative calm as the gusts of a growing storm started to rage above. Long past the event horizon, the point of no return, I had now crossed the threshold from hired hand to employer. No matter how hard I tried to adhere to the collegiate philosophy I had outlined to all and sundry, as production picked up pace I was discovering what comes with total control: total responsibility. Whether you want it or not. And when that is put to the test, when it is challenged, something else comes crashing in on you: the loneliness of leadership.

Often the challenges are not to your authority but to your judgement. How you react to the many and varied challenges that people throw at you. Like the time I was in the middle of a typical juggling session, answering a dozen different questions at once, when the Head of Personnel, who also happened to be a member of the Parole Board, came over and asked if he could have a quiet word. I could tell by his demeanour that it was something reasonably serious. We went into the only quiet space on the site. My office.

It's the gardener. I hope he isn't overspending that £25 budget I fought hard to give him? I asked, light-heartedly. No, he's doing quite well actually, but I'd like to lend him £200. That's up to you. No, I mean from the company. Er, we agreed no personal loans. This is a special case. Go on? Well, a bit of background. It started, as you may know, when we found him growing cannabis in the greenhouse . . . Er, no. This is me, zero tolerance on tobacco, I think I would have reacted, a bit? Perhaps we decided not to bother you with it. Guess you did. Anyway, it's all over now, the company's safe, but that's not the issue. Isn't it? No, it's the tragedy that lies behind it all. Which is? He was growing it to pay off his court fine. What court fine . . . for drugs? No, for selling his motorbike. Why'd he get fined for that? Because it was on HP and he'd stopped making his payments. Should I ask why he sold his motorbike? To pay for his girlfriend's abortion. I looked at him. HoP nodded. You are asking me to give a loan to some guy who got his girlfriend pregnant, then flogged off a motorbike he didn't own to pay for her abortion, but now needs to pay off his fine for debt by growing cannabis in our company greenhouse? HoP nodded again. Tragic, isn't it? No, it's wrong. And the best I can do is suffer from amnesia. About what? I don't know. Shall I find another solution then? To what? Ah. Yes, I get it. And off he went.

Was this the right judgement call? The easy bit was upholding the no-loans rule as that would have sent two obvious signals: the floodgates are open, and it's OK to flout both the law and company discipline. The harder bit was, having destroyed his crop, there was no real proof of what he had been up to, so what would have happened if we had taken a high moral stance and turned him in simply for some perceived risk to the company? Should he have been dismissed for gross misconduct? Perhaps. But I took my Parole Board member's point that the gardener was young, daft and well liked. I also knew most of our staff, citizens of the People's Republic, would soon find out and also support HoP's other point: if we sacked him, he'd have absolutely no way of paying his fine and would then face even greater temptation to turn to criminality. With the benefit of time and experience, I think my instinctive reaction was right and in line with the rest of the company's ethos of applied Scouse pragmatism, with the condition that he should never step out of line again. He had been given his last chance. Unfortunately, he did. And had to go for theft. Everyone knew. No one objected.

A bigger test came very early on after the shoot started when we started to slip behind. A little bit, then a bit more, then yet more, until we were three weeks in and two weeks behind. Instead of having six episodes recorded, we had something like 70 per cent of the first two, 20 per cent of the second pair and 40 per cent of the third pair. This was the result of a combination of inexperience, over-ambition and the hippy school of management. Still on the psycho-logical journey from working-class writer to production-company employer, I wanted everyone to buy into the vision and arrive at decisions collegiately. This had happened, by and large, as the company and production came together and everyone was responsible and focusing on their own particular area. However, when the shoot started there was no overall co-ordinating framework other than everything technical went to Colin and everything to do with the production logistics went to the Production Manager who had come across from *Grange Hill* (GHPM), but there was no overall creative control. While I was across the scripts and casting and could work with the designer, Leigh Malone, to make sure that the Grants and Collinses had the same kitchens, or that Gavin and Petra's house reflected the lifestyle of informal entrepreneurs, there were just not enough hours in the day for me to spin all the plates. In hindsight, we were short of a good project manager or site foreman of the sort I was used to working with in the construction industry. Someone like Graham Baker, from Broseley. GHPM was supposed to be doing this, but while fine at budgets and planning logistics, couldn't seem to keep up with the ever-changing demands of the production itself. This was an early case of *Brookie* shoot phobia: the fear of stepping on to the set and challenging what they were doing.

A production shoot can be quite an intimidating environment if you are not part of it. With anything from 50 to 100 people scurrying about setting, presetting, rigging or derigging all the equipment and getting actors and props in place, it takes a brave soul to step in suddenly and say 'Stop'. Once it starts to roll it can be a difficult beast to halt. Which is why shoots have to be kept on a tight rein. That is not an easy thing to do, especially with the adage 'time is money' echoing constantly in everyone's ears. The phrase 'walking the job' is often used in management, and for those managing production shoots it is vital. Rely too much on paperwork filtering back to the office and the beast can be away, out of control. That is what had happened on *Brookside*. Too many meetings, not enough observation, and because of this, it took too long for the real problem to be identified: Susi's Shepherd.

While Chris Clough was ploughing on with Episodes 1 and 2, sorting out the teething problems of being first time through, waiting for his camera, sound and vision engineers to fully understand the capabilities, limitations and tolerances of the technology, our Shepherd was supposed to be prepping and getting ready for Episodes 3 and 4, while Keith Washington was getting ready to take on Episodes 5 and 6. Our schedule depended on each pair of episodes finishing within their allocated week, to release cast and facilities for the following shoot. It was a challenge that we would face for twenty-one years, but in those early weeks of misplaced confidence we allowed just five days extra for Chris to hit teething problems. Which he did, and his two weeks started to extend to three, which meant the shoots collided at times, resulting in constant rescheduling, symbolised by the fact that the furniture van scheduled for one day's hire was still sitting on The Close six weeks later, waiting to shoot the arrival of the Collins family. It cost a small fortune, on top of which the inexperienced design crew then destroyed the company's real signage when they stripped off the fictional name. We had to pay for it to be redone, and by the time the 'one-day shoot' was completed, I could have bought the blasted thing. Elsewhere the shoot was falling behind because, well, The Shepherd was going AWOL, and when he was found he was taking an eternity to shoot anything.

It all came to a head one night when Colin McKeown and I got back to The Close late, having been off somewhere like visiting Sony in Basingstoke, to discover the neighbourhood still lit up and the shoot still going on hours past the set wrap time. We had promised the neighbours we would not be doing this without advance notice. Our Head of Cameras, Tony Caveen, spotted us and came hurrying over in a bit of a flap, saying he could not operate with 'this man'. He didn't know what he wanted and was incapable of giving clear instructions, was the gist of it. They'd been at this one shot for four hours now. Tony was a mild-mannered and gentle person, and for him to be in such a state of frustration, something must be seriously wrong. They were just getting ready to go for another take, so Tony hurried back.

We ambled over and found The Shepherd crouched down on the pavement, his long gangling legs folded like a praying mantis's, holding the camera monitor between his knees. He waved one arm grandly. Roll tape. Action. It was supposed to be a simple shot of Heather Huntington (Mandy Burton) arriving home in her Citroën 2CV, round the corner, up on to her driveway, lock car and go into house. It looked fine to the naked eye, but this was night and these were tube cameras. New technology or not, they couldn't cope with moving images in low light, and if you poured in a lot of light, the reflections from glass and chrome would produce hot spots and streaks on the recording.

As the car passed I noticed three things. One, it was practically covered in black gaffer tape, to mask out the reflective edges and try and resolve hotspots. This must have taken an hour or two to achieve. Two, watching the monitor, I immediately saw the reason for Tony's concern. All we were getting was white lights, the approaching headlights, traversing the frame, which then disappeared, to be replaced by two receding red lights, joined by a flashing orange one. The red lights suddenly grew brighter, then they all disappeared, and after a second or two a yellow light appeared top right-hand corner. Heather was home and had turned on the hall light. As an art-house experiment it was brilliant in its simplicity. As a piece of drama it was not going to win us any awards. However, the third thing I noticed was that The Shepherd was not even watching the monitor. He appeared to be asleep.

It was only after the floor manager asked him if he was happy with the take that he stirred and called 'Cut', then turned to Tony. How was it for you? Tony looked at Colin and me. Colin looked at me. I looked at The Shepherd. He was somewhere else. That's a wrap, I said. Tell everyone to go home; we'll regroup in the morning.

Colin went off to pacify, cajole and sympathise with the crews over the wasted effort, and time, while I went back to the office, pondering what to do next. Ever since Susi had first introduced me to our 'experienced director' in Teddington, I had had nagging doubts. These stemmed primarily from the fact that I'd noticed he carried a bottle of vodka in his briefcase. Was he another casualty of the sea-of-white-wine culture? I'd mentioned it to her at the time and asked if she knew whether he had a drink problem. She'd said she felt confident that he didn't but would check, later coming back to tell me it was a gift for someone else. He took us all in as eventually we found out he often used to carry these 'gifts' around with him, but on that night there was nothing concrete to go on.

Soon, though, the problems started to escalate and as his shoot fell further and further behind it was impacting on everyone. Finally we got him through his schedule but the real nightmare emerged from the edit suite when the senior editor, Ian Weston, came to find me. Equally mild-mannered and gentle as Tony Caveen, Ian now echoed his frustration. They didn't like having to come and say this, but they couldn't work with The Shepherd either. He couldn't make a coherent decision, and what he had already shot was rubbish. With the full realisation of what this meant, I went up to edit to have a look and, sure enough, although we could see who was on screen, most of the time, it was, well, rubbish. I thanked them and made the first of many of those lonely walks of leadership, back to the office to look at the production schedule.

We were now only four weeks away from transmission. I didn't have one completed episode and had just lost most of Episodes 2 and 3. These were supposed to be our chance to introduce and emotionally set up the Collins family: show how they were coping with enforced downsizing and would represent our middle-class demographic. But The Shepherd had not shot any of their scenes. Worse, the actors were now tied up with Keith Washington's shoot and if I pulled that to re-do their scenes, it would compromise the next pair and cascade forward. All eyes were on me. Expectant.

I said we'd carry on as best we could next week but I would take the scripts and have a think about what to do. While everyone went off for the weekend, I stayed on in the office, put Kim Carnes' album *Mistaken Identity* on the sound system, and with 'Bette Davis Eyes' on full volume, started editing the scripts. After I had done that, I went into the Production Office, prepared a new production schedule and sat on the floor, constantly shuffling the scenes back and forth across the week. If we did all Grants one day, then the Collinses, then the Taylors . . . but they're needed together at that location, which will take them out for a morning and we can only get it for Tuesday . . . but we also need them on Thursday . . . but we can't have the school then, only Wednesday . . . Round and round I went, trying to marry the logistics. An experienced production manager might have made shorter work of it or else come to the conclusion earlier that it couldn't be done. But what I had, which no production manager ever would have, was the ability to put a pen straight through the problem. I was, I realised, back to feeling the same frustration as being a writer on a series when the preceding or following script changes impacted on your own. What I was able to do on the floor of that Production Office was pick up all the scripts and change them, to make them work. No reason why that bit of information couldn't occur there instead of there . . . or Sheila tells Sharon instead of Bobby. This later turned out to be another of my guiding mantras: the public never know what you originally intended. They judge only by what they see. I stayed at this process right through from Saturday afternoon to Monday morning, without sleep, and then had to convince everybody it would work.

Initially there was astonishment that the entire week's schedule had been torn up and reorganised, with astonishment turning to disbelief at what I was asking them to do. I had reduced the Collinses to a minimum and rewritten more scenes for the Grants, which meant we had to pick up the shoot speed from the planned twelve minutes a day to something like fifteen, and one day needing to pick up twenty-seven minutes of the Grants, as that was the only day I could find to get them all together. Of course they all had to go off for a witter and examine what I had done, while I went into a huge row with GHPM. Why didn't you call me to do this? You were in London. I could have come back. Not in time. And you wouldn't, and couldn't, have rewritten the scripts. This is my job. No, your job means being out there, stopping us from getting into this position!

The biggest problem, though, was who would direct, as by now The Shepherd was known for falling asleep on set between takes and for going missing from location. It was too late to get anyone else in and no one on set had the necessary golden ACTT ticket. We don't need to worry about that, I said, just get him on the floor and he'll direct. I'll be there to make sure he does.

And that was how I ended up lying on the floor at the knees of Sue Johnston and Ricky Tomlinson as they went through a typical family scene, sitting on the settee watching the telly while the kids went back and forth delivering dialogue. Whenever I saw Sue and Ricky in *The Royle Family* in later years, it always brought back this early day in *Brookie*'s development. I had the camera on one side of me and The Shepherd on the other, getting closer and closer as the day wore on, until I practically had him in a headlock, pinning him down so he couldn't disappear off set. I'd given everyone the scripts and they knew what to do. All I had to do was get him to direct. 'Say "Roll Tape". Now . . . "Action". Say "Cut".' And he did. All day until we got that twenty-seven minutes I needed — a record that was never beaten, and not something I ever wanted to do again. We always knew, though, that if we were ever in a hole, shooting in the Grants' house would get us out of it.

Despite Sue's power as an actor coming through that day, the drama was a bit flat, but the chemistry between her, Ricky and the kids lifted it. The Collinses' characterisations, on the other hand, suffered throughout, from not having enough time spent on their set ups, and probably never actually recovered from this. There was too much focus on the Grants initially, which resulted in the programme becoming skewed towards them. This was something writers, actors, crews and critics reinforced by building upon what they perceived to be the focal point of the programme. It took a while to correct this but we got some powerful drama on the way, and I experienced once again how wrong academics and critics can be in their interpretations of a drama's intent. While some viewed what they saw as a harsh, gritty and realistic updating of *Corrie*'s 1960s portrayal of working-class life, I was as frustrated as Tony Caveen that my balanced representation of the changing nature of Britain's social issues had been scuppered by someone with a social issue and, in doing so, brought me into direct conflict with the ACTT. Still, the production was back on track.

We soon learned that a delegation from the ACTT London HQ would be visiting the site to look into working practices, manning levels, and that I had been 'reported' for directing on the programme. This sent a bit of a tremor round the place as, like employing an actor without an Equity card, directing without the ACTT director's ticket was a 'blacking' issue.

I asked security to intercept the main ACTT representative and ask him to come and see me when 'the delegates' arrived. I then welcomed him to the site and said I had heard they had a few concerns. Despite our past cordial relations he went into official mode so I knew we were now in their sights as one of Margaret Thatcher's 'Trojan Horses', as they referred to the independent sector.

He started talking about our not having any agreed manning levels and I repeated our mantra. We only crew to the level required by the technology and needs of the shoot, one of which was safety. He looked at me. Too many people in too small a space with all the cabling can be dangerous, I explained. This didn't carry as much weight as it would in today's H&S society, but it bought us both time to consider the next item: working practices. It had come to their notice that certain grades were doing other grades' jobs. Like what? A maintenance engineer was known to be operating the VT machines and, as I knew full well, they were two separate grades.

I did indeed know, just as I knew that the VT Operator on our 1-inch machines was nothing like the VT Operator in the bowels of the BBC or Granada or LWT or ATV, which is what the ACTT Agreement covered. The broadcasters were still operating 2-inch machines that needed a lot more engineering input than ours. I also knew that our VT operator had complained from day one about doing the 'most boring job on earth', which, basically, consisted of loading a tape at the beginning of the day then sitting on a stool with a clipboard in front of our recording machine and pressing Record when the director called 'Roll Tape'. He would then write down the timecode. When the director called 'Cut', he had to press Stop, then write down that timecode. At the end of the day he would unload the tape and hand the clipboard sheet to the PA. That was it.

Within days a request had come in for someone else to do this while the VT operator got on with something useful. No. That's your union agreement and we are not going to break it, he was told. Eventually the engineers came back with a plan. Could they put a small workbench close to the VT machines so that, while waiting for the five minutes of magic, the VT operator could get on with a bit of routine maintenance? I said, fine, so long as you police it yourselves. This was what the union was now here to investigate.

I ran through the history of it all, ending on a line about it seeming to be offering more job satisfaction, whereupon the full union-speak came out and I got a mini-lecture, complete with a finger stabbing the desk to make the point about 'job satisfaction being a tool of capitalist oppression'. If this was meant to provoke a reaction, it did, as I could feel the post-Marxist sociologist in me starting to emerge. So, I asked him, what would he prefer? That we all got back into the dark satanic mills in case we started actually enjoying what we did? Should we go outside and tell them that? He probably realised he'd pressed the wrong button and said he didn't want to get into meaningless debate as there was something else far more serious which he had to investigate. Which was? Something that made everything else 'pale into insignificance and could bring the company to its knees'. I still remember the exact phrase. By now the Scouser was pushing the sociologist to one side. And what's that? I challenged. The fact that one of your members put every other member's job here at risk? By being unfit for work on set, not having a clue where he was, never mind being able to do the job that your director's ticket is supposed to guarantee he can do. Is that it? Is that the principle and dignity of labour we are going to fight over?

He hesitated for a moment. Did you direct? No. I was told you did. I stood on the set one day and told them to shoot the scene when your member walked away. I then supervised him on another day. What does that mean? I made him do the job I am paying him to do. The union man hesitated again. And I'd do it again to protect both the company and the jobs of your members, I told him. I then gave *him* a mini-lecture. There was nothing he or any of the others could tell me about the trades union movement, or why it had not helped and supported Ricky Tomlinson and Des Warren, or indeed done anything to prevent my own dad being made redundant not so long ago. I reminded him where we were, and why we were here. This was not Teddington or Elstree or the South Bank of the Thames. Nor was it Soho Square where his union had its head-quarters. He and the union couldn't promote the benefits, rewards and authority of a closed shop if they were not going to accept the responsibility for policing it. With power comes responsibility. He pondered all this for a moment and then nodded and said he had better take it up with the local shop. Off he went, as did the issue. We moved on. Things became cordial again.

The only other major clash with the unions also came early on and was a residual result of The Emperor 'not undercutting' the unions' speech. After having to arbitrate in the cultural clash between London's brown rice and seaweed activists and the massed ranks of the crews demanding chips and beans, arguments over portion size and whether there should or should not be smoking in the canteen, Christmas brought something else NATTKE had warned me about: not running our own canteen. Our first 'chef' had his own mantra: a couple of bricks and an oil drum, and I can feed an army. With an alleged military background, he was obviously used to adopting the scavenger mentality, which was why he scavenged the takings from the till along with the 'Christmas Club' money people had been giving him to buy them cheap booze. He was also obviously used to retreating under cover of darkness because one morning he just didn't turn up and was, as far as I am aware, never seen or heard from again. Neither was our or the staff's cash. This seemed the time to accept that NATTKE had been right. This was also, from their point of view, another concession – the relaxation of their strict 'no sub-contracting' stance.

However, that was before The Emperor had issued his decree. This was now. Well, it was now, then, if you know what I mean. If then was now, there wouldn't even be an issue, but the now then was that, despite the early concessions, everything now came under the 'sorry, Phil' phone-call protocol. No undercutting meant no sub-contracting.

The real problem was not with the national union officials, it never was, but rather with some of the idealistic, well-intentioned but perhaps naive recent students who were now working for us but still caught up in 'the workers' struggle against Thatcherism'. One such armchair warrior decided to take up the cause of the canteen staff who might, just might, face the remote possibility of not having their jobs transferred to any new operator.

Despite the shoot carrying on as though nothing was happening, we found ourselves losing more and more time to something akin to *The Young Ones* or 'The Famous Five Do Industrial Relations', to the extent that they had wound the national officers up to the point of considering a national instruction to strike. This caused genuine concern to the staff, as people's natural tendency is not to break ranks or go against the principles of their union's closed shop. If they did, they would have their union card withdrawn. And with that went the right to work elsewhere.

Our hero of the class struggle was the same one who once left a note under Personnel's door at 8.00 one night, after everyone had gone home, informing them that he had called a strike for first thing the following morning. Attached to it was a holiday claim form, for the following day, as he was going to London to join a demonstration about cuts to the education budget there. Needless to say, none of his comrades joined in the class struggle to bring our bastion of capitalist oppression to its knees the following morning. Or the morning after. But it did give me the impetus I needed to call the national union official direct. I tracked him down to a union conference in Jersey.

I asked him if it was right that if I now went the route they'd advised me to go in the first place, and did not get rid of but guaranteed jobs by transferring them to someone else who could provide better training and job prospects, then they would call a strike that would jeopardise everyone's jobs? The reply was that the original advice was private, off the record. But it won't stay off the record long, I replied. You've got to understand, Phil; if we let you do it, all the ITV companies might do it as you operate the same agreements. I asked if he was serious. Did he really think Granada or LWT or Thames would risk their ad revenue because we got someone in to sell sandwiches? He said it was all about precedent, I must understand that. I said I did, but that he had to be careful not to set a precedent by putting a gun to my head unless he was fully prepared to pull the trigger. Meaning? Meaning that there is one person here who will never have to worry about where his next job will come from, as I don't need your union card. I worked long and hard to get to where I am, but I can walk away. There is no one else I need to consult or ballot. Just me. I believe what I am doing is right. I believe the people working here think it's right, apart from one clown . . . your shop steward. I understand that you must do what you think you should do, but I'd suggest you get up here and talk to people first. A pause for consideration. Then: OK, but I'm in Jersey at a conference. I know, I replied, but I think we can wait. Honest.

By the time he arrived the classic cooling off period had happened naturally. We worked out the sub-contracting arrangements and all moved on. There were no further major issues with the unions as I think a few things had become clear. One was that while I was discovering how lonely leadership can be in facing up to strong unions, I was also learning that most potential industrial relations issues have at their root either personnel matters, like our gardener's domestic problems, or things not being managed properly. Another was that I swore never, ever to get involved in the canteen again. A promise I kept for twenty-five years. Above all, though, I was on a fast track to understanding that management is not too dissimilar from walking the streets of Huyton. If you show weakness before the herd, you become vulnerable. If you don't protect the vulnerable, you become more vulnerable. In Scouse, if you don't take out the clown, you become the clown. I was learning that management is about more than pure logic. It is about how you interpret life. It's not about rules and regulations but arbitration, collaboration. With a bit of *Respice Finem*, or else.

In the end, though, it always seems to come down to car parks, toilets and canteens.

Nothing demonstrates this better than the smoking ban I implemented. Alcohol was never allowed since I'd already witnessed too many liquid lunches with characters like Dennis Vance. While I have always been an anti-smoking zealot, perhaps because I'd seen so many aunts and uncles ravaged by its effects, as so many of my generation did, I initially agreed to allow it, but not inside the set houses, offices, or downstairs in the canteen near the food. Eventually tensions rose to the point of a fistfight between one of our senior technicians and a soon-to-be-household name who refused to stop smoking near the food. It was finally outlawed when the actors, quite rightly, refused to sit amongst the sea of cigarette butts that littered the gardens. We had to bring in the entire Design Department on overtime one weekend to clean them up.

Tensions such as these have to be managed, but it is rarely as simple as instigating a workplace rule when dealing with a social issue about addiction. Even recognising this may not be enough as we found later, after carving out 'various smokers' enclaves' on our new 13-acre, 80,000-square-feet production base. A non-smokers' delegation demanded the same terms and conditions as 'the addicts': a five-minute break every hour and designated 'non-smokers only' areas. Fortunately, by then we had the European Court of Human Rights and it was illegal for us to discriminate in this way. In other words, management is about managing what you have. And as the shoot progressed it became more and more clear that we were not managing as well as we should be.

We did not have robust management systems in place to stop things drifting or being derailed by the 'I just thought . . .' mentality. We were wasting too much time and too many resources on things that shouldn't have happened or should have been obvious. The canteen was like a London bistro, with a healthy salad bar and vegetarian options, but the crews just wanted pies and chips to maintain their energy levels; more food was going though the canteen than was being eaten, and the cash return appeared less than expected, which NATTKE had warned me would be the case; we were hiring dollies and cranes we couldn't physically use in the houses; a taxi account had been opened and was already being abused. But perhaps the daftest example of all was that after having gone to all the trouble and effort to design the site to save labour time and cost in rigging and derigging cables, we were now losing hours a day manhandling furniture in and out of the houses. This was partly to do with some of the furniture chosen being too big for the rooms, but mainly to do with the fact that each director wanted it all rearranged to suit his or her particular shot. This had two consequences. One was that every time we saw one of the characters' living rooms, all the furniture was in a different place. It was totally disorientating. One episode would have the Grants watching the telly facing the window; the next they would have their backs to the window.

This impacted on the TV mantra of 'time is money'. The more hours we lost faffing about like this the less we shot and the further behind we fell. The call immediately went up for more people to handle the workload. It always does. Because that's the easy option. But the plan had always been for a freelance designer, Leigh Malone, another find from the *Grange Hill* movie project, to set the design in place and then leave it for our own in-house designer, Carol Shearon, to maintain. I had expected that, as in the real world, once the characters had set out their furniture the way they liked it, it would stay in one place until the next major makeover. No one moves their furniture every day. Not even, I suspect, TV directors. There was an easy solution in the end. A photograph and floor-plan was pinned to the wall in every house. This is how it is to look.

These kinds of things might not sound much coming off the page, but they are all simply examples of the bigger 'I just thought . . .' problem. It is incredibly hard to get bright, intelligent and committed people simply to just go along with things. They all want to try and improve them, but as each new person joins the process they run the risk of negating all the work and creative input that has already gone into the project. It's exactly the same problem as people fiddling with, amending or adding to scripts once they're signed off for production. The other example I used to give, when people tried to dismiss what we and the other soaps did as 'simply production lines', was to say that, yes, it was a production line but it depends which factory you are standing in. You could be making Ford Fiestas or Aston Martins. What you didn't want was someone deciding a Fiesta radiator grille would look great on an Aston, or vice versa. The challenge was to build production systems that let people feel engaged, but focused on what they had to do within and for that system. But no more improvements, please. No constantly looking for a better 'angle'.

The biggest priority, though, was budgetary control, and I was feeling more and more nervous that GHPM was not coping with the scale and speed of both the shoot and the company's development. This was not, as I kept emphasising, a six-week film shoot. We needed the sort of constant cost-control monitoring I had been used to providing as a QS, and which was part of C4's contractual requirements. While they had given us a bit of leeway as we had gone through the setting-up period, now that we were in production it would become more critical for us all. The one thing I wanted to avoid was the curse of the building trade: historical accounting. The financial state your project or business was in four weeks ago. I wanted to know exactly when someone committed us to expenditure, not when the bill was due. Above all, I wanted the right person to make the right cost decision.

I had already been caught out like this myself when I took a phone call from GHPM who was in London and had found the 'perfect' meeting-room table. It was a bargain and on sale in Heal's. Could they buy it? Fine. Great. If you think it's right . . . It was a nice table but it wasn't right. The veneer scratched every time you threw a file on it and the accompanying chairs turned out to be suedette mock-Bauhaus. It was the wrong choice and I had been the wrong person to say 'fine'. My head was elsewhere, the QS bit fretting about the critical path analyses. I also knew we needed more professional advice.

I took the example of the table and chairs to Arthur Andersen, one of the biggest and most respected accountancy firms in the world until they collapsed under the weight of the Enron scandal — proving the point that no matter how big or robust you think your internal management systems are, people can always get round them and crash the company. However, at the time they were the model of sobriety and financial acumen, with the arrogance to match. Leon fixed an appointment for me to meet their two senior northern partners, John Milbourn and Eric Kilby, at their Liverpool offices in one of the city's finest Art Deco buildings, Martins Bank Chambers. Into this financial temple I went, in my jeans, trainers and American football shirt, to meet these two suits: one sharp and cutting, Eric; the other a bit more relaxed and comfy, John.

I told them what I wanted: a full systems review from top to bottom. Proper project management, live financial monitoring and responsibility accounting. I did not want to be told I'd gone bust four weeks earlier, and I wanted everyone who could commit the company to expenditure to be aware of the full implications, by actually being responsible for controlling their own budget and cost-centre. Unlike the BBC and ITV, when we spent a pound it was gone. There were no other budgets to re-assign. We talked a bit, and they probed a bit more about what I was doing, and I had to go through the whole process again of explaining that C4 was a wholly owned subsidiary of the IBA; it would commission, not produce programmes; it would be funded by advertising, but would not sell the ad-space; that would be done by ITV who would have no control over the programme content or schedule but would be taxed by government to give a subvention to Channel 4.

They exchanged looks. You say ITV pays for this channel, sells ads on it but has no control over the content? Yes. Then how can they be sure they will get a fair return against the subscription tax the government is taking? No wonder AA were rated one of the best firms of accountants. They can't, I said. But that's like asking John Lewis to build a corner shop next door, then provide the finance for someone else to buy, manufacture and sell merchandise that they don't like or which could compete with their own products. They were good. It's lunacy, said Eric. It's culture, said John. I liked them both.

We then agreed that they would send someone in to review everything and come up with a report for me based on the principle of responsibility accounting. The next step was telling everyone back at base. GHPM was not too keen, seeing it as a direct reflection on their own ability. Which it was. What do they know about running a television company? Who are they anyway? Oh, only one of the biggest accountancy firms in the world. What'll they actually do? Come and talk. Watch, listen, and make recommendations. And we have no say in this? No. Well, I guess it's happening then, isn't it? Definitely.

While Author Andersen started the preparations for their review, the shoot was staggering on and the management machinations were unfolding, something else was starting to consume a lot of time, or cause me to lose a lot of sleep: the *Brookside* titles. While searching for the visual idea, I started working with a pair of musicians called Dave Roylance and Steve Wright. TV was the new rock 'n' roll, and if you were to be taken seriously in rock 'n' roll then you had to go to Strawberry Studios, originally set up by the legendary 10cc, and where all four of their albums, and eight top-ten singles, including their biggest, 'I'm Not In Love', were recorded. So we went. As did Joy Division, The Stone Roses, OMD, Happy Mondays, The Smiths, Simply Red and Saint Winifred's School Choir. Apparently Paul McCartney and his brother Mike also recorded an album there back in the 1970s, so anyone wanting to be taken seriously in northern music had to go there. We had used Amazon Studios in Kirkby for some of the background music, but for the theme we had to be seriously grown-up.

Not only that, but we had Mike Timoni working with us, who, I had been told excitedly by the musos, had put that extraordinary synthesiser sound on 'I'm Not In Love'. He was a fantastic session musician. After the day's shoot was finished, and once I'd viewed tapes, attended post-mortems and re-scheduling meetings, I'd get in the car about 11 p.m. and drive over to Strawberry to spend a few hours there before heading home. It was just brilliant sitting and listening to Mike demonstrate the real art of playing a synthesiser. He would play a string section as most synth players did, which sounded passable. He would then play it his way, putting in false finger slides. For wind instruments he'd put in false breathing pauses, so that it was extremely difficult to differentiate between his synth and a real orchestral section.

It seemed to take for ever, probably about two months, to build up the theme as it evolved along with the scripts and early production process. It was probably not the most efficient way to put it together, but it was great fun. Finally, in true rock 'n' roll style, we sat in the car park at Strawberry and played the multi-tracked production through the car cassette player, to hear what it sounded like through a domestic speaker. This was the same trick our sound engineers employed after completing the final programme sound-dub, to make sure it would still sound great through a domestic television. The music sounded brilliant then, on the way home in the car, and for every one of the 2,932 episodes over the following twenty-one years. Music's power rests in its ability to conjure up memories and emotions of when you first heard it, or being part of some memorable moment in your life. That piece of music encapsulates so much of what went on in my life around this time, and how *Brookie* changed it completely – which was why I later chose it as one of my eight pieces of music on *Desert Island Discs*.

The title sequence itself came to me while driving back and forth to Stockport on the motorway. I used to think how the look and feel of the country was being changed by these strips of concrete and tarmac that were helping to speed things up, increasing not just the pace of traffic, but also the knowledge exchange that goes with allowing people to move around quicker, to meet and swap ideas. They were part of the developing communications grid, a concrete and tarmac variant of the wire ribbons found inside computers, joining all the components together. I would never have been able to put *County Hall* together, let alone *Brookside*, without these ribbons allowing access to almost anywhere in the country within a few hours. Well, within a few hours of London – something else that hasn't really changed in thirty years.

What occurred to me was that we were slowly losing sight of the countryside between our towns and cities, dropping into motorway cuttings or shielded by sound or safety barriers. Leaving one town or city, you would find yourself on a tarmac and concrete ribbon that would deliver you into the heart of the next town or city where you would pick up the suburbs and supermarkets and gradually melding high streets of wall-to-wall Boots and McDonald's and building societies and banks and, eventually, phone shops and opticians. Disappearing were the occasional views of cows grazing and farmers gathering, the trees and fields and ponds of our green and pleasant land. It was becoming too easy to slide into the mindset that the country was being concreted over. That before long there would be no space left between cities, just one huge urban sprawl. Even today, when around 50 per cent of people live in cities, the corollary is that 50 per cent do not. They live in the 70 per cent of our land mass not covered in concrete and tarmac. From these late-night musings came the idea of using the title sequence to show exactly where Brookside was located. In Liverpool. In the suburbs. And not in the kind of terraced streets I saw back in Stockport, which were still reminiscent of *Coronation Street*'s title sequence.

So, in a world before Health & Safety, Colin, cameraman Ken Horn and myself all hung on to each other while sheltering from a gale-force wind on top of St John's Tower, Liverpool, now home to Radio City. From this high vantage point we shot *Brookie*'s title sequence with its views of the river and city centre. It took a while trying to work out the best position to prevent the wind from buffeting the camera during the pulls and pans, but eventually we got it and survived. We then went in search of the linking shot from city centre to the suburbs, looking down on to a busy road junction, taken from a third-floor council flat in Tuebrook. It was easy in those days. If you had a camera on your shoulder, you could knock on someone's door and ask to shoot out of their window. As in my QS days, provided you weren't 'from the Council' you'd more often than not be offered a cup of tea. As TV expanded and the city became a hub for TV production, it wasn't long before those in prime locations practically had a rate card pinned behind their door. So much for the BBC, twice as much for ITV, but *Brookie* always got a discount. Today you'd have to show a full risk assessment and insurance indemnity cover too. And so you should, to stop madmen like us from climbing on your roof and being blown off in a Force 8 gale. But we got our title sequence to go with our music.

Along with my title sequence I also had my systems review. The guy from Arthur Andersen had duly arrived, talked, watched, listened and was bamboozled. Upon seeing his report, it was clear to me he had fallen hook, line and sinker for the traditional view that television and film, especially film as we were closer to that with our single-camera shooting, was somehow different from any other industry in the world. That it was so fast-moving, and subject to so many vagaries like the weather, that traditional systems and procedures couldn't work in it. How could you give inexperienced people a budget when that budget had to be manipulated daily to get through the schedule? It worked only if budgetary control was held by one experienced person, who could look right across the whole project. As I read on, I could hear the voice that must have dictated these passages . . . something confirmed when GHPM popped in to ask if I had read the AA report too.

I said I had – and called the AA double act. I told them: one, the report was supposed to come to me, no one else. Two, it is not objective. Three, send me someone else, with a brain. Four, you are paying. We agreed a new strategy. They would go back and start the process again but this time report direct to me.

While AA went off to find a brain, I began to think through what this was all going to mean. Changing the way you do things in business often means changing personnel. Just as Susi Hush had had difficulty coming to terms with a new way of approaching production, the two people most likely to be affected would be GHPM and the current Financial Controller – a legacy of my early chat with Justin Dukes about finding someone solid who would manage the financial reporting for C4.

Recruited with the help of David Scott he was indeed solid, but not much else. Our chosen candidate soon earned himself the Scouse nickname of Fish, because as a devout Christian he wore the silver fish symbol on his suit lapel. While he did seem competent enough to pull together the monthly reporting pack, his wider management and political skills soon came under scrutiny. Once in the middle of a management meeting I turned to him to ask how things were going, meaning with the budget. It seemed like a reasonable question to ask your accounts manager, but instead I got a ten-minute rundown on how his family, health, the kids' schools and their holiday plans were going. Another time he asked to come in and see me. Got your car keys handy, Phil? Er, yeah, why? Just popping over to the bank and thought I'd see what it was like. My car? Well, it is a company car, isn't it? Er, yes, but I own the company. Ah. Yes, ah, indeed.

Life, perhaps moving in curious ways, often throws up solutions to what appear intractable problems. I was beginning to fret about how I would handle the now expected ramifications of the next AA review. As soon as they arrived Fish probably knew he was heading for the departure lounge as even the first aborted report had flagged up the weaknesses in financial controls. After all the early turbulence created by the departure of the first potential FD and the Susi Hush débâcle, I had decided to make the current team directors and give them a small percentage of any secondary income the programme might generate. It was also a legacy of the years of collective bargaining and a desire for a more collegiate and consensual management style. The one that was now under review.

Some of this was playing at the back of my mind during a

particularly long and late-night management meeting when we were trying to address the perennial issue of lack of space. We had totally underestimated the number of people we would actually need and how much space they would require. The joke round the office was that you always ended up sitting on someone else's knee, it was just that you couldn't get to choose who. Susi would never have coped. We had cut and diced, carved up and partitioned every space we could, until there was only one area left as originally planned: my office, always meant to double up as a boardroom, meeting and entertaining space. My desk was now the recycled Heal's dining table, and we used the chairs for meetings. Around 1 a.m. I gave in to the recommendation that we should subdivide it. The needs of the production had to come first. It was only when I was driving back in the next morning after a couple of hours' sleep that I started to think about that decision. It was daft. We had to have somewhere to hold meetings meet and greet, conduct confidential conversations with C4. And, above all, it was my company. I was *not* going to be stuck in a cupboard.

When I got to the office I sent word that it was to stay as it was, we would find another solution, and went off to the shoot. The solution I had in mind was to buy another of the one-bedroomed flats being built adjacent to the site. Around lunchtime HoP came to see me, more concerned than he had been about the gardener. Er, I thought you should know that GHPM is organising an emergency management meeting at the end of the shoot. I was puzzled. What does that mean? He went on: the directors are going to ask you to step down as chairman of the company as, apparently, your overriding last night's decision has not gone down too well, especially coming, well, after the AA report was forced upon us all. I was now becoming irritated. And who is 'all'? Er, the company directors. Of which you are one? Well, yes, but I think it should be debated properly. From memory, I then went in search of Colin and found him perched, as so often, on the wall at the end of The Close talking to someone. They must have seen my body language as whoever it was scooted off and Colin immediately said he was going to warn me. When? Look, it's all daft. I know that. You know that. But they need to be told its daft. Great Scouse logic. It just needs to be talked about, he added. I assured him it would be.

I then called Leon. They'll probably be trying to invoke Section

184 of the 1948 Companies Act that gives the directors the right to remove any other director, including the chairman, if he is acting unreasonably, he explained. For wanting to keep my office? Well, it does seem a bit thin, he agreed. Whose idea was it to make them company directors anyway, Leon? I think it was yours, Phil. Part of your collegiate approach, I think. Like the canteen you mean? Well . . . He left it unsaid. I knew. I had been warned. But what should I do this time?

He ran me through everything I should prepare for, and when the appointed time arrived, in they all shuffled, including Colin and Fish, who was carrying a couple of legal tomes, including a copy of *Butterworth's Guide to the 1948 Companies Act*. They all perched at one end of the room. I stayed behind my desk. Symbolic. We usually congregated around the desk, or rather the too-expensive Heal's dining table. But collegiately.

Let's hear it then, I opened. GHPM said it was becoming intolerable if not impossible for them to function if I kept overriding their decisions. Even if they are daft? I asked. Then it came. From GHPM. The Arthur Andersen report clearly said that I should be running the company. Only because you told them that, I replied, and looked to the others. HoP repeated his earlier line, hesitantly, under the icy stare of GHPM, that things needed to be discussed. Colin agreed. Fish claimed to be there as Company Secretary, holding up his copy of *Butterworth*. I interpreted this as a plea for impartiality but such fence-sitting did not seem to go down well with GHPM. It was coming down to a one-on-one. After a physical nudge, Fish gave the obviously prepared line. Having been asked by the directors, I have confirmed that under the Companies Act the Directors do have the power to remove you as chairman of the company. Really? I asked. One defiant stare in response. GHPM. One academically curious. HoP. One oblivious. Fish. And Colin, looking almost apologetic.

People close to me tell me that they know when I am about to 'go off on one' as my top lip tightens. It was probably very tight right then, as I gestured toward Fish's pile of tomes. Turn to the section about shareholder rights. Puzzled looks. Fish thumbed through, found it and started to read, to himself. Eyes were now darting back and forth. Their turn to be puzzled. Does it not say that the shareholders can remove the directors? I prompted. And that the shareholders' views and wishes are paramount as – my voice rising now — *they* own the flamin' company? Shocked looks. Well? Well, yes, Fish confirmed. So consider yourselves all removed. Whether you have jobs is something else again. Do you want to get out of my, unpartitioned, office . . . now?

Well, the last two lines are the sort that always come to you later. The kind of thing you wished you had said, but when writing a script realise is unnecessary. Never over-dramatise an already dramatic situation. As soon as they realised what they had just walked into, the emergency meeting ended. Nothing more to say, is there? asked GHPM. I shook my head and they all shuffled out. Then I reached for the phone. Leon was waiting to hear how it had gone. As you predicted, I told him. What will you do now? Not sure, except I know one thing. What? The hippy school of management has just gone out the window.

Driving home that night, as the night before, to an empty house and a half-finished kitchen, my emotions were flipping back and forth from outright anger to anxiety. Anger with them for doing it; anxiety that I had not listened properly. Anger that I didn't see it coming; anxiety about our future relationships. By the time I got home and discovered the kitchen fitters had put the cooker hood too low, I knew that things would never be the same after the failed palace coup. The obvious and dramatic thing would have been to ask them all to go, but not the pragmatic response. I'm not sure I ever sat down and thought deeply about it but my instincts told me that it would create even more turmoil. Not just with C4 but within the company. I was still dancing with the unions and it was not that long ago since the *Sunday Times* had run their 'chaos at *Brookside*' piece, the main thrust of which was that I was an egomaniac refusing to listen to anyone. It would be a great follow up if I then cleared out my management team. Like all coups there had to be a ring leader and I knew who that was. HoP had tipped me off, so that guaranteed survival. Fish had probably just been bullied into providing info while Colin, well, he had given me the Scouse line, when asked. Unfortunately, while folk can pass the two-second, seven-second test that is not to say they won't let you down. You may like someone but not agree with their actions. And, they had all let it happen. I couldn't get past that. No matter how pragmatic I was about the loneliness of leadership; no matter whether I felt it belonged more in a Shakespearian play or not, loyalty mattered.

But to make a business work you do have to be pragmatic. Be aware of people's strengths, their weaknesses, their fallibilities, as much as their capabilities. Occasionally their indiscretions. You can forgive those. But never forget. I never did. However, I had to move on and the other thing in my mind was that it had happened behind closed doors and the only people who knew were us, and Leon. I probably rationalised it as a problem but something I need not address now, so they were stripped of rank and returned to their day jobs. What was needed 'right now' was reading and editing the next batch of scripts; agreeing to the location of the telephone exchange upgrade; the four-page list of production queries like can they change Annabelle Collins's dress as Doreen Sloane doesn't like stripes, or can they get extra security while shooting on a council estate known locally as Cannibal Farm; and could I get in about 7 a.m. to look at the final edit so we could get the first episodes down to C4? It was 2 a.m. I would be back at work by 7 a.m., which meant, above all else, I now had to mark out exactly where I wanted the cooker hood so the kitchen guys could get it right this time.

Arthur Anderson had also been busy and I got a call to ask if they could bring someone over to meet me. The meeting was set for around 6 p.m. as whoever it was, was working on another job and would need time to get there. It was of course the future Mrs Redmond, something not even suspected by either of us for quite a number of years.

Alexis always says I kept her waiting for forty-five minutes the first time she visited *Brookside*, with the most interesting thing being how she couldn't understand why her line manager, not known for his patience, was happy to sit and watch the comings and goings as the shoot reached its usual end-of-day frenzy, and production sched-ules were updated and call times worked out and given for the following day. I was probably caught up in some crisis or other so by the time I finally got to meet Alexis she had formed the impres-sion from the photographs hanging on the wall in reception that she was about to meet a fifty-something arty type with a bushy beard. She was both irritated and annoyed that instead all she got was some assistant – me. (She had been looking at a photograph of David Rose from the signing ceremony.) However, we seemed to pass each other's two-second, seven-second test and I ran her through what I wanted this time, stressing what I hadn't got from the first report. She just nodded and said it sounded very similar to other industries, like advertising electronics and pharmaceuticals, which I took to mean they too had their fair share of creative primadonnas. She got it.

After an hour or so we shook hands and I hardly saw her again for a few weeks except from a distance. I would occasionally notice her going from office to office to talk through what everyone was doing, what resources they had, what they needed, and behind her there would sometimes be a small crocodile from Make-up, Wardrobe and Design. Mandy Burton's character, Heather, was of course an accountant, so every time Alexis turned up on site they would make a note of what she was wearing, carrying, how she did her hair, and then feed it back as Heather. Alexis seemed able to win everyone over, except GHPM who was unable to see past the comparison with other industries. We were art, not industry.

Before long the new report was done. For me. No one else. It made perfect sense. There were all the usual purchase-ledger controls, cash-claim forms, capital-expenditure limitations, but budgets would be devolved to everyone who could commit to expenditure. As they would have weekly Accounts reports, we would take and analyse those. We would then have weekly, not four-weekly, interim reporting. They could carry over savings but could not forward commit. This meant that if our gardener got all his plants for £20 instead of £25 one week, he could roll over the £5 saving to the following month. If he accumulated enough to buy something he really wanted, he could do it out of these savings. However, he could not trim his budget merely to 'save up' for something, without prior approval. This worked across every department and gave managers an opportunity to maximise their own budgets. People rose to the responsibility or, even more enlightening, realised they didn't want to and handed it to someone else. All the while Accounts had a firm hold and a live feed on everything. No longer would I dread being told I had gone bust four weeks earlier. Now, I would know at the end of each week if something could, possibly, go awry. This was unheard of in television and film at the time, and over thirty years we never once had a problem.

David Rose had been up and sat in on a couple of the shoots and editing sessions, and, while I could sense he was disappointed with the programme's look and feel, he was complimentary about the

content and performances, as well as understanding about the difficulties and teething troubles with the shoot and equipment. I noticed
he had a mischievous grin on his face when he kept saying, 'These
things take time.' Perhaps he was enjoying the 'realistic language'
that Jeremy had said he would support, while knowing what sort
of storm it was likely to cause. It's hard to say with the passage of
time, but I think we had all got ourselves into our own fictional
reality, our own small community of people who understood. This
was C4. It had to be different. It was meant to be different. It was
not ITV, and *Brookside* was not *Coronation Street*. My overriding
memory was that C4 were nothing less than totally supportive in
the run up to transmission. As we exchanged the mutual good luck
messages, I was more worried about how people back in the city
would react.

It wasn't just the language and content of the programme I worried
about, but the fact that it would look and sound different. For one
thing, the only piece of British kit within the system was the one
that didn't turn up on time: the all-important gate compressor for
the sound. As a result the sound was crisp and harsh and did seem
as though it was recorded in real houses. And while real, it was a
bit like hearing a real gunshot, which is more akin to a pop than
the full-throated powww the sound departments dub on to make
it sound 'right'. Like the movies rather than the news. The picture
would look different too, for two reasons. Better technology, but
also lack of experience in using it.

Regardless of the technical complexities or explanations, when
the programme went out on air, as I've said so often to others, the
audience would not know what we intended, only what they saw
on screen. That was what they would judge. It was for this reason
that I decided to invite all the people who had helped us to date
to a special preview. I wanted the guys from Broseley, the Liverpool
Development Office, and MERCEDO and DTi and the Council,
along with the local media, to have seen the programme before
anyone else, so they would be ready for other people's responses
without having to knee-jerk defensively. We got everyone in for a
pleasant lunch and then ran the first episode. They loved the titles
and the first few minutes, but then the expressions started to stiffen
as we got into the Collinses' arrival and the discovery of the 'bollocks'
graffiti on the bathroom wall. The temperature in the room dropped

considerably, but they all remained polite and resorted to the usual platitudes like 'different', 'unexpected' and 'Is this new channel all going to be like that?' Gradually they all made their excuses and left. The others asked me how I thought it went. I put on the bravest face I could. Well, I think they now know it's not *Coronation Street*.

At the next viewing, at a club in the city centre, there was no need to worry about the reception. This was for the cast and crew and we had hired the club so we could watch the programme go out live on Channel 4. I was nearly late because I was working with the editors on the following week's episodes, the stitch ups of The Shepherd's last attempts, and I got there just in time to hear the continuity announcer say that the next programme was *Brookside*. A big cheer went up, and then faded as the actors' strike caption went up, saying the next programme would follow shortly. It was like waiting nervously in a doctor's waiting room until, suddenly, there it was. That wide shot of the Mersey we had risked our lives to get and the slow gentle build of Mike Timoni's synth bringing up the theme. The pan on to the city and the drum fill and then one of the editor's tricksy ideas of mixing two shots of the different cathedrals into one. Someone asking where we got that shot from, and then we were on to the milk float coming in to deliver milk and the paperboy setting off the Huntingtons' car alarm and a naked Roger coming out to switch it off, to be caught by Sheila Grant . . . And the beginning of a twenty-one-year saga.

All I could see was the missing shot, the clunky edit, the milky pictures and how much that furniture van had cost and a hundred other things you fret about and one or two you should have spotted in the twelve versions of scripts and half a dozen viewings beforehand. No matter how hard you look, a transmission viewing is always different. The things you fretted over seem fine and things you thought were fine seem to creak. It is, you learn, just the way it is. Just as the other thing I noticed that night was how many people were actually involved. Even in a relatively small company as we were, suddenly having over a hundred people in one place is quite surprising. And humbling. Did all these people actually come together as a result of an idea in my head? This was another of those moments that everyone else seems to enjoy, while I always felt under too much pressure to relax, preoccupied by what still needed to be done or what was coming next. There was also a sense that, since the attempted coup, I didn't have anyone I wanted to share the moment with. That little drama still hurt but I was beginning also to learn that everywhere I went within the company, I would be under scrutiny. Under the eyes of the herd, watching every gesture and every bit of body language for any clues as to what was going on at any one time. Watching the co-conspirators getting into the party mood, I decided to avoid the body-language scanners and head back to the relative sanctuary of the edit suite on site, wondering how the press would react. In a time before 24/7 news channels and preview tapes to critics, I had one last evening left before the nation's verdict. Finishing the edit in the early hours, I went home and for the first time in years actually slept past eight o'clock. It might have been a bit of an adrenalin come-down after actually getting across the line the night before, but it soon kicked in again. Not only was there a media firestorm threatening to consume C4 but during the night my house had been burgled.

11

Shoot – Part 2 (1982–83)

'No matter which way you look at it, the overall trend is down'
– *Justin Dukes, first* Brookside, *1983*

The first night of Channel 4 and *Brookside*, 2 November 1982, is naturally a key historical date. However, just as 1980 turned out to be the pivotal year in my own career development, the day after C4's opening, 3 November 1982, was probably the most important for Channel 4, *Brookside* and television in general: Judgement Day.

Channel Swore was the most obvious play on Channel 4 in the headlines of the national press, but for *Brookside* the locals tended to play off the soap links, with things like 'Foaming On 4' and 'All in a Lather' being common, probably because most local newspapers carry nationally syndicated stories from the Press Association. However, although the language was the main story, the stories were angled right back to the circulation and advertising war. It wasn't so much that there was swearing in one programme, the press implied, but that the entire channel was a flop and, by implication, no decent advertiser would want to be seen on it. How better to illustrate this than to report that senior figures were walking away from its flag-ship programme? The figure they found was none other than our Shepherd.

Someone else who had discovered this, apparently, was The Shepherd. Having managed to get through Episodes 3 and 4, he was now causing chaos on his next pair of episodes. I had already been down to location several times to try and coax him not just through the schedule, but actually to shoot the drama I wanted. Then I got word that he had gone AWOL again, to be found after an hour asleep in one of the crew vehicles. No matter what his personal problems, he had to go. We got together over the weekend before transmission and I suggested that the programme was probably not his kind of thing. He agreed. Having learned from the Susi Hush separation, I also suggested it would probably be best all round if we publicly kept to that line. He'd come to help us get set up, it was never meant to be a long-term appointment. He agreed. And that was it. Or so I thought.

Now, there he was, the guy I had fired for the chaos he had caused on set, on the front page of a tabloid, now scrubbed up in a black polo-neck jumper with something like a chain and cross round his neck, looking like an Anglican cleric, a 'Good Shepherd' passing sanctimonious judgement on the programme and describing how he couldn't bring himself to shoot scenes containing gratuitous bad language and violence. Nowhere did it mention that he didn't know where he was half the time. The headline was: *Vulgar! TV Director Quits in Four-letter Row.* That was something else to be framed and hung on the wall behind my desk, as a constant reminder. Trust, like respect, has to be earned. We had both agreed not to say anything, so why did The Shepherd do this? I could understand Jimmy making what he probably thought was a throwaway line to a *Sunday Times* journalist about the teeth gag, but our Shepherd knew why we had parted company. Why did he, well, lie so publicly? I know the answer, of course, but seeing that on the front page of a national newspaper and knowing how it would help embed the negative perception of *Brookside* and C4, made me feel angry on behalf of everyone involved. While I took anything that was thrown at me, that was my choice, but the rest of the company didn't deserve this sort of nonsense. In trying to protect his own sense of self-worth and reputation, The Shepherd had shown a total disregard for his former colleagues.

But then again, while I might have understood all the sociological aspects of the situation, it was still infuriating at the time, to the extent that that front page stayed on my office wall to serve as a constant reminder of the fallibility of people as well as of the phrase: get your retaliation in first.

That meant damage limitation became a new skill to be acquired, along with learning how to control the information flow, by being proactive and releasing information first, rather than merely reactive, as anyone who has suddenly had the news media descend on them will understand. Apart from the odd exception, most journalists come to a story with very little background understanding of the subject and are already working to an agenda dictated by their editors. 'We know this is going on, go and find something to back it up.' It takes a very brave, or exceptional journalist, to come back and say, 'You know, boss, I think we got this one wrong.' It is a lot worse now than it was in 1982, as the recent judicial inquiry into journalistic practices has indicated. The 24/7 rolling news agenda has increased the pressure to be first with the scoop.

At the time the agenda was, 'Get Channel 4.' To have a 'senior director' quit conjures up a much better story of boardroom disarray, rows, or, even, attempted coups. The latter is a great example of how, when following a pre-set agenda of their own, the press often overlook the real stories all around them.

Locked in their own mindsets, the news media constantly recorded the failings of others, including the early days of C4, almost as a vindication of their traditional positions. In doing so, they missed the trend. Where did they think all this new technology would lead us to? In missing the trend they also did not initially see 'this internet thing' as a real threat to themselves, mistakenly believing that you couldn't make money out of something that was free — completely overlooking the rise and profitability of their own free local weeklies. It was no longer about cover price, but advertiser reach.

They also made a second fundamental error: the 'just in case play'. They decided to adopt the tactics they had always used to see off competition: colonise the space. It is a tactic that has been used by the BBC many times over the years. As soon as a perceived threat becomes a reality, move into the space yourself and steal the potential audience. The BBC was first to dominate breakfast, morning and afternoon television, twenty-four-hour broadcasting, digital channels and television and radio online. There was a case for public-service broadcasting in these areas, but the print media thought that if they launched their own websites then their readers would arrive and help them see off the competition. Well, the readers did arrive, as did their competitors, to their own websites. What their old mindsets had been unable to see was that there is no such thing as real estate in cyber space. It is impossible to colonise. You can control the gateways, which is what the likes of Google, Facebook, Twitter, Apple and every ISP and telecoms company are trying to do – which perhaps calls into question whether those geeks back in 1960s California really knew what they were unleashing when they built the ARPANET.

On that pivotal date, 3 November 1982, we just knew that all this was coming together and they were out to kill us. The Good Shepherd might have been the headline but he wasn't the story. We hoped it would die down, but with C4 also allowing late-night programming like *After Dark* to have, well, after-dark language, alongside running films like *Semi Tough*, a hard-hitting Burt Reynolds movie about American pro football which had, of course, hard-hitting sports heroes using hard-hitting language, the *Storm Over Four*, Jeremy Isaacs's favourite headline and title for the book he wrote about it all, seemed to be gathering pace. Worse still, the audience had finally discovered, as I had been trying to tell them, that *Brookside* was not ITV2's new version of *Coronation Street*. They came in numbers, 4.2 million, and left in droves – at the rate of about 200,000 an episode, so that by the turn of the year we were down to around 1 million viewers. Something had to change. It turned out to be the audience, but first we had to do something to make that happen.

Following the principle of mutuality, messages and calls went back and forth to the channel. We believed in what we were doing and would ride the initial expected storm until people had time to watch the channel and develop their own informed opinion, not swallow the press agenda. But the storm kept building, right up to Force 11, Hurricane. Although Sociology Professor Laurie Taylor took a look at us for Ludovic Kennedy's *Did You See* . . . BBC TV review programme and gave us a must-try-harder pass, the rest of the press struggled with the idea of so many disparate social groups living in the same street, again indicating how little they knew of the changing face of Britain. Unlike Broseley's marketing and sales team. Some couldn't understand how the management figure Paul Collins had managed to keep his car, having just been made redundant, or how the working-class Grants could afford such a large house. I wanted to refer them all to Laurie who might have been able to talk them through *The Affluent Worker in the Class Struggle* by Goldthorpe, Lockwood, Bechhofer and Platt, then the live piece of research on the increasing wealth of factory workers. (This was something I would be unable to resist in later years when I sent some of the 4 wannabes copies of the then current A-level Sociology textbook.)

By the end of the month, when the second set of ratings came out, the *Sun*, probably never having seen the Wenham Report, that found every television slot having the same demographic as its own readership, was on the attack and kept up the Channel 4 gags in its headlines. From *Channel Swore* sprang *Channel Bore*, and *Channel Snore* before they switched to the much more prosaic *The Channel That Nobody Watches*, until Jeremy had a go at the then editor, still persona non grata on Merseyside after Hillsborough, Kelvin MacKenzie. He pointed out that even a zero rating on TV equated to 200,000 viewers, but the channel was actually being watched by many millions of minorities that neither other TV channels nor MacKenzie's newspaper actually reached — exactly as intended by its remit.

That seemed to calm MacKenzie down, but there was increased pressure from ITV and the IBA, also regulator of Channel 4. John Whitney, Director-General of the IBA, kept nagging Jeremy to kill *Brookside* after a couple of weeks. That was seen off by Jeremy's citing interference in editorial control, while also not losing sight of the financial and contractual implications to us all if he did. We had a three-year agreement, even if it did have a break clause after twelve months. The cost would have been prohibitive, as well as leaving a two-hour gap in the schedule every week. We managed to survive and win John Whitney over, I think, as he later came up to *Brookie* and had a very jolly lunch with us all. What I didn't appreciate until much later was how much some of Channel 4's own Board were set against the programme, in particular its Chairman Edmund Dell, who never wanted the channel to commission a 'popular programme' in the first place. He wanted it to be for a certain kind of minority. More 'upmarket', as it was put. He had also not been keen on appointing Jeremy as Chief Executive.

What we all knew, though, was that the storm was not abating, and because the press had set out their stall against Channel 4, anyone and everyone was given a platform. It seemed like any disgruntled or offended viewer, bishop, MP or member of the lunatic fringe, from any member of Mary Whitehouse's National Viewers' and Listeners' Association campaign down to disappointed *Coronation*

Street fans, were given a loud hailer. I had quite a few run-ins with the Mary Whitehouse brigade, either her own or copycat disciples over the years, and while actually appreciating that Mary Whitehouse herself had a passionate belief in what she was doing, I found many others just used controversy as a convenient way to grab headlines. I once ended up having a 'discussion' with one of her gang on Radio 1, which was where the bulk of the *Brookie* audience was at the time, and halfway through realising the guy opposite me didn't know anything about the programme. I asked him live on air if he had actually watched it. Well, no, but . . . But what? But I'm going on what other people have told me. Collapse of moral outrage. And this was my main bugbear. It's fine to have an opinion about television. To disagree with something that is transmitted. But if millions of other people are watching, why try to have it banned immediately? Why can't you just reach for that often derided, but very effective, off button? Or, these days, channel surf with the remote? Many of our initial viewers did. And that was the main problem. It wasn't long before the call came from Channel 4. Come in and talk.

We were all determinedly upbeat going in and out of the building, but in the privacy and calm of Jeremy's office we slumped in our chairs, tense but exhausted by the fight. Justin was being his usual calming, business-as-usual, shirt-sleeved self, while David Rose was chewing on his beard. Justin suggested we needed to agree a way forward. We all nodded. The Emperor gave me his imperial stare. You are our most important commission. You are our flagship. We have to do something. I felt like a commander summoned back from the front. How long will it take to turn things around? Justin asked. Turn what around? I responded. Your lighting is awful, the pictures are lousy, the sound is terrible and it feels empty, said The Emperor. It's supposed to, it's a new estate. The lighting is fine, it's not *Coronation Street*, and we're still waiting for the gate compressor I countered, and got another imperial stare. He shifted his eyeline. David, what do you think? I think these things take time, offered David Rose. The imperial eye was back on me again. We have to do something. What about the language? I stared back. I asked you about that at the outset. And I agreed, but we were both wrong. Emphasis on the *both*, so tensions eased. Justin asked what we could do about it. It'll take about three months to get the language out of the scripts, I told them. Too long, he said. I suppose I could try editing it out, I offered. We must. We have to do something. That imperial stare again. And from there I went straight to C4's own editing suite and started working through the existing episodes.

The main storyline at issue was the one centred on Bobby Grant and the union. The *Sun*, again, had now got on to this and ran a piece with the headline *Let King Arthur Reign on the Box*. The sub-heading was: *Union soap opera plan*. Again the headline bore little relation to content or reality, but as a Tory-supporting newspaper, at the time, it played to the pre-set agenda of union-bashing and residual concerns following the 'winter of discontent' of a few years earlier. The story quoted me as wanting to personalise trades union bosses: 'Someone like Arthur Scargill or Ray Buckton has to go home at the end of the day – they have families and everyday problems.' Which I did say, along with, 'Look at someone like former miners' leader Joe Gormley. He must have had hopes and fears at home as well – that's what I want to show. Trades unionism is almost totally ignored by television. I've included the character of Bobby Grant, a strong shop steward in *Brookside*, but I want to go deeper into the subject.' What I didn't say, though, was, '*Union leaders like militant miners' chief Arthur Scargill are set to be the star characters of a new TV soap opera*', which was how one article started, and went on to describe how I was planning a new programme called *Union*. Then again, why let a few facts . . . ?

They may simply have got mixed up as Channel 4 were looking for something about unions, and Granada later made *Union World*, perhaps after seeing how popular personalising trades union bosses was with an audience. What was not so popular was the 'realistic language' that those union bosses used on the shop floor. I had been careful to follow the social mores of men swearing at work but not in front of wives or families. I overlooked another social convention. Swearing was a matter of choice and trust. Apart from moments of anger, frustration or pain, we tend to swear only when we are comfortable with who we are with and in a trusted environment. We choose those environments and the people we trust. Transmitting fictional characters swearing, even though portrayed in their own fictional trusted environments, was not acceptable in living rooms across the nation. I was, inadvertently, removing the element of choice bar one: turn off. People repeatedly told me that they understood what I was trying to do, but they didn't want swearing in their living rooms. So, faced with that insight and the sight of a full-blooded trades unionist in full flow, looking straight into the camera while saying 'gobshites', what do you do? Edit it out.

Apart from the audience, there are two other constituencies you have to think about. Your family and your staff. My family were very supportive, although I had to take a bit of earache from my mum about making a 'holy show of them', and then a bit from my dad, but not much, about the earache he was getting from Mum. Most of the rest of the family said they enjoyed it, although I did have one auntie who went to her grave delighted to be able to tell people she had never watched it. But there is always one in every family. I was quite anxious about the staff and crews, especially those new to the media, and how they would react to all the negative reaction to what they had worked hard to achieve. I at least had experienced the earlier rows round *Grange Hill*. There was just a bit of anxiety about jobs, but once I had reassured everyone that we were OK until the twelve-month break date the following July, something they had all known from the outset, everyone went back to making the programme. I got a few 'I told you sos' from some, but the majority resented the suggestion that we should have to tone it down. Just as much as they resented the Good Shepherd's born again comments.

Another concern was how this might impact on the Arthur Andersen review. Having been given the imperial decree to get back and 'do something', this meant I would have to focus almost exclusively on amending every script that was in or about to go into production. I was nervous that, after one false start with AA, I wouldn't be able to give Alexis the time she needed and she might be sidetracked by the old mindset of my *Grange Hill* Production Manager. No chance. As soon as she stepped over the threshold she had everyone in their right boxes, and calmly and efficiently worked her way through the company. She had, she told me later, seen it all before except, she admitted, the press furore that broke upon transmission. However, by that time she was well into the review and her aim was to set up the company for what we wanted to do, not to be judgemental. She was more concerned about being stalked by Gill from Wardrobe.

No matter how robust your systems are, as the collapse of Enron, bringing down Arthur Andersen with it, and later Barings and Lehman Brothers Banks, illustrated dramatically, it is with the people operating, or to be more precise, not operating, them that the real risks lie. As the review progressed and confirmed that more robust systems of management would be appearing, the expected consequences began to materialise. I started to hear a bit of noise from the failed coup organisers, GHPM and Fish, about feeling undermined. It was still not the time for a clear out but I asked AA to widen their brief. When the systems review was complete could they help me recruit someone to manage the company, allowing me to focus on the programme? Serendipity then passed my way again. Alexis was camped out in the Head of Personnel's office. Towards the end of her stay with us, he answered a telephone call meant for her. When he asked if he could leave her a message, he was told it was about 'the job offer'. He then duly passed it on and in conversation discovered she was thinking of leaving AA when her assignment with us was over. He told me. I thought she would be perfect to run the company, but would she even consider it with all the furore going on around us?

She'd proved her suitability almost from the day she'd walked on to the site and started winning over everyone with a straightforward approach to life forged among the valleys, mines and steelworks of South Wales. Besides this, she had a strong grasp of the still-emerging personal computer technology. She 'spoke DOS', meaning she could operate them from the command prompt, the short sequences of computer code that were necessary then to make a computer do anything. This not only impressed the techies, but it also emphasised the gulf yawning between her and Fish. At a meeting to discuss the acquisition of a computerised accounts package, he was advocating something being developed for our Wang word processing system. There was only one small snag. It might not be ready for twelve months. It would though, hopefully, eventually, he was assured, do everything we wanted. With a bit of luck. Alexis recommended a new PC-based system familiar to AA and ready off the shelf. How much? I asked. Fish said £33,000. Alexis said £3,000. There was more than just the accounts system at stake. It seemed a simple choice.

With the review complete, and aware of what had happened on the previous report, we met to go through Alexis's findings formally, although I already suspected what the main conclusion would imply: GHPM and Fish did not appear to have the skill sets to initiate, run or manage the new systems required for a 52-week production process. I would have to find new people. The problem, though, was time. It was running out. I needed to focus on the drama and demonstrate to C4 that we were going in the right direction. To do that I needed the company running even more smoothly. If not, C4 would invoke the twelve-month break clause, which meant that in order to meet all the contractual notice periods they would be making their decision in March 1983. That was now only four months away, the time it would probably take to recruit a new Financial Controller.

Alexis suggested AA could second someone. I asked if that could be her. She knew I was fishing and confirmed that she was indeed negotiating to join a developing electronics company. I knew that with her AA background and obvious skill sets she could probably write her own package, but following the old Scouse 'worth a try' route, because if you don't ask, you don't get, I popped the question. Would she come and join me and run the place? She asked me why she should. She could have a good career at AA or take up a great job offer with the electronics guys, while *Brookside* was fighting for survival. She could have security – or risk it all folding in a few months. It would be gratifying to say that after offering to match anything she could get elsewhere I talked her into it, but after Alexis had put it like that, it did seem like an offer anyone could refuse. Eventually, though, and for reasons neither of us can recall, we got to the point where she said she would actually consider it, so I thought it might be a good idea to invite her along to the planned Christmas Party. There she would have an opportunity to meet everyone in a different atmosphere. Well, it was a good idea and certainly a different atmosphere, but not quite what I, or anyone else for that matter, was expecting. I thought that would be the last I would see of Alexis.

The venue, The Fur and Feathers Social Club, was just round the corner from *Brookside*, right next to the now notorious Cantril Farm estate or, as my production managers had discovered early in the shoot, Cannibal Farm. It was booked on the recommendation of Ricky Tomlinson and obviously someone had asked them to go all out to impress. There, in the middle of a fantastic buffet, was a huge plate of salmon and a pig's head, complete with an apple in its mouth. Then someone discovered the head wasn't actually cooked. A few of my Southern middle-class television types, the ones who had wanted the canteen to serve brown rice and seaweed, discovered reasons to be elsewhere and left, which was a pity because they missed the food fight that became the scramble for the salmon.

Alexis arrived to find herself immediately cornered by Mandy Burton and Gill from Wardrobe, both wanting to know where she got the chiffon top and trousers she was wearing, and again it was a bit odd to see my fictional and what I hoped would be my real accountant standing talking side by side. You could tell easily, though, which was which. I was soon dragged away to talk to other people, and in doing so realised we were not the only occupants of the club. We had not hired the whole place as I'd thought, but had simply been 'booked in' for a buffet. The Fur and Feathers regulars were also milling around on the edges, and on my way back from the toilets I found the narrow corridor to the main room blocked by three guys. I moved to the left to go past, but the apparent leader stepped to his right. I went right, he went left, and it felt like I was back on the streets of Huyton. Worse than that, I realised I wasn't. The club was only a few hundred yards from where I had been turned over by Digger for being 'on his territory'. What was all this about?

I looked at the guy blocking my path, who was about six inches shorter than me, and waited. It came. You don't remember me, do you, Reddo? As no one had called me that since school, I could only conclude that this was some form of long delayed retribution. That would really impress Alexis. I waited. Well, he said aggressively, you don't, do yer. It was more of a statement than a question. I looked at his two henchmen, both with that old familiar dead-eyed non-committal look. They could just as easily ignore you, kill you or eat you. Or possibly the last two. No, I said, honestly, trying not to appear nervous. Terry, came the response. It's me, Terry. I shook my head. You'll have to give me another clue? He looked at his two mates and gave an exaggerated sigh. Is he thick or what? This was not going well. Then back at me. Terry Jones. Seeing I still looked blank: From the Infants, knobhead. I was then thirty-three.

I looked him up and down again. No recall. But if I was going down . . . Sorry, mate, but there were no short fat baldy fellas with a moustache in our class. Another exchange of looks from the trio, before they burst out laughing. Had you going there though, didn't I? my newly rediscovered Infants classmate said with a huge grin. They had indeed. Good style. But after chatting to him for a few minutes I still didn't recall who he was. He was obviously one of the three thousand-odd people I have met over my life who swear they were in the same class at school. Including many women, but during my all-boys education, I think I would have noticed them. Later in life, when *Brookside* and MerseyTV became successful, 'I'm Phil's cousin' became a well-known phrase for people trying to gain access to the site. Alexis, having come to know just some of my Irish extended family, had to caution our security guards and receptionists that many of the folk making the claim, probably were. The skill lay in determining with which of them I was still in contact.

But for now it was time to declare the buffet open. Obviously both the salmon and the pig's head had seriously impressed the onlookers. No sooner had Ricky made the announcement than people swept forward – or perhaps swarmed would be a better description. While our staff started to form an orderly queue, the club regulars just went straight for it. Queues were not for them, nor plates. Hands were soon reaching out and grabbing bits of the salmon, which was when that too was discovered to be not actually salmon, but some form of mousse. Unfortunately, Alexis and Mandy, still chatting next to the buffet table, were caught in the onslaught as hands darted out between and around them. Both emerged from the scrum with salmon mousse smeared on their clothes. It was like a scene from a *Carry On* film. At any other time it would have been funny, but to me, looking across at both Mandy and Alexis, retreating from the table looking down in horror at their ruined clothes, it felt more like a tragedy.

Alexis said she would think things through over the Christmas break, and I remember leaving the site quite late on Christmas Eve, realising I was back in that familiar position: out on a limb. If she said no the New Year was going to be difficult, to say the least.

Sometime between Christmas and New Year I got a call from Alexis – with an offer I couldn't refuse. She would work for me, in Phil Redmond Enterprises (PRE), not MerseyTV. Part of the review process had included how Arthur Andersen would also manage my own personal finances, and she was now probably the only person apart from Leon Morgan who understood the legal structure we had put in place to protect *Grange Hill* from being threatened if anything happened to *Brookside*. She knew that the contract with C4, with its twelve-month break clause, could be terminated in three months, but even so, I would still be there and would be looking for something else. She could start after Christmas, if I also paid the dry cleaning bill to get rid of the salmon streaks. How could I refuse?

While Alexis had been pondering the job offer, I had been pondering in the edit suit about how to get rid of things like that full screen 'gobs★★★★', an Irishism that means, as the word might suggest, somebody who talks rubbish. One of Bobby Grant's fictional pickets had used it during a heated exchange in the Grants' house about what to do with people who crossed the picket line. It wasn't just trying to edit out all the swearing that was the challenge, but how to do it without butchering the scenes or disturbing the mood and passion of the drama. That in itself would become another issue as when I started to edit out the swearing in the scripts themselves, rather than it being a simple cut and paste job as it was with the finished material (in other words cut that shot and move that one from here to there), it became more a debate about content, story and character development. Following the social mores of people only swearing in certain situations or conditions, what began to happen was that we started to avoid those types of storylines. Having started on the premise of treating heated or confrontational moments as realistically as possible, including the realistic language, we got into a typical creative spiral. If we can't say that, we can't show or do that. How can you have scenes of trades unionists arguing on the shop floor, or teenagers messing about or villains fighting without the swearing? You can't, it's not real, I don't want to do that. So, let's not do it.

This sort of pressure came in waves over the years when at various times certain subjects became more contentious or sensitive. Guns and knife crime are fairly obvious recent concerns, but in the 1980s homosexuality ranked quite close to trades union activism, and although everyone probably remembers the first lesbian kiss being on *Brookside* between Beth Jordache and Margaret Clemence (aka Anna Friel and Nicola Stephenson) and *EastEnders* have claimed the first male gay kiss, that in fact happened on *Brookside* too, in 1985, between Gordon Collins (Nigel Cowley) and his boyfriend Christopher (Stephen Parry). Well, it was more a peck on the cheek as that was about as far as I thought we could push it. Having decided to include the storyline, as a middle-class thing of course, I remember asking the writers to include signs of affection, the first of which was to have Christopher arrive to see Gordon and, in front of his parents, say hello with a peck on the cheek. That was it. But both our own and Channel 4's switchboard went into meltdown. It caused outrage, with one call to Channel 4 being logged twenty-four hours after transmission because the caller, a man, had spent the day after 'traumatised' by what he had seen on British TV.

Descriptions of what had happened in the callers' recollections ranged from the innocuous peck itself, which was bad enough, to some form of male homosexual orgy. It is incredible what the power of imagination can do, especially for those who probably never watched the episode at all, but this was demonstrated in greater detail when we decided to force the confrontation between Gordon and his bewildered and disapproving father, Paul (Jim Wiggins). As this was a big story I wanted a big moment as an episode hook so decided on Paul discovering Gordon and Christopher actually in bed together. To illustrate this, but being aware of the sensitivity of the storyline, I also insisted that they be shown back to back, with a clear gap between them. This was so as to observe the 'child of eight' rule from *Grange Hill*, where I said that nothing should be included that couldn't be explained to a child of eight, in terms they would understand. In this case, Paul was to walk in looking for Christopher, look horrified, then cut to boys in bed, back to Paul, horrified, and roll credits. To the child of eight, because of the back-to-back separation, the explanation was that Gordon had not asked his father's permission for his friend to stay over. For everyone else, obvious.

Except to Channel 4. They insisted that we cut the scene actually showing the boys in bed. Result: audience know from previous scene that boys have gone to bed; Paul walks in; shock and horror . . . roll credits. Channel 4 said the audience would use its imagination. Which it did. The same people who interpreted a peck on the cheek as a preliminary to full-blown sex. Switchboards everywhere went into meltdown. The regulators piled on the moral outrage pressure to the point where I was in a script meeting one day and found myself saying it would perhaps be best to avoid saying the word 'homosexual'. To assuage the writers' moral outrage, I suggested that the character could start saying 'Hom——' and then be interrupted. To his credit, Bob Carlton, creator of theatre hit *Return to the Forbidden Planet*, who was directing that episode, looked me in the eye and said, '*Redmond, you have sold out.*' It came as a shock. So I agreed that we could say 'homosexual' and went back to fighting the forces of taste and decency. We, or I, had been on the brink of falling into the trap of self-censorship. From then on I always made the point to Channel 4 that it was not my job to self-censor, but to fight their sense of bureaucratic survival. It worked well for many years, until they lost sight of what their bureaucracy was surviving for.

At the same time as the backlash against the swearing, there was a deluge of further moral outrage after the episode shot on 'Cannibal Farm'. Sixteen-year-old Karen Grant was shown at her boyfriend Demon Duane's house offering him a cup of tea but discovering he had other things on his mind. There was nothing ambiguous for the viewer about the way he picked up the steel teapot and held it to her face. Another offer she couldn't refuse. Sex or a scalding. It was, as I intended it to be, a harrowing moment, dramatically intensifying something many teenage girls experienced. The pressure for sex, especially when getting out of their depth. The other element was the romantic notion of big brother Barry saving the day. Having warned Karen about hanging around with 'Demon', Barry turns up just in time to give him what he really deserves. Sibling antagonism is displaced by support and lessons learned all round, about talking to each other rather than thinking they know best all the time, while also agreeing not to tell their parents. While this episode helped define the characters, it brought down the wrath of the taste-and-decency brigade and gave more fuel to the IBA's John Whitney who was still asking Jeremy to cancel the programme.

Just as on *Grange Hill*, when the biggest affront to public taste and decency had been working-class accents and storylines, so it was beginning to appear with *Brookside*. On *Grange Hill* one of the sacred cows, or taboos as the media started labelling them, was that teachers were not the paragons of virtue that the establishment, and especially the NUT, wanted the BBC to portray. While the BBC didn't want me to end a scene with the kids noticing beer on the breath of their form teacher, nor end an episode on the word cow, then neither did some sections of society want to show that sports teachers habitually humiliated kids over either not being fit or not having enough money to buy the correct kit, as Frosty Foster had done with young Benny. Even though he had already demonstrated that he was one of the best football players, he was still castigated in public because his family couldn't afford to buy him football boots. If the public weren't ready for working-class accents and poverty in an inner-city comprehensive school, how would they cope with the swearing and harsh realities of life's dark survival codes on an inner-city council estate? That was the view of the moral minority, and a sizeable part of the audience at the time. But neither the moral minority nor the post-*Coronation Street* viewers were our intended audience. They switched off, creating our crisis of confidence, so the challenge became not to win them back, but to find the mums and dads of the kids that loved *Grange Hill*.

First though, how to get rid of that offending gobs★★★★. While we managed to cut away from most of the characters when in full flow, then overlap dialogue from another character to drown out a lot of the swearing, I had agreed with David Rose the swear words that might appear most offensive and those that we could 'live with'. However, this full screen was the biggest challenge. Fortunately though, Channel 4 had the latest version of the 1-inch recording machines, the ones that I had wanted but they had vetoed during the negotiations on the equipment levels they would fund. It would play at slow speeds. Amazing. It sounds so primitive now, looking at what most people have in their living rooms or on their pocket cameras or phones, but our recording machines at the time did just that. Record. At one speed. With C4's machine I could look for other shots to use as potential cutaways. Back and forth we went, scene after scene, until after a while I spotted something. Go back. There. When he tuts. No, no, there. Yes. It was just a shot of one of the other committee members tutting at a comment in another scene entirely. Copy that. Go back to gobs★★★★. OK, when he says, '. . . *and if those GS's* . . .' Drop it in there. So we go to him to a reaction on the use of the word. Yes. Play. It didn't work. Too quick. I can slow it down. Can you? Yes. Let's see. 79 per cent. No, 60 per cent. No, until we got to about 30 per cent. By now the reaction had gone from a quick 'tut' to a much slower raising of the eyebrows-type gesture. It worked. Go back to GS. Cut in as, '. . . *and if you think those . . .*' Lose the GS completely, drop in a cough, and we'll be on him for what is now a reaction, not to language, but to the young Turk looking for a fight. It was compiled, a bit grainy, but it worked. And no one noticed.

It was the first time I had ever done this. The first time the C4 editors had done it, and we think the first time anyone had ever fixed things like it in video editing. Soon it would become common practice as the technology developed and the editing suite became known as 'the resuscitation unit'. It was even better a few years later when we could afford to buy our own slow-mo machines. And, they could even run the tape backwards. Real technological frontier stuff. But all the time these sessions were going on I would be telling the press that no changes were being forced on me or the programme, as I was a willing accomplice, and that although we had said we wanted to include realistic language in realistic situations, the storyline would evolve and so would the language used by the characters. And so it would. I just never added, as fast as it possibly could.

After the call from Alexis over Christmas I had started to convince myself that she obviously couldn't resist the chance of being part of a start-up. To be there at the dawn of a new era of television and so on . . . until she later told me it was a lot more prosaic than that. At AA's own Christmas party her senior partners, John Milbourn and Eric Kilby, had asked the question that would come to frame our later shared management doctrine: 'Why not?' AA would have been tracking the way technology was developing, both in the UK and across the world, and would have known that television was the new and developing sexy industry. They said Alexis's current experience and CV would always ensure that she could step back on to the professional career ladder, so their advice to her was simple: 'Go and have some fun.' I'm glad they did. I'm glad she did. Because we did. Just as we remained lifelong friends with John and Eric. And after having pondered what to do about GHPM and Fish, I came up with my New Year's resolution: act quickly.

With this in mind, I called Justin Dukes over the weekend to let him know that I was going to be making changes. Out would go GHPM and in would come Alexis. Having himself recently taken on a couple of people on secondment from another of the big eight accountancy firms, to supplement C4's finance department, he saw the logic of this, was reassured by the AA reputation, and said he admired my ability to make tough and brave decisions. There were few people who could, he said, in such a way that I got the impression I had been included in some form of management club. I met GHPM on the Monday, 2 January. It was the New Year bank holiday and the rest of the company were still off. There would be the three-month notice but I wanted GHPM gone immediately. Fish was to follow soon after as the more the new systems were introduced, the more his shortcomings and inability to change became apparent. The whole ethos of the company was beginning to evolve, rather than change, towards the level I had been striving for.

Within a week I had a spare black BMW, an office, and the flat GHPM had been using. I suggested Alexis move into the office but she said no, she would go and join Linda Farrell, who would become her long-standing company accountant, when Accounts moved into the vacated flat. When I went over to see how things were going a short while later, I found everyone set up and happy, and Alexis surrounded by the techies, all negotiating hard for the level of budget they would now be given to administer. She was working off the draining board in the kitchen. She really did get it. Absolutely.

While things were speeding up in terms of getting the company sorted out, allowing me time to start getting on top of the production process without worrying if I'd have an office to come back to, things on the press front were starting to calm down, although we did get a late flurry in January when the episode featuring Danny Webb's early exit, which brought on the fictional Gavin Taylor's death, was approaching. The departure of GHPM was then linked to this by the press, and Peter Kerrigan and Susi Hush got another outing. Things were obviously still in chaos at *Brookside*. Well, for that day's paper at least.

In reality, the programme was now becoming a lot more organised and we had even got to the point of being the first television company in history where management had imposed tea and meal breaks on the labour force. Alexis had even got the canteen running well, even if the shoot was killing us with good intentions. Ever since the late-night Close Encounter scenario, we had been trying to rein in our crew's youthful enthusiasm. I didn't want to kill the energy that went with the tool of capitalist oppression, job satisfaction. As a young company with a low average age – at thirty-three I was probably one of the oldest – they were quite prepared and willing to go on working beyond the allocated tea break or lunch timings, just to get 'one last shot'. Unfortunately the food wouldn't keep, so gradually whinges and moans started coming in about food being cold, baked or stewed by the time they got there. While the 'great scene' that had caused the over-run was fine, the ones following to make up the schedule often suffered. So, floor managers were told the tea and meal breaks were not advisory, but time-markers in the schedule. They had to complete what they needed to, as per the schedule. Finally, things were beginning to fall into place. There was only one cloud on the horizon. Valentine's Day. The Chairman of Channel 4, Edmund Dell, wanted to make a personal visit to check us out. Ahead of the contract review.

At the time, with the arrogance of youth, I thought Dell was a typical establishment shoo-in. Someone who had served his time somewhere and was now given a reasonably interesting sinecure to while away his twilight years. A view not altered by his visit to *Brookside*. There before me was an ancient white-haired member of the Oxbridge mob. He was in fact sixty-one, younger than I am now writing this, but then again, as Bob Dylan reminded us in his track 'My Back Pages', we were all so much older then. I was surprised to discover that he had been MP for Birkenhead. Even more so that he had been a Labour member, but had resigned because it was too 'left-wing', something I thought he should have spotted when he joined. He was probably part of the early swing towards New Labour, though in its absence later joined the new Liberal Democratic Party.

What I was not surprised by, though, was Justin letting me know that his Chairman's visit was part of the whole Channel 4 review process. Justin initiated the visit, as he wanted Dell, one of the sceptics, actually to see the scale of what was going on and what we had achieved. This was something we would always encourage people to do, especially the respective Chief Executives who came and went at C4, as it was too easy otherwise for them to overlook what a logistics exercise putting *Brookie*, then *Hollyoaks*, together actually was. We had to make them aware that when they sat in their comfy, air-conditioned, offices in London, firing off memos asking for this and that, it all had to be weighed against the logistical impact.

Unfortunately, as the years passed and more and more people rose up the executive ladder at C4 and elsewhere, even this started to lose its impact as they simply had nothing to compare it with. Fewer and fewer of them had actually ever made a programme. So it was with Edmund Dell. A career politician who had never worked in television was now Chair of what was probably the most exciting opportunity for innovation in the UK's cultural history. This may help explain why, with the whole industry lining up behind Jeremy Isaacs, Dell had not been keen on appointing him to the post of Chief Executive.

With Dell and Justin Dukes came Paula Ridley, then the IBA's North West Regional Board member, who happened to live in Liverpool and, as a piece of trivia, was married to the Politics tutor I'd had while doing my Social Studies degree. She was probably there out of courtesy and protocol, but I knew the IBA themselves had negative feelings towards us. To counter this I invited along the Chief Executive of the Merseyside County Council, Ray O'Brien, to offer a positive view from the region, as well as Leon Morgan, who got on well with Justin and spoke establishmentese.

I have no great recollection of the lunch, except that it was held in the Collinses' house, which I'd thought would be more appropriate. Dining in the houses became a regular event when people came to visit the site, mainly because we had nowhere else. It was also more interesting and fun for a visitor to be taken on a quick tour of The Close and then suddenly walk into one of the houses and find the table set for lunch. They would often comment later that it was weird but added to their interest in viewing the programme at home, to say that they had actually eaten there.

Sometimes, because of the shortage of space, to get away and read scripts I would go down and sit in one of the houses. There was always a tension between Design, who would set up the houses as they should be, and the shoot, who would crash in and move things here, there and everywhere, only for Design then to have to come back and redress. After Design had cleaned up after the shoot, the houses not only felt as real as their fictional owners, they also smelled like them. It was something I hadn't expected, but all the houses had their own individual smell, which came from the collection of furniture, ornaments and bric-a-brac we had filled them with. I'm sure it helped, even subliminally, the cast and crew get back into character as soon as they came in the front door. The houses felt so real that standing there making a cup of coffee or sitting reading quietly felt like being in someone else's home. And at any moment they might come in and kick you out.

I was not the only one who did this, I later discovered, as directors, PAs and various members of the crew could often be found there going through their scripts or schedules away from the noise and bustle of the production offices. This multi-usage of space became part of the programme's ethos. Nothing would be built or converted, if it couldn't double or triple up as a shoot location, admin or entertainment space. On later moving to our bigger base at Childwall, the 80,000-square-foot former college, the canteen was also the Grants' restaurant and our Christmas Party venue, linked as it was to the Hollyoaks pub, The Dog in the Pond. We built a courtroom, initially to keep the infamous Jordache storyline verdict confidential, but planned for later use in both *Brookside* and *Hollyoaks*, and this became the main storyline and first draft meeting space. And there were other assignations that went on in the houses, that again I wasn't supposed to know about, but with a young company and a lot of single people the bedrooms were obvious targets for multi-use, one or two actually being slept in overnight. One of the biggest issues, though, was the amount of toiletries that used to go missing from the bathrooms, not least when members of the cast started using 'their' bathroom to get ready for a night out.

Three things came out of the lunch with the Chairman. The first was that he showed no real interest in anything except when we got to the top of the canteen on the tour and I was explaining how we had, as in number 7, worked with Broseley to redesign the building's structure so that, in place of the three bedrooms, we'd created a larger eating and meeting space, toilets and artists' Green Room. Halfway through this explanation, fascinating to any QS, I turned to find him bent low over one of the electric storage heaters. Where did you get these? Er, they came with the houses. Could you send me details? Er, yes. Just what I'm looking for at home. Shall we go?

The second thing was that we were left in no doubt that the key date for renewal would be in a few weeks' time when we were due to meet to discuss progress. That didn't sound too promising, judging by Dell's apparent lack of interest.

Third, Justin met Alexis for the first time and, while he had been impressed with the Arthur Andersen pedigree, was a bit surprised to discover that I had entrusted the company to a financial director he later described to me as 'nothing more than a slip of a girl.' She was twenty-eight. I was thirty-three. He was forty-one. David Scott, his own FD, was twenty-nine. But I guess he was a man. That didn't sound too promising either. As a Valentine's Day lunch, it was pleasant enough, but it could have gone better.

If 1980 had been more significant than 1982, and 3 November more eventful than the official launch date, then the hardest day of my *Brookside* journey was probably that review meeting in March 1983. The audience figures had continued to slide from the opening night total of 4.3 million. By the time we got to the meeting, the weekly figure was around 500,000. However, ratings is not a simple or exact science, but more of a black art. Or so the schedulers would have us believe as they appear with their market research, audience analyses and demographic data, to suddenly pronounce that 8.30 on a Tuesday night is the ideal time for . . . well, something. The truth probably owes more to what is happening in the lives of the viewers – whether they are willing or available to view. One of the most frustrating things for any programme-maker is knowing that no matter how fantastic your programme is, approximately 70 per cent of the TV audience will not even bother to turn up to watch it. They will either be already locked into their chosen viewing or simply doing something else. Television is a second-choice activity, amply illustrated by the overall fall in ratings when the clocks go forward in the spring and people decide to start gardening, go for a walk, or just simply stay out later.

Understanding this makes it easy to interpret and accept the occasional dips between high spots as events happening elsewhere to pull the audience away to another programme, resulting in the overall ratings graph looking like a typical saw-tooth chart with the peaks and troughs clearly visible. What is more important is the trend: rising, falling or flat. By the time we got to March, the print-out showed a very clear saw-tooth pattern, up and down from week to week, but Justin Dukes, to make a point, placed his pen diagonally across the chart. From one end to the other the trend was clear: down.

At the same time it was also obvious there was no cliff edge. The audience had not suddenly disappeared, but was drifting away. It seemed a bit like a crowd leaving a football match when they've decided they've had enough, but stopping and glancing back, hoping something is going to happen. It might also have been that the spikes were indications of new viewers coming to try out the programme, or resulted from more publicity, as in the week that Danny Webb left. Publicity always arouses viewers' curiosity. What was also becoming clear, was that the swearing had been a huge turn-off for the initial audience who, it also emerged, had been drawn to the programme on the common misunderstanding that it was to be son or daughter of *Coronation Street*. What we needed to do was becoming clear. We needed to increase the number of spikes. To do that we needed to put more resources into publicity and marketing. We'd started to recruit but this would be another agenda item on the rapidly approaching, make-or-break, review of the programme.

The day actually started the evening before when I had dinner with David Rose to give him a more in-depth briefing as to where we were. We both wanted to be sure we were at least reading from the same script, no matter how harrowing, as there was, and hope-fully always will be, a special affinity between members of the crea-tive community as opposed to 'the suits'. I have always been able to switch, slip between or change hats in this way relatively easily, which many in the business have found difficult to grasp or deal with. Those who worked closely with me would know when to ask, 'Which hat are you wearing now?' It was not uncommon to hear Alexis in particular say, 'Could you just switch hats for a moment?'

Over the years, culminating in my playing ringmaster during European Capital of Culture 2008, I have come to understand that creativity is not something confined to a particular activity or endeavour, but is found across and within all walks of life; all aspects of what we do; all areas of human interaction. It happens as much in a lab as it does in a studio. The search for the Higgs boson at the Large Hadron Collider at CERN, for instance; Tim Berners-Lee and the World Wide Web; the ARPANET geeks; and back beyond them to Einstein, Galileo, and their predecessors . . . all different aspects of human creativity. In our fairly recent past, the twin pres-sures of Church and State in their never-ending quest to control the way people act, behave and ultimately think saw creativity as something dangerous because it challenges bureaucracy's prime directive: the maintenance of the status quo. It is no coincidence that most oppressive regimes target intellectuals first and burn books second. The thinking mind is a questioning mind, and that in itself is the basis of creativity. Why is that? What is that? Why should it be so? Why don't we change? Why not, instead of why.

David Rose understood this, as his own CV indicated, so while he was not reticent in his criticism, it was always with the caveat that 'things take time'. He once said he didn't quite understand why *Brookside* worked, but it obviously did and so did I, and that was all he needed to know. He was the epitome of what Channel 4 set out to create in its commissioning editors: facilitators who were there as critical friends, to prod, probe and push occasionally, but generally to let you, the person they had asked, commissioned and empowered, get on with doing the job you had both agreed on. This was what was lost in the 1990s, when the control mindset of a typical broad-caster started to creep in, take hold and stifle creativity. What David had to come to terms with, which he did rapidly, was the difference between the two currencies: BBC and ITV cash, and Channel 4's allowance. He soon grasped that if he asked me to put more back-ground actors in scenes, I would have to ask for an increase in budget and 'the suits' – his suits – would say no. He never had that problem at the BBC. We left dinner that night with an understanding that we were heading in the right direction, something I then reported back to Alexis as we spent the rest of the night rehearsing the case, and arguments, for the following day.

The next morning we had breakfast with Leon Morgan at a slightly later start than our old contract meetings in the Sutton Row caff. It was also in the more salubrious setting of the top-floor restaurant of St George's Hotel, overlooking the adjacent city roof-tops, close to BBC Enterprises, the reason I knew of its existence. Leon was attending because if things went well we would be into a new round of contract renewals. If they went badly he would be involved in the subsequent arguments. We were joined by our new line producer, Nick Prosser, who had stepped up from programme production manager to help manage the shoot since the New Year reorganisation.

Nick was a great guy with a lot of production experience, but an ambition to direct. The deal we did was that he would act as line producer for a year or so until we were rock solid and could appoint someone else who would know what they were taking on, not what they wanted it to be. He was also a terrier when pursuing an objective, and he coined another phrase I would come to dread: site geography. Space and where people sat was a constant Rubik's cube on *Brookside* but Nick was always determined to find solutions. As soon as I saw that on an agenda, I tried to find a reason not to be there. Like the canteen, it was something else I was happy to pass over to Alexis. To this day I have never met anyone with such spatial awareness. She can get a quart into a pint pot.

Having prepared as best we could, with scripts rehearsed and roles agreed, we headed off to Channel 4, went through all the rigmarole of being signed in, and watched the media souk that doubled as Reception for a while, then were collected. But instead of heading upstairs, we were guided down to the boardroom on the lower floor. This was obviously serious and, knowing what Justin was like with his management mind games, I also knew that this was the 'keep them waiting moment'. It is while waiting that doubts and nerves start to build. Our ratings were down, no doubt about that. But they kept spiking. But only when there was increased publicity. But we couldn't keep doing that. We didn't have the budget. Then there was all the personnel churn. How were they reacting to that? How were they reacting to pressure from elsewhere? A glimmer of hope lay in the fact that it wasn't just *Brookie* that was taking flak. But it was the most expensive programme, after ITN News, they kept telling us. And I'd said it would deliver big audiences like *Corrie's* for ITV. This must be bad news. How would I tell everyone back at base? And what about the future? How would I move forward? Then the door opened and in they came.

As Justin led the charge across the room to shake hands and introduce himself, I could see him counting heads and making sure he had his usual majority. Alexis was dragged off by David Scott for a session on finance while Justin stayed with David Rose and Paul Bonner, someone who had been Edmund Dell's preferred candidate for Chief Executive but was now instead part of the Holy Trinity, or triumvirate, that ran the Channel: The Emperor, who had just popped in to say hello and add something imperial, Justin, who ran 'everything not creative', and Paul, who ran 'everything not creative or financial' as far as I could figure out, which was quite a considerable portfolio. It really meant making sure the channel got on the air and ran smoothly. He did a good job.

We spent an hour going over where we were to date and what we thought needed to happen with the programme. More resources, more actors, more time, with Justin consulting his charts and graphs and me talking about the scale of the achievement to date. I suppose, looking back, while we were all consumed with the detail and fighting our respective corners, there was not actually any real sense that this was the end of anything. As the meeting went on it became apparent that what we were talking about was how to build on what we had, so by the time Alexis and David Scott rejoined us and he confirmed that he was happy with the new financial monitoring systems, it was clear from the body language that the 'slip of a girl' had made a connection with the 29-year-old head boy. They were, after all, both not long out of professional practice and tackling this alien world of TV finance together.

It was now time to get down to the nitty-gritty. Justin then produced the ratings chart again, and for everyone's benefit reminded us, through the demonstration with his pen, that the trend was inexorably downward. I argued that it was in line with the channel's performance as a whole, but of course he had another chart showing the same saw-tooth pattern, this time with his pen noticeably horizontal. He reminded me that I had said *Brookie* would deliver ratings. I reminded him that it was wrongly marketed and we had all agreed that we, emphasising the imperial we, had got the language issue wrong. He conceded this and explained that was why we were actually sitting round the table: so as to move forward. He could easily have just issued a termination notice as required under the contract, which he was sure Leon would confirm. He did. And with that irrefutable fact made, I had to sit on my Scouse hands as three key points emerged that we needed to agree on. How to improve the programme; what that would require; and, as C4 were at the point of being able to terminate, was the current deal actually the best structure for moving forward? The great 'ah' moment. The Phil Redmond Schedule had resurfaced. They were going to chip the deal.

This was when Alexis really took control. I think she sensed that my blood was beginning to boil as they were trying what Yorkshire, the BBC and Peter Kerrigan had already tried: the ransom play.

Whether it really was the Phil Redmond Schedule, or residual resentment about the additional £150,000 the year before, or simple opportunism, I can't be sure, but what they wanted was to reduce the production fee paid on top of the budget price. Alexis probably sensed my instinct to argue so moved forward in her seat. Without her having to say anything, I read the body language. I sat back in my chair, she took over, and while I sat brooding and festering she slowly and methodically took them through what she had learned since joining from AA. How I was already subsidising the budget through the purchase of the 'party house', although she didn't describe it as such then, and the flats adjacent to The Close to use as accommodation for freelance directors and extra office space. None of this was being recharged to the programme, but carried by the company as an overhead. She said that if they were insistent on reducing the production fee, then the overheads would have to become line-budget items. They agreed. We would need more to cover the additional background artists David Rose had asked for. Agreed. We would need more in terms of publicity to help deal with the increased calls coming in for programme information that C4 couldn't handle but in themselves proved there was a growing audience interest. Agreed. And then she asked for a £25,000 uplift in the capital budget to buy a Steadicam.

This brought a few puzzled looks as it was a relatively new piece of camera kit, in the form of a counterbalanced harness that the operator wears to allow the camera to stay perfectly level and smooth while running with the action. As far as I was aware it had never been used in television. In fact, its acquisition meant another minor skirmish with the technology priests who had deemed it a film tool, and were convinced that as such no one would sell us one for *Brookie*. Until I called the guy who had invented it, Garett Brown, in California and did a deal to have one shipped over. It had recently been used in the *Rocky* movies; particularly the famous scene when Sylvester Stallone runs up the steps of the Philadelphia Art Museum and the camera goes round and round him. Nowadays it is the piece of kit used to get those close-ups of footballers coming off the pitch at the end of the game. For us, it would be an ideal tool to replace the need for all those traditional dollies, tracks and cranes we couldn't get into the confined spaces of the houses.

After hearing what it could do for the programme, David Rose concurred and the purchase of the Steadicam was agreed as a budget item. It still gives me a kick when I see a Steadicam operator running the touchline, for Sky Sports, to think I was the guy who first brought it to British television. Alexis then took them back to the fee and suggested that in return for a change in the fee structure, company overheads for things like the use of the accommodation house and flats would be a rechargeable item. That was agreed too. Justin looked across at me. I was still slumped back in my chair. 'Cheer up,' I remember him saying with a grin, 'we've got what we need, you've got the programme renewed . . . and you've got your Steadicam.' I looked at Alexis, then Leon, and they both nodded.

Time to be pragmatic. I could accept all their arguments and see that there was a sense of growing camaraderie built in to our joint defence of the programme and the channel itself; in those Channel 4 edit suites and these no-holds-barred negotiation sessions. I nodded. I could forgive, but never forget. I didn't need to. Later Alexis walked me through what she had actually done. The amount the production fee had been reduced would be compensated for by the increase in legitimate overhead recharges. I quickly changed hats. The creative had got too emotional but had ended up with a Steadicam and more actors. The entrepreneur approved and had ended up with a now strong and viable business and someone he could finally trust to run it.

After that meeting I felt secure. The programme and company grew and went from strength to strength. I knew at the time it was going to be a hard day, but the more I look back, the more tempting it is to think that the outcome was inevitable. Both sides had invested too much in each other to walk away. But these moments are often about the chemistry in the room. Sometimes gelling. Sometimes catalytic. Sometimes toxic. But there is no question in my mind that if Alexis had not been in that room that day, things would have been different. I doubt they would have been as harmonious. The key point, though, is that she was. Slowly, she would come to play a bigger and bigger role in my life, but that particular moment marked a massive milestone in my career. I had finally and irrevocably evolved from writer to major employer in the industry.

12

Reviews and Results (1983–84)

'You sod!' – *Heather Huntington to Roger – and out*

Almost from the day she joined I handed over the running of the company to Alexis. She was from the valleys and therefore, while never allowing anyone to grind her down, was a bit more pragmatic and tempered my Scouse mindset of 'us' against the rest. Not to overlook the comic irony, the biggest independent production employer no longer felt alone in his 'class struggle' against the London-based Marxist wannabes. With Welsh steel and coal grit in her veins, Alexis knew all about the real labour movement, which was actually about employment, individual dignity and self-empowerment – not about whether the workers could travel first class, be paid ten times their daily rate for a weekend or get a £150 allowance for a waterproof coat. I had at last found someone I never had to doubt.

This left me free to get on with figuring out how best to make *Brookie* and how to stop and reverse the decline in ratings, for there was one additional condition attached to the *Brookside* renewal agreement: to rebuild the audience and have a rating of over 1 million by the time of the next renewal in twelve months' time. Otherwise C4 would cancel. But they had taken a second great leap of faith. They had given me a second, albeit last, chance.

With that came the double-edged sword of relief and responsibility. While we were relieved that C4 had renewed, there was also now a growing sense of responsibility. Not really to C4, but to the people in the company who had put their faith in me. For C4 it was a gamble on one programme and one programme-maker. At the time they could afford to give it another twelve months as their income was secure through the taxation on ITV. However, for the people around me it was more pressing. It was about their jobs and mortgages.

That sense of responsibility was something neither Alexis nor I ever forgot and it ran deep, underpinning nearly every decision made at MerseyTV. It was a community as much as a company, and as such we had asked for a counter condition. If we hit the 1 million rating, C4 would pay for the celebratory staff party. By the time the next renewal came round we were over 2 million, and by the time we organised the party, the ratings were over 3 million. Invitations went out to attend a '3-Mega Binge' on 25 May 1984.

To let everyone know what had happened with Channel 4, and that we had one more year to prove that the programme would work, we decided to call an all-company meeting. The meeting was intended to give everyone as much advance notice as we could. Those on fixed-term contracts had to decide whether they wanted to sign on again or leave; and those on full-time staff contracts would know that their jobs were secure for another year at least. Out of this came the renewal of the actors' contracts and everyone decided they wanted to stay on, including Rob Spendlove, who played Roger Huntington. Or so I thought. He later came to see me and said that although he had fully intended to stay, he now wanted to leave. As soon as possible. From memory it was for another job, something that he really wanted to do and that would require him to leave on or before the end of his first contract period, let alone any extension to give us time to write him out. What this meant contractually was that we had to get him out a few weeks ahead of his contract end date, in case we needed to reshoot anything. What it meant in practice was that we would have to amend the scripts already in the system, and we had only a few weeks to do it.

In later years we would often greet such moments with 'it'll be better this way', as losing a main character often allows the storyline and writers' imaginations to travel in ways and areas prohibited by the demands of continuity. A character would not do that or this because they have always done this or that. The frustration only comes when you are forced to do it quickly. Like then. But that is also part of the problem-solving creative fun. Like, how do I lose Rob and keep Mandy? Heather would have to discover that Roger was having an affair. Not only that, but she would have to do this and throw him out within four episodes, Episodes 91–94. It was also not a moment to ask the writers to do it as there just wasn't time to get everyone in, go through things and agree the changes. I would have a week to change the scripts.

So I went off and locked myself away in one of the flats I had bought behind The Close and started to edit. Episode 91 took two and a half days; 92 two days; 93 one day, and 94 was done in four and a half hours, the fastest I had ever written.

Around the same time as this, the storyline we had already scripted was Bobby and Sheila celebrating their 25th wedding anniversary. This was the anchor point. So Heather discovering Roger's affair would play on an emotional level what I had originally wanted to do with social issues. Have different characters from different backgrounds and different views, exploring different facets of the same issue.

While Heather the professional accountant was throwing Roger out and facing a future without him by choice, next-door neighbour Petra Taylor, the wife of a scally entrepreneur and desperate for a child, was still coming to terms with widowhood; while over The Close Sheila was the epitome of the idealised form of marriage and motherhood. To further explore the inter-generational attitudes, I brought in Roger's dad to reveal to his son how he now couldn't stand his wife, Roger's mother, but he had taken the 'for better for worse' vow and would stick by it. That scene, along with the one where Heather actually throws Roger out is among my top ten list of favourite *Brookside* moments, thanks to an extremely powerful, hell-hath-no-fury performance from Mandy.

The dialogue was minimal, relying purely on the actors' performances. Years earlier, around the time I was doing *Going Out*, I had been renovating the house James Fox stayed in, looping the ring main for a couple of new sockets in the hallway, when I realised that I was following the plot of a drama series on the television in the lounge. I couldn't see the pictures but I knew everything that was going on. I distinctly remember stopping and thinking that I shouldn't have been able to, otherwise it was radio. Television, like film, should convey the story through what's on screen, though the picture. From that moment I worked harder to make sure that everything I wrote had to rely on the pictures as much as the words. Neither could tell the story alone. And both should rely on the audience's imagination.

We back-seeded Roger being seen to be having an affair with one of his clients. The audience knew what Heather didn't, and would be waiting for the moment when she found out. They had probably already envisaged what might happen. All I did was accelerate that moment by having Roger on the phone in the living room and Heather come in from the kitchen. No secret notes or hotel receipts or lipstick on collars. Just her face, as she realised from his body language and tone that this was neither a business call nor someone she knew. She stood. Watched. Waited. Then, on the fateful line, 'Of course I love you,' he turned round. His wife was there. It all came down to her next line. '*You sod!*' There was no need for anything else. Everything encapsulated in those two words. The lies, the betrayal, and the end of a marriage.

The actors' performances were brilliant, but the shot that sticks in my mind is the one I really had to talk the director, Richard Standeven, into shooting. Heather bundles Roger out of the door and then goes and gets his briefcase, the symbol of his life and worth as a solicitor, to hurl out of the door after him. Richard, from memory, thought the bundling out was sufficient and that we only needed to see the crest-fallen, guilty and banished Roger before going back to end on a shattered but determined Heather. But before we came back to her, I wanted a symbol that indicated all the bridges were burned. The story was now going to be about Heather and how her neighbours reacted to her. I wanted something that made the audience aware that everyone knew Roger had cheated on his wife. It would then be more understandable and acceptable for him to go and never return.

To do this I had one of those writer's moments that many directors hate. When the situation and image in your head is so clear that you write it down exactly how it should be shot. Blow by blow. Edit by edit. Almost frame by frame. Over the years I've encouraged other writers to do this in their first draft scripts, and if we liked it we'd keep it. I probably drove Richard mad insisting that this briefcase had to be hurled up and out so that it would fly across The

Close and come to a sliding halt right outside the Grants' house, where Sheila, Bobby and Barry Grant were talking to next-door neighbour Alan Partridge while, across The Close, Marie Jackson looked on from her front window.

Having hurled the briefcase that far, Mandy would have been immediately selected for the Olympic shot put team, but the magic of production allows you to cheat every now and then and that sliding briefcase ended up exactly where I wanted it, right in front of all the neighbours, so the exposed adulterer had to meekly walk over and recover it, before heading off with his tail between his legs.

Having completely re-written four episodes to break up the relationship, we then had to pick up the existing scripts. In Episode 95 Heather and Roger were scheduled to attend the already-planned and scripted silver anniversary party for the Grants. The only change we made was substituting his dad for Roger, amending a few lines to explain why. In the following episode, a couple of scenes were re-written to show Roger being thrown out by his lover. He was last seen waiting for a bus to, as the final stage direction said, who knows where?

The storyline worked well in terms of audience and media reviews, concentrating on the fiction itself rather the production. In fact, Heather's line '*You, sod!*', perhaps not on the cutting edge of offensive language despite what the purists who monitored *Grange Hill* would claim, was the first expletive heard in *Brookie* for almost nine months, since the early frantic re-editing. I had decided to include the line as one of those moments when the only realistic form of articulation is scatology. But we didn't get one complaint. Not even from the kill C4 lobby.

Adrenalin is a great drug. It can keep you going long after you should fall over, but sooner or later you either have to stop or run out of energy completely. Alongside the *Brookie* contract and programme renewal, *Grange Hill* was approaching a critical time in losing its first iconic cast and moving on to the new teenage spin-off, *Tucker's Luck*. No matter how confident I felt about *Brookie*, I also had to be pragmatic. I still only had twelve months to convince Channel 4 *Brookie* would work, and if I didn't it would fold. If that happened, then at least *Grange Hill* would still be there. Besides, having had all the creative arguments while setting it up, I was not simply going to let go.

I wanted to keep control, especially as the new front-line characters of Gonch, Hollo, and Imelda and the Terrorhawks needed to step up and into the shoes vacated by Tucker, Trisha & Co. This meant I was working twenty-hour days trying to write all the *Grange Hill* storylines as well as the opening script and storylines for *Tucker's Luck*, alongside keeping on top of things like the *Grange Hill* novels, annuals and merchandise. Taking on the scripts for the Heather and Roger break-up was probably the final straw. On reflection, it was bound to happen: total mental and physical collapse.

Having seen the scripts through production and watched the rough-cut edits, I was feeling pretty tired so I decided to try and spend the weekend catching up on sleep. I now know that it is the worst thing to do, at least for me. Coming to a halt only exacerbates the adrenalin come down. It's probably why people often get the 'flu as soon as they take a holiday and the action stops.

Another difficult thing to do is suddenly to sleep when you have been getting by on four hours a night. It seemed like a sensible idea, but I couldn't do it. So I found myself taking a weekend off to catch up on my sleep and then not being able to, worrying over wasting time, and then ultimately worrying about wasting time being unable to sleep. The next obvious thing then was to 'do something', so I moved on to the mountain of books I had piled up waiting for the great mythical moment when I had time on my hands. This was it.

It was a hot sunny summer Saturday so I went through all the rigmarole of getting the sun lounger out, a drink, something to eat, and then had to decide what to read. Near the top of the pile was a copy of the Beatles biography by Hunter Davies, still unread. Like a lot of people in Liverpool I probably bought this at the time it was published because I felt I should and then left it on the shelf along with the pristine vinyls; as no matter where you went, you wouldn't go too long before hearing them. The city was like a form of crowd-sourced iPod shuffle before we even knew the term.

It was not long before I began to skim the book. I was probably too tired to concentrate, just as I had probably left it too late to read. A lot of it was now in the public domain since its original publication in 1968. Perhaps it was tiredness, perhaps even heat stroke, as I don't know how long I was in the garden, just as I don't know why I became fixated on wondering why things happen the way they do. How had I ended up here? In this house that had brought a tear to my dad's eye? And why was I now here alone? And after that came the 'What's the point?' moment. I might have fought for and won total control over my work, but what was the point if it left me so tired and alone?

It might not have been as dramatic as Agatha Christie's disappearance, but in my own life story this was a bit of a lost weekend. I really do not have much recollection of how long I was in the garden with the Beatles before I realised that I actually wasn't, as I was back in the lounge and Alexis was crouched down next to me on the floor.

I was sitting propped up against a chair. How had I got there? There was definitely something not right. I could have been lying there all night for all I know, but I had, apparently, managed to phone her. This was telling in itself. Alexis was probably the only person I felt able to trust at that time.

She had brought the company doctor, assuming I would prefer that to a 999 call. With *Brookie* and C4 still on the media hit list, a tale about the 'ailing soap' having an ailing exec producer would have made some freelancer a few quid. Her next call was to my brother Larry. By the time he arrived I had been pulled back from the abyss after the doctor ran me through the usual health checklist: what had happened; what had I been eating; how long had I been working; when did I last have a day off? And as I gave the responses, between being prodded and poked and my blood pressure taken, the concerned expression gave way to one of incredulity. No wonder I had collapsed.

On the medical form the doctor simply wrote 'exhaustion'. It did not seem that dramatic to me, but although we are all guilty of flopping down at times and saying something along the lines of 'I'm exhausted', I did gain a better medical understanding of the term that day, and how it differs from fatigue. The symptoms can include numbness, delirium, confusion and inability to stay awake or even to fall asleep. All these things can often be brought on by long-term and hectic schedules, and is the reason we often hear of touring artists having to pull out towards the end of a tour. Another symptom is the desire for complete withdrawal from other people.

Recalling the doctor's questions and listening to his diagnosis, it was obvious the warning signs had been there. The sense of loneliness was no doubt due to the all-consuming nature of the previous two hectic years spent trying to set up both company and programme. Then there was diet. That usually consisted of an early-morning bowl of cereal, a sandwich on the go at some time during the day, supplemented by coffee and Mars Bars. I'd obviously been brainwashed by the Mars 'work, rest and play' media campaign. In fact, a very obvious sign should have been my birthday, when the staff gave me a cake shaped like a Mars Bar. After working twenty-hour days, seven days a week, with a bad diet for nearly two years, what else did I expect?

Having spent a few days at my brother's I felt strong enough to go off on a delayed trip to visit my sister, Kathy, who was now living in California, not too far from where I had met Sony in Palo Alto, and to grow a beard. After a few weeks in and around the developing Silicon Valley I came back, if not fully refreshed then with the realisation that no matter how crazy you feel, there is always a home for you in California. I was also determined to rebuild my fitness by eating more sensibly and getting more exercise, yet I seemed to be going from one cold to another until towards the end of September I had another bout of wondering if God really did move in mysterious ways.

Back at my brother's, I was lying in bed recovering, I came across a story in the press about how local children with leukaemia had to travel to Birmingham for treatment because, although the Royal Liverpool Hospital had recently found the funds to build a Bone Marrow transplant facility, they couldn't actually afford to staff it. It wasn't the idea of building something that you couldn't afford to run that intrigued me, so much as the sum of money they needed. It was around £80,000, or the cost of approximately two episodes of *Brookside*.

I'm not sure you can get a wake-up call if you are already sitting in bed reading, but it was definitely time for me to get up. Here I was, feeling fragile because I had exhausted myself making nothing more than a television programme, while spending more in one week on the antics of fictional characters than it would take to run a critical-care unit for terminally ill children. I got up and went downstairs to 'borrow the phone' which, recalling that moment, makes me wonder if the real reason for the increase in national obesity is the mobile. How many miles did we have to walk in those days, to find a phone tied to a wall by wires? The call was to

Alexis. What did she think? The main burden would fall on her, managing the logistics of running two productions side by side, if only for a few weeks. There was no hesitation. Her Welsh Methodist background of self-help and determination got it immediately.

We called together both cast and staff. They too all readily agreed and so we booked the Everyman Theatre for a ten-night run, to put on *An Evening With Brookside*. The show was in two parts. For the first I wrote a light satire about how the programme itself was made: the actual production process, from the actors receiving their scripts to finally recording a scene. From actors enthusing if they were central to the scene, to complaining when they were seen, yet again, 'putting the milk bottles out', one of Sue Johnston's pet hates. It went on to illustrate the creative tensions we experienced every day, as actors, directors and crew would be constantly trying to 'improve' the script, while the evil script department was ever-present to discourage them. The second part was a Q & A with the actors on-stage. By the end of the run we'd managed to raise over £20,000. More importantly, we discovered that we had helped the Bone Marrow Trust raise awareness and hit their initial target early. The unit's future was secure.

It was great fun to do, a bit of a welcome release for everyone to get away from the demands of the daily production schedule, and it laid the foundations for much of the charity and community work MerseyTV became engaged in over the years – driven, I have to say, by that same Welsh Methodist determination. We would cover all the out-of-pocket expenses and the staff and cast would give their time free, so every penny made would go directly to charity. No overheads.

My mum used to have a saying about relationships: God made them; God matched them. Across that Everyman run I think he also pushed the Irish Catholic and the Welsh Methodist a bit closer. Having spent my childhood supporting my mum and dad in their attempts to raise money for the church, whether I wanted to or not, I suppose I expected everyone else to have the same 'Why not?' ethic towards charity. Alexis shared it. And she also shared something else – the sense of disappointment when the Everyman Bistro decided 'charity begins at home'. Theirs. Despite us delivering full houses for the run, they found it difficult to make a donation to the charity. We had to make do with the box office, which between us all we managed to oversell. Alexis stepped in and took over. It was with some amusement that I arrived at the theatre one night to find this highly qualified Arthur Andersen chartered accountant manning the box office, and explaining to the TV-loving audience why they were now on a chair in the aisle instead of one of the posh seats.

That Everyman experience laid the foundations for both the Script to Screens sessions, when we took the cast and crew on the road to illustrate how we actually made the programme, and for the annual charity balls that became such a feature of the year for everybody. Both were great occasions and an informal way for the whole company to come together, even allowing people from different departments to try out different jobs.

There were quite a few people who changed careers and advanced more quickly after they had shown everyone what else they could do during those get togethers. Lasting memories for me include great duets between Sue Jenkins and Dean Sullivan, as Jimmy and Jackie Corkhill; fantastic solo rock performances from Mickey Starke aka Sinbad, one of life's natural impersonators; from *Hollyoaks* Jimmy McKenna (aka Jack Osborne) doing Sinatra; and Will Mellor (aka Jambo) and Ben Hull (aka Lewis) performing anything. Then there was the comic genius of Vince Earl (aka Ron Dixon) as compère, although he had a bit of the Ken Dodd about him, refusing to leave the stage until he would see me walking down the hall and looking at my watch. Two bitter-sweet moments I will never forget were seeing a young Jenny Ellison (aka Emily Shadwick) doing a better job of Britney Spears than Britney herself, and standing unnoticed at the back of the hall when Claire Sweeney (aka Lindsey Corkhill) did a sound test, singing 'Don't Cry For Me Argentina'. Both performances were electric in their own way, and I knew the day would not be far into the future when I would have to face up to losing these performers.

Yet everything might have come to a premature end in February 1984, not through anything we or Channel 4 had done or were doing, but thanks to the vagaries of fate, which meant that Alexis and I were in the wrong place at the wrong time. On the M56 motorway, hit from behind and pushed into the central reservation. At 70 m.p.h.

We were on our way back from London from another round of

finance and legal meetings, probably still trying to finalise the never-ending contract negotiations with Channel 4. It was late, around eleven at night, after a fairly sedate journey up. Mainly, as fate would also have it, because I was having to behave myself and keep the BMW 323i under control. I had nine points on my licence.

I was holding the speed at 70 m.p.h. when I noticed a set of headlights in the rear-view mirror closing on us quite rapidly while weaving from side to side on the carriageway. From hard shoulder to outside lane, then back again. Just as I mentioned it to Alexis and she turned to look, I also realised that whatever it was, was in danger of running straight into us, so I dropped a gear and put my foot hard down in an attempt to outrun it. I knew the 323i could outrun almost anything, but it was too late. Whatever it was, hit us. And we were now heading flat out directly towards the central-reservation crash barrier.

These were no ordinary crash barriers. We were on top of the Weaver viaduct, alongside Frodsham, high up above the River Weaver and Bridgewater Canal. There was a gap between the two motorway carriageways so the barriers were high and obviously designed to stop cars like ours hitting them and flying over the edge into the river and canal a couple of hundred feet below. The old cliché of life going into slow motion at such times is true. I could see the safety barrier approaching. I saw the car hit it. The front edge of the bonnet began to crumple, fold back, and bits of paint flew off and past the wind-screen as we seemed to be going through the huge square heavy metal grilles. They reminded me of the potato chippers we used to have at home and I remember thinking, quite calmly, So *this* is what it is like to die.

The next thing I remember is seeing the engine block through the windscreen. I wondered why I could do that. Then I saw, rather then felt, my right arm moving to turn the ignition key and I was thinking, but again not feeling, that my feet seemed to be having trouble finding the pedals. They were not where they should be. The engine groaned and moaned but wouldn't start. Then, again watching but not feeling, I saw my left arm come up and reach for the hazard-warning light switch in the centre of the dashboard. It started to flash and as it did I heard the most awful rasping and spluttering sound coming from my left. Alexis.

Fortunately it was only the sound of her regaining consciousness and fighting to get air into her lungs. We were both apparently in one piece but hardly able to move. I then noticed the flow of white lights coming towards us, but slowing and diverting. We had been hit and spun round so that we were now facing into the oncoming traffic. Within the white headlights I thought I saw a set of red ones, moving in the opposite direction. As we regained our senses I kept trying to get my seat belt off to get out, but Alexis kept fighting me to keep it on and stay put. She thought it was safer in the wreck than on the carriageway. The traffic would eventually stop, she said. But it didn't. Vehicles would slow down and skirt round us, but none of them stopped.

Eventually we decided we should get out so, in what we thought was a break in the traffic, we managed to climb out and support each other across the carriageway. It was only when we were on the hard shoulder and leaning against the safety barrier that we realised the traffic was actually quite minimal. The flow of lights, it was later explained, was probably the compression of time as we were still in the process of recovering full consciousness. So there we were, a car wreck in the outside lane and two human wrecks leaning against the safety barrier. Relatively safe, but, in the pre-mobile phone days, totally isolated.

Then, as it often does, well, if you are one of life's dramatists, the scene from the movie came along. Over on the other carriageway a car came to a sliding stop. A figure came out and round from the passenger side and, as the car sped away, then scaled the high barrier, leaped the gap between the carriageways, dropped down on to our side and ran towards us. As the figure drew closer all we could see was an old army greatcoat and a mass of long tangled hair and beard. A sight I had seen many a time on building sites across the People's Republic, and for an instant I wondered if we had just avoided death only to fall into the clutches of a refugee from the Charles Manson Family. However, Samaritans should not be judged by their coats. He was more super-hero.

Whether he was trained in nursing, first aid or trauma recovery I don't know, but he did a great job of reassuring us that help was on its way and took his coat off to wrap round Alexis. It was February and we had been travelling in a heated Beemer. His mate finally arrived in what looked like either an old Morris Oxford or an Austin A55, like the one I had lovingly restored only for it to be sunk in the River Dee. He said he'd called for an ambulance and threw open the doors for us to sit down inside and warm up a bit, to reveal the seats were covered in some form of fluffy but badly matted blanket material. I remember wondering what could be living in there and if that was why they were both wearing thick overcoats, so as to insulate themselves. That's probably unfair and part of my mental disorientation, as we never got a chance to find out who they were or thank them as the first blue lights and sirens to arrive belonged to the cops. As they approached, our Samaritans, in true super-hero fashion, decided their job was done. They helped us out of the car, wished us luck and sped off into the night. I'd seen that many times across the Republic too.

The cops slowed to have a look at us, but, seeing we were upright and in one piece, drove past. What? They then positioned their Range Rover in front of the BMW, attached a chain and dragged it off the carriageway and on to the hard shoulder. As this was happening the ambulance arrived and took over where Swampy and Charles Manson had left off, but they were local so I then had the Eric Morecambe moment. He had recently told the tale of how he had had a heart attack and, as he was being rushed through A&E, people were asking him for his autograph. He would die a few months later of another one. As I huddled at the side of the motorway, in agony now, and the guys put me in the ambulance, one of them said the line that was starting to become very familiar: 'You're him, aren't you? That bloke that does *Brookside*?' Alexis always tells the tale, still with the Valleys edge to her voice, of how at the hospital I was ushered through like royalty, while she was practically left to stagger in by herself.

Upon examining us, because there were no visible injuries, the typical on-duty-eighty-hours-plus doctor, obviously coming to the end of his shift, reckoned we had only severe bruising from the seat belts, and with a couple of painkillers could probably head home. However, the eagle-eyed Casualty sister wasn't having that. She kept pointing out to him the way we were both holding our chests. She thought it was something more serious and we should be X-rayed. He did not, especially as there was no one in X-ray at that time of night. She insisted. A radiographer was on call. He hesitated. She gave him a look that said, I'm more experienced than you. And I'm telling you. He decided to give me another check up and started tapping my chest, until he tapped my sternum and I went up and clung to the ceiling. OK. Get him down to X-ray. A voice was heard from the cubicle next door. Er . . . What about me? The developed films showed we had both fractured our sternums and would probably have whiplash.

The now-solicitous doctor explained that the only treatment was painkillers, bed rest, and wrapping our arms round our bodies if we felt we were either going to cough or laugh – which actually made me laugh and proved his point. He went on to explain that we had what were now the most common injuries in our sort of accident: damage from seat belts. He said it seemed like a reasonable result. Either that or be killed flying through the windscreen. I tended to agree. We thanked the diligence of the A&E nurse and were released carrying our possessions in plastic bin liners.

It turned out that the car that hit us had been driven by a guy who had just been made redundant but had been allowed to keep his company car for a few days, in which he had gone out and got drunk. The red lights I thought I had seen amongst all the white approaching the car as I regained consciousness were indeed his tail lights. After hitting us, he too had spun round. Facing the wrong way, he had driven back up the motorway and exited down the entrance ramp. We knew all this because later he had gone into a police station, and said he thought he had hit something on the motorway the previous night. He had obviously realised that the damage to the company car would be queried. Once he sobered up.

It took a long time for my anger to subside, not just because we were hit by a drunk, which did nothing to soften my views on alcohol, but due to his total irresponsibility. Within a couple of seconds he had inflicted so much damage and injury on Alexis and me, most of which took years to heal while being managed with painkillers. But I was also left with residual problems to my back, neck and knee that caused occasional incapacity, meant a change in lifestyle, and which are now a worsening problem. During our follow-up medicals, we were both told that things would gradually heal and be fine for probably twenty-five to thirty years. After that, we would start falling apart. And, as though set on a timer, that has proved to be true.

There was another major concern too. If I had been anxious not to let anyone know about my exhaustion six months earlier, I was almost paranoid that C4 in particular would discover I might be bed-bound for six weeks. Although *Brookie*, as the medical staff's curiosity had demonstrated, was beginning to build its audience, we had still not consolidated our position with C4. We were approaching the all-important second-year renewal negotiations and, although we had exceeded the ratings target, we still considered these fragile. And I was the key man on the insurance policy. If they, the staff, or the press, got wind of how bad the crash had been, or could have been, they might have become anxious about the renewal. It seems strange now, looking back at that age of innocence – almost – considering the digital web of information and social media that surrounds us all today. We'd have been Tweeted by the side of the motorway, Facebooked in A&E, with a live YouTube feed from the X-Ray Department. It would have been impossible to keep things low-key, never mind under wraps. Yet that was what we managed to do.

Against medical advice I convinced myself I did not need six weeks' rest. If there was no treatment except painkillers and self-hugging every now and then, I was sure I could cope with 'just talking to people'. It seems ridiculous now, as I couldn't even get to the bathroom without help initially, mainly because with a fractured sternum any arm movement is agony. I couldn't turn a door handle or even push on a light, a task I eventually discovered I could do by pressing my nose against the recently installed modern rocker switches.

I called Alexis to see how she was doing and found she was experiencing the same difficulties but, as usual, also going through the same thought processes. We had calls scheduled with our respective links at C4, with one of mine being to The Emperor himself to reassure him that all was well going into the renewal and that the ratings curve would continue up. I couldn't tell him I would have to hope for the best, as I would be at home recovering. So I didn't. And made the calls from my bed.

The next hurdle was the staff. Although we had to say we had had an accident, due to things like having to notify the insurance company and have the car collected for repair, cancel a few meetings and so on, it was important to make it seem inconsequential. So, despite being told to stay in bed, five days later we were both back at work attending a Heads of Department (HoD) meeting that had been called to discuss the production requirements attached to that all-important second-year renewal. The staff were all anxious about it due to the possible impact on their families and mortgages. We might have overdone the inconsequential bit, but dosed up on strong painkillers we managed a couple of hours in the office before attending the HoD meeting, though by the time we were drawing to a close I was instinctively starting to self-hug.

A couple of the staff noticed, notably the senior production assistant, Angela Mocroft, who was always highly attuned to any political or personal developments. As such she would become a great stalwart of the company, handling community liaison on our behalf, but she asked if we were really all right in a way that outdid both the Samaritan brothers and the medics for concern. We managed to convince her we were OK and Colin McKeown, displaying his own highly tuned conspiratorial genes, said he thought we had overdone the sympathy bid. He assumed we were playing it up, not down, to get everyone feeling more sympathetic to us and not expecting too much ahead of the Channel 4 negotiations. Perhaps he had a point.

Alexis and I then went back to our beds of recovery, agreeing that we should take a week off. As it turned out this was not enough medically, and emotionally way too long. I began to realise how much I was missing my daily contact with this 'slip of a girl'.

13

What Now? (1984–86)

'Is Jesus bloody Christ a swear word or a blasphemy?' – *Paddy O'Neal*, Daily Mail *TV journalist*

It turned out that 1985 was to be another stepping-stone year as I became involved in two different drama series, one being developed at MerseyTV, the other not. The one at MerseyTV was a six-part drama series called *What Now?* The other was a small project the BBC was developing, a fifty-two-week twice-weekly to be known as *EastEnders*. Both needed me as a writer. With *What Now?* I would be writing the scripts and making my directing debut. With *EastEnders*, the BBC needed my signature to get started.

A call came from BBC Copyright asking me if I could forgo the now traditional annual arm wrestle over the *Grange Hill* contract and sign it quickly. Why? Because we are buying the old ATV Studios out at Elstree. I've heard. Yes, for training. You need four studios and a back lot for training? Yes, but we need a production to go there to allow us to open it up. And that's *Grange Hill*? Yes, you know all the aggravation we've had trying to use real schools. I did. After each series they had had to move on as the schools used for locations had complained about the disruption. These days, we'd probably find a school with media as its specialism and build it into the coursework. However, then . . . So, we thought it would be a good idea to give it its own dedicated set, a bit like *Brookside*. Oh, yeah? What's really going on?

It turned out that David Reid, still Head of Drama Series and Serials, was searching for a long-runner. The BBC was now the only broadcaster without a regular twice-weekly, but was actively looking for one, and whatever it was, it was going to be made at Elstree. But the first programme to be made there would be *Grange Hill.*

The programme was now in its eighth production year, accepted for what it was – entertainment with a point – and on the verge of crossing another generational threshold as Pogo Patterson (aka Peter Moran), Gripper Stebson (aka Mark Savage), Claire Scott (aka Paula Ann Bland), Roland Browning (aka Erkan Mustafa) and Suzanne Ross (aka Susan Tully aka Michelle Fowler in *EastEnders*) were starting to make way for the class of Gonch Gardener (aka John Holmes), Jackie Wright (aka Melissa Wilks), little brother Robbie Wright (aka John Alford), Ronnie Birtles (aka Tina Mahon), Calley Donnington (aka Simone Hyams), and Imelda Davis (aka Fleur Taylor). Into this generational, rites-of-passage mix came Anthony Minghella, having joined the series in 1983 as script editor. Probably best known for directing *Truly Madly Deeply*, *The Talented Mr. Ripley* and *The English Patient*, and for becoming Chairman of the BFI, Anthony worked on *Grange Hill* for three years, which included probably its best-known storyline, Zammo McGuire (aka Lee McDonald)'s decline into drug-taking and rehabilitation from it, a storyline that would help ease the generational transition as it was spread over two series.

Remembering this time is tinged with great sadness for me as Anthony joined the series with a new producer, Kenny McBain, and while they both brought a new and fresh energy to *Grange Hill*, before both going on to make their own considerable mark on the world, both men would die too soon and too young. Kenny stayed with *Grange Hill* for two seasons and then went on to develop *Inspector Morse* for ITV, but died in 1989 at the age of forty-two. Anthony would die in 2008, aged fifty-four, a great shock to everyone. It came not long after we had bumped into each other at a Bafta event, spent a short time reminiscing and promised not to do the typical media thing of saying we would 'do lunch' and then finding our respective careers keeping us at opposite ends of the earth.

While I'm sad that we didn't rekindle our friendship as we had planned, the memories endure. I knew Anthony was a 'real one' when I first met him. He had the aura you pick up in the presence of talent. I remember reading the obituary tributes from people like Jude Law and Tony Blair, saying he was 'a wonderful human being, creative and brilliant, but still humble, gentle and a joy to be with'. I too still remember fondly the moments we shared, especially when he used to come up to *Brookside* and camp outside my office until he'd squeezed the new storylines for *Grange Hill* out of me.

'Consider me your amanuensis,' he used to say, and I would respond that since I went to a comprehensive school, he'd better speak English, but if he wanted to be my writer's assistant then he would have to wait until after the shoot was finished. Which he did, much to the delight of the girls in the office. They all developed a soft spot for him, which I used to say was because he was the male equivalent of the girl whose dad owns a pub. His parents owned an ice-cream factory in the Isle of Wight, making Anthony second in popularity only to Willy Wonka. In our late-night sessions we would talk through the *Grange Hill* storylines and he would go off and knock them into shape for us to review again over a snatched lunch the following day. From these sessions came the Zammo drugs storyline, played brilliantly by Lee, with Anthony supporting my desire to have it run over two seasons: one to show the decline into drugs, the other to show a possible route out.

I felt strongly that the '*thou shalt not*' anti-drugs message pushed by both government and health authorities was pointless and counter-productive. The overriding theme was that if you took drugs, you died. End of. That was obviously not the life experience of many living in the social conditions that fostered the drug culture, including the media. More pointedly, those most at risk, vulnerable teenagers, were unlikely to be sitting at home, happily watching TV, waiting for a government information film to pop up and change their entire outlook on life. This, for me, was another symptom of the sociological divide. Those in authority knowing they had to be seen to be doing something but not quite knowing what, while constantly fearful of being seen to be doing the wrong thing.

Health advisers and anti-drugs counsellors were saying that the '*drugs bad: you die*' message was not working, obviously, as drug-related problems were increasing. A more sophisticated message was needed, the real message, about the lack of life opportunities, which is predicated on eventually entering the employment market. Sweeping statement, I know, but, unfortunately, one of life's simplistic truisms that was and still is too sophisticated for government. '*Jobs good: you live*', or, we can create meaningful employment that binds people into a community with social status and self-esteem. Both are difficult election promises to deliver. Both sides of the sociological divide know this, but neither have the capabilities to deliver on it. Neither can simply conjure meaningful employment from thin air. Otherwise, why have teenage unemployment and illiteracy levels remained fairly constant, discounting the constant reclassification of suspect youth schemes, courses and stretched education?

While developing and running the Zammo storyline in *Grange Hill*, we were also in *Brookie* running the Damon Grant storyline about Youth Training Schemes (YTS). Both were about teenage despair. When Damon had done everything asked of him, had worked hard, been diligent, and was then sacked at the end of the scheme, all he could do was return home and fall sobbing into his mother's arms, totally bewildered. It is a scene that always comes up in other people's top ten lists. It was shot back in 1986. It would be just as relevant today. Yet, while we took Damon in a different direction, perhaps pointing up something Zammo didn't have, a more long-term reflection is that perhaps there is another addiction at work here: that of our policy-makers in always reaching for a short-term 'fix'. A scheme that temporarily alleviates the boredom, despair or pain, while only masking or displacing the underlying problem.

We worked with SCODA, the Standing Committee on Drug Abuse, to include positive information. The *Grange Hill* cast released the 'Just Say No' record that reached number five in the charts, raising over £100,000 to help with SCODA's work. Out of this came the idea of releasing a more commercial single and album. BBC Records wanted to do cover versions, but I wanted to keep to the philosophy of the books and offer something more original, an extension of the series and better value for money, so Steve Wright and I put together six original tracks. However, someone from Records didn't take someone from the Children's Department to lunch in time, and just like the *Grange Hill* movie the project foundered on inter-departmental rivalry.

There was one great media moment, though, when I went on BBC's *Breakfast Time* to promote the single from the album and found we had been booked for a couple of minutes before the news at eight o'clock. This was our one and only spot, but just ahead of us was a guy coming on to trail a major item after the news about whether the Turin Shroud, one of the Catholic Church's most precious relics, was authentic. We went on, did the knock-about spot on the programme, cast and single, and went back to the Green Room to gather our things and leave. Just as we were about to go the floor manager came hurrying along the corridor, shouting, 'Keep the kids. Great reaction from the audience about the *Grange Hill* single. We're ditching the Shroud!'

The entire basis of the Catholic faith had just been rocked, but the *Grange Hill* single got the viewers' vote. That's media. Not that it made much difference. With the promotion now scuppered by in-house politics, the album bombed . . . until being re-released in 2007 when it did reasonably well as a nostalgia buy, probably to people who were kids back in the 1980s. And that's media too.

While the series was applauded and the cast were flown to the White House to meet Nancy Reagan, who was patron of the US Just Say No campaign, we were still getting flak because we had shown Zammo at one point enjoying taking drugs. And therein lies both the tension and the hypocrisy at work in reflecting social issues like drugs. Fine to show an anti-message, but not actually to try and educate by fully explaining the issue: that it may be a pleasurable short-term high, but one that carries long-term consequences. Twenty years later I was fighting the same argument all over again with the Jimmy Corkhill drugs storyline. Despite, this time, *Brookside* being aimed at adults. More policy addiction at work.

Drug addiction is a theme I returned to many times over the years in my writing simply because it is one of life's constants. It affects great numbers of people. It is also something that pervades all sections and elements of society. Around the same time as *Grange Hill* was running the Zammo storyline, in *Brookie* we had Heather discover that her new husband, Nick Black (aka Alan Rothwell), was a user. The point of this storyline was to explore a different aspect of drug-taking. While reinforcing the point that death was all too common among addicts, we showed it didn't have to be if they sought help. Nick, as a respectable architect, had done so and had managed his addiction for years through a network of sympathetic suppliers. It was another of those storyline points we wanted to keep for as long as we could, but under the twin pressures of

Mandy Burton wanting to move on and the need to abide by the TV Regulations, he had to go. In other words, Nick the user had to get his comeuppance. So he did. Drugs bad: he died. Which gave Heather the rationale to leave *Brookside* and set up a new life, allowing Mandy to go off and enjoy the glittering career she deserved.

If by now you are wondering why character exits always have to be so dramatic, it is not all to do with ratings, honestly. It is because the audience feel dissatisfied, almost betrayed, if one of their regular characters just decides to up and go. It's almost, for some, a form of desertion. People often asked me why I let actors like Mandy, or Sue Johnston, or Anna Friel, or Will Mellor from *Hollyoaks*, just leave. Why didn't I keep them? The answer I usually gave was that slavery was abolished in 1833, and that when the actors decided they wanted to leave, their characters had to go with them. It was much easier for the audience if there was a strong and compelling storyline accompanying the departure. Interestingly, off-screen Mandy's next jobs were on *Inspector Morse* and *Boon*, with Kenny McBain and Anthony Minghella.

The tension between what you want to show, what you should show and what you can show was something we had to juggle constantly, and something which I think gradually eroded television's power as a tool for social intervention as the regulations became tighter and tighter throughout the 1990s. I rank the Jimmy Corkhill drugs storyline as one of *Brookie*'s best, but it was a constant battle with Channel 4 and the ITC to keep it on air. At times I felt as though I was the only one in British television the regulators were monitoring, and at times I probably was, but in 1985 *EastEnders* arrived to help take some of the heat.

It wasn't planned that way. I think David Reid's original brief was based around a Southern *Coronation Street*. However, he chose Julia Smith and Tony Holland to come up with it. They were the obvious choice, in fact, having worked together on *Z Cars* and *Angels*. The latter, written by one of my WGGB mates Paula Milne, created a few waves with its 'gritty portrayal of nurses'. In other words she showed the reality of the job. While David might have been thinking *Corrie* with a Surrey accent, with their heritage Julia and Tony were bound to come back with something a bit more challenging. As the Southern *Corrie* was going to be filmed across the road from the

Grange Hill school, I soon received another call asking if I would be prepared to spend a bit of time with Julia and Tony, to share experience. Why not? *Brookie* was seen as a progression from the BBC-nurtured *Grange Hill*, and *Z Cars* was, fictionally, based on Kirkby where I had gone to school.

We got together at a wine bar in Wood Lane, just off Shepherd's Bush. By then they had really nailed down what they wanted to do. Although admitting that they were initially thinking about a Southern *Coronation Street*, this was soon dismissed as they thought it would look and feel dated against *Brookside*, now regarded as the more 'realistic' programme. At the same time, though, they would be studio-based. They needed the traditional set up of a central set, like The Rover's Return in *Corrie*, to get all their characters together easily. Putting that and the hard edge of the *Brookie* scripts together seemed both sensible and inevitable. Which is why the nation was soon enthralled by Dirty Den and Angie knocking seven bells out of each other in the Queen Vic.

Brookie was already settling into its twelve-month story and script process. Long-term planning meetings (LTPM) twelve months ahead of transmission; storylines five months ahead; first drafts four months ahead; production scripts two months ahead; and the actual shoot six weeks ahead of transmission. Editing was three weeks ahead, and delivery two weeks ahead of transmission. And, for anyone reading who was part of it all, I know . . . but that is how it was supposed to be. Provided we all knew that, we could work round it. Couldn't we? This need for logistics planning was something emphasised to Julia and Tony. Running a continuous soap was like piloting a supertanker. It took a long time to respond to commands. If you spotted anything wrong it would take six months to fix and six months to show on air.

When Julia got to Elstree she imposed an iron rule there that made me look soft and cuddly, or so I was told. I only ever saw nice Auntie Julia, but I got all the gossip from *Grange Hill*. She never quite got over the fact that they had been there first and 'bagged' all the best offices on the first floor, while she had to go up a couple of flights. She was like the unofficial school headmistress, who would tell off the kids and crew if she found them loitering on the stairs.

She and Tony came up to spend a bit of time at *Brookie* to see the way we were doing things, and whenever I went down to *Grange Hill* I would call in if she was around. That was quite odd at times. I sometimes found myself in the same rooms as I had been in while working on *The Squirrels* or *Dan Dare*, and could never quite shake the memories. I would expect to see Bing Crosby or Val Doonican or to hear the ghostly strains of Val Parnell's Orchestra drifting along the corridors. I used to bore people like Anthony Minghella by constantly referring to what used to be at Elstree. Where the old water tank was under Studio C which they used while making *The Muppets*, and how the Henson gang had painted Miss Piggy and Kermit on the ballet mural, but it all gradually faded as Lew Grade's marble and stardust was swept away under BBC Health & Safety rough-cord institutional carpets.

Two other things were always odd at Elstree. One was the reaction of people seeing the exec producer from a so-called rival soap hanging about the *EastEnders* set, until the penny dropped that I was there with *Grange Hill*. The other was, that having been asked to share experience with *EastEnders*, and having come down from *Brookie* where I had total control over everything, I had to sit on my hands and bite my tongue during the *Grange Hill* script meetings as I could see resources being wasted unnecessarily. There, I was back to being a mere writer and creator, but I respected their protocols just as I would expect them to respect ours.

By this time, and as a direct consequence of my physical burnout, Alexis had recruited Andrew Corrie, despite his surname, to be my creative assistant. He had been working as a script editor at Granada and was recruited to take the weight of *Grange Hill*, all its merchandising and spin-offs and everything that was 'not *Brookside*'. Andrew would be the go-between who saved both my own and many other people's sanity by stepping up, like Alexis, to say, '. . . *what Phil really means* . . .' For that, I am eternally grateful. Like Alexis, he worked directly for Phil Redmond Enterprises Ltd, and from the first day until he left many years later, he carried that weight with the patience of Job – along with his blue checklist file that he would try and run through whenever he could pin me down. As the years went by it would be Andrew who would attend those *Grange Hill* meetings, but one is permanently etched in my mind, not because of the script content but because it was filmed for some documentary or other. It keeps popping up in retrospectives, with the main focus of attention being the green shoes I was fond of wearing at the time. They will come back in. One day.

On 19 February 1985 *EastEnders* finally arrived. *Emmerdale Farm* was also networked across ITV, and on the other side of the world, Reg Watson, one-time producer of ATV's *Crossroads*, was launching *Neighbours*. *Brookie* was not only no longer the new kid on the block, but soon it would be having to fight its corner against a whole new gang. This was not going to be a ratings war. No two soaps ever go head-to-head as the audiences overlap. The only time it ever happened, when Albert Square went up against The Street, they both lost 50 per cent of their ratings. The fight ahead of us was going to be for press coverage.

Just as there are four dimensions to television – the idea, the production, the broadcaster and the politics – there are two currencies: ratings and media impact. To maximise either there are a few standard tools an executive producer needs to keep on the tool belt. The two most obvious are casting and spectacle. And for times of real emergency, on the wall in the 'break glass' box, there is the timely explosion. This is exactly the same philosophy that drives any marketing campaign: the grab. It may be the music, visuals, front cover, headline or star presenter, but from selling a new soap powder, alerting people to health threats, promoting a party leader to raising money for charity, it is always about arresting attention. Getting people to stop and take notice.

This strategy had developed after the first renewal and the need to increase ratings. Every new arrival in the programme was an opportunity to publicise the programme and reach a wider audience. So, still in the afterglow of the white heat of IT82, young Francis and his Xerox script printer were kicked out of number 6, the bungalow, to make way for computer programmer Alan Partridge, aka Dicken Ashworth. This was in order to tap the growing 'geekaverse'. Cuddly would be seen with the latest gizmos and gadgets, including the boy-racer car of choice at the time, the Ford Escort XR3i, that could, almost, give my 323i Beamer a race away from the lights. He also had a cutting-edge sound system that had speakers the size of small dinner tables, which I commandeered when the character left and strapped to my Writers' Guild prize-money sound system, which is still keeping people away from the door thirty years later. He also came with a ratings and publicity-grabbing former Miss UK, Dinah May, as his girlfriend.

Next door, at number 7, the house with no walls upstairs, one of our all-time legends arrived, Harry Cross, aka Bill Dean, bringing with him his own backstory and existing publicity as one of Liverpool's best comedians and actors. His fictional wife, Edna, aka Betty Alberge, was already part of the UK's social history, as she was the lady who spoke the first words in the venerable *Coronation Street* itself, playing Florrie Lindley in the corner shop. That definitely got media watchers talking.

With *EastEnders* coming, we and C4 were going to have to face a BBC media blitz across all its, then, two TV and five national radio channels plus the regional and local radio networks. Whether we liked it or not, the nation was going to be told that *EastEnders* was the best thing since the BBC had been created. And they did. And the nation did as it was told and watched. ITV did the same with *Corrie* and *Emmerdale*, and C4 agreed to give us a mention every now and then, caught on the horns of the same dilemma as always: whether to promote the corporate entity of the channel or its programmes. However, we had to do something to maintain *Brookie's* profile, so we also went back to what we knew. If we couldn't buy the publicity, we had to get editorial coverage. We had to get people taking about the programme again. And we would have to be heard above the increased tide of chatter, surrounding soaps.

Although 1985 is known for what is regarded as our first big high-profile storyline, 'the siege', when Harry Cross's tenants, the two nurses Sandra Maghie (aka Sheila Grier) and Kate Moses (aka Sharon Rosita), together with hospital porter Pat Hancock (aka David Easter), were held at gunpoint by an increasingly deranged gunman, John Clarke, played brilliantly by Robert Pugh, it was in fact the second news-grabbing attempt after the Free George Jackson campaign we ran at the end of 1983. That began as a device to allow Cliff Howells, who played George Jackson, to leave by having the character wrongly convicted and sent to jail.

When discussing the social justice element of his wife campaigning to prove his innocence, the idea developed of doing something loosely modelled on an earlier real-life campaign in London: Free George Davis. This had caught the imagination both of the media and the public, as well as their support, to the extent that it was mimicked and adapted across the UK by other campaigners. We decided to ride this wave and printed T-shirts, car stickers, and even issued a record around the theme – many of which I think are still stacked in a warehouse somewhere – as well as having a huge banner hauled up to the top of what is now the Radio City Tower. It worked. The ratings went over 4 million for the first time since the initial launch.

We learned then, as others must have done, that a high-profile storyline would attract more visibility and column inches, so it often puzzled me why some media practitioners used to criticise us for adopting high-octane storylines, as though there was yet another sacred rulebook somewhere that said if you made a programme of a certain length that fitted a certain transmission slot then it had to be called a soap, and therefore had only to cover a certain type of storyline involving certain types of characters in certain settings. This was the same sort of narrow perspective that could not conceive of C4 as anything other than ITV2 and would therefore insist its continuing drama was going to be a soap like *Coronation Street*. The other puzzling thing was how they didn't quite get the link between a long-runner and its audience. Whenever we ran a 'special', the figures went up. The audience enjoyed them. Yet this too was something to be scorned apparently.

Over the years critics would often try and hurl the accusation that we were simply engaging in 'cynical ratings-grabbing exercises', while we were often left wondering, 'And your point is . . . ?' That was what my programmes were meant to do. They needed to reach the highest possible audience they could for the sake of the broadcasters. Ensuring this happened was just part of my role as executive producer, and it was also what I had set out to do creatively: create a relationship with as large an audience as possible in order to explore contemporary issues. Intriguingly then, the relationship with the audience actually became an issue in itself, another form of class division, as soap audiences generally conform to the demographics of that ill-fated Wenham Report, correlating to the readership of the tabloid *Sun*, while most of the critics instinctively saw themselves as *Guardian* readers. Even if they wrote for the tabloids.

What that meant was that while the television audiences were predominantly working-class, the commentators were predominantly middle-class, and therefore separated at birth in terms of cultural experience, reference points and expectations. This also applied, by and large, to the broadcasters themselves who were still very much of the Oxbridge ilk. So while they would fret about the opinions of the middle-class critics, they gave too little attention to what their own audiences wanted. They thought a lot about what was good for the audience, but not about their actual experience of the story. It would be nice to think twenty-odd years on that this gap has narrowed, but I do not believe it has.

The siege story revolved around the fact that Clarke believed the nurses had in some way failed his mother who had died while under their care. It was more the story of his own deteriorating mental health than any failure on their part and eventually culminated in his suicide, but not before the killing of Nurse Moses during a struggle. It was well written by Andy Lynch, well acted, well directed, and very well received by the audience . . . but not the critics. We had, apparently, transgressed and broken the unknown, let alone unwritten, rule that we shouldn't do storylines like this. *Brookside's* audience disagreed, over 8 million of them. It earned the highest rating we had ever achieved. We got the column inches. We were heard, and we kept our place on the corner of the block. And after that, spectacle would become part of *Brookie's* DNA.

Something else happened. *Brookie* was finally becoming 'cool' in its own right, another of those strange moments when you suddenly realise that the tide has turned. Instead of fighting it you are suddenly being swept along by it. With *Grange Hill* it happened around the fifth series, when the critics realised it wasn't going to go away and the campaigners realised it was reaching an audience they hadn't been able to. Suddenly, it seemed *Brookside* was the place where people wanted to see and be seen. *The Tube* visited, with Jools Holland on The Close while Paula Yates was filmed out in a rowing boat on Liverpool Docks with Shelagh O'Hara, aka Karen Grant. Among the overseas broadcasters and UK indies was a very young Michael Jackson, the epitome of cool, who would later become Chief Executive of C4 itself, but was then producing *The Media Show*. We became a mandatory destination for all the local MPs. We were so cool I was even asked to speak at a Coal Industry Association Dinner, as requests for me and the cast to appear on the developing chat-show circuit increased. Although we were always careful which actors we let loose on the airwaves. So many people made the assumption that because an actor played a particular role they were expert on the associated subject, so we would get requests for the cast to go and discuss abortion, rape or unemployment, as though they were expert counsellors. We used to offer the researchers or writers instead, but in the ratings-driven world of television, they wouldn't have attracted any additional viewers. There were actors we did feel comfortable to have talking on behalf of the programme, like Sue Johnston or Dean Sullivan, or later Terri Dwyer or Jeremy Edwards from *Hollyoaks*, I always knew they would do their research before discussing anything other than their own roles and careers. While the actors did peak entertainment or breakfast shows, I would be invited on to the late-night news and current affairs programmes.

With *Brookie* going from strength to strength, and Andrew in place taking the weight of *Grange Hill*, I was looking for another, bigger challenge, and despite the popularity of the younger characters like Damon and Karen Grant in *Brookside*, I still felt I hadn't quite cracked teenage drama. *Going Out*, successful as it was artistically, had not received the exposure we had all wanted due to Southern TV losing their franchise. *Tucker's Luck*, although a scaled up *Grange Hill*, was still a tamed down early-evening offering, caught in a BBC limbo, being neither children's nor adult drama. As *Going Out* had also helped shape the early discussions about what *Brookie* could be with David Rose and his then assistant Walter Donahue, the obvious idea to pitch to him was another teenage drama that would let us go where we had originally intended: into the late-night territory first chartered by *Going Out*. And return to 'realistic dialogue'. On top of this, it would also be my directing debut.

Just like my other projects, the name was changed as we got into production. Originally called *Streetwise*, it became *What Now?* Perhaps as familiar a teenage phrase as *Going Out*. And perhaps a play on my own musing about what to do next . . . *What Now?* That question was also posed about the technology, as due to our continuing relationship with Sony, we were both ready to take the next quantum leap. Just as we had introduced *Brookside* with 1-inch C-format tape instead of 2-inch, now we were going for the next generation. We would use the new Betacam half-inch tape, and in cassette form rather than reel-to-reel. The cameras would have built-in recorders which had again been developed with news-gathering in mind and were therefore becoming known as ENG (Electronic News Gathering). While they offered even greater mobility and flexibility, we soon found that, as with the 1-inch format, drama's requirements had been left out of the development brief. The sound quality was not good enough.

The idea was that the sound would be captured from either a camera-mounted mic or one held by a reporter, and cabled to the camera back. Fine for live news interviews on location, but there was not enough bandwidth on the half-inch tape for clean drama recording. Even if there had been, it would mean cabling from floor or boom mics back to the camera, thus negating the whole purpose of the cameras being lightweight and portable. This time there was no quick trip to Palo Alto to talk to the software engineers, so Colin McKeown and Ray Palfreyman, Head of Sound, decided to resolve this by adopting the film practice of taking separate sound. We would link radio mics back to portable Nagra recorders, synching the sound in post-production. To do this we would use a 1-inch, sixteen-track machine from an audio recording studio, another first in the UK, which had the union diehards scratching their heads about whether this was an audio- or video-grade editing process. I don't think we cared much by then.

From a creative viewpoint what I was pushing for was a refinement of what we already had at *Brookie*. But while smaller, faster and more technically advanced than anywhere else, it was still cumbersome in terms of the actors having to hit their 'marks' and confine their performances within the limits of the sets, lighting and cable lengths attached to camera and sound. Every location shoot still needed a quasi-military reconnaissance exercise or 'recce'. Were there enough toilets, phone lines, power, car parking, and so on? The new Betacam promised us the ability to turn up, roll out, point and shoot. Battery-powered and carrying everything we needed. We probably achieved, as you normally do, about 60 per cent of what we wanted.

Due to production being a collaborative process and subject to so many vagaries and uncertainties, if you achieve 55 per cent of the original intent you are doing well, 60 per cent means you are ahead of the pack and 65 per cent is terrific. Seventy per cent is almost perfection. Anything above is some form of miracle. If you think you are getting better than that then you are setting your sights too low at the outset, which is the critical point. You have to aim high because occasionally, very occasionally, you will almost get there and, when you do, it comes in third on the emotional scale, after love and sex. To conceive a fictional universe and then actually see it unfold in front of you doesn't happen too often. On any shoot, that is what everyone wants to be part of. That magical moment when you shift dimension, from reality to the imaginary.

Or else you become so absorbed in what you are doing that you forget you are actually in the middle of someone else's universe. You finish shooting and walk off to lunch, talking through things with cast and crew, only to realise halfway through coffee that you are sitting at a table in the middle of an underground car park. Or you turn to complain about a loud bang that has just ruined a romantic screen moment, to discover someone has wrecked their car by driving into a traffic island while rubber-necking your shoot. The best example I had on *What Now?* was during the typical baddies-chasing-goody sequence. It was planned to have our romantic lead, Ray (aka Vic McGuire), being chased by Digger Johnson (aka Tim Dantay) and his gang through Liverpool city centre: from a shopping precinct, across overhead walkways, rooftops, and down through an underground car park to emerge into Williamson Square. The idea was to show off the Liverpool skyline and end up outside the picturesque Playhouse, where Ray, during the chase, would knock over a new love interest, but then come back to find her, apologise and ask her out. Simple.

Once again I was trying to incorporate as much reality as I could by setting the actors in public spaces and just letting the public react as they might to similar events happening in real life. The first sign of trouble was that when we turned up to 'point and shoot', the Playhouse was being repainted and wrapped in scaffolding. Never mind, it was too late to move. Although a simple story point, it involved choreographing the chase sequence for Betacam and Steadicam to run along with the action, with the final set up being in the square itself and involving four hidden cameras. I wanted this to be as real as we could make it and when all cameras were in place we went for a slow walkthrough. Cue Ray; cue Digger; cue gang; up and out of the car park towards Playhouse; cue girl; Ray touches her to simulate clash; she turns to simulate fall; Ray walks on; Digger goes past girl; gang past girl; all round corner and cut. Great. Reset.

We made sure everyone knew that the next one would be the take or the public would catch on and start searching for the cameras to stare at. This was now a constant problem for *Brookie*, as the actors were so well known by now, to the extent that we sometimes positioned someone like Sue Johnston in one place and let the crowds gather round her while we shot the real scene just round the corner. On *What Now?* though, with a relatively new cast, we hadn't had to engage in such diversionary tactics.

Everything was ready to go. Action. Cue Ray; cue Digger; cue gang; up and out of the car park towards the Playhouse they came, the hounds after the fox, Digger now roaring abuse and threats; the public stopped and looked at this apparent outbreak of street violence; cue girl; she starts walking past the scaffolding outside the Playhouse and looking in her bag; Ray also looking back, right on cue to run into her; the girl bounces off him and turns and falls; Ray hesitates but the gang are approaching, hurling more threats: Ray takes off again, heading for corner; girl cowers; Digger jumps over her; gang go round and over her; Ray about to go round corner; it's looking great until . . . Ray is brought to a dead stop by a sharp fist to his face. What? Cut! What the . . . ?

The closing hounds now arrive and confuse the gathering public as instead of attacking the fox, they set upon his assailant, who turns out to be a public-spirited painter who had seen the drama unfold from the scaffolding. Thinking our hero Ray was mugging the girl and the other lads were giving chase, he scaled down the scaffolding to land in front of Ray and give him a smack. He was now looking absolutely mortified as the production crew had surrounded him and were pointing to the cameras. My first line into the walkie-talkie was: 'How's Vic?' The second line was: 'Can we go again?' After an hour of ice-packing over lunch, during which we hoped the public, who had seen everything, would disperse, Vic's face had gone down, nothing broken, and he was game to carry on. So we got the sequence and moved on, cursing the hero who had cost us an hour or so in shooting time and could have badly injured our leading man.

However, we later discovered that the painter himself had gone off to hospital and been signed off for a few days with a fractured hand. I wasn't quite sure what the moral of the tale was when I heard that news. From his point of view, it was a noble and brave thing to have done. Something we should have perhaps expected, if we had not been too wrapped up in trying to create our own fictional reality. Looking back, I guess we should have at least told those painters what we were up to. And the character name Digger? Well, why not?

Other high points from that shoot were working with the young Vic McGuire and Ian Hart, two actors who had come through the Everyman Youth Theatre and had a power and presence few others possess. Vic later went on to play Jack Boswell in Carla Lane's *Bread*, and to feature in series like *Peak Practice* and *Casualty*. Ian went on to focus on more concentrated one-off or mini-series roles, including becoming Professor Quirrell in *Harry Potter*, and more recently playing Hitler in *The Man Who Crossed Hitler*, for BBC films. While Vic played the disenchanted main lead of Ray, trying to make sense of a world which seemed to offer no prospects for what we now term NEETS, Not in Employment, Education or Training, Ian played his mate Gosgo, facing the same problem while also being an unrecognised and unpaid carer for his abusive father. Their lives were typical of those spent in inner-city housing estates, where the only breaks from the monotony and boredom of unemployment were sex, drugs and the occasional street fight. Where the only routes to status, as the Playhouse chase symbolised, were who you dated, hung out with or could fight.

For every episode, we filmed another variant of the three main male characters trying to decide what to do to alleviate the boredom and monotony of unemployment: *What Now?* Instead of these deliberately repetitive scenes being set in the same place, as originally intended, I decided to make a theme of the series a tight opening shot that gradually widened to show that they were, in fact, trying to fight the boredom by appearing in a series of odd or unusual places.

A shot might start on one of them apparently lying down, but pull back to reveal he was actually on the high retaining wall of the M62 motorway. Another might pull out to reveal the actor sitting leaning against a wall . . . but on the main supporting structure of a flyover in the middle of a busy traffic junction. We would place them there, on radio mics, and then have the cameras on a crane above, or with long lenses across the road. Often I would spot these locations on the way in and then phone and ask the crew to get clearance for the following day, or sometimes the same day. The next variant was what would they be doing, rather than just sitting. Where can we get some fish and chips at eight o'clock on a Sunday morning? I would ask, and Design would suddenly have to conjure some up. Just like that. And they did.

This is in fact how I got to know Mal Young, who would later go on to take over running *Brookie*, then move to Pearson to oversee *The Bill* and develop *Family Affairs*, then move to the BBC as Controller of Continuing Drama Series, where he took *EastEnders* to five nights, created *Doctors* and resurrected *Doctor Who*, before going on to work with Simon Fuller at 19. Not a bad run from finding fish 'n' chips at eight o'clock on a Sunday morning. Trained as a graphic designer, he was working in Design as a Props Assistant on *Brookside*, but had been assigned from there to work on *What Now?* His creativity and natural talent for problem-solving soon became apparent, and in the end I was trying to think up more and more things I wanted on set, just to see if he could do it. But he always did, and even ended up having a Temporary Bus Stop sign in the back of his van, knowing that if we were ever stuck, I would suggest finding a bus stop somewhere to prop the characters against.

It saved the schedule a couple of times. We used it on the roof of the Sun Alliance Building when we shot a video to go with the title track, having the band The Touch lined up next to it then pulling back to reveal it was, in fact, on a high-rise building roof. Not knowing of the band before the production, I was amazed, and delighted that its main member and the composer of the theme tune was actually a guy called Andy Wilson with whom I had been in the sixth form at St Kevin's. The lead singer, though, was really special. Known as Connie Lush, she had an amazing blues/jazz-rock voice that should have taken her beyond the loyal following she still has in Liverpool and Europe. She later performed in the opening concert for Capital of Culture and, although virtually unknown to the world's media, held her own with or outperformed many of Liverpool's rock glitterati.

From the actual production side of things we learned a great deal that fed back into *Brookside*'s development, as *What Now?* was also a form of technological field experiment. How better to use and find the limits of the ever-developing technology like the use of Steadicam. It also gave us an opportunity to experiment with wireless technology, despite some of it not actually being licensed for use at that time.

As a director or producer on a shoot, if you can listen in to the chatter going back and forth you can often stop or forestall people heading off up blind allies on the 'I just thought' path. Unfortunately, our open TV and sound transmissions also meant that when we were shooting on some of the estates, the residents soon picked up on what we were doing. We found them sitting in their living rooms with TVs tuned to the cameras and their FM radios tuned into our sound channels. Probably the first ever experience of true reality TV.

While this technology amused people on one location, we got a bit of grief at a different location for different technology on another late-night shoot. As I was still wanting to get wide shots at night, we had decided to mount several 5Kw lights (big) on a high cherry picker crane platform and have it light up the entire neighbourhood. A bit like floodlights at a football stadium.

Everything went well and around midnight we called a wrap, reaching the moment of switching realities or universes. Stepping from fiction to reality. Just as it is momentarily disorientating after stepping out of a nightclub going full tilt, into bright sunshine, then the moment you are plunged into darkness when they kill the main overhead lights is similar. The sparks send a warning round the crew to tell everyone to get ready and then kill the power. After a moment or two eyes readjust and everyone gets back to the derig. We had just done this and I was about to leave when a guy came running up the street in a bit of a state. Me birds. Me birds. You've killed me birds! What birds? My birds, in me shed with your lights, you've killed them. What? How? Eyes were rapidly exchanging looks. What was he up to? Or, what was he on?

Keeping birds. In an aviary, that's what. It turned out that because the lights had been on so long all his birds had thought it was dawn and woken up. They had been sitting chirping away when they were suddenly plunged into darkness and, well, fell off their perches. They normally sense the dusk and then get ready to settle down and fall asleep, but the sudden black out also disorientated them. He asked if the lights could go back on. I nodded. Let there be light. And the area was in daylight again. We sent one of the floor crew off with him with a walkie-talkie to let us know what the casualty rate was but fortunately the crackly voice came back to say that all seemed OK, but could we now simulate dusk? I looked to the sparks, John McCormack and Paul Taylor. They looked at each other, then nodded, went back to the cherry picker and started to slowly lower the lights while still lit. It was quite a tricky manoeuvre making sure all the cables didn't tangle and yet another of those moments I wished we had had the camera still on, as we saw the artificial sun slowly set over that neighbourhood. All birds were reported safely snoozing.

Above all, though, projects like *What Now?* allowed staff and crews to develop, especially people like Mal, who thrived on that daily point-and-shoot philosophy. We discovered that life was not about problems, but merely challenges to be overcome. This would become another MerseyTV mantra. We never have problems; only challenges we rise to meet.

Some of these were obvious, like the high costs attached to anything that had a film or TV order form. The specialised cameras and editing equipment and associated parts were perhaps understand-ably expensive, but the high costs even applied to the more everyday things like portable generators and scaffolding, something I still knew a bit about from my time in construction. When a TV lighting company quoted £1,200, we found a construction scaffolder who would do it for £200. As Alexis had said, we were no different from a lot of other industries, but the enduring lesson learned from the series was that creativity extends beyond the scripts, acting, directing and editing. It was in everything we did.

To make the separation of *What Now?* from *Brookside* clear, we decided also to have the press launch of the all-location programme on location, and chose the swimming baths where we had shot yet another clash between Ray & Co. and Digger and his gang. This was actually the Harold Davies Memorial Pool in Dovecot. Built in 1936 to reflect Art Deco influences, it was one of two similar baths, the other being in Norris Green. While very modern and striking in their day, by the time we got there in 1985 they were beginning to show their age. Or, perhaps, more correctly, lack of Council maintenance. Like a lot of great buildings in Liverpool they were legacies from a former and more prosperous age, but still helped to imbue that sense of specialness in young people growing up among and within them.

This great bathing palace was no exception, with its pre-Olympic thirty-three-yard competition pool, a ten-foot-deep diving pool and a learner pool. It was only a couple of miles from where I had lived in Huyton and it was our weekly junior school treat to walk the three miles there and back, starting to undress about half a mile away, trying to be the first ready and in to break the still water. As a teenager I'd also spent many an evening and weekend there because it was virtually free, warm, and you could get a cup of Oxo and a round of toast for threepence. I wanted to show our central characters trying to fill their empty days by going to use the Council-funded gym and pool, hanging out, hunting for women, and, inevitably, getting into another of the ongoing and relentless run-ins with Digger.

Just as outside the Liverpool Playhouse, I had choreographed a chase sequence that would have Digger pursue Ray through the building – alongside the pools, up and along the large seating galleries, until eventually it would look like he was cornered on the balcony overlooking the pools. As Digger and his crew were closing in, Ray was to climb on to the hand rail and leap straight into the diving pool below. He'd be out and away by the time the more faint-hearted Digger had found the stairs. It was a jump my mates and I had done many times as teenagers, when the lifeguards weren't looking, which was why it was in the script and why Vic McGuire had said he was happy to do it himself. However, when we got to it, despite the fact that we had built a small set of steps to aid his balance, it did seem a bit higher than I remembered it some twenty years earlier.

When lunch was called I went back and had another look, and then asked the floor manager to go and find Vic. As they returned I was waiting on top of the steps. I said to Vic, 'Look, like this.' And then leaped into space, to land right in the middle of the pool, exactly as I used to all those years ago. When I surfaced they were both laughing. More so because the shoot photographer had got wind of it, but had arrived too late.

The photographer always had me in sights after that, in case I pulled off another stunt myself, which I didn't as I'd aggravated the residual problems I had with my back and shoulder after the car crash. But I couldn't tell them, as they'd have told Alexis and she would have killed me. I'd been specifically prohibited from any kind of action that would shock my neck or spine. Like diving or jumping from a height into water.

The photographer did manage to catch me out, though, during a tea break when I'd flopped down by the side of the pool. I saw him snapping away but thought nothing of it until he came into the office to show me the contact sheets, a huge smile across his face. Only then did I realise I had been by the kiddy pool and right behind me was a huge 'Learner' sign. It summed up my first directorial stint and was another photograph that would stay on my office wall for a long time.

The picture didn't go in the press pack for the launch event although we had Andy Wilson, Connie and The Touch in to perform a set. We took over the gym area, brought in the viewing screens to play the first episode, but before we had even reached the Q&A, never mind the party, I knew we were going to have another media skirmish on our hands over the programme's language. As the episode progressed there were two journalists not really watching the visuals, but listening very intently to the sound. I stretched over to have a look at what they were scribbling but this was in the days when all journalists took shorthand notes, so it was indecipherable. However, the clue was in the timing of their scribbles. Every time a swear word was used, a mark would go down on a pad. This was confirmed when the guy from the *Daily Mail* leaned over to Roy West from the *Liverpool Echo* and issued the immortal line 'Hey, Roy, is Jesus bloody Christ a swear word or a blasphemy?' Here we go again, I thought.

14

Other Things (1987)

'If the VAT man calls, just hide under the kitchen table until they've gone' – *IPPA Council Member*

With *EastEnders* embedded in the British psyche, and just across the car park from *Grange Hill*, the end of the 1980s began to take on an air of anticipation reminiscent of a decade before. Then the industry was positioning and shaping the expected ITV2 that became Channel 4. At the end of the 1980s it was Channel 5, the ITV regional licences and satellite looming on the horizon. Back at Mersey we were still pondering that vexed *What Now?* question. Where next? The answer, the 1990 Broadcasting Act. Like the asteroid that wiped out the dinosaurs it was a long time coming but, unlike their biological counterparts, the ITV companies could actually see its approach even if they didn't plan very well for the moment of impact. Ultimately seismic shock waves were to rock the temples of the industry, and the weakest built collapsed, while most of the rest were left with structural damage that is still being patched up twenty-two years later.

The asteroid was made of many elements, with the franchise renewals, Channel 5 and independent access to ITV and the BBC high in the mix. After the Act was passed both the BBC and ITV would be under a regulatory obligation to take 25 per cent of their programmes from independent producers like Mersey. Although I had been persuaded by C4 to join the industry trade association, the IPPA, the Independent Programme Producers' Association, I had done so more out of respect for C4 than any obvious need. I could see the argument that their biggest independent commission should be helping to develop the sector. In fact, I had the same misgiving over the IPPA as I'd had over the WGGB: that it was not properly focused on its core objective. Just as the WGGB saw itself as a trades union when it was in reality an association of self-employed people, so the IPPA saw itself as a trade body when it was in reality a collective of self-employed freelancers. They had more in common with the ACTT than the CBI.

The tensions were soon obvious, as although generally supportive of the broad aim of industry representation and a workable copyright framework, the issue of which employment agreements to work under brought us into immediate conflict with the rest of the membership. Most, understandably, worked and wanted to remain under the freelance contracts derived from the film industry, while we were now managing very well under the ITV staff employment contracts. This meant MerseyTV's cost base was much lower and more controllable, and on the issue of copyright our directly nego-tiated contracts were much stronger and more rewarding than the industry standard. Due to this it sometimes felt like we were more in tune with the fifteen ITV companies than with the IPPA itself, and at times actually felt like the sixteenth ITV company. We were bigger than Channel Television.

When we did join, I found myself on a committee cycle again as a member of the IPPA Council. It was not long before the different needs, aspirations and requirements of Mersey TV and the rest of the membership became apparent. On discussing what advice to offer members concerning VAT and its implications, one almost venerated producer said we should just tell everyone to ignore it. I laughed, thinking it was a joke, but was told quite firmly that it was his strategy, and if they ever came to inspect his books he hid under the kitchen table until they went away.

I again thought this might have been a North–South humour divide problem, but a couple of other nodding heads seemed to suggest it was not. If this was the level of professional advice our new trade association was going to dispense, political expediency with C4 or not, I couldn't see this getting past Arthur Andersen, let alone my new MD.

A compromise was worked out. Brookside Productions Ltd, as C4's commissioned independent, would join, but MerseyTV, the holding company, would not. This seemed to satisfy everyone, especially as one of the conditions of joining the IPPA was that a 0.5 per cent levy was raised on all productions. We didn't mind *Brookside* paying, as it became a direct-line item to C4, but with other aspirations bubbling, we didn't want to set up an open-ended direct debit. Especially as 0.5 per cent of *Brookie's* budget went a long way towards fully funding the entire thing. Which was why I had ended up on Council, with full voting rights.

One consequence of being on the IPPA Council was that I was forced to spend a day or so a month in London, during which time I would catch up on the industry gossip and briefings. What became clear in all the rounds of media and ministerial meetings, conferences and seminars in the 1980s was that there would be no expansion in capacity until the early-1990s when satellite and a new Channel 5 might be possible. Despite creativity needing opportunity, there would be no great explosion of airtime as we had had after ITV, BBC2 and C4's arrivals. We would all have to make do with the typical Buggins' turn approach to C4's limited airtime, plus whatever we could persuade the government to squeeze out of ITV and the BBC.

Mersey could expect nothing much else from C4 as they were under both commercial and political pressure to spread what resources they had as wide as possible, something they were naturally keen to do in their own quest to try and support the development of a robust independent sector. Understanding something and being pragmatic enough to accept political reality, doesn't make it any less irritating or frustrating. While I fully supported the balanced ecology of the C4 schedule, some parts supporting others, I would often mutter about how hard we worked to earn the ad revenue in and around *Brookie* only to see it go to ITV and then a proportion of it be fed back to C4 who would, from my Scouse perspective, blow it all on some self-indulgent, esoteric minority of all minorities London-centric project. I wouldn't care how much or how little was spent on anything, provided it was in support of a national agenda on a national public-service broadcaster. London *isn't* the nation. And this was something I did bang the drum on: making regional quotas a part of the future.

It was a long and sometimes solo drumming session, so our own immediate agenda became to see how much we could stretch *Brookie* itself, as well as what we could do around the periphery. Having seen the impact of the 1985 siege episodes on both ratings and media, there was obviously an audience appetite for such high-octane storylines, so we decided to think about what else we could do to enhance the programme. I knew we couldn't just keep escalating the drama, as that would take us away from the programme's 'extraordinary things happen to ordinary people' ethos, and besides I already had the sobriquet 'master of the mundane' – a back-handed compliment if ever there was one, and something originally attributed, I think, to American photographer William Eggleton. Having seen some of his work, I consider it a title worth sharing.

There was at the time a great deal of industry noise about what had happened in one of the biggest global TV hits of the decade, *Dallas*, which had ended the 1984–5 season with one of its main characters, Bobby Ewing, played by Patrick Duffy, seen to have been killed when run over by a car. Realising that losing one of its biggest characters was not one of their better audience-grabbing ideas, they then came up with a better one: his wife, Pam, played by Victoria Principal, woke up to find him in the shower. The whole incident, and previous series therefore, had been nothing more than a dream. Professionally it was a brilliant ploy, but the sleight of hand was not slick enough and the expression '. . . *and then he steps out of the shower and it was all a dream*' became industry code for a terrible idea.

Dallas became a valuable touchstone on the dangers of escalatory drama, where the temptation is to top what you have done before. It is hard to resist doing sometimes, especially when your broadcaster starts adding pressure for more and more ratings – something we probably fell foul of ourselves in the mid-1990s. But towards the end of the 1980s we were all very conscious of the need to stay within the now-accepted conventions of *Brookie*: the mundane, occasionally sparked by something extraordinary happening to ordinary characters. In terms of our existing characters we needed something that would appear as extraordinary to the viewers, but would remain faithful to the characters. The solution was the 'soap bubble', a phrase coined by David Rose to describe taking a few characters and letting them float away from the main programme, while remaining connected by the same storyline. At 8 p.m. we would have Sheila and Bobby worrying about where Damon was, and at 10 p.m. we would show what he was up to. This would be another industry first.

It did not come as a typical light–bulb moment, but rather a convergence of ideas, or part of a cascade. The siege episodes boosted the ratings, so C4 wanted more. *What Now?* had given us both a creative and technological boost, so we wanted more. And the typical catalyst: one of our most popular cast members wanted to leave. This time it was Simon O'Brien (aka Damon), who not only wanted to leave but had also asked if I would kill off his character.

This was an unusual request as most actors want to retain the safety net of coming back to a secure and regular lifestyle if things don't work out elsewhere. Simon's view, though, was that he had already become too comfortable and now wanted to go out and test himself. It would be a big loss for the programme, but I really admired and respected him for arriving at this decision. The only thing to do now was make sure we maximised the opportunity.

And there was one other element to take into account. It was *Brookie*'s fifth year on air. Simon O'Brien's departure would be the catalyst for the UK's first 'soap bubble': *Damon and Debbie*. It would air alongside the programme from 4 November, two days after the fifth anniversary of the programme that IBA Director John Whitney had asked Jeremy Isaacs to cancel.

To help us celebrate the fifth anniversary of the programme, we decided to celebrate the fifth anniversary of MerseyTV. In a re-run of the original 10 August launch day we would invite back all those who had helped get the company and programme off and, in Broseley's case, out of the ground. We would have a party on The Close. Whereas in 1982 we'd had to ask Broseley to knock up a podium, by 1987 we could afford to hire a marquee. We now also had our own publicity department so started thinking about how to mark the occasion with something a bit more exciting than the usual press release.

We had the *Damon and Debbie* bubble to talk about, which was three extra hours of drama for the company. Normally, for both broadcaster and producer, that would have been a press event in its own right. However, we were already living under the long shadow cast by *Brookie* itself. In terms of media awareness it would be just a few more episodes. It needed something else. A marketing grab. Something to arrest attention. Or, as our publicists were now fond of saying, 'What's the angle?' This was, at the risk of making a pun, becoming the acute question. More and more national newspapers were reducing or closing their regional offices and losing their regional reporters. The media's slow retreat to London had begun. To get them to send people up to Liverpool now meant providing them with a really good story – or else paying for their travel.

This seemed the logical way to go. If we didn't pay they would simply write about Damon and Debbie and we wouldn't get the opportunity to demonstrate or remind them that *Brookie* was more than just another programme.

Accepting this, Alexis asked the publicity department to come back with the costings for bringing up the London mob, which they did, prompting the immediate response from me that I could hire a train for that. Which was the light-bulb moment. Why not? It appealed to my post-Marxist sense of humour. Like the sealed train that took Lenin from Switzerland to Russia in 1917, we could collect the London bourgeois and escort them to the Scouse Republic. Alexis made sure that bit didn't go in the press release, but we did hire jugglers and magicians to keep them occupied on the journey. C4 came along to show support, which really surprised some of the journos, especially seeing the triumvirate of Justin Dukes, David Scott and The Emperor himself, Jeremy Isaacs, on board. However, the biggest surprise of all was when we got to Liverpool Lime Street. We walked everyone to the front of the train where another engine was standing waiting, and together with the British Rail Regional Manager I pulled a cord to unveil its nameplate: *Brookside*. We now had a train named after us. That was the angle.

From Lime Street we piled everyone on to a coach and, with police outriders, went on a short tour of the city towards the recently refurbished Maritime Museum, then the jewel in Liverpool's tarnished crown, where the City Council and Merseyside Development Corporation hosted a civic reception to reinforce the message of the city's regeneration. They had also, with our prompting, invited Granada along and I was genuinely pleased to see both David Plowright, its Chairman, and Andrew Quinn, the Managing Director, although I did wonder if they too had come on their own sealed train from Manchester.

If the Big Five ITV companies sometimes acted like a bunch of teddy boys, then Plowright was definitely up for leader of the pack. In my speech I said something about how grateful we all were to the City, the MDC, the DTi, and our 'regional supporters'. I also thanked Channel 4 and said how proud I felt, which I did, of having been given the opportunity to achieve something in my own city. Then Jeremy responded by saying how proud he too felt of Channel 4's role in making it all happen.

We started to usher everyone back to the coach – only to discover that The Emperor was returning to the Senate. I was amazed. He had come all the way up but wasn't going to bother even coming out to the site to see and, more importantly, be seen by the people who worked so hard to deliver his biggest programme. Alexis had to take me to one side and tell me to keep focused on the rest of the day. He was Chief Executive of the channel and we didn't know what else might be happening back in London. We had most of the senior management with us and it might have been a huge effort for him to even do the morning and, probably more important on a corporate and civic level, he was seen to have done that for the region's great and good, including Granada.

It was, as always, good counsel, so I shook hands, wished him a safe journey back and took Alexis's next bit of advice. Enjoy the day. I did, as did Justin and David, especially when we noticed the Granada lot, now with their Head of PR, David Highet, had the British Rail manager backed up against the side of the marquee and were giving him a good ear-bashing. It later turned out that they had been trying to get a train named after *Coronation Street* and were demanding to know how come BR had given one to me and not them. But I knew. We had originally been turned down because official policy was not to name engines after television programmes. But we'd gone back and said *Brookside* wasn't just a programme, it was a regeneration project and a separate company now employing around 150 people. The teds obviously hadn't been listening to the anniversary speeches.

British Rail also gave us a replica nameplate which we had mounted and hung behind Reception. It stayed there until 2005 when Alexis and I sold MerseyTV, but not the nameplate. We wanted to keep it as a reminder of that day. A few years later we received a call from Network Rail to say the engine was coming to the end of its working life and would I like the nameplate? It would only cost me a donation to charity. I went back and said yes, if I could have a ride in the front of a train, something I'd been promised in 1987 but had never had time to do. Deal. So one day Alexis and I went to Crewe to collect the nameplate and got a lift back in an engine they were repositioning to Liverpool. Now there are two great memories attached to that nameplate.

The train-naming might have come from what we had learned about maximising media impact, but we still had to deliver something special on screen to celebrate five years of *Brookie* and Damon's departure. With the prior experience of *Grange Hill* I was also beginning to feel we were approaching the 'Tucker's leaving' moment, as Damon had been his Scouse reincarnation. Although Mandy Burton had by then left, Simon leaving was a bigger event. He was part of *Brookie*'s first, if not royal, family, the Grants. While the rest would stay, his going would probably signal the beginning of the first-generation exodus, the time the original cast moves on and you have to rebuild and reshape. Whatever we did, it would have to be good. It would also have to adhere to the central principle of impacting on the characters left behind. Damon's end would have to be the beginning of something else. Something that took Sheila and Bobby in a different direction.

Recently, we had had them both in Rome reaffirming their marriage as a consequence of the biggest and most iconic of the Grants' storylines: Sheila's rape. The subject itself is probably on every writing team's list of must-do storylines, but when it was proposed at a long-term story meeting, my instinctive reaction was that if we were going to do it, we should look at the issue for what it was: an act of brutal violence. To keep people focused on this, I did not want to risk any chance of tabloid titillation by allowing them to use any sexy or glamorous publicity shots of the younger actresses next to the story. I put it to the writers that we should not ask the male-orientated question: 'What if it was your wife, girlfriend, daughter or sister?' but something even more sacred: 'What if it was your mother?'

There was some initial resistance, as they knew this meant changing the character for ever. Would we still be able to retain Sheila's character of feisty matriarch once she was brutalised in this way? That,

I said, is entirely in our hands. It's our universe. We can make her saint, sinner, victim or survivor, just as we can with every character. What it would do, though, is open a dramatic avenue we had never contemplated before. Eventually there was consensus, but the next thing I wanted to do was talk to Sue herself. We could write what we liked, but she would have to carry it forward. It would be harrowing and it would be long-term.

When she came to see me she listened to what I had to say and why, and, as she relates in her own memoir, *Things I Couldn't Tell My Mother*, then shocked me by revealing that she herself had been attacked when she was young. It was my turn to sit and listen as she told me about it and how, if we were going to do it, it had to be done properly, and sensitively, but she thought we should. It was not a subject that was dealt with often in mainstream television so we would be treading new and difficult ground again, but working with a local Rape Crisis centre, we put the storyline together.

Come the day of the shoot everything went well despite Sue telling me how nervous she felt, and then afterwards as if a weight had been lifted off her — a form of release from the fears she had been carrying around for years. The audience's reaction was fantastic, including many, many women who contacted us, and Sue, simply to share their own experiences. Some had been raped but had never spoken about it. For the first time they felt there was a forum in which they could talk. This was something that would become an integral part of *Brookie*, a touchstone by which people knew that if we were covering a story or issue, then we must have got the idea from real life and there would then be somewhere for them to go and get help with a similar issue. For this reason we started putting helpline details on the end of the relevant programmes.

It was also the beginning of another rule used at all storyline conferences. No matter how far out or controversial a storyline might seem, if we did anything we had to make it as realistic as we could, in the fictional universe, and never just throw issues up in the air without offering at least some explanation, solution or path to help resolve them. If we were to deal in our fictional world with rape, or dyslexia, or domestic violence, then we had to be able to point people towards professional support in dealing with these problems in real life.

Over time I discovered that no matter how hard or harrowing

the issue we covered, provided we did it as honestly and realistically as we could, the audience supported us and appreciated it. Even – and this is crucial to understanding the value of contemporary drama – if occasionally they didn't enjoy, or feel comfortable with, particular moments or events. They appreciated that others would derive benefit or support from them. That there must be differences, as there must be tolerance of those differences.

The weak link, unfortunately, and too often, was C4 itself, though to be fair to them they were under pressure from the television regulator, the ITC. The call about our handling of Sheila's rape caught up with me at Radio 1 where I was on one of the afternoon shows so, before mobiles remember, I had to drag the BBC telephone out into the corridor as far as the cord would stretch, away from the big ears of the crew. You need to edit the episode for the Omnibus, the Saturday repeat. Why? Because we have had forty complaints. About what? The rape scene. There wasn't a rape scene. All we saw was a coat going over Sheila's head and then she was dragged into the bushes. You're always talking about the audience's imaginations. True, but what about their intelligence? You have to change it. Someone from the BBC radio show popped out. On air in two minutes? OK. Back to phone. Different tack.

How many complaints did you say you've had? Forty. How many watched the programme? About four million. I thought we lived in a democracy? The audience doesn't get to vote, so why should the ones who phoned up? Because they complained. We should stand up for the four million. We can't. I can. What? I'm not cutting it, it's daft. Then we will. Fair enough, but I'm not agreeing to it. OK. OK. I hung up, feeling livid. After all we went through to get the story and scripts right . . . Talking it through with Sue, who had agreed to do it, reliving her own ordeal, and now they were going to cut the key scene. And for what? Forty people out of four million. The radio head popped out again. You, er . . . ready? Yep, fine, let's go. Now, about Sinbad . . .

After the chat about whether *Brookie* was still going to tackle difficult subjects – of course it was – I dragged the borrowed phone back out into the corridor to call back to base and let everyone know what C4 were planning. And in particular to let Sue know. I knew she would be disappointed, which was short-lived when we saw the response not only to the mid-week episodes but the Saturday programme as well. At the back of my mind I hoped C4 would realise when they got into the edit suite that it would be a difficult cut without the original rushes, which were back in Liverpool. I should be so hopeful! It looked like they'd just brought in a local butcher who'd chopped the tape and butt-jointed it. No finesse at all. The original had Sheila walking home. A voice calls. She stops. As she turns, a coat comes over her head and the camera goes with her as she is dragged into some bushes. Roll credits. C4's cut had her walking. The voice. She turns. Jump cut to thrashing bushes. Roll credits.

Again, this may seem like a small thing, but these moments take a lot of care and attention to get right. You want to take your audience with you and let them share some of the character's feelings. Apart from it looking really naff after the edit, the audience's imaginations had also been sent on a different and sharper trajectory. Instead of the surprise, then concern, then open-ended speculation about exactly what had happened, it was now abundantly clear that she had been attacked violently, and by a flesh-eating bush for all we knew. And the complaints came in again.

This time, around one hundred and forty. Everyone wanted to know why on earth C4 had made the cut. I phoned and asked them what they would do now? Reinstate it on the next episode? I was even more annoyed than I had been about the original cut, so much so that I agreed with C4 that even if we fell out about things like this, in future *we* would do the butchering. The only other time we had a higher audience response was when Barry Grant threatened to kill a dog, which received two hundred complaints. What does that say about the sort of democracy we live in? The dog was, naturally, safe and sound in the next episode. Even Barry, his own life in danger from local gangsters, couldn't ever hurt a dog.

This was probably the beginning of the slow but crushing 'taste and decency' drive that would grow worse and worse after the passing of the 1990 Broadcasting Act. That included among its measures the establishing, on a statutory basis – probably the worst piece of nanny state legislation ever conceived – of the Broadcasting Standards Council (BSC) alongside the Broadcasting Complaints Commission (BCC). These two quangos were designed to vet, monitor, establish and maintain standards of taste and decency in broadcasting. The BSC, effectively, was to decide what we could and could not watch; the BCC was meant to provide the mechanism for complaint if someone did not like even the sanitised version. Because you can probably guess on which side of the sociological divide the standards for taste and decency were set – not with the bulk of the audience, living on council estates in inner cities. However, Sheila's rape was before the all-encompassing 1990 Act so C4 had no excuse for its clumsy censorship except its own timidity in the face of forty complaints.

Not too long before that, we'd had Damon's YTS storyline. The drama in Sheila's rape is more obvious, but when Damon came home and collapsed into his mother's arms after being given the sack, it was very difficult to keep dry-eyed, seeing the powerless mother trying to comfort the usually cocky young man, now reduced to the crying child she had borne and nurtured, desperately trying to understand why he had just lost the job he had worked so hard at. Scripted by Barry Woodward, it is one of the *Brookside* scenes people most often talk to me about.

Both these stories, in their own way, highlighted what *Brookie* was all about: personifying social problems that were affecting a great number of people who were unable to get their voices heard. The role of the programme was never to attack anything directly, but to provide as balanced a view as possible in order to allow the real campaigners perhaps to receive a more sympathetic hearing.

With all this backstory invested in the Grants, Damon's death would have to be something a bit special. It would also have to propel the drama back on to the remaining characters and extend into their future. It would have to be seen as part of a continuing story arc, not something that simply flew out at a tangent. It seemed that it should be rooted in the parents' characters, and with Rome, the Vatican and Sheila's Catholicism fresh in our minds, the most logical story arc appeared to be about challenging Sheila's faith. How could the God she believed in allow her to be raped? Where was the fairness and justice in what had happened to her son? And, ultimately, why was he taken from her? We had to focus on what the consequences of Damon's death were going to be, following the rule that characters exit to history; our remaining characters are our future. So how would the death affect Sheila, Bobby, Barry and Karen?

The storyline was put together and woven in and out of the main serial. Damon's girlfriend Debbie was played by a very young Gillian

Kearney, later to go on to *Hope and Glory, The Forsyte Saga, Shameless* and, more recently, *Casualty*. It was a tender love story wrapped in a mini road movie, with scripts from Frank Cottrell Boyce. Billed as a modern-day *Romeo and Juliet*, Damon's death came just when everything was looking right for the young lovers, who had even been through a mock wedding ceremony of their own making. On his way back to a canal boat they had rented, Damon bumped into a guy on the towpath, only to find that he had been stabbed and to die in Debbie's arms.

While Simon made a great job of the hero's death, Gillian's performance of grief-stricken shock and horror came a close second to one of the best moments in *Brookie's* twenty-one-year history. That was Sue Johnston's expression at the moment when Sheila first realised Damon was dead. We choreographed it with nothing more than a police car drawing up outside number 5. The audience already knew, and, as soon as Sheila saw the young police officer hesitate to compose himself, so did she. Just as Mandy had portrayed Heather's world falling apart on overhearing Roger's phone call, so Sue brought every mother's nightmare home in a single look. The puzzlement, realisation, disbelief, denial and the horror. Words were redundant. That one shot is probably the best of *Brookie's* entire run.

The generational shift was now underway. People still tell me, thirty years later, that *Grange Hill* was never the same when Tucker and Trisha left. Similarly, for some, *Brookside* was never the same after Gavin and Petra, Heather, Bobby and Sheila, and Billy, or even writers like Jimmy McGovern, Frank Cottrell Boyce, John Godber and Kay Mellor, had left. But these were all before the Jordaches, Bev and Ron, Jackie and Jimmy, and Anthony and Imelda were even thought about. It was true that, for some viewers, things would never be the same, but a programme is inevitably different for different audiences at different times. The golden age of anything is the one you personally enjoyed the most. That's why I could never answer the perennial journalists' question about who my favourite character was. They all meant something different to me at different times. They all formed part of the same whole.

Sometimes you plan for these moments, sometimes they happen naturally, and sometimes they are forced upon you. The rejuvenation of *Brookside* soon accelerated when news came that 'Ricky's done one'. There had been some tension for a while over the direction in which we were taking Bobby Grant. When we first met Ricky in the Playhouse rehearsal rooms I'd talked about wanting him to personify, perhaps humanise, the role of trades union official – and that was still the aim. Having covered the union–management dynamic over the preceding years, what I wanted now was to explore the politics of the trades union movement itself.

In real life at the time this was reflected in the bitter divisions within the TUC between unions like the left-wing National Union of Miners (NUM), led by Arthur Scargill, and the perceived more right-wing Electrical, Electronic, Telecommunications and Plumbing Union (EETPU), led by Eric Hammond. Both men of strong principles, the two leaders were brought into conflict through their differing approaches to labour negotiations, with Hammond coming to national attention when he refused to agree to his members stopping work at power stations in support of the miners' strike, accusing the NUM of being 'lions led by donkeys'. The EETPU had also become the first union to accept private health insurance for its members, widely seen as a betrayal of the principle of universal health care through the NHS. Hammond dismissed this as hypocrisy as some of the TUC's own leadership had private health care employment packages. These sorts of pragmatic dilemmas, dogma over benefit, seemed an interesting area for Bobby Grant to become embroiled within as his career as a trades union official developed.

Just as Paul Collins had been there originally to represent the other side of the union–management debate, we now brought in the character of Billy Corkhill (aka John McArdle) as an EETPU-type electrician, to react to and argue with Bobby, who was definitely in the NUM camp. However, it was not to be. As Ricky had, indeed, 'done one'.

There was a lot of talk in the press about us falling out over the character, which had some truth in it but not enough to force such a rapid exit. As I had talked to Sue first before we committed to the rape storyline, I was even more aware of Ricky's past and politics and would probably have amended the storyline to take into account his views and experience. In hindsight, although his decision to leave probably resulted from a combination of things both on and off camera, I realise he was unhappy with the way Bobby was scripted in the aftermath of Sheila's rape. We might have concentrated too much on Sheila, and not enough on her husband.

I might have spent time talking things through with Sue, but perhaps not enough with Ricky debating where this would lead his character. Just as it changed Sheila Grant for ever, it also, inevitably, changed her husband, but we did not get Ricky's buy-in to those changes. I should also have been more aware of his deeply held trades union convictions and not put him in the position of having to walk away in such a manner, if that was indeed the cause or part of it. Whatever it was, I regret it happened, and although we remained distant for a time we are back on hugging terms again now. We've probably both mellowed with age.

For such a major character to disappear, especially halfway through an episode, initially seemed like a huge challenge. This was not Arthur disappearing from a picket line. The solution, though, became very simple and arose out of everyone's real-life puzzlement as to why he had suddenly gone. Why? When? How? All questions Sheila might ask if Bobby also 'did one'. What if he just didn't come home from work one day? Sheila would start to get worried; start looking for him; start asking questions . . . and then discover he had had to rush off in support of trades union activity, in Gdansk. And that was the new story twist.

Why? When? How?

If this was dealt with relatively smoothly, the fastest-ever departure was probably the loss of Tracy Corkhill's boyfriend Jamie (aka Sean McKee). It came after I got word Sean was refusing to do a particular scene. This was a teenage comedy story in which his character had done his own washing, shrunk his favourite sweater but to save face insisted he had done it on purpose as tightness was the next big thing. I went to the set. The adjectives were already flying. He thought it made him look daft. I said it was his character, not him that was daft. He said he wouldn't do it and, fatally, in front of the entire crew, said there was nothing I could do about it. Time froze. Perhaps he *was* daft. He'd just crossed universes, from fictional teenage face-saving to the exec producer's reality. I said there *was* something I could do. Like Ricky, he could also 'do one'.

With the crew sent to lunch, I went back towards the office, recalling the script from the memory bank. Then I only had to carry about fifty episodes in my head, from storyline to transmission. When the programme expanded and *Hollyoaks* came along it was two hundred, all to be recalled at a moment's notice whenever I received a question passing someone on the stairs, in the canteen or loos: 'You know that scene when . . .' As I was doing the mental global search, wondering how we'd fix this one, a taxi drew up at the security barrier out of which stepped Allan Swift, the writer of the episode they were shooting.

Allan, thank God it's you. If it was anyone else, I'd worry . . . He knew the code. What's happened? We have a problem with your script. Go on. One of your characters, Jamie, has just left. Oh, shh . . . ugar! How much needs fixing? Probably most of the episode, but . . . Go on? Jamie's only there for Tracy to talk to, really. Go over to Scripts and flick through, see if it will work by putting 'Uncle' in front of all his lines. Allan laughed. What, Jamie becomes Uncle Jimmy? I nodded. So long as there's no sex involved. And off he went. Within half an hour I got the call. Jamie was history. Uncle Jimmy was now Tracy's confidant. And Dean Sullivan was on his way in to start shooting. It had been forty-five minutes since I'd had the call from the shoot. These were moments I really enjoyed: having to deal with issues from the fictional universe alongside the real one. Whatever happened in one would impact on the other, but I felt totally secure knowing that while I manipulated the fiction, Alexis would handle reality. At the same time, she always knew that if we faced difficulties in reality, I would bend the parallel universe so as to accommodate them. It was a good job she was into *Star Trek*, something else that endeared her to more than a few of the techies who were also Trekkies.

If we were running behind on the schedule, or needed building work done, or were spending too much on extras, she knew all I had to do was pick up the scripts and move ink around on the page: scenes reduced, locations switched and extras cut. Just as I knew that if I ever had to face down anything on the shoot, or build a new set, by the time I got back to the office, she would already have been told and the Starship would be safely on its new heading.

Pushing the *Star Trek* metaphor, after Ricky's exit we had to determine where we would boldly go where we hadn't been before, and that came to me in one of those rare, almost magical moments when you find yourself drawn from the real into the fictional universe. A production gallery or an edit suite can feel a bit like a Starship bridge: all the monitors, lights, panels, a crew ready to take commands, and of course the big swivel chairs. Everything is ready to take you wherever you want to go in the fictional universe, but the reality is that you are more than likely too focused on achieving the fiction, to enjoy the journey. You should have done that at script stage. Once there, in the big chair, you are usually concentrating minutely on everything that is in the frame. Not just how it looks and feels, but how it's shot, framed, each edit cut, the sound quality, the design, costume, hair, make-up, continuity, choice of music, sound effects . . . and any number of other things that twenty other people have already checked.

And even then, when you have seen it several times and signed off the final edit and it's been sent to the broadcaster, you can sit and watch the transmission at home and spot something that you and twenty other people have looked at about half-a-dozen times already, and all missed. But sometimes, very occasionally, something breaks through all that and you suddenly find yourself focused on the drama itself as something almost magical happens. Or rather this time it was not so much the moment itself as what it could lead to: putting Sheila Grant and Billy Corkhill together. Sue Johnston and John McArdle.

Although I can't recall the exact scene, I know it was something very simple. It could have been the first scene they ever played together, as it was not uncommon for actors to be in the same programme for some time before they both actually played a storyline. But immediately I saw them, I knew this was something special. Just as the Grant family revolved around Sue Johnston's dramatic energy, so did the Corkhills around John's. I just knew if I put these two characters together we would find something perhaps even more special than Sheila and Bobby.

The reaction from the writers was one of outrage, with Jimmy McGovern his usual vociferous self, saying he couldn't even contemplate 'St She' (my words) taking up with an electrician scab (his words). Jimmy was also definitely in the Ricky and Arthur Scargill camp. In a replay of the film *12 Angry Men*, I found myself in a minority of one. New producers could initially find the bear pit atmosphere among the writers slightly intimidating, though the better ones quickly realised that the free flow of debate between them was actually their strength and, like cabinet responsibility, once a consensus had been reached they would all go with the storyline.

Eventually I talked them round to the challenge: taking Sheila on that same journey again. Why? How? When? And, to his credit, Jimmy wrote some of the best lines for Billy and her, just as he had done for the middle-class Collinses, whom he detested. He couldn't suppress his own innate ability to write about people and their emotions, whoever they were.

For the next couple of years I got what I wanted out of the new generation, and we built up to the five-night special when Billy and Sheila first kiss. They were great episodes with Sue once again taking everyone through all the desires and doubts, the conflicts and angst, of not knowing how exactly she is feeling or even if it is right for her to have feelings for Billy . . . to the extent that most of the audience were willing them finally to get together.

However, proving my point that putting two of our best actors together would create something special, they soon wanted to push themselves further: all the way to the Bolton Octagon Theatre where an old friend, Andy Hay, the Artistic Director there, wanted them to do a new two-hander, written by Jim Cartwright and called, appropriately, *Two*. They knew my view on releasing people for panto or extended theatre runs, but I knew this was partly my own doing. If they had reached the point of needing another dramatic challenge then they would be likely to go anyway. With my own sorties out beyond *Brookside* to recharge my own creative batteries, I also fully understood why.

Alexis and I went up for the play, but all I could see was the end looming for Sheila and Billy. Like I would later stand and watch Claire Sweeney singing Evita, and know she had to move on beyond Lindsey Corkhill, so I realised that Sue and John had a talent that needed a life beyond *Brookie*. The genies, or actors' genes, were out of the bottle. Sheila and Billy would soon move off *Brookside* and another generation would replace them.

While it's always a sad moment losing old friends, worse was the untimely death of Doreen Sloane who played Annabelle Collins, a sad loss across both universes. Doreen had become a stalwart of the company, and although we had already had to face the loss of members of the production crew and staff, this felt much more personal. She had become, like Sue, a friend. Her departure meant that we had to lose the rest of the Collins family too, by sending them off to the Lake District.

This, together with Sue and John leaving, definitely marked the end of an era, but the first rule in storylining is that every day is day one, the point you start telling the story. Everything that's gone before is backstory. All the end of any era signals is the beginning of the next. Jimmy and Jackie Corkhill would come to number 10, Ron and 'DD' Dixon to number 8, and Frank and Chrissy Rogers would inhabit number 5. Life, as they say, goes on. And as it did, something else came with it: a change in attitude and perception. As with *Grange Hill*, people started coming to the company and looking at the programme for what it was, rather than what it used to be or what they thought it should be. They knew exactly what they were signing up to. And one of those was a man with a bus stop sign. Mal Young was about to step up to the co-pilot's seat.

15

Comparisons (1987–90)

'The thing about the press, is that you can give them a button, and they'll sew a shirt on to it' – *Sara Keays*

It wasn't just *Brookside* that was stepping into the next generation, but Channel 4 itself, as we saw the passing of The Emperor. In an emotional valedictory speech to the Edinburgh Festival in 1987, Jeremy Isaacs gave a summary of his time at the channel which included a rather poignant passage on how media has a tendency to consume people. The work becomes the life, and too often family and friends take second place. This hit home with me, thinking back to my physical and emotional difficulties in the summer of 1983. I am sure it did with many others too but I was feeling a lot more secure and settled now, another great legacy of the 1985 *Brookie* siege storyline: Alexis and I were 'stepping out'.

It was another moment when a wormhole opened between the two universes . . . sorry, I've already done the *Star Trek* metaphor. Still, the fictional nurses, Kate and Sandra, who shared a house in the fictional universe, crossed over into the reality of three actors, Sharon Rosita and Sheila Grier, along with David Easter (aka Pat Hancock), sharing a house; they decided to have a barbecue and invited me to drop in. I usually ducked out of these social events, as it felt both unfair and uncomfortable to go into someone's home and accept their hospitality when I knew, as I often did, that the writers and I were already planning their exit from the show. This was always a hard line to walk, keeping a professional distance, especially with people I really respected.

Because for me accepting such an invitation was all mixed up with trying to figure out where the work, social, employer, employee boundaries were, along with an early awareness that my every sentence, word, or even nuance of body language was always under constant scrutiny, I was verging on my default apology . . . until Alexis said she was thinking of going, but didn't know whether she should. Before long we had debated this and decided that we could go together, as 'management', that divisive phrase we refused to allow within staff-company matters.

Out in the car park we wondered if we should meet there or go in one car? That seemed logical. We could leave together then. That too seemed logical. Get back for a meeting. Just dropping in. Almost as a courtesy. Again, logical. That would be fine. It wouldn't be read as anything else, would it? So we did. And it was. We had a great time because everyone treated us matter-of-factly as a couple, to the extent that when it was time to leave we wondered if I should drop her off or . . . ? We ended up shrugging our shoulders and going home. Together. It seemed very, well, logical.

Over the following weeks and months we still kept up the pretence of leading separate lives, never quite sure how people would react. It was left to Carmel, my Production PA, once again to burst the bubble of denial. For God's sake, why don't you just stop all the nonsense and go in the same car every day? Everyone knows. What? Knows what? When? A Scouse look. Well, I knew before you two probably did, but it's taken you long enough, so can we just get on with it now and co-ordinate your diaries properly? Fair enough. As to how people reacted, everyone made it perfectly clear that I was lucky to have her. I've never argued or denied it.

When Jeremy signed off, leaving his successor Michael Grade a note saying that if he messed it up he'd come and strangle him, this was a sentiment shared by many in the industry, both outside and inside C4, including the man then with responsibility for *Brookside*, Peter Ansorge. On hearing of Michael's appointment, he was reported as being seen running round the office like Private Frazer from *Dad's Army*, declaring that they were all doomed. This was of course a bit of media hyperbole, linked to the view that Michael was a populist in the grand tradition of his uncle, Lew Grade.

Those who know Michael realise that, first, he is a great supporter of talent, and second, he knows that talent is not enough. It has to be packaged and marketed properly. No matter what it is — as a more than cursory glance at the history of ITV, with its Bernstein-Grade box-office principles, would have shown. While Lew Grade's ATV was delivering some of the best and most innovative drama, like *The Planemakers* and *The Power Game*, Bernstein's Granada was delivering programmes like *World in Action* and *What The Papers Say*.

I got to know Michael while he was still Controller of BBC 1. He had made an industry announcement about wanting more comedy and I went to see him about a sit-com I was working on. I'd sent him a script and when we first met he caught me out by actually having read it and started grilling me on it, in between looking at the bank of TVs he always used to have on in his office, one for each channel. It wasn't so bad in those days with only four, but whenever you went to see him you had to accept that you would be the third person in the room. We didn't progress that idea but out of it came a first-look deal, under which the BBC would pay a small amount of development money for me to come up with a range of formats.

He was thinking around what to do in the 5.30 p.m. slot, into which he would drop *Neighbours* as a bridge between the early-evening schedule and the end of children's programmes, coming out of *Grange Hill* and *Byker Grove*. This was always the holistic approach he took, like delaying transmission of one series of *Grange Hill* for a few weeks until *Wogan* was ready, so that he could market a 'new look BBC1'. The ideas I went back to him with ranged from a new version of the old BBC favourite *Ask the Family*, where families competed against each other in observational games, to regional sports competitions, to a weekly fightback against the tabloids called *Hold That Story*. I also threw in the idea of doing a more teen/grown-up version of *Grange Hill*.

Michael agreed to fund two pilots, the family quiz show and *Hold That Story*, with the proviso that the latter should be the front-runner. We both had enough experience of being in the media spotlight to know this could be something really interesting. Anyone who has ever been interviewed by the press, or knows a lot about a specific subject, always wonders. 'Why did they use that bit?' on seeing it reported. Many people also experience the 'I never said that' moment, and the programme was going to be a straightforward approach to the process of news-gathering. The whys and hows of getting and publishing the story, not the story itself.

It is important to remember that 'tabloid journalism' in the 1980s was not what we know today but it was starting to head that way. That's what we were interested in. Just as Channel 4, by adding 30 per cent more airtime, had opened up television to new people with new ideas and new ways of doing things, so the print media was going through a similar expansion and state of flux. Due to the same technological revolution that had made *Brookside* possible.

The Times, the *Sunday Times*, the *Sun* and the now-defunct *News of the World* had been reinvigorated by coming under the common ownership of News International, but two new kids had also arrived on the block. The *Independent* and *Today* were both launched in the mid-1980s, bringing with them opportunities for journalists to move between more titles. Alastair Campbell, well-known Burnley football supporter and adviser to Tony Blair, was political editor of *Today*, while his partner, Fiona Millar, was the news editor. Over at the *Sun* a young-ish Kelvin MacKenzie was starting to make his name and presence felt.

The arrival of new printing technology was making the news itself as it led to large-scale and bitter union demonstrations outside the *Today* and News International printshops, based around the time-honoured opposition to new technology displacing human labour. In other words, jobs. One irony in all of this was that the print unions' struggles, including a fight with the EETPU, who agreed to install and operate the new electronic presses that would displace traditional print workers, was exactly the sort of scenario I had wanted to explore with Bobby Grant's character. It was a tense time for the industry, and the cultural impact of it all was that the nature of daily newspapers began to change. The emphasis was shifting, from the 'news' bit to the 'daily' bit. The main driver seemed to be to fill the pages. If you can't find something, make it up.

There is probably an academic study of when exactly this started to happen, but I began becoming aware of it personally when Alexis and I found ourselves the target of a couple of local news hounds. Word was beginning to circulate that we were more than chairman and managing director, which we now were, and one morning the doorbell started ringing around seven o'clock. They probably hoped to catch one of us in that offguard time after just waking up, like they caught Cherie Booth on the morning after Labour won the election in 1997. Or maybe they thought they would catch us coming out together on the way to work. Fortunately, I was as usual working on scripts early so I was wide awake and could see the front door from my office.

I went up and told Alexis we might have to work from home that day, then phoned Larry and asked him to come and do 'the minder thing': in other words, get rid of them. By the time my brother arrived they looked to be on the verge of giving up, but were still there when he pulled into the drive, which was enough to send them scooting over, blinding him with flashes, before real-ising they didn't know who he was. In his best Scouse he asked them if they had any legitimate business being on the property and suggested that if not perhaps they'd like to go and do something useful elsewhere. They started quizzing him about who he was, and did Alexis and I live in the house? By this time he was at the front door. He took out the set of keys he kept, waved them at the journos and photographer, opened the door and stepped inside. Scratching their heads, they wandered away.

When Larry gave the all clear, Alexis and I went off to *Brookie* having arranged to do a house swap for the night. The next morning the bell went again at 7.00 a.m. and Larry went down, so he tells me, in a pair of boxers and string vest he'd bought for the occasion, and threw open the door while wearing a pair of sunglasses to save his eyes from the flashes. We had to take his word for it as we never saw the photographs, just as we never saw the doorsteppers again, for a while. His boxers had obviously worked a treat.

However, with the journos not wanting to lose a good story or let a few facts get in the way of a good fee, we still found ourselves in the newspapers. They published a photograph that looked as though we were out at a nightclub, but was actually cropped from a picture taken at a civic reception. This was probably the only time that the press broke the informal understanding that I wouldn't talk about my private life, after the *Grange Hill* incident of years earlier. It may just have been because I was boring the rest of the time, and Alexis made me a bit more interesting, but doctoring photographs with new technology was coming into its own and starting to distort the news agenda. Just as a good picture is worth a thousand words, then a good cropped or composite image can generate a further thousand pounds.

I knew Michael Grade had suffered his own fair share of journalistic speculation and, while we had to accept it as part of the game we were in, we both agreed that this sort of thing was probably the tip of the iceberg. What else might be being 'manufactured'? It seemed like a perfect fit for the BBC's impartiality and public-service remit and my own sociological interest in 'reading the media'. Each week we wouldn't just report what the newspapers had been reporting, we'd ask why. And every now and then take a closer look at the coverage and point out that things might not be quite the way they seemed – and then suggest they *Hold That Story*.

The pilot for *Hold That Story* was made in Manchester as the BBC studios there and MerseyTV were at either end of the M62. While we were cutting-edge at one particular programme, stepping into the BBC at the creative coalface, as a producer this time and not just a mere writer, I was reminded of the sheer scale of its technical potential. Almost anything you wanted or needed could be found in some far-flung outpost or at the end of a dark corridor, if you found the right people to guide you. It is often said that while you are never more than seventy miles from the sea in the UK, you will never be more than fifty from a BBC outpost.

The original proposal for the programme was to reverse the old gag 'Never let a few facts get in the way of a good story' by adopting a new principle: how many facts does it need to make a good story? The programme would do this by showing how to construct a good story out of as few facts as possible; to demonstrate how slight stories can be built up by exaggeration; the value of unsubstantiated gossip; and how fabricated pictures, like the one of Alexis and myself, were becoming commonplace with the advent of new technology. Considering the recent revelations around the 2011–12 phone-hacking scandal, it's interesting to remember that we were doing this in 1986 and that the basic idea owed a lot to a book that journalist Henry Porter had written in 1985, *Lies, Damned Lies and Some Exclusives*.

By the time I got to Manchester to make the pilot I had met Porter, as I was interested to see if he would present the programme, but while supportive of it, he felt that he had said all he wanted to say. We then started looking elsewhere, including the then young(ish) Jeremy Paxman, but while feeling he had 'the aura', I was looking for someone less traditional. I don't think he'll mind my saying this, as he seems to have done all right for himself since, or hearing that he lost this investigative journalism slot to Helen Madden, who had not long before been known as 'Miss Helen' while fronting the Ulster TV programme *Romper Room*.

What I was looking for was a softer, more gentle, elder sister or mum figure who would coax people into talking about their experiences and activities rather than feeling the need to deflect questions and defend themselves during a typical inquisitorial, even adversarial, current-affairs interview. A style that didn't seem to inhibit young Jeremy.

Within the pilot we planned a form of 'answerback' interview during which people who had been in the media spotlight could come on and tackle the 'Why did they write that?' element. There were two people being demonised by the press at that time, from opposite ends of the political spectrum but both finding themselves in conflict with the Thatcher Government, one for waging class war, one for refusing to have an abortion. We wanted Arthur Scargill and Sara Keays to come and tell their side of the stories.

Helen, with her Northern Irish lilt, could charm the birds out of the trees if she wanted to and we were within a whisker of getting Arthur Scargill to come and talk about his treatment at the hands of the media. I was interested in Scargill because he really did encapsulate what I had set out to investigate at the beginning of *Brookside* with the character of Bobby Grant.

Helen nearly coaxed him in as he was aware of who I was, and of *Brookside*, and of the way Sue and Ricky had been so supportive of the miners. However, we were still doing the programme with the BBC and, as if to prove the point of it, Scargill said he felt they had totally misrepresented him and the NUM in the past, and refused our invitation.

Although we were unsuccessful with him, we did manage to get Sara Keays. Her backstory was that she had been the personal assistant of MP Cecil Parkinson, they had had a long-standing affair, and when she became pregnant he asked her to have an abortion. She went public with the story, which led to his resignation as Secretary of State for Trade and Industry, and from that moment she found herself the focus of sustained and intrusive media interest. Again it took a lot of coaxing and cajoling from Helen and the assurances that this was not the 'usual BBC', but more MerseyTV who did *Brookside*, before she would consider agreeing. It was beginning to feel as if the BBC was viewed like 'the Council' was back in Liverpool. She couldn't, or wouldn't, come all the way up to Manchester, which was fair enough, so we arranged to do the interview at the hallowed news studios in Lime Grove, just off Shepherd's Bush, part of the original BBC estate.

When we all turned up we found they had let us have the Newsnight studio for 'a few hours', so we actually got there before Jeremy became Paxo. Sara was still nervous, glancing at the *Newsnight* logo, the belly of the beast, but after further assurances from Helen that she was only there to listen, she relaxed. We also agreed that we would not transmit anything we'd recorded until she had seen it.

The interview started and I stood at the back of the control room which, from memory, was unusually placed as you could go directly out to the studio floor rather than be perched high above as at the original *Grange Hill* studios. It was probably something to do with the age of the estate, as they closed it a few years later, but I remember thinking how much more sensible it was than having people continually dashing up and down staircases. The big advantage was that the floor manager could amble across and pop his head in as a reminder that the interview had been running for five minutes, ten minutes then fifteen, getting twitchier by the minute as I don't think they had ever shot anything longer than five minutes before. I just kept nodding and saying fine, so in the end they all did an eye exchange and a shrug and gave up. I distinctly remember the racks and lighting engineer just falling back in his chair. The quiet sigh. The folded arms. Not quite a shake of the head, but his gloomy silence said it all.

However, one of the great things about working in those old studios with those old(er) guys was that there was such a level of expertise that it could just happen in front of you. And just as you get those seemingly magical, unexpected moments in the edit suite, sometimes in a studio the atmosphere changes, stills to a quietness you can almost touch, caused by everyone becoming focused on something extraordinary.

As it did here. Helen made Sara relax, and then she talked freely about how journalists would pretend their cars had broken down and ask to use the pre-mobile phone just so they could get into her house; about hearing voices and finding a journalist in the kitchen talking to her little girl; or being at a private dinner and becoming upset as she had had some bad news about her daughter's health, only to discover the following day that a fellow guest, a newspaper editor, had sneaked out and phoned the story back to his paper. And as she talked and the clock ticked round to thirty . . . thirty-five . . . forty minutes, I noticed the cameras sensing the right close ups and our jaundiced engineer and the hard-bitten floor manager were actually engrossed in this human tale of persecution and despair.

Helen brought it to a close at about forty-seven minutes, with no one moving for another thirty seconds before everything seemed to click back into place. The engineer turned to me and said, 'I thought that was going to be naff, but, y'know, I think that's the best thing I've ever seen come out of here. Good luck with it.' The floor manager nodded, shook hands and said, 'Longest we've ever recorded, anyway.' In the middle of her story Sara had come out with a sentiment that was the essence of the programme, and something I have remembered ever since. 'The thing about the press, is that you can give them a button, and they'll sew a shirt on to it.' Quite.

The first-look deal with the BBC was one of my continuing attempts to discover life beyond *Brookside*, knowing that opportunities would remain limited at C4 because of the politics there. Part of the rationale was also my belief that independent production could consist of anything, from licensing a format to delivering the entire programme. Too often in life people fall into the either/or trap. If it can't be this, it must be that. Along with 'Why not?' instead of 'Why?' we also adopted the 'never mind either/or, let's have it all' principle, picked up from the storyline process. Every stage of every story has another story attached to it. Someone arrives at a location. How did they get there? Where from? What happened when they woke up? Who did they meet? Who did they sleep with? Every character, like every situation, can be peeled back, like an onion, one skin at a time. Every location is a maze of tangents. Every issue is a moral maze. We adopted the same approach to independent production.

We could develop ideas, package scripts, hire facilities, crews, locations, or even act as consultants. In the late-1980s I enjoyed the role of latter-day electronic brush salesman, travelling the length and breadth of the UK extolling the virtues of MerseyTV. This took me to Aberdeen to meet Alex Ferguson, before he was Sir Alex, and Mandy Rice-Davies long after she had featured in the Profumo affair. To Belgium, Canada, New York, Italy and Dublin, to advise on drama and hear how RTÉ got cheesed off when BBC Centre in London would assume they were on the BBC network grid and call up to say they needed extra recoding capacity so would be coming to them in thirty minutes.

These sorts of trips Alexis and I used to put at the beginning of a planned break as they helped us wind down. We'd recognised and worked through the catatonic fatigue syndrome, usually experienced in the first few days of any holiday. Being at the centre of the maelstrom, most of our time and energy was spent meeting people and fielding questions. After intense periods I would find myself reaching a point of not wanting to make another decision, no matter how inconsequential or trivial. I just didn't want to decide whether to have coffee or tea. The standard response was that great teenage refrain that can become the most annoying thing in the world: whatever. It was what Jeremy had alluded to in his valedictory speech at Edinburgh. How media consumes you, and as the social side is mixed with the business it is usually family who suffer.

After Alexis and I got together, this mix was much easier to handle, as we would both be at the same level of fatigue. Initially we carved out time to go off to places like the Greek Islands, with the idea of 'leaving work behind'. But of course 'the work' was what brought us together, so we would struggle through two irritable days before we accepted that what we found most enjoyable was being away, together, and sorting out all the company issues in peace. Once we acknowledged that, we sorted out more problems on holiday than when we were back at base. And had a great time doing it.

We had a funny moment in France one time, when the media

company we went to visit had a small conference facility with a few bedrooms attached. They put us up in separate rooms, as Chairman and Managing Director, but when we were caught emerging together the following morning there were raised eyebrows, then smiles and Gallic shrugs.

If Alexis and I weren't on the road we'd get people turning up at *Brookie* from South Africa, Israel, East Germany as it was, and even China. Everyone wanted to know how to make their own soaps, but the best at obtaining information were the Japanese. One day my PA, I think it was Diane by then, brought me a fax and asked if I knew anything about it. The fax appeared to come from the Japanese advertising agency Dentsu, based in Tokyo and one of the biggest in the world. It simply said, 'Greetings. Our representative will call on you at 10.30 a.m. Tuesday. Please tell him everything you know.'

Like spam e-mail, anyone could make up a dodgy fax and send it, so we figured this was some form of wind up and forgot it. Until Tuesday when, sure enough, at 10.25 there was a call from Reception. 'Security say there's a Mr Dentsu from Japan to see Phil.' Intrigued I went down and there was the Dentsu representative, with assistant, who bowed and asked if I had received the fax. Still thinking this could be a Jeremy Beadle-type *Candid Camera* wind up, I took them into our reception area, a conservatory we'd had added to the side of number 13. There we had a few more bows, sat down, and I asked them what they wanted to know? Everything, please. Everything? Everything, please. I couldn't resist, so started talking about being born at home in Huyton and . . . but soon realised Scouse humour got lost in translation. Tell me exactly why you are really here? I asked eventually.

It turned out that Sony had put them on to us, after they had been commissioned by the Japanese Government to do a global mapping exercise on production processes. Media had been targeted as a growth sector they wished to expand. We spent a pleasant hour or so as I told them a lot, if not quite everything I knew. They then bowed, gave me a small replica samurai sword, and left. A week later Publicity got a call asking if I would do an interview for the Japanese state broadcaster NHK about *Grange Hill* next time I was in London. When I got there they did the interview as normal and then stood up, as did I. Then they asked me to stay seated while they shifted the camera, bowed and asked me if I would mind doing another interview, for the Japanese Government this time.

They then ran through a set of questions I immediately recognised as being supplementary to Mr Dentsu's. I answered them, but still didn't tell them everything. When the interview finished there were more bows. Deeper bows. Government bows perhaps but I was given another sword. I said I already had one so they gave me a banner instead. As I left, I pondered whether or not the BBC World Service conducted this sort of industrial espionage, and if they didn't, perhaps they should, even granted that I hadn't told them 'everything'. It must be easier and cheaper than sending Bond in. A few weeks later when I was with my dad, I couldn't help wonder if Mr Dentsu was at home with his father. And whether our dads had been trying to kill each other just over forty years earlier.

On the basis of always having at least twenty projects under development, while we were waiting for the 5.30 formats, as we now referred to the ideas I'd put to Michael Grade, to work their way through the production cycle, I was still busy casting the net elsewhere. *Brookie* and *Grange Hill* were both in their 'golden years' and were ticking along well with established production teams. Creatively I was looking to stretch myself, and despite the backstage, or rather front-of-house, problems at the Everyman I had really enjoyed the different buzz that theatre offers: the instant and live interaction with an audience that changes every performance, and is impossible to achieve in television.

I had two further theatrical adventures. Both were linked to the programmes and the idea of trying to bring the television audience in and introduce them to theatre. Put another way – the cynical, ratings-grabbing way – to see if we could attract the larger television audience into filling theatres. It worked, but not quite. The first attempt was at the Liverpool Playhouse, *Soaplights*, with Ian Kellgren, then Creative Director. The second, a few years later, was *Grange Hill: Tucker's Return* at Hornchurch with Bob Thompson as Creative Director – another Scouser.

Soaplights was fun and we managed to get good houses, but this was another experience marred by the clash in cultures. Even on our tight television budgets, with our actors (like the writers) being on the Equity national union rates, they were paid far in excess of what the theatre could offer. While accepting that it was a different form and a different market, nevertheless, as I was directing, I felt obliged to make up their fees to the level they would receive from us. Two positives emerged though. The production designer, Candida Boyes, joined MerseyTV as Head of Design, becoming responsible for the *Brookside* Parade, the Jordache courtroom and all of *Hollyoaks*. The other new arrival was Tony Wood, who would go on to become Head of Continuing Drama at ITV and Producer of *Coronation Street* before becoming Creative Director of Lime Pictures. Yet on his way to doing all that, he came to work at *Brookside* as a trainee because, although he wasn't working on *Soaplights*, he was passing through and managed to conjure up a missing, but vital prop at the eleventh hour, with all the resourcefulness of Mal Young finding fish 'n' chips at 8.00 on a Sunday morning.

Tucker's Return at Hornchurch was a completely different experience that reunited me with Todd Carty and Terry Sue Patt (aka Benny), as well as Hollo, Gonch, and Imelda and the Terrorhawks. The plot revolved round Tucker returning as a teacher, and Steve Wright and I re-worked the music from the ill-fated *Grange Hill* album to include in the show. Not quite *Grange Hill: The Musical*, but not far off. It ran for four weeks to 97 per cent attendances and it was amazing to discover mums and dads explaining who Tucker and Benny were, while their kids were telling them who Gonch and Imelda were.

Another aspect of my life started to develop around this time: education. After discovering that first *Grange Hill* and then *Brookie* were being used, both formally and informally, as teaching aids, I started putting more time into answering questions from schools and academics, but, more significantly, into trying to correct some of the misconceptions about them. This led to more guest lectures in schools, colleges and universities, and more Script to Screen sessions, taking cast and crews the length and breadth of the UK. Whether in Falmouth or Glasgow we would do the first day for media students and the second day for the public, which always threw up the hardest Q & A sessions: for that was the point. The audience were the only critics I would listen to.

It was a way of keeping in touch and hearing from them. Getting our mid-term reports direct from the people I was making the programmes for. This predated what would become almost the dark art of market research, but a live, unvetted audience offered a much more honest feedback mechanism than any number of carefully selected 'representative samples'. When all's said and done, you can never hand-pick your audience, but they wouldn't have been there if they weren't already followers of the programme. Their views were honest, and invaluable in helping us make sure we were keeping in touch. It was just a pity the broadcasters couldn't get themselves out on the road too instead of relying on 'mediated research'.

Back in Manchester with *Hold That Story* we were turning our attention to the 'every picture could be worth a thousand pounds' trend that had Alexis and me featuring in the tabloids. We had put a call out for people to contact us if they knew of any photographs that had been doctored. It didn't take long to uncover exactly what we wanted, proving the point that anyone is only ever six phone calls away from absolutely anyone else on the planet. Once you have worked in media, you know that there is no such thing as confidentiality.

The Royals, and especially Princess Diana, were always in demand, and one photograph arrived on our desks showing the young Princes, Harry and William, on a beach holiday with their mother and apparently staring at a topless bather. A priceless picture. However, the word 'apparently' was the key here as there was another photograph taken from a different angle showing that the boys were staring at a sandcastle twenty metres away. A pretty boring picture. But, hey, if it was a slack day for news. And if the Royals were fast becoming a tabloid soap opera then two other subjects closer to home, *East-Enders* and *Brookside*, started to feature regularly.

There was a story running that 'BBC executives' were forcing *EastEnders* to radically tone down their storylines and to curb the antics of Dirty Den, fearful of the proposed new Broadcasting Act going through Parliament. Quick calls were made to all concerned in the BBC. No one had said or done anything like that. On *Brookie* the tale was that 'ITV bosses' not executives, were in talks to buy *Brookside* from C4. I'm sure I would have known. When querying the stories with the newspapers that had run them, we were told that the BBC *was* bound to be worried about *EastEnders*, and that ITV *should* buy *Brookie*. But they're not true stories, we protested. Yeah, but it's only telly, isn't it? It was. But also people's livelihoods and businesses.

Another story we picked up on was featured in the *Guardian* and concerned a young(ish) Kelvin MacKenzie, who had the *Sun* running a campaign against Everest Double Glazing. It turned out that this champion of the consumer was himself a disgruntled customer unhappy with the fact Everest wouldn't return a £450 deposit he had put down as part of a contract, later cancelled. Everest said he had left it too late, and MacKenzie had admitted not having read the contract. I think we all know and sympathise with that feeling, but he was personalising a press compaign. Perhaps there was nothing wrong with that, as we would all love to have a national newspaper defend our consumer rights, but was it the right subject for a national campaign? It also appeared that the Office of Fair Trading was dragged into it and Everest then had to spend time on damage limitation, even writing to all 650 MPs to spell out the exact position. This was more than 'just telly'. It was about our taxes being spent on what seemed more a personal argument than the public interest. It was also meant to be a 'C'mon, Kelvin', as part of the media's knockabout relationship. We ended the item with two recommendations: Never believe what you read in the papers – and never, ever sell anything to Kelvin MacKenzie.

As we put the pilot of *Hold That Story* together, the doubters started to whisper. Was this wise? Yes, it's about balance. Should the BBC be doing this? Yes, it had a public-service duty to highlight bad practices. Weren't we antagonising the newspapers? Only a few. We were sure the *Guardian* and the *Independent* would support it. Michael remained robust and said, Press on, but when I was ready to show him the pilot the meeting was cancelled at short notice. Then the next one. Something was going on, but not with our project. He had decided to jump ship and go and take over from The Emperor. Great. I was with the BBC trying to get more work away from the Channel.

Within days he phoned me and said I should just bring the project over to C4. I said he knew the deal. Under the first-look agreement, the BBC had six months to make its decision. He said they'd never do it without him, but to call as soon as they'd confirmed that. Which I said I would, and then waited and waited and waited until Michael's successor there was announced. This was Jonathan Powell, previously Head of Drama, who didn't 'get it'. In the meantime Michael got fed up waiting and commissioned his own show for C4, on the usual basis that there is no copyright in ideas. It was called *Hard Talk*, fronted by Ray Snoddy from the *Financial Times*. Ray was a print journalist and, while the *FT* was above all the tabloid antics, there was still a familial pull there. The reporting was slick instead of sharp. It was caustic but it wasn't cutting.

There are always things you look back on with regret, missed opportunities and disappointments, and *Hold That Story* is a big one for me. Not just because it was a good idea, but also because it was the right idea at the right time. If we had managed to get it on air it might, just might, have made the tabloids pause for thought every now and then. If we, on the BBC, with the same demographic as the *Sun*, had given Kelvin a gentle and friendly nudge in the ribs about his double-glazing, might things have been different? If they had all known that dear old Auntie at the BBC was watching, well, perhaps the press wouldn't have developed that sense almost of impunity that seems to have emerged from the phone-hacking scandal and subsequent Leveson Inquiry. Listening to J.K. Rowling describe finding notes put into her child's school bag by journalists was very reminiscent of hearing Sara Keays talk about finding a journalist talking to her own little girl in the family kitchen. The warnings were there as far back as that. And if we had, it might also perhaps have toned down the *Sun*'s despicable coverage of Hillsborough, which still casts a shadow over Liverpool today.

Elsewhere I was still trying to find other creative outlets; more so after Michael had left the BBC to go to Channel 4. One possible new platform was satellite television. The government, through the Independent Broadcasting Authority (IBA), reverting to the intentions and aims of IT82, were still in thrall to new technology. Although the cable revolution had stalled and the 'sunshine industries' were still in the first light of dawn, satellite was the new 'next big thing'. Unfortunately, as is so often the case with governments and their regulators, being bureaucracies themselves, all they can see is like-minded solutions. Big bureaucracies need big bureaucracies to deal with. That means big solutions with big companies with big deep pockets. So usually they opt for the gee-whizz-bang solution, i.e. go with the most technically advanced, complicated and expensive, option.

As this time they did: high-definition D-Mac, which had a square rather than the already available round satellite dish. They called it the Squarial, to be funky, and said it would be an additional stimulus to get people watching the as yet non-existent high-definition TV sets. This was to be a quality service. They had obviously not been watching the videocassette wars where the best and most expensive brands, Philips and Sony, were being crushed by the cheap and cheerful JVC VHS. Someone else had, though, and that was Rupert Murdoch who, as he had done with LWT in the 1960s, had recently bought a struggling venture, Sky Satellite, which was operating on an existing telecoms satellite and utilising easily available satellite dishes while transmitting in the standard PAL 625 lines television system so that it could be watched on existing TVs. It was meant to be a cheap and cheerful service. He put £40 million into the operation and everyone said he was mad.

The new regulatory venture was to be called British Satellite Broadcasting, and from a distance we could see Granada gathering forces to go after the official licence as the main plank in their developing aim to dominate the UK market. It was a big-ticket, deep-pocket consortium and they recruited the usual suspects from BBC and ITV. Big salaries and big offices were established at the soon to become infamous Marco Polo House, a glass and marble edifice close to Battersea Park. They were building the temple before founding the religion. I went to talk to the then Chief Executive, John Gow, another ex-BBC man. With many of the resonances of my initial contact with Channel 4, we met at the old IBA Building in Brompton Road, where I had first met and talked to Jeremy Isaacs about getting *Brookside* started. John Gow and I had a similar conversation about the need for programming on tight budgets, but unlike Channel 4, British Satellite Broadcasting had no guaranteed income from ITV. They would have to earn it in the marketplace. I came away feeling not quite as sure as I had been of Jeremy, but hopeful that we could work together on something. However, as things progressed it became obvious that not only did they not have a properly formulated religion, they hadn't yet even a vision.

We were promised some development cash and did make some pilot programmes for them, although in the end they proved too innovative. My description, as BSB said they thought we were not offering what others were, i.e. the same old same old. But what was the point of that for a brand new technological platform? They thought they needed to remain 'new but not different' in order to win over the existing television audience. Our view was that they needed to be 'new and innovative' or they wouldn't get the established, and older, television audience to cough up around £400 for something they were already getting for free from terrestrial channels. It was eight-track audio cartridges against the smaller and cheaper cassettes all over again. Sony Betamax or VHS? We wanted to make programmes like 'women at lunch' and fly-on-the-wall reality shows. Things that would eventually, unfortunately, come to dominate mainstream television.

Two years and around £200 million later, the long-expected crash and burn of BSB occurred. Despite forced grins and attempted spin, by calling it a 'merger', Rupert Murdoch's Sky Satellite acquired the company for the proverbial song and the name was changed from British Satellite Broadcasting to *BSkyB*, which probably saved on the letterheads and corporate branding. BSB was therefore consigned to history and its Squarials became collectors' items. Once again a triumph for regulatory imposition: structures and procedures valued over creative drive, consumer demand or even need. The temple at Marco Polo House was ditched and ultimately became the home of QVC, a shopping channel – not exactly what the guardians of broadcasting quality originally had in mind.

The lasting significance of all this was that it once again threw into stark relief why government regulators shouldn't meddle. The original D-Mac licence they issued for BSB was both well-intentioned and far-sighted, supposed to usher in the age of high-definition television, but in their technological zeal they decided to develop a different standard from the rest of Europe. The unintended consequence this time was not only the delayed introduction of HD TV but the accelerated development of pay-TV, sports rights and Premiership Football profligacy. Amazing what one daft decision can lead to!

At the polar opposite of the creative spectrum, I received a call from my old Southern TV commissioner friend Lewis Rudd, now at Central TV. He asked if I would 'do him a favour' and write a half-hour children's drama. Initially I thought this was a pilot for a new series, but it turned out to be ITV's contribution to a drama festival they were obliged to support as part of the European Broadcasting Union. It didn't seem a big deal so, knowing that I owed Lewis the favour, for *Going Out*, I thought about the challenge of appealing to all the different European territories and languages, then sent him an outline for a short film with a twist. It would be a silent movie. With no words, we wouldn't have to worry about multiple translations.

It was a simple premise. The opening shot would be of a young lad getting a surprise birthday present of a bike; he's overjoyed; out and about thoroughly enjoying himself; seen by a scally; scally follows; young lad leaves bike unattended; scally steals bike; scally also seen overjoyed and experiencing same sense of enjoyment; but then scally sees young lad being beaten for losing bike; both once again experience same emotions – remorse and regret; scally experiences sympathy; returns bike; happy ever after.

It was a simple moralistic tale. With no dialogue, it would need sensitive direction and performances. Initially Lewis was reluctant. He was paying a writer and writers are supposed to write dialogue. No, writers write drama, I told him. Directors interpret. Actors perform. Eventually he accepted, we developed it, the director shot it, and it won first prize at the festival.

About the same time Film 4 were experimenting with shorts: eleven minutes of drama. I suggested to David Rose that we could try a silent movie, like the old London to Brighton railway films, proposing to do one around either the emotional highs and lows of going for an interview or medical, or else something like the cradle-to-grave journey of life. Changing times, changing looks, changing values. He thought silent movies had had their day. As did most people, until the 2012 Oscars and Bafta hit *The Artist*. But, like any other idea, it was only as good as its execution. First someone needed it make it happen .

That someone at the BBC was Michael Checkland, then Head of Resources but soon to become Director-General. I received a call from his deputy Keith Anderson to ask if I would meet them for a drink next time I was in for *Grange Hill*. It turned out that they knew I had spoken to Julia Smith and Tony Holland when they were setting up *EastEnders*, that they had been up to *Brookie*, but a review of all programming costs was now underway. They wondered if I would be up for a confidential comparison of their costs with *Brookside*. I said I would if they opened the books on *EastEnders*, but I would have to think round the confidentiality issue with Channel 4, which they accepted.

Alexis and I discussed it and decided to adopt the same principle of consultation that both C4 and the BBC itself adopted: we would tell them after the event. So we found ourselves in a secret conclave away from both Elstree and *Brookie*, in the anonymity of Television Centre where we could all arrive at the same meeting room from various routes and not actually be seen together: initially Julia was very protective and defensive until it looked like the *EastEnders* costs were not too bad compared to *Brookie's*. They said they had to factor in premium payments to 'star performers', etc, until Alexis started speaking accountant and it appeared it was the same overhead cost recovery issue we had had with C4 in the early days. The *EastEnders* budget was looking favourable because while the *Brookside* budget included absolutely everything that would be a cost to the programme, *EastEnders* did not. It excluded the BBC's central overhead costs for things like security, canteens, studios and, most significant of all, make-up and wardrobe which were then considered a central resource. When these central resource costs were added back it looked far less favourable.

It might have been worse as the BBC didn't really know the true cost of their central overheads and Julia was getting more and more depressed until the accountants, including Michael Checkland, reassured her that the point of this exercise was not to see whether she was running *EastEnders* less efficiently than we were running *Brookie*, but more to investigate the hidden BBC overhead costs. Things like how much of BBC Copyright's budget was spent dealing with *Eastenders'* legal issues. Then there were the difficulties of like-for-like comparison. We shot single-camera, they were shooting multi-camera studio. Shooting our way, on their cost base, would have seen their cost double. The very reason for starting *Brookie* the way I did.

Yet that was in fact something of a red herring. The real point was that in terms of the BBC's remit, *EastEnders* was delivering more viewers at a lower cost per viewer, and therefore licence-fee payer, than any other drama or perhaps department. Great value for money! Whether they could reduce overhead costs was really a separate issue, and something I think they lost sight of when they decided not to renew Michael Checkland's term as DG and to opt instead for a non-accountant who seemed to revel in business consultancy. The days of Producer Choice were ahead, which should really have been termed Hobson's Choice – and the beginning of the end of public–service broadcasting as we knew it. Then there was *Waterfront Beat*, one of the first indie commissions from the BBC. They too could see the new legislation on the horizon and knew they would be 'forced' to help create a better market for the sunshine industry promised at the beginning of C4 but now stalling for the lack of a proper market, something that was compounded by the regulatory failure that led to the satellite TV débâcle. Although slow to change, like all large-scale institutions, once the BBC sense the prevailing wind they are quick to move and colonise space, so they were the first to open the door to independent production. It was probably a combination of my continuing relationship with them through *Grange Hill* and the fact that they would have known *Brookie's* cost base after the *EastEnders* audit comparison, that helped get me a lunch with Mark Chivas, then Head of Drama. It was decided that Mersey TV would be part of the first wave of independent access.

Initially things went well, but a sense of déjà vu soon started to materialise when the appointed producer began giving off signals that this was not really what he wanted to be doing. It was starting to feel like *County Hall* all over again, although at least there was no script editor lurking in the background. That no-no was probably flagged on my BBC file. An early warning sign came when the producer started to query scenes in which senior officers were to be seen talking politics. The main objection seemed to revolve around the fact that I had one reading the *Guardian*. Surely police officers don't read the *Guardian*? Why wouldn't they? Because, well, they're all right-wing, aren't they? How many cops do you know? What's that got to do with anything? Do you actually know any? Well, no. Then how can you assume you understand their politics? Because I know someone who knows.

I would have this same conversation with every writer and director and at every casting session. What do you think of the police? Bastards. (These were artistic people.) Why? Because they are, aren't they? Everyone knows. OK. But have you, personally, ever had any direct contact with the cops? Er, well, no. Then why do you say they are 'bastards'? Because I know someone who was arrested, right?

And this was the sociological issue I wanted to tackle. The fact that, apart from when stopped for speeding, or while they were asking directions or the time, 95 per cent of the population never come into direct contact with the police. Their opinions are formed third-hand from other people or, more usually, from media misrepresentation. The remaining 5 per cent are either perpetrators or victims of crime, neither category being ideally suited to appreciate what policing is all about.

As with *County Hall* I had spent the previous couple of years researching, in this instance spending time with the Merseyside police force. I'd been out on the beat, with traffic patrols, in the custody suites, following the drugs and serious crime squads, attending the training college, sitting in the control rooms, as well as with finance and HR. I even spent a twenty-four-hour shift in one of the Divisional HQs in order to get a feel for the changing atmosphere and challenges faced during the day. As part of this, I asked them to gather together all the paperwork they had to process and we spread it out on the briefing-room floor. It eclipsed my rug of contracts and actually surprised some of the officers, who had never seen it collated in one place before. At the end of the research period, even the cynic from Huyton, who'd had a couple of typical teenage run-ins with the local cops, felt these were far from 'bastards'. Neither were they saints. They were nothing more nor less than the usual Wenham Report demographic, people having volunteered to do a 'bastard' of a job.

The British police still operate on the founding principles of Robert Peel: the police are the public and the public are the police. In other words they are part of society, not something separate, and policing only works effectively with the full support and co-operation of the public. It is this basic relationship that has been put to the test in recent years after the G20 Summit and Student Grant demonstrations, followed by what I described earlier as the 2011 smash'n'grab riots. Yet an irony within this is the fact that when Peel, as Home Secretary, introduced the 1829 Metropolitan Police Act, which laid the foundations for modern British policing, he did so as part of a reform agenda that reduced the number of crimes punishable by death and reformed the corrupt prison system by introducing paid staff and education for the inmates. It was never about command and control, more about community co-operation.

This is what I wanted to make a programme about. How the police are the public and the public are the police. How we all, as a society, wanted the cops. How we wanted them to keep us safe in our beds. To be there to defend or apprehend and remove the need for our homes to be, literally, our castles. Yet at the same time how we probably expected too much from them: to act as saints when confronted by real 'bastards'. To be Arnold Schwarzenegger and Stephen Hawking and Gandhi and Mother Teresa all buttoned into one uniform. To take on more and more social nannying when politicians found it too difficult to find real solutions or too easy to formulate new legislation . . . I didn't really sense any great enthusiasm within the Drama Department. The clue came in the proposed transmission slot: 8.00 on a Saturday night. Blue lights, car crashes, shoot outs and, er, *Casualty*.

Once again the very reason I'd wanted to make the programme, as with *County Hall* – to explore a bureaucracy that very few people understood – was also going to contribute to its limited success. Unlike *County Hall*, however, although it wasn't bringing in ratings suitable for a Saturday-night slot, we did get a second series and, in fairness, it came with a commitment to move the programme from the weekend to a more favourable Wednesday night transmission time. We were publicly upbeat about this, but I remember coming back from the BBC and telling Alexis that my instincts said no matter how well the programme performed from then on, I thought that would be it. The BBC could demonstrate that it was embracing the independent sector, through working with us, but would then feel obliged to spread the work around a bit. We would be back to Buggins' turn.

Like all productions, it left me with some good memories. We had a great cast, including Jimmy McKenna who would later go on to became a stalwart on *Hollyoaks* as Jack Osborne, obligatory car chases, better technology, boats and helicopters. There were also the typical location moments, like when we discovered our outside catering bill was escalating because we were also feeding the homeless of Liverpool who were just ambling up to join the queues, everyone assuming they were extras.

Another came when we had to reshoot a sequence about sheep rustling. This was inspired by a trip back to Alexis's family in the Welsh Valleys where the local bad guys were backing furniture vans into the fields, using a couple of dogs to round up the sheep, and within an hour or so the flock would be at a market, sold and gone. To counter it, the local cops put mounted officers on trains. If they spotted any suspect activity they would pull the communication cord, stop the train and then leap off on their horses to give chase. It was real Butch Cassidy and Sundance stuff, and hilarious to the city slicker Merseyside cops. Until they checked with their St Helens Division. Sure enough, they had had a couple of 'unauthorised removals' also.

The reshoot involved four mounted policemen galloping across a field, being shot from the back of a horse-racing camera truck just ahead of them. The rushes looked great. Except for two things. Better quality from the new digital cameras we were using meant we could clearly see the camera truck's car tyres flattening the grass, and the horses kept veering to one side. We cured the tyre-track issue by reframing the shot but discovered one of the horses was blind in one eye. As it veered away, the others followed. It was placed in the middle so the others kept it on the straight and narrow.

Then, when the mid-week slot was announced, we discovered we would be up against ITV's indestructible ratings offer, *Inspector Morse*, developed by ex-*Grange Hill* producer Kenny McBain. Perhaps I should have taken it as a compliment that the BBC thought *Waterfront Beat* would be the police series to arrest John Thaw and *Inspector Morse*, when everything else had failed, but I was more inclined to think, as I am now, that if you were only commissioning a second series because you were told you had to, then why not give it a proper try and see what happens?

However, even if there was anything in my own conspiracy theory, we didn't stand a chance in the numbers game. Either in ratings or in terms of media impact. Three weeks in, when we should have been consolidating our audience, everyone's attention shifted to a much bigger drama: the first Gulf War. When Operation Desert Storm was launched, someone at the BBC had the idea of providing news updates at, well, 8 p.m. This was a good public-service move by the national broadcaster, but it meant *Waterfront* would start at 8.10 p.m., meaning most of the intended audience for a police drama would definitely go to *Morse* and then catch ITV's *News at Ten*. I think this was when I started saying that we were 'only making telly, and if we stop doing it, no one dies'. You do need to keep things in perspective sometimes.

As the 1980s drew to a close I found myself with two certificates to mark the end of the decade: one for a professorship, the other for a marriage.

Since discovering both *Grange Hill* and *Brookie* were being used as teaching aids, I'd started to focus on the key message, which was that the only agenda is to show life as it is, not as we would like it to be. If we could do that, and real-life campaigners could use what we did to gain a more sympathetic or understanding hearing, then we were happy to help. Part of that lay in accepting more invitations to talk at universities and colleges as interest in Media Studies started to grow, including going over to Leeds to talk on one of Laurie Taylor's courses.

As this two-way link developed between the programmes and educationalists at all levels, accepting the offer of a professorship at John Moores, still Liverpool Polytechnic at the time but heading towards university status, felt like a natural progression for me. I was all the more pleased as it was seen as a second-chance institution. Even before the phrase 'life-long learning' had become a political slogan, it had more mature, i.e. older, students than the usual 18–21 coterie. It seemed to be geared to offering the chances I had benefited from, which had helped me to achieve what I had now accomplished. So when they asked me if I would accept the Honorary Chair of Media there, my initial reaction was one of delight. The next was to ask what it actually meant. In terms of prestige, quite a lot. In terms of time, not a lot. Oh, yeah?

They came out to *Brookside* to confer the Chair on me, in the same conservatory where I had met Mr Dentsu. I didn't get a sword this time, but a scroll, a hat, and virtually a new career as, having an all-in-or-all-out approach, I'd decided that if I were going to hold this title, whether Honorary or not, then I would do the best I could to help, which eventually led to Alexis and me funding a building for the International Centre of Digital Content (ICDC) and writing a guide for a new degree course, Media Professional Studies (MPS), the purpose of which was to put the word 'professional' firmly into the media context. The course probably has the highest employability rating in the UK, at over 100 per cent, as its past graduates are now recruiting the current crop. All of this was encouraged by the university's inspirational, energetic and constantly vibrant Vice Chancellor, Professor Peter Toyne, always supported by his wife Angela. Peter came to a poly, left behind a university, and in 2003 delivered Liverpool's bid to become European Capital of Culture in 2008. He instinctively understood the Bernstein-Grade principles of circus and box office. It's no good having a great product, programme, or, even, a university, if you don't tell anyone about it.

Now that I had gone from sociologist to social phenomenon; from studying education to being studied; from student to professorship, perhaps there was another transition that should be made: from business partner to marriage partner. That was to become the next big project for Alexis and me: the how, where and when? We already knew the why.

16

The Franchise Affair (1991)

'We liked your quality, Phil. It just wasn't the quality we were looking for' – *George Russell, Chairman, ITC*

We were in Vancouver when I proposed to Alexis. We were in the penthouse suite of the recently opened Pan Pacific Hotel, overlooking the rapidly developing harbour district. The only other people to have stayed in the suite were Charles and Diana, so they said, but as they had been there over a year before, for Expo '86, I thought this was either marketing spin or else it was no wonder they did a great deal on the room rate. No matter, the link to the Prince of Wales and Alexis's oft recounted tales of attending his Investiture as a child with her school would probably have been enough to spark a romantic flame, which had me handing her a single rose while gazing out over the harbour lights and asking her to be my princess. It would have been, but it was more along the lines of the Scouse, 'What d'you reckon? Shall we get married or what?' 'Er . . . why not? What time's that meeting with the Head of Tourism?' We were there setting up *Brookie*'s location trip to Canada. As always, business and romance were close bedfellows. And it was, actually, two dozen roses.

One of the things I still miss about having a large production company is being able to get things done both quickly and exactly the way you want them. Or, even better, the way you dream about them. The researchers and designers you employ will find a way to make it happen, in either universe. The other great advantage is that you can ask people to do things as part of the fictional universe without worrying that they will start to wonder why. We really wanted to get married as privately as possible so I had the researchers start investigating how that could happen if, say, Sheila and Billy decided to get married on The Close.

They soon came back and said that they had looked at everything, from private chapels to university colleges, and had even discovered that the age-old belief of the captain being able to marry people on his ship at sea was a myth. The only way for Billy and Sheila to get married privately was in a church, a register office, or else to convert to Judaism or become Quakers, since both religions were exempt from the provisions of the Marriage Act 1753. While it seemed like an interesting storyline for Sheila and Billy, it seemed a bit extreme for Alexis and me.

Neither of us wanted a church wedding so the next thing was to look for a small, isolated and 'romantic' register office. This would not be a mission to entrust to our location managers, so we spent many a weekend between antique fairs, garden centres and architectural salvage yards popping in and out of various council offices that were within easy driving distance from home, until we eventually found one that did not look like the back of a 1960s library building. That done, we then had to organise the reception itself, which we could hold at home, but keeping in mind the media mantra of 'the only way to keep a secret is by not telling anyone', we fibbed.

The caterer thought he was coming for a large family lunch to celebrate an industry award; the photographer thought he was coming to do a few quick shots of the family together, and the driver of the Rolls-Royce we'd hired thought he was coming to take my sister Kathy back to the airport, while the mini-bus driver was told just to follow the Roller. At any family occasion the kids are there to wreck the carefully choreographed itinerary, so when the various nieces and nephews saw the Roller they all piled in on top of Alexis's Elizabeth Emanuel dress – and David was Welsh – and insisted on riding to the wedding with us. Why not?

When we got back to the house the kids insisted on being taken round the block in the Roller again while we organised everyone for a group shot outside the house, which was when both the photographer and the caterer realised what they were really there for and the wedding cake we had bought separately could now be revealed and placed on the table inside. It had taken some doing but went off as planned, and created, we think, a much stronger and more enduring family memory. Alexis and I had a lot of fun putting it all together but our security cordon was breached twice: first by the postman arriving to deliver the mail, to find himself dragged into the family group shot, and then by Frank Cottrell Boyce.

Frank lived not far away and was jogging past when he noticed the Roller, the people, the flowers, a photographer . . . and wondered. He then called Colin McKeown, in London, to see if he knew anything about us getting married. Colin didn't. He started phoning round but got nothing back as the only people who knew were family and close personal friends, and they were all now at the house. Even as people arrived in the evening, for 'a party', they were surprised. Life was so much more romantic before mobiles, Twitter and Facebook.

For the honeymoon we flew to Los Angeles, to talk about making *Grange Hill* in the US. Because why go off to some exotic location and be bitten by insects when you can go to an equally exotic and more luxurious location and wrestle with sharks? Well, that's not wholly true: we were going on a prearranged trip to visit Hannah-Barbera where we would meet the legendary Joe Barbera himself, one half of the duo who had created *Tom and Jerry, The Flintstones, Yogi Bear, Scooby-Doo, The Jetsons, Top Cat, Huckleberry Hound*, and nearly every other non-Disney cartoon coming out of Hollywood. When they discovered we had just got married, the dinner and lunch venues all went up a notch or two. We stayed at the Bel Air Hotel on the recommendation of David Puttnam and they told us that the suite we were in had just been vacated by Tom Cruise. I later found a sports sock under the bed and wondered if it was Tom's. I tossed it in the bin. Perhaps today I might have put it up on eBay.

Hannah-Barbera had contacted me because they were starting to diversify into live-action drama, probably a result of the two original founders now no longer running the business. They were also interested in *Grange Hill* because the new 'big thing' was the teen market. Everyone was still looking for a new *Happy Days*, the reason I had been out to LA with *Grange Hill* five years earlier, but due also to the success of the more recent *Saved by the Bell*. There was talk that Hollywood production legend Aaron Spelling, creator of programmes like *Charlie's*

Angels, Dynasty, Starsky & Hutch and *The Love Boat*, also had a new teen show in production. Something called *Beverley Hills 90210*.

We went round all the networks doing the pitch and every meeting was prepped and rehearsed to a level unknown in the UK. It was fascinating trying to keep up with their version of the 4D chess game. I quickly appreciated that I was there as 'the curio from Brit TV, but he knows how to make live action drama for kids, hence the absolute phenomenon of *Grange Hill*, now being replicated by the colossal success of *Brookside*, with its fantastic demographics for kids . . . Phil, tell them how amazing it is . . .' and I'd nod and throw in something typically idiosyncratically British about how the kids had taken *Grange Hill* to their hearts . . . Yeah, but it's even more amazing than that. What is it, Phil, seventy-five per cent . . . gee, what's that? Three-quarters of all British kids . . . can you believe that Cheryl, Merv or Hank? Or whoever we were talking to at the time.

The routine was the same everywhere. At the beginning of every meeting HB would ask what they were looking for, then tailor the pitch to suit. If they were looking for action, then *Grange Hill* was about the feuds and fights in the playground; if they wanted comedy, it was a sit-com about the japes and scrapes of teenage life; if they wanted drama, then it was about, what it was about. I came out of one pitch asking what it would be next . . . a war movie? The networks would listen, nod, smile at me, but they made ITV look like a teddy bear's tea party. They had the second-best media answer down to a premonition. You heard the word 'no' before it was even uttered. It was refreshingly stimulating, as was the universal supplemental, 'But what else you got?'

The US networks, like their British counterparts, make great play of being oversubscribed, which they are, but great ideas don't come along too often. That is why a few producers in the US, like Norman Lear or Steve Bochco, of *Hill Street Blues*, *LA Law* and *NYPD Blue*, reputedly ended up with 'put deals'. A network would give them exclusive contracts but whatever idea they 'put' to the network, had to be made. I filed that away in my 'if only' box, as in the UK we were still fighting for 'output deals', when the broadcasters guarantee to buy so many hours – but only of what they wanted you to make. By the end of every meeting, the guys from HB, having assimilated and synthesised the discussion round the *Grange Hill* pitch, would have created an entirely new show, ready for that 'What else?' question.

We came pretty close at one meeting, so much so that we were asked back the following day to meet a few more people, but halfway through the phone went. The guy took the call and said, great. Then turned to us and said, sorry. They'd just bought a school show from New York. He looked at me and grinned. Guess it's closer than London. Who could argue with that? We left with a 'that's show business' shrug, but on the way back to the hotel one of the guys, knowing I'd been in construction, insisted on showing us a house that was being built. It was his own four-bedroomed house, which from the plans, the development itself and its timber-framed construction, looked amazingly like the ones on *Brookside*. Which was why he showed it to us. Neat, eh? Perhaps we should start thinking about . . .

While still searching for both creative and business growth beyond the 'colossal success of *Brookside* and *Grange Hill*', as the HB development guys pitched it, nothing came of this latest foray into the US market, as once again things back home started to get interesting. The ITV franchise bids were now on the horizon and the cascade of events that led to the 1991 bid against Granada probably began while we were still planning the wedding back in 1988. In October, John Fairley, then Programme Director of Yorkshire Television, came over to visit *Brookside*. John had with him his Head of Science, Duncan Dallas, to talk about whether we would be interested in making a series of thirty-minute drama–docs about major scientific breakthroughs.

By now the main players in the industry had accepted that independent producers could produce high quality at a price level they themselves could never match, with their costly in-house union agreements; aside from which, as a consequence of the IPPA lobbying, the government was preparing legislation to force them to commission from independents – always a convincing cultural imperative. John's idea was to commission a series of drama programmes about scientific achievements or milestones, to see if the subjects could be made more accessible. Because of what we had been doing with *Brookside*, he wondered if we could do it at a rate that would match the documentary-slot cost from the ITV Network. The obvious answer was, why not?

It came at a perfect time for us. We were shooting *Waterfront Beat*, while Alexis and I had just concluded a five-year search for another production base. This had taken us across the North West and into North Wales, even viewing the old seminary in Up Holland I had last seen as a boy, before acquiring the now closed College of Further Education just round the corner in Childwall, Liverpool. This was being sold off by the Council as part of yet another education 'rationalisation'. A rambling institutional building, it would serve us well as a reservoir of different locations. It even had the old science labs intact, which still sent a shiver down the spine of most who entered them, but they would be perfect for the proposed YTV drama–doc series that was eventually called, of course, *Science Fiction*. The series covered things like the discovery of the ozone hole and pulsars, when scientists initially thought they had discovered alien communications. One programme looked at how a British physics teacher, Geoffrey Perry, at Kettering Grammar School, had become something of a household name in 1966 by tipping off the world to the existence of the world's first satellite, the soviet sputnik.

However, in the 4D world of media politics you should never consider anything to be pure coincidence. The fact that only a few weeks earlier we had been in conversation with Steve Morrison, Director of Programmes and Pippa Cross, Head of Film, at Granada, about a potential output deal, should have been enough for conspiracy theorists to start speculating that the ITV companies were beginning the groundwork to protect their extremely lucrative broadcast licences. The game was either to buy in or buy out anyone considered a credible threat. We were on the list of people to be neutralised even though, as I now know, they didn't know that we didn't appreciate that at the time. I used to enjoy baiting Granada whenever I could, but that was just a continuation of the Scouse sport of having a pop at the pompous.

My jousting with Granada went all the way back to the early days of *Brookie*, when I'd asked them if we could use the *Corrie* titles and theme tune. If I was trying to make my fictional universe as realistic a portrayal of life in the UK as possible, then my characters should be seen to be watching the UK's favourite programme on their TV sets. C4 shared the humorous intention until Granada got all sniffy and leaned on them to lean on us, and in the end we decided there were too many thngs going on in the maelstrom to worry about giving Granada a bit of free promotion. We then made our own lookalike title sequence and later sent the shoot to

Manchester to use the Granada building as a rendezvous for Heather to meet Roger after work. Granada went ballistic and sent security guards out to try and move the crew on. Why? I have no idea, but it did make me smile at the time.

I think this was the same sense of humour which encouraged me to name Phil Redmond Enterprises after BBC Enterprises and why I always called myself Chairman instead of CEO or MD. Apart from the obvious dictatorial connotations, that also appealed. Titles are transitory, often meaningless, as authority stems from a person's ability to earn respect, but they can be used to make a point or have a bit of fun. I know these things are daft but they appeal to and encourage the Scouse mentality: even when we know we are actually being daft for doing it, which in turn makes it even more fun knowing that other people think we are really daft, which is daft in itself as how daft is it that they should think we care? You may have to be Scouse, or daft, to follow that, but basically I just didn't 'get' why Granada had to act so precious about everything. Especially as I genuinely had great respect for Granada and what they had achieved. You couldn't ignore *Coronation Street, World in Action, The Cuckoo Waltz, University Challenge* and Michael Apted's brilliant sociological documentary *Seven Up* (now the *Up* series) that had followed the lives of fourteen British children since 1964, revisiting them every seven years to see how they'd done in life.

I also respected the fact that Granada's legendary founder, Sidney Bernstein, had insisted every office should have a picture of P. T. Barnum on the wall. The Barnum from Barnum and Bailey's Circus. ITV was not the BBC. It was not created to follow the Reithian doctrine of inform, educate and entertain, but rather entertain, inform and educate. That suggested they'd be having a bit of fun along the way. How had they become so, well, po-faced and serious?

By the late 1980s I felt they were suffering from two problems: ageing technology and ageing ownership. Large regional transmitters, cumbersome equipment and restrictive working agreements all mitigated against innovation, compounded by a second-generation management that was beginning to believe in its own self-promoting publicity. There was no need for change, according to them, as they genuinely believed they were the bastion of quality within the ITV Network and, in some areas, like current affairs, they undoubtedly were. But not everywhere. There was also a prevailing belief among them that they provided most of the programming for the ITV Network. But they didn't. Among the other ITV companies there was a growing perception that they were starting to throw their weight around a bit and become the bully boys of ITV. And they were.

One example of this overbearing attitude was when Bafta decided to set up a Northern branch and I found myself press-ganged into becoming a founder member. Once in, I started on my usual agenda of agitating for civil rights for the North, a good step towards which would be to bring the Academy Awards to Manchester. That way we could sell tables to Northern businesses who would pay a premium to have a glitzy dinner with the Academy's Patron, Princess Anne. Ignoring the sharp intakes of breath from the London lot, the Northern block votes carried the day and I quickly figured out that if Granada hosted it and flogged it to ITV, paying a facility fee to Bafta, even with one dinner, we could clear around £250,000 and that would have set up the Academy in the North for ever. They said they'd take it back to London for t'Committee to consider.

The next stop was Granada and a guy called Peter Ridsdale-Scott. A senior commissioning editor at BBC Manchester and one of the nicest men you could ever meet, he had been deputed as Chair of Bafta North. He was a bit nervous of meeting Granada and soliciting their help, knowing of their fierce industry reputation, so whether he asked or whether I offered to go along for moral support, we both found ourselves ushered into the presence of the great grandee himself, Granada Chairman David Plowright. He could be quite gruff and domineering, if you allowed him to be, but I found that if you pushed him back he had a reasonable sense of humour.

Peter stammered out the plan. Plowright sat listening in silence and then nodded. OK, but it'll be a Granada show. Quick. Pacey. And no long boring speeches. We'll intersperse it with variety acts that the viewers will actually want to watch. A real programme. No speeches, OK? He held his gaze on Peter. Peter looked at me. No speeches? I could almost see the twinkle in Plowright's eye. No, I told him. He turned his stare on me. You are supporting the industry, especially here in the North West. And when these people win their awards, it could be *the* highlight of their lives. You have to give them their moment in the spotlight. This is not Granada's show, it's the

Academy's show. He held my eye for a moment then turned and gazed out over the Manchester skyline for what seemed like a couple of minutes. Then he said, still staring out over the city, 'You know, Phil, humility doesn't come easy to Granada.' Then he nodded. Deal.

There was a grin when he said this but I'm not sure whether he had just enjoyed the moment or whether he had been working through the 4D chess game in his mind, and smiled when he realised I was one move away from checkmate: the media interview to tell everyone how big bad Granada wouldn't support the industry. However, more than likely he was ahead of me, and had just been working through Granada's schedule to find out when they were likely to get a ratings hammering off the BBC. They could place the programme there without wasting a real one.

The way it turned out none of us should have bothered. In London, t'Committee thought that if an awards ceremony were to be held outside London then it was only fair it should move from city to city. Buggins was also an Academy member. Out went the idea of annual repeat bookings. Because a lot of the performance awards went to the film industry, and most of that was London based, it was also felt 'better' if only the Craft Awards travelled. Out went the box-office draw of the film celebs. Then, because of the logistics of getting everyone up from London, it was considered 'more efficient' to hire a plane and fly everyone up. Oh, and down again, which meant keeping Manchester airport open a bit longer. Out went any chance of making money. In the end, instead of making the £250,000 endowment I'd envisaged, the event cleared under £10,000 and most of that came from Granada's facility fee. So, in a way, Plowright did help out the industry: by giving its own grandees a jolly good night out. No wonder they got away with so much.

I was so angry when all this unfolded that I felt like withdrawing from my newly anointed position as a founder member of Bafta North. Yet again the metro-centric mob had hijacked what should have been a regional initiative to create a self-sustaining centre for creativity and knowledge exchange. However, a more considered opinion came from the other side of the kitchen table. What good would walking away do? It'll make me feel better. But not help anybody, and the Academy is right to think about using its position across the UK, not just in Manchester, where Granada and the BBC would hijack it anyway. Hmmmm. I then became a fully paid up life member, made a few donations here and there, and supported the 'national vision', particularly when the Craft Awards were held in Cardiff.

But while Granada might have been able to bully people in the network playground, the boast about them supplying most of the programming to ITV didn't stand up when we analysed the schedules. Nor did the frequently aired argument that *Coronation Street* was the network's cash cow, as a closer look showed that of the approximately £120 million advertising revenue, only around £9 million was directly attributable to The Street. This was because ITV ad sales are based on random time slots within the peak hours between 6 and 10.30 p.m. Advertisers would have to pay double or even triple the going rate to guarantee a particular slot, which most wouldn't. What that meant was that whatever programme was in that slot would have attracted around £113 million in sales. We worked out that a programme tuned to the needs of the growing financial services sector would actually have brought in the same, if not more, with an audience of only 350,000 against The Street's alleged 15 million viewers.

It wouldn't have been as sexy, I admit, as Granada later made great play of the fact that it was the whole schedule that had to appeal to advertisers, which was true, and that the schedule without *Coronation Street* would not be as attractive, which was also true. However, as we tried to point out, the same legislation that would enable us to take a tilt at their franchise, the 1990 Broadcasting Act, would also provide the mechanism by which we could acquire their programming, like *Corrie*, as part of the new obligation to take 25 per cent from independent producers, as they would then be. As indeed Thames TV became after losing their franchise and selling *The Bill* back to ITV. However, Granada's programming supremacy was too great a myth to dispel, which caused me publicly to declare that if we won the battle, one department we would guarantee jobs to would be the publicity department.

However, the one area their publicity department couldn't bamboozle, as others have found, is the People's Republic itself. Liverpool had always been the weak spot for Granada, which was why they had only recently poured a lot of investment into both a new News Centre and *This Morning*, both based at the new regenerated Albert Dock. But this was always seen, at least in Liverpool, for exactly what it was: a political box-ticking exercise for the London-based regulator, the IBA. Two years ahead of Granada's franchise renewal.

For me, it was an easy target to attack, knowing that no matter what Granada did, they could never satisfy the demands of Liverpool for parity with Manchester, never mind adequately cover the whole North West Region. That structural flaw had existed since 1926, and no amount of spin, marketing or regulatory sops would change the feeling at grass-roots level. And that, I am now aware, was why they were always so wary of me. I might only have been another Scouser with a big mouth, once described by a Granada apologist as being 'very well balanced, with a Scouse chip on each shoulder, but with an inferiority complex to match'. I liked the two chips bit, but thought I had done a reasonable job of masking the inferiority complex before I ever came to their notice. The charge more usually levelled at me was that of arrogance, as I had both Mersey and *Brookside* and that, in their eyes, gave me a much bigger platform to shout from. I can see the logic now, or maybe paranoia, but even with the arrogance of youth, or perhaps because of that, I didn't quite see it at the time. I just thought they were a bunch of pompous grandees. And I think we both played our parts well.

MerseyTV's growth in size and higher profile, achieved through things like Waterfront, Science Fiction, and even the purchase of the Childwall College, meant that as the ITV franchise positioning got underway the phone started ringing. Throughout 1990 the ITV companies were jockeying every which way, trying to make sure they had all the political bases covered and bureaucratic boxes ticked. One of these, a big box, was regionalism. This was always termed 'local programming', despite the fact that the Crawford, Beveridge and Lloyd triumvirate had made that almost impossible as far back as the 1950s. With one transmitter at Winter Hill to cover the entire North West, an occasional three-minute bad news item in a thirty-minute Manchester-managed news bulletin was never going to convince the good citizens of Preston, Blackpool, Chester or Southport that they were receiving quality local programmes. This would be one of the main targets, as the key vulnerability in any ITV franchise bid. For Manchester-centric Granada, due to the historic television tensions with the city, Liverpool was like having a huge black hole at the edge of their universe. Tugging. Threatening to consume them.

Consequently all the ITV incumbents and potential bidders would aim to demonstrate as much local support as they could, especially among the local MPs. It was all part of the game. Always had been. But post the 1990 Act, there were a few new things to consider, including plans for embracing independent production companies. This was even more problematic for ITV than the BBC, as the arrival of C4, or perhaps loss of their 'ITV2' was still relatively recent history. Not only had C4 opened the gates to the Trojan Horse of low-cost production, but Michael Grade had done a great job in negotiating total independence. The new King had become a freedom fighter.

He had convinced everyone that it would be far better for C4 to sell its own airtime and raise its own advertising revenue than be dependent on a tax on ITV. Under the 1990 Act C4 would change status from a wholly owned subsidiary of the then regulator, the Independent Broadcasting Authority, to become a public corporation in its own right. Channel 4 Television would become the Channel 4 Corporation and control its own destiny, while ITV got back the cash they were paying to fund it. It made complete sense, at the time.

What it meant, though, was that ITV received something of a dividend which swelled their coffers and brought them instantly to the attention of the very folk who had levied the Channel 4 tax in the first place: the government. A Tory government moreover that was no great admirer of ITV, described by PM Margaret Thatcher as the 'last bastion of Spanish Trade Union practices'. There was plenty of talk at the same time of ITV, and Thames Television in particular, doing themselves no favours by broadcasting a controversial documentary, *Death on the Rock*, about the SAS shooting dead an alleged IRA bomb squad in Gibraltar, just when the government was trying to deny 'the oxygen of publicity' to terrorism. However, the real antagonism towards ITV was probably more to do with the Conservative government's deeply entrenched commitment to the free market.

This can be traced back to Selwyn Lloyd's minority report on the 1948 Beveridge Television Committee, when he outlined proposals for a more competitive television market that would see not one, but two, independent broadcasting channels, ITV1 and the now supplanted ITV2. For a free market to operate properly it needs

competition, and what ITV represented to the Conservative government was exactly what it was: a privileged and protected monopoly
that had encouraged the worst practices of cartel and unionisation.
The move to grant C4 its independence as a public corporation in
its own right would not solve this economic, as well as ideological,
point due to the apparent ceiling on C4's audience reach, then
around 10 per cent of the total. With no market mechanism available to regulate monopolistic profits, the government economists
proposed the classic solution, and a continuance of what had already
been happening: additional taxation.

Due to the high profits ITV was making, the effective taxation
rate, a combination of standard tax and special levies, including
funding for Channel 4, had crept up to around 98 per cent – the
proposed space helmets for *Dan Dare* were budgeted at £3,500
because the perception was that it was only costing £75. Even paying
tax at such a punitive rate, broadcasting was still a licence to print
money and to maintain a very high-end lifestyle for those privileged
few who were members of the club. The government knew this
and, following the established policy of auctioning off or privatising
high-value state assets like BT, BA and British Gas, it was inevitable
that the high-value, but state-owned, television licences should also
come under scrutiny from the economists. Why not auction them
off too to the highest bidder? It made perfect sense. To everyone
outside television. Outside the club. Those inside it were not only
pompous but completely divorced from reality. In fact, as the *Dan
Dare* space helmet story illustrates, they inhabited their own special
universe. But finally it was under threat. Their licences were now
going to be offered to the highest bidder.

The politicking began and throughout 1989 and 1990, leading up
to the passing of the enabling Act in November of that year, the
formidable power of the ITV corporate publicity machinery was
harnessed to deliver one message: the blunt instrument of 'highest
bidder' would attract the 'wrong' sort of members to the club. The
previous beauty-parade system, where applicants had needed to show
good programming ideas, was to be replaced by highest-bidder
auctions to determine the winner of each ITV regional franchise.
This element of the franchising process was extremely controversial,
with widespread unease about the 'tabloidisation of television' that

was happening elsewhere, the most commonly given example being the 'stripping housewives' gameshows from the Berlusconi channels in Italy. Normally, 'the club' would have been able to rely on their own membership committee, the IBA, to make sure that those unsuitable for membership would never cross the threshold, like that pesky Australian Murdoch who had tried to rescue LWT back in the 1960s. But under the 1990 Act they too were being asked to step down in favour of a less intrusive, 'lighter touch' regulator, the Independent Television Commission (ITC). All anyone had to do in future was turn up and show they could afford the membership fee. Imagine that.

Still, the devil you know is always better. Even at MerseyTV we felt an open bidding process was probably going a step too far, and joined the industry campaign to persuade the government at least to introduce some provisions on programming content. I spent quite a bit of time lobbying on this.

There were three main areas of interest to the 1990 Act: greater independent access, the ITV franchises, and the promised new fifth channel. This was what took me to an industry dinner at The Admiralty with Home Secretary Douglas Hurd and the other goverment figures with broadcast responsibilities, after which the *Financial Times* reported me as being 'tieless as usual'. Perhaps they were trying to tip off the Membership Committee, but there was little else to report. The dinner started late and, just as the discussion got going, the Parliamentary Division Bell went and all the politicians got up and left.

It was safer having lunch with David Mellor, which I did a few times. Despite his famously supporting Chelsea, I always seemed to get on well with him as he was open to new ideas, like the one that Channel 5 should be based outside London as a counterbalance to the London-centric BBC, ITV and Channel 4.

By the time the bill became an act most of the industry lobbying had been successful. There was to be 25 per cent independent access to the BBC and ITV, a new quality threshold for programming for the ITV franchise, and new ownership rules that meant that pesky foreigners like upstart Aussies and stripping housewife-loving Italians, could not hold more than 20 per cent of any licence. Unfortunately the point about Channel 5 not being London-based was lost because, David Mellor told me over another lunch, a free-market-espousing

Conservative government couldn't prescribe where any business should base itself, and in any event the intellectual argument about a cultural counterweight to London was now widely accepted. I thought the first point a bit thin, as they had no problems telling the ITV companies where they should be, as well as foreigners where they shouldn't, but was persuaded on the Channel 5 point. Still, we live and learn, and he didn't, to be fair, give me his word on it. But what more could either of us have done anyway?

With the 1990 Broadcasting Bill grinding its way through our democratic processes, the media lobbying, and briefing lunches and dinners underway, the ITV game was either to buy in, or buy out, anyone considered a credible threat. Granada should by then have been aware that I had officially named the company The Mersey Television Co. Ltd; because the river flowed all the way up to their back door. I had said it often enough, with the implication that one day we might, just might, take a tilt at their franchise. At that stage, though, the idea of joining forces with Yorkshire was not even in our thoughts. We never dreamed that one ITV company would go after another, and the best Alexis and I thought was that if we kept them all guessing we might, just, end up with the coveted 'output' deal.

It was not long before prospective suitors started to turn up on our doorstep either offering output deals or membership of a consortium. From traditional broadcasters like Anglia and Yorkshire, to newcomers like Virgin Media and the Guardian Media Group, and even heritage names like Marconi, who had been in on the original foundation of broadcasting as part of the British Broadcasting Company back in 1926. Like a lot of big industrial conglomerations they were, I think, pondering if there were any synergies to be found as there had once been between content production and equipment manufacturing. Attached to the obvious and public debates about terrestrial television, its quality and the risk of foreigner owners, there was a parallel but not widely noticed technology debate continuing around the potential of cable TV and what Tim Berners-Lee had unleashed at CERN, satellite and high-definition TV. All of this would require 'kit'. And that 'kit' would require content to drive consumers to it.

But the industrial investors soon lost interest and moved on, being unable, like the DTi in 1981, to make sense of the regulatory regime as a business model. We stayed close to Virgin for a while, but both ultimately decided that we could not add value to each other's aspirations. They wanted to remain in London and the South East, and it would seem daft them having us, the great regionalists, as part of their consortium or bid. We parted with an understanding that we could always meet again on the 'other side'.

The Anglia approach was interesting, if also a bit odd, partly for the same reason as with Virgin, the geographical split, but also because Anglia was one of the regions Virgin were targeting. Our take on this at the time was that we already knew Virgin through having talks with them in the past about *Grange Hill* merchandising. We also felt that our corporate cultures probably had more similarities, having met them while they were moving into offices in an old warehouse in Ladbroke Grove, which had brought back memories of *Brookie's* own early days. They had the same type of Habitat kitchen furniture and phones on the floor. Anglia, on the other hand, gave us a very nice dinner in a smart flat just off Baker Street, but while we listened appreciatively to their pitch about us being the best, biggest, etc., etc., that geographical spread still seemed a bit odd.

However, our energies at that time were fixed on trying to secure an output deal, if we could. Geographically speaking, the ideal partner would be Granada, something we put to Steve Morrison and Pippa Cross, and then to Yorkshire as part of the *Science Fiction* discussions. After all, they would need to source 25 per cent from the independent sector once the Act was passed. To counter this, from Yorkshire's perspective, they would have a host of indies in their own region clamouring for work. The same was true of Anglia, but these would be regional independents. We wanted to make drama, so part of our pitch was that our programmes would contribute to the network 25 per cent. At the Anglia dinner, they had asked us about our aspirations in the North West but we remained non-committal, mainly because we didn't know what we were going to do, while always remaining aware that they were part of the ITV club and might just be fishing on Granada's behalf.

Back in the North West the on-off conversations with Granada continued, with a real opportunity to work together seeming to present itself in a new daytime drama that ITV Network wanted to commission. Since our fifth anniversary we had also kept in touch with Andrew Quinn, MD at Granada, who seemed the most pragmatic of them all. We had had a couple of meetings with him, Steve Morrison and their Head of Business Affairs, Jules Burns, about the notion of an output deal through which we would take the *Brookside* model and tailor it to produce twelve movies a year for their subsidiary, Granada Films. The key to it lay in having the critical mass to guarantee employment, then we could bring down the costs as we had at *Brookie* but make movies instead of continuing drama.

It seemed to us a perfect fit and we were open about the fact that it was the way we really wanted to build our business, but after a meeting in Manchester to talk through terms, Alexis told me she thought they were not really serious. She couldn't put her finger on why but felt there was something else going on. Just as my creative antenna had picked up something at the BBC about *Waterfront Beat*, she was doing the same about the business and finance. I put this down to the usual problem of mindset. They still didn't believe that we were making *Brookie* cheaper than they were making *Corrie*, because like the BBC they were excluding their own corporate overhead. If they didn't understand we could make television cheaper, then they'd have even greater problems believing we could make films at the rate we were proposing, simply because films cost them so much more.

Instead, Andrew Quinn suggested we could make the afternoon drama we'd also proposed to them. At that time, our Head of Development was Philip Bowman, an Aussie (although we didn't tell the IBA, just in case), who had worked for a stint on ATV's *Crossroads*. I had got to know him at a 'soap production conference' in Italy, and at the time, due to *Neighbours* and *Home and Away*, anyone from Oz was worth a few bonus points at any pitch meeting. He had an idea called *The Family* which he had been developing, about Australia's long but little known role in Vietnam. The premise was a soldier who went back and forth between the countries and had two families, one in Oz and one in Vietnam. The drama would be about how he juggled both lives so that instead of the 'neighbours' being on the same street, they would be 'home and away' in different countries, with him the central linking character. Since being in the UK, and seeing the success of Aussie soaps here, he had started adapting it to work between the UK and Australia as a co-production. We told Andrew, he said it sounded perfect, to send him the outline and he would pass it to 'the programme people'. We did. And waited.

In the meantime we had a visit from Graham Benson, then Head of Drama down at TVS, the ones who had taken over Southern's franchise. He'd produced Trevor Preston's series *Fox*, at Euston Films, then gone on to do *Rules of Engagement* and *Perfect Scoundrels* at TVS, and much later the *Ruth Rendell Mysteries* at his own company. Alexis and I had bumped into him in Los Angeles, although we didn't tell him we were on honeymoon, and had done the usual thing of inviting him up to see *Brookie*. We were sitting, in Colin McKeown's old office, in the sunshine on the wall next to the brook, watching the shoot, when he asked if we would be interested in making the proposed ITV daytime drama on behalf of TVS.

Surprised but pleased, I asked why. He said he thought I was the UK's only hyphenate. I thought he was taking the mick, but he said he wasn't. He had been thinking who he could ask to have a go at it and had come to the conclusion that it was me, as the UK's only writer-producer. The hyphenate. Although a common term in the US, it wasn't in the UK, and he had just encapsulated a lot of the awkwardness I often encountered when people couldn't quite put me in a box, or deal with me swapping hats, from one role to the other. We were sitting across The Close from where I had had my picture taken on being made Professor by Liverpool John Moores University. But earning Graham's informal accolade, the UK's hyphenate, meant almost as much to me.

However, before we went any further, I told him about the potential deal with Granada and said I would check if anything was happening. I asked Philip Bowman. He called Granada. They said they were still thinking and would get back to us. They didn't, but we got back to Graham. Sod 'em, let's get on with it.

What I had in mind was taking the original principle of *Brookie*, portraying how people lived in the UK now, not thirty, twenty or even ten years ago as *Brookie* itself had done. If it were to be based on the South Coast and for the afternoon audience, it should be a bit more escapist, a bit more glam. In other words, just as people would watch *Brookie* as a suburban soap mid-week, like they would *EastEnders* and *Corrie* too, a new soap should be about what people wanted to do at the weekend. Include the sun, sand and sea. This was also a new growth area for housing developers on the South Coast in the form of marina villages. Our '*Brookie-on-Sea*' would be called *Ocean View*.

After a couple of months or so, still with no news from Manchester, we had a pilot shot and were in post-production with TVS, getting ready to go to the ITV Network pitch session. I was at yet another 'future of broadcasting' conference, which seemed to occur every six months, when I met Graham and he asked me how things were going. Fine, I said, just as Andrew Quinn from Granada came over and also asked me, enthusiastically, 'Hi, Phil, how's our daytime soap going?' I was a bit wrong-footed by this and asked if he was talking as part of the ITV Network or Granada? He said Granada of course, about the programme with the Australians in. Graham and I exchanged a look, then Graham grinned and sidled off. Andrew picked up on the body language. What? We never heard anything back from you, so we're working with TVS, I explained. His turn to be wrong-footed. And genuinely shocked. But we've been out to Oz, I signed off all the expenses . . . Not with us, I told him. He asked me again if I was sure no one had contacted us? I said I was sure. Really sure. We had double-checked. We were still waiting for the call back. There was no deal between us.

He said he would find out what had happened and get back to us. He didn't, but I would soon discover why. When we turned up to the pitch session at ITV we discovered we were in the semi-finals. Keith Richardson, Head of Drama at Yorkshire, was nervously pacing the waiting area, I think Central was there, and, surprisingly, Granada. Even more surprising was another of those incredible coincidences that happens when several people get the same idea at the same time. Just as ATV discovered someone was already working on a schools programme after they turned down *Grange Hill*, then, amazingly, someone at Granada had come up with an idea for a drama about two families linked by a bigamist. One in the UK and one in Australia. And just as ours was called *The Family*, theirs was called *Families*. Astonishing how these coincidences happen. Even more astonishing was the fact that no one at Granada had been able to find our phone number. At any time.

As if that wasn't amazing enough, we then heard that Yorkshire and Central were out and we were now head to head with Granada, fighting a remarkably similar idea to the one we had offered them. The judges were tied. They couldn't make a decision, so they went 50-50 and phoned a friend, Thames. They had not submitted so were not conflicted and were tasked with undertaking market

Above: Simpsons incest – Nat (John Sandford) and Georgia (Helen Grace). All the regulators were against this one. Channel 4 were forced to apologise, but it was the timing we got wrong, not the storyline.

Left: Another challenging storyline *Brookside* became famous for: Dean Sullivan portraying Jimmy Corkhill's mental breakdown.

Right: The first pre–watershed lesbian kiss: a dramatic moment which became so iconic it was beamed around the world as part of the London 2012 Olympics' opening ceremony.

Left: How to attract male viewers. The gas explosion stunt allowed us to 'redevelop' the Brookside Parade.

Below: The Jordache trial. Filming in a real court was problematic… so we built our own.

Right: Beth's outburst was a brilliant TV moment – unfortunately, though, we couldn't keep Anna Friel under lock and key…

Above: Using the
Steadicam Mk III
with Sony HD for
the last ever episode
of *Brookside*.

Right: Production
planning with
David Hanson,
final-year producer.

Below: That poster
campaign…

Left: The first open call for *Hollyoaks*, which had kids queuing round the block and Channel 4 running for the hills.

Right: The original cast looking remarkably fresh after their weeks of casting sessions… I lost most of them over the years but still have the car bonnet.

Below: With Jo Hallows at the Hollyoaks 5th Birthday Awards – by which time *Brookie* was 18!

Celebrating Liverpool as Capital of Culture with, *right*, some of the *Brookie* crew: Pauline Daniels (aka Maria Benson), Philip Olivier (aka Tim O'Leary) and Alex Fletcher (aka Jacqui Dixon).

Above: The Superlambananas. And I'm in there somewhere…

Right: The mechanical spider that clanked through the streets and stole Scouse hearts.

Left: Save Our Samaritans: Dean Sullivan with Sue Jenkins (aka long-suffering Jackie Corkhill). The cast were always willing to turn out for charity…

Above: …just as they would turn out to encourage young people to vote. David Blunkett and Hazel Blears with members of the *Hollyoaks* cast.

Above: The first outing for the shirt I'm wearing on this book's dust jacket…

Right: …and it has already outlasted one PM.

Right: 'Oh yes, you're the window cleaner… Sinbad.' Mickey Starke, lost for words for the first time, when the Queen asked about the Brookie Basics literacy scheme.

Below: Of course, there's more than one Queen.

Above: At the CBE lunch with *Brookie* writers Andy Lynch and Roy Boulter – also drummer with The Farm.

Below: At the opening of the Museum of Liverpool.

Right: I'd never have got this close to Spielberg as just a writer, but for a university…

Above: With Cherie Booth as Chancellor of Liverpool John Moores University, Vice Chancellor Michael Brown, and then Director General of the BBC Greg Dyke… plus digital friends.

Right: All there to celebrate, with Alexis and me, the new home for the International Centre for Digital Content: Redmond Close.

research to predict likely audience reaction and outcome. We lodged a protest when we discovered that Granada had spent well above the agreed slot rate, trying to impress, whereas we had stuck rigidly to the rules to prove it was deliverable. This was noted, but we were told we had to wait for the Thames market research to come back.

When it did, apart from criticising us for not having either enough cats or seagulls, considering it was by the seaside – which no one really understood – *Ocean View* was generally liked and people thought they would watch it. Thames thought it would be either a massive failure or a massive hit. Granada's *Families* was rated as probably watchable and safe. They opted for *Families*, having obviously forgotten their own founder's view that everything should be about circus and box office. That the trick is giving the audience not what they already have, but what they really want. Surprises. You don't do that by playing safe.

Mind you, could we argue with such a great idea? And we did crack a smile later when we heard – I think it might even have been from Andrew Quinn – that the network would only pay at the agreed rate, but insisted Granada maintain the higher-level production costs. And how could the guardians of quality television argue with that?

By the time the 1990 Act became law we were beginning to suspect that we were not going to make much progress with an output deal in Manchester, so turned our minds to whether we could actually take a tilt at their franchise instead. It would be a big game to play. Too big for us alone, but there were no major players circling. Nobody with a big enough gang to take on the teds in a turf war. We knew Trinity, publishers of the *Liverpool Daily Post* and *Echo*, reasonably well, but their view was that Granada was unassailable, even if you could figure out how much to bid.

Our thoughts then turned to Border Television. Despite Granada making a pre-emptive move to take a stake in Border ahead of the 1990 Act that would relax cross-ownership rules, Border's licence would still have to be advertised separately. Mersey was now a similar size and we could probably raise all the capital we needed without taking a partner. The only thing we would have to work on would be the local angle, but at least it was closer than Anglia. The Lake District, like North Wales, was considered part of Liverpool's wider cultural offering. More so than Manchester. The trick, we thought, was to get a seat at the ITV table. No matter if it was at the far end.

Despite Border's size and history of being treated as not just second- but third-class citizens, like Channel Television, Tyne Tees and Grampian, the 25 per cent access rules would be a game-changer. If we could offer both better regional access and network drama, creating another *Brookside* with accompanying jobs and skills up in Cumbria, then that might just swing it. At least it was a plan. The next turn of the cards was totally unexpected. The call from John Fairley. How would we fancy joining Yorkshire in a go at Granada?

All conspiracies and attempted coups need a secret place to meet so we agreed to meet Yorkshire just down the road from their offices in a city-centre hotel. When we arrived we knew we were in the right place by the sign in Reception: 'Welcome Mersey Television and Yorkshire Television – Room XXXX'. We quickly had it removed and the conspirators outlined their plan. They were a bit cheesed off that Granada, along with making a move on Border, had also attempted a raid on Tyne Tees in the far North East. This was because both Yorkshire and Tyne Tees had been under common ownership until 1980 when the IBA had ordered them to demerge and become separate. It still rankled and their overall plan was to apply for both franchises and merge the companies once again, using the same changes in cross-ownership rules that Granada had been trying to exploit. In short, the Lancashire teds had strayed on to the Yorkshire teds' turf. All's fair in love, war and franchise battles.

Within an hour we had a plan and a potential consortium. Yorkshire could hold 20 per cent under the ownership rules, but would put up most of the bid cash. We could hold 20 per cent without losing our independent production status, which would be important to C4. Yorkshire said they could line up the banks to spread the rest, but it would be good to have another big media partner, preferably someone from Liverpool or the wider North West, so it was perceived as a regional bid against Manchester, with Yorkshire's assistance. We knew someone. Someone based in Chester. I picked up the phone to David Sneddon, Chairman of Trinity, and asked: 'Do you think Granada would be unassailable if we had another of the big five ITV companies in a consortium?' 'It's worth a conversation,' was the reply. Not quite, why not? But for a canny Scot, not bad.

★

Things then started to happen very quickly and it was not long before we were all high up on the old Barings Bank Tower in the City of London, staring down at Richard Rogers' Lloyd's Building, an architectural masterpiece that I would sit and study as Alexis argued the maths with the merchant bankers. The first big getting-to-know-everyone meeting got off to a great start when we arrived and found an unknown OAP sitting at the end of the table, looking like he'd lost his bus pass. He gave me, tieless as usual, a cursory once over, neither imperial nor regal in nature but more colonial grandee, and moved on to Alexis, giving her a brief smile. At least he was polite, although it might just have been wind. Hi, I'm Phil. And this is Alexis. He nodded. Briefly. I looked at Alexis. She gave me the 'Be nice' look. So, being nice, 'Who are you then?' I asked. He hesitated for a moment. Just long enough for me to realise that it was the wrong ice-breaker. Another look up and down. Then he spoke. If, he emphasised, you can get into the IBA Library, go to the History of ITV index. Thomas, Ward. Then you'll know who I am. I looked back at Alexis. That told me. But what?

It turned out that this was the legendary G. E. Ward Thomas, once MD of Grampian Television in the 1960s. He'd then founded Yorkshire TV, and created a vehicle called Trident Television to control both Yorkshire and later Tyne Tees in the 1970s. Thomas's idea was that the third prong of Trident would be Anglia TV but the IBA blocked that and later ordered Trident to be broken up as well. It wasn't his bus pass he'd lost, but one of his television companies. No wonder he looked a bit miffed with life. He also, to give him his due, played a key role in launching satellite television, back in 1978. It lasted five years, was called Sky and was sold to Rupert Murdoch for £1. Once again, it's not the idea but the execution that counts, and although this venture was imbued with a sense of history, I felt Trinity would make sure he kept his mind on the future but his wallet on the table.

Generally, though things went very smoothly as we spent a few long nights up the tower, with its twenty-four-hour, money-never-sleeps dining room, slowly and relentlessly working through the deal; arguing about things like the cost of my mobile communication platform or who had tag-and-drag minority shareholder rights or why wouldn't we be daft enough to sign an unfair contract as, regardless of what it said, it would make us very rich? Because we already were very rich, considering where we came from, was the sensible answer. Granted, not compared to some of the multinational clientele we'd pass wandering the tower floors looking for fresh toast and marmalade, but we were very comfortable, thank you, so let's keep the deal as we originally said.

It was also great fun going round the City, from bank to bank, investor to investor. It was like the *Grange Hill* pitches in LA, but far, far easier. They're expecting you, they've seen the deal, they just want to look at you. Fair enough. In, do a verbal twirl, and out. Next. What do you think of the *Coronation Street* question? Red herring. Granada have shareholders too. They'll want to keep selling it. We agree. £20 million. Do you think this regional model will work? Yes. Quadruple the hours, on a lower cost base, and we should double the current regional revenue. OK, we'll do £15 million. Is there really any money in programmes? Don't tell Yorkshire, but Mersey doesn't sell ads. Can we do £20 million too? What do you think the ITC will actually do? Dunno. They should play by the book, but this is Britain. True. We were thinking of going to £20 million, but we think we'd like to stay at £10 million. And within two hours we were called back as we'd raised £80 million.

So having been paraded round the investors, financial journalists, analysts and PR advisers, we then got on with the actual bid document, put together mostly by Philip Reevell, now our Head of Corporate Affairs, slowly building up the case to turn the traditional ITV model round. Instead of running a network company that felt obliged to do a few regional programmes, the vision was to run a regional company that would also offer network programmes. With the obligation to take 25 per cent from independent producers, it seemed logical simply to replicate on a regional basis what C4 was doing nationally. We also had Mersey, Yorkshire and, in our minds, even Granada available to make network programming. The emphasis would be on building the capacity in the region, through the concept of timeshare television, which would make sure that every town in the North West would get a guaranteed place in the schedules, as would their local advertisers. It was also aimed at building the sense of regional identity and brand awareness that local radio had, but not television.

We commissioned market research with the obvious aim of making Granada look like complete wastrels, which, of course, it didn't – as a network ITV company. But as a regional entity they were almost invisible, except perhaps from the halo of TV rentals, bingo and motorway cafés. Despite their spending millions building regional centres, most people still saw them as a Manchester-focused company. When asked to name Granada programmes, only 58 per cent named *Corrie*, with the next highest response being *This Morning* at 3 per cent. The biggest surprise, though, was that *Granada Reports* and *Granada Tonight*, two of their major regulatory 'must haves', with the company name in the title, only registered 2 per cent and 1 per cent respectively.

Asking if they would watch a substitute of similar quality to *Coronation Street*, the researchers were practically run out of town for even daring to pose such a question, with 67 per cent of respondents saying they would definitely be opposed to such an idea. Better not labour that one then. At the same time 56 per cent said they would like to see more regional and local programmes at the weekend, and when asked what type, 60 per cent said more on the environment, indicating that the public, once again, were ahead of the policy-makers on such issues.

The biggest challenge of all, though, was keeping everything under wraps. Yorkshire in particular knew that if Granada found out they would go nuclear and the fallout within the network would be difficult to manage, so the plan was to seek forgiveness later. Right from that first meeting in Leeds we had been running a disinformation and distraction campaign. When we realised Yorkshire were serious and we had signed the confidentiality agreements, we told them that we were thinking of going for Border. They could see the logic but really wanted us to go after Granada with them, and in exchange would give us the output deal we had been manoeuvring for.

Back at Mersey, Alexis and I knew we still had one problem to resolve. We trusted our management team implicitly, except for one person, an ex-Granada hand who had joined us not long before. While having got past the two-second, seven-second test and being likeable as a person, there was just . . . something. As the 1990 Act came and went and the clock started ticking down towards the franchise application dates, the level of interest they showed in what we were considering became more and more pronounced. My dramatist's mind was ready to believe that this was a mole put in place by Granada, but Alexis felt that was pure ego or paranoia, on my part, and that in fact it was more likely to be a case of someone looking for a useful angle to advance their own career. Whatever it was, we initially decided to keep them out of the loop, but once we had been to Leeds decided we would put our suspicions to the test. We called the management together, including the suspected mole, and informed them of the plan to go after Border, saying it must not get back to Granada as we wanted to keep the pressure on them.

Within a matter of weeks another of those amazing media coincidences occurred when our manager was headhunted for an almost dream job. Something they had wanted to do for ages. Would we mind if they left early. Where to? Oh, it's only in Manchester. Oh, who with? Oh, er, it's Granada actually. Where you came from? Yes, but . . . But what about confidentiality? Yes, but . . . Don't worry, it's in your contract. We know you won't say anything. Then, it's OK? Yes, go, with our blessing, I thought.

Within a matter of a few more weeks I was getting off the train in London when I realised I must have caught one of the Scottish trains, which also stopped in Carlisle, as there in front of me, walking along the platform, was a raiding party from Border Television. As we reached the ticket barrier one of them noticed me, nudged one of the others, and they all turned round with fixed smiles on their faces. Phil, how are you? Long time, no see. You should come up and visit us. Find out if there is anything we could do together in the region. We had a pleasant chat and parted with the usual promises to get together. Now, I thought, as I went off in search of my mobile communication platform, I wonder what little bird has been talking to them.

Although some of the Granada die-hards insist to this day that they knew exactly what we were up to, they didn't. Until, perhaps, about three days before the bids were due in and we got a call to tell us that a *World in Action* crew in London had happened to spot me going into Barings. For the final couple of days we would arrive and leave through the loading bay and stay away from the windows until the bid document was sent to the bank's own high-security printers. They would deliver it at the appointed time and we would wait for ITC to announce the list of interested parties.

And if anyone wants any proof that Granada didn't know, then they need only go to either the BBC or ITN news archive and pull up the news from lunchtime on 15 May 1991. David Plowright was leaving a business event he was hosting at Granada Manchester when the cameras caught him and asked for his reaction to the news that we had bid, with Yorkshire, and £26 million more than Granada themselves. You will not see the picture of a man who knew exactly what was going on. You will see a picture of a man, to use the Scouse phrase, who is utterly gobsmacked. If you could have seen my expression that day it would have shown my utter delight. Gotcha!

We all enjoyed that day and the ones immediately following because we knew that before long Granada would rally and start fighting tooth and claw to protect what they thought of as rightfully theirs. No doubt we would have done the same, and before long they were rubbishing our bid as expected. They criticised our plan to have a weekly original single drama, fifty-two weeks a year. All they could think about was the way they made single plays or films, not grasping that that was exactly what we were already doing with *Brookie*, and what they were doing with *Corrie*, but they also didn't understand *Brookie*'s cost base, now itself ten years old and due to be updated when costs would be reduced even further. We could have made all fifty-two dramas for less than they spent on *Brideshead Revisited*, but we would have had fifty-two hours of drama against their twelve, and would have been making contemporary drama that reached a much bigger audience.

The signs were there with the *Brookie* siege's 8 million viewing figure and Damon Grant's funeral attracting 7 million on a minority 10 per cent audience share. What could we have done with ITV's 35 per cent? Granada just didn't want to believe it. They couldn't. And how could we blame them, as even Yorkshire TV who had asked us to front their bid didn't really believe you could make money out of programming?

Granada also tore into our idea of building a greater regional identity by quadrupling regional programming. This was going to be put in the slots they currently filled with cheap imported material. They also didn't grasp the point that we were going to do this by allowing and encouraging people to make their own programming, presaging the whole user-generated content revolution. The levels of antagonism and vitriol thrown at our regional plans were, on the one hand, unsurprising and understandable as they were a direct indictment of Granada's, ITV's and the IBA's failure to deliver a proper cultural strategy, hiding behind the euphemism of 'local programming' when they meant regional. Although I suppose the view from Brompton Road, opposite Harrods, would encourage the IBA to view Southport as local to Stockport.

On the other hand, their negativity was as surprising as it was hypocritical, as in only 1990 they themselves had conducted a media experiment, the Television Village, in Waddington in the Ribble Valley, North Lancashire. They had installed satellite dishes and then cabled the entire village to see how its inhabitants would react to an always-on TV world, including having their own local TV channel. Funnily enough, the village they chose just happened to be where the new Home Secretary, of the same name, lived, the one now in charge of the approaching 1990 Act. Another of broadcasting's coincidences.

However, the main finding, and a shock to Granada, was that the locals opted for their own rough-and-ready local channel over all other offerings, including, gulp, *Coronation Street*. It was as though no one had told them that TV was a second-choice activity. Yet, after receiving this massive shock to their collective wisdom, Granada still didn't appreciate why we were going for more local programmes. That was the real shock to us. That they hadn't learned or grasped this from their own 'experiment'. But they were still searching for the wrong outcome. They were looking at it as a purely techno-logical experiment. Expensive technology at that, and therefore still a long way off in the future. They had completely missed the point that what had made it so compelling was not the technology, but the fact that the villagers used it to make their own entertainment. Programming didn't have to be slick, it just had to be relevant. That was the real meaning of quality at grass-roots level.

Despite the fact that once the bids had gone in we were all supposed to observe a period of purdah and not contact the ITC unless asked for further information, we learned Granada had sent a 'dossier' on our bid to the ITC. What was in it or if the ITC ever read it we never knew, as we were never asked for comment. Perhaps it'll come out some day.

Knowing they were out there rubbishing us every chance they got, Philip Reevell and I went on a series of road shows, criss-crossing the region to explain our bid and encourage people to write in to the ITC and demonstrate support, but hardly anyone bothered turning up. To the public it all seemed like a bunch of telly folk rowing amongst themselves. They had a point. At one public debate I found myself under sustained feminist attack for calling two of our proposed dramas *King Cotton* and *The Railway King*, recognised historical references to the North's industrial heritage. I came away realising we were no match for the Granada publicity machine.

Granada were still looking, sounding and acting nervous as they kept up the media and political campaign to reinforce the message that, if they went, life as we all knew it would come to an end. At one of the university graduation ceremonies at Liverpool's Anglican Cathedral, I bumped into Mark Fisher MP, then Labour's Shadow Arts Minister, who should have been a natural ally on our jobs and access agenda. Yet he was hesitant. Have you looked at what we are offering, Mark? I asked. Yes. It's good but . . . I don't know. He glanced round. Life without Granada, Phil? It's too difficult to contemplate. I watched him walk off to mingle with the great and good. I suppose we were, in some eyes, razing the temple.

Then, suddenly, things changed. In midsummer the mood music flowing down the M62 became a bit more upbeat. One of the Sundays ran a story saying they had heard that Granada was going to retain the licence. The guys in Yorkshire said to ignore it, it was just speculation. We agreed, but were left wondering what could possibly have put a smile on those previously glum faces in Manchester.

We never found out, but rumour and conspiracy theories abounded as the stakes surrounding the new, even if reduced, 'licences to print money' remained high. So much so that we, like some of the other companies, found ourselves the target of a conman purporting to have evidence that Granada were bugging our offices. He would provide proof, for a fee. If we met in Amsterdam. We went to the Merseyside police instead. They swept the offices and our home, found nothing but eventually caught him through Interpol. A drama within a drama that had me, Alexis and Philip Reevell gathering evidence at Schiphol airport.

Yet there was one obvious frustration with the whole process. We were supposed to be in purdah, unble to make any contact with the ITC about our franchise bid, yet around the time the mood music changed, Alexis and I were in a small restaurant in London one day when I thought I saw someone with a remarkable resemblance to George Russell, the ITC Chairman, having lunch with someone who looked remarkably like Alex Bernstein, Chairman of our rival, the incumbent ITV company Granada. I nudged Alexis and nodded towards them. Was it them? Surely it couldn't be as we were all supposed to be in purdah and the ITC wouldn't put themselves in such a position of perceived conflict of interest. I wondered whether to go over and say hello, just in case it was them, but decided against it. Even if it was them, even a Scouse conspiracy theorist would have to accept that two such high-profile industry figures would have had many other things to talk about. The frustration, though, was that non-incumbent bidders like ourselves couldn't even have coffee, never mind lunch.

16 October 1991, Franchise Day. And the announcements were to be made at 10 a.m. We would be advised by fax a short time before the main announcement in London. This would come through at MerseyTV and John Fairley had come across to join us. He was in an upbeat mood, believing we were going to win. If the ITC and the government wanted radical change and innovation, he maintained, then that was what we were offering.

As is the way of things, everyone managed to find something to occupy themselves until about thirty minutes before the fax was due, but then everyone involved started to congregate in and around my office, perching on the ends of desks or settees, and generally engaging in that aimless, superficial chit-chat that helps push the hands of the clock round. Every now and then someone else would arrive and, as though no one had thought of it, religiously check the paper, toner, and even the phone line behind the fax in the outer office. Everyone moved from my office, closer to the fax. Willing it into action. Finally the time came. 09:47. The connection click. The whirr of the machine as it warmed up. And then the paper slowly fed out. We had lost. On the very thing we had all lobbied so hard to have written into the Act: quality. Silence. Someone else looked and confirmed. They had ruled us out at the Quality Threshold. I turned to hug Alexis, and then looked towards where John had been but he was nowhere to be seen.

I went back into my office and he was sitting alone, staring out of the window. If I was disappointed, here was a man who was almost desolate. I closed the door and perched on my desk. It took a good few minutes before we could each find something to say. 'I really thought,' he said, turning back to the window, 'that they would play by the rules this time.' All I could do was nod. Even the news that YTV had retained their licence in Yorkshire did little to lift the mood as Alexis came in to see if we were both OK. She then told us word was already out, probably from Granada, and the media were waiting downstairs. John stood to give her a hug and said that he had better get back to Yorkshire and face it all over there. Especially how they were going to survive with what they had bid. We would regroup with Trinity Mirror the following day.

Next in was Philip Reevell ready to brief me on who and what was downstairs, the main warning being that the pack had positioned themselves at the end of the corridor that led to where they were supposed to be waiting in the canteen. They were getting ready to get 'the dejected body language' shot. I said I would tell them Granada had bid £9 million, £26 million less than us. So that was £26 million the ITC had just cost the Treasury. He advised us not to go down that route yet, as YTV had just handed them £37 million for Yorkshire and £15 million for Tyne Tees. Insane amounts of money, partly, we thought, attached to the prospect of having the North West franchise as well.

Going down to face the media, I was getting my head in order when, through the glass panels in the corridor, I saw what Philip had meant. At the other end of it was a bank of cameras, wall to wall, floor to ceiling, as this contest between us and Granada had been the one to watch. If it had been a Sky football game it would have been in the 4 p.m. Sunday slot. I paused and considered going back and coming up behind them, but thought that was probably a bit unfair. They were, after all, only doing their job, and if there were that many, then a few column inches must already have been set aside. Best make the most of them. The thought processes were not quite as rational as they might appear written down, it was more instinctive at the time, but I threw open the doors and strode through, hands outstretched, hoping the body language was more about disbelief than disappointment.

I think I just about got away with it as it was this shot that mostly appeared. It accompanied a piece *Today* had asked me to write, under the headline, 'Ageing Toffs Have Killed Off People's TV'. I think it made the point quite subtly. Richard Branson must have thought so too as he gave me a call and asked what did I think about this Quality Hurdle business and should we join forces to have a go at the ITC? He had been backing CPV-TV, with David Frost and Chrysalis, bidding for Anglia, Thames and Television South West. They were outbid in Anglia and the South West but, like us, had been ditched at the Quality Threshold for Thames. We chatted for a while and decided that it was probably pointless as there was no formal right of appeal. The other potential course of action was to go for a full Judicial Review, an expensive option and only possible if they had got the process wrong in some way. We both knew they were too good a set of bureaucrats for that. However, all bidders had the right to go and ask for clarification and feedback on the decision, so we agreed that if anything came out of that we would talk again.

By the time we got to the regroup meeting with YTV, Trinity and Barings I think there was a common sense of both anger and frustration. This was not just about our particular decision in the North West, but looking at what had happened across the country. Of the fifteen regional licences, twelve were returned to sitting incumbents; four had been the highest bidder, three had been unopposed, five had been outbid but, fortunately, their opponents were disqualified by the so-called quality assessment. This meant, in effect, that the ITC was saying that they, rather than five consortia that ran the likes of Virgin, Chrysalis, Trinity and MerseyTV, all of whom had businesses based on selling to or attracting large numbers of the public, would decide what was good for that same public.

There was a wider sense of disquiet at the way the bids had been handled. The new consortium Sunrise Television (later GMTV) had bid £34.6 million against TV-am's £14.1 million. It seemed odd then that the incumbent Television South West (TSW), making the highest bid at £16.1m, was disqualified for an over-ambitious business plan, allowing Westcountry to gain the franchise with a low £7.8m bid. Why did one high bidder fail and another not?

This had ramifications for us and for YTV. After all, we were the only new consortium that actually had one of the Big Five ITV companies backing both our programming and business plan. At the same time, YTV had been one of the highest bidders with its combined bid of £52 million for YTV and Tyne Tees, but that business plan had not been challenged. If that was fine, against the TSW bid, it left us wondering how the ITC could perceive our programming plans as having failed when they had been drawn up in consultation with one of the Big Five companies, to sit alongside what they were successfully planning to do in Yorkshire and the North East.

It began to feel, and look, as though the ITC had focused too much on the state of the overall network rather than, as they should have done, each individual region. Our ambition was expressed in the name North West Television. We were expecting to work alongside YTV and a surviving Granada Productions, as Thames later did, to provide network programmes, including the sacred *Corrie*. Just as Thames continued to sell *The Bill* to ITV. It was soon apparent, and later obvious, that the ITC had worried too much about network stability, partly because of changes at Thames TVS and TV-am, and partly because of the financial precariousness of the high bidders, incumbents and newcomers alike. There seemed to be general consensus with Mark Fisher, that life without Granada was impossible to contemplate. TSW wasted a lot of money launching a Judicial Review on this suspicion but as Richard Branson and I had figured, the ITC were too good at their jobs to lose that.

This became blatantly apparent when we finally ended up sitting in front of them in the old IBA offices in Brompton Road. David Sneddon, Chairman of Trinity, accompanied myself and Philip Reevell. From the ITC there was George Russell, Chairman, David Glencross, Chief Executive, and Michael Redley, Head of Licensing. They were obviously well prepared and rehearsed as they immediately ran through the process they had followed, making the points that the needs of each region had been addressed differently and that all decisions had been double-checked by lawyers, at every stage. They had been through this process with other disqualified bidders by then, and when George Russell read out a note of the formal findings of the Commission we all realised it was meant for Richard Branson's CPV-TV bid. He apologised, but carried on. The facts were standard for everyone, no doubt double-checked by the lawyers.

David Sneddon queried how Granada had got over the quality threshold relating to news-gathering. As Chairman of Trinity Newspapers, which was bigger across the region than Granada, he considered their news-gathering abysmal. The reason Trinity had become involved in our bid was that they wanted to develop a quality service for the viewers. Philip Reevell pressed this point, reminding the ITC that they themselves had been critical of Granada on this front. There was no real answer except a line about not being interested in history, only the future.

After a bit more huffing and puffing, prodding and probing, we came away with two very clear facts. The big negative was that we had been failed on the provision of quality network programmes, despite the fact that our bid proposed we would buy those in as necessary, even from Granada. More positively, we had not failed, but actually been complimented, on our finance plan, as the ITC was sure we could have delivered what we promised.

From my contemporaneous note of the meeting, later circulated to the North West Board, two other things emerged. When asked at what stage the decision had been made about the North West, they said it was probably initially around late July. Around the same time that the mood in Manchester turned more upbeat. The other thing the ITC wanted to make clear was that we would be considered 'fit and proper' people if thinking of any future licence application. Whether this was the proverbial nod, wink or nudge, towards Channel 5 perhaps, none of us knew, but it was a clear sign that we had passed the club membership criteria.

Having made that clear, they also appeared to be expecting our sympathy for the fact that they had been put in a no-win situation. It was a horrendous task they had just had to perform, they said, even at one point reminding us that they had had to lose some 'friends'. While appreciating what they were trying to convey, I for one had never assumed their position to be one of win or lose. They simply had a procedure to oversee.

Nor was sympathy at the forefront of our minds, considering we had just lost over £500,000 on something that was, in the end, all about exactly what the government had tried to avoid: subjective interpretation. As George Russell explained: 'We liked your quality, Phil. It just wasn't the quality we were looking for.' It was left to *Private Eye* to explain it all pithily, picking up on the Toffs' and People's TV angle, to report that we had failed to notice a little-known but long-standing establishment rule, that 'television couldn't be run by long-haired gits from Liverpool'.

★

With the benefit of distance and time, Alexis and I look back on that franchise decision and realise we had a lucky escape. The day after the announcement we woke up together, got up together, got dressed together, drove in to work together, and it felt . . . just great. Never for one moment had we wished for it not to happen. We both believed in the vision. Yet the only way to keep Mersey's independent production status would have been to keep Mersey and North West apart, which meant *we* would have been apart. We had got used to working together, being together, eating together and sleeping together. If we'd won, it would inevitably have put distance between us. And would we really have wanted that?

As a postscript to this, at around the time of the sale of Mersey TV itself, in 2005, we discovered that some of the old guard at Granada had sat festering for years claiming I personally had cost them £9 million a year that could have gone into programming, while Central got away with paying just £2,000 because they were unopposed. As if! Leaving aside YTV's part in the game, here's another take on it all. We were looking for a £5 million a year output deal, around ten hours of ITV drama. If they had given us that they would have been able to bid low, like Central, and save themselves the £9 million. That would have put them £4 million ahead on our deal, but they would also have had the programming refunded by the network's part of the Secret Santa committee − or internal market programme supply − and, on top, all the ad revenue around the programmes we delivered. In other words, it would have cost them nothing; they would have been at least cost-neutral, but probably making a profit.

Something else we only discovered in recent years was the real reason Anglia had invited us to dinner. Granada were making a move on them. They were trying to make a pre-emptive strike ahead of the 1990 Act, just as they had with Border and Tyne Tees. Anglia's response was, apparently, that if Granada tried, they would form an alliance with Mersey to have a go at the North West. So Granada backed off. Whether that made me a poison pill or a white knight I am not sure, but it worked for Anglia. Coming away from our dinner with them feeling puzzled, we remained blissfully unaware of these backstage machinations until years later. It was a great time. A difficult time. It cost us all dear. And all because we didn't really know how to talk to each other. And all because they wouldn't let me have the *Corrie* theme tune back in 1982.

Reviewing everything again for this book, it is amazing how the lens of time can lend things a much sharper focus. Granada were already on their predatory path to dominate the UK media industry. Even if unsuccessful with satellite, they had their eyes on the rest of ITV. Yorkshire felt threatened and wanted to peg them back and dominate the North, while we were on our People's TV mission. We were not interested in the 'great game' of the ITV Network, with all its trappings and politics. We were interested only in making drama and offering greater public access. We were all speaking different languages and no common tongue.

Granada must have seen our consortium's bid as a challenge to everything they had built and held dear, but while I can understand that, I feel no sympathy for them, only for the people they eventually let down: the staff they shed and the audience they deprived of better access. One could have served the other, but rather than more local television being developed, there was even less regionalism as they slowly regrouped and went about their aim of total ITV domination. In 1997 they acquired Yorkshire-Tyne Tees and by 2004 they practically owned the ITV map, which now looked remarkably similar to the BBC's, with a presence in England, Northern Ireland, Scotland and Wales. So much for localism.

Yet . . . what else could they have done? As David Glencross said at our ITC meeting, it was really a politically determined no-win situation. The ITC came out of it with little credit, but the television companies and structure had to survive. Individual fortunes differed greatly. Granada's ringmaster, David Plowright, was famously 'thrown overboard' within eighteen months, while Alexis and I came away with the output deal we went looking for initially. I didn't know David Plowright very well, but I would have liked to as we seemed to get on whenever we met. It was unfortunate that we ended up in different corners, and it was a sad moment when I heard he had passed away. He might have been of a different generation from me, but he too believed in what television could be, and the power it could wield. There are too few people like him today.

The fight we really had with Granada was not about the right to own a licence to print money, but about the privilege of being allowed to use a scarce resource. A resource that, at the time, belonged to the people who paid for it – the viewers. They seemed to have forgotten that it wasn't theirs to keep in perpetuity. But this was the last time that these state-sanctioned monopolies would be up for tender. The last time there would be the opportunity to influence social change through the power of mass communication, instead of 'just telly'. Once awarded, these licences could henceforth be renewed on request. This was a change we could not get anyone to take any notice of in advance. After all, it just sounded like telly folk arguing among themselves. Its consequences are by now apparent.

A further consequence of the 1990 Act was that Channel 4 could sell its own advertising airtime and keep the revenue. That meant it could make programming decisions based on what they meant to its own income, not ITV's. One immediate result was that *Brookie* would go from two to three episodes per week, so on 9 October, five days before the franchise announcements, the brand new Brookside Parade of shops was unveiled to mark our one thousandth episode.

17

Emmerdale (1991–92)

'You can have anything, Phil. Whatever it takes. Just fix it' – *John Fairley, Yorkshire Television, on* Emmerdale

Coming out of the franchise affair, we at least had the comfort of knowing we were 'fit and proper persons' which, at least in television regulating circles, is quite an important concept. While the franchise consortia disbanded and ITV began the slow meltdown we had foreseen and tried to warn the government about, Alexis and I were still enjoying that sense of relief we had felt the day after the decision. Whether it was the atmosphere of peace and goodwill I don't know, but coming out of Christmas '92 I had that old feeling that there were mysterious forces at work. Our New Year's resolution was to 'enjoy what we have'. We had the output deal with YTV, *Brookie* was now occupying three nights a week and *Grange Hill* was running quietly in the background, now approaching its fifteenth year.

There were also other aspects of the 1990 Broadcasting Act to think about, like the debates about Channel 5 and the 25 per cent access to independent producers. However, Channel 5 was still some way off, we had already been given our Buggins' turn at the BBC and the output deal with YTV was taken care of, so with a few hours to spare here and there I started to become more involved in life on campus. Alexis was already a Governor and the Chair of Finance at Liverpool John Moores University, which had now given me both a Professorship and Fellowship, so I agreed to become Honorary Chair of Media as well as a Trustee. This sounds a bit grander than it actually was, as the Board of Governors is, as the name suggests, the governing body, while the Trustees were, as I would describe them, the Tombola and Raffle Committee.

For some arcane bureaucratic reason that eluded me it was felt necessary to establish a separate trust fund, with a separate Board of Trustees, detached from the university, who would then be free to raise money on their behalf and gift it to the university, all of which would require a separate staff at additional cost, which would be a legitimate expense against the running of the trust and therefore deductible from any money raised, but to maintain probity and strategic linkage the Vice Chancellor of the University and other senior staff would attend Trustee meetings. You can probably guess where this is going? Fifteen years later the government finally realised how daft all this was and made it possible for universities to run their own fund-raising departments.

In case you may be tempted to assume that the example given is just that, a small example, it may be worth bearing in mind that it is, like many of the reflections in this book, formed by the passage of time and experience. The same bureaucratic mindset I'd encountered in television – that we have the best governance systems in the world so let's not change them – was also awaiting me in education, local government, politics and museums. It was even lurking when we acquired our new corporate HQ, the old College of Further Education in Childwall, Liverpool. But this time bureacracy became its saviour. The Council could either sell it to us, or let it go to rack and ruin as they had no resources either to protect it or knock it down, and the land had so many restrictive convenants on it that it had no value for development. It had something more valuable for us, though, a past covered by Crown Immunity. This is a concept no longer in general use, but at the time it meant that any public building was exempt from planning and building regulation regimes. This meant that over the years, when making additions to the building, the council had simply added an odd classroom or office here and there with what appeared to be leftover materials from other projects. To anyone else it looked like a dog's breakfast; for us it was the perfect collection of different-looking location façades.

Naturally, as soon as the building passed into our hands the Crown Immunity disappeared. Whereas a few months earlier there had been around eighty staff and 500 students coming and going there, before we could move in thirty people we had to install twelve sets of fire doors and a fire-alarm system. We would have done this anyway, but arrived to discover the canteen kitchen that had been included in the price wasn't actually included in the building. The Council's Estates Department had efficiently removed it to store, meaning they had to buy us a new one. It was quite tempting after that to keep the truckload of toilet rolls and paper towels that arrived every month for about a year, as 'Procurement' had not cancelled the contract.

We should have had a bit of warning about this, though, as just before the sale was completed we had discovered there was actually someone still living on site: the old caretaker who used to be there for security purposes, but was now deemed to be occupying a council house and therefore had the 'right to buy'. Fortunately, he didn't have any interest in starting up a TV company, he just didn't want to be thrown out on the streets. He was found somewhere else to live and we started to move in, only to discover that the site had become a recreational oasis for both local druggies and dog walkers.

There was a great movie moment after we decided to use the still-empty college as a location for a *Waterfront Beat* drugs bust. Just as we got set up, the real cops arrived on a real bust, and for a short while it was pandemonium as the two universes collided and real cops mixed with pretend cops, all shouting and asking who was who. That was the last we ever saw of either local users or the real drugs squad, but the local dog walkers took a little longer, and a large fence, to turn away.

Childwall was bought once the notion of growing *Brookie* from two to three episodes per week was floated, and it is hard to believe, looking across the weekly soap schedules now, that making the decision was such a big deal. But there was much hand-wringing and fretting about whether it could be done and whether the audience would actually be there for another episode. It was left to the bastion of quality, Granada, to show that it could be done by taking *Corrie* to a third episode in October 1989. The world didn't come to an end.

We and C4 watched this development closely. We were already running our shoot from 8 a.m. to 7 p.m. five days a week. Adding an extra episode would mean we would have to find two and a half more working days, but by the time the call came we had run over the design specification for our own soap supertanker and reckoned it could be done, by stretching the hull. However, almost as the order was placed and work began in the shipyard, a structural problem was spotted. We were beginning to take on water, or, to drop the analogy, losing viewers.

While Michael Grade was not as imperial in style as Jeremy Isaacs, he was equally, well, regal. He had a right to be. He was part of ITV's royal family, coming from the Grade-Delfont dynasty. Instead of an Emperor, C4 now had a King, and I invited him up to see *Brookside* and asked him what he wanted to do with the channel. If he gave me his vision I would make sure the programme came behind it, as that was its original purpose. He didn't hesitate. He spoke at length, telling some great stories along the way, the essence of them being that he was not there to make radical change, but wanted to see a more cohesive channel that promoted and marketed itself better. This chimed with what I had experienced at the BBC: packaging the talent rather than imposing his own tastes. From this and other conversations, we took it that we should carry on what we had been doing, which we did.

The only trouble with this philosophy was that the publishing model of C4 meant he would have to rely more on his commissioning editors as go-betweens. This was a completely different relationship from at the BBC or ITV, where the channel controllers, heads of department and producers all worked for the same organisation, so there was a direct line-management system. At C4, and for us, the relationship was based more on procurement and supply, so the skill set was different.

This ethos went right back to the establishing of the channel itself. The original advertisement for commissioning editors included the sentence: '*What is essential is that Channel 4's Commissioning Editors should share a willingness to experiment and a concern to broaden the range of British Television.*' It went on: '*If you think you know a good idea when you see one and could help others realise it on the television screen, write now to Jeremy Isaacs . . .*' In his memoir, the former Emperor makes the point even more forcefully when he explains that they were not looking for traditional heads of department or even executive producers who would want to make their own programmes, but that he set great store by the inventiveness of the programme-makers themselves. C4 was there to publish, not produce. More specifically, commissioning editors were not there to second guess producers or run their programmes for them, but to facilitate their ideas. That was the ethos around which our common bond had been built.

David Rose, following the original brief, had been totally hands off. Peter Ansorge, his successor, had followed suit until put under pressure by Michael to get more involved. This was probably the first subtle shift in culture at C4, moving from publishing other people's ideas towards commissioning their ideas from other people. A slow shift to the mindset that had dogged both *County Hall* and *Waterfront Beat*. There is nothing wrong with this, provided you have the right people in place. But it turned out that at *Brookie* we didn't.

As the architect of the phrase 'Britain's only true hyphenate', Graham Benson at TVS was one of the few people who could cope with me switching hats between creative writer and business entrepreneur. In the early years this had led to some intense creative friction, resulting in C4 commissioners being banned from the set for a short while until we also had our go-between producers. And, like Michael, I do believe that if you appoint someone to a job, they have to be allowed to get on with it. Until something goes wrong.

When we were approaching the three-nights-a-week launch and losing audience, a bit of noise started coming out of C4 about us taking our eye off the ball because of the 'franchise affair'. The typical metro media chaterati nonsense. Michael came out with some jibe about me having to be kept on a golden choke chain, to which I responded that he only spent C4's money, I actually earned it for them. But that was all part of the media knockabout. Our relationship never suffered because in every criticism there is always an element of truth, no matter how small. Things had changed around the time of the ITV franchises. I had let C4, through Peter Ansorge, get more involved. And the programme had become boring.

We were on the cusp of another generational change with Sheila and Billy on their exit trajectory, as Sue and John headed for theatreland, and the Collinses, through the death of Doreen Sloane, on their way to the Lakes. The audience were waiting to see who we would replace them with and didn't quite take to the new family who had moved centre-stage, the Chois. Unfortunately, while our then producer and Peter Ansorge enjoyed the well-acted and well-written drama based around them, all the feedback and audience data made it clear that the audience was frustrated with the Chois, to the extent that I invoked my executive producer right of veto and issued an edict that no episode or part of an episode could begin or end with a scene in which they featured. It was something I would have to do again a few years later, with the Simpsons, to much greater consequence.

As things were, it was not too traumatic for the programme, even when our then producer decided to leave, as Mal Young had been shadowing. He'd been progressing through the company since *What Now?* and it was obvious his natural storytelling ability and energy could drive the programme. Mal always says that I took up the reins for a while, but then, one day, I went to the loo and never came back. So by the time C4 had spotted that the ratings were drifting away, we had worked out the reason and fixed it. The Chois left and Mal took over. And all before that call came from John Fairley and the franchise adventure began.

Our real problem was that we were shedding viewers because the programme had become boring. Instead of on Bobby and Sheila or Sheila and Billy, it was focusing on a new family, the Chois. The audience just did not take to them, and when that happens it is time for radical intervention.

The Dixons and Farnhams arrived, the Corkhills were built up, and the Rogerses started coming more centre-stage, with Sammy's drinking and Geoff's dyslexia. Both these storylines helped the Rogerses deliver the second major currency after ratings: media impact. Sammy ended up in a teenage car crash, helping to highlight the dangers of teenage joy riding, while the family were featured at the Houses of Parliament in support of a dyslexia campaign. The programme was making noise again and being seen because of it.

What did come out of the franchise débâcle was the resolution to 'enjoy what we had', so we decided we'd take the writing team to Majorca for the next long-term planning meeting. We had been doing this for a while. The entire writing team, together with the script department, would go off for the weekend, away from phones and the pressure of the shoot, to spend time talking about the programme and characters and where they should be in the next twelve to eighteen months. We usually went to typical UK locations like Wales or the Lake District, but just as the shoot had started to go to places like Portugal or Rome or even Canada, it was easy and sometimes cheaper to fly the team from Liverpool. We would give the script department the budget and they would hunt for the best package they could get, so come March we were all heading for Majorca.

The night before we were due to travel Mal and I ran through the agenda and I told him about an idea I had been formulating, then sent him a fax with the outline of a story I'd like to include. It was headed 'New Family − No. 10 − SHACKLETONS' and described how a new family would arrive and, although appearing slightly odd initially, would gradually be accepted by the rest of the residents. The story would then develop to reveal the horrors of domestic violence and sex-abuse, resulting in the mother and daughter killing the husband and . . . you guessed it, surely? . . . burying him under the patio. This was to become *Brookie*'s biggest-ever storyline.

The name Shackleton was used as a bit of a red herring at first so as to explore a secondary issue, the NIMBY factor of most people being willing to support things like refuges for victims of domestic violence and rape, or safe havens for the homeless or refugees, so long as they are somewhere else. The Shackletons were part of a charity trying to rehouse victims of domestic violence, and it would only be when Louise (later Mandy) Jordache and her two daughters arrived that the truth would come out.

When Mal and I outlined the story arc to the writers they kicked back, particularly the bit that said, '*They then bury him in the back garden of number 10 and . . . leave him there. We should then not discover the body for at least two years and only then by accident . . .*' Mal and I looked at each other; we'd been through this often enough, as with Billy and Sheila, to know that it usually meant we were on to a winner. This is because a good writing team, no matter what its literary or liberal leanings, should also reflect the views and mores of society as a whole. If the writers are shocked, then so too will the audience be. As executive producers, the primary need is to convince the writers, take them on the journey, or how can you expect them to convince your audience? To most people the idea of killing someone and burying the body in the garden is way outside their comfort zone, never mind their moral boundaries, yet as our police research contacts would say, 'Where else would you bury it?' However, the main objection was, why did I want to keep the plotline going for two years?

The straightforward answer was that I had got the story from the same place we tended to get most stories, from 'reading the media'. The incident that had caught my eye involved someone trying to plant roses against their garden fence and discovering what was at first thought to be a bit of old carpet. Scratching away at it, they then discovered it was more in their neighbours' garden than theirs and was wrapped round the remains of a body. After doing a bit of research by phoning a couple of contacts from *Waterfront Beat*, it seemed this was the typical pattern. Bodies could remain in gardens for years until they were disturbed by accident. It seemed like an interesting story for *Brookside*, and of course I was still searching for characters who would give us the same depth of storylining we had had with the original Grants and then with Sheila and Billy, characters who would take us into complex yet socially relevant areas. Like the complexity of abusive relationships. Why they happened. Why people put up with them. What they did to cope and survive.

As with many previous issues we had looked at, like Sheila's rape, these events set off a chain reaction, leading from one storyline to another. My feeling was that anyone being driven to murder would already have undergone a dramatic journey that we could explore, as well as the inevitable consequences of trying to keep such a terrible act secret. In Majorca, I explained that we could build to the murder over a year and keep it a secret for another, considering the impact it would have on the mother and her two daughters, all trying to live a normal life while dreading discovery at every moment. I also felt sure we could provide quite a few narrow escapes before discovery, and that we would then have a third year of consequences.

Alongside the dramatic rationale was, as always, the pragmatic one. We were there to get ratings. Going into long-term planning, we always kept one eye open for the big headline-grabbing storylines. The ones that would get people talking and become those cynical ratings-grabbing exercises, once we had worked out and agreed a realistic story arc. Why or how could they bring themselves to do it? Through provocation. Sustained pressure and abuse. Why under the patio? As the police advised, where else? I don't believe that bit. Well, what about this? Or that? It takes six months to feed an idea into the script process, in this case around September, and then another six months for it actually to be seen on screen. As it turned out, we started the story in February 1993 and found the body in January 1995. The two years I'd originally suggested.

Not long after the Jordaches appeared on screen, a call came from John Fairley. Never mind our output deal, there was something else he'd like me to consider. Could he come and talk to me about *Emmerdale*? He outlined the challenge. *Emmerdale* had lost ratings and YTV were under heavy pressure either to fix it or lose it. They had been given three months to turn things round. This was a big issue and more than the fate of one programme was at stake for, as *Brookside* was to MerseyTV, *Emmerdale* was to YTV. It was their financial keystone. Take it out and the whole company would collapse, along with the lives and livelihoods of everyone working there.

By 1993 *Emmerdale* had been running for twenty-one years since its beginnings as a daytime programme. It moved to an early-evening slot in 1978 but only became fully networked across ITV in the mid-80s when Thames and Anglia agreed to take it. There was therefore a lot of history but the issue now was that one of the newer ITV companies, Carlton, who had taken over Thames Television's London weekday franchise, had objected to the programme. They had the new-kids-on-the-block disdain for old ITV politics and had undertaken market research that indicated it wasn't working either for them or for ITV as a whole. The side chat was that it didn't quite fit the cool media image of Carlton, where David Cameron used to work in corporate affairs. They had pushed for the three-month deadline, which was, whether knowingly or not, an impossible timescale to turn a soap supertanker round, as I had previously counselled Julia Smith and Tony Holland about *EastEnders*.

Fairley asked me what I would do if I were running it. He didn't like my first suggestion, which was to scrap it and commission a new series from MerseyTV as he thought that was what Carlton was hoping for in the great 4D industry chess game. He did like my next suggestion, which was that although you couldn't turn the programme round in three months, you could probably do it in six. How? By introducing a high-octane storyline that would come out of the blue, get everyone to take notice, and from that reshape and remodel the programme, just as I had done with the *Brookie* siege storyline back in 1985. I told him it would take six months to set up and then six months to embed the changes.

He then asked me would I do it. Could I do it? As John was a great horse-racing man, it felt more like being asked to train a twenty-year-old war horse not only to run the Grand National, but to win it. The National, so I am told by those who know, is a race in a category of its own. It is not necessarily the best and fastest horse that wins; a combination of serendipity and stamina usually carries the day. Like the race itself, John's challenge had quite a few fences, jumps and ditches for me to fall at, but Mal was now driving *Brookie* with the Jordache storyline as the rocket fuel, so the biggest concern was a personal one. Going back to John's simple question: could I do it? If I didn't, the critics would have a field day and the industry would be unforgiving.

But it was too great a challenge to resist. Yes, I could do it. Given twelve months. And total control plus the same sort of freedom I had at *Brookie*. John gave me a great broad grin, and said he'd expected nothing less. 'You can have anything, Phil. Whatever it takes. Just fix it.' With responsibility only to him and the main YTV Board through our old franchise co-conspirator, Managing Director Clive Leach. The situation was that desperate. Alexis then made sure the deal reflected the financial significance of the series to YTV. If it worked, they would be financially secure and we would be very happy. The first thing to find out, though, was how fit the war horse was.

A box of tapes and a pile of files soon arrived on my desk and I spent a week immersing myself in the programme. It was not long before I was in the Carlton camp. What should have been the programme's USP was being totally ignored: the countryside. The thing that most townies have wistful and idyllic thoughts about but never visit because it smells. The thing that makes up our green and pleasant land, and the place where, in the early 1990s, nearly 70 per cent of the population lived. Instead, the programme was full of characters acting out the births, deaths and marriage staples that could have been in *Corrie, Brookie, EastEnders* or *The Bill*.

We agreed that I would invite the current producer and script team over to Childwall, knowing that as soon as I stepped into YTV the rumour mill would pick up speed. Nor did we want a repeat of the franchise incident, with any secret meetings being advertised on a hotel reception board. On the other hand, everyone at Mersey was used to seeing the whole industry passing through Childwall. It would be seen as yet another showcase or fact-finding mission. As expected, the current team of *Emmerdale* felt undermined, threatened, were defensive, and made it clear that they'd find it hard to continue if I were brought in to sort out the programme. It was understandable and I was sympathetic . . . until I asked them to run through all the programme's strengths, weaknesses, and to map out for me where the locations were and the layout of the fictional village. They couldn't do it.

No one could draw me a map of where the characters' houses were in relation to each other. Just as number 5 of The Close was opposite number 9 and you got to the Brookside Parade of shops along the footpath between numbers 8 and 9. They couldn't do it. I was both surprised and appalled, knowing the amount of time and care we put into every detail. If we didn't, how could we convince an audience to accept our fictional universe? It was now understandable to me why Carlton couldn't understand and didn't want the programme.

I have lost count of the number of meetings I have sat in where someone has said 'the audience won't remember', or 'the audience won't care about that, provided what's on screen is terrific'. What that too often means is that *they* don't care. That *they* want to make *their* show, not the audience's programme. Too many people do not understand, especially on long-running serials, that the audience are better versed in the programme than they are as newcomers. While it is true that the audience only judge by what they see on screen, which you can use to lose characters or move storylines on, they will view it in the context of their shared past. Having invested large chunks of their time watching the programme, they will come with you on a different path, but they will do it more willingly, and stay much longer, if they believe the characters' lives run true to previous history. Gavin Taylor's cookers on the lawn had more impact because the audience could see they were right next to the fusspot Roger Huntington, so that every time Roger came home, saw them and gave a frown of anger, the audience could imagine rows over the garden fence that we never needed to script.

There is one other important factor. You may create or end up running a soap, but there comes a time when the audience considers it theirs. It is their programme with their characters, and you become the custodian. That was how I felt about *Emmerdale*. I might have been given the authority to 'do what it takes', but I had to do it and remain faithful to its audience. That was the lesson I had learned in the first few weeks of *Brookside*, when individual directors started rearranging the furniture. Real people do not do that. The fictional universe has to be as rigid as, and follow similar rules to, its real-life counterpart.

The other thing about having a fixed and rigid fictional world for your characters is that it makes it easier for writers, actors, directors and designers to know how the characters interact. Who can see what from their windows and front doors. How long it takes to get from, say, where Seth lived to The Woolpack. Or how far Home Farm was from the Tates' mansion. The *Emmerdale* team could tell me this in terms of location travel time, which became an issue in itself, but not from a fictional character's point of view.

The next step was to find the big idea that would act as the marketing grab. Arrest the public's attention and get media and audience talking about the programme. Something that would have a huge impact, force all the characters together and allow character-changing, as well as storyline-developing, moments. In *Brookie* we had used the siege in 1985 to double the audience instantly. In *Grange Hill* it had been things like the Zammo drugs storyline, but with *Emmerdale*'s fictional location supposed to be quite rural, almost isolated, that ruled out things like drug-related warfare, motorway pile ups or even a train wreck, as *Coronation Street* had done in 1967 when a train fell from the viaduct on to the end of the street (and were to do again in their fiftieth anniversary year). So what else could happen to have a similar and isolating impact? Something external. Something that could be instant. Which eventually took me to something, quite literally, falling from the sky.

I arranged to meet Keith Richardson, Head of Drama and *Emmerdale*'s executive producer. The last time we had seen each other was when we were both in the semi-final for the ITV daytime soap. We met at Yorkshire's London offices and over a cup of tea I told him what I had in mind. We would drop a jumbo jet on the village. It would be the best and biggest stunt ever pulled off in soap and would arrest everyone's attention. It certainly got his. I can still clearly recall the look of shock on his face. I've often joked that he went grey as the blood ran from his cheeks. That's probably a bit of poetic licence built up over the years, but the shock was genuine. Whether it was because he thought the idea was crazy, or I was, or both, wasn't clear at the time. I just pressed on with how it would attract attention and get people talking in reality, while in the fictional *Emmerdale* we could push the characters together, end or start relationships, demolish or build new sets.

Probably the real reason for his initial shock was the immediate realisation that we were talking about a £1 million stunt. Would Yorkshire sanction it? But I'd already had my brief from John Fairley. Whatever it takes. Still, over the next few days Keith kept phoning me to ask if I was sure.

I told John Fairley that as the existing scripts took us up to Christmas, we should aim for that as the timing for the spectacular as there would be more people off work with time on their hands and available to view then. Not just that, but having seen the impact of *Damon and Debbie* and the five-nighters we had run on *Brookie*, I suggested he should start badgering the network to let us do it over five nights. If we were going to spend the equivalent of around twenty normal episodes on a single stunt, we needed to get the maximum impact out of it. This meant I would have about seven, rather than the normal twelve, months to get on air, but it was worth pushing for. I could get the writers working straight away, treating the plane crash itself as the opening episode of a brand new soap, *Emmerdale: Resurrection*.

To make this work I sought out Nick Prosser, and asked if he would do what he did for me during the early days at *Brookside*, and take on the day-to-day line producer's role of shepherding the scripts and episodes that were already in production towards the crossover point. That would leave me free to work on the 'resurrection scripts' and create the future direction of the programme. Thankfully, he agreed. With Nick on board and support from the existing production supervisor, Tim Fee, a calm, efficient and politically astute fixer, we got to work. The first stop was the production centre, located in a disused woollen mill, Sunnybank Mills, at Farsley near Leeds, to meet the cast and crew. I was hoping to reassure them that I was not there as the proverbial axeman, but wanted to spend a bit of time looking at everything and then talking to them as we went along. As expected, they were a bit reticent at first but gradually seemed to relax, with a couple seeking me out to tell me it was about time something was done. The shop floor is always the first to know.

The next task was to reassure the researcher and script assistant that they were secure while seeking their opinions of the writers. Like the director roster, I felt there were too many of them really to take ownership and feel part of the actual production process. I slimmed down both teams, melding three of the writers from *Brookie*, Allan Swift, Andy Lynch and Kathleen Potter, with the two main writers from *Emmerdale*, who between them possessed all the programme's history, Bill Lyons and David Joss Buckley. With those five writers we ran the programme for almost a year as we rationalised the character list and locations, then developed new characters.

I discovered that my old sparing partner from *Tucker's Luck*, Mr BBC himself, Darryl Blake, was already on the directors' roster so I kept him, again retaining some of the programme's history, and persuaded Colin Cant, who had kicked off *Grange Hill* and *County Hall* for me, to come up and join the team. I then asked Ken Horn, who had shot *What Now?* but had progressed to directing at *Brookie*, to come over and take control of the actual plane crash itself.

The actual idea for the plane crash came not from the Lockerbie tragedy, as the tabloids were quick to assume, but from a crash that had happened eighteen days later. The British Midland Flight 92 that had crashed at Kegworth just off the M1 in Leicestershire. This was the one that was more prominent in my mind because British Midland flew in and out of Liverpool Airport and I had a frequent-flyer card. I might well have been on that very aircraft at some time. These things do stay with you. The Air India Flight 118, in June 1985, is believed to be the first jumbo jet to be blown up by a terrorist bomb. It was en route from Montreal to Delhi, via London, and came down in the Irish Sea. All 329 people on board, including 280 Canadians, were killed. It was only when deciding to go for the Christmas scheduling option that similarities with Pan Am Flight 103 would become apparent, along with the unfortunate timing of the Kegworth disaster only eighteen days later.

Appreciating that there would inevitably be some comparisons, I asked the researchers to get me a list of all such crashes since 1972, when British European Airways Flight 548 went down in Staines killing all 118 people on board and making it the world's then biggest air disaster. That research showed that there was a plane crash about every six days, somewhere in the world, excluding classified military operations. In 1993 there were sixty-seven. We all had to keep reminding ourselves of the number of flights across the world and the number of miles flown. It was still by far the safest way to travel. We also had to keep reminding ourselves that although Pan Am 103 had entered the public's consciousness, with the graphic news footage showing the almost complete nose of the downed jumbo, it was the result of a major terrorist incident and not mechanical failure or pilot error.

Tragic though it was, a plane dropping out of the sky was perfectly feasible and would make for compelling drama. If we got it right. And we would do that by remaining true to the principle of endeavouring to make our fictional universe as realistic as we could.

I would leave Ken Horn, Nick Prosser and Tim Fee to figure out how best to portray the crash, while I worked with the writers on what consequences we wanted to stem from it all. From my early viewing I thought we needed to pull back together the Tates and the Sugdens, who had been allowed to drift apart under the twin pressures of wanting to keep the cast but still find new stories for them.

Something else that had been allowed to fade from prominence was the character of stalwart Seth Armstrong (aka Stan Richards), who was to *Emmerdale* what Harry Cross was to *Brookie*. He would be revived, along with a few others as we went into *Emmerdale: Resurrection*.

We tweaked the existing scripts for the week before to place everyone where we wanted them, in and around The Woolpack, and then just started with the plane dropping out of the sky. The first five episodes would be taken up with the shock and aftermath as people came to terms with what had happened and started to put into perspective what really mattered in their lives. Out of this we would bring the families back together. Like *Brookie* and *Hollyoaks*, much of this is detailed on Wikipedia and the numerous fan sites, so there is probably no need for me to go into detail about what appeared on screen, but the aim was not, as the tabloids automatically reported, to 'kill off most of the cast', so much as to put them back together.

The Tates, for instance, were by then all estranged. Frank and Kim (aka Norman Bowler and Claire King) were the *Dallas*-style power couple – with Claire able to beguile the male audience every bit as well as Mandy Burton – but they had separated. We decided that their twelve-month arc would be a typical romantic storyline, starting with the plane crash making them realise what they had lost, then struggling to come back together and ending in a form of soap Royal Wedding at the end of the year. Zoe (aka Leah Bracknell), Frank's daughter and Kim's stepdaughter, would similarly come back into the family fold after seeing the horrors of the crash. To play against this, we would put their son Chris (aka Peter Amory) in a wheelchair, just as his wife, Kathy (aka Malandra Burrows), was about to leave him. She would stay with him, and we would then explore Chris's frustrations, anger, bitterness and coming to terms with sudden disability as he would know that Kathy had only acted from pity. She too, like Bobby after Sheila's rape, would be another victim of this life-changing moment.

To bring the Sugdens back together we used the traditional family gathering, and Sheila Mercier (aka Annie Sugden) was persuaded to come back for a few episodes as she had been with the programme from the first scene of the very first episode in 1972. If we were going to 'start again' it would be both fitting and newsworthy to have her back. As for Seth, well, he was safe but his dog Smoky was condemned to perish in the plane crash. There's a terrible gag in there but I'll leave it to other people's imaginations.

By the time we had gone through the cast and character list the eventual death toll was to be four, three of whom had already decided to leave the programme. That left the production death toll at one, not counting Smoky. Not quite the 'cast wipe-out' everyone was predicting or fearing. The real drama is always in those left behind, so it was the consequences and after-effects we were primarily looking at. Every family was touched in some way and, in returning to the programme's USP, we also focused on something that *Brookie*, *EastEnders* or *Corrie* couldn't: the animals. We saw the desolation of Jack Sugden walking among his dead sheep, alongside Joe sitting next to his unconscious mother, alongside Frank and Kim trying to save the horses in the barn. We even had Samson the horse find and then help rescue Chris Tate from the wine bar wreckage. Stretching it a bit, but the townies went for it.

With production looming around November, Ken Horn and Tim Fee came and told me they had been in touch with the Air Accidents Investigation Branch part of the Department of Trade, at Farnborough, and through them would be able to 'borrow' bits of other aircraft to use for the crash location. Apparently we could have anything from tail fins to fully intact engines. Aware of public sensibilities I asked them to make sure that we did not end up with anything from a civil disaster, especially Kegworth or Lockerbie. They assured me that wouldn't happen, and by the time I went out to see the dressed location, the designers had done their usual work of sculpting a part of the fictional universe. It looked exactly like any plane crash site seen on any news network anywhere in the world. When it came to the shoot there was one fantastic shot of a wing tip coming directly at Joe Sugden's car, causing him to swerve off the road.

They had achieved it by using two cranes. One to suspend the wing, and another to pull it backwards and high into the air. When it was released it did as it was designed to do, and glided down towards and level with the ground. As I said, easy. If you know how. Just as they had spent days walking across fields scattering debris on the ground, in the trees and hedges, forming the trail and shape of where the plane had impacted. They had aircraft seats placed at odd angles, always shot from the rear, and one really harrowing detail from one of the research documents: a baby's cot perched high in the trees. We decided it was too much for ITV at 7.00 p.m. and brought the moment home by having Frank Tate carry a dead baby into the temporary morgue. It was meant to shock. To remind everyone, just as the very first episode opened in 1972, at the funeral of Annie Sugden's husband, that something life changing for these characters had just happened.

To reinforce this I also had the name of the fictional village changed from Beckindale to, well, Emmerdale. It was scripted as a form of commemorative symbol, but was really to clear up Production confusion. Originally the programme had been about Emmerdale Farm but then the focus moved to the nearby village, Beckindale, and then, because it was not about a farm any more, the producers decided to drop the 'Farm' bit, so it became a programme called

Emmerdale about a village called Beckindale. A bit like *Brookside* being about Meadowcroft Close. With a changed village name, we cleaned up the titles, keeping the shot of the spring lambs playing in the fields. The townies loved them too.

With everything now coming into place, John Fairley called me and said they were having a bit of trouble with the network. Transmission was going to be over the New Year holiday. The first episode would go out on 30 December in its normal 7 p.m. slot, and then pick up the following Tuesday for three nights. This was far from ideal, but it did have the advantage of having the actual crash as the Thursday hook, and a whole weekend of media specu-lation and, therefore, promotion, to follow. However, there was a snag. Carlton – who else? – wanted to opt out of the agreed four-night run and play the first episode at a different time from everyone else. But if it didn't hit the media in London at the same time as everywhere else we would lose impact, as most of the media over New Year would be London-based. It would be *Going Out* all over again.

Paul Jackson was then MD at Carlton, but before joining their bid against Thames had been a powerful force for independent production. I gave him a call and said Fairley must have got hold of the wrong end of the stick as he thought Carlton were trying to block the four-night run. Surely that couldn't be the case, as I had lost out to Granada because the ITC said I was not focused enough on the network. Now, here I was, an independent, trying to help the network and hearing some garbled story that Carlton, his Carlton, which had won its franchise on the independent publishing model, was trying to scupper the best soap storyline ITV had ever had. Well, why not? We sparred a bit, but in the end I said it would either work and he would get his ad revenue, or it wouldn't and he'd get the headache of trying to make a programme of his own. He said he thought Fairley must have got it wrong.

I later told Fairley that he must have been mistaken, as I'd spoken to Paul and was convinced he would never do anything like that. He gave me one of his grins. I gave him one back. We left it at that, and then grinned more broadly as the network confirmed the episodes would run as planned. As if any ITV company would miss out on a cynical ratings-grabbing exercise!

Whatever anyone called it, it worked. Within seconds of the credits going up on transmission the kitchen phone rang. It was John Fairley. A very happy John Fairley. You did it. You actually did it! It's a bit early to know, John. Listen, I've been around this game long enough and the French have a word for people like you. Do they? Yes. *Réalisateur*. And you're one. And worth every bloody penny. You've made all our New Years happy.

And so I had. When the figures came in *Emmerdale* had actually hit 18.5 million, double the previous week and the highest rating the programme had ever had. With that one episode, it had it gone from being pretty much ignored by the national press, to stepping out of the shadow cast by *Coronation Street* once and for all.

Back at *Brookside*, I don't think any of us really knew what we were signing up for in Majorca when we embarked on what became known as the Jordache saga. By the time the plane had come down on *Emmerdale*, Trevor had been buried under the patio for six months and Mal was spinning every narrow escape from discovery he could. It had got to the point when the critics had started to mutter about it going on too long and even at storyline conferences the writers were beginning to agitate about digging up the body. However we resisted all these calls, as we wanted to carry on as long as we could, as in the original outline I'd faxed over to Mal. Still the pressure kept building, with words like 'ridiculous' starting to creep into the comment pieces, until around February 1994. Then police started to search the home and garden of serial killer Fred West.

Suddenly we went from ridiculous to prescient, and even to tame as more and more horrific details emerged about what the Wests had been up to. Almost overnight everyone started to take a different perspective on the Jordache storyline, as though finally getting the point that Mandy (aka Sandra Maitland), Beth (aka Anna Friel) and Rachel (aka Tiffany Chapman) were not killers, but victims. The cries to bring up Trevor abated slightly, although the writers were always champing at the bit, eager to get on to the next phase of the story. However, as long as we could keep spinning it, we would hold off. Until we needed a ratings-grabbing exercise.

The plan for the twelve months I had agreed with John Fairley was to include the initial impact, a mid-year spike, and then another big storyline on the anniversary of the first to maintain momentum. The mid-year spike came from an armed robbery and siege at the village post office, which also brought YTV's first-ever regulatory reprimand.

As we had now done two stories that brought outside threats to the village, I wondered if the next one should come from inside the community itself and returned to the notion of Eyam: a plague-like disease that would infect and affect the entire village. Just as the Black Death was brought to the Derbyshire village by the fleas on a piece of tailor's cloth, then perhaps we could develop something around the farm animals infecting the village.

To me it was another great 'what if' story. What would the village do? Would they seal themselves off? Who would organise things? Who would stay, come in or break out to be with their loved ones? Perfect situation again, for an isolated village community to explore these great human dilemmas. Or that's what I thought. YTV panicked. Well, some of them did. Keith Richardson knew that my time was coming to an end and was hunting for a new series producer. He had also had YTV's factual department come up with a research document that proved, conclusively, that animals could not pass any disease to humans.

I was never quite sure why he was so terrified of the story; perhaps he thought it would bring them into conflict with the regulators again. Plagues at 7 p.m. on ITV? Perhaps he was right. I'm still not sure. But at least they now had the Dingles. I handed over my custodial armband as, after all, it was not my show. It now had a steady audience of around 14 million, 50 per cent up on what it had been twelve months earlier, and was taken more seriously by network, press, and, most importantly, the audience. I left them and took the plague story back to *Brookie*. Everyone laughed. Then came Mad Cow Disease and Swine Flu.

18

Hollyoaks (1996–2003)

'The ITC have deemed *Hollyoaks* a children's programme.'
– *Channel 4, 1996*

In spring 1994, the *Brookside* long-term planning meeting was in the Lake District. While we pondered what would happen in 1995, the main item on the agenda was the Jordaches. On one of my trips back and forth to Emmerdale, passing the farmhouse in the middle of the M62, I wondered, as I suppose many do, as to why whoever lived there never moved but instead let the motorway be built around them. That had taken me back to the Jordache research that indicated that if people were driven to kill someone and bury them in their garden, they never moved. They remained to protect the evidence of their crime. A form of self-imposed house arrest. The fear of discovery had been a fascinating part of the story arc, but Mal had spun that as far as we could.

If the actors chose to go then we would be left with two unsatisfactory outcomes. One was that they might take the evidence with them. Macabre, but interesting for a week or two and then the story would be all off screen. The other was that they would leave it behind. We would then still have the discovery moment, but it would also be short term, with the main story off screen. We would have the story of the rose gardener who discovered a carpet, rather than the murder investigation it led to. Time to dig him up while we still had the cast.

Once that decision had been made timing was important, in both universes. We felt that if we were going to get the most out of the story then we would have to have a guaranteed run with the characters and, tracking back from the dates that we would have to lose the actors, the box on the Storyboard for Jan '95 became the focal point. Everything would then flow from there. On 31 January 1995, 8.95 million people watched Eddie Banks (aka Paul Broughton) and Jimmy Corkhill (aka Dean Sullivan) discover Trevor's body. Whether this or the kiss between Beth Jordache and Margaret Clemence (aka Nicola Stephenson) was the biggest, best or most-remembered moment of the whole Jordache saga still keeps weekend seminars busy, but in raw numbers the 'body under the patio' is generally regarded as having achieved the highest viewing figures. It would be nice to be able to say that everything went according to plan, that we got the timing absolutely right, but fate, as it often does, played its part. On 1 January 1995, Fred West killed himself.

While I have never denied that part of the job of driving a soap is to have one eye on the viewing figures, this was one 'cynical ratings-grabbing exercise' that we could not claim. We had killed and buried Trevor before even the news of Fred West's crimes broke, and we had decided to exhume him months before West killed himself. It was the mysterious workings of fate at work again, but what West's suicide also meant for us was that we were released from the strictures of regulatory impartiality. While he was still awaiting trial we were caught under the *sub judice* rules, which meant we had to double-and triple-check every word in the Jordache scenes to make sure that we were not in any way offering an opinion that could be prejudicial to his receiving a fair trial. But as in the mysterious ways of British bureaucracy, while we were now free to comment publicly, a bigger question soon emerged. By running such a storyline were we inciting people to murder their abusive spouses? It would be fine for us now to comment on one of history's most infamous mass murderers who committed his crimes long before we thought about our story, but now we were being challenged about whether we were likely to encourage people to do something similar. We had stumbled on to the developing regulatory concept of 'imitative behaviour': television should not portray any anti-social behaviour that people can imitate.

This was another of those well-intentioned but not thought-through concepts that came out of the 1990 Broadcasting Act, to try and reach a common understanding of what was and was not 'acceptable' viewing. I do not doubt for one minute that the people who act as our regulators are sincere in their intentions, but the trouble is, like the police, they end up having to impose and enforce regulations that can sometimes seem daft.

There were quite a few of those moments as we progressed the story, like being told we could show a stabbing so long as we didn't show the knife. The on-screen Jordache saga is well documented and could keep anyone at their search engines for days on end. It has been called a great piece of drama, and one that helped change the way the law treated women accused of fighting back against abusive husbands. That is not what we set out to do. It was never the primary purpose. Nor has it ever been my purpose in writing about social issues. I'm not sure that television can have that effect. But what it can do, and what I have always striven for, is to highlight an issue and in doing so perhaps, just perhaps, help provide a more sympathetic environment in which real campaigners will receive a better hearing. Policy- and law-makers, as that never-seen Wenham Report indicated, are part of the general television audience. If they are touched by a piece of drama they may, just may, listen a bit more attentively.

For me then, the off-screen Jordache saga was equally fascinating, veering as it did between receiving establishment praise and establishment sanction. While we would be getting into trouble with the regulators for portraying domestic violence, we would also have Sandra Maitland (aka Mandy Jordache) appearing on the front page of the *Independent* with QCs Cherie Booth and Helena Kennedy, to attract media exposure for the legal arguments as to why it needed to change. The argument revolved around the concept of provocation. At the time, to truncate and paraphrase a complicated legal concept, if a sixteen-stone body-builder came home and found his wife in bed with someone else and killed her, he could claim a defence of provocation and be found guilty of manslaughter. However, if the same body-builder came home drunk and beat his eight-stone wife unconscious every night until she could stand it no longer or feared for her children, and she stabbed him in his sleep, she could claim no defence of provocation and would be tried for murder. The concept hinged purely on timing. A man acting instantly out of passion . . . a woman having to wait for the right moment. One provocation. One premeditation. Such is the stuff of law. Such is the stuff of drama.

Yet, despite good intentions all round, we found ourselves in the same moral maze Zammo and I had stumbled into on *Grange Hill*. How can you adequately explore the issue of drugs without showing why people use them? We saw Mandy and Beth receive months of provocation, until they were driven by despair and fear that Trevor was starting to abuse his younger daughter Rachel to the point where they planned to kill him. From that moment on we were in trouble with our regulators, and Beth was condemned to death although, in the real universe, we didn't fully appreciate it at the time.

Having failed with weedkiller, they then tried crushing up tablets and spiking his food, but when that didn't work and he turned on them, threatening to kill Beth, in the heat of the moment Mandy picked up a kitchen knife and stabbed him. This was the real crime in the real universe: not the murder itself, but using a knife. We had broken a rule that said common household implements should not be used in television scenes of domestic violence.

The bureaucratic reasoning was, and probably still is, that as the most common weapons in domestic violence are household implements, especially kitchen knives, television must not be seen to reinforce this by illustrating events that could easily be imitated. I hope, like me, you can see both the good intent and the absolute nonsense of this circuitous logic. The point is, surely, that people are driven to violence not by the availability or proliferation of kitchen utensils but by psychological disorder, whether short- or long-term, induced or inherent.

Although some critics said we had shown an ABC guide on how to kill someone, was *Brookside* the first drama ever to think of poisoning a character? Were we the first to think of stabbing a character? What does that say for the teaching of British history or Shakespeare? Yet this was not the problem. Nor was the actual murder. The precise charge was that we had included a shot of Mandy dropping the knife she had grabbed to stop Trevor battering Beth. We went back and forth with esoteric arguments about how short the clip was, or that the knife didn't have any blood on it, but in the end it was down to, 'Thou shalt not show a knife.' We had.

Channel 4 got a yellow card. One more and it would be red, the equivalent of being sent off, and a fine. Up to 3 per cent of their ad revenue. At the time, that was around £24 million and this was enough to make them for ever nervous as there appeared to be no clear guidelines on how long the yellow card would apply.

It was for this reason that in one of the *Brookside* videos I had Jimmy Corkhill reach for something to defend himself when he thinks someone is about to break into the house. It turns out to be Barry Grant, and Jimmy is shown to be holding a potato peeler. Barry looks at it, then at Jimmy: 'What you going to do with that? Peel me to death?' It was a poke at the regulators as, to me, a lot of this sort of intervention was a complete waste of everyone's time. It was also an insult to the audience's intelligence, which was often proven when talking direct to the public at the Script to Screen events we used to run.

Through those Q&A sessions and subsequent debates, it would become clear to us that the public neither knew nor agreed with a lot of what the well-intentioned regulators were doing on their behalf, and, lest we forget, at their expense. Still, I'd like to repeat what I have emphasised so many times in the past: that I do not believe in total deregulation as there are common responsibilities we all must share in a democratic society that values free and open debate. Total deregulation allows the irresponsible, or plain stupid, free rein to cause harm to others. What I have always pressed for is sensible and proportional regulation that reflects life as it is, rather than how we may wish it to be in our own personal universe.

That means there are certain times of day when certain types of programming are likely to cause offence to certain groups. I learned this lesson early on with *Brookside*, but I also learned that the audience is discriminatory in its choice of viewing. The aim then should be better information, to allow the audience to make informed choices as to what, on what channel and at what time, to watch so that they do not simply stumble across content they may find inappropriate. That will always happen, of course, but should be met with an element of common sense. If forty people out of 4 million complain, it should not be treated as cause for official concern or action.

At the time of the Jordache saga, we, along with other programme-makers, suffered because there was no degree of proportionality or selectivity in the regulatory response. Even if just one person complained, there would be no effort to determine who or what they were. It could quite easily have been a journalist up to mischief, but we would all then have to go into a full quasi-judicial process of providing 'evidence' as to why we'd included the incident in question. When I once challenged the regulators on this, their response was brilliantly bureaucratic: we are empowered to investigate but we have no resources to do so. The real cops could make great use of that.

That sense of proportionality and common sense should have been widely extended. People coming to watch *Brookside* knew it was not *Coronation Street*, but the regulatory regime dismissed this notion by adopting something called the 'family viewing policy'. This deemed, in effect, that programme-makers had to assume that families could be watching together and therefore content should not include anything that might upset children. Initially this did not cause us too much concern as we had always operated the 'child of eight' rule: if you could explain a scene in terms a child of that age would understand, you should not offend anybody. The problem came when the age-old, almost ancient concept of 'the watershed' was reinterpreted. There is academic work to be done on this whole subject but, broadly speaking, there was always an understanding that 9 p.m. signalled the switch from 'family-oriented' programming to more challenging genres, perhaps reinforced by *Brookie*'s problems with language in 1982. However, people being people, this began to be treated as a finite threshold so programmes began to appear with swearing or violent content featured just after 9 p.m. With three regulators, the ITC, BCC and BSC being available to complainants after the 1990 Act, it was not long before this became an issue and the decision was made to 'suggest' that 9 p.m. should not be seen as finite, but only the start of a progressive move to more challenging content; 10 p.m. was 'suggested' as the new finite threshold, when most young people would, or should, be away from the TV, safely packed off to their bedrooms . . . with unlimited and unmoderated access to the internet.

Once the watershed was rolled back like this, for *Brookie* it meant we were now in even shallower water, as there was no consideration given to different watersheds for different channels. Except on Sky. Those of you with a Sky Movies subscription might have spotted that they started putting up warning captions on different channels highlighting their own watersheds, some as early as 8 p.m. This seemed like a common-sense approach from Rupert Murdoch's outfit, the man once deemed not 'fit and proper' to run LWT, yet here were we, MerseyTV, the makers of *Brookside*, deemed to be 'fit and proper' people during the franchise rejection, now starting to come under intense scrutiny for doing what we had always been doing at 8 p.m.

It didn't stop there. Throughout the 1990s regulatory pressures intensified so that we ended up with another bizarre concept, that of the so-called 'susceptible adult'. This was supposed to stop anything going out that might offend or affect a susceptible adult, but a definition of that was hard to come by. I suggested, tongue very firmly in cheek, that Liverpool FC being beaten by Manchester United at Anfield might generate 40,000 susceptible adults for a few hours, only for a 'regulocrat' to come back and say they agreed, if a film about football violence was shown immediately after. The really daft thing about this sort of debate is that you can sometimes see the point. Which obscures the real issue. What makes these adults susceptible in the first place? Is that not the issue? The minority with a problem. Not the majority who see no problem. Unfortunately it's a bit like unemployment. Easy to mask. Difficult to eradicate.

Now, if you've been sticking with this you should have grasped that as a drama producer you have to be aware of the so-called 'light touch regulations' concerning impartiality, socially unacceptable behaviour, the portrayal of social and anti-social drugs and stimulants, undue prominence, the rolling watershed, imitative behaviour, susceptible adults, to say nothing of things like libel, obscenity and blasphemy, but, to top it all, there is one more card to play: 'cumulative effect'.

This, as far as I can recall, started out as a concept related to language. Going back to the Southern TV 'defuckification memo', saying 'bloody' once may be OK, but saying it six times in the same scene escalates its impact and creates a cumulative effect. Basically the more you say it the worse it becomes. Again, I'm not really sure I agree with that as it could equally be argued that the more common something is, the more devalued it becomes. The key phrase though is, 'could be argued'. As with most of these sociological interventions, like surveys, it depends on who is saying it and who is paying for the research.

We ended up with an army of compliance officers checking, double-checking and then, worst of all, second-guessing anything and everything. They in turn start putting pressure on everybody else to be vigilant so that in the end it filters down the chain until you end up in the situation of self-censorship, as I had found myself in the early days fretting about saying the word 'homosexual'. I eventually took the stance that we were not there to do the regulators' job for them, as people will always err on the side of caution. If in doubt, take it out. But we would do what we thought was accurate and reasonable and the broadcaster would have to convince us that it was unacceptable by, if necessary, challenging the regulator. That, I think, is a more healthy relationship. If everyone simply accepts the status quo then we make no progress.

Earlier, I outlined problems encountered with the *Grange Hill* and *Brookside* anti-drugs storylines, but let me share a couple of other examples of the sometimes confusing world of regulation that I got personally involved in:

- Early in Tracy Corkhill (aka Justine Kerrigan)'s relationship with Jamie Henderson (aka Sean McKee), he of the shrunken sweater incident, we did a typical rites of passage story of parents finding their teenagers' contraceptives, but were asked by the regulator to explain why we had given 'undue prominence' to a packet of Durex. We'd held the shot for about 1.5 seconds. I wrote back and said it was to help illiterate young people recognise at least one brand image. We got a tick.

- One of our actresses was pregnant and wanted to keep it as private as she could for as long as she could so we shot round the developing bump, until the paparazzi caught her on a long lens at the Brookside shops. To stop this happening again we put up advertising hoardings to the side of the petrol station. In order to make these appear fresh and contemporary I asked Publicity to offer the sites to charities on a rolling four-weekly basis. If they supplied the posters we would give them free space. It worked well for a time until the regulator queried it. Why were we giving 'undue prominence' to some charities over others? We weren't, it was open to all. Ah-ha, not ones who are not big enough to advertise. I was not charitable in my response. It went away.

- Eleven-year-old Josh McLoughlin (aka Jack McMullen) was seen cooking himself some beans and the regulatory challenge came. Imitative Behaviour. It might tempt children into cooking for themselves and they could get burned. True, until David Hanson, who took most of the weight of the last few years of *Brookie*, pointed out that his own son, the same age as Josh, had just won a badge at the Cubs, for cooking beans. It went away.
- The same Josh climbed out of a window at 8.00 p.m. Imitative Behaviour. Children might climb out of windows. We challenged it as the very same week we had exactly the same scenario in *Grange Hill* at 5.00 p.m. No reply.
- Ron Dixon (aka Vince Earl) put a sign up in his shop saying 'Only Two Kids at a Time'. It was a comedy scene illustrating shopkeepers' frustrations and worries about kids nicking things, but the regulatory call came. Undue Prominence. Why had we used the back of a Flora margarine box? I wrote back and said it was for one shot and a random choice of packaging by the Design Dept but Flora was legal. Why hadn't they had a go at *Corrie* a week earlier when Vera Duckworth was seen standing in front of the cigarette display for several scenes? Tobacco advertising was illegal. The reply was that they saw us and didn't see *Corrie*.
- But probably my favourite was when Max Farnham (aka Stephen Pinder) thought new wife Jacqui (aka Alex Fletcher) had been killed in a road accident and they were so overjoyed to see each other they had sex, in a hospital bed. Taste and Decency: 'inappropriate content.' Because, I am not making this up, '. . . *the wife was seen to be enjoying it too much.*' I wrote back and asked if it would have been satisfactory if she had not enjoyed it. Silence.

It did occur to me that we had a harder time than others because our regulators actually watched, rather than reviewed, *Brookie*, but mostly these things were sorted out in private exchanges behind the scenes, usually between the production and legal departments. Occasionally they became more difficult to deal with, as when the regulators, all three, took against the Simpsons' incest storyline. That culminated in another official censure, not quite a yellow card but the Broadcasting Standards Council forced Channel 4 to broadcast an apology in 1996 for showing brother and sister Nat (aka John Sandford) and Georgia Simpson (aka Helen Grace) in bed together. At the time I was widely quoted as saying 'we got it wrong', which was taken to mean the storyline. What I was actually talking about was the timing.

This was an interesting debate because, again with the benefit of hindsight, it is clear that it marked the beginning of the end of the old Channel 4. Michael Grade, who had acted in many ways as a benevolent custodian of Jeremy Isaacs's original vision, was getting itchy feet and a new wave of management was about to descend. Channel 4 would abandon the role of facilitating publisher of independent ideas and adopt the command-and-control mentality of a producing broadcaster with a centralised corporate agenda. Instead of standing alone and slightly nearer to the public-service ethos of the BBC, Channel 4 would try to become a global media company and come to see the BBC as a competitor. As such it made them, in my view, more compliant when challenged by regulation. This had more to do with personalities than structure. It had more to do with personal ambition than public service.

The first signs of this should have been the subtle but discernible requirements on us to keep up the ratings, though that was, after all, part of the television game. But the underlying build up of pressure probably started when the programme went from two to three nights a week back in 1991. The same year, coincidentally, that Tim Berners-Lee unveiled the world's first website, as well as the first year that Channel 4 started collecting its own advertising revenue instead of relying on a tax on ITV. Ratings became more important. However, in another typically British bureaucratic fix, to ease the transition Channel 4 had to pay ITV 50 per cent of any surplus income over and above their historic running costs, while in return ITV would provide a safety net should income fail to cover those costs.

The idea was to make Channel 4 more commercial, but not too commercial, while providing a guaranteed income to protect its minorities and public-service remit. But this changed the nature of the channel, and it was probably no coincidence that *Brookside*, its biggest revenue earner, then increased its output by 50 per cent. This was never formally discussed with us, but was implicitly understood. That was another part of the game, and the reason why the introduction of the new Brookside Parade was accompanied by a whodunit high-impact storyline: Who killed Sue Sullivan (aka Annie Miles) and baby Danny? This shift in both the channel's and the programme's intent was not seen, never mind identified, as an issue at the time; merely as part of a continuing and mutually supportive relationship. It was what we did. Together.

In fact, over the next few years, with Jimmy Corkhill (aka Dean Sullivan)'s drug problems, the Rogers family continuing to face issues like Geoff (aka Kevin Carson)'s dyslexia, Katy (aka Diane Burke) being bullied at school and Sammy (aka Rachel Lindsay)'s alcoholism, and the Farnhams' nanny Margaret being romantically involved with a young priest, the programme continued to deliver familiar, challenging, but lower-key storylines. Slowly, though, things began to shift, with the advent of the Jordache storyline, driven by Mal Young, incorporating the first pre-watershed lesbian kiss, together with a rating of 6 million viewers.

This dramatic moment came from Mal and became so iconic that it featured in the 2012 Olympic opening ceremony, written by ex-Brookie Frank Cottrell Boyce. But it emerged once more from research. It came out of the advice we were being given about sex abuse and how it was not uncommon for abused teenage girls to turn to, or experiment within, the perceived safety of same-sex relationships. At the same time we had the emotional and sexual confusion swirling round Margaret's teenage relationship with Father Derek (aka Clive Moore), so the two stories collided within that momentary relationship. It created a real media sensation, with the actresses instantly propelled to gay icon status as part of the then recent discovery of and fascination with the term Lipstick Lesbian, used to describe, or perhaps label, gay or bisexual women who dressed and acted in a feminine manner. In other words, not the boiler-suited, Doc Martens-wearing caricatures, but people who looked like Anna Friel and Nicola Stephenson.

No one was uncomfortable with all this and I do not recall too much of a reaction from either public or regulators, while C4 loved the ratings. The Jordache storyline then took centre-stage, and by the time we reached its conclusion towards the end of 1995, the programme's ratings were running at their highest-ever averages. Naturally, everyone wanted more. And pressure built on to us deliver more. That was where we got it wrong. We went too fast, too soon with the Simpsons incest storyline.

By the time we got to the Jordache trial, media speculation was at an all-time high so we knew we would have a really difficult time trying to keep secret what was probably our biggest story twist, the trial verdict. We also knew that the shoot, post-production and C4 were the three most likely leak points, simply due to the timings of past press stories. To keep the trial verdict as secret as possible, Mal and I would plot at least two, possibly three, separate outcomes for the trial, and from that moment we would storyline and script alternative plotlines, right down to the shoot, post-production and delivery to C4. At no stage would anyone except he and I know the final verdict. If anything leaked it could only be that Mandy and Beth were either guilty or not guilty, and that didn't sound too much like a front-page exclusive.

Mal and I loved the idea, of course. Philip thought it would make more column inches than any leak, but Alexis was already punching her calculator. You do know how much this will cost? I looked at Mal and grinned. How can you think of money at a time like . . . ? Because that's what I'm here for. But I get it. You figure the storylines and scripts; I'll work on the production logistics. And that's one of the reasons I love her. A 'yes' accountant.

Gradually we pushed and pulled and agreed with C4 that they would not know either, until as close to transmission as possible when they would do all the usual technical and compliance tests. Then another problem came up. To shoot on location meant working when the courts didn't, at weekends. This would mean working over eight successive weekends, which would be too long and increase the risk of leaks. Driving home one night, Alexis and I talked over the idea of actually building our own courtroom. The cost of sixteen days' location catering, travel, overtime, etc. might not be that far off the construction costs. By the time we drove back in the following day we knew where the court would be. The Design Dept would be moving out of their prop store.

Not only would we now have decoy scripts, but we would have total control in a locked-down location. It was one of the best sets we ever built and was designed to double up as a large meeting room, in which the storylines, scripts and production meetings were held from 1995 until 2003 when *Brookie* finished and it became the courtroom for the afternoon drama of the same name, *The Courtroom*. Amortisation of costs at its best.

Come the day and we actually got away with it. Just. There was only one scare, when we had to tell the floor manager and director of the verdict scripts which one was 'likely' to be used, to make sure we really got the reaction we were looking for. They shot the decoy first and everyone was pleased. Then the floor manager asked everyone to reset with the immortal line, 'Places, everyone, while we go for the real ending . . .' A moment's frisson. But not many had heard. They then went on to shoot with the words 'Make it as real as we can, please . . .'

No one apart from me, Mal and Peter Ansorge at Channel 4 actually knew the real verdict until it was transmitted, and then there was uproar. How could we send both women to jail? Everyone knew they were right to do what they did. Trevor deserved it. All true, except that was the point of the *Independent*'s front-page story: no matter what they pleaded in mitigation, the law could not accept provocation as the women's defence. They had plotted and conspired to kill him and that was a separate charge, conspiracy to murder. This was what condemned Beth to an early grave.

There was outrage about the verdict. Press, critics and public all railed against it. It was wrong. Not fair. Set the course of equality back. There was even a demonstration outside MerseyTV's gates. C4's own *Right to Reply* decided they'd come up and do a 'special' from the courtroom. When they arrived we discovered they had invited a couple of the demonstrators to sit in, which got my media antennae twitching. What were they up to? I found out as soon as I was 'called' for interview. The techies told me they had set every-thing up to focus on the dock. The 'members of the audience' were in the jury rows. Nice try. I entered through the main doors so they couldn't even get a shot of me entering the dock, and said I would sit down at the front to one side. As I did I turned three-quarters on, so the camera had to come round to get me, without the dock shot. All I would say was that the story was accurate but not over, so stay tuned. The audience did.

While the Jordache Saga was unfolding in the fictional universe, the debate around the new Channel 5 was contracting. Once again we were courted by various consortia, including some of the names like Virgin and Marconi we had talked to in 1990 about the North West. The big issue could once again be traced all the way back to 1926: frequency availability. From the mapping exercise done back in the early 1950s it was clear that there would only be enough frequency spectrum to allow for four national channels: the then current BBC, proposed ITV, and possible BBC2 and ITV2. What channels would be left would only be available to about 70 per cent of the population. It took until 1990 for this to be 'allowed,' utilising Channels 35 and 37, nominally dubbed, unsurprisingly, the Fifth Channel. Even with this, there was still enough spare space to provide coverage for around 60 per cent of the population, nominally dubbed, unsurprisingly, the Sixth Channel. Since 1983 I had been asking, unsuccessfully, various Broadcasting Ministers to allow us to trial a TV station for Liverpool utilising one of the available frequencies that would allow these two new channels. The answer was always the same: they were 'not minded' to consider local television at that time.

If there were many opportunities missed in the 1990 Act, local television was certainly a big one. But it was felt to be too much of a challenge, both technically, which it wasn't, and from a legislative view, which it was. It was completely ignored in favour of Channel 5, despite the time I had spent lobbying David Mellor, who would later come to fame for wearing a football shirt with someone he shouldn't have done. Local television was finally offered in 2012, sixty years after being mapped out in the 1950s.

However, there was another complication with Channel 5. As well as only being available to 70 per cent of the population, Channels 35 and 37 would clash with many people's videocassette recorders (VCRs). This was because when VCRs played back recordings, they did so using Channel 35. Why did they do this? Because historically Air Traffic Control in London had used that frequency. Once they upgraded their systems the frequencies could be released and thus provide the basis for a national network. Because of this London was going to be the most expensive region to start up a new fifth channel as whoever was awarded the new licence would have to take on the task of retuning the VCR of any affected household.

I remember sitting in the House of Commons Members' tea rooms, trying to explain this to a Chair of the Media Select Committee on Broadcasting, and wondering if the problem was not actually with the technology but sitting in front of me. I also remember having yet another lunch, this time with the Permanent Secretary at the Department for Culture, Media and Sport, Hayden Phillips, a mandarin's mandarin if I ever met one, still lobbying to get Channel 5 based outside London. I remember this lunch particularly well because I splashed tomato sauce from the spaghetti on to my white shirt. Not a good thing to do in front of a mandarin.

Still, I was from the North and left him with a map, prepared by Philip Reevell after he'd analysed the franchise awards and the winning companies' aspirations. It showed how ITV would probably look by the mid-1990s. Basically, four or five companies dividing up the Network as North, Midlands, South East and South West, probably dominated by Granada. He smiled. Surely not? It happened in 1997. Shouldn't they know this stuff if they are forming the regulation that governs it?

Recognising that local TV was dead 'for the time being', which turned out to be another twenty years, we then lobbied hard for Channel 5 to be based outside London so as to counterbalance the London-centric focus of the BBC, ITV Network and Channel 4. It would also mean that, if it started, as we suggested, along the M62 Corridor, Liverpool-Manchester-Hull, then there would be no need for so much VCR retuning and it would therefore be much easier and cheaper to start up and grow. It would also create, as we had done at Mersey, badly needed jobs. We pressed hard to have this condition inserted into the 1990 Act, but it didn't go in and Channel 5 didn't come north. The counterbalance to London-centricity was thought to be best placed . . . in London. The most expensive region to try and start it up.

By the time the ITC got round to advertising Channel 5 in 1992 we, like many others, had decided that, as with BSB, they had opted for a deep-pocket, deep-consortium operation that made little business sense. We, like many others, decided not to bother. They only received one application so decided to withdraw the offer and try again in 1994, finally awarding the licence to Channel 5 Broadcasting in October 1995. It would take them eighteen months to solve all the transmission and retuning problems and launch at 6 p.m. on Easter Sunday 1997. It has struggled ever since, and along with BSB and ITV is another example of how a heavy-handed, over-prescriptive regulatory regime has stifled growth and innovation in the UK's television industry. We could have had sixty local TV stations instead. We would have had the M62 corridor up and running in 1993. In fact, by the time Channel 5 was launched, *Hollyoaks* had been on air for six months.

As we approached the post-trial storylines on *Brookside*, the moment I had pondered alongside the M62 farmhouse arrived. Anna Friel, probably the hottest name in the UK at the time, indicated that she was thinking of moving on. Instead of just facing this moment with our long-standing friendly and subtle suggestion that 'the signed contract should be returned by 5 p.m. the following day, or be written out', things were allowed to drift. I think it was because no one wanted to face up to losing her, while C4 were piling on the pressure that we 'had to keep her', with the typical broadcaster's lack of understanding about the abolition of slavery.

With the end of Anna's contract approaching, I reviewed where we were with Mal and we both agreed we were going to lose her. Not only that, but the latest legal advice had confirmed something we had known for a few months. It all hinged on that very dramatic moment everyone had loved, Beth's court outburst when she said, basically, that they had killed Trevor, they planned it, he deserved what he got, and why wasn't he punished before? It was a brilliant television moment. We'd remember it for ever. And it meant she was guilty. We could get the murder charges reduced on appeal to manslaughter and then get them off by pushing, perhaps stretching, the provocation defence. Unfortunately, there was no defence to a charge of conspiracy to murder. There was also no judicial discretion. The only sentence was mandatory life. Beth would have to go down.

Finally we got to the crunch moment. If we couldn't keep Anna in the programme, her character would have to go off-screen. We could say she was serving life somewhere and see Mandy and Rachel going back and forth, writing letters, etc., but we had already been round the houses on whether to repeat what *EastEnders* had done when their iconic character Dirty Den (aka Leslie Grantham) went to jail. When Leslie Grantham decided to leave they concocted a story that had him sent to jail, then shot a year's worth of storyline in five weeks, which they then fed into the programme across the following year. It was a neat idea but as the year progressed this storyline began to look like a universe within a universe and further and further away from the main programme. The hope was probably that they would persuade Leslie to return, but they didn't. My gut told me that when Anna left, that would be it. She would fly. She has the aura.

Ideas for Beth's exit involved her slipping out of a conveniently unlocked external door during the Appeal hearing to a gang of militant 'lipstick lesbians' storming the court and spiriting her away, which did have a certain chaotic and poetic appeal, but I somehow felt that it would appear too easy and in many ways undermine all the effort we had gone to over the trial. The other consideration related to the rest of the cast. We wanted to keep Sandra Maitland and Tiffany Chapman (aka Rachel), and already had them signed up. We also had to avoid the audience wondering why they didn't just move away, which would be a bigger and more pertinent question if Beth were still out there somewhere. To counter this we already had something developing between Mandy and Sinbad (aka Mickey Starke), who tended to be overshadowed during the whole Jordache phenomenon, though he put in some terrific performances over this period. The only possible outcome was to ask Research to come up with some form of 'sudden teenage death syndrome'.

They came back with Hypertrophic Cardiomyopathy or HCM, which causes an excessively thick and often scarred heart muscle. High blood pressure is therefore needed to pump the blood out of the heart. Most people – the majority – can live with the condition, but because it can cause Arrhythmia (when the heart beats too fast or chaotically) there is a risk of sudden cardiac arrest. HCM had been in the news recently, as a year before Daniel Yorath, son of Terry and Christine Yorath and brother of Gabby Logan, had collapsed and died because of the condition.

So, in the same courtroom set now turned meeting room, I put on the metaphorical black cap and passed sentence. That was how Beth would go. While Mandy would be freed on appeal, she would still lose her daughter. The research also revealed something else. HCM can be hereditary. So Trevor did, in the end, kill Beth. Not only that, but Rachel would now have to live knowing that she too might be affected. The curse of Trevor would linger on. We knew this was not satisfactory, but it was the best we could do in the time available, and while it is easy to look back and say we should have known, or we should have done this, it was probably more the same problem that affects most long runners. The same thing that had *EastEnders* trying to keep Leslie Grantham. The fear of losing your star performers. I had done it with Sue Johnston and John McArdle. The lesson of all this is that the programme, in the end, is bigger than any one character. It's tough losing old friends, but when it happens, try and make sure they go with a great storyline that rapidly switches back to those left behind. And we did. As usual. We still had the Bankses' gambling addiction, the Farnhams' surrogacy, the Johnsons' euthanasia, the gas explosion on The Parade, Jimmy Corkhill's mental breakdown, Ron Dixon shooting a burglar and Anthony Murray killing Imelda Clough, all to come.

During the time when we were sorting out the Chois and developing *Brookie* for three nights a week, Michael and I were having a chat in his office . . . well, me, Michael and his TVs . . . about the relationship between C4 and Mersey TV and the industry in general. I think we were in bridge-building mode again after another light skirmish over access and control. A renewal contract had not been signed, as it never was, and a new eager beaver in finance had had a great idea. He would suspend all contract payments unless it was returned, signed, the following day. This was an interesting reversal of our own 'sign or be written out' policy. Unfortunately, it was not too clever when the Channel itself needed our tapes to keep coming on a regular basis.

I sent a note to Michael saying that I had suspended delivery of the programme until the cash was turned back on, knowing they would run out of programmes before we ran out of cash. Within thirty minutes a call came through to say it was all a misunderstanding.

With tapes and cash flowing again, I think Michael and I were smoothing things over. He said he wondered why I spent so much time on the minutiae. He reckoned I was bored. 'You know your trouble, Phil? You need another show.' I think he meant it as friendly advice, but I also remember his nonplussed expression when I asked him why would I want that? There was really nowhere else to go unless he commissioned another one and we both knew Buggins and his gang would go mad if he did, so where else was I to go? Besides, *Brookie* was not just a show. It was my programme, my company and my platform. It was a part of me as I was of it. This was probably the first time the C4 producer conundrum appeared. They always wanted me to have one, but when I did, and loosened control and let the Choi dynasty develop in collaboration with their commissioning editors, the programme suffered and I was criticised for letting someone else run it. Then, when I sorted it out and brought it back on track, I was told I needed a producer.

Of course, a few years later I did find another show, the updated version of the outline I had sent him at the BBC as part of the 5.30 format pack: a teen drama. However, once again, by the time I delivered it he was on his way elsewhere and did not see the actual launch of *Hollyoaks*.

Hollyoaks should have been a no-brainer for Channel 4, but as always with them it was a struggle. With the benefit of distance, hindsight and reflection, I can now say, hand on heart, their behaviour seems as myopic today as it did then. They told us that we would have to prove we could do it. What!?

Since 1976 I had been writing for a young audience, beginning with the scripts for ATV's *The Kids From 47A*, Southern TV's *Sally Ann, Grange Hill* and *Tucker's Luck*, and *Going Out*. Then came *Brookie* and its appeal to Yoof TV, out of which came *What Now?* and *Damon and Debbie*, all of which seemed to demonstrate some continuing interest. You could say I had form in this area.

The pitch for the new series was the same as for *Grange Hill*. A take on Kevin Costner's line from *Field of Dreams*, 'If you build it they will come.' The initial resistance to *Grange Hill* from all five major ITV companies was that kids didn't have an attention span and why would they watch a progamme about school anyway? With the teen generation, the resistance line was that 'teenagers don't watch TV' as they never sit still long enough. How hollow that all sounds now.

Something that helped with *Hollyoaks*, though, was the rise of the copycat culture. Just as one hit sci-fi progamme spawns a whole generation of wall-to-wall aliens series; or, just as the BBC needed its own soap opera after we developed *Brookie* for C4, then suddenly it seemed Aussie and US imports were all over the channels. *Neighbours, Home and Away, Beverly Hills 90210, Heartbreak High, Saved by the Bell* and *Friends*. The influx followed the same ten-year inno-vation curve that Philips electronics had indentified: five years for people to get used to an idea and five years for them to accept that it worked and wasn't going away. *Hollyoaks* aired almost exactly ten years after *Neighbours* had arrived on the BBC.

So, despite my past form, I was asked to pitch an idea. As if this wasn't galling enough, it seemed that we were also becoming victims of our own success as Mal had recently put together his 1960s drama *And The Beat Goes On* for C4. Featuring Jenny Agutter and Stephen Moore in the cast, alongside *Brookie* stalwarts like John McArdle and Danny McCall, it seemed that having this and *Brookie* would prove too much for C4 to hand the teen commission to MerseyTV. Perception over pragmatism. Again. I told the channel that while appreciating that politically, diplomatically and financially they had to be seen to be open, transparent and fair, I was not going to join the Buggins' turn lottery, or line up with all the other soap wannabes outside the Crystal Palace. Old arrogance resurfacing or increased business experience? A bit of both probably as, having gone through the back catalogue, there could not have been many other people with more experience in the genre or who could compete on price, and there was definitely no one who could shoot and amortise costs alongside *Brookie*. Not only that, but having been through previous beauty parades for the ITV franchises, BSB, and ITV's afternoon soap, then found our ideas ripped off by other people having access to our publicly available proposal documents, we were never again going to give someone else a great idea for no return.

They kept insisting that we had to take part in the formal process if we wanted to bid for the project. I talked this over with Alexis and we agreed that, while we could see Channel 4's problem, to be open, transparent and fair all they needed to do was be open, transparent and fair — and tell everyone no one could match our track record or cost. We did get a bit of coaxing and cajoling from both our own people and C4 to go through the process as, if we were right, then we would be bound to emerge with the commission. I couldn't do it. Perhaps it was my Irish Catholic upbringing, but honesty and an ethical sense of what is right and wrong are in the DNA. Channel 4 was, by now, a public corporation, like the BBC, and although it is hard to spot in broadcasting at times, there is an accompanying responsibility to administer public funds wisely.

What was about to happen on the teen soap tender was the classic bureaucratic scenario of wasting not only resources and money but also the time of so many people who were tendering, all to satisfy some perceived notion of impartiality. This is something that continues to bedevil every part of public life.

Besides, I knew that slot was meant for me. I knew I could do it. I had been arguing for it ever since 1981 when pitching *Tucker's Luck*. Yet I had also been round the block enough to know that we were not dealing with a rational market-place. We were in the 4D world of media politics, and decision-making could just as easily be subjective as objective.

The only tactic left to us was to withdraw. So that is what we did. We let C4 know that we didn't want to take part in an open tender process but that we would send them a briefing note on what they should be looking for. And that, really, was our pitch. I wrote a four-page document that basically outlined all the things MerseyTV could offer but without saying what we would make except that it would be as inspirational and fun as the US-Aus imports. There were actually young people like that in the UK, it was a no-brainer that a similar series would work, but our strategy allowed C4 to scan what else was on offer and then ask us what we would do. I told them: *Chester CH99 1DS*.

It was an obvious play on *Beverly Hills 90210* but to differentiate it from *Brookside*, and to some extent what *Grange Hill* had become, I suggested we should set it in a non-urban city environment. Somewhere a bit more leafy and suburban but with lively shopping and nightlife. A bit more Richmond, Teddington, Esher or Cobham in Surrey, the closest the UK came to Beverly Hills. In other words, going back to the very beginnings of *Grange Hill* and *Going Out*, to 'somewhere in the UK' and not 'media London'.

To get this message over I sent a crew out into Chester on a Saturday and asked them to cut me something that showed the nightlife, the rowers on the river, the Roman city walls, Tudor shops in the historic Rows, buskers and street entertainers, many of whom came from the University or College of Law. The idea was to show the money, and that it was a young people's city. I then sat down, put Bon Jovi's *These Days* album on, and wrote the pilot script and character profiles. By the time this and the Chester tape went down to C4 the working title had changed to *Teentime*.

John Willis, who was Director of Programmes at C4, called me and said they liked it and we should do it. I went next-door to

Alexis's office with a wide grin on my face. I didn't need to say anything. She jumped up to get to me. This is what business series never show: the thrill of the deal. It was even better than seeing that look on David Plowright's face.

The programme would come under the remit of Dawn Airey, then Controller of Arts and Entertainment, which was good news for us as behind the Girton College, Cambridge education was a lass from Lancashire with parents from Liverpool – giving her a forthrightness that wasn't everyone's cup of tea. Unfortunately she then went off to Channel 5 and left us with a children's commissioning editor I found to be a real jolly hockey sticks Head Girl type, who obviously hadn't read or didn't even know the original Channel 4 job spec. From day one she didn't quite get that we weren't actually employed by C4, or that we had already been through the fight she wanted to have. We were going to make the programme as commissioned, not what she thought the programme should be. It was déjà-vu back to *County Hall* all over again.

When we got to the point of dropping the working title and finding a real one, she hated *Hollyoaks*. Why? She didn't understand it. It should be something like *Saved by the Bell*. Why? Because everyone gets that. They get *Beverly Hills 90210*, and *Brookside*, and *Grange Hill* because they're all about a place. What does *Hollyoaks* mean? Well, you could have the Holly from Hollywood, or the holly bushes you find in every posh suburb across the UK, and then oak trees, so holly and oaks gives *Hollyoaks*. Kids won't get that. They don't have to! Kids in Sevenoaks don't spend all day fretting about why it's called that. It just is.

When we set up the company that would actually produce the programme, like we did with *Brookie*, the one that got us our train nameplate, she didn't like the company logo either. Why and where do broadcasters find these people?

Alexis sent me home to work on the scripts while she smoothed over all that and sorted the deal. What I was aiming for was something that would fit comfortably within Channel 4's 'happy hour', alongside the *Beverly Hills*, *Saved By* and *The Fonz* crowd, so I focused on comedy. Same boy-meets-girl, first-date, best-friend scenarios as ran through *Grange Hill* and *Brookie*, but with more laughs. And I wanted to borrow the US-style 'Next on . . .' sequence at the end of the programme.

On *Brookie* I had introduced the grab sequence, three short menu scenes at the beginning of each episode that would let the audience know which characters would be featured, having learned with the Chois that if you opened on a longish scene of a set of characters the audience didn't take to, they would soon start channel surfing, and during that time they might miss the scene with their favourite character. If they did, as soon as they came back they would be off again. However, this was the first time I'd tried the 'Next on . . .' end sequence, perhaps a first in the UK.

Although the green light from C4 was to build a new twice-weekly, we were now in the world of programme finance committees and the developing dark art of market testing, so the initial commission was for thirteen episodes only. This then went to twenty-six, then fifty-two and eventually 104 as each batch of episodes was tested and the audience grew and held. We decided, though, that to make it work and keep the costs within the agreed slot cost, we would build the main set as though we were going straight to a twice-weekly. This was to be The Dog in the Pond where one of the central characters lived, the ultimate male fantasy of a beautiful girl whose dad owns a pub. We took the view that even if *Hollyoaks* folded we would still have a great set we could use for *Brookie* and anything else, including meetings and our own Christmas parties, as it was built right next to the canteen so the whole area could, and did, become a great hospitality and party venue.

Casting sessions started and as usual went down to the line as I kept looking for my ideal Kurt Benson and Natasha Anderson. I needed actors who would bring their own aura to the characters I had created. As usual there was a great array of talent to see and the characters could have been cast many times over, as individuals. What I was looking for was the 'gang', the group of characters who had gone through their own natural selection process so that when you looked at them, their body language, shapes and attitudes would convince you they were a real social alliance, not a bunch of actors pretending to be friends. Production was banging on the door by the time I settled on who would become our Kurt and Natasha, the trans-Atlantic/mid-Pacific couple I was searching for to pit against the US-Aus imports.

Partly because we were gearing up for a thirteen-part run, rather than the full twice-weekly schedule, production itself was running very smoothly, just another extension of *Brookie*. But it was also because of who and what we now were. There was none of the maelstrom of creating something new like *Brookside*. We were all a little older but a lot wiser.

After the intensity of the final few days of casting, I'd decided that Nick Pickard had both the talent and the sociability off-screen to be the hero's best friend Tony Hutchinson; Shebah Ronay had the almost unapproachable beauty that fitted her to be Natasha, the focus of Kurt's teenage passion; Will Mellor was quirky enough to be Jambo; Lisa Williamson was down-to-earth enough to be the sensible Dawn; Yasmin Bannerman sassy enough to be our female entrepreneur Maddie Parker; Brett O'Brien New Age enough to be Louise Taylor; and Jeremy Edwards had both the model's body and the cool head required of Kurt. I gathered them all together with Dot Andrew, our casting director, and gave them the 'welcome to the world of soap' speech.

That was to remind them that they were signing up for something that 'may go as big as *Brookie*' and, if it did, their lives would no longer be their own. Part of them would have to remain dedicated to the shoot. Work there never stopped and could be quite relentless, as Terri Dwyer (aka Ruth Osborne) always illustrates with her story of coming to a casting session and then going straight on to the shoot. For two weeks. With only the clothes she'd travelled in, she had to keep sending out for new underwear. The actors would have to plan the rest of their lives around the time off we gave them. And even when they did, they couldn't come back with a deep suntan or a different hairstyle, as it would upset the programme continuity.

I also emphasised that the biggest change they would notice was that part of them would become public property: the part that carried the characters the public saw on screen. They would say hello to Natasha, not Shebah. They would ask Kurt, not Jeremy, about how Tony was getting on, not Nick. This was something they had to live with, and they must remember to stay in character until at least after the initial introductions. 'Don't bother me, I'm on holiday', or 'I'm "me", not "them"' doesn't go down well with the public, the ones who ultimately pay our wages.

I'd lost count of the number of letters we had had to send out apologising because one of the actors had refused to give an autograph somewhere. Granted, it can be a bit trying at times. The worst example I ever had personally was when I was in the Gents somewhere, busy at the urinal, and the guy next to me asked to shake my hand. I asked him if he'd mind waiting a minute.

As I could see all the heads nodding, I also reminded them that they would probably agree to anything at the moment, but they should think about this and we would remind them of it as time went on: publicity is a powerful drug. We would also be reminding them that they were there because of what they had just gone through and what the writers, directors and crew gave them to do on screen, but that they should also enjoy every moment of it. Fame is fabulous if fleeting. They would be in the public eye, so should never do anything they wouldn't want their mothers reading about in the Sunday newspapers. And they should remember that one of them in this room would turn into a monster. One of them — we didn't know who yet, but one of them — was bound to start believing their own publicity. It was the sociological 5 per cent deviancy point. It always happened. And it did. But I'm not telling you who it was.

So we were into production reasonably smoothly, but not until after the typical nonsense from our regulators. The central premise of the programme was the typical and not-so-typical lives of a group of teenagers, one of whom, Natasha, lived in a pub. We cast Alvin Stardust as her dad, to give it a bit of media impact, and he would let the kids come into the bar and hang out, so he could do the 'protective dad thing' of always knowing where his daughter was. My office at Childwall overlooked the space where we were building The Dog in the Pond. Just as they were pulling up the hand-painted pub sign we had commissioned, the call came. Phil, bit of a problem.

What now? It was becoming a catchphrase. The ITC have deemed *Hollyoaks* a children's programme. They haven't seen it yet. I know, but we are, as you know, putting it through our Children's Department. So what? It's for 16 to 24-year-olds. We know, but as it's coming at them through Children's, the ITC have deemed it therefore to be a children's programme. Does that mean if we go to a Chinese restaurant and order steak and chips that'd be deemed a Chinese meal? Oh, er, well . . . but that's not the issue. It is really. Can't you tell them it's only an administrative exercise?

I knew the answer, just as I knew the consequences. This designation meant *Hollyoaks* now came under the Children's Regulatory

Code, which meant 'no alcohol'. I watched the pub sign drop into place. Brilliant. This latest development had serious implications not just for the content, but for the production schedule. Unlike *Corrie*, *EastEnders* or *Emmerdale*, *Brookie* never had a regular pub set, believing that our mixed characters would never go to the same one, but I knew that teenagers would. The Dog was meant to be our Rover's, Queen Vic or Woolpack, the main time- and cost-saving central set.

To help get round this I wrote in a couple of lines here and there, with Natasha's dad laying down 'no alcohol' rules, and had Design get a whole stack of glasses frosted so no one could tell what they were drinking and accuse us of flouting the regulations. But by the time we got to the press launch the main story seemed to be about teenage pregnancy, or rather why we didn't have any in the programme. It was a mini-*Brookie*-as-*Corrie*-offspring moment, as without asking us or waiting to see the programme the tabloids had assumed that because I was the writer it would be full of swearing, drugs and teenage pregnancy. I suppose I did have form in that area too.

To test the reaction we had a small launch at Childwall where I fielded some of these questions by pointing out that it was about the more aspirational side of teenage life, the British equivalent of the Aus-US imports; that more teenage girls had mobile phones than pregnancies, so which was the more important issue to kids? The unemployment rate was then around 10 per cent, which meant 90 per cent were not unemployed so to them passing driving tests and buying clothes were bigger issues. In any event, *Grange Hill* and *Brookie* could deal with the angst of rites of passage; *Hollyoaks* was about the fun side of growing up.

By the time we had the main press launch in a packed canteen at C4 the media message was out, and it was a great, almost jubilant, celebratory atmosphere after we'd shown the first episode. That was a first for me. John Willis seemed as pleased with the reaction as John Fairley had been after the *Emmerdale* plane crash had aired. We were on opposite sides of the canteen and gave each other broad grins and he blew me a mock kiss. That was definitely a first, but not a patch on Alexis's reaction when she heard we had the deal. However, the big test still lay ahead. What reaction would we get from the intended audience?

19

Time to Go (1997–2001)

'Let me get back to you on that, Phil' – *Michael Jackson, Chief Executive of Channel 4*

Hollyoaks opened with all the usual circus elements of mystery and surprise. Joyriders, guys on motorbikes and leggy blondes were all introduced as gradually, without dialogue, our hero Kurt Benson (aka Jeremy Edwards) is seen on his trail bike outrunning the cops to almost, but not quite, catch up with the girl of his teenage dreams, Natasha (aka Shebah Ronay); the joyriders turn out to be Kurt's irrepressible younger brother Ollie (aka Paul Leyshon) and his crew; the geek on the sedate Honda 125 is Mr Sensible, Tony Hutchinson (aka Nick Pickard); and the blonde bombshell lives in a pub, with a protective father and even more protective Alsatian dog.

So the rebellious and conventional sides of teenage culture were represented, set alongside the new materialism and eco-consciousness. Natasha, Dawn and Louise demonstrated that it was OK to like clothes and make-up while still caring for the planet and each other, and Tony and Maddie settled into the routine and rigour of employment and business. But the overall tone was one of light comedy, acting as both antidote and complement to the US–Aus imports as well as *Brookie*'s stories of teenage unemployment, pregnancy, crime and violence.

To help with this, the shooting style was more glossy, with a filmic look and a new generation of widescreen cameras, and like the opening of every *Brookie* script now had three short, fast menu scenes to set up which characters and stories featured in the episode – the opening of a brand new series needed something similar, but bigger. *Hollyoaks* opened with mystery and promise.

Having decided to shoot it in Chester, we then discovered an unforeseen problem: tourists. A great historic Roman town, the third destination of choice for most US visitors, apparently, after London and Stratford, we found that every time the cameras came out, so did an already curious crowd looking for anything and everything to photograph. The diversionary tactics we had deployed on *Brookie* by placing well-known faces in one place while we shot in another didn't quite work as no one knew who the actors were, yet. So we resorted to hiding the cameras in BT tents and even using a cherry-picker crane to enable the camera to come up over the rooftops and follow the action in the street below. Partly for style, partly for fun, partly for practicality.

Generally, though, the 'no cranes' rule applied as they inevitably eat into the production schedule, but on my way to the canteen one day I was accosted by a blonde in a Belstaff. It was Jo Hallows, one of the directors, looking as bright and mischievous as ever. Can I have a crane for Episodes 9 and 10? No. It'll pay for itself. How? I've looked at the scripts following mine and I could shoot all the night scenes with the Christmas lights on, save them having to go again. Easy. It was. And probably the first time I'd ever heard a director talk in those terms. OK, if I say yes, can I go and have lunch? Yes. Yes, then. We both went off grinning. She'd got her crane and I knew that if C4 committed to the programme long-term, I might have my new series producer.

I suppose the big stepping-stone for the programme came with the death of Natasha. Although the aim was for *Hollyoaks* to become a British *Happy Days* or even *Friends*, the audience started to signal that, while they liked it, they already had all that from the US-Aus imports. If *Hollyoaks* was British and it was by Phil Redmond, where were the issues? While this was a great compliment, it was also part of the creative frustration that everyone often overlooks when they start having a go about why this, that or the other happened in programmes. This was part of the reason I started to take more interest in Media Studies, to try and help explain the interplay between writer, production and audience.

In print, film, short-form TV or on the stage, you have the opportunity to write what you want to write. By and large, what ends up being put before the public is your creative vision. They either take it or reject it. On a long-runner there is another dynamic: the relationship with the audience. When you step back from being creator to becoming curator, and when the audience itself becomes part of the dynamic. They do so because they come back, week after week, and with them bring the shared narrative and history. You have to remain true and faithful to that.

What our audience were signalling was that they wanted to see their own culture, hopes, issues, ambitions and concerns played out, not those of their US and Australian counterparts. There was only one thing for it: a return to the high-octane, high-impact storyline. Someone had to die.

At the back of my mind I had the tragic but perennial teenage car-crash story that too often appears in the news, but at the time a bigger concern was the increasing use of recreational drugs like Ecstasy.

Following on from lessons learned on *Grange Hill* and *Brookside*, the bigger the character, the bigger the impact, so Natasha, the focus of Kurt's life, died in Episode 21. The storyline and strategy worked and the audiences started gradually building as we responded to what they had asked for. While the same elements of boy-girl-teenage rites of passage remained, a harder edge was brought in with bad boy Lewis Richardson (aka Ben Hull) and really bad guy Rob Hawthorne (aka Warren Derosa), the local drug dealer who got involved with Kurt's sister Lucy (aka Kerrie Taylor), turned her into an addict and ended up being left to drown by Kurt. It was a long way away from him chasing Natasha home for a kiss in Episode 1.

The storyline's added impact came from the fact that Natasha was the character who lived in the central set, so earlier we had already storylined in her cousin, Ruth Osborne (aka Terri Dwyer) who was not only to become Kurt's new love interest but also popular within the company, like her on-screen dad, Jimmy McKenna (aka Jack Osborne). Both were great to have around, and although Terri smiled a lot more, she was equally down-to-earth as her on-screen coun-terpart, Ruth, something one of the male members of the cast fell foul of one day. We got to hear about it when he complained that she had 'violated' him. This turned out to mean he had been thrown up against a wall and given a good smack in the mouth by Ms Dwyer, after he refused to stop pestering one of the other female members of the cast.

I'm not sure which was worse, the fact that he was 'violated' or that everyone then heard about it. Whatever it was, we had to keep them apart for a short while but he didn't pester anyone again and, naturally, no one messed with Ms Dwyer after that. He must have stepped over the line as we very rarely heard anything of the comings and goings in the actors' Green Room, looked upon as their own inner sanctum where they could get away and chill out as they preferred. In fact, when *Hollyoaks* started we had to be careful about mixing its young cast with the old *Brookie* regulars. The younger actors were fine but, as may be expected on a fifteen-year-old programme, some of the older hands had been around quite a while and claimed elder nation rights. By the time *Brookie* finished there was full integration, but a certain irony in the fact that the elders who had reacted against the new kids on the block saw themselves outlived. On the other hand, it was nice that some of *Brookie's* younger generation, like Alex Fletcher (aka Brookie's Jacqui Dixon), ended up on *Hollyoaks*. Alex became Diane O'Connor, a parent this time.

C4's long-term commitment to the programme was a long time coming. We were well past the days of 'gut instinct and experience', and had to go through first 13 episodes, then another, then 26 more, until finally, on 23 September 1996, Episode 53, the commitment was made to go twice a week, for ever. Well, at least, until it stops.

As life always has it – and why is that? – just when *Hollyoaks* went twice-weekly, Mal came to see me. He had just returned from the Edinburgh Television Festival, which I'd long given up attending as a talk shop and career networking event. Neither held much attraction for me, but Mal was heavily involved and supportive of the young people's part of the Festival. However, he came to see me to tell me he had been speaking to a not-so-young person, Greg Dyke, who was running Pearson Television as part of the Channel 5 consortium. He had offered Mal the Head of Drama job at Pearson, looking after both *The Bill*, previously at Thames before they lost their franchise, and their new soap, *Family Affairs*.

After driving *Brookie* for five years, through the Jordache saga and all its spin-offs, Mal was probably the hottest name in long-running serials at the time, so it was no surprise that Greg was after him.

Many times he'd arrived in my office, sometimes flopping down on the settee with the opening line, 'Guess what . . .' It could be anything from C4 acting daft about some script content to the time he came to tell me that one of the three phone boxes we had dotted round the site, so the shoot needn't go on location, had just been taken off site, to a location. Why? Why didn't they just go to a location with a phone box? Don't ask. There were never any satisfactory answers except 'I just thought . . .' and sometimes Mal, or Jo Hallows, would need to come and vent their frustration in the privacy of my office, knowing that I had been there, done it and still didn't have any real answers, but would appreciate the way they felt.

Today, though, was different. He was pacing. We went all the way back to that travelling bus stop on *What Now?* We had spent ten years wandering the shoots, trying always to find new angles we had not shot before, and new ideas, like the time we stood outside the *Brookie* admin block and reflected on how the vegetation had grown. What had started as twelve-inch bushes was now a two-metre-high hedge. We wondered if we could get a horse in, position it to look over the hedge, and get away with the idea that we were off in a field somewhere. It was always great to have someone like Mal to bounce the crazy ideas back and forth with.

Mal knew my body language as I knew his, and I realised as soon as he came in that he was off somewhere. I listened while he ran me through what was on offer and the only thing I could say was, 'Take it. You have to.' There was no question in my mind, this was the career move he needed to make, as both Alexis and I knew his ultimate goal was Hollywood. He could do that, but not with us. He needed to go to London, to work with a broadcaster, and forge links over in the US through the usual industry rounds of buying and selling trips. And he did it, first to the BBC as Head of Continuing Drama, resurrecting *Doctor Who*, creating *Doctors* and looking after *EastEnders* and *Casualty*, before joining Simon Fuller's 19 TV and being based in LA.

There were a lot of miles between us all, not least the long-term planning trips away, so it was the end of an era and a wrench for all of us as Mal Young left the *Brookie* Academy. Jo Hallows meanwhile had taken over at *Hollyoaks* College, where she would stay until we sold the company in 2005. She took the programme from two to three then five nights, something for which she never quite received the industry recognition she deserved. She probably suffered from living in that long shadow cast by *Brookie*, the first big innovator, and by the time *Hollyoaks* did go to five nights others had got there first. But none had done it on single camera, something that Alexis and I never underestimated and constantly appreciated.

Joining Mal at Channel 5 was Dawn Airey, who had been in on the commissioning of *Hollyoaks*. She became Channel 5's first Director of Programmes, one of her first moves being to see if she could poach *Brookside* from C4. Dawn's position was eloquently simple. Why go through all the pain and risk in building a new long runner, when she could just buy *Brookie* as an established brand, as she would something like *Neighbours* or *Home and Away*?

The dance went on for a month or two, concentrating more on whether it made sense for both Channel 5 and us rather than a contractual position. The weakness of all creative contracts, as football clubs find out far too often, is what happens when the creative doesn't feel like being creative. You might be able to force a player to put on the kit and run on to the pitch, but will they actually run, chase or shoot when they are supposed to?

In the end it made more sense for both us and C4 to stay together as although Dawn might see it as risk-free, we were, ironically, now in the establishment position of not knowing what Channel 5 was or was not going to be. What did come out of it in the process, though, was Channel 4 being forced to go back and revisit our constantly argued point that they undervalued the programme. We never quite got to our preferred position of linking it to the ad revenue, but we did get a reasonable improvement in our terms and conditions, including improved termination and penalty clauses to protect both sides from similar raiding sorties in the future.

Dawn had in fact done us a great favour, one that C4 would not fully appreciate until they came to termination a few years down the track. For her efforts, Dawn received our lasting gratitude, and a large bunch of flowers.

With *Brookie* tied down and more secure than ever, we all settled down to await the arrival of a new leader at C4. King Michael II, Jackson not Grade, was eagerly hailed by the new breed of wannabes, but greeted a bit more warily by the old guard, into which we had inevitably fallen, having been at the channel for sixteen years. He was our third Chief Executive and, despite three successful years at BBC2, by far the least experienced in managing a channel, let alone a commercial channel about to face an increasingly competitive digital age. This, of course, is what fired others with energy and enthusiasm as he was seen as the next rising star, so we all waited to see what would happen. He came very early on, as Michael Grade had done, to visit *Brookie* and *Hollyoaks*, and although obviously knowing *Brookie* from his visits there in the early days, confessed to not knowing much about *Hollyoaks*, laughing at the comment that he was, at the ripe old age of thirty-nine, outside the target demographics.

Later on we discovered that his initial plan had been to scrap it and put the money into expanding *Brookie*, until the C4 sales folk took him to one side and explained to him what it was, what it cost and how much it brought into the channel. From then on he was a fan. I believed this tale as it was similar to one told to me by the BBC during our time spent comparing *EastEnders* and *Brookie*. In their version Jonathan Powell, the new Programme Controller of BBC 1, decided he wanted to scrap the snooker and make more drama. Until he was taken to one side and shown how much snooker cost against drama, and how many viewers snooker brought in compared to drama. He then took up the sport.

Like Jonathan, Michael had been shown the pot of gold, but there was only sixteen years of tradition at C4, not the seventy the BBC could boast. Michael was also on a mission to move C4 forward – not an issue in itself, but with the departure of the old guard, like John Willis, Colin Leventhal and Peter Ansorge, he had no collective wisdom to draw upon. Only David Scott was left and it was not his role to tell his Chief Executive how to shape the channel. There was something else. C4 also changed its Chairman. The governance structure was in a state of flux. It was into this shifting corporate environment that the ex-media student, independent producer, BBC Head of Arts and short-term BBC2 Controller stepped. I'd had a cowboy outfit with a sheriff's badge when I was a kid, but it didn't make me a law officer. Into Channel 4 walked the new sheriff and, having been shown where the money machines were, proceeded to round up a posse of deputies to help wreck them.

After giving him time to get his feet under the desk, Alexis and I made another pilgrimage to the Crystal Palace and asked for the new vision for the channel. Whatever it was, we would reshape and put the programmes behind it. So what was his plan? Michael J seemed to flush, then turned away and stared at the floor for what seemed like an eternity. Alexis and I exchanged looks. Surprising. Interesting. Puzzling. Michael G would have been ten minutes into a soliloquy by now. Eventually the response came, 'Let me get back to you on that.' We are still waiting.

It would be relatively easy, perhaps tempting, to repeat here what I have said in countless interviews: that the seeds of *Brookie*'s eventual demise were sown on Michael J's arrival. But that would be too simplistic. In one sense it is probably the right analysis, in that there was no immediate vision, or sense, that *Brookie* and/or *Hollyoaks* were central to any developed strategy. From another perspective, that also suggests that neither was there a master plan to cut them. My guess is that at that moment he just didn't know. He was a great reviewer, analyst, trend spotter, and understood the circus principle of surprise, but I was never convinced he was a real innovator. He would take a long time over a decision, not react instinctively. Just as Steve Morrison from Granada had once said during the franchise battle that I was a good producer but not a broadcaster, perhaps Michael was a great Channel Controller but not a Chief Executive.

What then did we expect of the Chief Executive of a public-service corporation? Jeremy gave the channel its vision and identity; Michael G definitely gave it a coherent identity and financial stability; whereas Michael J, I think, became caught up in the whole dot.com digital bubble and forgot that the core purpose was its public-service remit, not to become an integrated digital media company. In my opinion the vision should have been a re-examination of the remit to cater for minorities not already catered for. That was not to be found in snatching cricket from the BBC at a cost of around £100 million, or burning another £100 million on a digital strategy that included full-blown film production.

The cricket caper perhaps best illustrates what went wrong at C4 around this time, as it was more of a macho, almost phallic, gesture between media players than a considered response to audience demand or need. Outside the home counties, plus Lancashire and Yorkshire, the appeal would be limited, with the channel virtually losing Wales, Scotland and Northern Ireland for the days it had to strip its entire schedule between 9.30 a.m. and 7 p.m. That was quite apart from the disruption it caused to *Brookside* and then *Hollyoaks*, as their scheduled times had to move to accommodate the cricket. One of the principles of a soap, in the pre-Sky+ or PVR days of easy time-shifting, was the 'appointment to view' whereby a regular audience schedules a programme into their lives and slots things in and around it. If they have been used to watching on a Tuesday night and it is suddenly not there, or two episodes are put on back to back on a different night, then it upsets their viewing pattern and they start to drift away.

The cricket coverage might have won awards and generally made the sport more watchable for existing fans, but this was achieved by losing other viewers for other programmes. The only people who really celebrated were the cricket authorities who pocketed C4's cash. And, more quietly, the BBC, grateful that they no longer had to lose swathes of the BBC2 schedule to such a minority interest.

I suspect C4's main strategy at that time was to drive people from the terrestrial channel to the new digital satellite channels like Film on 4, E4, At The Races and, later, More 4. However this appeared to be replicating the same mistakes as BSB D-Mac HD satellite and ITV's ill-fated OnDigital set-top box. The idea was well ahead of the Philips innovation and adoption curve. The audience, let alone the necessary digital equipment, was just not there in sufficient numbers to make it work. We had learned this lesson early, in 1996 when we launched our own website. It was great to be 'first in', but we had to use the university network and soon discovered that when you are first in, well, no one else is there. Why didn't C4 know this? As time goes by this has begun to seem less of a conspiracy or tragi-comedy and more of a failure of corporate governance. Who let the lunatics actually take over the asylum?

Channel 4, like many other companies, got swept along in the dot.com bubble of the late 1990s when everything was going to turn digital overnight. In that respect Michael Jackson should not be criticised too harshly as he was just one of many who called it wrong then. Those who probably have not been criticised enough, though, are C4's Board of Directors who allowed him to run away along the bits-and-bytes road to the digital universe. They should have been reining him back, in the same way the BBC Board of Trustees imposed a cap on how much of the licence fee the BBC could spend on its digital development. Even at Mersey, Alexis had capped how much I could spend in developing our own digital strategy by asking the obvious and most basic question: where's the revenue? Er . . . er . . . er . . .

The other people who seemed remarkably quiet during this time were my old friends the ITC. Having tried to manipulate the broadcasting landscape for the previous thirty years or so, they were now noticeable by their silence. Again, with hindsight, while they could perhaps have been nudging C4's Board to justify this massive and costly digital strategy, they were probably equally hidebound by the 1990 Act, having been turned into a reactive post-event agency, no longer able to intervene beforehand. Yet another example of well-meaning people acting with good intentions and bringing into play the law of unintended consequences.

So the contemporary view of Jacko the media studies kid at play in the toy shop, while seductive, is probably too simplistic. There were other factors at work that affected him and many others, just as there were others who should have been acting as wise counsellors if not putting a brake on his ambitions. From our perspective, though, no matter what the cause, he still ended up creating problems for us and in the end bringing down *Brookie*. Whether that was really necessary is still open to debate. What isn't is that it could have been handled better.

While we left C4 feeling unsettled, after the 'vision' meeting, we did at least have a promise that we would like the new Head of Drama Michael J was lining up. This turned out to be Gub Neal, another ex-Granada hand who had worked on *Prime Suspect* and *Cracker* with Jimmy McGovern. A good track record but, again, not someone we would immediately have associated with long-running drama. It didn't take long for oil and water not to mix when Gub and his drama crew arrived at Childwall. Whether they were or not, they looked every inch the popular image of the public-school Oxbridge brigade. These were not folk we could immediately see empathising with the likes of Jimmy and Jackie Corkhill, Frank Rogers or Jambo. They did, however, give us an evangelical presentation about how 'surburbia was dead', and, on the topical wave of New Labour winning the 1997 election, the pronouncement that 'we are all middle-class now'.

Sitting in the leafy grounds of Childwall, in a leafy suburb of

Liverpool, producing *Brookie*, set in another leafy suburb of Liverpool, and *Hollyoaks*, set in another leafy suburb of Chester, this went down like the proverbial lead balloon with my team of class warriors sitting round the table. Without me even having to say a word, class conflict was openly being played out round the table. Hallows instinctively laughed, as she is inclined to do when she hears nonsense being spouted, while Sue Sutton Mayo, not long in the job as a *Brookie* line producer, launched into a post-Marxist lecture about the class struggle of the kind that I would have been proud to give.

An alternative cultural view was that the term 'suburbia' was a borrowed media or political reference from either the US or Australia. People who live in the outlying districts of British cities tend not to use the term. At that time the film *subUrbia*, an adaptation of a Broadway play by Eric Bogosian, about a group of twenty-year-olds in New Jersey, was playing to the political subtext of disconnection associated with the term. That is, suburbs were viewed as outlying areas around cities that meant long commuting times and poor quality of life, whereas in Britain, as *Brookside* reflected, suburbia is more aspirational as areas are reinvented, or recolonised, as the city itself spreads out. Its inhabitants were not people who didn't want to live in the city, but people who saw themselves as still very much a part of it.

Of course this didn't go down too well with Gub and his team, who seemed to be suggesting that we needed to relocate *Brookie* from The Close to the Albert Dock, to appeal to younger viewers. This was spelled out specifically as 16 to 24-year-olds, the first time the channel's overall audience remit had been identified or defined in this way and which would become more significant as time moved on. Life from now on, we were told, was all about loft living.

There was no consideration of the cost or the practicality of this, of course, in either universe, but that was their considered opinion. We pointed out that it was actually only a very small percentage of the population, even in London or Granada's Manchester, who actually could afford to live in lofts, but that didn't seem to be a welcome view.

The meeting broke up. While there was civility on both sides, I think the subtext was that Gub was part of the next wave of media migrants to arrive at the channel bringing their own different culture with them. They definitely had the command–and–control mentality of the BBC and ITV, not the original Channel 4 commissioning editor ethos of being there to 'facilitate others'. From that moment we were on parallel but never-converging paths. Gub wanted us to make his programmes. We wanted to make mine.

Secure in our long-term contract, we continued making the programme as we always had, but took on board the point about the redevelopment of old dockland industrial spaces and warehouses. As this would no doubt keep coming back as a developing and constant campaign to 'yuppify' the programme, we decided on a pre-emptive strike by redeveloping the flats above the Brookie shops, to play out the debate the *Brookside* way and move in our own yuppies. We could then have the older residents giving the other side of the argument from The Close itself.

Unable to resist, I also sent copies of two sociology textbooks to all of the channel's drama department, which caused mass panic at the Crystal Palace for some reason, until I sent a note saying it was 'a joke'. I think they thought I was about to go public and disavow their 'suburbia is dead' nonsense.

Gub and his gang might have known how to make expensive ITV drama, but not how to connect to an audience or sustain a relationship that underpinned either a public service, as Channel 4 should have been, or a successful corporate brand, which was what they wanted to achieve. They looked at things from the channel's point of view all the time, as though with resonances of their Granada past, they had a God-given right to exist and didn't have to worry about audience appreciation so long as they made the overnights look good. In short, it was all about grabbing ratings through sensation rather than integrity; through the next big spectacle rather than through loyalty. Their buzz was from competing with other broadcasters, not delivering a public service to their audience. They didn't understand the concept of viewer loyalty upon which you build a sustainable business model. The audience, to them, was just a passing homogeneous crowd to be farmed, and one crop they wanted more of was young males.

Almost to prove this to them, and give us the opportunity to reshape the programme and provide space for their new 'Yuppy concept', which was nothing more than what Heather and Roger Huntington had been in 1982, or indeed what Jonathan and Laura had been later, I decided to blow up the Brookside Parade.

It was a similar tactic to the one I'd used on *Emmerdale*. To create high interest and media impact, to get young males watching TV and film, you simply need to blow things up. Turn up the 'adventure quotient', and alongside that crank up the emotional responses to keep the female audience, and then add the 'why/who/blame' debates and post-mortems. The ingredients are relatively simple. It's how you mix them that is the trick.

So soon Ron Dixon (aka Vince Earl) was blamed for a dodgy gas cooker that exploded and had Sinbad (aka Mickey Starke) trapped in the rubble, facing up to a life-or-death decision. The only way to get him out would be to amputate his legs . . . The tactic worked, and staved off Jacko's Killing Crew by delivering an immediate 700,000 upturn in 16–24s, and predominantly male viewers! The lessons were lost on Wacko's team, though, because while they exhilarated in the immediate overnights, almost echoing the Fairley *Emmerdale* and Willis *Hollyoaks* moments, they soon reverted to their pre-set agenda of changing the shape, nature and feel of the channel.

This was more toward artificially manufacturing 'event television' as it became known – or what I later dubbed 'the slut 'n' sleaze reality agenda'. It was easy to set up *Big Brother* and keep hinting that sooner or later there would be live sex on television. They could whip up a media campaign to create a 'me too/water cooler' moment, an event or programme you think you have to be seen to be watching, but it was quite another thing for them to maintain an audience base with intellectually challenging content. The output moved more to freak show than circus box office.

They started shifting *Brookside* round the schedule – first, I think, to create more space for *Big Brother*. We argued that they would be breaking the time-honoured concept of the audience's appointment to view. They said the brand was so strong the audience would find it, which they did to be fair, after a few weeks, but in slightly lower numbers than before. The longer this went on, the worse the figures looked until it became a self-fulfilling prophecy. The programme was losing viewers because it seemed as if the C4 schedulers were trying to shake them off.

It might not have been such a problem if they had advertised the fact or informed the viewers. But they did not. This was another abrogation of their public-service remit, in my mind. At the time I said being bumped round the schedule felt like 'death by a thousand slots', but this brought denials and expressions of outrage, with C4 insisting they were only doing it to 'protect the programme itself' from competing channels. That might have had some grain of truth in it, but if so it fuelled a growing anxiety that they'd lost faith in the appointment-to-view concept, because if they hadn't then they would have protected the programme by leaving it in the slot it had occupied for sixteen years. Of course, they hadn't. But they were now applying it to a different programme. After bumping *Brookie* from its fifteen-year-old slot to accommodate *Big Brother*, they then equally and vehemently refused to contemplate moving *Big Brother*, for fear of breaking the now four-year-old *BB* audience's viewing habits. Kafka come home.

While life at C4 was changing, we were getting involved in supporting the new National Year of Reading by developing the Brookie Basics literacy scheme. Working with Liverpool Community College and the Department for Education and Employment, co-ordinated by Broadcasting Support Services and the Learning Direct Helpline, we developed teaching packs and reading aids that went to 3,000 drop-in 'clinics' across the UK where people could go and ask for help with their reading and writing skills, at no matter what level. These included twenty-six prisons, and by the end of the scheme's run over 30,000 people had improved their literacy.

That fact really moved me. Although I often stood on platforms and talked about how *Grange Hill* and *Brookside* were not there to change the law but could help create a better environment for real campaigners, too often it was hope and hearsay. However, with Brookie Basics the results were real, tangible and documented. This was best summed up by two letters I received. One read: 'Dear Phil, I just wanted to say thank you for Brookie Basics. Now when I take things back to a shop I can write my own name and address.' Another summed it up even more succinctly: 'Dear Mr Redmond, Thank you for helping me being able to write this note.'

It still moves me just reproducing those words here. We may only have been making telly, but it was telly making a difference. Although something else I often say is that if we stop doing it nobody dies, every now and then you get letters that make you think a bit more deeply about that.

One such letter came from the son of a well-known TV

newsreader. It read: 'Dear Mr Redmond, My mum said I should write to tell you that while I was watching the *Hollyoaks* storyline on testicular cancer I decided to test myself, and found a lump. The doctor said that if I had not found it then it may have been too late. So, thank you, for saving my life.'

Brookie Basics was so successful we even got a call from the Palace asking if I could meet and brief the Queen. This soon went from my vision of a quiet cup of tea in front of the fire at Windsor and then of her paying a visit to the site when she was in Liverpool, to the reality of a small group assembling in Liverpool's Central Library during which apparently she would like to hear about me, the company, the programme, and all about Brookie Basics. Oh, and I'd have seven minutes to do that in. Excellent.

Come the day, we all turned up at Picton Reading Room, where I had spent many a night working on my A-levels. I would be first to greet the Queen. Everyone else was assembled in small groups relating to their various projects, and we all stood right in the middle of the large circular room. We had the Brookie Basics displays in position and were told Her Majesty would arrive about 10.05 a.m. By 10.12 it would all be over. A royal visit is usually very precisely timed.

Around 9.55 I looked around and saw our group had got themselves into a rigid line, almost like a football wall, blocking access to the displays. Everyone, despite being constantly in the public eye and having attended premieres and Baftas galore, was beginning to look nervous, so I started walking about, suggesting that they huddle together more in groups, so that the Queen could see the display as she walked by. I then started fooling around, trying to loosen everyone up, going down the line pretending to be with the Queen. When I got to the end I gave a fake pantomime bow as though it was all over. And just as I did the hubbub, commotion and background chatter in the room seemed to be switched off. Deadly silence fell. Still bending over, I glanced round and under my still-extended arm and saw a small figure standing in the doorway. HRH.

Straightening up, I scurried back to my position, glancing at the clock. She was early. She started advancing across the vast room and with every step she took I was trying frantically to find the right opening line. Should I go for the Liverpool 'All right, Queen?' Better not. By the time she reached me and offered her hand, all I could manage was, 'Welcome to Liverpool, ma'am.' I then quickly turned and introduced Alexis, saying, 'May I present my wife Alexis, Managing Director of Mersey Television. We too have a family firm, ma'am.' Her smile broadened as she exchanged a few words with Alexis and we then set off down the line.

I went along and told her about myself and the company. Two minutes. I introduced the actors who had taken part in the scheme, and in so doing realised that it is true what they say about the Queen. She does seem to have a magical effect on everyone. They were all grinning from ear to ear, and bowing and when I got to Sue Jenkins (aka Jackie Corkhill) she did the greatest curtsey I had ever seen. Four minutes. The Queen then stopped and pointed at Mickey Starke. 'Oh, yes, you're the window cleaner . . . Sinbad.' His face was a picture, and everyone else was amazed. In all the time we had known him, we had never before seen Mickey lost for words. His grin widened and he nodded. We moved on down the line. Five minutes.

I spent the remaining two of the allocated seven minutes explaining about the reading clinics and how many prisons had been involved. When I reached seven minutes I got ready to hand over to the next person by saying, 'So that, Your Majesty, is Brookie Basics.' She smiled and stood there. I glanced around. There was no one to take over from me. Nobody else was moving and the royal entourage was still some way away and seemed to be happy chatting to all the civic dignitaries. 'So, Your Majesty, the other thing about Brookie Basics . . .'

I walked her over to the display and then back along the line. Perhaps I had got it wrong and was supposed to wait for them to collect her. I talked a bit more about the campaign. Two, three, four, five minutes. Again no one was moving. 'So, Your Majesty, the most important thing about *Brookside* . . .' And the minutes ticked by. The Queen seemed to be either a regular viewer or else had been well briefed. Just as we were beginning to start a real conversation, they eventually came and guided her on.

With a sigh of relief I turned to look at the clock. I'd had more like twenty than the seven minutes they had originally allocated me. The civics were laughing. What was that all about? I asked. Well, she was running a bit early and we knew you'd be able to cope.

★

This period of constantly fighting the war of attrition over *Brookside* meant relations with the channel were not what they had been. We were getting to the point – maybe that should be I was – where it was difficult to have a sensible conversation with them. It was like trying to talk a teenager out of a daft haircut, even if my own hair suggested I knew that problem inside out. We got to the producer conundrum again. Perhaps the programme needed new blood, a new producer. Basically they wanted someone who would change it to something they really wanted to commission, not the programme they had inherited which was sitting more and more uncomfortably with what they were developing. Alexis and I had seen this scenario before somewhere: Carlton versus Yorkshire over *Emmerdale*. Elements of *County Hall* and *Waterfront Beat*. What we needed was to find a producer they thought would work whatever wonders they were expecting. So, for the first time ever, we let them nominate someone to the shortlist: Paul Marquess. Like Yorkshire, it would buy us time.

We ended up having dinner with Paul. He got through the two-second, seven-second test even though we suspected he thought he was there as C4's representative and this was just a formality. We listened and chatted and bounced ideas around, and out in the car park we decided that we liked him. Although he probably wouldn't have been our first choice, there were many worse and it would keep C4 quiet for a while. Our main priority was keeping the programme, the company and the community alive for as long as we could.

I did like Paul, and in hindsight regret the way he became caught up in the politics of the situation. It was to this moment in the hotel car park that I referred at a Nations and Regions Conference in Salford, when I talked about taking the decision to 'whore for C4 to keep the jobs alive'. The word amongst the chaterati was that he was put in to be C4's eyes and ears – to some extent true, but we had total hiring and firing rights. As always, once I had handed over the chair to a series producer I let them get on with it, sometimes having to allow them to make decisions I didn't agree with. On *Brookie* I let him shape, sometimes distort, both character and programme, and to some of the actors I probably still owe an apology for what happened to the characters they portrayed. However, I did it for the sake of the two hundred people whose livelihoods depended upon the programme.

To them too, I should say well done – they weathered some personnel changes over the years which in hindsight meant them having to put up with some real clowns at times, both in and out of the company. Fortunately, they always found discreet ways to let us know, like the writers inviting us out to dinner whenever they had 'concerns'. Our responsibility was to spot and act on the signals. The Scouse first rule of management: remove the clown or become one. Hopefully we never failed the challenge and we are still grateful to all those who helped us then.

Still, there is only so long you can live with yourself after a decision like that. My breaking point was reached after watching what seemed like a seven-minute scene of Ron Dixon filling his car with petrol. No spectacle, no impact, no drama – either on or off screen. I started to offer more support when his new best friends at C4 also started to play musical chairs or revolving doors as they went looking for pastures new. Paul was young, enthusiastic, and above all bright. It was not long before he too was off somewhere and came asking to be released from his contract. He was being headhunted to go and take over *The Bill*. Usually we would just have said OK, but because all of us had been the victims of C4's daftness, Alexis said she would agree if *The Bill* compensated us for the rest of his contract. Even I raised an eyebrow at this, but they did. Probably the first transfer fee in British soap history.

It was around this time that I started to get fed up with the wannabes C4 was starting to recruit and/or encourage. People who just wanted to be 'in telly'. I know I had often said that it was 'only telly, and no one dies', but that was to counter the pomposity of some of the commissioning editors. Now it was swinging the other way and they were forgetting the power and privilege that their jobs gave them. And even more so the responsibility. How they could help create the climate for social change, not just create mischief.

It was doubly frustrating trying to find new writers with something to say other than, I just want to write for telly. Why? Because I love it. But what would you write about if I gave you an episode of *Brookie* or *Hollyoaks*? Anything you want. Never mind me, what about you? I'll write anything you tell me. I just want to be in telly. How can you create a circus if all you've got is clowns?

This was highlighted in a different way when we covered the

topic of euthanasia. Mick Johnson (aka Louis Emerik) was seen to smother his mother-in-law in heart-rending desperation over her suffering. This hugely controversial storyline revolved around the availability, or not, of palliative care. All the advice we got was that it was hit and miss and another postcode lottery. But then *Right to Reply* decided to cover the episode and Ric Mellis, series producer at the time, who knew about this issue from personal experience, having had a relative go through the 'or not' scenario, went on to defend the storyline – only to discover that the medic opposite and opposed to him was one of our previous advisers.

Both the storyline and that experience, I think, had a profound effect on Ric, and they served to heighten my own conviction that Channel 4 was not taking overall corporate responsibility. *Right to Reply*, always the mischievous child of the channel, was there theoretically to be a platform for the viewers, but like each successive generation of commissioning editors they seemed to have forgotten the original remit and were more and more running their own current affairs agenda. The regulators kept surprisingly quiet. Two consenting siblings in bed together was an inappropriate storyline, but smothering your granny was, apparently, OK. I knew it all depended on who complained, and what the news agenda was at any given time, but I was frustrated by the lack of consistency and, at times, integrity.

And then, almost as suddenly as it began, the Jacko period came to an end. It was a surprise when he was made Chief Executive and his departure was equally surprising, but by then he had had different-coloured letterheads made, brought cricket to Scotland, and burned through £200 million, leaving the channel with an overdraft. What more was there to do? One more thing: leave it without a Chief Executive for a year. A year of what felt like, to me, drift and uncertainty spent under the direction of a man described to me before I met him as one of the 'poshest and brightest people' on the planet. Perhaps it was the preamble that did it. How could anyone live up to that? There was only one likely result. We soon fell out. Big style. And then Dawn Airey came back . . . this time looking for *Hollyoaks*.

20

Exit Route (2001–04)

'Say what you like about Phil, he always delivers' – *Michael Grade,*
Variety Club Tribute Dinner

Into the breach left by Jacko's departure stepped Tim Gardam,
Director of Programmes, and I think it's fair to say we never quite
had the best of creative relationships. It seemed to start OK but
went sour very quickly. Because of this I never got to know him
very well so my views and recollections of his actions might be
slightly distorted, but I do recall the tone of the calls and notes that
went back and forth between us. It was not good and Alexis had
to work hard to get between us.

What it probably all distilled down to was a complete separation
of vision. We didn't know what the channel was supposed to be any
more. I don't think we were alone in that. But what I did know was
how to produce *Brookside* and *Hollyoaks*, and what their audiences
wanted. Nothing had changed there; what had since the 'suburbia
summit' was C4 wanting more of a *Hollyoaks* audience, 16–24s, and
less of *Brookie's* 16–44 audience, especially the older end who had
been with the programme for nearly twenty years by that stage.

From Tim's point of view, I suppose he felt it was 'his channel'
and he wanted 'his programmes' on it, whereas I was now on my
fourth generation of commissioning editors who no longer shared
the collective history, relationship or emotion that grew out of those
early days. In the end, it became a power struggle over whose

programme it actually was, and because of that we all wasted too much time and energy fighting.

There were constant rows about the scheduling, or rather the constant moving of the programme around the schedule yet, with the benefit of time and distance, I can see this was probably not the real issue. The fact was the channel itself was changing and, as we had suspected not long after Michael Jackson's arrival, *Brookie* was no longer central to its purpose. And yet they needed the revenue, as the only remaining survivor from the early days, David Scott, must have told them. A Catch-22? Don't really like it, don't want to lose it. So they tried to change it, as they might have done at the BBC or ITV, by simply ditching the current producers and installing new ones, as Yorkshire had done with me and *Emmerdale*. But that was command-and-control ownership. This was C4 as procurement. We were independent and had a very strong contract in place devised for just such an eventuality: the whims of changing personnel.

I have no doubt that my own mindset did not help over this period, as by then I was at the end of my patience. This stemmed partly from having to nurse my now recurring car crash injuries through the rigours of production, but mainly from the exasperation I felt with each new generation coming in and further eroding the original intent and remit of our relationship with them. That was something I still feel the channel neither recognised nor addressed properly. We needed deeper and more meaningful conversations rather than attempted diktats, as we had been there doing the same thing for twenty years, yet it was left to us to make the overtures whenever they changed Chief Executive. It was their responsibility to deal with our mindset; to take us on their journey. They weren't the BBC or ITV. Why didn't they engage with us?

They might have thought they had with Gub's suburbia review, but that was too superficial. Almost flippant. We needed more from them. In all probability Tim's wife's terminal illness did not help either. I have no doubt that he coped remarkably well with it, but in calmer, more reflective moments I did wonder why no one at the channel had either the compassion or the corporate governance sense to intervene. Tim, like me, was a man who liked to be in control. But by trying to remain in control, no matter what, was he in the right frame of mind to make the best and right decisions? I know I wouldn't have been, so I believe someone else at the channel should have taken a more proactive role during this time. To help us all.

In fact they did, in one crucial area: *Hollyoaks*. Dawn Airey came back to us during all the media chat about what was happening with *Brookside* and suggested that Channel 5 would be a much better and more secure place for *Hollyoaks*. As always there was immediate chatter amongst the Met-Grouch-Ivy mob that if *Brookie* went we would take *Hollyoaks* too, but a moment's sane reflection in the real world of business would have ruled that out completely. If a large part of your business appeared to be under threat, why would you jeopardise the rest? Again the gossip came from those with no real production experience, let alone of anything on the scale of *Brookie* and *Hollyoaks*, or knowledge of the people who depended upon it. But it made for a good story. There was never any intention of moving the programme, but the Airey effect worked again. *Hollyoaks* would be going nowhere. No one else could afford it.

We would eventually be given the calm discussions we had been looking for with the arrival and anointment of Mark Thompson from the BBC. Neither an Emperor nor a King, Mark was more a Cardinal, working towards being Pope at the BBC Vatican. He at least had an understanding of what public-service broadcasting was supposed to be about. This included a sense of objectivity and a belief in not rushing decisions until they had been properly debated. As with all the previous Chief Executives, we extended an invitation to him to come up and actually see what *Brookside* and *Hollyoaks* were, as production centres, not just programmes on a scheduling board. They were, as was MerseyTV, a resource C4 should have made more use of, if they could ever have got over their anxiety that Buggins would kick off. We could have served as the umbrella for all the 'start again' productions they constantly had trouble with. The new indies they commissioned who then, inevitably, fell into all the same traps as their inexperienced predecessors, with the subsequent cost and resource implications for the channel itself.

Alexis and I met Mark very early on as my disquiet and unease about the direction of C4, and *Brookside* in particular, were a not-too-closely guarded secret. Our position was clear. Either kill *Brookside* or support it, but don't let it linger, dying the 'death by a thousand slots'. I wanted to know whether he was there as public-service saviour or, as the industry's collective consciousness suspected, a plate-spinner for the BBC's DG job? No matter which, he had to make an impact, so while Gradey's symbolic gesture upon taking over from Jeremy Isaacs was to move his office away from the public gallery at the front of the building to the back, and Jacko's was to play colouring-in with the logo, Mark took his tie off.

I brought away from that meeting a sense that we would at least be given the opportunity to reinvigorate *Brookside* as we had done several times before, the last occasion being the gas explosion stunt that allowed us to 'redevelop' the Brookside Parade.

For Alexis and me clarity was the imperative. Apart from the needs of the staff, we had decided to start the process of selling the company. While *Hollyoaks* was secure, the fate of *Brookside*, good or bad, was the main thing potential investors would be considering. We went looking for the second-best media answer: the quick no. What we came back with was what I later termed 'the football manager's vote of confidence from the Chairman'.

At the time, though, I genuinely believed that Mark had given us the time to prove *Brookie* could either sink or swim, with one last throw of the dice for a revamp on its twentieth birthday, due the following November. This was our own *Emmerdale* moment, and would also be a £2 million bet, front-loading the annual budget to fund a spectacular, headline-grabbing storyline, backed by a national poster campaign.

From March that year we started working on what was to become *Brookside*'s biggest-ever shoot. As the date approached we had to face a summer of press debate and speculation, almost on a par with that of 1982/3, constantly having to deny there was any cause for concern, and to reassure our staff that we had the 'full backing' of Cardinal Thompson.

Despite this we could scent the air of conspiracy at the channel and it was a long period of attrition, with the press obviously being briefed by 'sources within Channel 4'. It was now obvious that despite Mark's wanting to give us the chance he'd said he would, the forces of scheduling, marketing and sales were all battering at his door. The channel was losing share, but not because *Brookie* wasn't delivering; it was because their schedule was out of kilter with both their audience's viewing habits and their own game against their competitors.

They were haemorrhaging viewers because they had bought turkeys like live cricket and were having effectively to eat their own young, as they had to sacrifice more, day upon day, to a nowadays minority sport. Not only had cricket affected *Brookside* by often occupying its omnibus slot, usually with very little notice to viewers, it then started to hit *Hollyoaks* as the channel started to bump it from its regular 6.30 slots to create hour-long editions on non-cricket nights. The traditional 'viewing habit' ethos was being flouted again. It was ridiculous to think that a *Hollyoaks* audience would switch to cricket, and that the same audience would then switch to *Big Brother*. The common cross-promotion moments were being eroded.

Again, to give Mark his due, he knew this. He started slowly to unwind the cricket deal and, while not being able to cut it completely because of the penalty payments in the contract, he was able to reach agreement that they would actually stop coverage at 6.30 so that *Hollyoaks* could remain in its stable slot.

We fought our way through the press war and developed a great storyline reflecting the current social issue of the rise of gun crime in the urban drugs wars. After a Manchester drugs gang's visit to Merseyside goes wrong – well, it would, wouldn't it? – they inadvertently end up terrorising The Close after being chased into the cul-de-sac by the then new police helicopters.

It was a similarly high-octane storyline to *Emmerdale*'s crash, after going through the same thought processes. To find something that would impact on everyone and give us an opportunity to revamp the shape and look of the programme. We built a three-quarter-scale helicopter to crash into the shopping parade. Those who said this was a combination of *Emmerdale*'s plane crash and *Brookside*'s siege were right, but wrong to think it was mere repetition. That's like saying Hollywood should never do a remake or publishers should never reissue Dickens or commission new romantic novels or terrorist-based thrillers.

What was exactly like *Emmerdale*, was the production schedule. It was tough and demanding and we couldn't afford to fall behind, so the last thing we needed was a torrential downpour. We could cope with cold, heat, snow and wind, but not getting washed out. That was exactly what we got on one of the biggest shoot days when The Close's drains were quickly overrun and water starting backing up, literally flooding the place. News reached me at Childwall so I went over and out into the downpour in only my tee-shirt and jeans to assess things. It was a deliberate gesture to keep everyone motivated. While they were all standing about in their waterproofs,

I was wading through three feet of water, suggesting where we could tweak the scripts, relocate and change the angles so as to keep shooting. They knew exactly what I was doing – raising the ante – so slowly the umbrellas came down, they came out from under cover and things started moving again. As I'd never doubted that they would.

Over this period we had advanced negotiations with a number of potential investors as we were embarking on the exit route. This would mean we retained control but would get everyone used to the idea that we were now definitely on the exit route. The beauty parade for this was both interesting and funny, with some people being discounted for not being able to cope with my jibes at them about turning up in ties. Hadn't they done their homework? It is true, though, you can be judged by what tie you wear – especially by someone like me, who thinks they're ridiculous.

The guys from Lloyds Development Capital took everything, including the tie jibes, in their stride and we began negotiations to sell them a minority stake. Everything then, on- and off-screen, was set for a spectacular celebration and reinvigoration of the programme for *Brookside*'s twentieth anniversary. The high-octane story that would grab both media and public attention; the socially relevant storylines around drugs and gun crime flowing out of it; the emotional trauma that would focus and refocus the characters and drama. But then two weeks before it was due on air, the call came. Could Alexis and I go and meet Mark in London urgently? We knew what that meant.

By the time we got there we had worked through all the possible scenarios and were ready to discuss what best to do with the wind-out period. How to utilise the budget and penalty payments they would have to make, our preferred option being to go back and rewrite the scripts coming out of the twentieth anniversary episodes and then end on a high as a twentieth-year sign-off. We could later, perhaps, find another broadcaster for a scaled-down version and utilise the following twelve months to develop something else with the channel. It seemed like a plan.

Our rationale was confirmed when they changed the venue from the Crystal Palace to a hotel nearby, suspecting, I suppose, that I might revert to my earlier type and 'go off on one' in the midst of the channel itself. They were right. I did. Not because of the sudden decision to pull the programme, but because of the timing. They were not only going to pull the show at the end of its contract, they were going to move it 'out of peak' immediately and lose the mid-week slots – leaving only the omnibus at the weekend. This was manic behaviour verging on panic. After letting us spend the entire summer working eighteen hours a day and stretching everyone above and beyond, not even viewing the first cuts, let alone letting the public see the programme, made no sense at all, from a creative, business or political point of view.

There was only a brief conversation before Mark suddenly stood up and said he was going, leaving David Scott behind. Alexis and I exchanged looks. That was one scenario we'd missed. However, we walked back with David to the Channel and over the coming month he would be very hepful and his usual calm diplomatic self. Now having taken on the role Justin Dukes used to play. One thing was certain though: we had to control the information flow.

We had three pressing things to do: tell our staff, our prospective investors, and then the media. I had actually already written the press release from Mersey's point of view, reflecting what we'd suspected would be the probable scenario, so no sooner had we left David outside the Crystal Palace than I had word out that 'I now felt like every football manager feels when he has been given the unequivocal support of his Chairman'. The phone started ringing and the story played not on what C4 wanted, 'failing ratings for a failing show', but the fact that they 'had agreed a multimillion revamp and then had pulled the plug before that revamp could be unveiled or launched to the public'.

Even with hindsight and the long view of a retrospectivescope, reviewing the cuttings and ratings files, it was a daft decision. We said at the time that they should have allowed the anniversary episodes to screen as planned, then say the revamp hadn't worked and moved the programme out of peak. We would have gone along with that. However, to move it before anyone, even themselves, had had a chance to see any footage was bordering on irresponsible. That cynical Scouser in me which I try to keep suppressed always suspected it might also have been driven by fear that the new-look programme might actually have worked, and then that would have left this huge slice of hard social realism, the basic origins of the channel itself, sitting uncomfortably within what was now a schedule packed with reality and lifestyle froth. Everyone would notice and it would, in a cynical Scouser's opinion, expose the weakness of the rest of their schedule. I still suspect this was the driver, even if they couldn't articulate it properly at the time. It would be another, 'We liked the quality, but it wasn't the quality we were looking for' moment.

It was also probably no coincidence that our meeting took place just as the channel's ratings as a whole fell off the cliff with the end of that year's *Big Brother*, when the unholy marketing alliance with the tabloids lapsed. Industry gossip at the time had it that the channel's main media buyers had apparently called them in and told them that if they didn't show some signs that they were 'fixing' the schedule post-*Big Brother*, they were going to squeeze them hard. If true, which seems likely, the policy on *Brookie* might have been an immediate knee-jerk reaction to that. Because the programme was in the strange 'we'll wait and see but we don't really want it' category, axeing it was, I think, supposed to be a clear and positive sign that if harsh decisions had to be made, then they were not going to shy away from them. Good stuff. I had done the same with *Brookie*'s early management team. The only difficulty is, you have to make the right decisions.

The next stage, of course, was 'What now?' When all the industry kerfuffle around the decision died down, we were left with a year to run on the *Brookside* contract, including the termination penalties, which meant there were fifty-two ninety-minute drama slots to fill. And as C4 basically didn't care how we did it, we had one of our best years in terms of letting the writers/directors and actors enjoy making what they really wanted to, without fretting about ratings or a future with the channel.

We shifted the format of the programme to focus on a different house and family each week and, in my opinion, produced some of our best drama over that year, even if it was to a dwindling band of loyal viewers as, despite consigning the programme to the scheduler's equivalent of Room 101, the channel kept shifting the time slot also. But the viewers still kept finding it and coming back to us.

The final story arc stemmed from a combination of past frustrations and present-day interest in the level of disempowerment people were beginning to feel about social policy. It seemed that life was beginning to become a lot more centralised, with the real needs of local communities being overlooked within the national agenda. I had wanted to run a virus story first in *Emmerdale*, and then in *Brookie*. Both would have explored people's frustration with policy-makers to the extent of seeing them take matters into their own hands. Both times in the past my plans had been shelved. This time, though, I would have the time to focus on the theme properly, and this time we would make it a lot more tangible and something that had grown out of *Brookie*'s past: the drugs war.

It had been planned to rejuvenate the programme with a storyline about a Manchester drugs gang cornered on The Close, so it seemed a natural evolution to use the same theme to bring the series to an end. I also let the writers have their own form of creative exorcism by naming the drug dealer who came to infect *Brookside* Jack Michaelson. Contrary to media myth, when Michaelson was found 'lynched', that was not my idea but the writers enjoying a moment of literary revenge. As one of the sharpest think tanks in television, they too had watched the 'teenagers painting their own bedrooms' syndrome take hold from around 1998, and the way Gub Neal and his drama department had no empathy with long-running serials. In other words, they too were not fooled. There was also, interestingly, no comeback from C4 about the choice of name.

I got my own moment in the last episode when I had the iconic *Brookside* character, Jimmy Corkhill, sit and reflect on the state of world and UK TV. It was a long solo rant against a changing world, a vent for my own frustrations and a piece of self-indulgence that I would normally have put my red pen through. But with a last stamp of the creative foot, I refused to cut the programme to time. C4 indulged me by allowing a twenty-minute overrun. I suppose it was one minute for every year we had been sparring, but I really appreciated the gesture. They, like me, probably thought that after 2,932 episodes the audience wouldn't mind. So we sat back and let Jimmy slag off the world around us all.

That wind-out year was full of 'symbolism' and 'iconic moments'. The last storyline meeting; the last commissioning, first draft, second draft, the last script to be 'EPA'd; the last production meeting and casting; the final shoot, edit and sound dub and 'tech spec' before final dispatch to C4. By the time we got to the last day of shooting it had been dubbed the 'Famous Final Scene', a play on the Bob Seger track of the same name. As is customary at the end of a film shoot, the clapperboard was inscribed with the designation and presented to the director, Alan Grint, marking the final shot of the final scene of the final episode. I still have mine from when I finished shooting *What Now?*

There was one really big iconic moment: the final lunch with the final writing team on the actual anniversary of *Brookside*'s first transmission, 2 November 2003, when Alexis and I gave each of them a traditional carriage clock inscribed with the number of episodes they had written. The roll of honour read: Maurice Bessman (233), Roy Boulter (112), Judith Clucas (10), Peter Cox (227), Carol Cullington (8), Arthur Ellison (21), Neal Jones (23), Steve Lawson (8), Andy Lynch (174), Heather Robson (40), Barry Woodward (400). David Hanson (1) as series producer had also taken the strain of that final wind-down year. Andy Lynch and Barry Woodward had been there since that very first script meeting in the 'party house' behind Broseley's sales centre. While Peter Cox became our indispensable 'catering liaison officer' at all storylines and long-term planning meetings, he also played the equally indispensable role of 'father of the chapel'. It was also a thank you to them all for holding the drama together over that last year, when it would have been much easier simply to 'go through the motions', but they shared our own view that we would do our best with what we had, for the sake of the audience and staff. We also managed to surprise Alexis and present her too with a clock, inscribed with the number of episodes to which she had contributed: 2,932. Every one.

Despite all the preparations it was still an emotional moment when Alexis and I went on set to present bouquets to the final four cast members: Dean Sullivan (aka Jimmy Corkhill), Suzanne Collins (aka Nikki Shadwick), Philip Olivier (aka Tim O'Leary, aka 'Tinhead') and Steven Fletcher (aka Steve Murray). At the end, I also slightly distorted the storyline by opening up a worm hole between the two universes. Once the drama was done, with The Close compulsorily purchased for a refuse incinerator plant, Jimmy went round the houses daubing paint on the boarded-up windows. The camera pulled back to reveal he had daubed 'Game over', as it was. His final act was to put the 'D' on the end of the Brookside Close sign. We were now closed. But the final shot broke both the programme's twenty-one years of history and television convention by having Jimmy turning to camera and winking. Perhaps self-indulgent and heavy-handed symbolism, but why not? We would stop but no one would die. One game was over but others would continue. Including one last behind-the-scenes drama over the *Brookie* budget.

Throughout, neither Alexis nor I gave up trying to talk 'sense' into C4, on the basis that we could either just continue to burn up £20 million of public funds by simply running down the *Brookie* clock, or we could try and work together to use the money to develop another programme. We understood *Brookie*'s return to its sociological roots was not what they wanted in peak time, but why not use the cash and expertise to open up daytime drama again? The argument was the old one. We could produce at a rate they could afford, if we worked together.

Eventually, after banging on and on about public funds and public-service remits we did manage to convert the last few months of cash flow to develop a new daytime drama, as Mal Young had done at the BBC with *Doctors*. We would offer a legal series. Partly because we knew from Granada's daytime drama *Crown Court* to *Perry Mason* or the more recent US import *Law & Order* that courtroom dramas are a global scheduling perennial, and partly because we still had the Jordache court set at Childwall. With another quantum leap in technology we would be able to shoot at a rate well below the then current daytime tariff. *Déjà vu*. Again.

The format would use five fixed cameras, simultaneously recording on to hard disc, which would then be able to feed all five recordings direct to an edit suite. Although sounding similar to the way I had watched *Doctor in Charge* or *The Squirrels* or even *Grange Hill* being recorded using five cameras, these were all mixed to a single feed for recording. If a shot was missed or fluffed there was no going back for a better angle. This was the reason I had gone to single camera for *Brookie*. Twenty years later, I knew the technology was better, cheaper, and I had, as I had done at the birth of *Brookie*, a man who could make it work. This was Graham Deaves, now MerseyTV's technical director, who had built Granada's News Studio in Liverpool but, more interestingly, had come up with the technical solution that had made snooker one of the most-watched events on TV. He had negotiated slight changes to the colours, to make the balls more easily visible on early colour cameras.

What this all meant was that the editors would be only one scene behind the shoot, not two weeks as we'd been with *Brookie* or *Hollyoaks*. By the end of the day we would have an episode shot and edited in 10 hours as against the normal 110. Once again it seemed like a no-brainer, but . . . I'd forgotten: mindset. The reality check soon arrived in the form of Channel 4's new Head of Drama, who, like most modern commissioning editors, hadn't been given a copy of C4's original commissioners' recruitment advert and soon lost the perspective between 'commission', 'produce' and 'fiddling'. What I had in mind was a really simple, cost-effective, but very powerful one-set drama in a format that had been a success the world over, with the clue being in its title: *The Courtroom*.

Apart from the technical production bit, the tried and tested concept would have one case a week unfold over five days, taking or building an audience as it went. It even included the hot new idea of having the audience vote by text. They would be the jury. However, I think it is fair to say that our new drama head reacted exactly like the incoming producers of *County Hall* and *Waterfront Beat* and wanted to make *his* programmes, not someone else's. Like many who end up working for the broadcasters, he mistook 'difference' for 'innovation', and insisted that we should have a new case every day. This one creative request increased the budget by about 50 per cent, taking it outside the daytime tariff rates. It was therefore doomed from the outset.

This was a missed opportunity for everyone, as we had managed to cobble together out of *Brookie*'s ashes a format and technical platform that could have gone on to deliver a lot more lower-cost but high-quality drama. If, that is, you consider quality lies in the ideas, writing and performances, rather than sheer spectacle. With changing social patterns and the advent of downloading it would also, I believe, have opened up new audiences for both C4 and other broadcasters. Instead, their efforts went into so-called reality TV which is, in real reality, as scripted, cast, produced and marketed as any other piece of television. It has to be, to deliver the expected outcome.

By this time, I suppose I was feeling the same sense of centralised disconnect from C4 as the population at large was beginning to feel from social policy, and probably didn't put as much into fighting the creative battles as I would have done in the past. Balanced against this there was also a desire to let those who would be staying with the company past any sale develop their own relationships. Whatever it was, I stepped back from the day-to-day production and 'let them get on with it', pleased at least that we had managed to push the technology frontier. From my own viewpoint, I had enjoyed developing the format and pushing the techies to make it achievable. The creative moment, and buzz, John Cleese had talked about.

So another era ended on 4 November 2003. In one last technological leap, *Brookie* was shot in High Definition, the first time for a British long-runner. For me, that symbolised the whole ethos of the company. When one chapter ends, it signifies the beginning of the next. This time it was an expansion of *Hollyoaks*, from three to five nights, but perhaps more significant for me, *Grange Hill* was 'coming home'. In 2002, Bafta awarded the programme a Special Achievement Award for being on air for twenty-five years. At the ceremony, Alexis and I met the then BBC Head of Children's Programmes, Nigel Pickard, and the Executive Producer of Drama, Elaine Sperber. The conversation turned to what we did next. We were all a bit uncertain about the programme as the 25th Anniversary Award made us look back on what it was, had become and was now. We all felt that it had, like most long-runners, drifted away from its original intent and was perhaps reflecting a general trend in television by moving away from a radical social-intervention agenda. Out of that dinner came a decision to meet again and discuss the simple question: reinvent or end on a high?

We met and the decision was that we would reinvent, with *Grange Hill* becoming an independent production from MerseyTV. To make the cost structure work this meant relocating from Elstree to Liverpool, but by retaining most of the cast and spinning the typical, and in a broader social context well-known, scenario of schools being constantly reorganised, *Grange Hill* would be given a makeover at Childwall. The deal had to be sent out for approval to Greg Dyke, then Director-General of the BBC, who was on holiday in Barbados. This reminded me of its move to Elstree, when that time they'd had to track me down and get me to sign the contract. Fortunately, Greg must have had a good day's snorkelling as he gave the nod.

A new intake, Year 7, was recruited, to include none other than Togger Jenkins (aka Chris Perry-Metcalf), the legendary Tucker's nephew. Todd Carty agreed to come up and make a cameo appearance, and off we went. When *Brookside* finished, we then moved Jack McMullen (aka Josh McLoughlin in *Brookie*) to become Togger's younger brother, Tigger.

Initially the production was on a three-year deal, which was extended for a further three, but just as we reached the moment when our long-brewing, on-off romance between Togger and Tanya Young (aka Kirsten Cassidy) was coming to a head, the BBC had a similar change of direction to C4's. They suddenly announced that they were redefining children, for the purposes of their output, as 6–12 year olds. This, in effect, meant 9-year-olds, and we received this news just as we were sitting down to storyline the series that took Togger & Co. into the sixth form. Which put *Grange Hill* in almost the same position as *Brookie* had found itself in C4's frothy mix of reality TV. In other, words, nowhere.

We made a valiant attempt to refocus the programme on the Year 7s and make it more of a community, after-hours resource for 6–12s, as many schools were coming under the new Building Schools for the Future ethos, but it all came too late and once again it became obvious that in the BBC's 4D game, programmes such as *Grange Hill* were not now considered part of the children's mix. They suggested that teenagers were catered for by BBC Switch, but under the channel proposals agreed by the BBC Trustees, it was apparent that BBC Switch was going to focus on the 16–24 age band – in other words the Channel 4 demographic. That left out the crucial 12–16, rites-of-passage, teen years, the ones who had always found *Grange Hill* and *Byker Grove* and their like to be great social touchstones.

From a sociological, academic and practioner viewpoint, I criticised the BBC for this. I felt, as I still do, that they abrogated responsibility in this area by focusing on their own internal reorganisational requirements rather than the needs of the audience. However, by this time our exit deal was almost struck and it would be up to others to fight for the life of the series and that wider programming agenda.

Over this period we had also launched and were developing our new media division, Conker Media, through which Lee Hardman and I had Silicon Valley breakfast meetings to hatch plans like compressing an episode of *Hollyoaks* on to a Sony memory stick for use in the latest Sony Ericsson phones, before realising once again that it was pointless as there were not that many about. Yet through this we developed new models for online production and monetarisation, like buying a premium reusable memory stick complete with an episode of *Hollyoaks*. However, while the technology was there, the mindset in broadcasters and audience alike wasn't. We were only in year two of the Philips ten-year technology curve – five years for people to accept it is real and then another five to realise it isn't going to go away. Which was what Jacko's digital crew missed, and why, twelve years later, more and more content is now starting to proliferate on mobile devices.

Alexis has always been brilliant at keeping my feet on the ground during all the technological advances, as I have always wanted to be on the frontier, first with Sony and then with the university. She once said that I spend so much time in the future, I sometimes miss the present. She though kept a very keen eye on the financial here and now. Her view was 'bank as we go', taking out and locking up value as we earned it, removing the temptation either to blow it or see it drift through the silicon sands. She was always right.

Because of her vigilance and attention to detail, we had built up an iron-clad contract with C4 over the years, based on the simple premise that by engaging people on staff contracts, we had been able to deliver programming at a rate Channel 4 could not get anywhere else. It was only right therefore that the termination provisions included a guaranteed wind-down or penalty payment equal to the contract sum, so that people could be redeployed or given sufficient time to reorganise their lives. This meant that the termination of *Brookside* would not have any serious impact on the company for a couple of years, by which time we would have reduced the costs relating to it and/or put the assets, including the staff's intellectual potential, to use developing other programming.

Alongside this was the fact that we had been able to deliver *Hollyoaks* at a very competitive rate because we were amortising costs across the two programmes – a central point in the original argument about why we wouldn't tender and should be awarded the 'teen soap contract' outright back in 1995. With *Brookie*, general overheads like casting, legal, accounts, publicity, etc. were shared across the programmes, like any other group of companies. Obviously, with one programme going, the other would have to carry all the costs, which in turn meant that the cost of *Hollyoaks* would increase

– something the denizens of the Crystal Palace might have overlooked in their rush to judgement. Scrapping *Brookie* was an even more expensive exercise than they'd originally thought. Something the industry didn't quite get, but our potential investors, Lloyds Development Capital (LDC), did.

It soon became even more profitable as part of our negotiations was the redeployment of *Brookie* personnel and resources to expand *Hollyoaks* to five nights per week, so they would still be taking in the ad revenue *Brookie* should have been making. We would therefore be making the same number of episodes but, because *Hollyoaks* always cost slightly more than *Brookie*, at a higher rate of return. It was now a less complicated and more profitable business.

However, in terms of the company as a community, the greatest gain, to Alexis's great credit, was the way she managed the wind down. In the transfer of staff from *Brookside* to *Hollyoaks* and forthcoming *Grange Hill*, out of potential redundancies of over 140, she made sure we ended up only having to let around six people go. Difficult to lose even one, but a fantastic achievement on her part to keep so many jobs.

It was really interesting seeing LDC's response to all this. Nice people though they were, they were bankers and venture capitalists after all. They didn't waver. They were also surprisingly supportive of us, being genuinely appalled by the way C4 had made this important business decision, simply writing off both the programme and the £20-odd million it took to produce it. They, like us, could see that the final year and termination payments were opportunities to grow the business by developing new ideas, so they stuck with the deal.

Of course it had to happen. After killing *Brookie* – well, after being talked into killing *Brookie* – Cardinal Thompson received the call the industry had been waiting for. Would he return to the BBC Vatican as the next Pope? Even after publicly declaring that it was never in his thoughts, how could he refuse? How could he hesitate? Why would anyone expect him to?

So, Chief Executive number five arrived and the vision this time seemed to be: do nothing. Sit in the open-plan office and get on with things. It seemed like the best plan since Gradey had taken over from The Emperor. While we went through the normal courtesies, we never got close to Andy Duncan as we were already well on the road to selling MerseyTV. Like the franchise courtships, the number of suitors was long and varied as we and our venture capitalist investors hunted for a suitable buyer. This took us back and forth across the country and the Atlantic, from our arch-foes at Granada to a couple of the American majors.

Eventually, and by another of those twists of fate life constantly offers, I found myself sitting across the table from my old franchise sparring partner, Steve Morrison. We had always remained on good terms post-franchise and he was now part of a Granada in-exile group called All3Media. The All3 part stood for himself, Jules Burns, whom Alexis had been trying to tie down to that early output deal, and David Liddiment, executive producer of *Corrie* before becoming Director of Programmes and Channels at ITV as it slowly morphed into being Granada. Despite past rivalries, we all still got on well.

This is one of the things that people outside the media sometimes find hard to understand. How people who are apparently at war with each other one day can come together quite quickly on the next venture. It is part of that same philosophy that underpins 'the second-best answer is a quick no'. That great cliché: it's business, not personal. This is much more prevalent in ITV than in either the BBC or C4. It's harsher at Sky and even more so in the US, but at least you know exactly where you stand. It is also about delivery. Michael Grade has often said that there are many people who can open a deal, but very few who can close one. He also threw me one of the greatest back-handed compliments I've received at a Variety Club Tribute dinner: 'Say what you like about Phil, he always delivers.' I think that is why we always got on. No matter what the fallout, we each knew the other would deliver, when necessary.

So it was with All3. What we were looking for was to sell MerseyTV to people who would fully understand and know how to run and manage the business properly. Not just carry it on, but make sure it was done right. All3Media were more complete 'media animals' than any of us and consequently did exactly what we wanted of them: bend and meld with the broadcaster to keep *Hollyoaks* alive and thriving, thereby protecting the hundreds of jobs connected to it.

The final year was difficult as I had more or less signed off, having gone through all the emotional issues, and mental and physical traumas of selling up and moving on. It was on 8 October 2003 that it really hit me. I was standing in the kitchen at home fretting about something. I couldn't put my finger on it. It was eleven o'clock in the morning and I was becoming agitated. Something was wrong, but what? I kept racking my brains and wondering what it was I was overlooking. I called Donna and asked what was in the diary. Nothing. Was I supposed to be somewhere today? No. You have a clear day, that's why you're at home. Right. I put the phone down. And that was it. I had nothing to do. For the first time since 1972 when I had given up quantity surveying, I had literally nothing to achieve that day. No ideas, storylines, scripts, tapes, mail or phone calls to push or make. For the first time in thirty-one years, I did not have to do anything to a deadline. It was quite disorientating. What did I do instead? Got out my toolbox and started building a treehouse. I can still do this stuff.

Alexis, on the other hand, was getting deeper and deeper into the financial and management technicalities of lining up the company for the sale. That meant endless days and nights with round after round of bankers and lawyers, and facilitating due-diligence chats with C4 and the BBC about anything and everything, from the *Hollyoaks* and *Grange Hill* contracts to the covenants on the properties at *Brookside* and Childwall. I was dragged away from my battery-powered reciprocating saw and wheeled in as and when necessary, but she carried the bulk of the burden, with ease I have to say. It was physically exhausting, though, and not helped when every now and then I would have a brilliant idea, like: why didn't we keep the *Brookside* set and open it up as a themed motel? Wouldn't it be cool to be able to rent the house where Trevor was dug up? One look was usually enough, as the underlying, unflinching, unmoving principle was: a clean sale.

She was right, as usual. She didn't want, but even more so didn't want me, to go through the emotion of retaining and then selling the places we had put so much of our lives into. We didn't want to be walking around thinking what they used to be like. Remember that? Oh, what about that? And nor did I want to be that old guy at the end of the table, muttering, 'We never did it like that.' It was great to visit Hanna-Barbera and meet the likes of Joe Barbera still wandering the corridors but that wasn't for me. Time may inevitably move on, but neither Alexis nor I wanted to linger, nor was it what our Granada gang wanted. We all needed a clean break.

The actual deal with All3, devoid of the Barings all-night diner facility, ended up being fuelled all the way through on terrible coffee and stale biscuits served late at night. Why do they do that? We'd all been there before and knew from experience that late-night/through-the-night sessions only get rewritten the following morning, because both sets of lawyers are too tired to cover everything. All it does is run up fees. Perhaps that's the point, but I suppose it is more macho that way. So we reached the almost obligatory 6 a.m. signing session. But not before, just for devilment, I'd added a rider to the contract saying that if we ever had meetings with All3 again, I got to choose the biscuits, and they had to include ginger snaps. And Dundee cake.

Finally it was done. We all shook hands and went off on our different paths, Alexis and I smiling about one ambition we had kept to ourselves. We had always wanted to conclude the deal before her fiftieth birthday. And this was it. We went off and had breakfast at Tiffany's.

The day after we signed away the company we sat in the garden and reflected on the recurring moments in life. On how this felt similar to the day after what we had come to accept as the 'great franchise escape', and how we appeared to have come full circle. From trying to beat Granada to the North West franchise, we had now sold the company to what was left of their old guard. Both outcomes were right. For us. Mysterious ways again, perhaps, but we had left the company, the community, in good hands. If the old Granada gang knew anything, they knew how the industry worked. They would keep the place, and the jobs, going for as long as they could.

We had done a lot of the groundwork in the three years leading up to that moment in the garden, to the extent that the annual bonfire party in 2004 was soon dubbed 'Phil and Alex's leaving do', even if we were still half-denying it at the time. Karl Dolan, who was producing *Grange Hill*, had organised a brilliant firework display, set to music, which rose up from behind the *Brookie* shops and kept the entire south side of the city entertained for fifteen minutes. With a dancing robot and mini-fairground, everyone realised the budget had been increased for a reason. That's the trouble with building good teams of people. They react by instinct and their instincts told them this was probably the last big 'staff and family' party.

As we got down to the minutiae of the deal we decided to move out of our suite of offices. These had huge windows that had once been part of the college's art studio, looking out over what C4 had once declared to be dead: the leafy suburbs. They had also become, literally, with their self-contained studio flat, our second home. Where the kids had hung out when younger. Where we had dined and entertained and shared private moments together. We wanted to keep our memories both of the views and what went on in front of them to ourselves. We did not want ever to think back and remember other people with their feet up on our desks, looking out of our windows, at our views.

For the same reason, part of the sale agreement had been that All3Media should find a new name for the company. MerseyTV had been so much a part of us, our public and charitable commitment to the city. It was a name now inscribed on buildings and public gifts, but it was of its time. Within twelve months MerseyTV was consigned to history, while our offices went three months before that. Our furniture was taken away and the space was turned over to Production, to use as a set for the new *Hollyoaks* late-night drama. That had been arranged as part of the production slate we would leave behind, but allowing our offices to be converted into production space made it clear we were breaking the continuum.

Everyone had been prepared but when the actual moment came it was still emotional, walking round saying goodbye to friends old and new. Margaret Seiga, Alexis's long-serving PA; Joanne Bibby, our own legal eagle; Andrew Gossage in Finance; Graham Deaves in Technical; Sean Marley, who had joined us from Radio City; and Linda Hendrick in HR. We went to where our offices had been. Design had worked their usual magic and transformed the place, shifting it from the real to the fictional universe as a brand new apartment in Chester. But I could still see where the personal mementos had been. The pictures that reminded me of things like interviewing Steven Spielberg on the set of *Band of Brothers*, using multiple ISDN lines to create an interactive session with students back in the Media School; of Tony and Cherie Blair's town hall session in Bar *Brookie* during the 2001 election; my first credit board from *Doctor in Charge*, the early ratings charts, press cuttings, and of course the framed but yellowing front page featuring our Good Shepherd.

I stood at the window for one last time and looked out at the brand new Dog in the Pond sign, remembering I had been in this exact place when the telephone call came through to say *Hollyoaks* had been deemed a children's programme. That original sign was now at home, included in the long shopping list of things we would not leave behind. Then there was a last walk round the building, but keeping moving and busy so there was no further opportunity for tears.

A last look at the canteen, that had also been Grants Restaurant; the College hall that had been home to *Brookie's* Millennium Club, and assembly, examination, disco and rave halls for *Grange Hill* and *Hollyoaks* as well as used for countless staff parties and charity events – a reminder that every space in the building had to have at least three uses. Through reception, which had been Police HQ for *Waterfront Beat*; past Casting and Publicity and on to the science wing that had become Brookside Parade then Hollyoaks College before becoming *Grange Hill's* classrooms; to where the college gymnasium had become the staff swimming pool that was split down the middle as *Brookie's* health club and *Hollyoaks's* college pool; up to the old college classroom block that had Technical on the first floor, Accounts and Production on the top, and back down the stairs, passing the courtroom to go out and round to the old art block that became Hollyoaks Village; then back through the gardens where Anthony Murray (aka *Dancing on Ice* star Raymond Quinn) had strangled Imelda (aka Billie Clements), next to the oldest yew tree in Liverpool incidentally, and out to the car park to wave goodbye to security as we drove away. We said we would never go back. We never have. The clean break.

21

What Next? (2005–TBC)

'Liverpool, the best ever Capital of Culture' – *José Manuel Durão Barroso, President of the European Commission*

While I'd wanted time away from the perennial problems with 'car parks and canteens', I was also mindful of that moment of anxiety a few years earlier, upon discovering I did not have a deadline to meet. While I had often felt the loneliness of leadership, I had always had Alexis within arm's reach and home had been our sanctuary. She was already a trustee of National Museums Liverpool, a Governor of Liverpool John Moores University, a non-Executive Director at Riverside Housing Trust, and a few other things besides. She would continue with all that and, despite my own involvement with the Media School, I imagined being stuck at home like Billy No Mates.

So I too was ready for the next challenge. That took me on to chairing the Merseyside Entrepreneurship Commission, becoming Deputy Chair and Creative Director of European Capital of Culture, then Chair of the Knowsley Youth Commission and National Museums Liverpool. All of which would teach me that television is not alone in suffering from good people acting with the best intentions to introduce the laws of unintended consequences. I would also discover that just as 1980 had been a pivotal year in shaping the direction of my life, then 2008 would set me on a new course towards political engagement and the brink of standing for election as Liverpool's first elected Mayor.

However, both the Merseyside Entrepreneurship and the Knowsley Youth Commission reaffirmed my view that the biggest challenge in bringing about and managing change is mindset. Even where there is the insight and ambition to initiate change, it is often extremely difficult for most people to accept it is really necessary. Ironically, it is often politicians – who by definition should be inspiring people through idealism – who are the most resistant to change. Both Commissions shared a common problem. The subjects of the review, entrepreneurs and young people, should be valued for the very fact that makes them so difficult for policy-makers to understand: neither category likes following rules. Both want to be free to follow their dreams.

This was even more evident during Liverpool's time as European Capital of Culture 2008, particularly around my appointment as Deputy Chair and Creative Director of the Culture Company which was set up to deliver the programme of events. I had sidestepped earlier overtures to become involved, mainly because we still had the business to run but also knowing what a viper's nest local politics can be in any city, let alone the People's Republic. Only after it was becoming clear that the project was really – no, really – heading for the rocks did I decide I had at least to try and do something. It was my city too, after all.

At the end of 2006, when my time with the Entrepreneurship Commission was coming to an end, I agreed to join the Culture Company Board. The first meeting I attended felt like stepping once more into the rarefied atmosphere of the *Coronation Street* storyline conference. Despite the age gap now being a lot narrower, there was still a feeling of 'young Phil' being sent to the end of the table. And what a table it was. Walking into one of the grand rooms of Liverpool Town Hall, I found an aircraft-carrier-like table set out with microphones and place names, extra seats on all sides for advisers, and off to the side a separate table for note-takers. My immediate thought was that we must be about to plan an invasion. Was the People's Republic finally about to declare independence, reclaim Huyton and Kirkby and annex the Wirral? But no, it was more serious than that. We were discussing the route of the number 26 bus.

Out of the three hours allocated to the meeting, we spent nearly an hour on the route and potential bus livery and not once, from memory, did we discuss either culture or creativity. Being the People's

Republic, every potential stakeholder, from the Regional Development Agency to community arts groups, was represented, to the extent that the law of unintended consequences was at work. There were so many people with competing voices around the table that the quest for inclusivity had created a feeling of exclusion. No one was being heard properly. What was lacking was effective leadership.

By the time I attended the second meeting, in a slightly smaller but even more grand room, I decided that life was indeed moving in mysterious ways. For years I had resisted all the family's attempts to get a dog. We were too busy, constantly travelling, out all day and every other excuse I could pin on running the business. But now we had theoretically sold the company to be less busy, do less travelling and have more time at home. Instead of which I was sitting in this room as nothing more than a glorified extra in a reality TV version of *County Hall*. I'm not sure what else was resolved at that meeting, but I definitely decided to give in to the kids and get a dog.

The actual story of how I went from an extra sitting at the end of the table to a starring role in the middle is impossible to cover in this mid-term report. There is neither time nor space for the full tale, which needs to be the subject of a separate book, film or farce, even if only as a case study in cultural intervention. Also, if I have missed out people from my own life journey, the list of characters and clowns in the Capital of Culture circus was equally large so, again, I would probably upset a lot more people by omission.

Yet, like *Brookside*, it had such an impact on my life that I couldn't omit it completely. Here then is a much-truncated version of what happened after the main power-brokers in and around the city agreed that something 'had to be done'. The catalyst came during a specially convened board meeting to discuss the news that the long-standing Mathew Street Festival, Liverpool's annual tribute to the Beatles, had been cancelled due to 'Health & Safety' issues. It was all a bit of a nonsense as from memory only one of the main stages was at risk, but the climate of suspicion and expectation of failure was such that when someone, somewhere said the wrong thing to the wrong person, the media had done what Sara Keays had said they do: sewed a shirt on to the button. It was a totally unnecessary public relations disaster, but at least it acted as the trigger to gather together the power-brokers.

In between working with the Head of Communications to redraft the official press release, replacing the word 'cancelled' with 'revised', we were also hearing plans to stage the Paul McCartney concert, on a floating stage in one of the waterfront docks. It sounded brilliant, as a TV show, but putting my exec producer's hat back on I started probing the production plans. How is it going to be built? The dock is going to be drained; then disinfected to get rid of the salt and seaweed smell; then scaffolding built to carry the stage and seating; then about twelve inches of treated water will be reintroduced to give a sense that everything is floating in the dock; all shot on cranes, jibs, dollies and tracks, very mobile; it'll look terrific.

It will, I thought. But what about the fish? There's enough fuss about moving one stage for the Mathew Street Festival, we can't have shots of dying fish on the six o'clock news. Right, we've thought about that. We're going to stun the fish then carefully lift them out and put them in the adjacent dock, to be reintroduced later when everything is removed. OK. I thought about asking how they were going to stun the fish but dreaded the answer, so instead asked how big the floating temporary arena would be? 6,500 seats. Great. How long will we have the facility? One night. One night? Yes, there have been complaints from the neighbours. What neighbours? The only people next to the dock are the cops in Police HQ. There are a few flats nearby in the Albert Dock. OK. But, er, how much? Only £4.5 million, we think. You think? Thereabouts.

Everyone took this in for a moment but no one else commented as the spiel continued. It'll look fantastic and every time we shoot from the stage or pan round we'll get shots of the city beamed across the world, which will be a great promotional tool. And on and on it went. Sounding 'terrific' to everyone who had never worked in TV.

I thought I should try again. How deep is the dock? The standard eye exchanges began. Er . . . about twelve feet, we think. And with twelve inches of water, the scaffolding will be, what, eighteen inches off the dock floor? More eye exchanges. Er, yes. OK. So when sitting down, the audience will be about six feet below the top of the dock wall. Well, yes, suppose so. Perhaps they saw what I was thinking in my face or realised as soon as I'd asked the question. But the crane shots and aerials will look fantastic, came the hasty reassurance. All I had in my mind by then was a shot of a gigantic burial pit with the audience imitating the Chinese Terracotta Army. OK, two last questions. What time is the show and how many of the 6,500 seats will be going to the public? Eyes darted back and forth again, and shoulders sagged, before we were told: 10 p.m. and about 2,000. Where's the rest going? Corporate and sponsors.

I think they were beginning to get where I was going, but for everyone else I summed up. So we are planning to build a temporary arena in a dock, but to do so we are nuking the fish and lobbing them into the next dock. We will then pump out the water, scrub and disinfect the dock, put scaffolding across the floor, fill it with twelve inches of treated water, then shoot pictures either of sandstone walls or a black night sky, while allowing only 2,000 members of the public to see the biggest gig of the year, for one night only. Have I got it? Er, yes, but the global media coverage will be fantastic. Oh, no doubt, but do we actually have any TV coverage agreed? Er, well, no. So does that sound like a great bargain for four and a half million?

A motion was put forward, and passed, that we reconsider this piece of lunacy at the next meeting together with finding a more suitable venue to accommodate more of the public. Attention then turned back to the damage-limitation exercise and the redrafted press release met with full board approval, until it was pointed out that it was a pointless exercise. The politicians on the board had already released the original 'cancelled version', to explain the Council's position. The rest of the board began to appreciate how the fish in the dock might feel: stunned. The wave of negative media reaction was the very reason this special board meeting had been called. To defuse, not fuel it. What it did do, though, was ignite a revolution.

The politicians' decision might have had some political merit, as Mathew Street was a long-standing Council-run event, but it showed a clear misunderstanding of both the media and relationships with the major stakeholders who had come together to form the Culture Company. These stakeholders were actually putting in a lot of the funding and now they insisted on changes being made in order to protect that funding. Soon afterwards, in another grand room in the Town Hall, in the typically British way, the right people sat down and came to the right decision. *Respice Finem*: or else.

Bryan Gray, then Chair of the North West Development Agency, the biggest funder and power-broker in the region, became Chair of the Culture Company. The then City Leader, Lib-Dem Warren Bradley, would become co-Deputy Chair, alongside me. The politicians fought long and hard against this, not just because I was perceived as a 'friend of Labour', but because they too had learned what I had from following Sir Horace Cutler round the GLC: the power of the office. I could have been Creative Director without it, but the Deputy Chair title conferred the badge of authority on me. With Bryan Gray's hands on the region's political and financial levers, together with my relationships with the media and creative community, we began to reshape and drive things forward.

The first thing was to reduce the board from sixteen to just six members, as we now had only sixteen weeks until the official opening weekend: Friday and Saturday, 11–12 January. For the first time since joining the board almost a year earlier I now had access to the real programme plans, which were, actually, terrific, but for the two biggest and most important shows on that opening weekend, there was very little on paper and no scripts. It was a bit reminiscent of *Brookie* getting planning permission in February and needing to start shooting in July, but this time there could be no pushing back the dates. Before that, though, there was another small issue to be resolved. The programme highlights would be revealed to the world on 27 September 2007 – in a little over a fortnight.

While a world away from television, this was not too far from *County Hall* and the challenge was the same as on *Emmerdale*: changing people's perception, and quickly. While I'd used a plane crash in Yorkshire, the national media were expecting to watch a 'political car crash' in Liverpool. The not-so-hidden agenda was that there was a £20 million black hole in the Council's budget, so Capital of Culture seemed doomed from the off. The local politicians, for their own purposes, had stoked this agenda. The ruling Lib-Dems were trying to put pressure on the national Labour government to give them the money, while some local Labour politicians were myopically hoping Capital of Culture would fail so that it would precipitate a collapse of the Lib-Dem vote in the following May's elections. Lunatics fighting lunatics about who controls the asylum? That, then, was both the challenge and the solution. Get the media to think of the city as its people, not its politicians.

By the time the day arrived for us to launch the programme

highlights, I had been jousting with the media for two weeks. The story they wanted to cover was the financial black hole . . . oh, and was Macca signed up? I would need something good to get the press pack turned in a different direction. It had come to me a few days before when I had lost my patience with yet another sneering London-based journo. He had been going on and on about the budget-deficit issue and about everything being reorganised too late. We Scousers were going to cock it up, as expected.

I had got so fed up with him that I stopped the interview and said, Look, mate, you're making the classic mistake. You think we care what a bunch of media tourists might think? We don't. We don't care what the London chaterati think. You're always slagging us off. You've been doing it for hundreds of years, but as always we're still here. 2008 is our year. Our party. And we're going to enjoy it. He was a bit taken aback, but, to be fair, turned out a more balanced piece. So at the programme launch, I just adopted the same tack.

The event itself was stage managed very well by the marketing team and I had two production tricks to play: the reveal and the hook. The reveal was that not only did we have Ringo, but also Macca, and there he was, on video, to confirm that, yes, he was coming. How could he miss such a moment in the city's history? But no need to tell the media he'd only agreed the night before. For the hook I needed the right 'angle'. The budget-deficit story was old news after all. We needed something that would newly intrigue them.

Watching them listening to the two executive producers, Fiona Gasper and Claire McColgan, I could see they were halfway there, so when it was time to wrap up, I repeated what a great programme of events it was, what a great year it was going to be, and then, no matter what happened, what a great party we were going to throw. They might have thought or heard that all was disharmony and chaos, but in fact we were doing nothing more than organising a great party. It was like a wedding: who sits where . . . I'm not going if they are . . . Have you seen the state of him, her or that hat? . . . And so on and so on. But then, come the Friday night and everyone realises the big day is tomorrow, they all turn up and have a great time. And then I came out with the line: '. . . *it's nothing more than organising a great Scouse wedding!'*

As I did, we had one more production trick to play. I had the team line up a great Scouse anthem, The Farm's 'All Together Now'. It was cued to come in very low when I started talking after Claire and Fiona, and then build so that when I came off the stage the room would be filled with the chorus of 'All Together Now, All Together Now . . .' I'd obviously been hanging around New Labour too much, but it worked. 'All Together Now' became the unofficial slogan and the Scouse wedding quote went viral round the globe and created a lasting afterglow, to the extent that it is now being used as a metaphor for any culture-led urban regeneration. But it isn't. Every such project, from previous European City or Capital of Culture to the Olympics, goes through a similar cycle of initial euphoria, then the grind and reality of delivery and political in-fighting that causes people to wobble and run for the hills, and the final defining moment when someone takes hold and realises it has to be done, by a certain day.

That is also why most such occasions appear at best adequate, at worst mediocre, the best that could be done in the time. But this was the one thing I was determined I wouldn't let happen to Liverpool. It wouldn't happen because I would make sure that the media, which define the myth around any event, would at least look at it properly. On that day, at that launch, all I had wanted to do was produce a sound bite to counter and perhaps kill the media's preoccupation with Liverpool's internal politics. If there was any metaphor, or model, to come out of that year it was the spirit of co-operation that later developed. 'All Together Now'.

Right then, though, I had to focus on getting more positive column inches, both in Liverpool and outside. To get the external media perception turned around we didn't need live coverage of the opening events, just a few good column inches here and there. And I knew a man who would be able to help. Since our differences over *Brookie*, Mark Thompson and I had maintained a reasonable working relationship, so when I heard he was, as Director-General of the BBC Vatican, making a Papal visit to BBC Radio Merseyside, I arranged to meet him.

In a typical BBC cramped meeting room over a cup of typical BBC tea out of a typical BBC plastic cup, I asked for more typical BBC support. I thought they were overlooking the project as no one had really sold them the point about its belonging to the UK as a whole, not simply being a regional award to Liverpool. Unlike Glasgow, which had applied as a City of Culture, the new European

Capital of Culture designation was a rotational award granted by the European Union to its member states. It had been the UK Government's decision to run the beauty contest that selected Liverpool as the nation's host city, for an event that would not be back in the UK for at least twenty-six years. As the national public-service broadcaster, the BBC should be more involved. And if it were, every other broadcaster would follow. They always did.

To his great credit Mark got it straight away and while we both recognised that it was a bit late in the day, with all broadcasters operating on an eighteen- or twenty-four-month planning cycle, opportunities would just have to be identified wherever possible. That of course included things like *The Culture Show* and BBC News that would always be looking at current events. I'm not sure he ever sent out a Papal Encyclical, but within hours he had appointed one person to act as liaison and together we started encouraging the BBC to do more and more, wherever and whenever it could. It made a huge difference. Gradually the story started to move away from the periphery and more and more into mainstream, away from the stories of political shenanigans and towards those about creative endeavour and community engagement.

That is not to say that everything was rosy as one of the great challenges of working with the BBC is recognising the principles of impartiality and editorial freedom. Having the support of the DG, as management, can be as counter-productive as it can be rewarding, but the central truth always remains: tell the story as it appears. If various journalists or presenters had a negative view it was our job to change it, not ask them to ignore it. Attack the mindset, not ask for favours. Give them positive stories to eclipse the negative. Above all, though, remove the potential for the negative 'vox pops' in the street with which the media love to bolster their opinions. Or, in other words, find a local to confirm the bad news.

To avoid the latter eventuality, the internal challenge was to change the mindset locally. This challenge was linked both to an historical fear that anything connected with the Council was bound to be, well, less than innovative and to something even we Scousers share with the rest of the UK: an almost genetic predilection for disaster. We are, as most city-states and as a nation, never better than when we are battling some external foe, backs to the wall. And if there is no discernible enemy in sight, we invent one. Never let the lack of adversity get in the way of a good fight. Never waste a good crisis.

No sooner had I pinned on the badge of office than there was a line of people outside my door, wanting to come and 'talk' to me. These ranged from those hoping for a commission to those who who were piqued they hadn't had a letter acknowledged, but the overall point was the sheer volume of people who felt, in some way, disconnected, disenfranchised and disenchanted, including The Samaritans. The real ones this time, not the guys who had pulled Alexis and me off the M56 in 1984. The Liverpool contact number is 0151 708 8888, if you are ever in need, and they had put a banner up outside their offices using the Culture Company '08' logo as the '8' in 708. I thought it was really cool, to get this level of community support, but soon discovered they had then been sent a draconian 'cease and desist' legal letter from the Culture Company. The '08' was copyrighted, it seemed, and would cost them a £2 million sponsor's fee if they wanted to use it.

Fortunately, a few years earlier I had headed up a 'Save Our Samaritans' campaign when they had hit a funding crisis, so I knew them and the local media well enough to ask them both not to break the story, while I went to the board and suggested we change our policy. This was, after all, The Samaritans, people we might all have need of by the year's end. We got the change agreed, The Samaritans got their sign, and none of the other sponsors complained. To be fair to the previous administration, they had been overwhelmed by the scale of people's desire to be involved, something they themselves had engendered but had not managed very well after winning the original bid with the slogan 'The World in One City'. Everyone felt a part of it in 2003. By 2007, rightly or wrongly, it had become just another Council project.

Another early intervention was stimulated by a half-page story in the *Guardian* about the artists responsible for painting the highly contentious political murals on the sides of houses in Derry/Londonderry being turned away from Liverpool because they were not 'edgy enough'. This didn't sound too good so I got them in and said that no matter what they had been told in the past, this son of Irish immigrants wanted more of the City's Irish heritage in the programme and would like to see a couple of murals depicting the shared social history. They interrupted me in full flow and said that, well they really wanted to do the Beatles. Ah. Not quite as edgy as I had expected. In the end we settled on two murals, one reflecting social history and one about the Beatles.

The more time I spent meeting and listening to the dissenting voices, all the time using what became my standard greeting, 'Hi, there is no money', the more clear it became that all that was missing was the 'Scouse day in court'. No matter how harsh or bad the news, so long as people in the city are given a fair hearing and explanation, they will accept it. What they were really complaining about was lack of effective communication, or sometimes not even receiving a reply to their submissions. More and more, it became clear to me that all most of them wanted was to be listened to and told that they didn't need permission from the Council to do most of what they wanted. They could go out and raise their own money. Book their own venue. Organise their own event.

To counter this I set up two things: Cultural Clearing and Open Culture. Cultural Clearing was a mechanism for everyone to 'clear the air', by giving them a second chance to pitch their idea or express dissatisfaction with their previous treatment. It was also a way of making connections, putting people in touch with each other: a sponsor with an artist or a venue that could house a performance. Open Culture was a media alliance that included BBC Radio Merseyside, Radio City and the *Liverpool Daily Post* and *Echo*.

Having learned from the soaps that it is to no one's benefit, especially not the public's, to put similar programmes up against each other, we sat around the table and worked out what events in the programme would appeal to which audience. This was the first time we had ever sat round a table in this way, and I offered them total involvement and, more importantly, total openness. I would keep them as well as the Culture Company briefed on what was happening with the cultural programme, good, bad or indifferent, just as I would respect their independence and objectivity. We agreed to trust each other. And we all benefited as a result.

To manage both I needed someone who would 'get' what Jeremy Isaacs had been looking for in those early C4 commissioning editors: someone to facilitate other people's ideas. We found this in an arts officer from Knowsley Council, Charlotte Corrie, and from day one she was tasked with helping people 'create culture not simply consume it'. She did a great job and is now still running Open

Culture as a separate organisation, to help people 'create rather than consume'. In the early months leading up to the opening weekend it played a critical role in helping to turn round the mindset locally. Throughout the year it was vital in maintaining the momentum and keeping the media informed and onside.

The build-up to the opening weekend was frenetic, manic, crazy, paranoid, and schizophrenic. It was an amalgam of theatre, outdoor events, acrobats, stuntmen, aerialists, musicians, TV, film, radio . . . and as I seemed to be the only one who spoke all the tongues, I was constantly arbitrating between the light levels the theatre guys wanted against the needs of TV, and getting all their rigs to coincide and not overlap, and not seating the Secretary of State for Culture behind a speaker stack in the arena.

A few moments stand out for me from that opening weekend. On the Friday night, 'The People's Opening', our serial worrier, Claire McColgan, came up to me at 6 p.m., after we had closed Lime Street to traffic, fretting that no one would turn up, but by 7.45 was worrying that too many had done. As was the 'Gold Commander' in charge of public order and safety. So instead of the long-cherished 20.08 start, we gave the signal to go at 19.50. No one cared. As soon as things got underway the crowd was captivated.

Having spent too many years organising big shoots and events only to miss them as I was backstage or in a control room some-where, this was one I wanted to experience out front. I also wanted to gauge people's reactions. Twenty minutes later I felt the city's collective shoulders relax and saw a smile on everyone's face. As at the programme launch, I felt things were beginning to turn. There was one special face and one special moment in that crowd when I saw the BBC Director-General himself, Mark Thompson. I was quite moved that he had travelled up to attend the opening in person, and in doing so given us the best level of support anyone could ask from the BBC. It was a gesture the news crews all noted. He didn't have to do it. But he did.

From the arena show the following night, the memories are of unbridled energy, enthusiasm, chaos, and a host of brilliant perfor-mances by the Scouse glitterati during what I described as the second-best dress rehearsal I had ever seen. The first had been the previous evening. As for that, there had been neither time nor opportunity for us to have a full run-through with everyone and everything in place, so when the order to 'go' was given, a thousand fingers crossed.

There had also been only one trial run of the arena venue, when we asked our 4,000 volunteers to come in and help us test the fire and evacuation procedures, so that we could get the fire certificate that would allow the venue actually to open. I hosted the evening with local shock-jock Peter Price and we had the honour of instigating the 'first-ever' Mexican Wave in the arena, just as The Farm were the first band ever to play there, giving a live rendition of 'All Together Now', before we interrupted them with the fire alarm to test the evacuation protocols. Everything worked perfectly, as it did on the opening night when I looked round the crowd and saw them sitting enthralled by the sight of the Royal Liverpool Philharmonic Orchestra, suspended vertically on scaffolding, as the house band for the night.

And in all the creative madness there were also the bureaucratic moments to cherish. Like when it was realised that to get our near-septuagenarian Beatles' drummer into a cargo container on top of St George's Hall, he would have to negotiate a slippery staircase. Since it was too late for the Council's procurement procedures, one of the Regional Development Agency staff used their credit card to pay for a small piece of carpet, and later faced disciplinary proceedings for inappropriate use.

Then, as if to illustrate the point about how disconnected London is from the rest of the world, the Department for Culture Media and Sport (DCMS) officials, who had come with the Secretary of State, thought it would be a good use of their time to have a full briefing from two key Culture Company figures, Kris Donaldson, the Director, and Bernice Law, who had been seconded from the RDA as Chief Operating Officer. And they wanted to do this the afternoon of the arena opening. Consequently, instead of overseeing what was going on, they were sitting in a hotel room briefing a civil servant, and because of that the programmes and merchandise for the night were overlooked and we lost about £50,000 in badly needed revenue. Not what I'd call best value for public money.

Yet for every officious bureaucrat there are many creative stars, one of whom worked on the arena show. Jayne Casey (aka Big in Japan, Pink Military and Pink Industry) had diplomatic skills which allowed her to manage a task worse than herding cats: getting the various Liverpool bands together and keeping them in one place, on time and on cue. This included, I later discovered, keeping a few under house arrest to prevent them wandering off on some drug-induced walkabout. But what a performance they all gave, backed by the Royal Liverpool Philharmonic Orchestra with internationally acclaimed Vasily Petrenko as at home with Pete Wylie as he was with Beethoven.

As the arena show came to a close, despite the idea that there were to be no speeches, there was still an air of expectancy emanating from the audience. They needed something else. I'd sensed what it was the previous evening. There had been so much anxiety, so much negativity, leading up to this opening weekend, but it had gone really well. So I got up and made the producers, Jayne Casey and Nigel Jamieson, come out on stage so we could all say thank you to them for putting it together. Then I turned to the audience and said, 'Well, we did it! It's now going to be bigger, better, wider, deeper – but above all it's no longer something run and owned by the Council. It's going to be your Capital of Culture – 2008.' The cheers and applause proved my instinct had been right. The crowd wanted to express their own sense of relief. They wanted to know the event wasn't reliant on the Council, but that they too had permission to get involved. We were now definitely going to be OK.

While nowhere near the maelstrom of *Brookie*'s early days, probably because I was older and, if not wiser, perhaps a bit more experienced, this was nevertheless an extraordinary time. From getting Ringo on to the roof of St George's Hall to councillors leaking board-meeting discussions on their BlackBerrys; from being with local artist Alex Corina, who opened a gallery in Garston, to organising Irish President Mary McAleese's visit to the city; from getting the Council to pay Macca what he wanted for playing at Anfield, to getting someone else to pay for the Queen's lunch when they wouldn't; from sitting outside Tesco's with local artist Ruth Ben-Tovim getting shoppers to stop and tell a story, to sitting next to Rowan Williams, Archbishop of Canterbury, debating over lunch whether the Anglican Church really had ushered in the age of novel-writing; from unveiling a community mosaic, to taking Gordon Brown on a boat ride round the Liverpool docks; from encouraging city-centre pavement art, to swapping horror stories about public procurement with European President Barroso who was at the time struggling with his own bureaucracy over the choice of a new rug for his office.

And all the time, the writer's sponge was gathering material for a potential future return for *County Hall*. For instance, the Health & Safety police were not going to allow the British Prime Minister to enter the building site for the new Museum of Liverpool unless he wore a hard hat, which would exacerbate his already-impaired vision, until I came up with the perfect get-out ruse that the real cops, Special Branch, needed to be able to see him easily at all times. In a sea of hi-viz jackets and helmets, the guy without one would be the PM. The guy next to him would be me.

And getting a forty-ton spider to clank around the city, with all the arguments about who paid for the broken pavements, while keeping the untaxed and uninsured French support vehicles away from the cops, was nothing to what went on with the umbrellas after Macca's concert at Anfield, another saga in its own right, but for another time. Just as we thought it was safe to let out a sigh of relief, we discovered someone had 'just thought . . .' Oh, how well I remembered that phrase, and the 'good ideas' that invariably followed, like confiscating umbrellas from the crowd, just in case . . . Health & Safety? Perhaps. But what do you do then with a few thousand umbrellas? Bin them, of course. And, even better, in among all the catering waste. So when the complaints came in and people, quite reasonably, assumed their umbrellas were safe and sound in a Council repository, we had to pay for them all to be recovered, cleaned and put on display in St George's Hall so that the owners could come and reclaim them.

But my favourite example came after I was asked to play tourist guide for Gordon Brown's and the Cabinet's visit to Liverpool. Having spent two days with him at various events, including hitching a last-minute lift in the Prime Ministerial convoy when I realised I didn't have my pass to get me through the ring of steel round the convention centre, I was then pulled over on my way home and surrounded by cops. They had noticed that my car had been in close proximity to the Prime Minister for the past couple of days. Fortunately, before I was tagged and bagged and sent to Guantanamo, they recognised me. Nice to know they were paying attention though.

Yet although all the high-profile events were good for media headlines and the gradual shift in external perception of the city, they are, in fact, easy to stage, if you have the budget. You just phone up the professionals and ask them to do it and everyone lucky enough to take part has a great time. The real work, changing internal perception, was going on out in the communities, where I probably spent around 75 per cent of my time across the year. Much of it was a credit to Claire McColgan and her education and community teams, but a lot also came from local but nationally known companies like Boodles, David M. Robinson, Home Bargains, Beetham's, Andrew Collinge, Davis Wallis Foyster and others, who supported Open Culture and stepped in at the last minute to give their time, cash and resources to boost local community activities.

These were all illuminating, sobering and humbling experiences, from which there was feedback akin to the letters I received after the Brookie Basics literacy campaign. Real people, telling you something had made a real difference to real communities.

Things like the community *X-Factor* organised out in Croxteth, where gun crime had claimed the life of young Rhys Jones. Or listening to the residents of Kirkdale tell me that the public art installation, The Rotunda, that had been built through the culture programme was 'the first thing we've ever had off the Council'. This was from a forty-something mum who told me it had become such a positive focal point for all the so-called 'scallies', that they were spending much of their weekends gathered around it, instead of creating aggravation through boredom. She went on to say that some of them were so enthused by the year that they were even now going 'into town'. We were standing about 1,000 metres from the city centre at the time.

This was something I would hear about many times during my time on the Knowsley Youth Commission: young teens who had not ventured more than six streets from home in their entire lives. Looked upon as 'aggressively territorial', they were also classed as 'anti-social', yet twenty minutes in their company, speaking in the right accent, and they reverted to being just kids wanting someone to listen and give them something to do. At the same time there was research that indicated they were also among the happiest teenagers in the UK. Under-achieving according to national education benchmarks, but possessing a great sense of community and family.

It was not just young people who felt they had been given

something 'for the first time'. Whether it was a nostalgic photo-montage in one of the stroke recovery units to help rebuild memories, art and artists to enhance the waiting room for surgery at Alder Hey Children's Hospital, or a verbal history project to recall and record local memories, people were beginning to feel newly involved, perhaps reconnected to their local communities. And two things that did much to encourage this were *Go Superlambananas!* and the Open Culture project.

The Superlambanana, or SLB, is a piece of public art that has been in Liverpool since 1998. Created by Japanese artist Taro Chiezo, it is a bright yellow seventeen-foot-tall sculpture depicting a mythical creature, half-lamb and half-banana. It was supposed to be a comment on the dangers of genetic engineering, but heavily influenced by the history of the Liverpool Docks in importing both sheep and bananas. From that you may easily imagine how, due to the Scouse sense of literalism, for the first ten years of its life it was misunderstood, unloved, and the centre of general derision. Many a stag had been chained to it the night before their own individual Scouse wedding.

Then came 2008 and the excuse, or permission, for people to think differently. While many cities have staged cow, rhinoceros or elephant parades, when artists work with local groups to decorate white models, Liverpool decided to opt for its Superlambanana. It was a simple yet inspirational decision, taken long before I became Creative Director. The people of Liverpool finally took it to their hearts and soon there were SLBs everywhere, attracting hundreds of thousands of people to the city and, at the end of the year, when sold off at auction, they raised over £550,000 for the Lord Mayor's Charity, a record amount for any such charity anywhere in the UK. And that raised other issues. While it was always clear that the SLBs would only be temporarily on display, for the Capital of Culture year, people had grown fond of seeing them outside their homes or places of work. They decided they wanted them to stay, and like the mum in Kirkdale, told me that if the Council tried to remove them they would be out on the streets fighting. How's that for public engagement in culture? The Kirkdale Rotunda and the SLBs are still in place.

If public engagement with the SLBs was surprising, then Open Culture's projects also caught many off-guard. These were designed to close the gap in perception and engage the public in helping define 'Scouse culture', through media phone-ins, texts and website visits, to the Liverpool Map that set out where Scousers really think their city boundary is, to a region-wide talent competition held in the arena – Now That's What We Call Culture, to the *Liverpool Saga*, a form of Nordic saga based about Liverpool's 800-year history, celebrated in 2007. Eight hundred lines to mark eight hundred years sounded like a simple idea, but when the public was asked to send in a line or two about what they felt made the city and Scouse character, there were over 3,000 responses. My favourite two were: '*You can always tell a Scouser, but you can't tell him much*', and '*Scousers learn to read between the lines before they learn to read*'. With such a mass of material we needed to have some way of curating the project and I thought I might know just the man: my old Geography teacher, Roger McGough. Please sir, could you . . .? And he did. Working with local poets, Roger also topped and tailed the saga and later performed a public reading in St George's Hall Concert Room, where Dickens had given public readings.

So all this, the melding of high-profile media events to bring credibility and awareness to the community engagement, taught me how a simple 'badge of authority', or permission to get involved, could harness enthusiasm and achieve great things from very little in the way of resources. It was what had underpinned my own upbringing and involvement with our church-based community. The message was as clear as it was simple. Do what you can, where you can, when you can, how you can. That applied as much to individuals and groups through Cultural Clearing and Open Culture as it did to the power-brokers who came together to make sure the year of celebration was delivered successfully. And it was. And that £20 million budget black hole? It went away and we ended the year with a small – very small – surplus.

So having seen what was possible I was then tempted, perhaps swept along, into trying to make sure it carried on. Everywhere I went people wanted it to carry on. They wanted more community action. But without the badge of authority that came from the European Award, without the need for political expediency, what quickly resurfaced was the same mindset I had run into over *County Hall* and *Waterfront Beat*: the right idea at the wrong time with the wrong people. Tribal loyalties resurfaced, and the 'not invented here' syndrome prevailed, to the extent that the day after the final event I found that my electronic pass for entry into the Council Culture Company offices had been cancelled.

With their obvious desire to get back to the status quo, and already preoccupied with the next election battle, it proved difficult to maintain momentum among the local politicians. Nationally, though, the success of 2008 was not lost on the Liverpool-born Secretary of State for Culture, Andy Burnham. He had not just seen but felt the positive impact on the city, its people and its communities: a sense of rediscovered pride, confidence and ambition. They had seen that we Scousers had not 'cocked it up', but had set a new benchmark for the European Union's culture programme. All that had been lacking was leadership and continuing authority, so he readily took up the suggestion of giving other cities a similar opportunity by creating the UK City of Culture programme.

Both he and I invested a lot of time and energy in persuading all the major arts organisations to come together every four years to support one city, as they had in Liverpool. Mark Thompson was once again an early supporter, and once again with the BBC at the table, others followed. All agreed to ring-fence funds within existing budgets every four years. Following the example of Liverpool 2008 the event would have three guiding principles: there would be no extra government funding and people would need to come together and work from existing resources, to rally behind the badge of authority, exactly as Liverpool had done; it would be for each city to define its own culture, as Liverpool had done; and, once defined, it would be up to each city to define what step change they would bring about during their own 'wedding year'.

Above all, the event would give permission for people, organisations, institutions, agencies and bureaucracies to come together and unite behind a common goal. If there is such a thing as a 'Liverpool model' for culture and regeneration, it is not that culture leads to regeneration, but that through a shared culture people can come together and actually talk to each other, then focus every agenda, whether civic, economic, social or political, on one moment in time. This was what had brought over £4 billion in investment to Liverpool between 2003 and 2008. It was what had brought to an end the twenty-five-year conversation about whether or not to have the arena and convention centre which eventually staged the second-best dress rehearsal I'd ever seen. It was what delivered a £750 million economic impact to the city, academically validated by a joint research project between John Moores University, the University of Liverpool and the City Council. And what led European Commission President José Manuel Durão Barroso to comment, 'Liverpool, the best ever Capital of Culture'.

It was also what led to our seeing Derry/Londonderry announced as the first UK City of Culture for 2013, and then accompanying a Tory Culture Minister, Ed Vaizey, there to witness the same sense of excitement, anticipation, expectation and ambition that had swept through Liverpool in 2003. They too 'got it'. It was this that made it easy for me to stand up and say that although I thought 'Big Society' was a naff political slogan, it was a good idea. After 2008 I felt that if we in the People's Republic could 'get it', then why were my media colleagues unable to grasp it?

The answer, I thought, was that it was due to the over-centralised media–Westminster agenda, where everything is about national political careers rather than local policies or even community needs. It was this that got me an invitation back to Downing Street and made it easy for me to invite and then introduce the first Tory Prime Minister, David Cameron, to enter the People's Republic for around thirty years. If there was one city that epitomised the Big Society it was, ironically, Liverpool itself. With a historical tradition for social justice and philanthropy hard to match anywhere else, despite the historical political divide, there seemed obvious common ground for Scouse pragmatism to explore. As I tried to get over to the political ideologues, it is better to have a seat on the sofa than be out in the corridor waiting for news.

So it was that self-confessed *Grange Hill* fan David Cameron diverted from his first meeting with President Obama to launch Big Society in Liverpool, and meet, in private, some of the power-brokers who had made 2008 the 'best ever' European Capital of Culture. Unfortunately, the Scouse wedding's honeymoon period came to an abrupt end when both national media and politicians conflated austerity cuts with the call for more community engagement. Such action was regarded as a substitute for public services. It was as politically convenient as it was daft, but the curse of centralisation struck again. Instead of looking at specific local needs, national party politics continued to dominate. The conversation ended and we were back to talking at, not to, each other.

Battle lines were drawn, mindsets retrenched, and Big Society turned from being a simple idea to encourage more community activity into a complex and top down, centrally driven and managed programme of agencies and agents who would 'train people how to be more collaborative'. It evolved into becoming a big scheme for big government, when all it means, I think, is 'do what you can, where you can, when you can, how you can'.

The more I have reflected on my own journey through life, the more I believe that social change is no more difficult than that. It just takes time, and people who are prepared to admit and accept that. We need people at all levels to do 'what they can'. Whether to pick up a bit of shopping for a neighbour, organise a school talent show, plan a village fete, a city festival, or think a bit more about things like car parking at our hospitals. Doing just a little bit more for whatever community we belong to.

There was, and still is, nothing wrong with the comprehensive education model itself, as the principle works in our primary schools. It tends to fall apart at secondary level, as does most education reform, due to the scale on which policy-makers repeatedly try to implement it. Like the Parker Morris standard in housing, the SCOLA building system or television transmission patterns, big government looks for big solutions though big schemes and big headlines. But, above all, at a big cost.

Yet most people live in small communities and desire small-scale solutions to their own local or personal needs, usually at very little cost. Dating from the Industrial Revolution and continuing to this day, there is an idea that the more people crowd into cities, the more need there is for centralised planning and control. What is often overlooked is that cities are not homogeneous but merely collections of urban villages. Suburbia lives and will never die. It only changes shape. It also comes down to this: it is all about jobs. Without them there is neither social cohesion nor a taxation system.

Social change does not stem from the big revolutionary acts, as they are usually the consequence of years of frustration and/or repression. Real change comes about through the slow but inexorable pressure that builds up through small, incremental changes. Consider this. *Brookside* did not come about simply because I wanted to write it and C4 wanted to produce it, but because of an act that took place on board a battleship on 2 September 1945. That was when the Japanese Empire formally surrendered and brought an end to the hostilities of World War II.

Sound a bit fanciful? But that act meant that my dad survived and returned home to start a family, which led to me being born in 1949. At the same moment a chain of events was set in motion that meant the Western Allies would help rebuild the war-ravaged economies of both Japan and Germany. That in turn would mean, thirty years later, they would overhaul our battered economies and in doing so create the social conditions I wanted to write about: the de-industrialisation of the UK. At the same time, the only company that could provide the technology to allow me to make *Brookie* was Japanese. I've reflected many times on this, since the day when the Dentsu representative arrived to learn 'everything I knew'. I have reflected on my dad's time with the Chindits in Burma, and my Uncle Paddy huddled in front of his electric fire because of the malaria he'd caught in Changi, and the ways in which Japan has always featured in my life story.

I have also reflected upon how social change and social issues arise from incremental change and as they do they also create and then embed a mindset that makes bringing about change too difficult. It makes people preoccupied with what they have, to an extent that inhibits their ability to go in search of what they might gain. It was this latter point that finally made me decide not to stand for elected Mayor of Liverpool.

It was tempting. I was pushed quite close to the edge by the encouragement of others, but in the end decided against it, despite the fact that whenever I hear a traditional politician give a speech about how they are going to 'fix' this, that or the other, I cannot help but wonder where 'they' were when 'we' got into whatever mess they say 'we' are now in. As with Open Culture during 2008, the underlying issue was not what the administrators of Liverpool City Council wanted, but what the people of Liverpool considered their city to be. That is, and always has been, Merseyside. It is the elephant in the room that can never be shooed away. It is a similar situation in most great conurbations like Manchester, Birmingham or Sheffield, but some are better at disguising it or better at working round it. Liverpool is, well, Liverpool, and has grown used to being disappointed by its politicians so tends to work around them.

While being Mayor of Liverpool would have been a great honour, cool even, I don't think the 'badge of authority', as it is currently empowered, is enough to tackle the real issue, which is that even as the biggest, Liverpool is still only one of six boroughs that make up the city-region, the real Scouse Republic. Any major change will require negotiation and co-operation from the other five boroughs, but more importantly with the major-power-brokers who reside in the public-service sector, like the police, mental health, fire and rescue and travel services who operate on a Merseyside basis that encompasses areas where other 'Liverpudlians' like Terry Leahy and Stevie G come from.

Neither could I suppress the thought that it took three hundred years for a port city to expand and encompass Merseyside, increment-ally, so it will probably take many years, if not decades, to bring about real change. Politics is, unfortunately, a short-term game or career. National politicians tend not only to want big ideas, but those that chime with national and international agendas. Yet often the problems they should be challenging are local.

Liverpool lost its industrial base over thirty years. Its social problems evolved over the same period. They will not go away with a six-, nine- or twelve-month training or mentoring scheme. We made this point on *Brookside* with Damon Grant's YTS storyline in the 1980s. However, even I can see that standing for election under the slogan '*Trust me, I'll take years to fix anything*' probably wouldn't win over the average floating voter. To fall back on an old cliché: if I were only twenty years younger. Now, if it was Mayor for *Merseyside* . . .

None of this is to say that the years since MerseyTV have not been stimulating, they have been, but they have also been more taxing and more tiring than the eighteen-hour days I used to spend at the centre of a production maelstrom. Fatigue is kept at bay when you can say yes, a very quick no, or simply make things happen rather than have to call for another consultation or stakeholders' meeting or go through 'procurement'. Nor does the adrenalin flow to keep at bay the daily niggles of pain and discomfort when checking for 'matters arising out of the minutes of the last meeting'. In 1984, after the car crash, the medics told me I would have about twenty-five years before I started falling to pieces. Almost like an alarm clock, my damaged knee, neck and back are now daily reminders that, no matter what that BBC script editor thought, Alexis and I had a Guardian Angel looking down on us that night on the Weaver Viaduct.

Since then, I've experienced some great times and met amazing people, more of these out in the streets than at ceremonial events. I've got close to four Prime Minister, which in turn has provided a whole raft of associated memories, such as the time when during one dinner at Chequers I turned to talk to someone and the back of the chair broke with an ear-splitting crack. All eyes turned to me, including those of the British Prime Minister, sitting on Alexis's left. I was able to use the old gag, 'Good job it wasn't a new one,' and then share a joke with QC Cherie that I wouldn't claim for 'whiplash compo', even though they hadn't given me 'adequate training on the use and handling of eighteenth-century chairs'.

As another legacy of 2008, I was offered and jumped at the chance to become Chair of National Museums Liverpool, not just because of the emotional bond back to my lost friend the previous Director, Richard Foster, but because the museums are like the Mersey Tunnels and the Liver Birds: part of every Scouser's DNA. Before that, in 2004, I received my CBE. The offer letter arrived in a cheap brown envelope, the sort that usually encloses a notice from the DSS. After initially thinking it was a wind up, I went through all the post-Marxist angst about whether to accept, but not for long. I knew you had to be nominated, and felt the citation 'for services to drama' indicated that it had come from the company and the community. Then I was really thrilled, and especially pleased to discover that the guy who took my top hat from me in the cloakroom at Buckingham Palace was originally from Liverpool.

I was even more thrilled when Alexis was awarded an MBE in 2011 for 'services to Merseyside', in recognition of all she has done there, quietly applying her time and expertise to public-sector finances across the region. While both my mum and dad had passed away by this time, I knew they would have been very proud, especially because we had lived up to our Welsh Methodist and Irish Catholic backgrounds by working hard and helping others along the way.

But I had one more honour granted to me that probably eclipsed even going to the Palace. In 1986, North Liverpool Comprehensive, now North Liverpool Academy, named one of the school 'houses' after me. At St Kev's the houses were named after saints. Now it was Liverpool writers. So alongside Redmond House, there is Russell, Patten and, er, McGough. Now, how 'cool' is that? So cool in fact that when the SLBs were in great demand and short supply across the city, I managed to 'find' a few . . . and guess where one ended up?

Finding out that I was old enough to have a school house named after me naturally made me think back to my time at St Kev's, when I was in St Gregory House, and how much both my Irish Catholic upbringing and education, the good and the bad sides of it, had shaped me. I might have turned away from the church's hierarchical bureaucracy, but its teachings have stayed with me. Do unto others as you would be done to. *Respice Finem*. Or, do what you can, where you can, when you can, how you can. More simply, instead of automatically fretting about protecting the status quo and asking 'Why?', think about the gradual change you personally can help bring about by simply asking, 'Well, why not?'

And, finally, life did another of its full circles. As part of the 2012 Diamond Jubilee, Alexis and I hosted lunch for the Queen at the Merseyside Maritime Museum and in my speech I said that, as Chair of National Museums Liverpool, it was a great honour to have her with us as not only had she opened the Maritime Museum in 1993, when it was the first symbol of Liverpool's renaissance, but she was also there in 2011, to open the new Museum of Liverpool, the latest symbol of progress. Yet for me there was a more personal memory. The very first television programme I remember, when I crawled up that street with the sewing needle in my foot, had been her Coronation. It introduced me to the wonders of television. And so, in a way, she was not only responsible for my career, but also had to take some part of the blame for *Grange Hill*, *Brookside* and *Hollyoaks*. I don't think anyone back then would have believed that sixty years later I would be sitting next to her at lunch. Nor that she would giggle to hear the tale.

And with that it is time for me to offer a final apology to anyone I have missed and stick with the idea that I have not named the clowns in my own particular circus, but if they want to stand up and identify themselves, that is up to them. And another apology for the fact that I have not had time or space to talk about the forays into radio that saw MerseyTV become the first independent producer for Radio 4, live on location at *Brookie*, and then later, like the BBC, wonder what was the point? Just as I had once vowed never to make radio with pictures, why did we not just enjoy the fact that we needn't have fretted over the location logistics? Still, why not?

And lastly an apology to my kids who I know I have frustrated over the years by not taking them to some of the 'cool stuff' through my desire, following the troublesome *Grange Hill* incident, never to break the rule of not opening up my private life to the media. They are older now and understand why I did it; at least that's what they tell me. And even if they are humouring me, I love them all the more for it.

If this was a script it would now be time to cue the end theme, low but slowly building under the final dialogue, because as I have said in many interviews, one of the reasons *Grange Hill*, *Brookside* and *Hollyoaks* ran for so long was that I couldn't think of a good ending. The end of one episode automatically became the backstory and beginning of the next, which is why this book is called a mid-term report. It's the story so far. There was life for me after *Brookie* and *Grange Hill*, and even apart from *Hollyoaks*. Who knows where the next chapter will lead me? Life at MerseyTV was always lived following that very simple adage: 'Why not?' We never stopped answering it. I hope I never will.

And with the theme music now building . . . having spent seven years 'volunteering' in the public sector and having flirted with politics, the overriding conclusion of this mid-term report is that it is time for me to return to what I know best, perhaps what I do best, and write about social issues, not try to solve them. In doing so perhaps, just perhaps, I'll return to helping the real campaigners win a more sympathetic hearing.

Just like when they dip the music at the end of a programme and the continuity announcer tells you what's coming next . . . '*For those interested in the work of Phil Redmond, next year will see him returning to writing contemporary drama with the launch of* Highbridge *– a novel about life in a typical northern town, with typical schools, typical housing estates and typical teenage traumas.*' Then the credits come back full-screen to signify The End . . . Or . . . To Be Continued . . .

Index

(the initials PR refer to Phil Redmond; AR to Alexis Redmond)